Handbook of Gender Studies in the Dutch Caribbean

Handbooks in Caribbean Studies

VOLUME 01

The titles published in this series are listed at *brill.com/hcbs*

Handbook of Gender Studies in the Dutch Caribbean

Edited by

Rose Mary Allen
Sruti Bala

BRILL

LEIDEN | BOSTON

NWO (Dutch Research Council) Caribbean Research Programme (Grant number ALWCA.2016.030) (2017).

Library of Congress Cataloging-in-Publication Data

Names: Allen, Rose Mary, editor. | Bala, Sruti, 1973- editor.
Title: Handbook of gender studies in the Dutch Caribbean / edited by Rose Mary Allen, Sruti Bala.
Description: Leiden ; Boston : Brill, [2024] | Series: Handbooks in Caribbean studies, 2950-2993 ; volume 01 | Includes bibliographical references. |
Identifiers: LCCN 2023057707 (print) | LCCN 2023057708 (ebook) | ISBN 9789004690875 (hardback) | ISBN 9789004690882 (ebook)
Subjects: LCSH: Women–Caribbean Netherlands--Social conditions. | Sexual minorities–Caribbean Netherlands--Social conditions. | Women and the arts–Caribbean Netherlands.
Classification: LCC HQ1525.8 H35 2024 (print) | LCC HQ1525.8 (ebook) | DDC 305.409163/65–dc23/eng/20240205
LC record available at https://lccn.loc.gov/2023057707
LC ebook record available at https://lccn.loc.gov/2023057708

Typeface for the Latin, Greek, and Cyrillic scripts: "Brill". See and download: brill.com/brill-typeface.

ISSN 2950-2993
ISBN 978-90-04-69087-5 (hardback)
ISBN 978-90-04-69088-2 (e-book)
DOI 10.1163/9789004690882

This book is printed on acid-free paper and produced in a sustainable manner.

Printed by Printforce, the Netherlands

Contents

Acknowledgments

The *Handbook of Gender Studies in the Dutch Caribbean* would not have been possible without the collective efforts of so many people collaborating across continents. When we presented the project to potential contributors and colleagues in the field, it was received with enthusiasm, and we were consistently made to feel confident that this is a worthwhile and long overdue undertaking. Our first thanks are therefore due to all the contributors to this volume for their time, commitment and generous suggestions and recommendations. We thank the legal heirs and family members of the deceased authors, whose works are included in this volume, for granting permission to reprint a selection of their works. Our gratitude further goes to Eva Abraham-Van der Mark, Florencia Cornet and Ieteke Witteveen, whose participation is much appreciated, though their work could not be featured in the book. A big thanks to the Dutch and Papiamentu translators Marcus Ferley, Hein van Maarschalkerwaart and Wernher José Suares for their painstaking and sensitive work.

We are indebted to Liesbeth Echteld, director of the University of Curaçao Research Institute; Adriënne Fernandes, dean of the General Faculty; Desiree Manuel-Eliza and Rosemarijn de Jong, former and current coordinators of educational activities at the Bonaire office of University of Curaçao and Francis de Lanoy, Rector Magnificus of the University of Curaçao, all of whom supported the broader research project, from which this publication ensued, from its very early stages. Margo Groenewoud and Stephanie van Heijningen are due thanks for hosting and successfully conducting the pre-doctoral training program. We thank the Amsterdam School for Cultural Analysis and the department of arts and culture at the faculty of humanities of the University of Amsterdam for supporting the projects' doctoral candidates. Noor Breuning and Thomas Hazewinkel patiently answered our questions and attended to book order requests at the library.

Our deep gratitude goes to our research advisory board members Vanessa Agard-Jones, Kamala Kempadoo, Patricia Mohammed and Gloria Wekker. They have each been immensely influential in shaping our analytical frameworks. We greatly appreciate their participation in the project at various stages and their mentoring and advice at crucial moments. Josef Stuefer, Niels van den Berg and Arnold Lubbers from the Caribbean research program team at the Dutch Research Council have been supportive throughout the project and enabled us to make changes in the plans where necessary and have facilitated contacts with other researchers in the Caribbean and in the Netherlands.

Angelo Christiaan, Neifi Hussein, Lisanne Kniese, Ghanima Kowsoleea, Samantha Pires Vianna and Berit Zandbelt contributed to the project and the publication at various stages as reliable, energetic and creative research assistants. Martin Essemann has offered invaluable research support and editorial assistance, most efficiently and pleasantly communicating with all the contributors and maintaining the overview of all the steps in what turned out to be a complex publication endeavor. Our copyeditor Mariëlle Smith remarkably combined speed, sensitivity and an eye for detail in taking on this massive task. A huge thanks to all of you!

We warmly acknowledge the feedback, guidance and support offered by colleagues and dear friends: Miriyam Aouragh, Maayke Botman, Judith Brekelmans, Noris Doran, Heidi Dorudi, Layal Ftouni, Liliane de Geus, Francio Guadeloupe, Rivke Jaffe, Peter Jordens, Esther Krop, Wayne Modest and Wim Rutgers.

We are grateful to the entire team at Brill for a smooth publication process and for their enthusiastic support of the volume.

Rose Mary Allen and Sruti Bala

Figures

Notes on Contributors

Rose Mary Allen

is extraordinary professor of culture, community and history at the University of Curaçao and a pioneer of oral history research. She is the author of *Di ki manera: A Social History of Afro-Curaçaoans, 1863–1917* (2007) and coeditor (with E. Captain, M. van Rossum and U. Vyent) of *Staat en slavernij: Het Nederlandse koloniale slavernijverleden en zijn doorwerkingen* (Slavery and the state: Dutch colonial slavery history and its legacies, 2023). She is a recipient of numerous awards, most recently the Cross of Merit from the government of Curaçao in 2023 in recognition of her contributions to research on the Dutch Caribbean.

Oliver Antczak

is a Venezuelan and Polish doctoral candidate in the Department of Archaeology at the University of Cambridge. His research focuses on the relationship between heritage and identity and particularly how it is impacted by different colonialisms. His area of research is the Southern Caribbean where he currently employs a comparative perspective between the islands of Trinidad, Margarita and Bonaire. He received his BA from Leiden University College (2016) and an MPhil from the University of Cambridge (2018) and is affiliated to Unidad de Estudios Arqueológicos, Universidad Simon Bolívar, Venezuela.

Jean Antoine-Dunne

is an academic, critic, painter and filmmaker. She codesigned the BA in Film at the University of the West Indies, St. Augustine, and was its first coordinator from 2006 to 2009. She is the author of *Derek Walcott's Love Affair with Film* (2017) and editor of "Where is Here? Remapping the Caribbean," a special issue of the *Journal of West Indian Literature* (April 2010), and *Interlocking Basins of a Globe: Essays on Derek Walcott* (2013). Her film documentaries include *Rivers of Sound* on Gordon Rohlehr (2010), *Walcott as Poet and Seer* (2014) and *Dis-Abled/Mis-Labled* (2015). She has written extensively on the interface between film and literature.

Gilbert Bacilio

is a poet, performance artist, writer and director from Curaçao, also known as Gibi Bacilio. He was director of the street theater group Teatro Foro, producer of the TV program *Kachu* and is a member of the band *Palabra Musikal*. His writings include the poetry collection *Kueru marká* (2000) and the play *Chakutoe* (2019). He is vice-chairman of the foundation for the national park, Parke Lucha pa Libertat, editor-in-chief of the board of Fundashon Publikashon, member of the Curaçaoan association for the promotion of historical awareness of the legacy of slavery and a representative of Curaçao in the interinsular consultative body of the Kingdom of the Netherlands.

Sruti Bala
is associate professor in theater and performance studies at the University of Amsterdam. Her research interests are at the intersections of performance and politics, which have taken shape in various projects on nonviolent protest, participatory art, artistic activism, translation, feminist and postcolonial theories. Publications include *The Gestures of Participatory Art* (2018) and *The Global Trajectories of Queerness: Re-thinking Same-Sex Politics in the Global South* (coedited with A. Tellis, 2015). She was principal investigator of the Dutch Research Council funded project "Cultural Practices of Citizenship under Conditions of Fragmented Sovereignty: Gendered and Sexual Citizenship in Curaçao and Bonaire" (2017–2023).

Judith Brekelmans
is an HR professional, trainer, coach and storyteller. She is cofounder and chair of Fundashon EQ Bonaire, an LGBTQ+ rights group in Bonaire. With a Dutch mother and a Curaçaoan father, she is culturally connected to both places and has been living in the Caribbean for more than fourteen years. Her love of history and curiosity about her roots led her to join the oral history research masterclass with Rose Mary Allen in 2019, following which she conducted numerous oral history interviews with extraordinary women in Bonaire.

Aart G. Broek
is a consultant and independent scholar based in the Netherlands. He received his PhD from the Vrije Universiteit Amsterdam in 1990 and lived and worked in Curaçao from 1981 to 2001. He has published extensively on Dutch Caribbean social, political and cultural matters and researches the wider Caribbean context, particularly in relation to (post)colonial developments in the Netherlands.

Beatriz César Loureiro
is a Venezuelan-Portuguese scholar of the Venezuelan Caribbean. She graduated from the University of Amsterdam with an MA in Art and Performance Studies and completed the Predoctoral Honors Program at the University of Curaçao in 2022. Her research interests lie in postcolonial cultural anthropology and the cultural aspects of diasporic experiences. She is currently working on a doctoral study on ritual performances in Venezuela and the Leeward Islands and their interconnection to the cultural, political and social dimensions of displacement in the broader Latin American and Caribbean regions.

Lysanne Charles
is a writer of poetry, short stories, calypso, soca and carnival road march. She is also an activist and educator focusing on the empowerment of marginalized persons and groups. She is a PhD researcher affiliated to the research project "Island(er)s at the Helm," in collaboration with the University of Amsterdam, University of St. Maarten and University of the Virgin Islands. The words of Audre Lorde, "There is no such thing as a single-issue struggle because we do not live single-issue lives," inform her pursuit of liberation on many fronts.

Joceline Clemencia (†2011)
was a Curaçaoan writer, linguist, feminist and independence activist. She was a long-time advocate for the official recognition of the Papiamentu language and was active in efforts to standardize and promote the language. She was founder and director of the Instituto Kultural Independensha (Institute of Cultural Independence) in 1996 and the Skol Nobo (New School), dedicated to teaching the Papiamentu language, cultural history, art, sport and ecological issues that were not part of regular school curricula. She was an active campaigner for political independence from the Netherlands.

Sonia M. Cuales (†2018)
was a Curaçaoan feminist activist and researcher. She authored several academic articles about women and feminism in the Caribbean. She cofounded the Caribbean Association for Feminist Research and Action (CAFRA) in 1985 and the Caribbean Network on Studies of Masculinities in 1997. Cuales was part of launching the Annual Female Leadership Conferences in Curaçao in 2004 and was involved in advocacy on reproductive rights through Development Alternatives with Women for a New Era (DAWN). Cuales worked for the United Nations for eighteen years on development projects in the Caribbean and Latin America.

Frida Domacassé
writes poems and short stories in Papiamentu and Dutch under her mother's name, Domacassé. She tells intercultural stories on various stages. She is a member of the writing groups *Divers* and *Simia Literario*. Together with four other poets, she organizes the poetry stage "Ongehoord!" (Unheard!) in the Central Library of Rotterdam and "Poetry at the Home of" in Gouda. Her themes revolve around the Caribbean, longing, farewell, music and social photography. Her work has been featured in various anthologies and magazines. She has self-published a few poetry volumes.

Nadia Dresscher-Lambertus
is an interdisciplinary researcher in sociology, communication sciences, digital methods and arts-based methodologies and teacher at the Faculty of Arts and Science at the University of Aruba. She is a doctoral candidate at the University of Amsterdam as part of the Digital Methods Initiative. As a Caribbean intersectional (eco)feminist, she is committed to creativity and interdisciplinarity as life-giving modes of be(com)ing and decolonization, experimenting with registers such as (online) social cartography, autoethnography, collages, zines and poetry.

Elisabeth Echteld
is full professor at the Faculty of Arts of the University of Curaçao and chair of the University of Curaçao Research Institute. She obtained her PhD from Utrecht University in the Netherlands. Her dissertation focuses on Spanish Literature in Curaçao from the second half of the nineteenth century. She is coeditor of a multi-volume book series on the languages, literatures and cultures of the Greater Caribbean and beyond, jointly published by the University of Curaçao and the University of Puerto Rico.

Eric A. Eliason
is professor of folklore at Brigham Young University in Utah. His publications include *The Island of Lace: Drawn Threadwork on Saba in The Dutch Caribbean* (2019); *To See Them Run: Great Plains Coyote Coursing* (2015); and *Black Velvet Art* (2011) (with Scott Squire); *The Fruit of Her Hands: Saba Lace History and Patterns* (1997); *This is the Plate: Utah Food Traditions* (with Carol A. Edison and Lynne McNeil, 2020); and *Latter-day Lore: Mormon Folklore Studies* (with Tom Mould, 2014). His US Special Forces chaplain work in Afghanistan is featured in Hachette's *Hammerhead Six*.

Ryan Espersen
is a researcher whose work has focused on the historical and pre-Columbian archaeology of the northeastern Caribbean, with particular attention to how power structures and ideology relate to the material record of the Dutch Caribbean. He received his PhD from Leiden University in 2017, lived on the Dutch island of Saba from 2011 to 2018 and founded the Saba Archaeological Center (known as SABARC) in 2012. Since February 2022, he is a Marie Curie fellow with the McDonald Institute at the University of Cambridge. His research has been published in *Antiquity*, *Historical Archaeology*, the *Journal of Archaeological Science* and the *International Journal of Historical Archaeology*.

Liliane de Geus
obtained a bachelor of fine arts from Florida State University, an MA in arts administration and cultural policy from the Gallatin Division of New York University and an MSc in tourism planning and development at the University of Surrey. She has held high-ranking governmental and NGO positions in tourism and cultural and natural management in Bonaire and worked in the private sector in the area of downtown development in Curaçao. She was the UNESCO representative for Bonaire (2010–2014) and currently leads the UNESCO working group in Bonaire. Since 2012, she runs a consultancy focusing on policy issues, strategic management and sustainable development.

Margo Groenewoud
is a Dutch Caribbean lecturer and researcher working at the intersection of the humanities and social sciences. She specializes in the twentieth-century Caribbean, with an interest in social, cultural and intellectual history, migration histories, social justice and the strategic development of digital humanities. In 2022–2023, she was a Fulbright Scholar-In-Residence at The City College of New York, working on twentieth-century Dutch-Spanish Caribbean affairs with the CUNY Dominican Studies Institute. In her work, Groenewoud provokes thinking about the Caribbean beyond language barriers in efforts to achieve a deeper understanding of social strengths and resilience in the region.

Jeanne Henriquez
is an educator, historian, activist and mother of a son. She is currently director of Museo Tula in Curaçao and president of a women's shelter. She completed her second master's degree in the Women's Studies program at George Washington University, Washington, DC, in 1991. Henriquez is the author of the books *Kòrsou su muhénan pionero* (Curaçao's women pioneers, 2002) and *Historia oral ta historia di pueblo* (Oral history is people's history, 2013) and the editor of a series of historical films. In 2015, she was awarded the Cross of Merit from the government of Curaçao for her activism for women and the Afro-Curaçaoan community.

Wigbertson Julian Isenia
is assistant professor of anthropology at the University of Amsterdam. His work focuses on the concepts of gendered and sexual cultures by analyzing cultural practices such as archives, literature, theater and cultural performance. He cocurated the 2019 exhibition *Nos tei* (We are here) as well as a response to the exhibition "With Pride" and "House of HIV" in 2021, which commemorated forty years of Dutch HIV and AIDS activism. He is coeditor of the special issue

"Sexual Politics between the Netherlands and the Caribbean: Imperial Entanglements and Archival Desires" in *Tijdschrift voor Genderstudies* (2019).

Nanette de Jong
is professor of socially-engaged ethnomusicology at Newcastle University and a research fellow with the University of South Africa. Her research centers on the impact of decolonization and related issues of positionality and power on Black music across Africa and the African diaspora. She is the editor of *The Cambridge Companion to Caribbean Music* (2022) and author of *Tambú: Curaçao's African-Caribbean Ritual and the Politics of Memory* (2012) as well as numerous articles and book chapters, including explorations into the remembrances of homeland among Caribbean and African migrants, diasporic musical fusions and music interventions around HIV stigma and gender inequality in southern Africa.

Lucia Kelly
is a social worker and has headed a community development NGO in Aruba focused on women's empowerment for over three decades. In the 1970s and 1980s, Kelly was active in women's rights groups and the campaign for equal pay for women. She has published studies in the field of cultural heritage with the Aruban National Archives, including *Participacion di muhénan Arubano na e proceso laboral den e periodo 1900–1927* (Aruban women's participation in labor processes 1900–1927, 1999) and *Custumbernan rond di embraso y dunamento di lus na cuminsamento di sieglo 20* (Customs around pregnancy and birth in the early twentieth century, 2005).

Paula Kibbelaar
is lecturer, researcher and policy worker focusing on sustainable inclusive development within the context of the Kingdom of the Netherlands at the Aruban Teacher Training College. She was founding dean and associate professor at the Faculty of Arts and Sciences at the University of Aruba (2009–2013). Her research interests include diversity, equity and inclusion, SDGs, Dutch Caribbean Island studies, financial and economic security, organization and governance research. She is a board member of the Gender Steering Committee in Aruba and Women In International Security. She obtained her PhD in 2005 at the Utrecht University School of Governance.

Mario Kleinmoedig
is cofounder and spokesperson of Curaçao's LGBTQ+ foundation FOKO (Fundashon Orguyo Kòrsou/Pride Curaçao Foundation) and its predecessor

Asosiashon Orguyo (The Pride Society). He has been the main spokesperson for LGBTQ+ rights advocacy and awareness since 1996. In 2022, he was honored by the Curaçaoan government with the Cross of Merit for being an activist for close to three decades. He studied social sciences and media studies and has been a journalist and policy officer in the areas of human rights, ecology, culture, education and HIV and substance abuse prevention.

Maria Liberia-Peters
served three terms as prime minister of the Netherlands Antilles (1984–1986, 1988–1990 and 1990–1993), becoming the first elected female head of state in the Kingdom of the Netherlands. During her tenure as prime minister, she worked to build bridges between the English, Spanish and Dutch-speaking Caribbean. She initiated her political career as the first woman appointed in the local executive government of Curaçao in 1975. Liberia-Peters thereafter served as member of parliament and as acting lieutenant governor. In 2017, she was accorded a Lifetime Achievement Award from the Women Political Leaders Forum (Reykjavik) for her contributions to leadership at the highest political level. She is currently a member of the Council of Women World Leaders, an international network of current and former women presidents and prime ministers.

Troetje Loewenthal
teaches Spanish at the University of Curaçao. She was born in Bonaire and spent her childhood in Curaçao, later moving to the Netherlands. She was involved in the black women's movement and was a board member of the black women's information and documentation center Flamboyant. She was strategic policy adviser at E-Quality, an expertise center for gender and ethnicity. She has written columns and articles, a textbook on Spanish grammar and is the coauthor with Meindert Fennema of *La construcción de raza y nación en la República Dominicana* (The construction of race and nation in the Dominican Republic, 1987).

Pedro Pablo Medardo de Marchena († 1968)
was an anticolonial writer and orator, born in 1899 in Curaçao to a Jewish father and Afro-Curaçaoan mother. He travelled to the US where he became acquainted with Marcus Garvey and other black communist activists from the Caribbean. In the late 1920s and 1930s he became known in Curaçao as a public speaker and published articles in local newspapers opposing capitalism and colonial rule. He is most prominently remembered for his pamphlet *Ignorancia ó educando un pueblo* (Ignorance, or educating the people, 1929). He was charged with sedition and placed in an internment camp in Bonaire.

Fridi Martina († 2014)
was a Curaçaoan artist. She trained as an actor at the Academy of Theatre and Dance in Amsterdam in the 1970s and worked for ten years at the HKU University of the Arts in Utrecht. She worked in a diverse range of media as actor, dancer, musician, poet, writer, teacher, trainer, director and producer and was fluent in Papiamentu, Dutch and English. Together with her partner Margareth Adama, she cofounded the theater group Adamaria in 1980 and the intercultural art venue Villa Baranka in Amsterdam. She continued her artistic career in Curaçao after her return in 1997.

Kristen Martina
is a policy adviser on youth affairs at a municipality in the Netherlands. She previously worked on domestic violence and violence against women at Regioplan, a Dutch policy and research bureau. Martina grew up in Curaçao and moved to the Netherlands for her studies. She studied criminology and completed an MA in policy and law enforcement at Leiden University and an MA in intervention criminology at the VU Amsterdam. Her research interests include violence, gender, inclusion and decolonization. She has particular experience with criminological research on the Dutch Caribbean (diasporic) community.

Jacqueline Martis
is a trainer in gender-based violence and human rights and researcher in gender studies. She works for the government of Curaçao and teaches sociology at the Police Academy. Martis received her master's degree in sociology from the New School for Social Research in New York. She has researched and published on trafficking in persons in the Netherlands Antilles for the International Organization for Migration and on sex and tourism in Curaçao and St. Maarten with a contribution to the volume *Sun, Sex and Gold: Tourism and Sex Work in the Caribbean* (ed. Kamala Kempadoo, 1999).

Stella Pieters Kwiers
is a cultural anthropologist and international development specialist who worked as senior researcher for the United Nations in sub-Saharan Africa, Latin America and Asia. She studied international development at Fordham University and cultural anthropology at Columbia University. She is the author of *Afrika, un kontinente yen di sorpresa* (Africa, a continent full of surprises, 2023), *Nos kultura* (Our culture, 2022), *Famia i spiritualidat* (Family and spirituality, 2011), *Kreensianan afrikano* (African beliefs, 2000), *A Woman Alone: My Twenty Years of Work as a Single Woman in Developing Countries* (1996) and *N'Sobolo Balari: The Balari on the Road to Change* (1983).

Gladys J. do Rego-Kuster

is a writer and editor, with contributions and columns in diverse Papiamentu-language media, including *Bosero* magazine (1977–1984), *Agenda U.M.A.* (1981–1983); "Dos plaka di palabra" (Can I say something?) (*Extra*, 1982–1984) and the radio program "Bati Bleki" (To gossip) (Curom/Z86, 1985–1987). She was president of the Union di Muhé Antiano (Union of Antillean Women, UMA) from 1975 to 1986, local representative of the Caribbean Association for Feminist Research and Action (1985–1989) and head of the Center for Information and Education on Sexuality and Pregnancy, Maternity Clinic Rio Canario (Sentro INFESE) from 1992 to 2002.

Linda Richardson

has been active in the field of education for over four decades. She served as minister of education, culture and women's affairs for the government of the Netherlands Antilles. She was head of the Windward Islands' section of the Antillean Linguistics Institute, president of the University of St. Martin and interim head of the insular department of education. She founded the women's theater group The Oualichi Players in St. Maarten. She is a sworn translator and interpreter for the Joint Court of Justice for the islands of the Dutch Caribbean. Richardson was awarded two honorary doctorates for her contributions to education.

Yolanda Richardson

is lecturer in the Faculty of Arts and Science at the University of Aruba. After obtaining her degree in political science at Leiden University, she worked for the island territory of St. Maarten and the government of Aruba. In 2008, she co-organized the exhibition on Aruban slavery heritage at the National Archaeological Museum of Aruba. She also served as researcher for the temporary exhibition *Rancho – nos bario* (Rancho – our neighborhood) at the same museum. She currently researches migrants of the Dutch Leeward Islands and their descendants in Aruba and Curaçao.

Angela E. Roe

is a Dutch and Curaçaoan anthropologist, lecturer, writer and filmmaker. She coordinates and teaches a minor in sustainable business at The Hague University of Applied Science. Her research interests revolve around race relations, identity, colonial heritage, the African diaspora and social and environmental sustainability. In 2014, Roe produced and directed *Sombra di koló* (The shadow of color), a feature documentary on race relations in Curaçao, which was awarded the Boeli van Leeuwen prize in 2015. Roe completed her PhD in global and sociocultural studies at Florida International University and holds MA degrees in cultural anthropology and comparative sociology.

Jessica V. Roitman
is full professor of Jewish studies at the Vrije Universiteit Amsterdam. She received her PhD in Jewish history from Leiden University. Her first book deals with intercultural trade and the Sephardi community of early seventeenth century Amsterdam. Subsequently, she has worked on the history of Jews in the Atlantic world, Caribbean Jewry, the history of (Dutch) colonialism in the Caribbean, slavery, free people of color and the intersections of race, religion and colonialism in the Americas. Her current research looks at the interaction of "minority" groups with each other in colonial spaces.

Louis Philippe M. Römer
is a lecturer at Vassar College whose research and teaching lie at the intersection of linguistic anthropology, political anthropology, media studies, Caribbean studies, Latin American studies and Africana studies. His research focuses on populism, language and media and the construction of decolonial and anti-capitalist political futures. Römer is currently working on a book titled *Strategic Ambiguities: Race, Class, and Populism on the Caribbean Airwaves*, an analysis of how politicians and activists engage in populist discourse on talk radio to redefine racial and class identities, build coalitions and reshape the public imagination of what is politically possible.

Nolda Römer-Kenepa
is a Curaçaoan historian and was an archivist with the National Archives from 1980 to 2013. She was appointed national archivist of the Netherlands Antilles in 1991. She spearheaded the organization of the National Archives, the evaluation of the archival diploma, the realization of the national ordinance on archives and the construction of a modern archive depot. She was president of the Caribbean regional branch of the International Council on Archives (2001–2006) and vice-president of the International Council on Archives (2006–2012). She served as acting governor of Curaçao from 2013 to 2019. She was knighted in the Order of Orange-Nassau in 2013.

Wim Rutgers
is professor emeritus in literary history and philology with a focus on Papiamentu at the University of Curaçao. He received an MA in literary studies and completed his PhD at Utrecht University. He has taught courses and published widely in the areas of Caribbean, Antillean and Aruban literature. He has long

been a literary reviewer in the local press in Aruba and Curaçao. He is the author of textbooks and manuals on literature for different educational levels. He was born in the Netherlands and lives in Aruba.

Chelsea Schields
is associate professor of history at the University of California, Irvine. Her scholarship explores the entwined histories of sexuality, race, energy and empire in the twentieth-century Caribbean and Europe. She is the author of *Offshore Attachments: Oil and Intimacy in the Caribbean* (2023) and, with Dagmar Herzog, coeditor of *The Routledge Companion to Sexuality and Colonialism* (2021).

Crisèn Schorea
is a sociologist by profession and a writer, singer-songwriter and actress in her heart and soul. In 2017, she published her first poetry book in Papiamentu titled *Sinti mi sintí*. The verb *sinti* means "to feel," while the noun *sintí* means both "the feeling" as well as "the brain." *Sinti mi sintí* reflects the constant courtship taking place in her head between her reason and emotions. In 2018, she released her first album titled *Morde mi, kome mi* (Bite me, eat me). She lives and works in Curaçao.

Vincent Sleebe
is a social historian who has published on various aspects of Dutch social history. He currently works as archivist for the Dutch city of 's-Hertogenbosch. In the 1990s, he was a member of the editorial board of *XL*, the magazine of COC, an organization for LGBTQ+ rights in the Netherlands.

Imelda Valerianus-Fermina (†2005)
was a poet and writer who also went by the name Shon Me. Her poetry collections in Papiamentu include *Mi pensamentu* (My thoughts, 1985) and *Komunikashon* (Communication, 1988). She also wrote *Mente i kurason* (Mind and heart, 1990), the short story collection *Bolo pretu* (Black cake, 1992) and acted in the film *Almacita di desolato*, directed by Felix de Rooy (1986). She was actively involved in the women's suffrage movement in Curaçao in the 1940s and often invited to recite poetry during International Women's Day celebrations on March 8 and commemorations of the slave resistance on August 17.

Philie van Veen
is an independent consultant supporting nonprofit organizations and governments in policy development in Curaçao. Her work focuses on individual and organizational development. Important themes for her are patterns of oppression and victimization, transcultural communication and cooperation as well

as personal and professional leadership. She obtained degrees in developmental psychology and learning and development and various professional and managerial qualifications in the field of education and development. Van Veen grew up in an interracial family of eight children in Aruba, Curaçao and the Netherlands.

Imelda van West-Davelaar (†2009)
was an active member of the National People's Party (Partido Nashonal di Pueblo, PNP) and one of the founding figures of the Damanan di Djárason (Wednesday Women), an organization that was active in the 1940s. Also known by the name of Mena, she grew up in a working-class environment in Willemstad, Curaçao, and worked as a hairdresser and ran various small businesses. She was married to Frits van West, a former worker of the Royal Dutch Steamship Company (Koninklijke Nederlandse Scheepvaart Maatschappij, KNSM).

Evelyn Wever-Croes
is the first female prime minister of Aruba, having entered into her second term in 2021. She is the leader of the Movimiento Electoral di Pueblo party (People's Electoral Movement, MEP) and was first elected member of parliament in 2009. Wever-Croes studied law at the former University of the Netherlands Antilles and Leiden University, specializing in tax law. She served the tax authorities of Aruba (1994–2004) and was tax adviser in the firm Croes Wever Tchong. In 2021, Wever-Croes was awarded an honorary degree by the Xavier University of Medicine in Aruba for her leadership efforts during the COVID-19 pandemic.

Editors' Introduction

Rose Mary Allen and Sruti Bala

1 Why This Volume?

The *Handbook of Gender Studies in the Dutch Caribbean* seeks to introduce readers to five decades of scholarship, historical source texts and literary and cultural production from the six Caribbean islands of the Kingdom of the Netherlands in the broad terrain of gender studies. The selection of texts in this volume foregrounds voices from the region and features key texts that illuminate the diversity and complexity of gender history, culture and politics in these islands.

The volume is part of a research project on cultural practices of citizenship in the Dutch Caribbean, a collaboration between the University of Curaçao and the University of Amsterdam from 2017 to 2023.[1] The project examined citizenship in Curaçao and Bonaire from the intertwined perspectives of culture and gender. Departing from theoretical frameworks that regard citizenship not only as a legal category but also as a concept informed by cultural practices, the research examined how especially marginalized citizens articulate their struggles for political subjectivity, focusing on women and sexual minorities in the islands. The need for a broader historical overview and for taking stock of existing approaches in the region provided the motivation to publish this research and reference resource for studying gender in the Dutch Caribbean islands of Aruba, Bonaire, Curaçao, Saba, St. Eustatius and St. Maarten.

While the constellation of the "Dutch Caribbean" is itself mainly a category of governance and, similar to the "Kingdom of the Netherlands,"[2] by no means unproblematic (more on that below), it nevertheless represents an under-researched region of the broader Caribbean as well as an often overlooked part of the kingdom, most acutely in discussions of questions relating to

---

1 The research project "Cultural practices of citizenship under conditions of fragmented sovereignty: gendered and sexual citizenship in Curaçao and Bonaire" was funded by the Dutch Research Council (Nederlandse Organisatie voor Wetenschappelijk Onderzoek, NWO) in the framework of their Caribbean research program.

2 Since October 10, 2010, the Kingdom of the Netherlands consists of four constituent countries: the Netherlands, Aruba, Curaçao and St. Maarten. The so-called "BES" islands, Bonaire St. Eustatius and Saba fall under the jurisdiction of the Netherlands.

 | DOI:10.1163/9789004690882_002

gender. Although there is a well-established gender studies tradition in the Caribbean at large, with journals, book series, research institutions and networks in the English, French and Spanish-speaking Caribbean, the islands under the jurisdiction of the Netherlands remain an underrepresented subregion in this field of scholarship. The islands of the Dutch Caribbean also receive less scholarly attention in comparison to Suriname. Similarly, the Dutch Caribbean at best receives a peripheral mention in the disciplinary settings of gender studies in the Netherlands. A knowledge of gender-related historical and socio-cultural developments on the islands on the other side of the Atlantic is not mandatory in Dutch school or university curricula. The handbook aspires to fill the enormous knowledge gap regarding the Dutch Caribbean islands and serve as a useful resource for present and future scholars. It seeks to offer a multi-faceted and complex picture of the region and invite further research and study. It is our hope that this volume will feature on reading lists responding to the call for decolonizing the curricula of gender or cultural studies.

2 Studying Gender in the Dutch Caribbean

Gender studies is an increasingly important conceptual arena in the social sciences and humanities. It is an umbrella term for an area of research which attends to the role of gender in various dimensions of human existence. Understood in the broadest sense as the social, historical and cultural arrangements through which meaning and distinction are allocated to biological or sexual differences, gender crucially pervades people's lives on personal, psychic, symbolic and institutional levels. It is ever present in the contours and commonsense understandings of behavior, emotions, and dispositions. Gender distinctions form a core feature of cultural (self)-definitions and of how societies mark who belongs to or is excluded from their purview. Societies are orchestrated in ways that build gender preferences and privileges into their institutional mechanisms.

Historically understood as a binary system, by means of which society socializes and dynamizes biological difference, the operations of gender tend to appear as natural and pre-determined. It has been the task of gender studies to unravel these operations and analyze their underlying mechanisms and power dynamics. Contemporary gender research goes even further, critiquing this binary system that focuses on and thereby reifies differences between male and female or heterosexual and homosexual. It also questions the notion that gender is a social category as opposed to sex being a biological category, instead calling for a historically and contextually nuanced interpretation of how both sex and gender are taxonomized, performed and manifested in a wider spectrum of identities and social situations. In doing so, gender research has augmented an awareness of local gender expressions and struggles.

In the context of the Dutch Caribbean, the study of gender remains closely connected to women's studies. To speak of gender issues thus most often implies speaking of women, turning attention away from men toward women, questioning the universality of the male perspective, or indeed the dominance of a middle-class, heterosexual female perspective, and instead inquiring into historical developments from the perspective of the experiences of women and sexual minorities subject to patriarchal norms. It implies an emphasis on studying women's contributions to public life and to societal development, with a view to influencing policy, knowledge production and challenging stereotypes. Such an approach can thus be reclaimed as an explicitly feminist scholarship as it aims to address gender inequalities and foster greater freedoms. Areas such as labor, migration, reproductive rights, political participation, social movements, sexual violence, education and family or kinship structures form longstanding concerns of feminist scholarship in the Dutch Caribbean and are thus centrally featured in this volume.

The six islands of the Dutch Caribbean must necessarily be understood as deeply tied to the histories and legacies of colonialism and slavery. Any study of gender must therefore take these histories into account. This necessitates an intersectional approach to gender, i.e., an analysis of gender in terms of its intersections with other categories of power, in particular race and class. While many scholars from the islands represented in this volume may be academically trained in universities in the Netherlands or elsewhere in Europe or North America, their approach to researching the Dutch Caribbean has required a recalibration and critique of some of the assumptions of a universalist, i.e., white feminist approach to gender studies. Whether it is sexual violence or the history of social movements or the analysis of masculinity or spirituality, an appraisal of the racialized dimensions of gender and their entanglements with class differences become paramount. It is thus our hope that the studies featured in this volume will inspire and influence scholars in gender studies internationally to pay closer attention to the Dutch Caribbean, not only to learn about its specific historical and contemporary features, but also to learn from the indigenous perspectives and the modalities and forms of intersectional gender studies that emerge from these islands.

3 Problematizing the Dutch Caribbean

The present volume zooms in on the six Caribbean islands of the Kingdom of the Netherlands: the Leeward or "ABC" islands of Aruba, Bonaire and Curaçao, located off the coast of Venezuela in the southern Caribbean and the "sss" or Windward islands of Saba, St. Eustatius and St. Maarten, located almost a thousand kilometers away in the eastern Caribbean. Although they are not all geographically proximate, they have been historically grouped together in one way or another for purposes of governance. As editors we are acutely aware that the geographical and political constellation of the Dutch Caribbean is problematic for historical and social-cultural reasons. It has emerged out of the Dutch colonization of the Caribbean, where the Netherlands was the "colonial motherland" and the islands in the Caribbean, along with Suriname, were once colonized entities and eventually acquired different political and constitutional statuses over time. "Dutch Caribbean" also hardly reflects any linguistic, cultural or social unity, as most people from the islands would rather affiliate themselves with their own islands or by means of a pan-Caribbean or Antillean identity, rather than refer to themselves as "Dutch Caribbean." The reasons for specifically focusing on these six islands thus have less to do with establishing an imagined cultural commonality across the islands, and more to do with addressing the scant attention they have received in gender-related scholarship to date.

The clubbing together of these six islands can be traced back to their unification in 1954 as the Netherlands Antilles under the Charter (*Statuut*) of the Kingdom of the Netherlands, thereby establishing the Netherlands Antilles as an autonomous, i.e., internally self-governing territory within the broader kingdom, next to Suriname and the European part of the Netherlands. In the wake of various international decolonization movements in the twentieth century, which no doubt left their impact on Dutch colonial territories in the Caribbean, the Netherlands Antilles enabled inter-island cooperation of varying intensity in diverse areas of administration and governance, the traces of which remain palpable in the present. The constellation of the Kingdom of the Netherlands has changed several times since the formation of the federation. Suriname became independent in 1975. Aruba separated from the Antillean federation in 1986 to become an autonomous entity within the kingdom. The remaining five islands eventually ceased to exist as the Netherlands Antilles on October 10, 2010, a date popularly referred to as "10/10/10", marking the political dissolution of the Netherlands Antilles. Curaçao and St. Maarten, following Aruba, each obtained the status of autonomous entity within the kingdom, whereas Bonaire, Saba and St. Eustatius became overseas municipalities directly ruled from the Netherlands. The present volume attends to the impact of the constitutional reforms that came to the federation on the islands on issues such as labor and employment rights for women, tourism, the struggles of sexual minorities for social acceptance, asylum policies and the treatment of migrant sex workers.

Questions of (non-)sovereignty and national identity connect the Dutch Caribbean to other parts of the Caribbean, including both the countries that have obtained full independence as well as territories that continue to be governed by France, the UK or the US. As in the rest of the Caribbean, the construction of the Dutch Caribbean islands has taken place in a context in which the historical wounds of colonialism and slavery, with their attendant racial dimensions, are yet to heal. The asymmetrical link to the metropolis and the constraints evolving therefrom have shaped the often-ambivalent attitudes of citizens of the islands towards the Netherlands. Even as people may not desire full political independence for the islands in the near future, the question of what autonomy means for citizens of non-sovereign small islands remains intensely debated and explored, often through cultural and artistic avenues. Of interest to this volume are the gendered dimensions of this question. When the very category of citizen has historically excluded women, the enslaved or formerly enslaved, as well as other subjects deemed as "abnormal" from equal citizenship, deploying arguments based on notions of propriety and respectability, the handbook is interested in analyzing how these discourses emerged and continue to hold ground, albeit under the benevolent mantle of development or in policies toward migrants and asylum seekers.

The differences among the islands and their inter-relations are also of relevance. Curaçao, the largest of the islands and historically the center of Dutch colonial rule, has enjoyed a position of privilege and political dominance relative to the other islands, a fact that especially Aruba and St. Maarten have agitated against. This dominance extends to the realm of knowledge production in the humanities and social sciences, where there is far more research on Curaçao in comparison to other islands. Our strategy in composing the handbook has been to include a broader range of topics and purposefully invite new contributions from the other islands wherever possible, simultaneously acknowledging that this inter-island disparity needs more time and dedicated research and can hardly be adequately redressed with just one volume.

4 Introduction to the Four Sections of the Handbook

The selection of texts in this volume includes both academic writings as well as a range of other valuable resources for gender research in the Dutch Caribbean, such as primary historical sources, speeches, extracts from personal memoirs, poetry and other literary writings. We imagine the book as a solid first entry point into the field, offering readers selections from established and much-cited scholars, respected prominent activists as well as a younger generation of scholars and feminist activists. In addition to prioritizing the translation of texts from Papiamentu and Dutch, hitherto unavailable in English, we also invited scholars to contribute to specific themes and areas. The texts in the volume represent a wide – though by no means exhaustive – range of viewpoints and methodological approaches in gender studies, including oral history, ethnography, archival research, discourse analysis and sociological research. We have prioritized qualitative and interpretive approaches over quantitative studies, not least guided and limited by our own disciplinary expertise as editors. The volume is divided into four thematic sections, which however intersect in many ways. The division of sections is by no means watertight, as authors repeatedly address issues in sections other than the ones their contributions have been slotted in. We thus view these sections as being in conversation with each other and have included editors' notes indicating overlaps and convergences between contributions.

We would like to add a note on language here. For the sake of consistency, the language Papiamentu is uniformly spelt throughout the volume, although we are mindful of the fact that distinctions are made between "Papiamentu" in Curaçao and "Papiamento" in Aruba; these are highlighted wherever appropriate. We have avoided racialized terminology to the greatest extent possible, with the exception of texts by deceased authors and in instances where it was necessary to stay close to their historical usage, acknowledging that these terms are pejoratively connoted today. Older publications have been minimally edited for purposes of linguistic clarity.

5 Section 1: *Gender, History and Society*

The first section introduces readers to critical moments in women's history in the Dutch Caribbean on the one hand and appraises the gendered dimensions of colonial and postcolonial historiography on the other. The contributions in this section are ordered chronologically from the eighteenth century to the present. What were women's daily lives, social relations and working conditions like under colonialism and slavery? How were gender relations monitored and disciplined? Nolda Römer-Kenepa examines the differences and commonalities in the daily lives of white, colored and enslaved women in Curaçao in the eighteenth and nineteenth centuries. Jessica Roitman uses an archival case of an eighteenth-century dispute involving adultery to shed light on gender relations in the Portuguese Jewish community of Curaçao. Ryan

Espersen investigates trade, census and emancipation documents from Saba to interpret how gendering and racialization intersected in the lives of African-descended Saban women.

The section features for the first time in English translation a 1934 pamphlet originally written in Papiamentu by the anti-colonial orator and writer Pedro Pablo Medardo de Marchena, wherein he challenges the conservative social order and calls for integrating women into the quest for modernity. Margo Groenewoud introduces the text and contextualizes Marchena's political career, including his interactions with the black communist labor movement and Marcus Garvey's organization in the US.

Another remarkable historical document is a speech by Imelda van West-Davelaar, a founding figure of the Damanan di Djárason (Wednesday Women), a women's organization that campaigned for women's suffrage and social emancipation in Curaçao in the 1940s, wherein she proudly commends the women for seven years of involvement in struggles for liberation.

Aruban women's protests against the brothel called Campo Alegre (Happy Camp) in the 1950s present an interesting instance of the differences between the islands. Whereas the "camp" for sex workers from abroad was legalized and even supported by the Catholic church in Curaçao in the late 1940s and regarded as economically necessary, as well as for keeping public immorality and the spread of venereal diseases in check, Lucia Kelly charts a rather different dynamic in Aruba, where years of coordinated women's protests led to the dismantling of the camp on the island. Protests against similar camps for migrant sex workers in Bonaire also feature in the contribution by Rose Mary Allen, Liliane de Geus and Judith Brekelmans. Using oral history interviews with three generations of women, the contribution charts various turning points in the women's movement in Bonaire, thereby offering glimpses into a longer history that is intertwined with developments in Latin America and other parts of the Caribbean.

In another contribution, Groenewoud offers an extended examination of the strategies adopted by women's suffrage movements in the 1930s and 1940s and traces the legacies of these movements in various phases of women's activism in Curaçao throughout the twentieth century. Jacqueline Martis approaches the subject from the perspective of policy and legal reform, examining institutional shifts, policies and actions taken by governments both on central and island territory levels in dealing with women's equality and rights. Stella Pieters Kwiers zooms in on the pioneering role of the Women's Development Center (SEDA) in setting the agenda for governmental action on women's rights in the Dutch Caribbean as well as in transforming the public perception and understanding of women's issues. Gladys do Rego-Kuster's contribution situates the women's movement in relation to the broader societal changes in the wake of the uprising of May 1969 in Curaçao, focusing on the struggle to abolish the National Ordinance on Material Civil Servants Law, which legally incapacitated women.

The section concludes with a seminal text by the late feminist scholar, Sonia M. Cuales, reflecting on the task of memory in recuperating and reviving a women's history of the Dutch Caribbean islands. Methodologically it traces the historical shift in research from an outsider perspective on gender to critical, self-reflexive studies that view the researcher and the researched as equal partners.

6 Section II: *Gender, Race, Class and Coloniality*

The second section grapples with questions of gender in relation to class identity, heritage, and the legacies of colonialism and slavery in the contemporary moment. If the first section mainly featured the work of historians, this second section foregrounds scholarship of anthropologists and sociologists. Racialization, labor and migration form three thematic clusters in this section. Opening with a poem addressed to the mansions (Lanthùis) of the former slave owners, a prominent architectural feature and tourist destination of the islands of the Dutch Caribbean, the feminist poet Crisèn Schorea sardonically teases out their supposed innocence and recalls the history and legacy of colonialism and slavery that they stand for.

The relation to Indigenous histories in Bonaire is the focus of Oliver Antczak's contribution, which uses the concept of the *Sentimento Indjan* to reflect on how Indigenous legacies are memorialized and remembered on the island, whereby physical features such as long hair exceed gender stereotypes and become markers of an Indigenous identity. How are colonial power structures reinforced or resisted in the realm of intimate relations? Angela Roe investigates this question through digging into family narratives, colonial ledgers and news clippings to explore how gender and race are entangled in the distribution of power in the colony. Troetje Loewenthal's contribution is based on a lecture originally delivered at a women's studies conference in 1983. It offers insights into the rifts and transformations in women's studies and in feminist movements in the Netherlands against the backdrop of the rise of right-wing political parties that explicitly embraced a racist and anti-immigrant ideology.

The gendered dimensions of labor and the impact of labor opportunities especially on women's lives is another concern of this section. In a groundbreaking study undertaken in 1977, the late Sonia M. Cuales investigated the impact of labor opportunities on the lives of women employed by Texas

Instruments, an American electronics company which established its factory in Curaçao in 1968. Jeanne Henriquez explores the daily lives of working-class women in Curaçao in the 1990s, inquiring into their attitudes toward different forms of oppression. Analyzing their writings on the mother–child relationship, Henriquez problematizes attitudes toward single motherhood and the barriers faced by unsupported female-headed households. Paula Kibbelaar employs the concept of the glass ceiling to investigate the reasons for women's underrepresentation in managerial positions in business and government enterprises in Curaçao, with recent changes in labor regulations in Aruba offering promising positive developments for gender equity in the labor market. Yolanda Richardson's contribution on the daily lives of the Rancho neighborhood in Aruba offers a picture of the changes that the traditional fishing community underwent, the memories of people's involvements in political and labor struggles in the 1940s and 1950s as well as the unique relations of the community to the coastline.

The effects of migration on gender relations extend from transformations in law and governance following the dissolution of the Netherlands Antilles in 2010 to violence in intimate partner relations. Kristen Martina's contribution belongs to a larger body of work in criminology on domestic and partner violence among diasporic communities from the Dutch Caribbean. It employs the concepts of machismo and marianismo to assess the relationship between gender and emotion regulation in partner violence. Beatriz César Loureiro's contribution considers Venezuelan mass migration and its correlation with human trafficking and sex work in Curaçao, revealing the urgent need for a humane migration policy.

The section concludes with contributions from former prime minister of Curaçao, Maria Liberia-Peters and current prime minister of Aruba, Evelyn Wever-Croes. We invited them to reflect on what being the first female head of state of Curaçao and Aruba respectively implies for their political leadership and what their aspirations for gender justice are.

7 Section III: *Gender and Sexuality*

The third section features a range of texts about the interplay between gender and sexuality in the politics of integrating the islands into the kingdom. The adoption of legislation concerning equality in the realm of sexual and reproductive health as well as rights for women and sexual minorities following the model of the European sites of the Kingdom of the Netherlands is one aspect of the social transformations accompanying constitutional reforms on the islands. Same-sex marriage laws, sex work, abortion, adoption, euthanasia and surrogacy rights are all regulated on the model of Dutch laws in the Dutch Caribbean. Even if the local island government does not legally offer the possibility of same-sex marriage on its territory, as is presently the case in Curaçao, it has an obligation to ratify and acknowledge marriages performed in the rest of the kingdom. The implementation of legislative frameworks on the islands based on the European Dutch model is celebrated by some as the long-awaited arrival of a universal rights-based citizenship and regarded by others as a re-colonization by the Dutch without popular legitimation. Between these two extremes lies a vast knowledge gap relating to the specific processes of transformation and cultural histories of the islands.

The section features discussions of the transformations in the rights of sexual minorities and the ways their struggles have taken shape over the decades. Chelsea Schields closely reads the political discourses in the run-up to the first same-sex marriage officially performed in the Caribbean on the island of Saba in 2012, arguing that although politicians were keen to integrate same-sex marriage rights into legislation, they simultaneously blocked economic rights, thus de facto disadvantaging Caribbean sexual minorities. Vincent Sleebe charts the emergence of an organized voice for the rights of homosexuals in Curaçao in the 1990s and comments on the cultural and linguistic peculiarities surrounding the place of gays, lesbians and trans* persons on the island. Mario Kleinmoedig self-critically reflects on his journey as long-time LGBTQ+ activist in Curaçao, arguing that queer emancipation has for long been understood by local activists to be about personal emancipation and self-identification and not enough about societal, communal and intersectional emancipation of the collective self. Wigbertson Julian Isenia reviews the state of research on trans* and same-sex loving people in the Dutch Caribbean, offering readers an annotated overview of key studies since the 1950s and proposing avenues for future research.

The politics of respectability and (in)visibility form another thematic cluster within this section. Rose Mary Allen asks how, on the one hand, colonial cultural and institutional policies shaped the gender attitudes and behaviors of black working-class men and women in Curaçao after the abolition of slavery in 1863, and how, on the other hand, the quest for class mobility and social acceptability was expressed through notions such as *drecha bida* (to morally improve one's life). Aart G. Broek analyzes the depiction of female same-sex desire in Papiamentu-language serial novels in the first half of the twentieth century, arguing that they provide evidence of non-conforming forms of relationships existent on the islands in colonial times, albeit presented in a distorted manner. In what way do practices of naming become practices of self-liberation? The late feminist scholar Joceline Clemencia explores this question through discussions of the attitudes of different generations of women and men toward homosocial and homoerotic relations, arguing for the importance of the right to reject categories such as "lesbian" and use indirect, coded language in naming sexual practices and preferences. Louis Römer takes inspiration from the work of Clemencia and her engagement with the late anthropologist and public intellectual Elis Juliana to investigate the importance of *forma di papia* (ways of speaking), understood as a stylized language practice informed by poetic structures and discursive norms, in the study of sexuality in the context of the Dutch Caribbean.

In addition to these texts, the third section features poems by Lysanne Charles, Frida Domacassé, Gilbert Bacilio and Crisèn Schorea, which speak of the experiences of coming out and navigating social norms and of their intimate relationship with the islands.

8 Section IV: *Gender, the Arts and Popular Culture*

The fourth and final section of this volume showcases perspectives on gender through the lens of literary, artistic and popular cultural expressions. Elisabeth Echteld and Wim Rutgers offer an inventory and historical contextualization of women's literary production in the Leeward and Windward Islands of the Dutch Caribbean, highlighting key studies and recurring thematic concerns. The late Joceline Clemencia analyzes the life and work of the Tambú singer and poet Elia Isenia, discussing how she challenged the male-dominated cultural field through her songs and poetry. Tambú and the ritual's deity, Princess Diyani, is central to Nanette De Jong's contribution, which examines the complex relation between history and myth and how the deity allows practitioners to destabilize the masculine narratives surrounding Tambú. Jean Antoine-Dunne engages with three films of the Curaçaoan artist Felix de Rooy, exploring the relation between sexuality and spirituality in a postcolonial context.

The section features an extract from the play "Chakutoe" by playwright and poet Gilbert "Gibi" Bacilio, based on the life of Felix Chakutoe, who led the harbor strike of 1922 in Curaçao and mobilized youth and women from the working classes to revolt against the authority of the church. In a poetic and autoethnographic essay, Nadia Dresscher-Lambertus uses the *calco* or Caribbean queen conch as an inspiration to articulate her relationship to her ancestors, to her native island of Aruba and to the life forces of the ocean. A poem and a literary essay by Fridi Martina, introduced by Philie van Veen, speak to the fraught relationship of the writer to the island and to the Netherlands and to the quest for freedom through language and writing. Writer, former education minister and court interpreter Linda Richardson reflects on her involvement in various cultural activities in St. Maarten, starting from her founding of *The Oualichi Players*, a women's theater group. Anthropologist and folklore researcher Eric Eliason traces the history of Saba lace, its importance for Sabans through the late nineteenth and twentieth centuries, pointing to the social hierarchies and gendered divisions of labor that the craft laid bare. The volume closes with the well-known poem "Muhé" by the late Imelda Valerianus-Fermina celebrating defiant and resilient womanhood.

We hope this handbook will be widely used and remain a key resource for all future scholars of gender and culture in the Dutch Caribbean. The volume strives to contribute to ever-expanding knowledge about the region and to a meaningful inclusion of the islands in transnational gender studies scholarship.

SECTION 1

Gender, History and Society

CHAPTER 1

Curaçaoan Women in the Late Eighteenth and Early Nineteenth Centuries

Nolda Römer-Kenepa

Abstract

Using travelogs, colonial records and municipal archives, this contribution traces and reconstructs the living conditions of women in Curaçao in the eighteenth and nineteenth centuries, including both white women and women born into slavery. The sources offer insights into women's daily lives, working conditions and social relations. The author concludes that women in this patriarchal society worked hard and sought independence despite social barriers, and that women, white and black alike, despite belonging to different social classes, suffered different kinds of oppression. White women, although the more privileged, suffered legal, social and sexual limitations. Colored, black and enslaved women, on the other hand, experienced racial discrimination as well as economic and sexual exploitation. This contribution challenges the male perspectives inherent in the historical sources, arguing that they do not entirely correspond with the reality of most women's lives, especially the most exploited groups of enslaved and freed women.

Keywords

enslaved women – white women – living conditions – eighteenth and nineteenth century – Curaçao

The following is based to a great extent on works by authors of the late eighteenth and early nineteenth centuries: travelogs, descriptions and official reports by civil servants on the situation on our island.[1] We shall look here at

1 Algemeen Rijksarchief (former name of the National Archives, hereafter referred to as ARA), Archive of the States General until 1795, inv. 9425, Memorie van de West-Indische Compagnie, Willem August Syrtema van Grovinstins en Willem Cornelis Boey op het rapport van

 | DOI:10.1163/9789004690882_003

the writers' views on women and relate them to the position of women in a society underpinned by slavery.[2]

At the end of the eighteenth century and up to the middle of the nineteenth century, Curaçao was known for its division into separate self-contained population groups based on economic and legal positions as well as skin color. There were three main groupings: white citizens, freed people and enslaved people. It is therefore necessary to describe the status of women in each of these groups in order to form a picture of their lives.

1 Women of the White Citizenry

Women of Western European Protestant origin and women of Portuguese Jewish origin belonged to the white citizenry. The Protestant women were further divided into two status groups depending on their family's economic position. In the upper classes were the wives of planters and the wives of senior government officials, military officers and wealthy merchants. The lower class of Protestant women included the wives of junior civil servants and soldiers, small businessmen, sailors and artisans.

The wives of planters lived in mansions on the plantations where all the work was done by enslaved people. They lived on what their plantations produced, which in fact, in many cases, was not all that much. Among the planters, there were also those whose main income came from trade, carried out from their second homes in the city, where they lived. For Curaçao's elite, therefore, possession of a plantation with a country house and staff of enslaved people was not only a means of income but a status symbol.

The wives of senior government officials, military officers and wealthy merchants were also the most prominent citizens and formed the social circle of the island's director or governor. As far as possible, marriage to someone of lower status was avoided. Many women married newly arrived military men and civil servants, who were then immediately taken in by the group. Most of the upper-class Protestants lived in the city—what is today Punda—and a number of them owned country houses.

---

de commissarissen van Prins Willem V naar de koloniën van de Staat in West-Indië inzake het veranderen van de regeringsvormen aldaar [Memorandum by the West Indian Company, Willem August Syrtema van Grovinstins and Willem Cornelis Boey, on the report by the commissioner to Prins Willem V on the state colonies in the West Indies regarding the changes to the government structure], 1792.

2 ARA, Verspreide West-Indische stukken, inv. 792. Rapport W. A. S. Grovinstins, W. C. Boey, 1791.

The wives of more junior civil servants, small businessmen, sailors and tradesmen lived in what is now Otrobanda, on the other side of the city. Although their superior economic position meant the upper-class Protestants kept themselves apart from the lower-class Protestants, the lower classes still considered themselves as being among the leading citizens on the ground that they, too, were white-skinned and therefore enjoyed higher status than dark-skinned people. Lower-class women were occasionally chosen as wives by higher-class Protestant men, which gave those women the opportunity to change their status but led to a shortage of marriageable lower-class Protestant women. As a result of that, lower-class Protestant men began to marry women from the Latin-American population.

The other group of white women were the Portuguese Jews. As the wives of the island's wealthiest traders, shipowners and insurers, those women were members of a second aristocratic elite, alongside the upper-class Protestants. However, there was no social contact at all between the two elite groups. In fact, a stretch of water between them in the center of the city meant that Protestants and Jews lived separately from each other in Scharloo, and, in Pietermaai, the Jews lived outside the city gate. The Jews did not have full citizens' rights until 1824 and, being non-Calvinists, could not work in the civil service. For Jewish women, marriage to non-Jews was similarly out of the question.[3]

2 Freed Women

The group of freed people included both brown and black women. These freed people made up a sizable part of the population of Curaçao in this period. There were 2,776 freed people in 1789 and, by 1816, that number had increased to 7,329. Freed people were also divided into status groups based both on the economic positions they assumed and skin color. The division according to skin color came about because the white people in authority used it as a distinguishing feature for social categorization.

Freed colored and black people were recorded as strictly separate groups in official sources.[4] There were even separate colored and black citizen militias, with a group of lighter-skinned people among the colored group, most of whom were related to Jews and who had found in trade and craftsmanship a chance to improve their positions. They were described as *voorname kleurlingen*

3 Editors' note: see contribution by Roitman in this section.

4 Editors' note: we have opted to translate racialized terms such as *kleurlingen* with "colored" to stay close to their historical usage and acknowledge their pejorative connotations.

(prominent coloreds). Here, it was indeed skin color that prevented them from occupying the same social position as the lower-class Protestants and excluded them from social contact with both Jews and Protestants.

Among the "prominent coloreds" were women from the coastal areas of Latin America because they tried to keep this group as light-skinned as possible by marrying mestizos from the mainland if there were no other suitable candidates. Prominent colored women were able to raise their status by marrying men from among the lower-class Protestants. Like the Jews, the more prominent colored people chose to live in Pietermaai or Scharloo.

Ordinary colored people included those who came from poor families of agricultural workers, people who worked for artisans, shop assistants, sailors or fishermen as well as unmarried women who did any and all sorts of work to earn a living. The latter could change their status by marrying colored men from a higher-status group. By entering into a relationship with a white man and bearing his children, a woman could improve her own economic position, at least if the man took care of the children. In this way, too, change of status could be effected, for a poor woman could join the ranks of the more distinguished colored group either by such a relationship with a white man or by contracting a formal marriage with a distinguished man of color.

Ordinary colored people lived in small houses in and outside the city, or in rural areas.

Freed black women were distinguished from colored people by their "pure" African descent and, therefore, the darkest skin color. They belonged to the lowest status group. Their economic position was as weak as that of freed colored people of ordinary status. While they had the same chances as the colored people to better their economic position by marrying men of higher status or embarking on relationships with white men, they would still belong to the lowest status group because of their skin color. Only their children—being colored—had a chance of moving up in this hierarchical society.

3 Enslaved Women

It is difficult to discover the precise geographical origins of enslaved people. The countries and places mentioned are usually related to the territories on the African west coast, where the West India Company held a monopoly on slave trading: in modern-day Ghana, Congo and Angola. It is of course highly likely that not all enslaved people came from coastal areas but were captured deep inland and transported to the west coast. It is certain, however, that, right from the start, there was a great diversity of ethnicities, languages and cultures among the enslaved.

In the terms of the international slave trade, fully certified enslaved persons of 1.65 m in height, estimated to be between fifteen and thirty-five years old and "without physical defects," were certified as *pieza de Indias*, which assured their status as "salable goods." A number of enslaved women were also certified as *pieza de Indias*. Their value was determined by their number of children. Enslaved people with physical disabilities were known as *macarons*, derived from the Spanish word *macarse*, meaning spoiled or rotten.

Among the enslaved people, there were two criteria to determine their status: the type of work they had to perform and their skin color. The categories were so-called household, artisan, garden or plantation slaves.

Persons enslaved in households were of the highest status. This was because of their close contact with their enslavers. Some enslaved women working in the house developed close and intimate relationships with their enslavers. Other enslaved people looked up to them. The next best status was that of the enslaved artisan, whose trade was a source of income for his master. Enslaved artisans enjoyed the greatest liberty because they were often hired out, and a man might even work entirely independently on condition that he pay his master a daily or weekly sum. Enslaved gardeners and plantation workers were of the lowest status, being required to perform agricultural labor on the plantations or to tend cattle. They had the least liberty, having to work under the eye of a slave overseer.

Skin color came to be the second distinguishing category of enslaved people because enslaved women were also subject to sexual abuse. The children begotten by the white masters were in many cases favored by those fathers, being given easier work or allowed to learn a trade, while darker-skinned people had to do the heavier work on the plantation. It was from here that status differences came about between women enslaved in households and on the land. Enslaved household servants working in the master's house and who were required to assume responsibility for the care of the children of the house tended to have lighter skin. Such women were put to "light women's work," such as pottery, spinning yarn, sewing and repairing clothes and weaving baskets and hats.

Enslaved women working in the fields were required to do a certain amount of plantation work as well as take on the burden of feeding and clothing the male plantation workers and caring for the enslaved children. The women plantation workers lived in small dwellings on the edges of the plantation, while the enslaved domestic servants lived in the mansion or, if they worked in the city, with their master in his house there. Marriage was forbidden for all enslaved people. The master could designate a man with whom an enslaved woman could beget strong and healthy children. For the enslaved, there could be no status improvement through marriage.

4 Education

Little attention was paid to the development of girls and women. For each social group, there was a one-room private school in or near Willemstad, most of them run by a single individual from home and which could educate only an extremely limited number of pupils. The first official regulation on education, in 1819, stipulated the establishment of two public schools, and both public and private schools were attended only by boys of the white citizenry. The great majority of the population—most white women as well as all free and enslaved people of color—were deprived of any form of education.

The wealthy could afford domestic tutors who lived in one of the houses on the plantations but attended a small number of other families too, visiting at appointed times, rather like the doctor. This represented the only chance for girls from the upper classes to acquire any sort of education. Their mothers were always present as chaperones so that girls never had any opportunity to meet others of their own age. As a result of this isolation, these young women displayed a profound timidity.

In 1842, the Roman Catholic sisters of Rozendaal established their nondenominational schools especially for girls. Here, all girls from any class and any religion could receive an education free of charge. There were lessons in the Dutch language, reading, writing, drawing and useful handicrafts. Women's education emphasized their role in reproduction and propagating the species and for caring for others within the family context.[5]

5 Upbringing

Girls in white, bourgeois families grew up in a sort of isolation. Friendship, especially with girls from lower classes, was seen as abnormal and therefore forbidden by their parents. They might associate with other girls in their immediate surroundings—enslaved children on the plantation—but without approval. The negative connotation of the word *kambrada* is perhaps indeed

5 After the arrival of the nuns in Curaçao in 1842, Bishop Niewindt wrote: "[O]ur aim shall have been achieved when the female sex, so thoroughly neglected here, receive an education such that girls are taught the proper modesty fitting for their position in society so that they become at once good, competent and conscientious housewives, whatever their religious upbringing." Abbring, *Weemoedstoonen uit de geschiedenis van mijne leven of mijne reis naar Curaçao* [Melancholy tones from the history of my lives or my journeys to Curacao], 1834, p. 96.

linked to such friendships.[6] These girls had therefore few possibilities for social contact, so, besides their own families, the figure of their *yaya* (nanny) played an important role in their lives.

Socialization of children in Curaçao was strongly influenced by a moral double standard. Boys and girls were raised separately, with girls' upbringing designed to protect their reputations. Young men were expected to be sexually aware at a young age, while any kind of sexual information was kept from girls. Girls were brought up under strict control, while, with the encouragement of their families, boys were allowed to enjoy sexual relations with working-class women from the ages of fifteen or sixteen.

The same moral double standard applied to the socialization of the children of freed people. A great deal more self-control was demanded of girls than of boys. Roughly until she began to menstruate, a girl would be indulged, but thereafter she was placed under close control, and it was made abundantly clear to her that she was now a woman and must observe certain rules of behavior. She must also assist with housekeeping and looking after any younger brothers and sisters. By contrast, boys were far more spoiled than girls. A boy was to be a tough lad who, when there was no man in the house, had to take upon himself the job of protecting the honor of his mother and his sisters.

6 Motherhood

At the end of the eighteenth century, women's fertility was far greater in Curaçao than elsewhere in America. The custom of leaving a child in the care of another was common among freed people. They limited themselves not only to close family members but also acquaintances and even strangers. Such foster parenting, which sometimes happened at a very young age, did not mean that the mother no longer cared about the child. She would maintain an interest in the child's well-being, which sometimes led to difficult situations. Among freed people, the bond between mothers and their children was

6 Of these forbidden friendships, A. T. Brusse wrote: "Certain classes display the habit of maintaining a *kambrada*, a bosom friend, albeit always of a lower order than herself, by a woman who has chosen another as her *kambrada*. The deleterious consequences that are the most frequent result of such intimacy between girls and women of different upbringing and moral circumstances may easily be guessed at. Parents must indeed make it their business to resist such associations; a *kambrada*, whose arrival in the house invariably brings with it a host of disagreeableness, must simply be shown the door, with the warmest recommendations not to return." Brusse, *Curaçao en zijne bewoners* [Curaçao and its inhabitants], 1882, p. 55. Editors' note: see contributions by Broek, Clemencia and Isenia in this volume.

extremely close, and it remained so into adulthood and even after a child had left the family home. Sons were more highly valued than daughters because many of them supported their mothers financially. But if an adult son landed in difficulty, he would quickly return to his mother, on whom he could always rely for understanding and shelter.[7]

Mothers and daughters would remain close in the face of even the greatest misunderstandings. Indeed, many mothers lived in the house of one of her adult daughters. Her mother's presence during the day was of great value if the daughter had to go out to work. A grandmother would in such cases be heavily involved in the rearing of the children.

There is little record of the upbringing of the children of the enslaved. Owners had full say over any children and could sell them at will. Looking at the sources, one might very well receive the impression that there was very little parental affection among enslaved people.[8]

7 Women's Work

With all the work of looking after her family being done for her by servants, the life of an upper-class white woman was in fact very empty.[9]

Apart from extraordinary cases, it was not customary for people in Curaçao to visit each other during the day. Women were kept in economically straitened circumstances: the pocket money given to them by their husbands was usually meager, and perhaps this was why a number of upper-class women and girls made efforts to earn a little money by selling bits of jewelry, perhaps in a shop or by having their maid hawk items through the town in a basket.[10]

---

7 Ibid., p. 53.

8 In 1836, Teenstra wrote that, when children who had reached the ages of seven or eight were sold perforce, their mothers were not in the slightest downhearted, for, "the laden schooners left the harbor to general cheering, sent on their way with the time-honored 'Farewells!' of mother and family." Teenstra, *De Nederlandsche West-Indische eilanden in derzelver tegenwoordige toestand* [The Dutch West Indies islands in their present condition], 1836, p. 168.

9 In 1857, Van Dissel wrote this of a woman's daily activities: "The female sex will have been pretty busy until breakfast. Perhaps an early morning walk, if they have been outside; there is also the everlasting piano to be played, or she might take up a trifle of handiwork, a little small talk, or simply pottering. But everything comes to an end, and once breakfast is behind her it will invariably be time to 'take a moment,' as they call it—an afternoon nap, which must be three hours at least." Dissel, *Curaçao, herinneringen en schetsen* [Curaçao, memories and sketches], 1957, p. 54.

10 Van Dissel sought an explanation for this in the heat that was everywhere on the island. Ibid., p. 135.

The literature makes frequent mention of corrupt officials of the West India Company, who were legally forbidden from doing business on their own account but had their wives do it for them. The precise details of how such couples arranged their business was kept secret.

Many tradesmen's wives were obliged to take over the running of the business when their husbands were away. One sees in the sources cases in which men gave their wives power of attorney to take over their businesses while the men were absent, although, in most cases, a wife placed in that position would be supported by a male family member.

This is perhaps explained by the fact that women's lack of education left them poorly placed to express themselves in Dutch, neither in writing nor orally. There are indeed examples among the preserved notary protocols of cases where, instead of providing a signature, women placed a mark.

On the death of a husband, his widow took over the business. Among the planters' wives, there were many who ran the business on her own. It was out of the question for Protestant upper-class women to hold political and government positions. That world was not intended for them. However, it is possible that women might have had indirect political influence via their husbands. There are also examples in the notary protocols of Jewish women whose husbands authorized them to take over the running of their business when they were away. The names of wives as well as husbands appeared in documents admitting legal liability, and here, too, the lack of education of Jewish women is clear to see, with crosses and initials clearly showing their lack of literacy. In times of economic decline and scarcity, women from the most economically precarious groups were the ones who suffered most. Whether married or not, they had to contribute significantly to the economy of their household. These were the servants, market women, washerwomen, farm girls and manual laborers who did all the typical types of women's work, such as spinning, pottery, rolling cigars, raffia work and sewing. All these women had to work two or even three jobs every day.

It was difficult for free women to find employment.[11] Market women tended to be the wives of poor farmers or fishermen or were single women selling various handmade things, such as food and sweetmeats. A poor farmer's wife had a threefold duty to fulfill. First, she had to do some of the work involved in cultivating the smallholding. Second, it was a wife's job to take fruit and vegetables to market because her husband had to stay on the farm to do the

11 The Reverend Van Dissel described one aspect of housework: "All water must be carried up and, once used and adulterated, borne back down again; that was, naturally, heavy work for women servants (male servants are rarely available for household tasks) who carried everything on their heads." Ibid., p. 82.

heaviest work, and the walk to and from town took up most, if not all, of the morning. She then found the housework waiting for her when she got back in the afternoon. Fortunately, she would often have the help of her mother, who lived with her and could look after the children while she was out. The same was true of the wives of poor fishermen and other women who worked outside their homes.[12] There were no factories in Curaçao at that time, although a few items were produced to be sold locally—such as pots and pans, fishing nets, baskets, hats, cigars and cotton yarn—in the form of cottage industry. The handiwork done most commonly by both white women and women of color was basket weaving.[13]

The poorest women who could find no better way to earn their livings made cigars, using tobacco leaves imported from Cuba or Puerto Rico. The cigars they made were of lower quality than cigars from Cuba and were intended for the local market rather than for export.

Enslaved women did the same sort of women's work as freed women, in service, child care, market trading and farm work. A few worked in the salt pans.

The position of nanny in a master's family was an important one. A *yaya* cared for and reared children, rocked them to sleep and sometimes acted as wet nurse. She took the children to school and accompanied them everywhere, so it is no wonder that many children became very attached to their *yayas*. Indeed, a newly married girl would take her *yaya* to live with her in her new house.

The spinning of cotton yarn was one of the types of work done by enslaved women, along with mending and sewing clothes and making hats.

The women among the enslaved agricultural workers began work at six in the morning. There was a break between noon and two in the afternoon and then work continued until six. The market women took the plantation

12 Teenstra painted a shocking picture of a washerwoman; Teenstra, *De Nederlandsche West-Indische eilanden in derzelver tegenwoordige toestand*, 1836, p. 270. See also, Gaay Fortman, *Aantekeningen omtrent een verblijf op Curaçao in 1825 en 1826* [Notes about a stay in Curaçao in 1825 and 1826], n.d., 5n.

13 One source reveals admiration for women's work: "It is scarcely credible how many hands are turned to the work. One can hardly step into any house, and not just the poorest, without seeing the inhabitants all together at work making hats from a particular species of straw that can be bent. It is from the coast, where it grows in abundance. The material is dried, and given some preparation; then it is brought in, from Coro (Venezuela) for the most part. Many guilders are made from their work, and, indeed, if such industriousness were not to be seen among the lower classes, there should be only more want." Dissel, *Curaçao, herinneringen en schetsen*, 1957, p. 113.

produce to the city market, balancing it on their heads. Donkeys were used for heavier loads.

During the maize and aloe harvests, a number of enslaved workers would be hired out by their owners to the planters who were harvesting crops, and, in their daily rations, too, a distinction was made between men and women. In 1824, the government stipulated that, from the beginning of October to the end of March, each man should receive six jugs of corn per week and each woman five jugs; and, from the beginning of April to the end of September, men should receive five jugs and women four. Prior to that, each man had earned five jugs and each female four jugs per week the whole year round. If an enslaved man had to do extra work for his master on his days off, the master was supposed to pay for it with three jugs of corn or nine stuivers; a woman was to earn two jugs of corn, or one *reaal*.

The work in the salt pans consisted of men hacking out blocks of hard salt while women collected the pieces and carried them to dry areas and stacking them into small heaps.

8 Morality

There was a great deal of concern for the dignity of women in Curaçaoan society. As a result, there are many reports in the police records of insulting behavior toward women—such behavior was punished by fines.[14]

A good white woman was expected to be a chaste wife and to stay at home while her husband watched over her good morals because the slightest transgression by his wife would bring dishonor to a man. This perhaps explains why white women spent their days at home. Perhaps they dared not leave the house unaccompanied for fear of being seen with some random man they might have encountered by chance. If a woman were seen alone with a man, the rumors would start. Simple misunderstandings destroyed many a reputation in Curaçao's small and stifling social circle. Therefore, to ward off any difficulties, every outdoor task was performed by servants or enslaved people.

---

14 There was an occasion when a white lady accused a freed mulatto woman of calling her a prostitute. In another case, a slanderer claimed "that all and sundry could treat her house like a hotel, and do there as they wished, for it is a whorehouse." The plaintiff was of the opinion that "her daughters would be considered respectable girls as long as they didn't get themselves pregnant!" ARA, Archives of Curaçao and associated islands Bonaire and Aruba, 1828–1845, inv. 528, Criminal Justice, 23 Sept., 1835.

In contrast to the isolation of women, men enjoyed a very eventful social life with friends they met in clubs and, moreover, had sexual liaisons with a large number of common women.[15]

Men also noticed what they referred to as "the lover's time" in white women, a sort of jealousy caused by the untrustworthiness of men. Women always employed their friends and servants to spy on their men.

Among the Jewish community, couples who had indulged in sexual relationships before marriage were refused a religious marriage ceremony. Once a girl became pregnant, she received all the blame for her situation. If such a girl's father was working in the Jewish community, he lost his job immediately. If he was receiving community financial support, it was immediately suspended—unless his daughter could prove that she had been raped. The role of the father as protector of his wife's and his daughter's honor was quite clear. It was easier for white people to uphold such values not only because the social position of white women was more secure but also because lecherous white men always had freed or enslaved women available to them.

The freed people, too, assumed the same values, although the less well-to-do colored and black people were unable to sustain them. People saw marriage, and virginity until marriage, as the ideal, but this was usually not attainable. On January 1, 1833, of 2,701 free colored people, only 788 were married, and of the 3,830 black people, only 135.

If a young girl became pregnant and did not immediately marry the father, then her chances of marrying later were notably reduced. If she were to run into financial difficulty, entering into a relationship with another man might bring her respite, but this relationship might lead to yet more children. If this relationship, too, were to break down, then she could always enter into another with the next man. Sometimes such relationships became more stable or even permanent, leading to cohabitations or even marriage.

At this time in Curaçao's history, marriage between white and black or colored people was impossible, but affectionate relationships could take on permanent character.[16]

15 The Reverend Abbring wrote this of white women's morals: "white natives, both as damsels and women, have many excellent qualities and are of unimpeachable modesty," adding: "natural daintiness, innate moral sense and purity but above all timidity are the inheritance of the West-Indian girl." Abbring, *Weemoedstoonen uit de geschiedenis van mijne leven of mijne reis naar Curaçao*, 1834, pp. 94–95.

16 These women became white men's mistresses. The Reverend van de Bosch initially found the "Turkish" lifestyle, as he called it, extremely strange, "but after having been so many years in the West Indies, I was so used to it in the end that it came as no surprise to see that any Tom, Dick or Harry might have a few colored children running wild. And nothing

The cost of raising illegitimate children was low in any case since the cost of living was low in Curaçao.

If such children knew who their white fathers were, then they could take his name so long as they used the prefix *van* (of). The prefix *van* in a surname indicated that an individual was a relation of a certain person or family but was not allowed to bear the actual family name due to their illegitimate birth. The Jews, however, did allow their illegitimate children to use their true surnames unmodified.

Relationships among enslaved people varied greatly, from the short and purely physical to permanent coupling. However, all of them were entirely dependent on their masters, who could order them to establish ties or break them.

This must have given the impression that enslaved people were inclined to loose immoral sexual behavior, which was used as an argument against the movement to establish official marriages for enslaved people.[17]

9 Conclusion

Differences in social status among women in Curaçao during the first half of the nineteenth century were based on individual women's family circumstances, their skin color, their legal status and the sort of work they did. Distinctions were made between upper-class Protestant white women, Jewish women, white lower-class Protestant women, prominent colored freed women, ordinary free colored women and black women. Then came enslaved people working as domestic servants and enslaved people working on the plantations. Among freed women, distinctions were also made according to skin color and features. There was a difference in legal status between enslaved and freed

will change so long as the institution of slavery remains in existence in the West Indies and the division attendant on it between whites and colored or blacks; and so long as the first mentioned considers scandalous not the begetting of unlawful children with the latter, who are again despised for the color of their skin, but entering into lawful marriage with them." Bosch, *Reizen in West-Indië en door een gedeelte van Zuid- en Noord-Amerika. St. Eustatius. St. Martin. Curaçao* [Traveling in the West Indies and through parts of South and North America. St. Eustatius. St. Maarten. Curaçao], 1829, p. 103

17 The dependency that determined the sexual behavior of enslaved people was not mentioned by Commissioners Grovinstins and Boeys in their official report in 1791. They wrote: "Debauchery … has brought the mixing of colors to such a pass that you could not find half a dozen families on the entire island with no members of mixed race; there is thus a host of mestizos, castizos, and mulattos." ARA, Verspreide West-Indische stukken, inv. 972, report by Grovinstins.

women. Enslaved women were judged on their skin color and the sort of work they were required to do.

Marriage or a stable relationship with a man from a different status group allowed white and free women to change their status. By obtaining freedom, the slaves could also end up in another status group, the freedmen.

Nineteenth-century writers—all of them men because, at that time, no woman had exhibited literary skill—made passing reference to women in a few passages in their works. They concerned themselves mostly with women's appearance, character traits, moral behavior, attitude to work, social skills and how they spent their free time. Most writers saw white women as morally pure and blameless: they were tall and slim and rather pale from staying so much indoors. They had a reserved and timid air and had little conversation as a result of their inadequate education and isolated situation. White women led lives of domestic seclusion but were at the same time good, conscientious housewives and affectionate mothers. In their movements, there was a certain lethargy detectable—the effect of the warm climate—although there was no sign of it in a woman on horseback or one who appeared on the dancefloor. Nevertheless, there are traces of the participation of these women in public life.

Black and colored women were not particularly favorably portrayed by writers. Servants were never sufficiently diligent and the washerwomen were sloppy. Their personal hygiene was never good, nor were their clothes, and if they ever did try to smarten themselves up, they made themselves look like monkeys in a costume and would never even recognize themselves. Above all, they were noisy and uncouth and, from literary references, anyone might think their morals were quite beyond the pale. However, indolence, timidity and shyness would have been strange characteristics for enslaved women, market women, fishwives, washerwomen and craftswomen, all of whom had to work hard for their livings.

If we look at the lives of the women of those times, we conclude that they were conscientious, hardworking and independent and that all women were oppressed by a patriarchal society. The repression they experienced was not the same for all women, because it depended on their individual status. White women were heavily praised by authors, but they were subject to their own legal, social and sexual restrictions. Colored, black and enslaved women, by contrast, experienced discrimination on the basis of ethnicity and skin color and oppression in the form of economic and sexual exploitation. Nevertheless, nineteenth-century authors' descriptions of women in Curaçao paint an inaccurate picture of them. By studying their history, we can dispel such myths about women and, with the help of other data, correct the image we have of them.

Acknowledgments

This is a translated excerpt from an article originally published in Dutch as Römer, Nolda. "Curaçaose vrouwen in de slavenmaatschappij" [Curaçaoan women in a slave society]. In *Mundu yama sinta mira: Womanhood in Curaçao*, edited by Richenel Ansano, Jocelyn A. Clemencia, Jeanette Cook, and Eithel Martis, 30–47. Curaçao: Fundashon Publikashon, 1992. English translation by Marcus Ferley. The reproduction of this text courtesy of the author and Fundashon Publikashon.

Bibliography

Abbring, H. J. *Weemoedstoonen uit de geschiedenis van mijn leven, of mijne reis naar Curaçao, en vlugtige beschouwingen van dat eiland gedurende mijn tienjarig verblijf op hetzelve* [Melancholy tones from the history of my lives or my journeys to Curaçao and cursory reflections from my ten-year sojourn on that island]. Groningen: W. van Boekeren, 1834.

Bosch, G. B. *Reizen in West-Indië en door een gedeelte van Zuid- en Noord-Amerika. St. Eustatius. St. Martin. Curaçao* [Traveling in the West Indies and through part of South and North America. St. Eustatius. St. Maarten. Curaçao]. Utrecht: Van der Monde, 1829.

Brusse, A. T. *Curaçao en zijne bewoners* [Curaçao and its inhabitants]. Curaçao: Internationale Handelsdrukkerij, 1882.

Dissel, S. van. *Curaçao, herinneringen en schetsen* [Curaçao, memories and sketches]. Leyden: Sythoff, 1857.

Gaay Fortman, B. de. *Aantekeningen omtrent een verblijf op Curaçao in 1825 en 1826* [Notes about a stay in Curaçao in 1825 and 1826]. Curaçao: Uitgave Lux, n.d.

Teenstra, M. D. *De Nederlandsche West-Indische eilanden in derzelver tegenwoordige toestand* [The Dutch West Indies islands in their present condition]. Amsterdam: Sulpke, 1836.

CHAPTER 2

The Repercussions of Rumor: an Adultery Case from Eighteenth-Century Curaçao

Jessica V. Roitman

Abstract

In 1775, the Portuguese Jewish community of Curaçao, then numbering around 1,100, was rocked by a bitter dispute involving allegations of sexual misconduct or, as the sources put it, "unpermitted familiarity." The case threatened the social cohesion of the community and reminds us that the boundaries between the public and the private, especially in closely knit communities, could be porous indeed. The relationship between the adulterous lovers was conducted in plain sight of much of the city of Willemstad. Witnesses to their affair included a broad swathe of colonial society: housewives, merchants, doctors, colonial officials, enslaved and free people of color. They revealed their personal knowledge of the relationship and repeated hearsay, most of which was garnered on the streets of Willemstad after the affair became a matter of not only public interest but intense and long-running legal wrangling that spanned continents.

Keywords

Portuguese Jewish community – adultery – colonial society – rumor – eighteenth-century Curaçao

This contribution will examine the dynamics of the Jewish community of late eighteenth-century Curaçao through the prism of the court records resulting from a case of alleged adultery, with a particular emphasis on the role of gossip and rumor within and beyond the community. As in any small, densely packed community, gossip was an important feature of eighteenth-century urban life in Willemstad. Gossip—the exchange of information about the personal lives of third parties—was not merely "tattling" or idle talk, as the Oxford English Dictionary defines it. This contribution will argue that, within the Jewish community of Curaçao, just as in other societies with few other

 | DOI:10.1163/9789004690882_004

means of exchanging information, gossip functioned as a crucial means of transmitting vital data about others. If it involved sexual conduct, as it did in the case study to be examined in this contribution, it could also prove titillating and diversionary.

This reinforces what F. G. Bailey has described as the "quality of intimacy" in small communities and what Max Gluckman famously argued when he asserted that gossip helps to maintain the unity and the morality of the groups involved in it.[1] Gossip, in short, can be a positive force in communities. While it can damage social unity, it can help reinforce bonds of belonging and identity. It can also act as a mechanism for social control and buttress community norms. Robert Paine, conversely, saw gossip as a "genre of informal communication" and also "a device intended to forward and protect individual interests." This was especially the case, in Paine's view, for members of minority groups living inside larger "host" societies.[2] These anthropological observations apply well to eighteenth-century Curaçao. The present contribution will incorporate Bailey's, Gluckman's and Paine's perspectives on the function of gossip in societies and show that they were not mutually exclusive. Rather, they could work in tandem to both reinforce community norms while also bolstering individuals' statuses. Ultimately, this contribution will show how gossip highlights tensions in social relationships, flourishes in certain circumstances and, in turn, gives further impetus to these circumstances.

This contribution will also show that gossip did not appear to be a particularly female activity, in contrast to studies that do center gossip in the female sphere. In fact, as the case discussed below will show, men were the most garrulous. This is not surprising given the vital role rumors played in the realm of business and government. Historian Han Jordaan details how rumors of involvement in illicit trade led to a major problem on the island of Curaçao between Governor Faesch and colonial official Johannes Heijliger.[3] If men were at least as eager to spread rumors and speculate upon people's behavior, it is possible that reputed sexual conduct was intertwined with commerce and politics and that these spheres were not as separate as historians have heretofore thought. In any case, one deponent in the case discussed below testified that gossip related to sexual conduct had always circulated in Curaçao. In a community where many or most families were intermarried, gossip and

1 See Bailey, "Gift and Poison," 1971; and Gluckman, "Gossip and Scandal," 1968.

2 Paine, "What Is Gossip about? An Alternative Hypothesis," 1967.

3 Jordaan, "Samuel Fahlberg (1758–1834): De biografische contouren van een veelzijdig man" [Samuel Fahlberg (1758–1834): The biographical contours of a versatile man], 1994.

rumors must have created personal distress and divided loyalties that could not but impact trade and governance.

Every once in a while, a well-documented case provides us with a framework through which to view issues shaping the dynamics of a community or even of a society as a whole. Such a case occurred in 1775, when the Portuguese Jewish community of Curaçao was rocked by a bitter dispute involving allegations of sexual misconduct. The witnesses included a broad swathe of colonial society: housewives, merchants, doctors, colonial officials, enslaved and free people of color. Witnesses were asked to reveal their personal knowledge of the situation and also to repeat hearsay. The case threatened the social cohesion of the community and reminds us that close-knit communities could be rife with suspicions and simmering conflicts. It is also an example of how relatively clear-cut cases of adultery in the Dutch colonies could be manipulated in the defendants' favor.

The charges were dramatic and highly salacious by any standard. Sarah de Isaac Pardo was pregnant, but the paternity of her unborn child was the subject of much speculation in the Portuguese Jewish community, among its enslaved people and servants and even among the white Protestants on the island. In more than ten years of marriage, Sarah Pardo had never before been known to be pregnant.[4] Her much older husband, Selomoh Vaz Farro, was now gravely ill and had been for some time—so ill that the couple had twice been granted a conditional divorce in the preceding year by Haham (in Sephardic congregations, synonymous with rabbi) da Fonseca in expectation of Vaz Farro's imminent demise.[5] How was it, then, that an elderly man on his deathbed—whom two doctors had declared impotent—could impregnate his wife?

Vaz Farro claimed in a sworn statement that, one evening several months earlier, he had "found the strength" to have relations with his wife.[6] But this seemed unlikely to many within and outside the Portuguese Jewish community. Instead, suspicion immediately fell on Abraham de David da Costa Andrade Jr. After all, Sarah Pardo and Abraham Andrade had frequently been spotted in each other's company. This in itself was not particularly shocking. A certain

4 National Archives of the Netherlands [henceforth NL-HANA], Tweede West-Indische Compagnie (WIC), 1.05.01.02, inv. 223.

5 This divorce would have freed Pardo of the obligation to contract a levirate marriage to her brother-in-law. Apparently, Vaz Farro had recovered sufficiently enough for Da Fonseca to revoke the first conditional divorce decree. When Vaz Farro's condition worsened again, Da Fonseca issued a second divorce decree. Conditional divorce decrees in the Portuguese Jewish communities of both Curaçao and Suriname had mandatory expiration dates, hence the necessity for two decrees in Vaz Farro's case.

6 NL-HANA, Tweede West-Indische Compagnie (WIC), 1.05.01.02, inv. 223:1, 10, 30v; 26:1.

degree of intimacy between married people of opposite genders was permitted in a closely knit community in which nearly everyone was related by blood or marriage.[7] But Pardo and Andrade seemed to have pushed the limits of what was allowable by community standards. They were observed talking together on the porches of houses, exchanging small tokens such as flowers. Many witnesses had regularly spotted the pair strolling together outside the city gates. According to a few testimonies, Pardo and Andrade had even arranged a rendezvous during the small hours of the morning. Gossip about their relationship was rife and there was plenty of material to work with.[8]

The frequency with which the two were sighted together, their obvious familiarity with one another and Pardo's suspicious pregnancy flouted community norms and, eventually, incited censure. Sexual conduct was perhaps the single most important piece of information about a third party, as one deponent testified. Anthropologists acknowledge that a group's moral values are constantly reinforced, indeed policed, by gossip for gossip stories almost always have a moral edge to them.[9] Thus it is not particularly surprising that gossip related to intimate behavior, as the deponent asserted, had always circulated in Curaçao, whether among men or women, or between Jews, Protestants, enslaved or free people of color.[10]

In the Pardo/Andrade scandal, free people of color played a central role in information transmission. Even those unrelated to the families in question enjoyed a detailed familiarity with the case.[11] In fact, Samuel da Costa Andrade learned of his brother's suspected adultery when he overheard two black women gossiping in a narrow Willemstad passageway.[12] Other deponents admitted that they had listened in on conversations about the scandal from black people circulating in the marketplace and on the streets.[13] This could be evidence that, as Robert Paine has argued, gossip was conducted by individuals seeking to forward their own interests and was, therefore, an integral part of social processes of (attempted) advancement by minority groups.[14]

---

7 For more discussion of this, see the other cases discussed in Ben-Ur and Roitman, "Adultery Here and There," 2014.

8 NL-HANA, Tweede West-Indische Compagnie (WIC), 1.05.01.02, inv. 223:1, 11, 42, 50; 2:1, 41; 29, 1; 30, 1.

9 Wickham, "Gossip and Resistance among the Medieval Peasantry," 1998.

10 NL-HANA, Tweede West-Indische Compagnie (WIC), 1.05.01.02, inv. 223:2, 32.

11 Ibid., inv. 223:1, 29: 2, 4–8, 10; 4, 1; 5, 102; 15, 3; 29, 1–2; 30, 1–2.

12 Ibid., inv. 223:29, 1–2.

13 Ibid., inv. 223:15, 4–5; 30, 1–2.

14 Paine, "What Is Gossip about? An Alternative Hypothesis," 1967.

In any case, all of this brings to the fore one of the main features of this case: the entanglement of enslaved and manumitted peoples in the daily lives of white people. This is perhaps unsurprising given the geographical situation. Willemstad was a small walled city barely containing upwards of 11,500 inhabitants, who, by the mid-eighteenth century, had begun to spill beyond its gates and into neighborhoods such as Otrobanda.[15] In the testimony, people of color emerge as major actors and information transmitters. Informally, they absorbed and spread gossip across communal boundaries. White Portuguese Jews sometimes called on them to transmit messengers between the lovers. Sarah Pardo, for example, gave a letter to Antonia, a free black girl, to deliver to Abraham Andrade, who returned his own response via an enslaved girl. Clearly, these individuals occupied a central role in the Pardo and Andrade families, indicating not just intimacy and trust but also influence. This idea is further bolstered by the fact that, on other occasions, enslaved and free people of color played advisory roles to the parties involved, as we shall see. These roles could also point to the validity of Gluckman's claims that gossip contributes to the unity of the group, with these enslaved and free people of color clearly considering themselves, and being considered by the Portuguese Jewish community, as part of the community, playing a vital role in reinforcing its norms.

After her second conditional divorce from her dying husband, Sarah Pardo moved back to her father's house. However, Isaac Pardo's ploy of putting an end to his daughter's "shameless" conduct failed for Pardo continued to visit with Abraham Andrade sub rosa.[16] This he learned during the humiliating visit of Mrs. Clements, a prominent Protestant widow, who told him of his daughter's inappropriate conduct on the streets of Willemstad, a visit that illustrates how racial solidarity among white people overcame religious divides. It also illustrates the idea that rumor and gossip tend to form networks of communication in which fears and uncertainties emerge and challenges to existing power structures can be covertly made or, as would seem to be the case with Mrs. Clements' visit, overtly suppressed.[17]

15 Klooster, "Curacao as a Transit Center to the Spanish Main and the French West Indies," 2014. Klooster estimates that, by the middle of the eighteenth century, the number of Jewish families in Willemstad was nearly half that of white non-Jews. Based on WIC tax records, Klooster believes that, by 1789, there were about 6,000 free residents in Willemstad, which included free black and colored people—most of whom were Catholics— as well as 2,469 Protestants and 1,095 Jews. See Klooster, "Jews in Suriname and Curacao," 2001, pp. 353, 355.

16 NL-HANA, Tweede West-Indische Compagnie (WIC), 1.05.01.02, inv. 223:2, 7–10.

17 Ibid., 223:2, 14–16; and Paine, "What Is Gossip about? An Alternative Hypothesis," 1967.

Similar embarrassing social calls caused the situation at home to deteriorate: Pardo and her father were heard arguing loudly and frequently. Both friends and the family's domestic enslaved people attempted to broker a peaceful solution to this untenable situation. At last, Isaac Pardo's good friend Dr. Joseph Capriles, seconded by Pardo's "house slaves," persuaded Pardo to move in with her father, who owned a residence outside the city gates.[18] The "house slaves," although nameless, are listed alongside Capriles—Isaac Pardo's long-time family friend, business partner and prominent fellow Portuguese Jew—as key participants in persuading Pardo to change her domicile.[19]

Free people of color, referred to as mulattos, also appear in positions of intimacy or even friendship with Sarah Pardo and Abraham Andrade and other Portuguese Jews. Pardo was well enough acquainted with an unidentified mulatto woman whom she met on the streets to declare: "Everyone says I'm pregnant … I'm going to walk the streets now to show them that I'm not!"[20] Pardo also discussed her feelings for her ailing husband with this woman. She had "been hoping for two or three years for her husband to die … or for lightning to strike him."[21]

That these statements were made to a mulatto woman and that no one in the ensuing civil and religious litigation seemed surprised is again indicative of a level of familiarity between the free people of color and Portuguese Jewish populations that has not heretofore been explored for Curaçao's Jewish community.[22] For the purposes of this contribution, it may also show that Pardo was well aware of the important role of the free people of color in information transmission, either as sustainers of communal unity or as individuals seeking to forward their own interests, and therefore sought to influence them.

It was an enslaved girl who transmitted to Isaac Pardo the two love letters that would become centerpieces in the trial against Sarah Pardo and Abraham Andrade. According to Pardo père, these letters "came into my hands … from

18 Ibid., 223:2, 9–10.

19 Dr. Joseph Capriles was a prominent member of the Portuguese Jewish community in Curacao. He was listed as one of the wealthiest members of the community in 1769. Emmanuel and Emmanuel, *History of the Jews of the Netherlands Antilles*, 1970, p. 255. He owned at least one ship, La Dorada, valued at 800 pesos. See NL-HANA, Curacao, Bonaire en Aruba tot 1828, 1.05.12.01, inv. nr. 891, 395.

20 NL-HANA, Tweede West-Indische Compagnie (WIC), 1.05.01.02, 223:4, 1.

21 Ibid.

22 There is obviously secondary literature that discusses sexual liaisons between white Portuguese Jewish fathers and non-Jewish women of color, but these sources highlight the sexual and financial utility of such relations and do not consider friendship or trust. See, for example, Abraham-Van der Mark, "Marriage and Concubinage among the Sephardic Merchant Elite of Curacao," 1993.

a black girl I came across."[23] These two incriminating love letters were written in the island's creole language, commonly known today as Papiamentu, but are in the sources referred to as *neger spraak* (negro speech). They were especially damning for they provided actual evidence of an extramarital affair and compelled the parnassim (members of the powerful ruling board of a Jewish community, at this time usually drawn from the wealthiest congregants, who had the power to temporarily or permanently ban people) of the synagogue to act, in part because the contents of the letters had become so widely known to both Jews and non-Jews in the city. These letters—the oldest known documents written in Papiamentu—formed the lynchpin of the various accusations against the couple. It was in these letters that both the pregnancy and the attempt to abort the fetus were acknowledged.[24]

After these compromising epistles were made public, one of Sarah Pardo's brothers threw Andrade out of the synagogue.[25] In fact, feelings against him were running so high that Andrade had to request an armed escort from the governor in order to arrive home safely.[26] Pardo and Andrade claimed that they were innocent of the charges and that the adultery accusation was a conspiracy against them. They initially attempted to evade the parnassim when called to answer for their suspected crimes. Sarah Pardo disingenuously claimed several times that she did not realize she had been charged with a crime. Andrade's family also avoided appearing before the *Ma'amad* (lay board of directors of Sephardic congregations, which is often synonymous with the parnassim). His father feigned illness while his brothers suddenly found pressing business to attend to off the island. When Pardo and Andrade eventually came before the *Ma'amad* and were confronted with the letters they had sent to one another, they claimed them to be forgeries. Shortly thereafter, the haham and parnassim formally accused Andrade of committing adultery with Pardo and excommunicated both parties. Andrade was ordered to ask for forgiveness at the

23 This chain of transmission is related in NL-HANA, Tweede West-Indische Compagnie (WIC), 1.05.01.02, 223:2, 7–10.

24 Pardo wrote that she had sent her slave, a woman called Xica, to a Spanish doctor named Manuel de Estrada to procure an abortificant. NL-HANA, Tweede West-Indische Compagnie (WIC), 1.05.01.02, inv. 223:11, 1–2; 13, 1. Estrada later declared under oath that he was surprised that Pardo "trusted a black woman in business of such importance." Ibid., inv. 223:11, 1–2. When Estrada refused Xica, Andrade paid him a visit himself and was given certain herbs to end the pregnancy. Ibid., inv. 223:11, 1–2; 12, 1. Andrade's attempt to procure abortificants for his lover was a common response to an unplanned and possibly incriminating pregnancy.

25 NL-HANA, Tweede West-Indische Compagnie (WIC), 1.05.01.02, inv. 223:23, 1–2 (October 1, 1775).

26 Ibid.

synagogue altar, grow out his beard for six weeks, sit on a special bench in the synagogue, pay a fine of two hundred guilders and have no form of communication with Sarah Pardo. Pardo was not required to make the public penances in the synagogue like Andrade, but she did have to pay an equal amount to the charity fund, and it was Pardo that congregation president David Morales sought to have banished from the island, not Andrade.[27]

The reason for this harsher treatment could possibly be rooted in the family history.[28] Isaac Pardo had been one of the first community members excommunicated by Haham de Sola in the community-wide conflict that rocked the island two decades earlier. This could show how gossip may find its way into long-lasting networks or group contexts, where it can result in the storage of information that can lie unused for years but is a resource that can be pulled out in subsequent contexts of change and conflict.[29] This dispute was, in many ways, a continuation of other, long-running conflicts within the Curaçoan community. Like so many of the quarrels that plagued eighteenth-century Portuguese Jews in Curaçao, the case of twenty years earlier centered on delimiting the powers of the haham and parnassim. Disagreement arose when there was talk of building a new synagogue that would compete with the pioneering Mikvé Israel. Two "opposition" leaders, Moses Penso and David Aboab, and those who supported them, including Isaac Pardo, were excommunicated.[30] In any case, it also shows that talking about shared memories, what is sometimes termed social memory, especially what in a given context is the socially relevant past, legitimizes or gives meaning to the present for the group that commemorates it.

Andrade and Pardo turned to the civil authorities. They hoped their case would be judged more favourably than by the Mahamad. Andrade hired the lawyer Petrus Bernardus van Starckenborgh, who would later become interim governor of Curaçao, to defend him against the charges. On July 3, 1776, the governor and council acquitted Andrade and Pardo and ordered the parnassim

27 These events are detailed in NL-HANA, Tweede West-Indische Compagnie (WIC), 1.05.01.02, inv. 223:1, 1–25.

28 For a similar interpretation of underlying causes of interpersonal disputes, see Sullivan, *The Punishment of Crime in Colonial New York*, 1997, pp. 112–113.

29 Stewart and Strathern, *Witchcraft, Sorcery, Rumors, and Gossip*, 2004, p. 39.

30 For discussion of the case see, NL-HANA, Old Archive of Curacao, 1.05.12.01, inv. 825, 863/139; 1528; 818/47; 863/423; 867/79, 211; 180/132; 183/27; 821; NL-HANA, 1.05.01.02 (Second West India Company), inv. 243/53–61; 70–83; 135–136; 180–182; 316; 596/1261; 597/584; 765a–68; 596/1261; 403; 357/15; Roitman, "A Flock of Wolves Instead of Sheep," 2014; and Emmanuel and Emmanuel, *History of the Jews of the Netherlands Antilles*, 1970, pp. 188–212.

to remove the excommunications, annul the fines and have the son who was born to Pardo circumcised without discrimination (without the omission of certain words pronounced for sons of fathers leading moral lives).[31] The parnassim were ordered to seal all papers referring to Pardo and Andrade.[32]

Centuries later, the guilt of Abraham de David da Costa Andrade Jr. and Sarah Pardo hardly matters. What makes the case interesting today is the vivid light it throws on the social dynamics among the island's various population groups and polities. The Dutch colonial authorities' involvement in the case magnified long-standing tensions between Jewish communal autonomy and colonial hegemony, which illustrates a few important points, including the fact that it is the ideological and historical context rather than the words themselves that ultimately produces the effects from gossip. It also shows that gossip tends to emerge in conflicts over power. We may also perceive how information was transmitted within the Portuguese Jewish community and contemplate the far-reaching and decisive role of gossip, and we get a glimpse of the pivotal role of the colored population, whether enslaved or free, in one of the island's major scandals.

For the purposes of this contribution, though, one of the most important aspects of this case is to show vividly how rumors and gossip help in the production and outcomes of accusations that hit on fundamental but often badly defined areas of morality. Gossip, in and of itself, is simply talking about other people behind their backs. It is not gendered, although men and women often gossip according to different narrative strategies. It is not necessarily idle or arbitrary (much gossip is self-interested or manipulative or else essential

31 NL-HANA, Curacao, Bonaire en Aruba tot 1828, 1.05.12.01, inv. 916, 20; inv. 918, 206, 208–210; inv. 920, 315–316, 471: inv. 921, 150–151, 164, 226.

32 Nevertheless, the parnassim let the excommunication stand. In fact, David Morales, president of the community, tried to have Pardo banished from Curaçao, but the governor refused to comply. Public prosecutor Hubertus Coerman, who had been chief of police since 1773, also disagreed with the governor and the island council and took the case to the States General of Holland. But the States General ruled in favor of Pardo and Andrade on January 13, 1778. Prosecutor Coerman demanded a reversal. Andrade won again. The Amsterdam parnassim removed the excommunication immediately. On July 31, 1780, the Curaçao parnassim were ordered to circumcise the child—who was now nearly five years old—like all legitimate Jewish sons. They were also ordered to pay Andrade's costs to the enormous sum of 60,493:2 Dutch guilders. The argument over the payment of the costs dragged on until 1794. Abraham Andrade eventually moved to Jamaica and Sarah Pardo remarried and left for St. Thomas. See SAA, 1156 (Portugees-Israëlietische Gemeente Curaçao), inv. 44, unpaginated; SAA, 334 (Archief van de Portugees-Israëlietische Gemeente), inv. 95 ("Copiador de cartas" — Copies of outgoing letters, 1773–1784), 184, 237, 286, 323; 22 ("Compendio de escamoth" — Resolutions, 1728–1814), 171, 199, 229–230, 254, 268.

information exchange) and neither is it necessarily about secret behavior. As this contribution has shown, the feature that makes gossip interesting to historians is the way that it defines group identity. Groups construct themselves by talking. Some of it is gossip; indeed, in this respect, the group is actually constituted by who has the right to gossip about outsiders—or even absent insiders.

Gossip helps to maintain the unity and the morality of the groups involved in it. Pardo and Andrade were gossiped about and sanctioned for their behavior—a behavior that transgressed community norms. Gossip, in short, can be a positive force in communities. While it can damage social unity, as it also did in the case, causing conflict and fights within the community, it can help reinforce bonds of belonging and identity. Community members showed they belonged by transmitting information to each other about the case. Thus, it acts as a mechanism for social control and buttress of community norms. But none of what has been seen in the case contradicts Robert Paine's view that gossip served to forward and protect individual interests, especially in the case of members of minority groups living inside larger "host" societies. In fact, the clear entanglement of enslaved people and free black people in the case and their transmission of information confirms that they were advancing their own interests while also showing that they belonged to the larger (white) community. So community norms were reinforced while individuals' statuses were also bolstered. Ultimately, this contribution has shown how gossip highlights tensions in social relationships, flourishes in certain circumstances and, in turn, gives further impetus to these circumstances.

Acknowledgments

This contribution originally appeared in Studemund-Halévy, *A Sefardic Pepper-Pot in the Caribbean*, 2016. We thank Tirocinio for allowing us to republish this text. Part of this text has previously appeared in Ben-Ur and Roitman. "Adultery Here and There: Crossing Sexual Boundaries in the Dutch Jewish Atlantic." In *Dutch Atlantic Connections, 1680–1800*, edited by Gert Oostindie and Jessica Vance Roitman, 185–223. Leiden: Brill, 2014.

Bibliography

Abraham-Van der Mark, Eva. "Marriage and Concubinage among the Sephardic Merchant Elite of Curacao." In *Women and Change in the Caribbean: A Pan-Caribbean Perspective*, edited by Janet Henshall Momsen, 38–49. London: Ian Randle, 1993.

Bailey, Frederick G. "Gift and Poison." In *Gift and Poison: The Politics of Reputation*, edited by Frederick G. Bailey, 307–16. Oxford: Basil Blackwell, 1971.

Ben-Ur, Aviva, and Jessica Vance Roitman. "Adultery Here and There: Crossing Sexual Boundaries in the Dutch Jewish Atlantic." In *Dutch Atlantic Connections, 1680–1800*, edited by Gert Oostindie and Jessica Vance Roitman, 185–223. Leiden: Brill, 2014.

Emmanuel, Isaac Samuel, and Suzanne A. Emmanuel. *History of the Jews of the Netherlands Antilles*. Vol. 1. Cincinnati: American Jewish Archives, 1970.

Gluckman, Max. "Gossip and Scandal." *Current Anthropology* 4, no. 3 (1968): 307–16.

Jordaan, Han. "Samuel Fahlberg (1758–1834): De biografische contouren van een veelzijdig man" [Samuel Fahlberg (1758–1834): The biographical contours of a versatile man]. In *De horen en zijn echo. Verzameling essays opgedragen aan dr Henny E. Coomans*, edited by Maritza Coomans-Eustatia, 231–35. Bloemendaal: Stichting Libri Antilliani; Amsterdam: Zoölogisch Museum Amsterdam, 1994.

Klooster, Wim. "Curacao as a Transit Center to the Spanish Main and the French West Indies." In *Dutch Atlantic Connections*, edited by Gert Oostindie and Jessica Vance Roitman, 25–57. Leiden: Brill, 2014.

Klooster, Wim. "Jews in Suriname and Curacao." In *The Jews and the Expansion of Europe to the West, 1450 to 1800*, edited by Paolo Bernardini and Norman Fiering, 350–68. New York: Berghahn Books, 2001.

Paine, Robert. "What Is Gossip about? An Alternative Hypothesis." *Man* 2, no. 2 (1967): 278–85.

Roitman, Jessica Vance. "'A Flock of Wolves Instead of Sheep': The Dutch West India Company, Conflict Resolution, and the Jewish Community of Curacao in the Eighteenth Century." In *The Jews in the Caribbean*, edited by Jane S. Gerber and Miriam Bodian, 85–105. Oxford: The Littman Library of Jewish Civilization, 2014.

Stewart, Pamela J., and Andrew Strathern. *Witchcraft, Sorcery, Rumors, and Gossip*. Cambridge: Cambridge University Press, 2004.

Studemund-Halévy, Michael, ed. *A Sefardic Pepper-Pot in the Caribbean: History, Language, Literature, and Art*. Barcelona: Tirocinio, 2016.

Sullivan, Dennis. *The Punishment of Crime in Colonial New York*. New York: Peter Lang, 1997.

Wickham, Chris. "Gossip and Resistance among the Medieval Peasantry." *Past & Present* 160 (1998): 3–24.

CHAPTER 3

Gender Dialectics in Colonial Saba, 1780–1863

Ryan Espersen

Abstract

This contribution uses archival resources to discuss the racial and gendered relations on the island of Saba in the nineteenth century. It reflects upon the island's integration into the colonial economy of the Dutch Caribbean territories and the forms of social organization that this resulted in. It investigates census and emancipation documents to comment on the range of professions available to enslaved and freed people of color. The text also discusses naming conventions, religious groupings and purchasing practices, as they differed between different social groups, and the ways gendering and racialization intersected in the lives of African-descended Saban women.

Keywords

Saba – social organization – enslaved and freed people of color – naming conventions – religion – colonial society

1 Introduction

Studying powered relationships in a given society is often fraught with the issue of deriving inferences and conclusions for large populations based on a designated fraction that is arguably representative of the whole. As a single researcher, tracing the processes of ideological abstractions such as race and gender while accounting for the whole society can be a daunting task. It is facilitated, however, by studying social environments that are bounded through geographical limitations with small populations but with sufficient cultural similarities to the region to permit insightful contextualization of similar and divergent processes within their respective ideologies. Saba, at just 13 square kilometers in area and 872 meters at its highest point, never developed into a full plantation economy otherwise characterized by a large majority of enslaved Africans relative to free European-descent residents. Rather, the

 | DOI:10.1163/9789004690882_005

population of white residents compared to enslaved Africans and free Sabans of African descent fluctuated mildly around 50 percent respectively. Saba is therefore an excellent environment to understand the dialectics between race, gender and power throughout the colonial and postcolonial periods. This contribution will discuss the dialectics between race and gender throughout Saba's well-documented nineteenth century.

Generally defined, "dialectics is a way of thinking and a set of related categories that captures, neither misses nor distorts, the real changes and interaction that go on in the world or any part of it."[1] Dialectics "study the relations between two or more elements, in the sense that it is the relationship between the elements that define them, and they cannot otherwise exist outside of this relationship."[2] Race and gender are therefore understood as inseparable elements to understanding powered relations in colonial Saba.

A dialectical approach requires an awareness of the multiple social and material webs in which social agents participate. This is not to say that a complete understanding is necessary of all aspects of a given society, but the dialectic rather fosters an accountability to multiple lines of evidence for a given element. It is therefore impossible to study an element isolated from its relation to other social and material contexts. Ollman refers to this as the "Humpty Dumpty problem": "After the fall, it was not only extremely hard to put the pieces of poor Humpty together again, but even to see where they fit. This is what happens whenever the pieces of our everyday experience are taken as existing separate from their spatial and historical contexts, whenever the part is given an ontological status independent of the whole."[3] The elements comprising dialectical study of a society, however, do not always "fit" neatly together. The relationship between owner and enslaved person, for example, is ambivalent at best and violent, dehumanizing and oppressive as it approaches the worst. This relationship is also not static, as members of either will enter into a variety of different social contexts throughout their lifetimes where their race, class and gender matter more, less or are otherwise insignificant.

In mid-nineteenth-century Saba, for example, a person can be a free mulatto woman from Middle Island, a mother of three, Catholic and a small landowner living through subsistence agriculture who sells a small surplus in the village

1 Ollman and Smith, "Introduction," 2008, p. 4.

2 Wurst, "A Class All Its Own," 2006, p. 195; Harvey, *Justice, Nature, and the Geography of Difference*, 1996; Harvey, *Spaces of Hope*, 2000; Ollman, *Dialectical Investigations*, 1993; Ollman, *Dance of the Dialectic*, 2003; Sayer, *The Violence of Abstraction*, 1987.

3 Ollman, "Why Dialectics? Why Now?" 2008, p. 9.

of The Bottom on Sundays, but she is not simply the sum of these identities.[4] "At work, church, leisure or among friends, this individual will become reconstituted as a different social agent depending on the context since there is no pure context where we are dealing with only one set of relations."[5] Gender, along with race, are immutable elements of ideology that are imposed upon the individual by others from birth. It is this key element that separates class from race and gender. While one's class can change over time or according to the given social context, race and gender can never be transcended by the individual except through a radical shift in the society's ideology.

2 Plantations and Powered Landscapes

Saba's documentary record unfortunately lacks sources from the seventeenth and eighteenth centuries. This is in part due to the island's irrelevance to colonial authorities as a small colony that was neither profitable nor an expense to the Dutch West Indies Company.[6] Saba's landscape was divided very soon into plantation and non-plantation regions after Dutch colonization in the 1640s, with plantations occupying the majority of the flattest and most productive regions of the island. Half of The Bottom consisted of the Paris sugar plantation since the 1650s, and these lands were not subdivided into residential and agricultural plots until after the plantation was closed following the deaths of the last owners, Thomas and Joanna Dinzey, in 1829. This relegated Sabans to settle and farm the secondary lands across the rugged island.

The French Dominican friar Pere Labat visited Saba in 1701 and remarked upon the island's general state of order and cleanliness relative to its free white residents and noted that most of the island partook in shoemaking, with additional exports of indigo and cotton. Whether Saban cobbling may have included women, he did not specify. Later eighteenth-century authors

4 McGuire and Wurst, "Struggling with the Past," 2002.

5 Ibid., p. 89.

6 St. Eustatius governor Jan de Windt described Saba in 1773 as an island inhabited by poor people who subsist on fish and turtles as a means to support their families. Source: NL-HaNA 1.05.01.02 inv. 629: Feb 2, 1773. By the early nineteenth century, the only recorded annual exports were several head of cattle, although, during this time, government officials on the island participated in a clandestine smuggling and laundering network for pirates, privateers and illegal slave trading vessels with merchants and officials in nearby St. Eustatius, St. Barts, and St. Thomas. See: Espersen, "Fifty Shades of Trade," 2019.

noted that cotton was cultivated in Saba, spun into stockings and sold to other islands with considerable profit.[7]

Many subsistence agriculturalists owned small plots of agricultural land scattered across the island, far from their homes, which required long daily walks just to access. This irregular distribution of land across a small and steep island served to foster poverty across the island among subsistence agriculturalists as the logistics involved in maintaining and accessing small, scattered farming plots made it exceedingly difficult to transport surplus for sale locally or abroad. This encouraged men to work abroad, especially as captains and crew involved in the *kleine vaart* (regional trade) out of St. Eustatius but also St. Thomas and St. Barts. Due to the consistent lack of resident men in Saba, it became known regionally and even internationally as the "Island of Women."[8]

3 Race, Gender and Profession

The 1789 census shows 1,301 free residents and 564 enslaved Africans in Saba.[9] This census also shows the emergence of the free African-descent class on the island, accounting for just four adults and three children. Paying for one's emancipation is virtually unknown in Saba's documentary record, and, instead, they relied upon their owners for manumission. The population for 1816 included 656 "white," 27 free people of African descent and 462 enslaved Africans. The island was divided into six quarters, which included Palmetto Point, The Valley, Crispeen, St. John's, Hell's Gate and The Peak. Tradespeople on the island, all men, included four officials and one lieutenant governor, a school teacher, a cattle herder, fourteen carpenters and one sail maker.

Among these free men, two took to farming, one was a fisherman and seaman while the other was a carpenter. Shoemaking probably continued during this time, although on a much smaller scale than a hundred years prior as observed by Labat. In 1847, a court case was brought against the estate of the deceased John and Mary Hassell wherein the plaintiff, Henry Johnson, claimed that John Hassell, who was formerly enslaved by Henry, was to furnish him and his family

---

7 *The Present State of the West-Indies*, 1778, p. 91; Adams, *A View of Universal History*, 1795, p. 147; Thompson, *The Geographical and Historical Dictionary of America and the West Indies*, 1814, p. 359.

8 Raynal, *Histoire philosophique et politique des établissements et de commerce des Européens dans les deux Indes* [The political and philosophical history of the establishment and commerce of Europeans in the two Indes], 1782, p. 147. Editors' note: see contribution by Römer-Kenepa in this volume.

9 NL-HaNA 1.05.01.02 inv. 636:4391–4400.

with shoes so long as he was in existence.[10] In other instances, free people of African descent were also hired by white families as musicians during holidays or parties.[11] Most residents, known as "small landowners," continued to subsist on fishing and lived off the land, producing little more than some cotton, maize[12] and unspecified fruits and vegetables. Any surplus was generally sold to the Dinzey Plantation in The Bottom. Enslaved Africans owned by Sabans outside of plantation contexts were usually given to field labor, with smaller numbers working as domestic servants.[13] The 1863 emancipation list for Saba shows the professions of those mentioned in many cases.[14] The professions of cook and washer were exclusively the domain of women. "House servants" were mostly women, while field laborers were mostly men. In a few instances, enslaved Africans worked as "sellers" and even served as agents in St. Thomas for residents living in Saba.[15] Some owners took to hiring out their enslaved Africans to both white residents and free Sabans of African descent.[16] Sailing was exclusively the domain of men, mirroring the maritime culture of Europe in general. The ships' muster rolls for vessels calling into St. Eustatius reveal that sailing was not an uncommon profession for enslaved Africans, whether they were ships from Saba or elsewhere. The muster rolls for 1816 show at least ten vessels with enslaved African sailors, four ships for 1817 and twenty-one for 1818.[17] While porting was not specified as a profession in the 1816 review, it would have been a common task for enslaved Africans and later a source of income for free African-descent Sabans following emancipation. Both free men and women worked as porters; although they did not earn a great income from this profession, their resilience and endurance are often highlighted in oral history. "Big Jim" was known for his strength and endurance.[18] Another porter during the late nineteenth century, while carrying a forty-five kg sack of

10 NL-HaNA 1.05.13.01 inv. 540: Dec 2, 1847. This case is one of several examples of "conditional manumission," which was illegal under Dutch colonial law but permitted nonetheless by Saba's civil and criminal court, wherein an enslaved person could be granted manumission with a requirement to provide a certain amount of labor to their former owners for the rest of their life.

11 NL-HaNA 1.05.13.01 inv. 540: January 4, 1849.

12 Locally known as "Indian corn," "small corn" or "Guinea corn."

13 NL-HaNA 2.02.09.08 inv. 246.

14 Ibid.

15 Ibid.

16 NL-HaNA 1.05.13.01 inv. 540: December 14, 1848.

17 NL-HaNA 1.05.13.01 inv. 151, 152, 153.

18 Johnson, *Saban Lore*, 1994, p. 129.

flour on her head, stopped to give birth while ascending The Ladder and continued onward toward The Bottom with her load and newborn.[19]

By the mid-nineteenth century, Saban women continued to produce textiles on a small scale in addition to straw hats.[20] Drawn thread work, stitched by hand, introduced to Saba during the 1870s, became an important industry among women in Saba from this time into the twentieth century. The method and style are generally known as Saba lace but locally known as "Spanish work."[21] By 1907, exports of Saba lace totaled 712 guilders, and, by 1928, it reached a peak of 22,690 guilders, accounting for 30–40 percent of Saba's entire GDP. Spanish work was mostly shipped to customers in the USA, with women working for individual clients and zealously guarding their addresses from others on the island.[22] Literate women found great leverage in this enterprise, allowing them to find new American clients while keeping their addresses a closely guarded secret. Those who were illiterate, consequently, found themselves working for literate client-address holders to create a new working class in Saba exclusive to women.[23] Selling Spanish work abroad by mail provided steady income for households whose men and husbands were working abroad to send intermittent remittances, often for years at a time before returning periodically to the island. These sources of income benefited Saba beyond the household level; cash received through remittances from wage labor abroad and from mail-order payments for lace introduced new supplies of currency to Saba, where it was in chronic short supply during the nineteenth century. Women who had no trade or profession could take to subsistence agriculture on their own plot of land or a plot leased through another landowner for one-third of the crop.

Beyond the potential for lucrative profits earned through spinning cotton apparel or, later, through producing Saba lace, the culturally accepted professions for women were few and often relegated them to positions of subservience, economic dependence on their husbands and poverty. The restrictions were compounded by race and the association of certain professions with class. Washers, domestic servants and cooks were considered low class, and there are no known instances of white women occupying these positions. Porting was the exclusive profession of African-descent Sabans. Government positions,

19 Vito Charles, personal communication, 2014, 2022.

20 Koninklijk Nederlands Aardrijkskundig Genootschap, *Nomina Geographica Neerlandica*, 1885.

21 Editors' note: see contribution by Eliason in this volume.

22 Hartog, *History of Saba*, 1975, p. 65.

23 Eliason, *The Island of Lace*, 2019.

seafaring and most trades beyond tailoring were the domain of men. It is no small wonder that, in light of the few opportunities for women on the island, Saba lace production became so popular and lucrative. Notably, it appears to have been the near unanimous domain of white women, with a few exceptions later in the twentieth century.

4 Race, Racialization and Gender in Colonial Saba

Among the most revealing qualifiers of race, class and gender are titles, prefixes and racial designations that pervade colonial written discourse. Throughout the documentary records of Saba, St. Maarten and St. Eustatius, first introductions of individuals by name in a given document are often characterized by race when or if they are not considered white. This practice appears to have occurred with every instance of people of African descent in the seventeenth century, but the consistency appears to drop somewhat by the early nineteenth century in Saba, which is commensurate with a rise in free people of African descent on the island. In a similar vein to many Caribbean slave societies, the term "negro" is synonymous with slavery in Saba's documentary record, and, in the cases brought to court in the nineteenth century, it was never used to refer to free people unless hurled as an insult.[24] In the first case, the defendant, Miss Rebecca Horton, is purported to have called the plaintiff, Mrs. Eliza Simmons, "a thief, a whore, and told her she was no better than her negro woman Susanna."[25] The second two cases involved an ongoing dispute between John W. Dowlin and Jacob Every that was brought to court no less than four times between 1830 and 1831. It originated from an accusation that Jacob Every attempted to steal land from Elinor Beaks, wherein John called him a liar in court. Jacob Every brought the case back to court for a second time, accusing John W. Dowlin of saying that he was "a villain, and … that he was no better than a negroe."[26] The case was dismissed and brought back again two months later for an identical insult, which was also dismissed.[27] The case was brought back a third time on April 6, 1831, for the same insult, and the court eventually found John guilty, having to pay the court costs of six guilders "for the expression made use by saying he the plaintiff was not as good

24 NL-HaNA 1.05.13.01 inv. 540: July 20, 1827.
25 NL-HaNA 1.05.13.01 inv. 540: April 8, 1829.
26 NL-HaNA 1.05.13.01 inv. 540: June 9, 1830.
27 NL-HaNA 1.05.13.01 inv. 540: February 9, 1831.

as a negroe."[28] Referring to "blackness" or "Africanness" in a derogatory way also occurred among Sabans of African descent themselves. A court case dated February 5, 1827, which was dismissed for lack of evidence, was recorded as follows: "Celia Wood, a black woman, summoneth Miss Pleasant Hassell, free colour'd woman, to appear before an ordinary court held at the house of the vice commandant on Wednesday morning 9 o'clock the 7th instant, ten and there to answer for and make good what she had said by calling her a damn black thief for which she seeketh satisfaction."[29]

With regard to African-descent Sabans not in bondage, the term "free" always preceded the individuals' race: for example, "the free black woman Flora Wood" or "Mary Elizabeth Hassell, free coloured woman."[30] These terms were never employed when referring to white residents but appear with high frequency even when referring to free people of African descent. Adult white residents' names were prefixed with either Ms., Mrs. or Mr., depending on gender and marital status. In a few circumstances in the mid-nineteenth century, these prefixes were also accorded to free African-descent Sabans, such as the aforementioned cobbler Mr. John & Mary Hassell in 1848.

Fidelity among women carried a high social significance and formed the grounds for the divorce request by the husband in the earliest documented case.[31] The importance of fidelity is also characterized by the variety of insults in the nineteenth century that were directed at women who are described in testimonies in the Saba court minutes between 1812 and 1865. The term "whore" was employed in no less than eight occasions, used in such varieties as simply "whore" to the "blood of a whore," a "Martineller's whore," a "son of a whore" and "good for nothing whore."[32] Reputation relative to fidelity also extended to the household level. One colorful rant by Mrs. Mary Winfield is outlined in full below, which was unfortunately cut off prematurely by the court secretary: "Mr. Thomas Hassell summoneth Mrs. Mary Winfield to appear before the court ordinary held at Government House on Wednesday, the third Instant precisely at nine o'clock in the morning, then and there to make appear that the whores under his roof gave Peter Barns the drum to beat also that his house is a damn'd filthy house and all badness is carried on in it, and rouguishness [*sic*], and Peter Barns is one of the Rouges [*sic*]."[33]

28 NL-HaNA 1.05.13.01 inv. 540: December 29, 1831.
29 NL-HaNA 1.05.13.01 inv. 540: February 5, 1827.
30 NL-HaNA 1.05.13.01 inv. 540: September 16, 1827.
31 NAC 4 Gouverneur 103 RT: November 1, 1862.
32 NL-HaNA 1.05.13.01 inv. 540.
33 NL-HaNA 1.05.13.01 inv. 540: March 3, 1813.

Marriage in Saba was normally for life, but, in at least one case, a petition for divorce was filed.[34] The institution of marriage, though, was limited mostly to white Sabans prior to emancipation. The color line was also strongly observed in Saba during this time; as Gast observed, "the amount of mixed race people is very small in comparison to the so-called whites. It is extremely seldom that a white man will take a black woman as a concubine."[35]

The head of a household was primarily responsible for purchasing. In a married household owned by the couple, the household head was invariably the husband. The large numbers of Saban men working abroad for extended periods, sometimes years, provides an opportunity to interpret household goods and furnishings in probate inventories and archaeological excavations according to a woman's choice, in cases either as a single woman as household head or in the absence of her husband. Priorities for disposable income included house maintenance, clothing and furniture. Sabans prioritized their saved money to spend on furniture and especially clothing, although this would also have included house repairs.[36]

Being widowed carried its own social and economic hardships unique to women. Saban culture required a mourning period of three years in dark clothing for women following the death of their husbands, with minimal social activity, which would serve to foster poverty. The constant lack of currency in Saba was also characteristic of the region and fostered a system of debt holding and credit lending in its place that was often only resolvable on the death of the household head and subsequent public auction of the estate to repay debts. This left widowed women potentially homeless and dependent upon the charity of others.[37]

---

34 NAC 4 Gouverneur 103 RT: November 2, 1862.

35 Koninklijk Nederlands Aardrijkskundig Genootschap, *Nomina Geographica Neerlandica*, 1885.

36 Ibid.: "The craving for luxury in furniture, but especially in clothing, is great. It is therefore only for this that their money seems to be disposable."

37 Following Peter Simmons's death in 1785, for example, his debts amounted to 730 pieces of eight between twenty-seven creditors, which even included two enslaved Africans. He owed 517 pieces of eight alone to Saba's governor and resident planter Thomas Dinzey, which included two unspecified debts, two notes of hand, two half barrels of beef, two instances of a cash loan and eight goats. The auction of Peter's estate, which included a house with affixed land and cistern for 250 pieces of eight, along with two separate plots of land for 65 pieces of eight, was insufficient to cover his debt. While, in practice, the house lot could have been purchased by anyone, Thomas Dinzey purchased the estate and held the house mortgaged at 10 percent interest so that Peter's widow and children would not be left homeless. Source: NL-HaNA 1.05.13.01 inv. 542: May 8, 1785.

5 Race, Gender and Saban Naming Conventions

A collection of names was amassed from the 1705 census, Vendue Book 1780–1825, the 1780 census, the 1823 burgher list, the court records 1812–1868 and the 1863 emancipation list. Not all the 1705 census names were used as the scribe appears to have been Dutch and may have written English names in Dutch spelling, which makes their original form uncertain. Thus, these names were not included in the collection. The length of time between the creation of these documents together with the individuals' origin allows duplicates to be eliminated. In cases where a common name, such as "Peter Hassell," was mentioned in the court records without any other contextual information, the name was not recorded in the list. Name instances were recorded both for the total of each occurrence, so the names "Ann" and "Ann Elizabeth" count for two instances of "Ann," and one for "Elizabeth." The sample size of free African-descent names was unfortunately too small to derive any meaningful comparative data. Only two enslaved Africans, Mamboa and Tongerlu, bore West African names in the documentary record.[38] For white males, the data is based on 644 individuals with 57 unique name instances; for enslaved males, it is 413 individuals with 104 unique names;[39] for white females, 122 individuals with 26 unique names; and enslaved females consisted of 487 individuals with 203 unique names.[40]

The lists of names clearly demonstrate a strong white Saban tradition of naming children, probably drawn from family ancestry. Indeed, among white Saban men, only 8 percent of names fell outside the common names such as John, Peter and Thomas, and this trend was mirrored among white Saban women, wherein names other than the common pool constituted just 12 percent. White Sabans typically carried a first name and a middle name and were commonly addressed by their middle name. This small pool extended

38 Richard Ohene-Larbi, personal communication 2014; NL-HaNA 1.05.13.01 inv. 542.

39 Instances of names of white males from most to least prevalent: John (21%), James (14%), Peter (14%), Thomas (9%), William (9%), George (7%), Henry (6%), Abraham (4%), Daniel (4%), Richard (4%), other (8%). Instances of names of enslaved males from most to least prevalent: John (13%), Peter (13%), William (9%), George (6%), James (5%), Richard (5%), Thomas (5%), Abraham (4%), Simon (4%), Joseph (4%), other (33%).

40 Instances of names of white females from most to least prevalent: Ann (22%), Mary (13%), Catharine (10%), Elizabeth (9%), Maria (9%), Joanna (7%), Rebecca (7%), Elenor (4%), Margaret (4%), Jane (3%), Sarah (3%), Susanna (3%), other (12%). Instances of names of enslaved females from most to least prevalent: Ann (8%), Sarah (6%), Catharine (5%), Elizabeth (4%), Lucy (4%), Margaret (4%), Susanna (4%), Jane (3%), Nanny (3%), Frances (3%), other (56%).

to women, but men's names could also be employed as a woman's first name, which was most common with the name "Peter," such as "Peter Ann."

The naming conventions among white Sabans were significantly less pronounced for enslaved Africans, although the ten most common names among the former are also among the most popular for the latter. There is a larger discrepancy between males and females in this regard, especially concerning the variety of names given to female enslaved Africans. Several names given to enslaved Africans suggest that it were the owners who maintained control over naming, suggested through names such as "Black Betty"[41] and "Black Jinny."[42] In other cases, names of prominent figures, identities and places, both present and historical, were used for enslaved Africans. These male names included Yankey, William Wallace, Augustus, Titus, Don Carlo, London, Scotland, Washington and Wellington while a Cleopatra was noted among enslaved women.

6 Race, Gender and Religion in Nineteenth-Century Saba

For nearly two hundred years, from the mid-seventeenth century to the early nineteenth century, the surviving documentary records for Saba make no mention of a resident Christian minister with the exception of Hugh Knox for some years intermittently from at least 1759 to the late eighteenth century.[43] A Presbyterian minister, John Toland, took up residence in The Bottom in the 1820s, but his congregation was minimal, and he often found himself at odds with others in Saba's civil and criminal court.[44] By the time of emancipation in 1863, the "new" Catholic religion in Saba that was introduced in the 1830s and 1840s spread quickly across the island in every village except, notably, The Bottom.[45] The religion was adopted by considerably more women than men, whether free or enslaved. A total of 486 converts lived on the island by July 1 of that year, but only 171 were male.[46] The 486 Catholics also consisted of 183 enslaved Africans, of whom just 71 were male.[47] Sarah Mardenborough was winning many converts in Windwardside, while, by 1863, about three-quarters of Hell's Gate had converted, including both free residents and

41 NL-HaNA 1.05.13.01 inv. 540.

42 Ibid.

43 *Bibliotheca Peirsonaina of the Very Valuable and Extensive Library of the Rev. Thomas Peirson, D. D.*, 1815, p. 185; Saba Vendue Book 1783–1782, March 21, 1782.

44 NL-HaNA 1.05.13.01 inv. 319: December 18, 1834.

45 Saba Catholic Baptismal Records, Church of St. Paul's Conversion, Windwardside, Saba.

46 Ibid.

47 Ibid.

enslaved Africans.[48] Even Middle Island's sole enslaved African was baptized. Meanwhile, The Bottom only counted 25 converts, all white Sabans except for at least one free Saban of African descent, and 9 enslaved Africans.[49] The Catholic enslaved Africans, however, were all property of Capt. James Hassell and William Mitchell, who owned another 20 who were Protestants. Since The Bottom had traditionally been the village of residence for Protestant Christian ministers residing on the island, this may have turned the village into a sort of "stronghold" against the spread of Catholicism. The success of Catholicism in other villages, especially Windwardside, provided a means for residents to differentiate themselves from The Bottom. While no direct correlations between class can be confidently made regarding religion, its spread and adoption was clearly strongest among white women, and very few enslaved Africans and free Sabans of African descent had converted prior to 1857. This may have been a strategic move by Fathers Kistemaker and Gast. By focusing on converting white residents during the church's formative years, they could avoid repeating the errors of the Wesleyan missionaries in evangelizing among free people of African descent and enslaved Africans, which was perceived as a threat to social stability by officials in St. Eustatius.

7 Race, Gender and Purchasing Practices

There appears to be some regular purchasing patterns within sales records from estate and merchant auctions between 1783 to the late nineteenth century in document collections held between the Dutch National Archives and the Saba Planning Bureau.[50] Overall, most purchases were made by men, presumably the heads of households. The exceptions on large purchases appear to be widows and unmarried women with their own household. Items in quantities small enough to permit some inference, such as beacon stones, were bought exclusively by men, while there was no item below that quantity that was purchased only by women. Even those items that were associated with women's activities, such as tailoring, were mostly purchased by men.

48 Ibid.

49 Ibid.

50 The Vendue Book for Saba is irregularly split between both archives. Its holdings are NL-HaNA 1.05.13.01 inv. 542, 543 for the years 1780–1787 and 1814–1855. The Saba Planning Bureau holds a Vendue Book for the years 1816–1876. It should be noted that these books record estates, goods and enslaved Africans purchased at auction, not by a regular sale. Large, single purchases were otherwise recorded directly with the Island Secretary in other document collections.

In 1826, a popular regional merchant by the name of Robert Ferrier arrived in Saba and sold a wide variety of tailoring goods, clothing, tools such as knives and drills and miscellaneous goods such as books and umbrellas. This is the only recorded instance of a non-Saban merchant selling goods in Saba. From the 152 recorded sales by Ferrier, the goods sold consisted mainly of thread, patterned cloth and muslin, but, from this total, just 17 were sales to women. Among these women, one was known to be of African descent (Mary Ann Johnson) and two were probably such (Miss Bey and Susan Hassell). The last, Ann Horton, was probably white and likely either unmarried or widowed. Therefore, based upon the purchases by gender within the Vendue Books, married male heads of households among white Saban families, and probably married African-descent families as well, generally assumed control of finances and irregular purchases. Racially, most purchasers during estate auctions, with few exceptions, were white Sabans. However, regarding the estate of Sarah Gumbs, a free African-descent woman, all identifiable purchasers were of African descent, such as Daniel Woods, Pleasant Hassell and Charles Hassell.[51] The only other purchaser, H. (Henry) Hassell, was one of several with the same name during this time and thus cannot be identified. Otherwise, purchases by African-descended Sabans during auctions of white Sabans' estates were rare; Pleasant Hassell bought an enslaved African named Phetita in 1825 from the estate of Rebecca Simmons, and Charles Hassell bought four milk mugs and flower pots from the liquidated estate of Arthur Gozales.[52] Owning enslaved Africans was not limited by race, and there are several recorded instances of African-descended Sabans owning enslaved Africans. In Saba, enslaved Africans were not wholly barred from participating in auctions, at least by the mid-nineteenth century, but they did not actively participate either. There is only one recorded instance of an enslaved African as a purchaser by the name of Manerva, who bought two blue china cups for a small sum.[53] The aforementioned Peter Simmons also held debts to two enslaved Africans that were only payable upon the liquidation of his estate.

8 Discussion

The immutability of race and gender significantly restricted the ability of women in Saba to improve their social and material dimensions of class

51 NL-HaNA 1.05.13.01 inv. 543: November 14, 1853.

52 Saba Planning Bureau, Vendue Book 1816–1878: February 4, 1860. The Saba Planning Bureau does not have an index or cataloging system for its historic document collections.

53 Saba Planning Bureau, Vendue Book 1816–1878: October 10, 1847.

relative to the whole of the island's society. While one's class can change over time or according to the given social context, race and gender can never be transcended by the individual except through a radical shift in the society's ideology.

The interactions and complexities in the dialectic between class, race and gender-based analyses within nineteenth-century Saba are further tied to the quality, scale and setting of vectors that can be ascribed to them. This harkens back to the "Humpty Dumpty" problem described previously in this contribution.

A woman from Saba would generally be assumed to be poor by her contemporaries in the region by virtue of being from the island, regardless of her race. A woman from The Bottom would be associated with class on a local scale from the principle that residents of The Bottom and Windwardside considered Saba's other villages to be lower class. A white woman from The Bottom would not live in N-Town as it was exclusively associated with African-descended residents and would have been given a first name among a very narrow pool of female names probably derived from her ancestors. If married, her profession would have been mostly limited to weaving, Saba lace or subsistence agriculture. An African-descended woman living in Middle Island would have been considered lower class by virtue of her village and would probably have a first name outside of the narrow pool that otherwise characterized white Saban women. However, her name would be prefixed on documentation with "the woman" rather than Ms. or Mrs., which would otherwise be accorded to a white woman. Due to her African descent, she experienced somewhat fewer cultural restrictions upon her range of professions and could work as a porter, washer, domestic servant (mostly after emancipation) or seamstress.

The women described above exemplify the difficulties in understanding race and gender as separate when they are rather inseparably dependent upon one to inform the other. As immutable aspects of an individual in the colonial Caribbean, gender and race are further informed through their dialectics with powered landscapes, class and material culture. It is hoped that the approach and examples provided from Saba's nineteenth century spur further enquiries into the many facets of powered relations in the colonial Caribbean.

Acknowledgments

Three archives have been consulted for this contribution: the Dutch National Archives (hereafter referred to as NL-HaNA); the National Archive of Curaçao (referred to as NAC) and the Saba Planning Bureau, located in The Bottom, Saba.

Bibliography

Adams, Rev. J. *A View of Universal History, from the Creation to the Present Time*. Vol. 3. London: G Kearley, 1795.

Bibliotheca Peirsonaina of the Very Valuable and Extensive Library of the Rev. Thomas Peirson, D. D. London: Wright & Murphy, 1815.

Eliason, Eric A. *The Island of Lace: Drawn Threadwork on Saba in the Dutch Caribbean*. Jackson: University Press of Mississippi, 2019.

Espersen, Ryan. "'Better than We': Landscapes and Materialities of Race, Class, and Gender in Pre-Emancipation Colonial Saba, Dutch Caribbean." PhD Diss., Leiden University, 2017.

Espersen, Ryan. "Fifty Shades of Trade: Privateering, Piracy, and Illegal Slave Trading in St. Thomas, Early Nineteenth Century." *New West Indian Guide* 93, no. 1–2 (June 2019): 41–68. https://doi.org/10.1163/22134360-09301052.

Hartog, Johannes. *History of Saba*. Curaçao: Van Guilder, 1975.

Harvey, David. *Justice, Nature, and the Geography of Difference*. Oxford: Blackwell Publishers, 1996.

Harvey, David. *Spaces of Hope*. California Studies in Critical Human Geography 7. Berkeley: University of California Press, 2000.

Johnson, Will. *Saban Lore: Tales from My Grandmother's Pipe*. Saba: printed by author, 1994.

Koninklijk Nederlands Aardrijkskundig Genootschap. *Nomina Geographica Neerlandica*. Leiden: E. J. Brill, 1885.

McGuire, Randall H., and LouAnn Wurst. "Struggling with the Past." *International Journal of Historical Archaeology* 6, no. 2 (2002): 85–94. https://doi.org/10.1023/A:1016080520656.

Ollman, Bertell. *Dance of the Dialectic: Steps in Marx's Method*. Urbana: University of Illinois Press, 2003.

Ollman, Bertell. *Dialectical Investigations*. New York: Routledge, 1993.

Ollman, Bertell. "Why Dialectics? Why Now?" In *Dialectics for the New Century*, edited by Bertell Ollman and Tony Smith, 8–25. Basingstoke: Palgrave Macmillan, 2008.

Ollman, Bertell, and Tony Smith. "Introduction." In *Dialectics for the New Century*, edited by Bertell Ollman and Tony Smith, 1–7. Basingstoke: Palgrave Macmillan, 2008.

Raynal, Abbé. *Histoire philosophique et politique des établissements et de commerce des Européens dans les deux Indes* [The political and philosophical history of the establishment and commerce of Europeans in the two Indes]. Vol. 5. Amsterdam, 1782.

Sayer, Derek. *The Violence of Abstraction: The Analytic Foundations of Historical Materialism*. Oxford: Basil Blackwell, 1987.

The Present State of the West-Indies, Containing an Accurate Description of What Parts Are Possessed by The Several Powers of Europe. London: R. Baldwin, 1778.

Thompson, G. A. *The Geographical and Historical Dictionary of America and the West Indies*. London: J. Carpenter, 1814.

Wurst, LouAnn. "A Class All Its Own: Explorations of Class Formation and Conflict." In *Historical Archaeology*, edited by Martin Hall and Stephen W. Silliman, 190–208. Blackwell Studies in Global Archaeology 9. Oxford: Blackwell Publishers, 2006.

CHAPTER 4

New York, Cuba and the Birth of a Subversive Dutch Caribbean Writer: an Introduction to P. P. Medardo De Marchena's "Women and Modern-Day Life" [1934]

Margo Groenewoud

Abstract

As anticolonial writer and orator, Pedro Pablo Medardo de Marchena (1899–1968) was a unique phenomenon in Curaçao during the late 1920s and 1930s. This contribution introduces his life and work, following the young De Marchena on his journey as a writer, contextualizing his perceptions of "modern-day life," developed through his association with Marcus Garvey and other anticolonial movements of the time. The contribution introduces and analyzes the topical approach in De Marchena's pamphlet on women, published for the first time in English translation in this volume, subtitled "An Intimate Study of Women as Our Life Companions with Some Advice."

Keywords

Medardo de Marchena – biography – Marcus Garvey – Filogenes Maillard – Curaçao

As anticolonial writer and orator, Pedro Pablo Medardo de Marchena (1899–1968), widely known as Medardo de Marchena, was a unique phenomenon in Curaçao during the late 1920s and 1930s. Academic interest in De Marchena developed relatively late and long after his death in the 1990s, mostly through the work of the Dutch scholar of Papiamentu literature, Aart G. Broek.[1] His small but interesting legacy still leaves us with many questions, in particular

1 Broek, "The Rise of a Caribbean Island's Literature," 1990. Most recently: Broek, *Medardo de Marchena: Staatsgevaarlijk in koloniaal Curaçao* [Medardo de Marchena: A danger to the state in colonial Curaçao], 2021.

 | DOI:10.1163/9789004690882_006

about the development of his writing and formation of his ideas. This certainly holds true for the pamphlet published for the first time in English translation in this volume, subtitled "An Intimate Study of Women as Our Life Companions with Some Advice." After all, the topic and approach were neither mainstream nor part of any public discourse in 1934 Curaçaoan society.[2]

Studying De Marchena inevitably draws attention to the existence of subversive voices in the small but rapidly developing late colonial Dutch Antilles[3] and underpins the need to acknowledge the presence of Dutch citizens in anti-imperialistic transnational communities and movements.[4] In Dutch Caribbean intellectual history, the work of Medardo de Marchena does not stand out for its literary, rhetorical, ideological or philosophical value. His courageous and original work is primarily intriguing and historically important because of the uniqueness of his published anticolonial criticism in the late 1920s and 1930s Dutch Antilles. As was the case with anticolonial writers in Suriname such as Anton de Kom (1898–1945) and Louis Doedel (1905–1980), subversive actions in these decades met with harsh repercussions by Dutch authorities.[5] In Curaçao, De Marchena experienced police scrutiny and social exclusion on all levels, both public and private, in political as well as business matters.[6] Taken together with the history of continuous repression he faced, his writings assume a significant historical value.

In this introduction, I briefly present the life and work of Medardo de Marchena and follow the young De Marchena in his journey toward becoming a published writer. In exploring what experiences shaped his perceptions of "modern-day life," new insights are presented that bring us closer to understanding how he was influenced by movements such as the UNIA (Universal Negro Improvement Association) of Marcus Garvey, and how he started as a published author. From here, this introduction sets off to analyze the topical approach in his essay on women.

2 For a contextual introduction, see: Groenewoud, "Women's Mobilization in the Dutch Caribbean," 2019. An abridged version of this article is published in this section of the handbook.

3 The term Dutch Antilles refers to the six islands that historically formed part of the Dutch colonial territories in the Caribbean, prior to their formal constitution as the Netherlands Antilles in 1954.

4 This is one of the focus areas of my current research project "Unholy Alliances: Negotiation, Ideology and Morality in Twentieth-Century Dutch-Spanish Caribbean Affairs." See: https://unholyalliances.hcommons.org.

5 Groenewoud, "Decolonization, Otherness, and the Neglect of the Dutch Caribbean," 2021.

6 Family members testified of the long-term impact this had during a public lecture about De Marchena at Mongui Maduro Library, Curaçao, May 8, 2018.

Pedro Pablo Medardo de Marchena was born in 1899 in Curaçao as the first son of Delphina Wiel (1875–1906) and Abraham de Benjamin de Marchena (1850–1926). Although they had more children, they never married and it would take until 1918 for Benjamin de Marchena to register his fatherhood.[7] His mother, the Afro-Curaçaoan Delphina Wiel, was born in 1875 on Plantage Savonet, the child of parents born in slavery. She would legally change her name to Anna Delphina Martina in 1906. Benjamin de Marchena, was a typical Sephardic Jewish merchant of his generation, born in Santo Domingo in 1850 in a family that originated from Curaçao and held Dutch citizenship. As an adult, he followed the family tradition and became an active member of the Jewish-Masonic Caribbean-Atlantic network of traders, mostly working with Spanish-speaking communities and with close ties to relations throughout the Caribbean and in New York. Following the passing of Delphina, he permanently took residence in Cuba, where he would live and work in the sugar business until his death in 1926.

Benjamin de Marchena's children grew up at a distance from their father's world—both physically and ethnically—on a relatively small Caribbean island ruled by local Dutch colonial authorities, supported by the Catholic missionary church. Growing up in an Afro-Curaçaoan Catholic community in the early twentieth century implied that color, religious conformity and parental social status defined social mobility. With his parents not married, Medardo de Marchena could have been refused educational opportunities, as most males of unmarried black mothers were compelled to already start working at the age of twelve or thirteen. His father must have had some influence here since he finished school at sixteen. After that, he landed a job in retail and later also started to work for his father.

In the summer of 1919, young Medardo de Marchena sailed to New York to find an outlet for a stock of Panama hats produced on his birth island. According to the Immigration Office papers, he stayed here with a friend, Ernest Hanhest, at 396 Broadway. Hanhest was a widower in his forties, born in Switzerland and based in New York.[8] Archival traces indicate he was a trader in haberdashery and a former barkeeper. It was perhaps through this Swiss connection that Medardo de Marchena would soon meet his later wife Vivian, daughter of the

7 This was first done at a notary office in Havana in 1918. In 1920, it was formalized and changed in the Curaçao registers. Source: "WieWasWie." Available at: https://www.wiewaswie.nl/en.

8 Shipping details are from The Statue of Liberty – Ellis Island Foundation, Inc website - "Passenger Search – The Statue of Liberty & Ellis Island." Available at: https://heritage.statueofliberty.org; and also in the Library Edition of Ancestry.com, available at a few branches of the New York Public Library.

Swiss Albert Pfaffhauser and his Saban wife Rose Elvina Simmons.[9] Two years after meeting in New York, they got married in Curaçao on September 10, 1921, when Vivian was already pregnant with their first child.

Leaving the island, seeing other parts of the world and meeting people from various backgrounds must have influenced De Marchena's thinking. In the first decades of the twentieth century, passenger shipping was booming and thousands of young men and women set sail from the Caribbean to New York. Some of them were intent on migrating, whereas others traveled as laborers, adventurers or seafarers. All encountered worlds in which the approach to race and class differed completely from the colonial societies they left behind.[10] Many Caribbean migrants, both men and women, developed radical thoughts, such as the New York based Surinamese-Guyanese couple Otto and Hermina Huiswoud, who became active in the black communist labor movement.[11] The largest of all the black justice-seeking organizations in these decades was the Universal Negro Improvement Association (UNIA), founded by the Jamaican Marcus Garvey (1887–1940), with influential chapters in the sugar industries of Cuba and the Dominican Republic. It is in these chapters in particular that Dutch Caribbean labor migrants interacted with Garveyites.[12] Also, maritime communities and meeting places in harbor towns have brought Garveyism to the Dutch Caribbean as we know from the work of Manuel Fray and the life of Felix Chakoetoe.[13]

In April 1921, the *Negro World*—the formal journal of the UNIA—published the first and only article that had the Dutch Antilles and Suriname as subject, titled "Autocracy in the Dutch West Indies." It was sent to the editors for publication from Havana, Cuba, on April 7, 1921, by an author named Filogenes Maillard. The piece introduces the Dutch West Indies as: "[a colony with a population] of 150,000 souls of whose number eight-tenths are of the African race. And it is painful to state that this population is absolutely ruled by a half dozen Hollanders who are ignorant of the needs of the people. The inhabitants of these colonies, the Negroes especially, have entirely nothing to do with the

---

9 Saban Will Johnson wrote about the Simmons family on his blog. See: Johnson, "A Dream of Return," 2021.

10 James, *Holding Aloft the Banner of Ethiopia*, 1999.

11 Turner and Turner, *Caribbean Crusaders and the Harlem Renaissance*, 2005.

12 Muñiz and Giovannetti, "Garveyismo y racismo en el Caribe: El caso de la población Cocola en la República Dominicana" [Garveyism and racism in the Caribbean: The case of the Cocola population in the Dominican Republic], 2003; Davidson, "Disruptive Silences," 2017.

13 Allen, "Learning to Be a Man," 2011. Editors' note: See also the excerpt at the end of this section from a playtext by Gilbert Bacilio about the 1922 labor strikes led by Chakutoe.

government of their respective birthplaces. But it is their fault, as they also simply pass their lives 'fooling' with the bible."[14]

Although there is no evidence, I consider it very likely that Medardo de Marchena was involved in the development of this piece. The English text uses a Dutch word ("Hollanders") and some phrasing (e.g., "a half dozen" or "'fooling' with the bible") that indicate a Dutch-speaking author and clearly not a French one. This, however, could, in theory, also result from the fact that the presumed author—found in several records as Philogène Maillard (1882–?)—hailed from the French side of the Leeward Antillean island of St. Maarten, the other half of which was the Dutch colony of St. Maarten.[15] Most importantly though, the main arguments are fully in line with the other writings of De Marchena, and these were not mainstream Dutch anticolonial ideology and required insider knowledge of Curaçao. The article drew attention to two themes in particular: the role of the Catholic clergy and the power position of the black population as majority. Both themes—and I will come back to this later—are also central to the pamphlet we here discuss on women in society.

One week before the letter on "Autocracy in the Dutch West Indies" was sent to the editors of the *Negro World*, Marcus Garvey made his first Caribbean tour, speaking in Havana, Cuba, on March 31, 1921. With his father living there, it seems plausible that De Marchena stayed in Cuba at the time.[16] In that case, it could very well be that he was personally present at the March 31 rally and encountered Maillard, who lived in Cuba and wrote more pieces for the *Negro World* and *The Crisis*, here.[17] Given his St. Maarten's background and his connections with these US-based papers, Maillard was the perfect man to bring the subject of repression of the Dutch Afro-Caribbean population to the attention of the movement.

Back in Curaçao, as a married man with his own business, De Marchena became unstoppable in the late 1920s and 1930s, developing a critical voice on the island by speaking in public meetings and publishing articles in local journals and newspapers.[18] Although there were ample reasons in the Dutch Caribbean to fear repression and prefer anonymity, he did this under his own name, not really having a choice when speaking in public on a small island

14 Maillard, "'Autocracy in the Dutch West Indies,'" 1921.

15 See "Archives nationales d'outre-mer" [Overseas national archives], Tabelle annuelle des naissances [Yearly table of births], Commune de Saint Martin, 1882. Available at: http://anom.archivesnationales.culture.gouv.fr/caomec2.

16 According to De Marchena biographer Aart G. Broek, family members never referred to a Cuba visit. Email Aart G. Broek to the author, November 20, 2022.

17 See, for instance, Maillard, "In the French West Indies," 1922.

18 Mongui Maduro Library in Curaçao keeps a unique collection of these publications.

where everybody knows everybody. In 1929, the pamphlet appeared that would establish his name: *Ignorancia ó educando un pueblo* (Ignorance, or educating the people).[19] Several other essays followed, including the one published in this volume.

When the Second World War broke out, the Dutch government decided that, in order to protect the oil industries in Curaçao and Aruba, all people who may pose a risk would be isolated in a guarded camp in Bonaire. Among the people arrested and imprisoned in May 1940 was Medardo de Marchena. He would fiercely protest his fate for years, until eventually, in 1943, the government psychiatrist Dr. De Regt was assigned with the task to assess the mental state of De Marchena. After his verdict—stating that nothing was wrong with him—the government decided to grant him some liberties, provided he would "refrain from scribbling political pieces."[20] Like all other anticolonial writers in the Dutch Caribbean, De Marchena never received any apology or reparation payment, although his business was ruined by the repressive actions taken by the Dutch government against him.[21]

In "Women and Modern-day Life," the author presents himself as a well-informed, widely traveled man. Right from the start, he makes a comparison between Curaçaoan society and "the rest of the world." This approach is typical; the voice of De Marchena as author is impatient, often offensive and in constant disbelief regarding the apparent blindness or at least shortsightedness of the "people" he addresses.

After an introduction, the text follows a seemingly random path addressing seven subthemes: creation, capitalism, education, religion, fashion, sports and morality. This structured approach does not prevent the reader from being confronted with many associative jumps. The piece on "capitalism," for instance, moves from the elite to prostitution, to marriage and then to the church. The text uses two types of rhetoric: one of an accusing nature and one of a prophesying nature. The accusing pieces are the ones on capitalism, religion and fashion. Here, De Marchena tries to provoke women to look at themselves and their behavior and see how their supposedly backward, naive or shallow ways of living are standing in the way of progress and emancipation. His tone and messages are bold and often condescending, for instance when he accuses women of "using religion as their road of salvation or as something to help

19 P. P. Medardo de Marchena, *Ignorancia ó educando un pueblo*, Curaçao, 1929.

20 National Archive Curaçao, Collection Governmental Archives 1938–1945, letter dated August 25, 1944.

21 Groenewoud, "Decolonization, Otherness, and the Neglect of the Dutch Caribbean," 2021.

them achieve their convenience." And: "[religion] facilitates them with means for their corruption."

The pieces with a prophesying rhetoric are equally critical but emphasize the "way out" for women. Here, we see De Marchena at his best in his role as "man of the world," referring to other countries and customs and showing what we can learn from them. Again, diplomacy is not his forte. "Remember that sports will eliminate all kinds of worries, boost your blood circulation and make us forget about that habit of all small communities, which is gossiping."

In all cases, a deep disappointment underlies the text. From what De Marchena learned and read of the contemporary critical movements such as the UNIA, it must have included the conviction that if you want to change, you can, but you need to stand up and join forces. Marcus Garvey was known for the centrality of that message, whether he addressed world politics, the situation of migrants or competing with the white business world: numbers matter.[22] The reality of Curaçao, with a vast marginalized and silenced majority, seemed at quite a distance from the prospect of change.

It is interesting to read a text published on a very small and religious island in 1934 speaking openly about sexuality in a remarkably bold way—whether referring to pleasure, protection or morality. De Marchena's concern with prostitution is relatively early; historical sources indicate that this became a public issue on the island in the 1940s with the arrival of US-American soldiers.[23] Nevertheless, the population of the island had doubled between 1915 and 1935, and, with the large influx of single male migrants, it makes sense that urban life in and around the harbor and the refinery must have encountered issues with sex workers, clients and the disruption of family life already in the 1920s.

It remains unclear if, and to what extent, this essay was an attempt to support women's emancipation. De Marchena had shown keen support for this earlier in a 1933 lecture for the debating club published in *De Onpartijdige* (The non-partisan). In this, he shared his belief that "we haven't been able to achieve much of importance for our islands yet because we neglect women."[24] Throughout his work, De Marchena showed concern for the allocation of power in Curaçao and in particular for how that impacted the Afro-Curaçaoan population. This was by and far the majority and, in all situations, the least

22 James, *Holding Aloft the Banner of Ethiopia*, 1999, pp. 134–6.

23 Kempadoo, "The Happy Camp in Curaçao," 2004; Schields, "Eros against Empire," 2019; Kleijn and Schrover, "The Dutch State as a Pimp," 2013.

24 Original phrase in Papiamentu: "Considera si awe nos no a logra haci nada grandi pa nos patria ta pasobra nos ta descuida muher." *De Onpartijdige* 2, no. 27, September 13, 1933. Cited in: Broek, "Meer aandacht voor Medardo de Marchena" [More attention to Medardo de Marchena], *Antilliaans Dagblad*, May 15, 2018.

powerful of the population. There was no justification for that imbalance according to De Marchena but nor was there any justification for the fact that this was never challenged by this majority. This essay is no exception: here, the disbalance of power and the inability or unwillingness to change this by the oppressed are the central themes as well.

The choice of topic and focus on women seems directly related to his own travel experience and the result of seeing a completely new type of woman in places such as New York. De Marchena himself found his first wife there: a young Protestant woman with a transnational background. His repeated use of references to modernity and his examples from American marketing, tourism and general customs speak of a man enlightened by his own travel impressions. But, of course, this was not just about him: it informs us about the impact of large-scale transnational experiences in the mid-twentieth-century Caribbean societies and the risks of disruptive dynamics in the growing and transforming island societies that were still colonial at their core. In the fast-changing world of the 1930s, limited opportunities for formal education and social mobility for women on the island posed a major barrier to their emancipation. De Marchena had plenty of reasons for his concern with regard to a growing social divide, and he voiced them. Athough, indeed, his rhetoric might be read as undiplomatic, bold, unkind or sometimes downright offensive, De Marchena was among the first to show his concern about substantial rifts in this Caribbean society, and he did speak up, not only to address this in general but also to discuss how these rifts were related to gender. As such, again, he was the pioneer voice of his generation.

Bibliography

Allen, Rose Mary. "'Learning to Be a Man': Afro-Caribbean Seamen and Maritime Workers from Curaçao in the Beginning of the Twentieth Century." *Caribbean Studies* 39, no. 1 (2011): 43–64. https://doi.org/10.1353/crb.2011.0014.

Broek, Aart G. *Medardo de Marchena: Staatsgevaarlijk in koloniaal Curaçao* [Medardo de Marchena: A danger to the state in colonial Curaçao]. Haarlem: In de Knipscheer, 2021.

Broek, Aart G. "Meer aandacht voor Medardo de Marchena [More attention to Medardo de Marchena]." *Antilliaans Dagblad*, May 15, 2018.

Broek, Aart G. "The Rise of a Caribbean Island's Literature: The Case of Curaçao and Its Writing in Papiamentu." PhD diss., VU Amsterdam, 1990.

Davidson, Christina Cecelia. "Disruptive Silences: The AME Church and Dominican-Haitian Relations." *Journal of Africana Religions* 5, no. 1 (January 2017): 1–25. https://doi.org/10.5325/jafrireli.5.1.0001.

Groenewoud, Margo. "Decolonization, Otherness, and the Neglect of the Dutch Caribbean in Caribbean Studies." *Small Axe: A Caribbean Journal of Criticism* 25, no. 1 (March 2021): 102–15. https://doi.org/10.1215/07990537-8912808.

Groenewoud, Margo. "Women's Mobilization in the Dutch Antilles (Curacao and Aruba, 1946–1993)." *Clio. Women, Gender, History* 50, no. 2 (June 2019): 63–85.

Hill, Robert A., Marcus Garvey, and Universal Negro Improvement Association, eds. *The Marcus Garvey and Universal Negro Improvement Association Papers: The Caribbean Diaspora, 1920–1921*. Vol. 12. Durham, NC: Duke University Press, 2014.

James, Winston. *Holding Aloft the Banner of Ethiopia: Caribbean Radicalism in Early Twentieth-Century America*. London: Verso, 1999.

Johnson, Will. "A Dream of Return." *The Saba Islander* (blog), March 10, 2021. https://thesabaislander.com/2021/03/10/a-dream-of-return.

Kempadoo, Kamala. *Sexing the Caribbean: Gender, Race, and Sexual Labor*. New York: Routledge, 2004.

Kleijn, Mariëlle, and Marlou Schrover. "The Dutch State as a Pimp. Policies Regarding a Brothel on Curaçao (1945–1956)." *Tijdschrift Voor Sociale En Economische Geschiedenis* 10, no. 3 (2013): 33–54.

Maillard, Filogenes. "'Autocracy in the Dutch West Indies.' Letter to Negro World, April 23, 1921." In *The Marcus Garvey and Universal Negro Improvement Association Papers, Volume XII: The Caribbean Diaspora, 1920–1921*, edited by Robert A. Hill et al, 193. Durham, NC: Duke University Press, 2014.

Maillard, Filogenes. "In the French West Indies." *The Crisis: A Record of the Darker Races* 23, no. 3 (January 1922): 127–8.

Muñiz, Humberto García, and Jorge L. Giovannetti. "Garveyismo y racismo en el Caribe: El caso de la población Cocola en la República Dominicana" [Garveyism and racism in the Caribbean: The case of the Cocola population in the Dominican Republic]. *Caribbean Studies* 31, no. 1 (2003): 139–211.

Schields, Chelsea. "Eros against Empire: Visions of Erotic Freedom in Archives of Decolonisation." *Tijdschrift Voor Genderstudies* 22, no. 2 (2019): 145–61.

Turner, Joyce Moore, and W. Burghardt Turner. *Caribbean Crusaders and the Harlem Renaissance*. Urbana: University of Illinois Press, 2005.

CHAPTER 5

Women and Modern-Day Life: an Intimate Study of Women as our Life Companions with Some Advice [1934]

Pedro Pablo Medardo de Marchena

Abstract

This pamphlet was originally published in 1934 in Papiamentu with the title *Muher i bida moderna: Estudio intimo di muher como nos compañera den vida acompaña di algun consehos pa.* In this text, the writer and orator De Marchena addresses his own society and reflects on the status of women therein, calling for a modernization of conservative values and the equal treatment of women, comparing Curaçao to America. He criticizes the capitalist view of women's bodies as commodity. He also offers "advice" to women on issues ranging from religion to sports to fashion and morality. The text offers a glimpse into social debates and commonplace views toward women in the Caribbean in the 1930s.

Keywords

women – modernity – Curaçao – America – morality – conservatism

1 Introduction

Few people really value the actions that women, also known as the *fair or weaker sex*, represent, develop or have influence on in our lives, both regarding the opposite sex as well as regarding themselves as women. Daring to analyze or tackle this most delicate of topics for public opinion is not entirely to unburden myself in any way nor to give any unfair criticism or offend the female sex. Since women are invaluable in men's lives, just as men are equally invaluable for women, what I'm about to relate is nothing but a repetition of what is currently happening. Besides that, I'd like to rectify some errors that can always be found due to misunderstanding or stupidity while at the same time hoping to delight my readers with some strange and modern ideas, thus hoping also

 | DOI:10.1163/9789004690882_007

to move the rock of old-fashioned conservatism, which is keeping our nation behind in comparison to the rest of the world.

2 Women and the Time of Creation

If we have to believe the fantasy of history, we will find something very mysterious to solve, taking into consideration how people were created. According to this fantasy of history, the first man was created from mud and the first woman from man's rib, which shows us that women come from men and not men from women, a bit similar to the mystery of which was first, the chicken or the egg. I only intend to show this relationship, starting with women from the time of creation, regardless of whether the acceptance of the origin of mankind is correct or not. Using the word woman, I inform the reader that this expression is accepted by women in general.[1]

Departing from this point of view, the woman is described as the Mother of Humanity and it is from this that the woman has the symbolic name of Holy Mother of the Church, in acceptance that she represents the Incubator for reproduction or the source to populate the world. I will not waste my time writing about those who speak badly about women, something we can constantly hear all around us by both men and women. It is absurd, considering that a woman is our mother and that women are vital for us. Just as there are bad women, there are bad men, in the same way there are women who damage men just as there are men who damage women, yet we should never forget that women are the most enslaved of the two genders and who suffer the most contempt. History is something that changes and it's often written according to the author's taste, stubbornness and convenience. However, considering sources from ancient history, we can convince ourselves that women have always been men's common instrument, yet, thanks to the development of our civilization, this situation has changed, allowing more reciprocity between men and women, and, nowadays, we can even dare to say that women are enjoying many more advantages than before. The history of women changes according to their race and the laws made for them by men. Thus, women being from the

1 Editors' note: Medardo de Marchena wrote his text before there was a standardized official spelling of Papiamentu. The word *muher* (woman) is conventionally considered an inappropriate address, with the colloquial preference for *damas* (ladies). The term *Muher di bida or muhé di bida* carries a pejorative connotation of a prostitute. The title of De Marchena's text, *Muher i bida moderna*, plays on this, seeking to resignify and modernize the concept of woman in a positive way. In this sentence, De Marchena explains to the reader that the term *muher* (muhé) is, in fact, acceptable and ought not to be regarded as a negative term.

same species as men, it would be unfair if we stubbornly limit their wills and actions just for the sake of our convenience or selfishness.

3 Women and Capitalism

It's a very well-known fact that capitalism, or the system that most governments with power in the world are using, is a force based on money or capital. It mainly obeys the requirements or benefits of capitalists, the industry or commerce bosses and it has a lot of influence on women as well. If we refer to capitalism with regard to women, it shall not be based on what our capitalist laws grant them as rights in terms of worldly things, meaning money, property, in case of inheritance or divorce, but in the sense that capitalist laws favor the elite, allowing prostitution openly even though all governments pretend to defend morality.

It's almost certain that there is a punishment in our penal codes for having or maintaining brothels or houses of prostitution since only a few countries have laws that have not been made by the church (ecclesiastical laws). Under capitalist laws, prostitution was bound to flourish because every rich man can have as many sweeties as he likes, whether they are married or single. For government laws to be moralizing, they should be able to put an end to this sad system in which women are converted into money-making machines and, at the same time, a source of infection or disease for every innocent human being. Every decent person would like to see an end to this machine-like life, wishing for the government to introduce a companionship license system. Maybe my readers will now observe that it's impossible to get rid of prostitution because, even though prostitution is the system in which women rent their bodies to men, there would still be many more cases to solve because there are many married women who are living under the same circumstances as any prostitute. My readers would be completely right since it's difficult to control such actions. Capitalism invented marriage with the great objective of getting people to commit, frequently men, who are obliged to take care of their women and children (also forced by the capitalist laws of all governments). And they must actually be satisfied with the salary that the capitalist employer decides to give them according to circumstances. If the employer's pockets are full, the employee will get a loaf of bread, otherwise he will have to be content with a slice of bread. To give importance to marriage, the partner of capitalism, namely the church, has sanctified marriage as a sacrament, converting women into servants of men and men into instruments of these same women, giving special attention to children, so that this sacrament may continue its course for ever and ever, always at the primary interest of capitalism.

4 Women and Education

There's no reason why we should believe that women are inferior to men when it comes to education. This is one of the many exaggerated beliefs that can be found in Curaçao. In all places of our civilized world, women occupy the same positions as men, and all those who read foreign newspapers, from Holland and elsewhere, can read about female professors or doctors in the sciences, arts, literature and so on, who can be found in great numbers in several countries. Here, as a colony, even men are poorly educated, leave alone women being educated. It is at best hoped that they are useful for what is essentially necessary, meaning domestic life, and, unfortunately, it is because of poor instruction itself that our women are in so much obscurity. Our women are generally timid and sensitive. We can say that women inherently don't know much, almost nothing, and there are many cases in which a young lady, due to the mother's poor education (readers should realize that Curaçao has a mere eighty years of "civilized" life)[2], had to be content with the friendship of some classy prostitute or servants from their own class in order to learn something about their own sex or the male sex, resulting many times in the demise of these children because of corrupted people. Modern schools should equip their young ladies who are becoming young women entering puberty with sex education. A young lady must know about prophylaxis, about the opposite sex and learn how to protect herself and not become a victim of ignorance and avoid being infected with venereal diseases. It's easy to provide this education by means of cinematography as well as with adequate reading material on this matter.

5 Women and Religion

If women are called the weaker sex, it's not for any grace, but it's really because they are very weak and sensitive, and, therefore, all kinds of men, both civil and religious, exercise a lot of influence on them and dominate them as they see fit. If we pay proper attention to this, we will notice that, if it wasn't for women, religion would not be nearly close to where it is nowadays, let alone exist. Women are sensitive to things that cause pain, they cannot bear to hear

2 Editors' note: Here the author refers to the abolition of slavery in Curaçao in 1863.

someone moan or cry. They immediately pity him or her. This shows that they are a bit more humane than men, but, unfortunately, men take advantage of this weak and sentimental part of women so that they may take the most advantage out of them at their convenience.

Besides these actions for material benefits, the greatest dominion that women have over men is through religious people disguised as great benefactors and divine counselors who often take advantage of the influence on them so that they may let the husbands submit themselves to their will. It is well-known that men are always rebellious and will not allow any man or a man just like himself to trick him with any kind of fantasy and these divine counselors (priests) know that the husband, for the love of his sweetheart, is willing to do anything, thus giving them guaranteed success in attaining their objectives. The poor machos can't do without the love of their sweethearts, so for this reason they will surrender. If it wasn't for women, the donkey would have broken his bridle and never let them bridle it again. If women were able to assess how they are destroying their husband's virility, they would never force themselves to religious obedience, yet they would join with their husband, eliminating all third persons, the two of them forming one sound body, free from judgment and prejudice. Thus, the only advantage that a lot of women could get out of religion would be to hide behind the wall of religion so that they may pass as decent and thus cover up their evil deeds; as it happens in the evening in such action, during twilight devotions and at the communion table and for this behavior, we can thus observe that religion also favors evil deeds. Another case is that all women who kneel in front of the altar to get married must go for confession (many of them wearing a wreath and bridal veil) while they are on the family path. This action leaves us with two ways to choose from, to think that they are either violating this religious act to pass as pure or that they may be tolerated to do it. It's for us to conclude from this that women are really using religion as their road to salvation or as something to help them achieve their convenience. In these cases, we have to exclude matrons or young ladies secluded in age, in other words, those who have lost all illusion of marriage. We are tired of hearing our young damsels say: I'm not going to church because my dress wasn't completed and I don't like the others or because my suitor is sick etc., which clearly shows that they use the (religious) center as a place to show off their dresses or as a means to facilitate a "come and meet me there or wait for me" and hardly for the religious objective. If we dedicate ourselves to study the consequences of those most likable Aurora[3] masses, we will find many

3 Editors' note: Aurora masses are the Catholic masses held at dawn for the course of nine days before Christmas.

nice stories to fill up a novel, and funny things like setting the alarm clock etc. In these mentioned forms, religion does not constitute a stimulation for our women, but, in many cases, it facilitates them with means for their corruption.

6 Women and Fashion

I'm convinced that women are more inclined to spend time on their dresses than any other vice. Lately, your mouth can literally drop open when you see how well people, and especially poor people, dress up. We can figure out where the fire comes from, because you will soon see the smoke, nevertheless, it's very sad that this may be the only preference that damsels have, when the world requires many other things besides clothing. The misfortune of our people is that they don't want to learn anything other than imitation; for this reason, they keep having the same experiences. If our local women could understand that all illusion is only temporary, then they would not exert themselves so much, let alone expose themselves to criticism for such a vague pleasure of passing for something that they are not and which their situation doesn't allow them either. It would be so much simpler for a woman to dress better and be dedicated to developing herself in another sense, such as in educational rules and so forth, trying to be kinder to everybody. She will then gain more satisfaction than from wrapping herself up in clothes, twisting like a snake and pretending to rock the world. I will never forget a commercial for the car brand Ford, which says the following: Buy a Ford and spend the rest. We should therefore suggest to our ladies: Dress modestly and spend the rest on food.

7 Women and Sports

In Curaçao, excluding the few people with money, we can dare say that the only sports that our women engage in is that of dressing up and going to church. For this reason, you will notice that many of our ladies are in bad shape. Some are too fat, others are very bulky, others have a curved back, others have a very big belly and all these deformed figures are because of a lack of exercise. Some people don't like to walk and want to live in their cars. There are others who don't even know why we have so much seacoast around us.

It's really sad, my friends, remember that jogging is ideal for losing weight, bending your dorsal spine toward your toes ten times a day will flatten your tummy, stretching as an exercise will eliminate your hunchback and there are many other kinds of exercises that will help you protect yourself against diseases while, at the same time, they will give you a nice and elegant form. Notice the many American tourists and among them many elderly people who are still in good shape. Let's move forward, ladies, step out of those old people's habits and embrace modernism. Remember that sports will eliminate all kinds of worries, boost your blood circulation and make us forget about that habit of all small communities, which is gossiping.

8 Women and Immorality

Most women have an incorrect understanding of true immorality. If a woman becomes a victim of a man's lovemaking and must bring their fruit into this world outside of wedlock, we should not consider this an immoral act but only due to social prejudice by a society that condemns her because she got in this situation without legal permission, nothing else. Immoral is everything that people commit against their nature, for example, acts that sacred history recounts about Sodom and Gomorrah, which is the result of depriving a society and which forces people to fight the laws of nature just to comply with society's stubborn wishes. Immoral are all those who take the vow of chastity, either men or women, because they are actually going against God's commandment, which says: Go and Multiply. Therefore, our women should flee from these kinds of people because they are truly against morality. How is it possible that someone who has vowed to never get married or to have no sexual relationship with anyone can advise others to get married? What kind of knowledge does he have about the topic to do this? Sacred history once again reminds us about the passage of the appearance of the Angel Gabriel to the priest Zechariah, to announce in the name of God that his wife will give birth to a child and, because he doubted, he remained mute until the day the child was born (Saint John the Baptist). Every conscious woman knows very well that she has come to the world with the same mission as her mother and that she has to walk the same path, at least as soon as nature confirms this when she enters puberty (thus becoming a woman). If half of humanity is suffering nowadays, it's because society or the religious foundation puts it in this situation, introducing all kinds of deprivations and abstentions under the farce of morality. If we could see or read the hearts of many women, we would weep with them when they are in agony, when burning desire is suffocating them, because the bridle of selfishness or social intrigue is cutting their will to action. To alleviate their suffering souls, these social martyrs many times resort to homosexual vices, submit themselves to surgeries or make use of consolation devices (dildos) because their shame supports their cowardice of breaking this silence in a gesture toward a reformation or free love.

And still, in the full era of civilization, ignorance supports and allows this farce of morality to continue with its bleak ravages. Yet still, the baleful procession of all humanity continues slowly between the same narrow passage of marriage, between two abysses, under the influence of opium. It's sad to remember the great sinner Mary Magdalene, yet it's a huge relief for all women to also remember that their sins will be forgiven by the same Jesus Christ, and that He will extend the same hand that he extended to Mary Magdalene, saying: Rise woman, your sins are forgiven. As an example, I'd like to repeat the words of an elderly lady that go as follows: The decency or purity that society requires from us as women, leaves us with no just compensation, other than the simple consolation of people saying the following after your death: "Poor thing, she was a decent woman," and she'll hardly get a handful of mourners at her last resting place. On the other hand, we will see that, oftentimes, the victims of social censure, due to the simple fact that they followed their natural impulse, will abandon this world full of satisfaction, after contemplating their offspring, occupying the highest positions in our country and with a well-founded family. So, readers, what's the real difference between morality and immorality?

Acknowledgments

This text was originally published in Papiamentu as de Marchena, Pedro Pablo Medardo. *Muher i bida moderna: Estudio intimo di muher como nos compañera den vida acompaña di algun consehos pa*. Curaçao: Tip. Nacional, 1934. Translation by Wernher José Suares.

CHAPTER 6

We Have the Right to Break with that Custom: Speech on the Occasion of the Seventh Anniversary of the Organization of the Wednesday Women [1955]

Imelda van West-Davelaar

Abstract

The following speech was delivered by Imelda van West-Davelaar, one of the founding figures of the Wednesday Women (Damanan di Djárason), a women's organization that campaigned for women's suffrage and social emancipation in Curaçao in the 1940s. The speech marks the seventh anniversary of the organization and was delivered at the premises of the prominent Kas di Pueblo (House of the People) in Curaçao on August 17, 1955.

Keywords

Wednesday Women (Damanan di Djárason) – Curaçao – women's emancipation – suffrage

1 Editors' Introduction[1]

With the introduction of the so-called constitutional arrangement (Staatsregeling) in 1936, men in Curaçao above the age of twenty-three with a certain income and education level were given the right to vote and stand for elections through limited census and capacity suffrage. In contrast to this, women were given the right to stand for election but not to vote. To protest against this discriminatory law, women who were members of the People's National Party

1 Editors' note: the text was originally published in Papiamentu and in English translation in Allen, Rose Mary et al, eds. *Kas di Pueblo: Kas ku un mishon / House of the People: House with a Mission.* Curaçao: Fundashon Maria Liberia Peters, 2019, 249–51. Publication courtesy of Fundashon Maria Liberia Peters. Date formats, grammar and orthography have been adapted to the style used in this volume. We have opted to translate "damanan" as "women" rather than use the more literal term "ladies."

 | DOI:10.1163/9789004690882_008

(Nationale Volkspartij) joined forces to form the Wednesday Women (Damanan di Djárason) under the leadership of figures such as Clarita da Costa Gomez, Thelma Römer-da Costa Gomez and Imelda (Mena) van West-Davelaar. They convened every Wednesday in the premises of Kas di Pueblo (House of the People), the headquarters of the People's National Party and a popular venue for meetings related to the social emancipation and autonomy of Curaçao. The door-to-door lobbying activities of the Wednesday Women and their advocacy and awareness raising at a grassroots level was instrumental in achieving women's suffrage in Curaçao in 1948.

Imelda van West-Davelaar used to sew small collection bags from large used rice and cornmeal bags, which were passed around during the meetings at the House of the People for collecting funds. The expression used for collections was: "the sack is going around" (*e saku ta bai lora*).

The text of this speech is sourced from a handwritten transcript, signed by Imelda van West-Davelaar.

∴

My dear Wednesday Women,
Today, we gather again at the end of a fruitful year of work, which, at the same time, marks the beginning of a new year in the existence of our Wednesday Women's organization, in order to unite our strength, to continue on the same path that our women have taken over the past seven years.

Today marks the seventh anniversary of us coming together to commemorate that great day of August 17, 1948, when, on the initiative of our great leader, Doctor da Costa Gomez, a small group of women came together to form what is now known as this great organization, the Wednesday Women.

Our thoughts also reach out to the strong men, the leaders who, in those days, were known as the People's Committee, Comishon di Pueblo, who rendered us the necessary cooperation. Every year again, when we gather to commemorate the founding of our organization, we also commemorate the friends, deceased members of this organization who have passed on, and, as always, I request a moment of silence as a tribute of our appreciation.

Dear women,
It is with satisfaction and pride that we can talk about our organization of the Wednesday Women, celebrating its seventh year of existence today. I say with satisfaction and pride, for although it is not customary to brag about oneself, we nonetheless have the right to break with that custom and say that we are proud because, when we calmly analyze all that has occurred during these

seven years, we can say that we have seen many other organizations and different types of other meetings in this hall. But, in spite of all obstacles, it is our Wednesday Women that was the first and is still going strong; it is our Wednesday Women that has withstood seven years of struggle and is most willing to continue for another seven years.

In every organization one would find obstacles and we have encountered a lot, but in spite of all these obstacles,....[2]

Most appreciated women,
Today, we shall embark on a new year of work. Our Wednesday Women are willing to continue the fight in this line, marching forward for the advancement of our dear Curaçao, because, now more than ever, the cooperation of our Wednesday Women is necessary to fortify the existence of our National People's Party.

Signed: I. van West-Davelaar.

Bibliography

West-Davelaar, Imelda van. "'Nos si tin e derecho di kibra ku e costumber ey': Diskurso di Imelda van West-Davelaar, Presidente, den Kas di Pueblo na okashon di 7 aña di eksistensha di organisashon Damanan di Djárason" ['We have the right to break with that custom': Speech by Imelda van West-Davelaar on the occasion of the seventh anniversary of the Wednesday Women organization]. In *Kas di Pueblo: Kas ku un mishon / House of the People: House with a Mission*, edited by Rose Mary Allen, Maria Liberia-Peters, Emy Maduro, and Rose Mary de Paula, 249–51. Curaçao: Fundashon Maria Liberia Peters, 2019.

2 Editors' note: the rest of the sentence is illegible in the original transcript.

CHAPTER 7

Aruban Women's Protests against Campo Alegre [1950–1957]

Lucia Kelly

Abstract

Among the social transformations that characterized Aruba in the 1950s was the legalization of a site that came to be known as Campo Alegre (Happy Camp), which served as a location for sex workers from abroad, legitimized by the authorities as being economically necessary. The licensing of the camp led to nearly a decade of widespread protests, spearheaded by Aruban women and supported by leading figures from the church and civil society groups. This contribution, based on archival research in Aruba, summarizes the conflicts and protests around Campo Alegre, which ultimately led to its dismantling as well as the (temporary) withdrawal of residence permits for the sex workers.

Keywords

Aruba – Campo Alegre (Happy Camp) – protests – church – sex workers

1 Introduction

In the course of my work at the National Archives of Aruba, I came across information that dealt extensively with actions taken in the 1940s and 50s in connection with the construction of an "apartment building" in Aruba for sex workers from abroad, to be known as Campo Alegre (Happy Camp). [1] In addition, a great deal of information also proved to be available at the National Library of Aruba.

1 Editors' note: a similar legalized site for sex work already existed in Curaçao under the name Campo Alegre since 1949 and remained functional until March 2020, when it was forced to shut down due to the COVID-19 pandemic.

 | DOI:10.1163/9789004690882_009

In 1951, the women mainly came from Colombia and Santo Domingo, as well as from Venezuela and Haiti and, occasionally, from Panama and Ecuador.[2] They were employed as bar girls by owners of bars and hotels. Archival sources did not reveal how and under what circumstances they came to Aruba. However, both women's unions and the religious leaders pointed out the danger of human trafficking and the international regulations on combating trafficking in women and girls. This international regulation was also valid for Aruba. They stayed at two hotels in San Nicolas near Lago (an oil industry location). These two hotels, which collectively had rooms for a total of sixty-seven persons, were constantly full. Every week, about ten to twelve women were admitted while an approximately equal number left the island. The duration of their stay was set at about six weeks. The proponents of an apartment building to be built for the sex workers from abroad pointed out that each woman rents an apartment and leaves it when she departs the island. As a result, there would be no talk of a brothel, nor would there be profiteering from prostitution. Their working conditions in Aruba were not a point of discussion in the media. According to police reports, the hygienic conditions in the hotels were poor and the spread of venereal diseases could not be controlled. For a long time, sex work was carried out in public with all its possible consequences for safety and hygiene.

It became apparent from browsing through the documents that Aruban women were actively involved in the battle between proponents and opponents of a Campo Alegre in Aruba, which was reason enough to find out exactly what their role was and why ultimately no Campo Alegre came to Aruba. But the Aruban women did not act alone; they were supported in their struggle by religious and political leaders as well as other groups in society.

Plans for the Campo Alegre and the actions associated with them went on for a number of years, although few people in Aruba have heard of the affair and little is known of the role of Aruban women themselves in the fierce struggle against the construction of any such building, so it is important to rescue the events from obscurity.

The research into the problem of sex workers in Aruba covers the period from 1950 to 1957, seven years during which a fierce battle was fought between those in favor and those against the Campo Alegre and the allowing of access to and temporary residence in Aruba to sex workers from abroad. The most significant figures in the long conflict were the government and the owner-operators of hotels and cafés in San Nicolas as proponents of the construction of a Campo

2 Editors' note: for a discussion of the contemporary situation of Venezuelan sex workers in Curaçao, see contribution by César Loureiro in this volume.

Alegre and the admission of foreign sex on the one hand, and, on the other hand, the Aruban women and religious leaders who were against the idea.

This research addresses the role of Aruban women in this process.

2 Women's Protests in Aruba in the 1950s

By national decree dated May 16, 1951, the acting governor of the Dutch Antilles confirmed the grant of title to a parcel of real estate to Pereira, Debrot & Co. for the construction and subsequent ownership of a brick "apartment building." The land covered some 17,000 square meters in Aruba's fourth district (San Nicolas) and the grant was in response to a written application of May 9, 1949, from J. M. Debrot, who had written to the territorial governor of the island of Aruba seeking permission for the use of a hotel, which he wished to use to house sex workers from abroad domiciled in Aruba.

The decision of May 16 was taken despite the fact that, for some time, various groups had been protesting against the building of any such "apartments" for foreign sex workers. On March 29, 1951, a list of 1,200 signatures had been submitted to the territorial governor of Aruba in protest against the building project, known as a Campo Alegre, in Aruba. The protests grew and, on May 30, 1951, took the shape of a mass gathering at Oranjestad, in which, according to the territorial governor of Aruba, 1,300 women took part. The protests continued after 1951, with a further petition in 1953 along with another large demonstration at Alto Vista, on May 10 of the same year. There were reports of about 5,000 demonstrators, and, according to the organizers, the demonstrations took place because those in favor of a Campo Alegre and of allowing sex workers from abroad had been lobbying behind the scenes and had nearly achieved their aim.

In the early stages, letters of protest were sent to the governor of the Netherlands Antilles by the heads of Catholic schools, the chaplain of the army, the leaders of the Dutch, British and American girl scouts and the presidents of various Catholic men's unions. In the later stages, the Catholic society of teachers, the mental health organization and fourteen proprietors of recreational facilities in San Nicolas all protested against the admission of foreign sex workers.

Opponents of the Campo Alegre were obliged to deal with both national and island authorities. Allocation of land and permission to build a Campo Alegre were national matters presided over by the central government of the Netherlands Antilles, the island government's chief function being to find somewhere suitable to build a Campo Alegre, to propose it to the national authorities and then to oversee the admission of the sex workers from abroad.

The businessmen were a sizable group of traders and café owners who derived profits from sex work. All told, five individuals tendered for the construction of the Campo Alegre, of whom two remained who were the owner-operators of the Hotel Hija del Dia.

After the decision of June 1951, taken by Mr. Jas, then acting governor of the island, thirty San Nicolas businessmen made new requests for the admission of sex workers from abroad.[3] Mr. Jas had decided to no longer grant transit permits for sex workers from abroad and to not extend existing residence and work permits. As a result, the number of sex workers from abroad declined. Then, in December of the same year, a score of café owners let it be known that they were opposed to Mr. Jas's ruling. Some of them supported government plans to award permission to build the Campo Alegre to Pereira, Debrot & Co., but all were in agreement on one point: that sex workers from abroad should be admitted to Aruba. Despite their differences of opinion, the businessmen's main concern was to protect their trade and financial interests. An exception were the fourteen owners of recreational facilities in San Nicolas, who, late in 1955, protested to the island council against the business methods of the so-called "hoteliers" who were recruiting the women from abroad—ostensibly as domestic servants and "tourists." In the opinion of the fourteen complainants, their livelihoods were being fatally compromised by the activities of between four and six establishments where, according to them, women were being exploited. They insisted that foreign sex workers should be banned.

An enormous number of women opposed the building of a Campo Alegre and were against the admission of foreign sex workers to Aruba, and many thousands of people had already taken part in the protests in Oranjestad and Alto Vista.

Opposition to the Campo Alegre and the presence of foreign sex workers in Aruba came from the religious leaders of the various churches too. The Roman Catholic, Protestant, Reformed, Anglican, Methodist Reformed and the Lago Community Church, as well as the Norwegian Seamen's Mission and the Director of the San Pedro Hospital, signed one of the petitions.

The first letter of protest against the construction of a Campo Alegre in Aruba was sent by nine interested parties to the governor of Curaçao in

3 Kelly, *Protesten van Arubaanse vrouwen tegen een Campo Alegre: 1950–1957*, 2015, p. 75; and Alofs, "Onderhorigheid en separatisme, koloniaal bestuur en lokale politiek op Aruba, 1816–1955" [Subservience and separatism, colonial administration and local politics in Aruba, 1816–1955], 2011, p. 23.

September 1950. In fact, there had long been problems connected with sex work; since the 1930s, at least, there had been complaints about the spread of venereal diseases, public importuning, streetwalkers and inadequate police supervision of drinking establishments. Nevertheless, despite the many complaints from the general public, national and island governments allowed the admission of foreign sex workers. In Aruba, they lived in two hotels, the Hija del Dia and Hotel Hollywood, in San Nicolas. Campo Alegre was not intended for sex workers who were Dutch nationals, as they were free to set up shop in any rooms or houses in San Nicolas.

It so happened that, from the 1930s onward, in addition to the foreign sex workers, there were also local sex workers. Based on figures from the police and from women's unions, in 1950, there were approximately 91 known local and foreign sex workers in San Nicolas; in 1951, there were 125; and 132 in 1955.

At first, the Aruban government justified its decision to allow a Campo Alegre in Aruba by saying it wished to stop sex work in public places and to move sex workers away from urban and residential areas. Opponents were not pleased with this reasoning and took on actions of protest that continued for several years.

After various business operators had applied for permission to construct a Campo Alegre in Aruba, critical questions were asked within the administration about how to solve the problem of providing opportunities to sex workers from abroad. It was also remarked that government approval in this matter would bring with it enormous disadvantages and considerable danger in relation to sex work in general. It was felt that the government ought to tolerate but in no sense encourage sex work. But the government failed to take the warning to heart and decided to go ahead with planning a Campo Alegre for foreign sex workers.

The reasons for the business community of San Nicolas seeking to allow foreign sex workers were financial. A ban on foreign sex workers would be the end of San Nicolas's coffee houses and, in fact, would be a severe blow to trade of all kinds. The majority were also against the building of a Campo Alegre outside San Nicolas because that would put every café owner in San Nicolas out of business.

Aruban women opposed the construction of a Campo Alegre because they were against sex workers from abroad, fearing the social implications of this migration. In 1951, they demanded a ban on the arrival of any more of them, the deportation of those already there and the shutting down of the Hija del Dia and similar sites, believing that deportation would leave about fifty local sex workers to continue plying their trade in San Nicolas. The documents consulted show that the activists did not speak out against the presence of

Antillean sex workers on the island. The largely conservative community at the time relied on religious and traditional values. Sex work as a practice and as a policy was highly frowned upon. The consensus on the topic was that it was also a vile practice that led the men of the households to immediately spend a large part, and sometimes all, of their salaries on sex work, be unfaithful to their wives, contract venereal diseases and go against religious values. The protests largely began in response to the announcement of a Campo Alegre in Aruba. To give an idea of the social issues facing the community, based on oral historical sources: on pay day, women would wait for their husbands outside the refinery gate in hopes of obtaining some money to buy groceries before it would all be spent in the surrounding bars.

There was no indication in the archival sources of racial dimensions to the opposition to sex workers from abroad. The Aruban women were against sex work, but their initial goal was to abolish sex work from abroad as this was easier to obtain through immigration and policy reform. It is important to note that "local" sex workers were citizens from the Netherlands Antilles, thus including women of various racialized backgrounds. Citizens of the Netherlands Antilles at the time could freely migrate between islands without needing a residential or work permit. This was not the case for non-Dutch citizens. The fact that the foreign women were replaced by new women each time (every six weeks) made visits more attractive to the men compared to the familiar faces of the locals. This is the reason why the focus of the opposition was on foreign sex workers—it was not because of the color of their skin. Rather, opposing the importation of women when possible was the first step to fighting the issue of sex work on the island. The government faced criticism for putting the interests of the people who profited from sex work above the social impact it had on the community.

The focus of the movement against foreign sex workers was above all an implicit choice for an achievable goal, even if this goal would only solve part of the problem. Combating sex work by "local" women would have been a far more complex and difficult task to achieve. Strategically, this meant that the criticism of foreign sex workers was based on the argument that there was already a large group of local sex workers and that the presence of sex workers from abroad would increase their clientele among Arubans and other migrants living on the island. There was also severe criticism of how they operated, particularly the open-air activity and soliciting going on in front of the Lago Gate and in the main street of San Nicolas in front of bars. Women accused the businessmen of encouraging the patronizing of foreign sex workers and of wishing to improve their lot at the cost of bringing unhappiness to many thousands of families. The Aruban women said that the establishments in San Nicolas were visited not just by sailors but also by Arubans and the locals in general. In 1951, there were on average sixty-six foreign sex workers in Aruba.

Promotion of use of the night spots in San Nicolas and their sex workers had its adverse effects on families: there was less money left over for the family, and frequent visits to the nightspots and such women even led to abject poverty. The governor of Aruba acknowledged, in one of his letters to the women's union, that many who worked at Lago came home with empty wallets and nasty infections. Women who were short of money had no right to government assistance or any other such financial aid and were dependent on their husbands' incomes. This was a time when the vast majority of women in Aruba had no incomes of their own, leaving them financially bound to their husbands, partners or fathers, often with several children to take care of. Women felt that, by banishing the foreign sex workers, the government could make visits to San Nicolas's night spots less attractive. After Mr. Jas had made his 1951 ruling, the police commissioner wrote that "the better-off" were less inclined to visit sex workers in San Nicolas, allegedly because of the lack of "new material." At that time, too, it was known that government efforts to combat infectious diseases left a lot to be desired.

In their demonstration of May 30, 1951, women protested against the authorities' lax attitude to the abuses in the field of sex work, which were running rampant in an atmosphere of neglect. Police regulations concerning age limits were all too often disregarded. The women blamed the government for favoring certain entrepreneurs and their profit making instead of putting the welfare of Aruban families first. The urgency of the Campo Alegre was brought to the fore during—or at least just before—the upcoming election campaign. And the women complained in the strongest terms that attempts were being made to profit both politically and practically from it. In answer to the women, the governor admitted that this is one of the downsides of elections.

The women therefore found themselves up against powerful forces arranged in defense of the Campo Alegre and the arrival of sex workers from abroad: a group of influential people who could choose to take no notice of government regulations. The Hija del Dia and Hotel Hollywood indeed closed their doors following Mr. Jas's ruling in 1951, but, after considerable modifications, they opened again in August 1954 under new names—Florida and Las Delicias—and, by the end of that year, the foreign sex workers were back living in the two hotels.

In a letter to the Curaçao governing council, the secretary of the United Nations and nineteen agencies in the Netherlands, Curaçao and Aruba, religious leaders pointed to the legal and ethical side of the case and stated that Campo Alegre was based on unsound principles. They were of the opinion that the government was not legally empowered to collaborate in giving permission for a Campo Alegre, that the Campo Alegre in Curaçao was ineffective and that its attraction was greater because of its location outside the residential area. They protested against the plans to repeat this experiment in Aruba without any kind of prior enquiry into whether it was wanted.

Certain matters were highly sensitive in 1950s Aruba. At a time when Aruba was working hard for greater autonomy, people found it hard to digest the idea that the national government could ram through a Campo Alegre project and that the island government had no say in whether to build it or not.

Women demanded a general scheme to address the problem of sex work, free of any materialistic concerns and opportunistic profiteering, deeming it as obviously the responsibility of the authorities, but they also worked closely with representatives of local groups. They pointed to the importance of preventive action—for example, a ban on licenses to sell liquor—and as much material and moral support as possible for more dedicated accommodation for soldiers and sailors.

The government's efforts to deal with the problem of sex work left much to be desired. There was no transparency of government and no room was left for opponents to contribute to solving the problems, and it was only under pressure from the alliance of Christian religious groups that the decision was adopted to set up a commission. But this was far too oriented toward Curaçao, and, only after much insistence, was a woman from Aruba added to the panel. Of the five times the committee met, four times were in Curaçao, and only one minority opinion was recorded in the minutes—probably that of the female Aruban member of the committee—that the current situation in San Nicolas ought to be maintained but with a ban on the admission of sex workers from abroad. The rest of the committee members, who were from Curaçao, felt that the existing situation should be maintained—in other words, that the same number of foreign short-stay sex workers should continue to be admitted.

The actions of the Aruban women gave a clear signal that they were no longer prepared to put up with the refusal to listen to their complaints, their objections and their wishes. They repeatedly indicated that they would continue with their protest actions. In fact, the demonstration of May 30, 1951, by the women of Aruba occurred three years after they had been granted the right to vote—and they were perfectly aware that they had gained the electoral power they had so long waited for. There came a time, therefore, when the ruling parties were forced to reckon with the demands of women and others with opposing views or risk losing votes. The militancy of Aruban women fitted well within a time during which political and labor emancipation were very clearly at the forefront, something that had its origins in the 1930s. It was a time of great demonstrations and heated discussions in many areas.

The women's actions showed their great determination to stand up for what they wanted. They kept it up for seven years, and the Campo Alegre never materialized. Religious belief played an important role in the efforts. One of the prominent arguments raised was the moral well-being of children and families and a better quality and healthier family life. Two of the three women's unions that had taken the lead were Catholic, and, as the protest committee wrote in one of its articles: "We are Christian people; we have a right to a Christian government. So, no Campo and no foreign sex workers, because that's fighting one evil with a greater evil."

The demonstration of May 30, 1951, was the first time in Aruba's history that so many women took part in a public protest—long before the women's actions of the 1980s and 1990s—and is still the greatest demonstration by women ever held in Aruba. More women were present at the demonstration in 1953, but a number of men also took part in that one.

The women were certainly quite prepared to take large-scale action. It is well-known that, after the arrival of the Lago and Eagle refineries, the inhabitants of Aruba—both Arubans and migrants—began to organize themselves, both socially and according to their faith. The two Catholic women's unions and the Unitas women's movement had already been in existence for some time when the government announced its Campo Alegre plans, so they were able to take action without having to organize themselves first. The three women's unions, the Roman Catholic Women's League of San Nicolas (R.K. Vrouwenbond San Nicolas), Roman Catholic Women's League of Eucharistic Crusade San Nicolas (R.K. Vrouwenbond Eucharistisch Kruistocht San Nicolas) and the Asociacion Femenino Unitas Oranjestad (Oranjestad United Women's Association)—chaired by Marianita Chong-Croes, J. F. Emers and Angela Pietersz H. respectively—began to work together and formed a protest committee with Clara Villalba-Arends and Marianita Chong-Croes as chairwoman and secretary. These were women who dared to stick their necks out. We come across other names, such as Francisca Wernet from Juana Morto and Annie Ecury, who was on the research committee, Sara Oduber of Unitas and Carmen Harms, who spoke in Spanish to the crowd assembled in San Nicolas, and O. Maduro-Bislik, J. Bislik and C. Kock of the Liga di Maria.

The women also enjoyed the moral support of well-known figures in Aruba such as Laura Wernet-Paskel, who was the first Aruban woman to appear as a political candidate for the UNA party (Union Nacionalista Arubano [Nationalist Union of Aruba]). They were also reassured by their religious faith and by

Father Amado Römer, the Catholic chaplain of Curaçao, who also ministered in Aruba. The women were able to attract support for their actions from different social groups and, in doing so, to overcome language barriers and political and religious differences. After the action of May 30, 1951, the newspaper *Amigoe di Curaçao* wrote that women from all levels of society came together and that, in the movement against the Campo, the women found each other of one mind undivided by any differences and that their leaders had been punctilious in keeping politics out of it.

At first, the women were successful on both fronts. After seven years of protest, there was no Campo Alegre and Mr. Jas's intervention had made possible the removal of foreign sex workers, which remained the case from 1951 through 1954. The press wrote that, since Mr. Jas's ruling to deport foreign sex workers, San Nicolas was now completely peaceful. However, that situation proved to be temporary.

For the national and island governments alike, this meant that their plans for a Campo Alegre for foreign sex workers did not go ahead, nor was San Nicolas cleansed, and sex workers remained in the town center.

In 1957, it was the Foundation for Mental Health (Stichting Geestelijke Gezondheid) that protested against the arrival of sex workers from abroad, demanding the establishment of a permanent commission on "the question of prostitution," and critical questions were asked in parliament. Expressions of support were received from the Aruban Apostolic Center (Centro Apostolico Arubano) and 270 private citizens. However, in February 1957, the executive council denied that sex workers from overseas were again being allowed entry into the island. After seven years of effort, the women and their supporters proved unable to stop business interests in San Nicolas from transporting foreign women to Aruba with the authorities' approval.

There was never any media discussion of the conditions under which the sex workers were operating in Aruba—although there were certainly complaints about the way they went about it. Women's organizations were as keen as religious groups to point out the danger of human trafficking and to remind everyone of international agreements against the trade in women and girls, to which Aruba was also a signatory.

From the end of the 1950s onward, Arubans no longer showed open hostility to foreign sex workers on the island and discussion of sex work was no longer carried on in public in Aruba as it had been until then.

Sex work carried out outdoors, as it had earlier been practiced by women from abroad, disappeared and a large number of the local sex workers who did remain in San Nicolas disappeared from the picture along with it. Women continued to migrate to Aruba from the region, at first in the guise of touring businesswomen and later as nightclub hostesses. The government has maintained its policy of condoning the activities of sex workers from abroad working in the center of San Nicolas, although foreign sex workers work elsewhere on the island, so that streetwalkers are still a familiar sight on the sidewalks of Oranjestad and San Nicolas.

Acknowledgments

This contribution is an excerpt from a study originally published in Dutch as Kelly, Lucia. *Protesten van Arubaanse vrouwen tegen een Campo Alegre: 1950–1957* [Protests of Aruban women against Campo Alegre: 1950—1957]. Aruba: UNOCA, 2015. Translation by Marcus Ferley. Reproduction of this text courtesy of UNOCA.

Bibliography

Alofs, Lucas J. "Onderhorigheid en separatisme: koloniaal bestuur en lokale politiek op Aruba, 1816–1955" [Subservience and separatism: Colonial administration and local politics in Aruba, 1816–1955]. PhD diss., Leiden University, 2011. https://hdl.handle.net/1887/17992.

Kelly, Lucia. *Protesten van Arubaanse vrouwen tegen een Campo Alegre: 1950–1957* [Aruban women's protests against Campo Alegre : 1950–1957]. Oranjestad: UNOCA, 2015.

CHAPTER 8

The Women's Movement in Bonaire: an Introduction

Rose Mary Allen, Judith Brekelmans, and Liliane de Geus

Abstract

In the 1970s, women in Bonaire joined the wave of women's rights movements around the world and began to collectively and publicly address gender inequality and inequity. Over the years, this movement has gone through various shifts. This contribution traces the main currents within the women's movement since the 1970s based on women's experiences in the movement. It is based primarily on oral history interviews conducted in 2021 and 2022 with three generations of Bonairean women at the forefront of the women's movement, who have played an important role in the accompanying processes of consciousness raising. In addition to interviews, this contribution uses newspaper articles to offer historical insight into turning points in the progress toward gender equality and equity made by Bonairean women over the past fifty years.

Keywords

Bonaire – women's clubs – social movement – protests – oral history

1 The Historical Context of the Women's Movement in Bonaire

Bonaire shares with the rest of the Caribbean a history of colonialism and slavery that has shaped its development.[1] Unlike Curaçao, its first inhabitants, the Caquetio Indigenous people, remained on the island, to which other

---

1 Bonaire is an island with a surface area of almost 290 km^2. Since 2010, it has been a public entity administered as a special overseas municipality of the Netherlands together with the islands of St. Eustatius and Saba. It lies in the midsouth of the Caribbean Sea, eighty kilometers from the northwest coast of Venezuela.

 | DOI:10.1163/9789004690882_010

indigenous groups from the Spanish mainland, Dutch colonizers and African enslaved people later migrated.[2] The Dutch colonization of Bonaire was first executed by the West Indian Company (WIC). During this period, enslaved people were brought in from Africa to work in the salt and dyewood industries. Following the dissolution of the WIC, the Dutch government confiscated its properties and continued its operations, using the island as a kind of large ranch. The enslaved people were owned directly by the Kingdom of the Netherlands and were known as *katibu di Rei* (King's enslaved subjects), thus government-enslaved. The enslaved who harvested salt during the dry season would leave their huts in the Slave Village (as the village of Rincon used to be called) on Sundays and walk for about six hours to the salt pans in the south of the island. There, they were housed in small stone houses near the salt pans during the week. On Saturdays, they would return home, where they received their weekly rations. In the rainy season, the enslaved worked on the maize fields in what was euphemistically called the country gardens (*landstuinen*). Most oral histories about social life on the salt pans date from the post-emancipation period, yet even these stories relate the harshness of the work, which both men and women experienced.[3] Women played an important role in resistance against slavery, such as the slave revolt of November 10, 1834. On that day, thirteen enslaved persons, including six women, joined Martis di Katalina Janga and rose up against their brutal treatment by a *bomba*, a slave with a supervisory role over the other enslaved, on the plantation called Fontein.

After the abolition of slavery in the Dutch Caribbean colonies in 1863, the socioeconomic conditions in Bonaire hardly changed. Men left the island in large numbers to seek work elsewhere and occasionally sent money home. In the twentieth century, the oil refineries established in Curaçao (1915) and Aruba (1929) offered employment to male workers from Bonaire. Women carried the household while working on aloe fields, gathering *watapana* beans (*Libidibia coriaria*), harvesting salt on the salt pans in the south of Bonaire and in the Slagbaai neighborhood or weaving straw hats for a living. In his chronicle about the women of Bonaire, Boi Antoin mentions the names of several women who worked jobs traditionally held by men and defied the ideas of womanhood that were dominant at the time.[4]

2 Haviser, *The First Bonaireans*, 1991.

3 Antoin, *Muhé den historia di Bonaire* [Women in the history of Bonaire], 2020; Allen, *E Rincon di antes: Het dagelijks leven van vroeger, uitgedrukt in liederen* [The village Rincon of yore: Daily life in the past as expressed in songs], 1983; and Dalhuisen, *Geschiedenis van de Antillen* [History of the Antilles], 2009.

4 Antoin, *Muhé den historia di Bonaire*, 2020.

Bonairean women became more empowered when universal suffrage was introduced in Bonaire and the other Dutch Caribbean islands in 1948. During the first post-1948 elections, that is, those held for the Island Council on June 4, 1951, there were more female than male voters. Of the 2,362 citizens who could vote, 779 were men, suggesting a significant number of adult women who exercised their voting rights. It is important to mention that, as early as 1954, Rose Heitkönig-Rigaud was the first woman commissioner of Bonaire's Executive Council. In 1966, she was the island's first woman to become deputy island governor.[5] She was a schoolteacher, the spouse of the well-known businessman Jules "Heit" Heitkönig and sister of Adele Rigaud, one of the pioneers of women's suffrage in the Netherlands Antilles.[6]

2 The Start of the Women's Movement in the 1970s and 1980s

In the 1970s, women in Bonaire joined the wave of women's rights movements around the world and began to collectively and publicly address gender inequality and inequity. Over the years, this movement has gone through various shifts. The present contribution traces women's experiences in Bonaire and seeks to identify the main currents within the women's movement since the 1970s. It is based primarily on oral history interviews conducted in 2021 and 2022 with three generations of Bonaireans at the forefront of the women's movement, who have played an important role in the accompanying processes of consciousness raising.[7] In addition to interviews, this contribution

5 Cosijn and Van den Dungen Gronovius, "Bonaire door het oog van Heit" [Bonaire through the eyes of Heit], 2010.

6 Henriquez, Jeanne, *Kòrsou su muhénan pionero* [Curaçao's pioneering women], 2002; and "Politieke ontwikkeling Bonaire na 1945. Positief en zeer bepalend voor het heden NOCHI WILLEM" [Political development Bonaire after 1945. Positive and very decisive for the present NOCHI WILLEM], *Amigoe di Curaçao*, April 21, 1979, p. 1.

7 The oral history project of the women's movement in Bonaire was executed by Liliane de Geus and Judith Brekelmans in 2021–2022 and was guided by Rose Mary Allen. Twenty-eight persons were interviewed in total. The first group interviewed consisted of fourteen persons who were older than sixty years, some of whom were members of the different women's organizations and the Steering Committee Bonaire, the umbrella women's platform. Some of the women in this first group were not directly involved in a women's group but were activists and groundbreakers in their own right in the areas of politics, the labor movement, social affairs or culture and the arts. The second group consisted of women in the fifty to sixty age group, while the third group comprised women between the ages of twenty and forty-nine, generally called young professionals. The youngest woman interviewed was twenty-nine years old at the time and the oldest was ninety-two.

uses newspaper articles to offer historical insight into turning points in the progress toward gender equality and equity made by Bonairean women over the past fifty years.[8]

Around 1975, the UN International Women's Year, several women's organizations emerged on the island of Bonaire and were known at the time under the generic name of *damesclubs* (ladies' clubs), associations wherein women in Bonaire organized themselves around a variety of issues.[9] Many of these groups represented one of the neighborhoods of the island, some were religiously oriented, while others were labor unions or associations affiliated to political parties. For example, the UPB (Union Patriótiko Bonairiano [Patriotic Union of Bonaire]), a political party established in 1969, had a *damesclub*[10] that advocated for women's participation in politics.[11] Women also organized themselves to help safeguard cultural heritage, as in the women's club called Nos Kosecha (Our Harvest).[12]

There is no general overview available of the number of women's organizations that existed in the 1970s in Bonaire. A brief survey of local newspapers yields names of *damesclubs* such as Gold Finch,[13] RINFA (Rincon Femenina [Women's Rincon]), Flamboyant[14] and ORFEBO (Organisashon Femenino Boneriano [Bonaire Women's Organization]).[15] This last club was very active

8 The newspaper articles used in this contribution are from *Amigoe di Curaçao* and the Bonairean edition of the *Extra*, sourced from Archivo Boneiru, an archive built by Franklyn "Boi" Antoin, at http://www.archivoboneiru.com. The archival material consulted for this contribution is detailed at https://doi.org/10.21942/uva.23878791.

9 Rodriguez, *The Rise of Women's Rights in Curaçao*, 2015.

10 The organization is mentioned in the caption of a photograph in the *Amigoe di Curaçao*, May 25, 1977, p. 8. According to the caption, the young women hold frequent political discussions.

11 "Vrouw gevraagd voor Bonaire's politiek" [Women requested for Bonairean politics], *Amigoe di Curaçao*, January 20, 1979.

12 *Extra*, May 13, 1987. This item mentions the celebration of Nos Kosecha's 10th anniversary. The organization was started by women who regularly went to *fiesta di kòmbèk*, parties of the popular classes where Cuban music was played.

13 "Gold Finch wordt damesclub" [Gold Finch becomes a ladies' club], *Amigoe di Curaçao*, March 11, 1989, p. 15; "Gold Finch vol plannen" [Gold Finch full of plans], *Amigoe di Curaçao*, February 14, 1978, p. 2; oral history interview conducted by Liliane de Geus and Judith Brekelmans with Rudmila Koffy-Makaai, December 13, 2020, https://doi.org/10.21942/uva.21231395.

14 "Sint komt 27 nov. aan" [Saint Nicholas arrives on Nov. 27], *Amigoe di Curaçao*, November 17, 1977, p. 2.

15 This organization was founded in 1973.

and celebrated its third lustrum of existence with much publicity in 1988.[16] A slightly better overview of women's organizations may perhaps be gathered from a 1983 *Amigoe di Curaçao* article that mentions several clubs as signatories to a telegram sent in solidarity to like-minded women's organizations in Curaçao concerning November 25 as a day to combat and raise awareness about violence against women. These Bonairean women's organizations were: Asondra, DIASA (Dia Social i Alegre [Social and Happy Day]), ORFEBO, Organisashon Unife Bonairiano (Bonairean Organization Unife), the working women of the Antillean Airline Company ALM (Antilliaanse Luchtvaart Maatschappij), the working women of the Social Affairs Department, the working women of the Guardianship Council and the Bonairean Secretary Association.[17] These organizations were also mentioned during the oral history interviews conducted by the authors of this contribution, along with other clubs such as APRODA (Agrupashon pa Progreso di Dama [Group for the Advancement of Ladies]), Grupo Amistad (Friendship Group) and Yuda ku Amor (Help with Love).

One striking feature was that membership to groups such as ORFEBO was only open to married women.[18] By emphasizing the importance of marriage, these groups seemed to desire to conform to prevailing societal values and norms. However, by doing so, they excluded a large group of women. In the interview with Altagracia "Gacha" Pourier Jacobino, the founder of RINFA, she mentions that their group also initially followed this rule but later dropped it as they wanted to get a large group of women out of the isolation of their households.[19]

Most of these organizations adopted a mutual aid approach to addressing social problems in the Bonairean society. They would organize fundraising

16 "Bij derde lustrum vrouwenclub artikel Teresita Toré: Taak Orfebo nog niet klaar" [Article by Teresita Toré at the ladies' club's third lustrum: ORFEBO's task is not yet done], Amigoe *di Curaçao*, March 23, 1988, p. 9; "Damesclub viert derde lustrum – Trots op projecten als crèche en couveuse Orfebo: Ingezet voor eigen plaats vrouw in gemeenschap" [Womens' club celebrates third lustrum – Proud of projects such as Orfebo crèche and incubator: Committed to women's own place in society], *Amigoe di Curaçao*, March 18, 1988, p. 11; see also the oral history interview with Theresita Trickx-Toré, February 27, 2020, https://doi.org/10.21942/uva.21231266. Theresita Trickx-Toré was ORFEBO's first president.

17 "Damesclubs solidair met die van Curaçao" [Women's club in solidarity with those of Curaçao], *Amigoe di Curaçao*, December 2, 1983, p. 2.

18 "Bij derde lustrum vrouwenclub artikel Theresita Toré" [Article by Theresita Toré marking the third anniversary of women's club], *Amigoe di Curaçao*, March 23, 1988, p. 9; "Damesclub viert derde lustrum" [Women's club celebrates fourth anniversary], *Amigoe di Curaçao*, March 18, 1988, p. 11; and oral history interview with Theresita Trickx-Toré, February 27, 2020, https://doi.org/10.21942/uva.21231266.

19 Oral history interview with Altagracia "Gacha" Pourier Jacobino, April 12, 2022, https://doi.org/10.21942/uva.20750119.

activities to benefit the community, ranging from buying an incubator for the hospital or a new freezer for the mortuary[20] to addressing the need for a daycare center. For instance, ORFEBO conducted a survey to assess the need for a daycare center and subsequently started Kresh Bon Kwido [Good Care Daycare Center] in the capital of Kralendijk in 1979 to accommodate working mothers.[21] RINFA followed ORFEBO's example and established a daycare center in Rincon, Bonaire's second largest village. Women's groups also organized activities geared toward self-help and personal skill development, ranging from sewing and cooking to public speaking skills.[22] Such activities were aimed at helping women operate in meaningful ways outside the domestic sphere.

One of the highlights of women's mobilization in Bonaire was their protest in 1978 against the intended establishment of a brothel at Barcadera, to the southeast of Rincon. On the one hand, the protests were motivated by religious beliefs and moral objections, and the women's groups received support from Rincon's radical activist priest, the Ecuadorian Fr. Gilberto Alcívar,[23] as well as from organizations such as the steering committee in Curaçao and the Caribbean Conference of Churches in Barbados.[24] On the other hand, it was a successful effort to demand action on human trafficking issues, as the government later abandoned the idea of the brothel. It was a significant victory for the women of Bonaire and, in the same year, the island became the first in the Caribbean to organize a conference on the trafficking of women in the region, welcoming people from all over the world.[25] This also connected them with the women's movement in the wider Caribbean.[26]

---

20 "Actie voor freezer voor het mortuarium" [Action to bring a freezer to the morgue], *Amigoe di Curaçao*, October 06, 1978, p. 2.

21 "Bij derde lustrum vrouwenclub artikel Theresita Toré" [Article by Theresita Toré marking the third anniversary of women's club], *Amigoe di Curaçao*, March 23, 1988, p. 9; and oral history interview with founders of RINFA, April 12, 2022, https://doi.org/10.21942/uva.20750119.

22 Oral history interview with Rudmila Koffy-Makaai, December 13, 2020, https://doi.org/10.21942/uva.21231395.

23 Alcívar was threatened with expulsion several times; he left the island in 1979.

24 "Studiedag vooraf aan Prostitutiecongres gaat door" [Study day before prostitution congress continues], *Amigoe di Curaçao*, June 10, 1978, p. 2; "BC geeft organisatoren geen financiële steun – Prostitutiecongres op losse schroeven?" [Executive Council refuses financial assistance to organizers – Prostitution conference in doubt?], *Amigoe di Curaçao*, June 9, 1978, p. 2.

25 Kempadoo, *Sun, Sex, and Gold*, 1999, p. 15; "'Prostitutie' programma" ['Prostitution' program], *Amigoe di Curaçao*, June 22, 1978, p. 2; "Bijeenkomst Caribbean Church Women over prostitutie" [Meeting of Caribbean Church Women on prostitution], *Amigoe di Curaçao*, June 5, 1978, p. 6.

26 Editors' note: see contribution by Kelly in this volume on the protests against a brothel in Aruba in the 1950s.

Bonairean women's organizations were also active beyond their own island. Before 2010, Bonaire was part of the Netherlands Antilles, which had a governor and a federal government and parliament consisting of representatives from all five islands, seated in Willemstad, Curaçao. Changes in laws, such as the important country ordinance of May 7, 1975, on the lifting of the legal incapacity of married women, also applied to Bonaire. In addition, each island had control of its own local matters through an island governor, Executive Council and Island Council. Within the federal government constellation, and together with civil society organizations from the other islands, Bonairean women participated in the preparation and implementation of action plans of the United Nations World Conferences on Women in 1975 (Mexico), 1980 (Copenhagen), 1985 (Nairobi) and 1995 (Beijing). For the purpose of the preparation of the first world conference, a steering committee that served as a local umbrella organization for women's rights was set up in Bonaire following the model of the Steering Committee Curaçao. Women's groups with formalized structures, that is, with articles of association, were represented on the Steering Committee Bonaire. The committee organized workshops and conferences to discuss issues regarding women's rights and violence against women. In particular, the International Women's Day (IWD), celebrated annually on March 8, set the principal agenda on issues regarding gender equality.

The Office of Women's and Humanitarian Affairs, a body of the federal government set up in 1989, based on a United Nations recommendation, helped to connect Bonaire to organizations in the wider Caribbean and Latin American, such as UNECLAC (United Nations Economic Commission for Latin America and the Caribbean)[27] and CAFRA (Caribbean Association for Feminist Research and Action). At the civil society level, SEDA (Sentro di Desaroyo di Dama, which later changed its name to Sentro di Desaroyo di Hende Muhé [Women's Development Center]) in Curaçao also functioned as a coordinating entity.[28] Each of the steering committees of the islands of the Netherlands Antilles had a representative on that of the Netherlands Antilles.

---

27 See, among others, the overview on labor, education, health and human resources by the Bonairian delegate, N. Gonzalez in: Budike-Polak, *Preconference bundel. Preconference ter voorbereiding van de ECLAC-conferentie m.b.t. de integratie van de vrouw in het sociale en economische ontwikkelingsproces* [Pre-conference bundle. Pre-conference in preparation for the ECLAC conference on the integration of women in the social and economic development process] (Curaçao: National Archives of Curaçao), 1991.

28 Editors' note: see also contributions by Groenewoud and Pieters Kwiers in this volume.

3 The 1990s and the First Decade of the Twenty-First Century

In the 1990s, Bonaire became represented in the interdepartmental advisory group on women's affairs in the Netherlands Antilles (Interdepartmentale werkgroep vrouwenzaken), established in 1991 to monitor the intersection of gender issues with different governmental ministries and departments.[29] The year 1994 was marked by the Bonairean Edith Strauss-Marsera becoming the first woman to hold the position of minister of development cooperation of the Netherlands Antilles after the Partido Democratico Boneriano (PDB, Democratic Party of Bonaire) won the federal elections in Bonaire. She was also in charge of women's affairs. During her term in office, she adopted an extended Antillean approach by opening women's affairs offices on all islands of the Netherlands Antilles. The purpose was to facilitate the implementation of pertinent government policies, as these island offices could identify the specific challenges faced by women on each island and initiate projects to address issues such as gender equality, development and peace, education, health and labor. These had been the main recommendations of the final conference of the United Nations Decade for Women, held in Nairobi in 1985,[30] and the Beijing conference in 1995. Under Strauss-Marsera's policy, women's equality was no longer a stand-alone goal. The abovementioned central Office of Women's and Humanitarian Affairs located in Curaçao was later dissolved and in its place came the Department of Social Welfare, Family and Humanitarian Affairs.[31] This decision was partially motivated by considerations of the 1994 International Year of the Family,[32] which called for a broader societal response

29 "Door premier op Dag van de Vrouw: Oprichting adviesgroup vrouwenszaken" [On Women's Day: Establishment of a women's advisory group by the prime minister], *Amigoe di Curaçao*, March 9, 1991, p. 2. See also oral history interview with Ruthlyn Bernabela, who represented Bonaire in the advisory group, from February 29, 2020, https://doi.org/10.21942/uva.21231422.

30 "Minister Strauss-Marsera: Eilandelijke afdelingen Vrouwenzaken op komst" [Minister Strauss-Marsera: Island-specific women's affairs departments forthcoming], *Amigoe di Curaçao*, August 11, 1994, p. 3. See also oral history interview with Simona Edita Strauss-Marsera, February 27, 2020, https://doi.org/10.21942/uva.21230663.

31 "Hoofd deze week op de hoogte gesteld: Bureau Vrouwenzaken wordt per 1 oktober opgeheven" [Director informed this week: Office of Women's Affairs to be discontinued as of October 1], *Amigoe di Curaçao*, September 29, 1995, p. 2; "'In GOA besproken' – Minister Strauss: 'Personeel van Vrouwenbureau is correct behandeld'" [Discussed in civil service affairs consultation – Minister Strauss: Women's Office personnel matters have been correctly handled], *Amigoe di Curaçao*, ibid.

32 "Welzijnsnota over gezin naar Raad van Ministers" [Family welfare note sent to Council of Ministers], *Amigoe di Curaçao*, June 1, 1995, p. 4.

to gender inequality and a greater inclusion of men, both in their participation in women's emancipation as well as in addressing the adverse impacts of gender inequality on men's lives.[33] That year, women's organizations in Bonaire also focused on the celebration of International Women's Day.[34]

The oral history research that formed the basis for this contribution indicates that the pioneering women of the 1970s and 1980s gradually became less visible during the 1990s and 2000s as government welfare schemes integrated their concerns into state policy. This subsequently led to a shrinking of women's groups. Among the interviewees from the generation consisting of fifty to sixty-year-olds, only one interviewee is still a member (and president) of a women's group. The daycare centers that started as a result of the activities of ORFEBO and RINFA have, over time, become more professionalized, initially under the aegis of the SEBIKI foundation (Stichting ten behoeve van opvoedingsondersteuning [Foundation for Educational Support]), Bonaire's nongovernmental umbrella organization for daycare, which provides capacity building in child-rearing and training in parenting support.[35]

Although Bonairean society increasingly turned to the government for the solution of social problems, gender-discriminatory practices have persisted, in particular in the arena of labor relations. In 1993, based on labor union action and individual judicial cases, the federal government accepted the principle of equal pay for women and men, thus terminating gender-based discrimination as reflected in the salary discrepancy between married women and their husbands in government service, between male and female civil servants and the fact that married female civil servants were not allowed to enter into permanent labor contracts.[36] However, wage inequality in the private sector persisted and the lawyer Carlene Peterson argued in an International Women's Day speech in 1995 for a more women-friendly labor policy. Peterson's speech indicated that, despite greater participation of women in the island labor market, including in leadership positions, gender-discriminatory laws and traditions remained obstacles. Peterson singled out divorced and single mothers, who are confronted much more directly with these legal and sociocultural

33 Ann Philipps, former policy officer at the Office of Women's and Humanitarian Affairs from June 1994 to December 1995. Email correspondence with author, Rose Mary Allen, December 16, 2022.

34 "De kern van de gemeenschap: SCB viert Internationale Dag van de Vrouw" [The core of society: Steering Committee Bonaire celebrates International Women's Day], *Amigoe di Curaçao*, March 7, 1994, p. 11.

35 Oral history interview with Hermine "Mimi" Dongen, April 23, 2022, https://doi.org/10.21942/uva.21231167.

36 Rodriguez, *The Rise of Women's Rights in Curaçao*, 2015, p. 57.

hindrances; as mentioned earlier, they were initially even excluded from some women's groups.[37]

4 After 10/10/2010

On October 10, 2010, Bonaire became a public entity of the Netherlands, administered as a special municipality and governed by an island governor appointed by the Dutch monarch, an Executive Council with three commissioners and an Island Council with nine representatives elected by the people. In the island elections of 2019, Nina den Heyer received the highest overall number of votes, subsequently becoming the only female commissioner on the Executive Council. Den Heyer was responsible for social affairs (including youth and family), public housing, healthcare, education, culture, labor, the civil registry and the revitalization of the civil service. She resigned in September 2022 to become a top civil servant: director of the Caribbean Netherlands Ministry (RCN) of Education, Culture and Science.[38] As of 2022, three of the nine Island Council members are women. One of them, Désirée Coffie, is the first woman to start and lead a Bonairean political party.[39]

The relatively large number of women in party politics at the time of publication of this contribution marks a change in the perception of women as political actors. In one of the oral history interviews, council member Désirée Coffie[40] reiterated what another woman politician had said in 1995, that "women should not be afraid of politics."[41] Coffie questioned the assumption that politics is a man's world as women are, in her view, just as necessary in government as in, for example, a household because "they plan and organize better, are more caring, and are socially and emotionally more balanced. These

37 "Advocate Carlene Peterson: Streven naar een vrouwvriendelijke arbeidsmarkt" [Lawyer Carlene Peterson: Aiming for a woman-friendly labor market] *Amigoe di Curaçao*, March 10, 1995, p. 15.

38 Nina den Heyer received the highest number of individual votes in the last election, surpassing her own party leader in votes received. "Nina den Heyer verruilt politiek voor ambtenarij" [Nina den Heyer exchanges politics for civil service], 2022. See also the oral history interview with Nina den Heyer, April 26, 2022, https://doi.org/10.21942/uva.20585394.

39 Désirée Coffie established her own party, a first in Bonaire. See the oral history interview with Désirée Coffie, April 29, 2022, https://doi.org/10.21942/uva.20747314.

40 Ibid.

41 "Vrouwen moeten niet bang zijn voor de politiek" [Women should not be afraid of politics], *Amigoe di Curaçao*, March 7, 1995, p. 11. Adele Winklaar was number 4 on the electoral list of the political party Alternatief Sociaal Progressief (ASP, Social Progressive Alternative) in 1995.

are traits that men lack."[42] Although she appeared to justify women's political participation in terms of conventional gender norms and concepts of masculinity and femininity, her comment can nevertheless be interpreted as a call to change the status quo.

Since October 10, 2010, the national government of the Netherlands has been represented in Bonaire by the Kingdom Representative (Rijksvertegenwoordiger) and the National Office for the Caribbean Netherlands (Rijksdienst Caribisch Nederland, RCN). The latter interlinks with and provides support to the ministries of the Netherlands that are or need to be present in Bonaire (as well as in St. Eustatius and Saba, the two other Dutch Caribbean islands that have a constitutional status as public entities similar to that of Bonaire). Constitutional changes accompanied by new laws on euthanasia, abortion and same-sex marriage—similar to those in the Netherlands—have been enacted in Bonaire.[43] Since October 10, 2010, the island has experienced a significant population growth, induced by the establishment of the RCN and the expansion of the public apparatus and migration of civil servants from the Netherlands. The island also receives labor immigrants from Curaçao, Aruba, other Caribbean islands and Latin America.[44] These immigrant groups have contributed to the increase in the Bonairean population from 15,679 inhabitants in 2011 to 22,573 in 2022.[45] The gender balance has tipped, with more men than women on the island as of April 2022.[46] Since 2010, poverty has become a serious problem, especially for the elderly and for young people, even though, in theory, everyone is entitled to the same opportunities and benefits as their counterparts in the Netherlands.[47] Among the Bonaire-born inhabitants, there is growing discontent with the unequal treatment that they receive compared to municipalities in the (European) Netherlands. The interviewees have substantiated that many Bonairean women are presently merely surviving in the face of poverty due to the high cost of living and low incomes while dealing

42 See the oral history interview with Désirée Coffie, April 29, 2022, https://doi.org/10.21942/uva.20747314.

43 Editors' note: see contribution by Schields in this volume for a discussion of the complex responses to the laws.

44 Editors' note: see contribution by César Loureiro in this volume on the migration of Venezuelans to the islands.

45 CBS Statistics Netherlands, "Population of the Caribbean Netherlands up by over 900," 2022.

46 Statista, "Population of Bonaire in the Caribbean Netherlands from 2011 to 2022," 2023.

47 Nationale Ombudsman, "Ombudsman: 'Armoedebeleid voor ouderen in Caribisch Nederland moet prioriteit krijgen'" [Ombudsman: "Poverty policy for the elderly in the Caribbean Netherlands must be a priority"], 2019.

with a complex set of problems such as low self-esteem, mental health issues, burnout and/or drug addiction.

In this new Bonaire, it appears that challenges specific to women are not picked up by women's groups or by the women's movement more generally but are instead dealt with by a chain of organizations and agencies at both the national (ministry) and local (department) level, with each organization being responsible for only a part of the problem.[48] The government's approach to social issues is characterized by the so-called comprehensive neighborhood approach (*integrale wijkaanpak*). This approach is oriented toward covering the infrastructural and welfare needs of a neighborhood comprehensively, aiming to improve the overall living conditions of residents with a focus on areas where there is an accumulation of social and/or economic problems.[49]

Our oral history research indicates that there are hardly any women's groups on the island anymore. One active women's group is RINFA, which celebrated its forty-eighth anniversary in 2022.[50] They still cater to the needs of especially elderly women. Many of those interviewed in the oral history project attribute this decline to an increasing individualization within society, with women paying much more attention to their own individual needs than to those of women as a group. This observation warrants further research, including into Bonaire's connection to ongoing global processes, partially induced by its constitutional change in 2010.

5 Closing Remarks

This contribution seeks to historicize how women in Bonaire have approached gender equality and equity. In the 1970s, the island's nascent women's movement set the direction and pace toward greater equality for women in the labor market, in the domestic sphere and in political participation. This changed in the 1990s, when central and island governments took over some of the social welfare activities in which the women's movement had been engaged. With the constitutional reform of 2010, women's development concerns have become

48 UN Women, "Bonaire, Sint Eustatius and Saba," n.d.

49 Eilandsraad Bonaire, "Uitvoeringsplan integraal veiligheidsbeleid Bonaire 2018–2019" [Implementation Plan for Bonaire's Comprehensive Security Policy 2018–2019], n.d.; UN Women, "Bonaire, Sint Eustatius and Saba," n.d.; and Beek, "The Forming of a Community in the Heart of the Dutch Caribbean," 2013.

50 The interviewers were invited to their celebration, gathering at the house of their oldest member (aged ninety years), and later to interview the still active core group of four members (aged seventy-four to seventy-eight) and their younger president (fifty-three).

more intersected with other societal challenges, such as poverty and norms around sexuality.

The present study makes evident the need for additional, in-depth research into the roles that women of all age categories have played as agents of change in the small island society of Bonaire and the impact of the constitutional changes of 2010 thereupon. It further affirms the value of a feminist approach toward understanding gender discrimination and gender activism while simultaneously connecting the Bonairean experience to the wider Caribbean region and global economic and political developments.

Acknowledgments

The authors would like to thank the participants in the oral history research for their invaluable insights as well as Peter Jordens for commenting on the first draft of this text.

Bibliography

Allen, Rose Mary. *E Rincon di antes: Het dagelijks leven van vroeger, uitgedrukt in liederen* [The village Rincon of yore: Daily life in the past as expressed in songs]. Anthropological research report. Willemstad: Archeologisch Antropologisch Instituut Nederlandse Antillen, 1984.

Antoin, Franklyn. *Muhé den historia di Bonaire* [Women in the history of Bonaire]. Kralendijk: Fundashion Histórika Kultural Boneriano, 2020.

Beek, Julisa van. "The Forming of a Community in the Heart of the Dutch Caribbean." Master's thesis, Erasmus University, 2013.

Budike-Polak, I. "Preconference bundel. Preconference ter voorbereiding van de ECLAC-conferentie m.b.t. de integratie van de vrouw in het sociale en economische ontwikkelingsproces" [Preconference bundle. Preconference in preparation for the ECLAC conference on the integration of women in the social and economic development process]. Curaçao: National Archives of Curaçao, 1991.

CBS Statistics Netherlands. "Population of the Caribbean Netherlands up by over 900." CBS Statistics Netherlands, April 28, 2022. https://www.cbs.nl/en-gb/news/2022/17/population-of-the-caribbean-netherlands-up-by-over-900.

Cosijn, Christel, and Richelle van den Dungen Gronovius. "Bonaire door het oog van Heit" [Bonaire through the eyes of Heit]. *Antilliaans Dagblad*, June 23, 2010. http://www.bigbangexpress.com/wp-content/uploads/2010/12/BBE-Bonaire-door-het-oog-van-Heit-AD-230610.pdf.

Dalhuisen, Leo, ed. *Geschiedenis van de Antillen* [History of the Antilles]. Zutphen: Walburg Pers, 2009.

Eilandsraad Bonaire. "Uitvoeringsplan Integraal Veiligheidsbeleid Bonaire 2018–2019" [Implementation Plan for Bonaire's Comprehensive Security Policy 2018–2019]. Eilandsraad Bonaire, n.d. http://www.konsehoinsular.com/dsresource?objectid=10789&type=org&disposition=inline.

Haviser, Jay B. *The First Bonaireans*. Curaçao: Archaeological-Anthropological Institute of the Netherlands Antilles, 1991.

Henriquez, Jeanne. *Kòrsou su muhénan pionero* [Curaçao's pioneering women]. Curaçao: Archivo Nashonal di Antia Hulandes, 2002.

Kempadoo, K., ed. *Sun, Sex, and Gold: Tourism and Sex Work in the Caribbean*. New York: Rowman & Littlefield, 1999.

Nationale Ombudsman. "Ombudsman: 'Armoedebeleid voor ouderen in Caribisch Nederland moet prioriteit krijgen'" [Ombudsman: 'Poverty policy for the elderly in the Caribbean Netherlands must be a priority']. Nationale Ombudsman, September 10, 2019. https://www.nationaleombudsman.nl/nieuws/2019/ombudsman-armoedebeleid-voor-ouderen-in-caribisch-nederland-moet-prioriteit-krijgen.

"Nina den Heyer verruilt politiek voor ambtenarij" [Nina den Heyer exchanges politics for civil service], *Paradise FM 103.1* (blog), September 19, 2022. https://paradisefm.cw/nina-den-heyer-verruilt-politiek-voor-ambtenarij.

Rodriguez, Adaly. *The Rise of Women's Rights in Curaçao: The Potential of the Women's Convention to the Empowerment and Equal Rights of Women in Curaçao*. Amsterdam: Caribpublishing; Amsterdam: SWP Publishers, 2015.

Statista. "Population of Bonaire in the Caribbean Netherlands from 2011 to 2023." Statista, April 2023. https://www.statista.com/statistics/706799/population-of-bonaire-in-the-caribbean-netherlands.

UN Women. "Bonaire, Sint Eustatius and Saba." UN Women, n.d. https://data.unwomen.org/country/bonaire-sint-eustatius-and-saba.

CHAPTER 9

Afro-Caribbean Kinship Networks and the Emancipation of Women

Gladys J. do Rego-Kuster

Abstract

The present contribution was originally published in 1990 with the aim of exposing the dominant narrative on Afro-Curaçaoan girls and women as well as challenging prevalent notions of what constitutes a typical Afro-Caribbean family. It contests the emphasis on marriage and discrimination against single mothers, divorced or unmarried women and contrasts it with the unconventional realities of kinship networks. It reflects on the emancipatory processes that ensued in the wake of the uprising of May 1969 in Curaçao and the long struggle to abolish the National Ordinance on Material Civil Servants Law, which legally incapacitated women and did not permit women to be employed after marriage.

Keywords

kinship networks – women's emancipation – National Ordinance on Material Civil Servants Law – unmarried women

1 Preface

Words still matter. Words are a powerful tool. They can make you. They can break you. Even unspoken or voiced as rules of law. They may cause havoc in someone's life. They can free someone too.

At the end of the 1960s and in the wake of the aftermath of the uprisings known as Trinta di Mei, various narratives began to appear surrounding the day May 30, 1969. For some, it was a labor dispute, which spread like wildfire into a violent popular uprising. For others, it was the release of the wrath sedimented by ills encapsulated for years in a loaded Pandora's box. These narratives could

 | DOI:10.1163/9789004690882_011

mostly be traced back to local island politics and socioeconomic and racial legacies of colonialism.

On this date in 1969, I was just about a year away from finishing my college education in the Netherlands. It marked the end of my coming of age. Afterward, it also meant my entrance into a process of conscientization.

Trained in the 1960s in the Netherlands, my toolkit and scholarly registers proved to be inadequate. I needed to understand the fabric of my birth island, especially regarding girls and women's rights. Why was my mother so upset about me furnishing an apartment to live in with my soon-to-arrive boyfriend? Why would she, herself raised by a single mother, put so much pressure on me to get married? Why was I, a higher-educated, professional, female public servant, dismissed for getting married? Indifferent at first, I took it as a given, an acceptable rule of the National Ordinance on Material Civil Servants Law (LMA). So I moved on to the private sector. Within a year, I was fired again for siding with female health workers and their demands for a minimum wage. On top of that, my lawsuit was declared inadmissible since becoming a spouse had made me legally "incapacitated."[1]

It took several decades before I felt able to take a "real job."

I started to use my ears, eyes, voice and pen to explore and challenge the interaction between Dutch (post)colonialism, sex, race and class.

I discovered the increasingly popular phrase "the personal is political." It opened the window for me to understand why personal experiences of women are rooted in a system of power relationships that produces inequality and marginalizes women.

I wrote the following contribution at the end of the 1980s at the request of the journal *De Gids*. I wanted to expose and change the ruling narrative on Afro-Curaçaoan girls and women. Furthermore, I needed to voice a myriad of spoken and unspoken words. What was the ultimate meaning of the stereotypes, images and language used? What were the assumptions? Where were they coming from, and where were they leading to?

It almost seems like a never-ending story. Countless others followed in the steps of my generation. They all work hard to decipher those codes that objectively and subjectively produce and reproduce gender, race and class differences and discrimination. Be it in the 1970s or 80s. Be it in Curaçao or in its Afro-Caribbean diaspora in the Netherlands. It still matters.

1 Editors' note: according to the LMA, which was abolished in 1983, women were no longer allowed to be employed by the government after their marriage.

2 Introduction

One thing we aren't so forthcoming with is reporting births. In fact, I hardly see any in Papiamentu-language newspapers, although the three or four per week appearing in Dutch-language papers suggests that it is slowly becoming more common.

There are roughly 3,200 births per year in Curaçao. Fewer than seven percent of them appear in those little "newborn" ads in the paper, and almost all of them are alerting us to new additions to the delighted families of temporary residents on the island or those of the middle and upper classes. Most of them are returning *yu di tera* (children of the land) from the Netherlands or the US, and all are complete families, that is, all married. I've yet to see a notice of a birth to a so-called "deliberately unmarried mother." What you do see more often in the local, community newspapers are congratulatory messages complete with birthday pictures of babies and toddlers, from all kinds of family members, including several well-wishers living in the Netherlands. It is very likely that half of these children are born out of wedlock.[2]

Actually, public marriage announcements are even rarer than public birth announcements. I suspect that is not just because the *Curaçaose Courant* also happens to publish information on the Civil Registry in between the endless lists of business startups and failures, making it easy for the paper's readers to find out who's been divorced.

If I am not mistaken, it isn't considered appropriate in many places for couples to announce their divorce or intention to do so in a little notice in the paper. One can at best speculate on what might lie behind some pointedly worded notice by a Mr. So-and-So who wants it to be known in no uncertain terms that he no longer wishes to be held responsible for the current and future debts of his Mrs. So-and-So. Those announcements probably reveal less than the tiniest sliver of ice at the very tip of a whole iceberg of marital tension. Statistics suggest that one in three of Curaçaoan women who married in the 1980s could expect to be divorced.[3]

The severing of ties by death is of course something entirely different. The leading paper by far for that sort of material is the *Extra*, which boasts of a registered circulation of 25,000 copies. There can be as many as three or four whole

2 Calculated from figures from the population census of Curaçao. The percentage of children born out of wedlock to Antillean-born mothers rose from 37 percent in 1973 to 59 percent in 1989.

3 Leusden, "Indicators of Marriage and Marriage Dissolution of the Female Population of Curaçao," 1985.

pages per day of death notices. Actually, I've developed an almost embarrassing interest in their obituary columns. It's not like in the Netherlands, where you have the name of the deceased in capital letters, with the names of family members underneath, with just a plain white background. Not in Curaçao; here, you find whole lists of life partners and children, mum and dad, sisters, brothers, foster-siblings, grandchildren, aunts and uncles, their spouses, *kompader* and *komaders*[4] and godchildren, nephews and nieces, distant cousins, close friends and colleagues, friends from clubs and societies and many more. The death notice will invariably finish with a summing up of all the relevant family names; and that, too, is likely to be a long list.

Steadily, more announcements end with the words: "Despues di entiero no por risibí bishita di kondolensia na kas" (No home condolence visits will be received after the interment). However, it is more than self-evident that, as the mourning period progresses, family members know they can fully rely on each other's company.

The network of family relations spans birth and death. All the complexities spanning the time between those two events meanwhile offer inexhaustible food for thought for an army of researchers, who partly follow the path that missionaries once trod or chart their own new directions. They're not consciously trying to reinvent the wheel. It's just that the globe is not quite as round as Columbus imagined.

In my view, the most pioneering research and analyses of black Caribbean kinship networks and relationships came out of the US in the 1930s and the English-speaking Caribbean islands in the 1950s.[5] The characteristic strength of those studies is that the researchers weren't just passive observers but were themselves members of those communities. Nor did they adopt a moral high ground. They were not "moral re-armers" in the war against family arrangements that were "pathologically deviant from some the supposed 'norm,' itself characteristic of middle-class Western Europeans."[6] That "norm" was of course the monogamous nuclear family with the husband at its head. These researchers' greatest concern was not the accumulation of indications of "supposed indices of disorganization."[7]

---

4 The terms *kompaders* and *komaders* refer to the respective spouses of a godparent at baptisms, communions and weddings.

5 Frazier, *The Negro Family in the United States*, 1939; Henriquez, *Family and Colour in Jamaica*, 1953; Smith, *The Negro Family in British Guiana*, 1956; Clarke, *My Mother Who Fathered Me*, 1957; Solien, "The Consanguineal Household among the Black Carib of Central America," 1959.

6 Horowitz, *Peoples and Cultures of the Caribbean*, 1971, p. 401.

7 Ibid.

For those invested in the latter, there is more than enough evidence of such "chaotic" relationships: the high rate of extramarital births, the apparently weak bonding between fathers and their children and between men and women and the strong position of women in the household and broader kinship networks, which has led to a glossary of terms such as "matrifocal" and "matricentric"—even the contentious "matriarchal"—to describe such families and households. Frazier and his disciples were, however, primarily concerned with establishing how Afro-American and Afro-Caribbean kinship networks were composed and how they normally functioned. Their work provided the impetus for assessing, fully investigating and recording all parts of the Caribbean, including the Netherlands Antilles and especially Curaçao.[8]

It is difficult for new insights, their implied consequences and, above all, the tolerance required to acknowledge them to work their way into the minds of society's leaders and policymakers. Sometimes, it happens in contradictory ways. Indeed, even those who have close personal experiences sometimes find this challenging to accept.

To speak of kinship networks and the emancipation of women is to not only speak of their objective structures and patterns. We need to discuss behavior too. It is, of course, always difficult to quantify the wishes, ideals, motivations and, above all, the feelings that determine people's behavior. We shall therefore limit ourselves to a few examples of the nature of emancipatory behavior that has affected women in Afro-Curaçaoan family networks over roughly the last thirty years.

3 Exclusively for Married Women?

The history of modern women's organizations and groups goes back to the 1960s. Following in the footsteps of earlier societies of "Ladies belonging to well-to-do gentlemen," they called themselves "ladies' clubs." It's still difficult to eradicate this choice of words. The most appalling fact is that, even today, under the statutory rules of several of these clubs, only married women are entitled to be members. A word of explanation is needed here. Approximately ninety percent of our population is still Catholic, and, while secularism has had an effect on Catholicism, the mostly working-class women's groups show a remarkably strong tendency to religious belief. Yet, how many of those "ladies"

8 Abraham-Van der Mark, *Yu'i mama: Enkele facetten van gezinsstructuur op Curaçao* [Yu'i mama: Some facets of family structure in Curaçao], 1973; Marks, *Male and Female in the Afro-Curaçaoan Household*, 1976.

were themselves the daughters of women who had never uttered marriage vows? Although they had forgiven the sufferings inflicted through both word and deed on their mothers and grandmothers by *shon pastor*,[9] they had not forgotten their sins: marriage remains a holy sacrament.

That salvation can be earned while still on earth was clear from the advantages that came with being married. There was the flood of social security measures, introduced by the oil industry but available exclusively to married employees and their families. Other companies soon followed their example as did the government. And what of women's solidarity? Evidently, there was no notion of that. Probably all the more an emphasis on exclusivity. The label "exclusively for married women" matched the spirit of the times. Many a member of a ladies' club who parted ways with her spouse also parted from her fellow club members with much bitterness, albeit silently and submissively.

The uprising of May 30, 1969, significantly altered social accentuations. In January 1971, an advisory committee was installed on the elimination of discrimination against women. The committee was split into a social and a legal section. The legal section inventorized, all in all, fifteen examples of discriminatory laws and regulations that specifically pertained to married women. The committee highlighted ten provisions from the Civil Code, including Article 22, which stipulated that "the birth of a child must be registered by the father."[10] The committee's sole objection was that only fathers, and not mothers, were empowered.[11] Now, I, too, believe it's only reasonable that the law allows a birth to be registered by anyone who might have witnessed it; medicine men, healers, midwives ... But not even a single word of acknowledgment of the existence of single mothers ... ?

The LMA includes four articles 5(3e), 6(3), 95 and 96, the last of which clearly states that "the female civil servant who has entered into a relationship of cohabitation is honorably discharged." And what was the committee's response? "Ditto for articles 6 and 95." Let's read that again; "article 95 makes a distinction purely on the ground of the sex of the civil servant" (these words are underlined in the report).[12]

9 Editors' note: *shon* is a reference to someone with a high social status. Masters of enslaved persons used to be called *shon*. In this case, the Catholic priest is addressed as *shon*.

10 *Eindverslag van de commissie 'Uitbanning discriminatie van de vrouw'* [Final report of the committee for the elimination of women's discrimination], unpublished report (Curaçao: Government of Curaçao, Bureau of Women's Affairs, 1972).

11 Ibid., p. 4.

12 Ibid., p. 8.

Now, I was not present at those sessions, but the chapter delivered by the social section under the promising title "Social Discrimination" does reveal at least a little of what was discussed. Most striking is the committee's own ambivalence toward how women are valued in society and its attitude to sexual relations between men and women, unmarried motherhood and so forth, which they seemed to think constitute "an ever-present threat to women's physical and psychological health."[13] The fight against that danger had to be carried on by "reeducating both men and women about their social roles."[14] It's a plea that continues to resonate to the present day.

In fact, the movement to scrap discriminatory articles from the Civil Code gathered little momentum, not to mention practical results. One of the first articles to be removed was No. 1347 of the Civil Code, which stated that married women were considered as incapable as minors of signing contracts. In the second half of the 1970s, five years after the committee made its final recommendations and a decade and a half later than the Netherlands, the legal incapacity of married women was ultimately abolished. Despite that, it is still far from uncommon for shopkeepers to ask women—particularly working-class women—to provide their male partner's confirmation for purchases. Only in the mid-1980s, after numerous legal cases, appeals and campaigns by women civil servants and semipublic administrative organizations, the government finally decided to overturn legislation that discriminated against women, whether married, unmarried or cohabiting.

However, that is by no means the end of it.

For example, in the 1990s, the teachers' union (SITEK) began a monthlong bitter battle about child allowances for unmarried as well as married women whose partners don't receive the allowance in their pay packets. That battle has become polarized mainly around the general demand for unmarried employees to receive equal pay for equal work as their married colleagues. Married women, in turn, also earn twenty-five percent less than their married male colleagues. As well as basing their objections rather disingenuously on budgetary limitations, opponents also point to what they see as hidden attempts to legalize variations of procreative "normlessness."

Others view that as the other side of the coin. For example, the increase in the number of divorced women includes some who supposedly split up "deliberately." In fact, after acknowledging the most convincing reason for divorce, that is, adultery, the so-called "great lie" was soon exposed. The truth is that many lead their lives quite independently and even with greater affection for

13 Ibid., p. 12.
14 Ibid., pp. 3–4.

their former husbands while receiving a salary equivalent to those who are married as well as postdivorce benefits women civil servants are now entitled to. And that's to say nothing of their consequent evasion of tax laws that discriminate against married, working women.

It was soon obvious that improving the position of women and mothers in the Afro-Curaçaoan kinship networks could not be left to "reeducation," especially in legal and material terms.[15] This led to different kinds of outcomes. From the early 1980s onward, for instance, unmarried mothers no longer needed a guarantor to be eligible for social housing.[16] Guarantors had been required to have a reasonable income, which meant that most were male with some influence within the political patronage system. The applicant was then judged, to the point of sexual humiliation, on her political "credentials." And, for political campaigning purposes, newly built social housing was often held in reserve by powerful rulers. However, in mid-1978, twenty-four mothers set up a courageous campaign of squatting, and, thanks to their demands, the depoliticizing of social housing allocation began to gather momentum.[17]

The same year witnessed the establishment of the social housing association Fundashon Kas Popular (FKP). In the meantime, the government social services department stands as guarantor for welfare recipients by making automatic deductions from their meager benefits.

In November 1989, the law that prevented unmarried women from receiving welfare benefits and free pre- and perinatal care unless the child's father acknowledged paternity in writing to the social services was rescinded. The logic behind this law had been to attempt to make fathers responsible for their reproductive behavior. The government presented fathers in employment with a bill for costs incurred, but, in practice, that meant that more and more unmarried women chose to wait until they literally felt their contractions, notwithstanding the dangers that came along with it, as they preferred to spare themselves all the additional trouble.

15 The Union of Antillean Women (Union di Muhé Antiano) and Mama Soltero collected articles on single mothers published in the magazine *Bosero* from 1977 to 1982.

16 The loaded phrase used to denote this dependency in Papiamentu is "Hende pa para bòrg" (to stand surety for someone).

17 "Themanummer volkswoningproblematiek en bezettingsaktie in Seru Fortuna en Jan Doret" [Thematic issue on public housing problems and squatting actions in Seru Fortuna and Jan Doret neighborhoods of Curaçao], *Bosero: Portabos di Union di Muhé Antiano* 2, no. 4–5 (1978).

4 Idealized Norms of the Family versus Actual Kinship Networks

This brings us once again to the idealized norm of the family and the arsenal of weapons with which it is defended.

It doesn't take much to imagine the effect of Pope John Paul II's state visit in May 1990, with the mottos "More Christian families for a better Curaçao" and "A united family is a happy family,"[18] especially when accompanied by promotional television images of a nuclear two-child family, dining happily together and sharing jokes around the dining table.

History repeats itself, as the saying goes, and a new generation of "fallen women" must live their lives saddled with feelings of guilt and atonement complexes.

Of course, behind these media campaigns are efforts at preventing childbirth outside of marriage. But the question is to what extent it is based on objective facts. According to my own research and calculations, the percentage of teenage mothers fell from sixteen percent in 1973 to ten percent in 1989, yet this is read with overexcited clamor in the boulevard press as an indication that we're heading for the proverbial Sodom and Gomorrah.[19] Not that the effect of the press on the general public's judgment should be overestimated, but, in this case, I certainly think it shouldn't be underestimated.

The fact that more and more women are appearing in the general job market also creates the inevitable commotion from time to time. People have long forgotten that the majority of working-class women, especially unmarried mothers and grandmothers, have always had to work, often up to their last breath. That's always been true in the home and outside, on this island and everywhere else, and not only when there's a crisis. It's just as true in supposedly "easier" economic times. Approximately forty percent of women are estimated to be jobless, and they are part of a problem of structural unemployment recognized as long ago as the 1960s. That problem is to be solved. More and more unmarried mothers are moving to the Netherlands, sometimes leaving their children behind and sometimes sending them on ahead. Their

18 "Pa un mihó Kòrsou mañán, mas famia kristián" and "Famia uni, ta famia felis." Author's own translation.

19 The calculations are based on data from the Population Register of Curaçao (December 1989). I would like to leave open the question whether this was caused by factors such as migration, reduction of sexual intercourse between young people or a reduction in the desire to have children with greater use of contraception and abortion, including by adolescents. The downward trend is even more striking given that the percentage of women in the age group 13–19 increased from 6.4 percent in 1973 to 7.2 percent in 1989.

migration is not just an individual solution to the problem but, ironically, also the solution proposed by the Dutch Antillean state.

The need to earn a living and the lure of distant opportunities characterized the continuously reproducing Afro-Caribbean kinship system from the very beginning. But it is far from clear that physical absence equals the abandonment of those who stay behind. In fact, many migrants, both female and male, fulfill their financial obligations to family members back home as far as their meager and irregular income allows.[20]

The kinship network is thus not anchored to a place; in fact, it has shown remarkable resilience in extending far beyond its own geographical boundaries, branching out to spread far and wide. It's no surprise then that islands such as Saba and St. Eustatius earned the nickname "money order islands." Money orders were sent back home by sons and daughters who went to work in the oil and service industries in Curaçao and Aruba; there's a reason why so many rush to the island post offices. These days, it is as common to receive as to send not only modest sums of money but also parcels of food and supplies. The mutual interdependence of all family members, but especially women in kinship and household networks, actually only appears to be diminishing.

Unfortunately, all of this is not universally recognized, as proven by the severely limited social support offered to unmarried mothers and to caregiving grandmothers. Minimum wage levels in force for sectors specific to women are still discriminatory. We can surely all agree that the economic difficulties of the 1980s were another cause of the problems. But what are we to think of the feelings and other motives of our policymakers?

Consider the public moral sermons that make looking forward sound more like looking backward. They claim we need to return to how it used to be. But serious researchers and statisticians keep telling us this ideal-typical family has in fact never really been the norm.

The tendency to marry is decreasing in Curaçaoan society. That simple fact is just the latest in a long history of indicators that the typical Afro-Caribbean family is actually doing well in spite of many efforts to the contrary.[21] Freed from subjective views and idealized images, the continued existence of these kinship networks certainly cries out for more research. I also hope for more sensitivity toward the fact that working for the emancipation of women in Afro-Curaçaoan families is not equivalent to rejecting their varied social

20 Roberts and Steele, *Black Women: Bringing It All Back Home*, 1980.

21 Leusden, "Indicators of Marriage and Marriage Dissolution of the Female Population of Curaçao," 1985.

patterns and family relationships. And it's even more true that "reeducation" does not mean insisting on imposing the nuclear family at all costs.

A lot is possible once that insight is there, certainly in terms of policy. Only then will the position of the Afro-Curaçaoan woman in kinship networks no longer be merely glorified in words as a "strong woman" but rather that she will indeed be able to claim all her true rights.

Isn't that what emancipation ought to be about?

Acknowledgments

This is a translated excerpt from an article originally published in Dutch as Do Rego-Kuster, Gladys. "Het Afro-Caribisch gezinsweb en de emancipatie van de vrouw" [Afro-Caribbean kinship networks and the emancipation of women]. *De Gids* 153, no. 7–8 (July–August 1990): 542–47.. The author has written a new preface for this contribution. English translation by Marcus Ferley. Publication courtesy of *De Gids*.

Bibliography

Abraham-Van der Mark, Eva. *Yu'i mama: Enkele facetten van gezinsstructuur op Curaçao* [Yu'i mama: Some facets of family structure in Curaçao]. Assen: Van Gorcum, 1973.

Clarke, Edith. *My Mother Who Fathered Me: A Study of the Family in Three Selected Communities in Jamaica*. London: Allen & Unwin, 1957.

Do Rego-Kuster, Gladys. "Het Afro-Caribisch gezinsweb en de emancipatie van de vrouw" [Afro-Caribbean kinship networks and the emancipation of women]. *De Gids* 153, no. 7–8 (August 1990): 542–47.

Eindverslag van de commissie "Uitbanning discriminatie van de vrouw" [Final report of the committee for the elimination of women's discrimination]. Unpublished report. Curaçao: Government of Curaçao, Bureau of Women's Affairs, 1972.

Frazier, Edward Franklin. *The Negro Family in the United States*. University of Chicago Sociological Series. Chicago: University of Chicago Press, 1939.

Henriquez, Fernando M. *Family and Colour in Jamaica*. London: Macgibbon & Kee, 1953.

Horowitz, Michael. *Peoples and Cultures of the Caribbean: An Anthropological Reader*. Garden City, NY: Natural History Press, 1971.

Leusden, Hans van. "Indicators of Marriage and Marriage Dissolution of the Female Population of Curaçao, 1960–1962 and 1980–1981: A Multidimensional Analysis." Working Paper of the NIDI 66, Voorburg, Netherlands Interuniversity Demographic Institute, 1985.

Marks, A. F. *Male and Female and the Afro-Curaçaoan Household*. The Hague: Nijhoff, 1976.

Roberts, Margaret Prescod, and Norma Steele. *Black Women: Bringing It All Back Home*. Bristol: Falling Wall Press, 1980.

Smith, Raymond Thomas. *The Negro Family in British Guiana: Family Structure and Social Status in the Villages*. International Library of Sociology and Social Reconstruction. London: Routledge; London: Kegan Paul, 1956.

Solien, Nancie Loudon. "The Consanguineal Household among the Black Carib of Central America." PhD diss., University of Michigan, 1959. Microfilm.

"Themanummer volkswoningproblematiek en bezettingsaktie in Seru Fortuna en Jan Doret" [Thematic issue on public housing problems and squatting actions in Seru Fortuna and Jan Doret neighborhoods of Curaçao]. *Bosero: Portabos di Union di Muhé Antiano* 2, no. 4–5 (1978).

CHAPTER 10

Hidden Strengths: Intellect and Ideology behind the Women's Movement in Curaçao and Aruba, 1946–1995

Margo Groenewoud

Abstract

The present contribution offers an analysis of women's activism and political mobilization in Aruba and Curaçao from its early articulations in the 1940s in suffrage movements through to the critical legal victories achieved in the early 1990s. It examines the strategies adopted in effective mobilizations by women, arguing that, even though successes can be attributed to strong intellectual forces and a keen understanding of political tides, in the end the strengths of successful operations lay not primarily in knowledge, ideology or strategy but in the ability to find the right moment, to align and to cooperate and to ride the tidal waves of progress.

Keywords

Curaçao – Aruba – women's movements – mobilization strategies – legal victories

In the Dutch Antilles, emerging political movements in the 1930s and 1940s were radically emancipatory.[1] Yet, at the same time, nationalism aimed at full political autonomy was not part of the political reality. This article focuses specifically on the women's movement and political activism by women in the mid-twentieth century on the two larger and economically thriving Dutch Antilles islands Aruba and Curaçao. It examines how the specific circumstances of late-colonial politics, as well as Dutch cultural imperialism through education and religion, influenced the women's movement in Aruba and Curaçao. Research suggests a reluctance of the movement toward

1 Editors' note: In this contribution, the term 'Dutch Antilles' refers to the pre-1954 period, whereas 'Netherlands Antilles' refers to the period 1954–2010.

 | DOI:10.1163/9789004690882_012

intellectual and ideological development,[2] although, on the other hand, their successes have been attributed to sophisticated legal and political knowledge.[3] Studying the women's movement from its 1940s beginnings to the critical legal victories of the early 1990s, I am therefore particularly interested in the sources of strength of the women.

With the exception of a small number of middle- and upper-class social clubs, similar to those found elsewhere in the region, women in the Dutch Antilles began organizing themselves in the 1940s.[4] As June Castello observes about women's activism in the period from the 1940s to the 1960s, feminist issues across the Caribbean were "packaged within the wider nationalist struggles for political autonomy."[5] This also is true of the developments on the islands of Aruba and Curaçao, although each was shaped by a remarkably different political context.

In the 1940s, emerging political movements in Aruba and Curaçao argued for autonomy without considering independence a viable option.[6] Instead, local political leaders claimed as much autonomy as was feasible alongside efforts to optimize ties within the Kingdom of the Netherlands, fully accepting the idea of maintaining a nonsovereign status. Under the leadership of Moises da Costa Gomez, who left what was formerly called the Katholieke Partij Curaçao (KPC, Catholic Party Curaçao) and started the Partido Nashonal di Pueblo (PNP, National People's Party) in 1946, grassroots networks developed in Curaçao to prepare the masses for the expected arrival of universal suffrage and self-determination. Within these networks, people with informal authority in their neighborhoods disseminated basic information about government and democracy, issues that were completely unfamiliar to a majority of the population at the time.[7] Women played a vital role in this grassroots movement, both through affiliations such as the Wednesday Women and individually.

---

2 Horst, "Oecumenische vrouwengroepen op Curaçao gericht op strategie of praktijk" [Ecumenical women's groups on Curaçao directed toward strategy or practice], 1988.

3 Rodriguez, *The Rise of Women's Rights in Curaçao*, 2015; Schields, "This Is the Soul of Aruba Speaking," 2016, p. 211.

4 Ansano et al., *Mundu yama sinta mira: Womanhood in Curaçao* [The name of the world is sit and see: Womanhood in Curaçao], 1992; Henriquez and Berry-Haseth, *Kòrsou su muhénan pionero: Original na Papiamento* [Curaçao's pioneering women: Original in Papiamentu], 2002; Bailey and Leo-Rhynie, *Gender in the 21st Century*, 2004; Macpherson, "Toward Decolonization. Impulses, Processes, and Consequences since the 1930s," 2011, p. 178.

5 Castello, "Where Have All the Feminists Gone? Learning the Lessons of a Long Time Passed in the Women's Movement in the Caribbean," 2008, p. 146.

6 Oostindie and Klinkers, *Decolonising the Caribbean: Dutch Policies in a Comparative Perspective*, 2003; Jong, "Extended Statehood in the Caribbean: Definition and Forces," 2006, pp. 3–24.

7 Groenewoud, "Social Exclusion and the Entanglement of State," 2022.

They spread political messages and invitations for meetings through their informal contacts and convinced other women to participate.[8] For the first time in the island's history, women in Curaçao mobilized, and they did so for a political cause.

Scholarship on women's activism and mobilization in the Dutch Antilles remains limited, both in terms of the analysis of archival sources as well as dedicated publications.[9] However, there are noteworthy publications from the 1990s onward, guided by a critical feminist perspective, by scholars such as Joceline Clemencia, Sonia Cuales and Jeanne Henriquez.[10] Recent studies, such as those by Adaly Rodriguez and Chelsea Schields, relate the successes of women's mobilizations to the participation of educated critical thinkers who relied on legal and political knowledge, as well as on crucial interventions in the political arena, to pursue their efforts to improve women's position and rights in society.[11]

This article examines the specific circumstances of late-colonial Dutch Antillean politics, as well as the state of education and civil society, in relation to the emergent women's movement in Aruba and Curaçao, drawing on a diverse body of literature, reports and newspapers as well as material from the Curaçaoan National Archives and interviews with two key figures from the 1970s and 1980s. After an introductory presentation of the pre-war period, I will examine three phases in the development of the women's movement from its emergence in the 1940s to the early 1990s. For each period, the organizational characteristics of women's mobilization and the specifics of the sociopolitical environment from which they emerged are analyzed.

1 The Religious, Social and Political Background to Post-War Developments

When nationalist political movements emerged throughout the Caribbean in the late 1930s, the majority of the inhabitants of the Dutch Antilles held no

8 Allen, "Negotiating Gender, Citizenship and Nationhood through Universal Adult Suffrage in Curaçao," 2018; and Henriquez and Berry-Haseth, *Kòrsou su muhénan pionero*, 2002. Editors' note: see also the contributions by Pieters Kwiers and Martis in this section.

9 These limitations concern both available archival sources and publications. Editors' note: Also noted in the contribution by Cuales in this section.

10 Clemencia, "Introduction," 1992; Cuales, "In Search of Our Memory: Gender in the Netherlands Antilles," 1998, p. 86; and Henriquez and Berry-Haseth, *Kòrsou su muhénan pionero*, 2002. Editors' note: see contributions by Clemencia, Cuales and Henriquez in this volume.

11 Rodriguez, *The Rise of Women's Rights in Curaçao*, 2015, pp. 100–104; Schields, "This Is the Soul of Aruba Speaking," 2016, p. 211. Editors' note: See contribution by Schields in this volume.

voting rights, had received limited formal education[12] and had little access to information beyond that provided through the Catholic Church, schools and press. In the late 1930s in Curaçao, approximately seventy percent of the population still lived in sociopolitical isolation, far removed from an emerging civil society and with little means for social mobility.[13] This isolated majority of the population was largely Catholic and Afro-Curaçaoan.

The Catholic majority was the result of the presence of missionaries who arrived on the island to baptize the enslaved and free black inhabitants, and who played an increasingly vital role in Curaçaoan society following the abolition of slavery in 1863.[14] From 1868 to 1970, the Dominican Province of the Netherlands (Nederlandse Provincie van de Orde der Dominicanen) was responsible for this mission. Under their leadership, Dutch missionaries provided basic formal education and strict religious and moral training through their sermons, the sacraments and an active Catholic press.[15] Though economic and social circumstances in Aruba and Bonaire differed substantially from those in Curaçao, Catholic missionaries from the Curaçao-based congregations also served the non-elite populations of these smaller, neighboring islands.

From the 1920s onward, the predominantly Protestant colonial government officials and the predominantly Jewish merchant elite increasingly supported the role of the Catholic missionaries as their activities were seen as sustaining the social order and preventing labor unrest. The maintenance of social stability became of vital importance to the authorities once local economies started to expand with the establishment of the oil industry. In trying to avoid the formation of pressure groups, the oil companies employed temporary migrant workers and also set up ethnic- and class-segregated working conditions. In Curaçao, this resulted in the further social and economic isolation and repression of lower-class Afro-Curaçaoans, particularly those living in the rural parts

12 Because literacy was relatively high in the Dutch Antilles, education had a favorable reputation. In schools for the lower classes though, most of the teachers were not trained or certified until 1953; the curriculum offered was limited and opportunities for advanced education were restricted. Most children dropped out before the age of fourteen in urban schools and before the age of twelve in the rural schools. See Groenewoud, "Social Exclusion," 2022.

13 Allen, *Di ki manera? A Social History of Afro-Curaçaoans, 1863–1917*, 2007; and Groenewoud, "Social Exclusion," 2022.

14 Throughout the nineteenth century, this accounted for approximately 85–90 percent of the total population.

15 Groenewoud, "Social Exclusion," 2022.

of the island. Even when the economy was booming, social mobility remained limited for this group.[16]

In the 1930s, a growing number of Catholic urban organizations appeared in Willemstad in Curaçao and Oranjestad in Aruba, which were particularly popular among lower-middle-class women. Although modeled on Catholic social action, popular in Europe and the US, the Catholic organizations in the Dutch Antilles had a distinct patriarchal character serving colonial interests rather than social emancipation.[17] Activities within the new organizations took place under the strict auspices of priests who remained fully in charge of all decision-making. When voting rights were introduced in 1936 for a limited group of eligible men, and passive voting rights were introduced for women, active citizenship was close to nonexistent in the colony.[18] This was not challenged by women at that point in time. Changes in women's political status came later as part of the post-war anticipation of political autonomy.[19]

The war years (1939–1945) brought many challenges to the ruling establishment as a new political discourse developed, not only concerning changing domestic power relations and relations with the Netherlands but also relations with other Dutch Caribbean territories. The latter approach was prominent in Aruba. Here, the political focus in the late 1940s was on gaining as much autonomy from its former 'big sister,' Curaçao, as possible, with the intent of forging closer, direct ties with the Netherlands.[20] In 1945, a Dutch government survey reporting on post-war ambitions indicated that there was no demand for independence in the Dutch Antilles.[21] All the same, there was an undisputed need

16 A Dutch company named BPM, later CPIM and Shell, operated the refinery on Curaçao in 1918. The American Standard Oil company refinery was established in Aruba in 1926.

17 Groenewoud, "'Nou koest, nou kalm.' De ontwikkeling van de Curaçaose samenleving, 1915–1973: Van koloniaal en kerkelijk gezag naar zelfbestuur en burgerschap" ["Hush now, calm down." The development of Curaçaoan society, 1915–1973: From colonial and church authority to self-government and citizenship], 2017, pp. 71–73; and Groenewoud, "Social Exclusion," 2022.

18 At that point, only the Chamber of Commerce had a governance structure with voting members. The group of citizens eligible to vote in 1936 accounted for approximately six percent of the male population.

19 Groenewoud, "'Nou koest, nou kalm,'" 2017, pp. 221–24.

20 Alofs, "Onderhorigheid en separatisme, koloniaal bestuur en lokale politiek op Aruba, 1816–1955" [Subordination and separatism, colonial governance and local politics on Aruba, 1816–1955], 2011; and Schields, "Closer Ties. The Dutch Caribbean and the Aftermath of Empire, 1942–2012," 2017.

21 Try Ellis, "Rapport van de commissie, bij gouvernements-beschikking van 10 october 1945 no. 7981 ingesteld, tot onderzoek en bestudeering van de in het staatsdeel Curaçao levende politieke opvattingen en wenschen, ter voorbereiding van de rijksconferentie" [Report of the commission, established by governmental decision of 10 October 1945

for greater democracy in government and increased political participation of citizens.[22] In three Round Table Conferences (1948, 1952 and 1954), baseline agreements were made for a new legal framework for the Kingdom of the Netherlands.[23] This resulted in the introduction, first, of a series of new local laws for the Dutch Antilles in 1948, including universal suffrage, followed eventually by the formal ratification of a new constitution for the Kingdom of the Netherlands in 1954. It was in this context that women in Curaçao stood up for women's suffrage.

2 The 1940s: the Emergence of a Women's Movement

In the Dutch Antilles, in contrast to several other Caribbean territories, no political women's associations existed in the pre-war years.[24] Following participation in the nationalists' grassroots networks, petitioning for universal suffrage in the late 1940s was the first occasion on which women united for a common cause. In the campaign for the vote in the 1940s, women from different classes came together to achieve political equality.[25] The right to vote that they were claiming was a right that women in the Netherlands had obtained in 1918.[26]

Initially, there had not seemed to be any reason for women to stage a campaign, since active voting rights for women had been included in a 1944 draft

no. 7981, to research and study the political views and desires of those living in Curaçao, in preparation of the state conference], 1946.

22 As such, the analysis of nonsovereignty in the Caribbean, being much more than a "nonchoice," is relevant and of importance to the Dutch Caribbean. Bonilla, "Ordinary Sovereignty," 2013.

23 See Oostindie and Klinkers, *Knellende koninkrijksbanden: Het Nederlandse dekolonisatiebeleid in de Caraïben* [Oppressive kingdom relations: Dutch decolonization policy in the Caribbean], 2001; and Oostindie and Klinkers, *Decolonising the Caribbean*, 2003.

24 Throughout the Caribbean, a wave of anticolonial social and political movements emerged in the late 1930s. In the British territories, women activists found common grounds in their various struggles and combined their strategies to build stronger campaigns. Castello, "Where Have All the Feminists Gone?" 2008: p. 142. Puerto Rican anti-imperialism was inspired by the writings of Julia de Burgos and, in the Dominican Republic, the Mirabal sisters fought against the Trujillo regime. Robinson, "Women's Political Participation in the Dominican Republic," 2006.

25 Allen, "Negotiating Gender, Citizenship and Nationhood through Universal Adult Suffrage in Curaçao," 2018, p. 10.

26 Ibid., p. 1.

law concerning changes to the way the territories were governed.[27] During the debates in 1946, however, lawmakers introduced legal obstacles to women's suffrage: unlike for men, their eligibility to vote would depend on property and educational criteria.[28] The 1946–1947 developments made it clear that something needed to be done to ensure universal suffrage. By early 1948, 'women's wing' organizations within the major political parties united women in Curaçao as an institutionalized force. Adèle M. R. Rigaud, an educated woman from the urban middle class, led one of the most prominent of these organizations within the Catholic party, the Luchadónan pa Derecho di Voto pa Hende Muhé (Champions of the Right to Vote for Women). Her organization initiated a petition in favor of women's suffrage directed to the Dutch prime minister, with the endorsement of the women's division of the nationalist party, the Damanan di Djárason (Wednesday Women).[29] Rigaud wrote the petition with the support of the leader of the Catholic party, Isaac Debrot, and circulated it widely through local newspapers.[30] Soon, a growing network of women of all backgrounds canvassed in support of suffrage, resulting in over 1,000 signatures.[31] The campaign had a big impact. In March 1948, at the Round Table Conference, women's active voting rights were not incorporated in the draft constitution but listed as a culturally sensitive issue that should be addressed locally. In response, the Curaçaoan lobby in favor of women's rights contacted two politicians in The Hague who pushed the issue: Corry Tendeloo and Wim de Kort.[32] When the Dutch parliament accepted their amendments, universal suffrage for the Dutch Antilles and Suriname passed into legislation.[33]

---

27 "Het bestuur van Curaçao gedecentraliseerd" [Governing board of Curaçao decentralized], *Amigoe di Curaçao*, April 21, 1944.

28 "De staten van Curaçao, Minister Jonkman en het vrouwenkiesrecht" [The states of Curaçao, Minister Jonkman and women's voting rights], *Amigoe di Curaçao*, April 10, 1948.

29 Allen, "Negotiating Gender," 2018, p. 10.

30 In a report kept in the archival file of her parliamentarian uncle, Adèle Rigaud recalls: "On February 23, 1948, undersigned came up with the plan to write a petition to request the right to vote for women, and to have this supported by a whole lot of women.... On February 24, 1948, called Mr. Isaac Debrot. Drafted a request. Visited him personally. Received a new request in the afternoon. It is beautifully constructed. Powerful language, stating what people want to achieve." Archivo Nashonal Kòrsou (ANK), Collectie S. W. Rigaud, inv. 1045 (Vrouwenkiesrecht 1948).

31 Ibid.

32 Thelma Römer and Mirna West-Davelaar were instrumental in conveying letters to Dutch parliamentarians. See Henriquez and Berry-Haseth, *Kòrsou su muhénan pionero*, 2002, pp. 135–39; Allen, "Negotiating Gender," 2018, p. 10.

33 A detailed report of the parliamentary session was published in: "De West krijgt kiesrecht voor allen. Staatsregelen zonder hoofdelijke stemming aangenomen" [The West obtains universal suffrage. State's regulations passed without roll call vote], *Amigoe di Curaçao*,

Ideologically, the women's 1948 petition centered on the belief in a universal entitlement to citizenship, stating that, for women, their "education, employment and position were similar to those of the men and that they therefore should have the same civil rights as the men."[34] This was a considerable step, coming not only from a position of being discriminated against as women but also from being subalterns within a colonial administration. The women's challenge to the position of the local Catholic leadership, which effectively supported social and political inequality, made this protest movement truly radical. In the late 1940s, the leaders of the Catholic Church in the Dutch Antilles repeatedly and publicly expressed the view that a majority of the population was not considered ready for citizenship.[35] This majority was the core missionary target group: the descendants of the formerly enslaved, in particular those living in the rural areas of the island.[36]

Women's quest for equality was not just a matter of principle; it also stemmed from the pragmatic and apparently nationalist aspiration of these women to participate at all levels in the developing society and economy, or, as the petition phrased it: "to give their full commitment to Curaçao." With this argument, the campaign anticipated the objection that women were supposed to give their commitment first and foremost to their families. Again, this represented a radical stance, since this aspect of Catholic ideology was deeply ingrained in the island's population. The ideal of the nuclear family had always been a key element of the *mission civilisatrice* in the Dutch Antilles. With industrialization, this ideal became even more important than before.[37] By supporting women's suffrage, certain politicians, such as the Catholic party's leader Isaac Debrot, risked alienating portions of their constituency. They nonetheless supported the movement for obvious reasons: appealing to

---

March 23, 1948. For the full report: *Handelingen Tweede Kamer 1947–1948* [Parliamentary proceedings 1947–1948], House of Representatives, March 16, 1948, www.statengeneraaldigitaal.nl.

34 Allen, "Negotiating Gender," 2018, p. 11.

35 Groenewoud, "'Nou koest, nou kalm,'" 2017, p. 129.

36 The Catholic Church on the islands intensified its missionary activities in the post-emancipation period. In particular in Curaçao, the demographic situation called for a "strong hand" to protect the interests of the elite. This Jewish and Protestant elite in the late nineteenth century formed 10–15 percent of the population, as opposed to 85–90 percent Afro-Curaçaoans, who mostly lived in relatively deprived circumstances. Allen, *Di ki manera? A Social History of Afro-Curaçaoans*, 2007, studies the 1863–1917 living conditions of the Afro-Curaçaoan population.

37 Abraham-Van der Mark, "Continuity and Change in the Afro-Caribbean Family in Curaçao in the Twentieth Century," 2003; and Groenewoud, "'Nou koest, nou kalm,'" 2017, pp. 80–81.

women was the only way for his party to substantially strengthen the Catholic political base on the island. After all, of all those who were expected to gain voting rights in 1948 and go to the ballot for the first time in 1949, the majority were Catholics.

3 The 1950s to 1970s: Women's Activism in between 'Old' and 'New'

The 1949 elections resulted in a landslide victory of the nationalist party at the expense of the Catholic party. Despite this success for the nationalists, the center of gravity of political power remained largely unchallenged. As a result of shrewd inter-island coalition building, governments between 1954 and 1970 continued to represent and serve the 'old' establishment, in which the Dutch governor, the Dutch Catholic bishop and Dutch and American industry played key roles. The continuity of the 'old' power patterns was demonstrated in particular during a series of strikes in the 1960s, when the government staunchly refused to improve the working conditions of a diverse group of occupations, including teachers and dock laborers. This, combined with a deep economic recession and ongoing exposure to oppression and patronage, fueled growing tension in the mid- and late 1960s, eventually resulting in a violent revolt in downtown Willemstad on May 30, 1969.[38] In contrast to what happened elsewhere in the region, the growing discontent did not culminate in the development of a broad political movement claiming independence. Instead, protest focused on economic and social justice or, in the words of a popular slogan, on *pan i respèt* (bread and respect).[39] Throughout the 1950s and 1960s, women on the islands also found themselves situated between 'old' and 'new,' striving for progress, respect and respectability in a rapidly changing environment. Their activism leaned toward the 'old,' as in the case of the Happy Camp protest in Aruba, as well as toward the 'new,' as was the case with employment at Texas Instruments and the changes taking place in family planning.

38 Oostindie, *Dromen en littekens: Dertig jaar na de Curaçaose Revolte, 30 mei 1969* [Dreams and scars: Thirty years after the Curaçao Revolt of May 30, 1969], 1999; and Oostindie, *Curaçao, 30 mei 1969. Verhalen over de Revolte* [Curaçao, May 30, 1969. Stories about the revolt], 1999.

39 A similar popular slogan was *pan i rekonosementu* (bread and acknowledgment).

4 The 1951 Happy Camp Protest in Aruba

Religious factors not only defined the political landscape of the 1940s and 1950s but were also the catalyst for a wave of women's activism in Aruba in that same period. In 1951, an Aruban hotel owner requested a permit to establish a 'Happy Camp,' which turned out to be modeled on the 'Campo Alegre' brothel established in Curaçao in 1949.[40] In the case of Curaçao, not only the Netherlands Antilles government but also the Catholic Church leadership had supported the project, which they considered necessary to fight public displays of immorality and the spread of venereal disease. When, two years later, the Happy Camp initiative gained public attention, a fast-growing movement of Aruban women emerged, denouncing the government's support for the brothel.[41] The organizations involved—the Aruban Roman Catholic Women's League and the Maria League—soon succeeded in mobilizing the masses. The women claimed that their Aruban cultural identity was rooted in the colonial Catholic Church and its ideology, and their aim was "to defend families and public morality from government-sanctioned sin."[42]

The women's petition denounced not only the actions by the Aruban government but also the Antillean and metropolitan regulations that facilitated the introduction of prostitution on the island. Pointing this out was an effective move. Aruban parliamentarians in the Netherlands Antilles had no choice but to defend the case of the Aruban women. By calling on "the soul of Aruba" and the promise of morality, the women's protest against Happy Camp became a topic of general national interest, leading to a successful conclusion.[43] Soon after an impressive mass demonstration, acting Dutch Governor F. A. Jas joined the growing group of parliamentarians that by now wanted to prevent the government from facilitating Happy Camp and initiated changes in line with the claims of the women's movement. The protest movement's success thus resulted from a clever strategy, packaging its demands within a nationalist

---

40 In Curaçao, the government and the local Catholic leadership supported Campo Alegre. These initiatives were legally facilitated by a system of regulation introduced in 1944. Kleijn and Schrover, "The Dutch State as a Pimp," 2013.

41 Schields, "This Is the Soul of Aruba Speaking," 2016. Editors' note: see also contribution by Kelly in this section.

42 Ibid., p. 202.

43 Ibid., pp. 202–203, 215–17.

political agenda and effectively using the island's nonsovereign status and the layered sovereignty of the Netherlands Antilles.[44]

5 Empowerment and Oppression: the Case of Texas Instruments

Since the late 1950s, the Netherlands Antilles had been facing rapid and sustained economic decline as a direct consequence of increased competition in the oil industry. Throughout the 1960s, this crisis would affect society deeply. Since extended families often relied on the income of one wage earner, job losses had a profound impact. At the same time, overpopulation was a growing concern, potentially adding to the economic burden of the small islands. In this context, the establishment of a new assembly industry in Curaçao specifically interested in hiring female workers brought a spark of hope for many women in the late 1960s.[45] By the early 1970s, the largest of three new companies, Texas Instruments, was employing 1,600 women.[46] The job opportunities, however, came with a downside as working conditions proved to be deplorable. On top of existing legal gender inequalities, the government had agreed to special regulations in order to attract the industry to the island. These conditions not only included low wages, night work and health risks but also involved medical regulation and family planning facilities and the controversial implementation of these measures by a company doctor.[47]

---

44 Ibid., p. 221.

45 This was the result of a recommendation made by the Stanford Research Institute, who advised the Curaçao government to attract this type of industry by offering ample availability of cheap female labor. Abraham-Van der Mark, "The Impact of Industrialization on Women: A Caribbean Case," 1983, pp. 380–81.

46 The two other companies were Schlumberger and Rockwell. In 1960, approximately 500 women in Curaçao worked in industrial employment; by 1972, that number had increased to 2,400.

47 Cuales, *Verslag van een candidaats-leeronderzoek naar de positie van de Curacaose vrouw die bij Texas Instruments heeft gewerkt in de periode 1968–1976* [Account of undergraduate training-research into the position of Curaçaoan women working at Texas Instruments during 1968–1976], 1977, pp. 42–45; Ramdas, *De papegaai, de stier en de klimmende bougainvillea* [The parrot, the bull and the climbing bougainvillea], 2017 (originally published in 1992), p. 121. Traces of this controversial subject are also found in: National Archives Curaçao, *Archief kabinet van de gouverneur van de Nederlandse Antillen I* [Archive cabinet of the governor of the Netherlands Antilles I] (*1936*) *1951–1991*, 870h stakingen bij Texas Instruments [strikes at Texas Instruments], 1972–1973. A letter from the minister for social affairs dated June 29, 1972, in this file announces an inquiry regarding the position and activities of the medical doctor assigned by Texas Instruments. More research needs to be done on this issue. Editors' note: A translated excerpt of the study by Cuales is included in this volume.

Despite the manifest exploitation of the women in the assembly industry, stories recorded and narrated by Dutch-Surinamese social geographer, journalist and writer Anil Ramdas reveal that many women working at Texas Instruments felt *both* empowered and oppressed.[48] The fact that feelings of empowerment dominated in their interviews was related both to earning their own money and to profiting from facilities related to family planning. This profoundly liberating impact counterbalanced the experience of exploitation and led many women to a strategy of silent compliance.[49] By doing this, women again demonstrated their ability to ride the tidal waves of change.

The benefits of the new industry, in particular for lower-class women, would not last long. With increased pressure on the company by the trade unions, the industry started to cut jobs.[50] When the first strikes took place at Texas Instruments in 1972, male union leaders negotiated for better conditions, sometimes accompanied by female workers.[51] After the 1976 closure of Texas Instruments, most women workers had no alternative but to fall back on traditional ways of earning money, such as baking and sewing. Curaçaoan sociologist Sonia Cuales argues that the Texas Instruments episode shows how slow economic change was compared to cultural change. A large group of lower-class women had proved that they could adjust rapidly to new opportunities and adopt a new mindset. The closure left them without jobs but with the memory of what such paid labor had given them. They had changed, but society did not change with them, leaving them, as Cuales concludes, not only empty-handed but also mentally disoriented.[52] In analyzing these developments, anthropologist Eva Abraham-Van der Mark states that women in the late 1960s through to the mid-1970s had considerable social influence but lacked significant political or economic power. Voting rights had not in fact caused a substantial growth of

48 Ramdas, *De strijd van de dansers: Biografische vertellingen* [The struggle of the dancers: Biographical tales], 1994, pp. 121–51; fragment from Ramdas, *De papegaai, de stier en de klimmende bougainvillea*, 2017 also published in: Oostindie, *Curaçao, 30 mei 1969. Verhalen over de Revolte*, 1999, pp. 72–77, in which it was used to contextualize the May 30, 1969, violence.

49 Ramdas, *De strijd van de dansers: Biografische vertellingen*, 1994, pp. 129–30; Cuales, *Verslag van een candidaats-leeronderzoek*, 1977, pp. 60, 68–71. This strategy of silent compliance is not unfamiliar in colonial societies and has been observed in other situations in Curaçao society as well: Groenewoud, "'Nou koest, nou kalm,'" 2017, p. 218.

50 Abraham-Van der Mark, "The Impact of Industrialization on Women: A Caribbean Case," 1983.

51 National Archives Curaçao, *Archief kabinet van de gouverneur van de Nederlandse Antillen I (1936) 1951–1991*, 870h stakingen bij Texas Instruments, 1972–1973. Notes of the meeting of June 21, 1972, p. 3.

52 Cuales, *Verslag van een candidaats-leeronderzoek*, 1977, p. 71.

women's participation in politics in Curaçao or Aruba.[53] Nonetheless, a new generation of young professionals had begun to expect greater social and economic equality in a political climate that increasingly trumpeted equal opportunity regardless of race, class or gender.

6 The Politics of Social Justice and Family Planning

In the years preceding the uprising on May 30, 1969, in Willemstad, a growing number of young people from the Antilles obtained higher education in the Netherlands, returning to the islands full of new insights and often fierce criticism. In the mid-1960s, students and young professionals, with the involvement of some women such as Emely Henriquez, began to air their radical ideas in the influential magazines *Vitó*, *Kontakto Antiano* and *Kambio*.[54] Not only did they attack political injustice, they also addressed social injustice. Women's issues, sexual rights, homosexuality and reproductive health all fell within the scope of their attention.[55]

In the late 1960s, the issue of family planning became a hot topic in the Netherlands Antilles. Before Texas Instruments had implemented family planning policies, other organizations had considered similar initiatives.[56] It was believed this would encourage both economic and social stability on the islands, combating overpopulation, poverty and what was considered "irresponsible behavior," especially with reference to lower-class Afro-Curaçaoan women. In 1965, Famia Plania—the Foundation for the Promotion of Responsible Parenthood—was established in Curaçao and Aruba.[57] This was done with the help of local businesses, the government and the churches, including the Catholic Church, which supported the educational campaigns to promote responsible parenthood without changing its stance on contraception. Famia Plania successfully mobilized stakeholders in their activities, claiming this was

53 Cuales, "In Search of Our Memory: Gender in the Netherlands Antilles," 1998, p. 96; and Cijntje and Quirindongo, "De participatie van vrouwen in de Curaçaose politiek in de jaren tachtig" [The participation of women in Curaçaoan politics in the 1980s], 1992, p. 132.

54 Henriquez and Berry-Haseth, *Kòrsou su muhénan pionero*, 2002, pp. 155–58.

55 Schields, "Closer Ties. The Dutch Caribbean and the Aftermath of Empire," 2017, pp. 103–14.

56 Ditzhuijzen, *Anyway… Sergio Leon: Vrouwenarts en eilandskind* [Anyway… Sergio Leon: Gynecologist and island child], 2015, p. 80.

57 In Aruba, the spelling is Famia Planea.

a *need* for the islands without mentioning reproductive health as a *right*.[58] Although this organization was strictly speaking not part of the women's movement but a broad social platform working closely together with women's organizations, the approach is noteworthy. In mobilizing commitment by focusing on a social and economic need, here again we see that pragmatism, rather than overtly expressed ideology, defined the successful strategy. It was now only a matter of time before these progressive practices would be further supported by law, regulations and policies.

7 Progressive Politics and Legal Victories: 1971–1993

The eruption of violence in Willemstad on May 30, 1969, proved to be a catalyst for many political, social, economic and personal changes in Curaçao and in the Netherlands Antilles as a whole.[59] The Dutch government soon concluded that the Netherlands Antilles and Suriname were ready for full independence. A trajectory to anticipate independence started in 1970 but with reluctance on the part of the government in the Netherlands Antilles, which did not perceive the urgency and wanted to agree on the premises before setting a deadline for independence.[60] This deadline would never materialize. Several government bodies studied the option of independence but with little political commitment and little impact. Nonetheless, after 1970, a series of progressive policies developed with respect to domestic issues, with important repercussions for the position of women in society.

In early 1971, the government of the Netherlands Antilles installed an advisory commission to prepare for the elimination of discrimination against women. This issue had originally been raised in 1957 by one of the first female parliamentarians, Luisa van der Linde-Helmijr, but no follow-up occurred until 1968, when a legal report was issued on the subject.[61] Lucina da Costa Gomez, the minister of health and later the first female prime minister of the Netherlands Antilles, was responsible for seeing the subject through to completion.[62] When presenting the proposed new law to the press in 1972, she

58 Schields, "Closer Ties. The Dutch Caribbean and the Aftermath of Empire," 2017, p. 100.

59 Oostindie, *Dromen en littekens: Dertig jaar na de Curaçaose Revolte, 30 mei 1969*, 1999.

60 Reinders, *Politieke geschiedenis van de Nederlandse Antillen en Aruba* [Political history of the Dutch Antilles and Aruba], 1993, pp. 97–99, 113–21, 143.

61 Henriquez and Berry-Haseth, *Kòrsou su muhénan pionero*, 2002, pp. 125, 172.

62 Lucina da Costa Gomez-Matheeuws (1929–2017) was minister of health and environment, welfare, youth, sports, culture and recreation between 1970 and 1977 and briefly served as prime minister of the Netherlands Antilles in 1977.

proudly emphasized in her speech that "there had been no demonstrations of women so far in the Dutch Antilles to claim vocally their rights, and there shouldn't be."[63] Refusing to attribute the law to women's activism, Lucina da Costa Gomez effectively silenced the existence of a lively women's movement that functioned in Curaçao, and to a lesser extent in Aruba, from the 1970s until the early 1990s.[64] Although Da Costa Gomez emphasized the practical need for the law in that same speech, she adopted the narrative that gender equality was a commonly shared value in society, not needing much discussion. This narrative is found in all the official documents on the matter.[65]

With the 1975 abolition of the legal incapacity of married women, many other discriminatory provisions also lost their formal basis and were amended. Nevertheless, much work remained to be done. With the pressure and support of a range of women's organizations, further political progress was made in the 1980s and early 1990s, eventually resulting in key legal victories. In 1983, a new law banned discrimination based on sex and marital status against women in the public labor market. Ten years later, in 1993, pressure from women's movements resulted in the acceptance of equal pay for civil servants.

A range of activities in the context of the United Nations International Women's Year (1975) led to the establishment of the organization with branches in Aruba and Curaçao, formed to coordinate the activities of a range of smaller groups. Most of these smaller women's groups were religiously affiliated and nonpolitical, committed to providing social and educational activities for their members.[66] Many members of these moderate groups were elementary school teachers who joined the Steering Committee Curaçao because it was the only

63 See "Eindvergadering commissie ter uitbanning van discriminatie tegen vrouwen 1972" [Final meeting of the Commission for the elimination of discrimination against women 1972], *Amigoe di Curacao*, April 5, 1972.

64 For a concise overview, see chapter four in: Rodriguez, *The Rise of Women's Rights in Curaçao*, 2015, pp. 97–125. In Aruba, the organizational model was that of *praatgroepen* (chat groups), following a Dutch model ideologically based on the idea that "the personal is political." Two major groups existed from approximately 1978–1979, Anglo and Aloë. Source: email correspondence with Ini Statia, December 18, 2018.

65 *Memorie van toelichting bij de landsverordening opheffing handelingsonbekwaamheid van de gehuwde vrouw* [Explanatory memorandum to the national ordinance removing the legal incapacity of married women], Zitting 1973–1974, no. 3. ANK, Archives of the Advisory Board 1950–1990, Meeting on September 12, 1974. Committee report *Eindverslag van de commissie "Uitbanning discriminatie van de vrouw"* [Final report of the committee for the elimination of women's discrimination]. A copy of this report is available in Mongui Maduro Library, Curaçao.

66 Horst, "Oecumenische vrouwengroepen op Curaçao gericht op strategie of praktijk," 1988.

space where female teachers could meet. For want of an association or union for female teachers, the Steering Committee Curaçao functioned in practice as a platform for women to vent their general discontent and find an audience for their concerns.[67]

In 1975, also in anticipation of International Women's Year, an independent women's organization was established in Curaçao: Union Muhénan Antiano (UMA, Union of Antillean women). Although UMA and the steering committee had an effective working relationship, their ideology, profile and approaches differed substantially. Whereas the steering committee attracted mostly elementary school teachers, most UMA members were college and university graduates, active in the field of social work. This was reflected in their areas of concern, such as housing, domestic violence, sexuality and poverty. The UMA agenda was generally considered more radical; one of their targets was to incorporate women's equality in the struggle for "true national independence."[68] As Schields analyzes, UMA feminists integrated gender equality in their anti-imperialist agenda, in which they involved both men and women.[69] Throughout its existence, UMA refrained from partisan politics. In this it differed from the steering committee, which encouraged women to become politically active and had close ties with several women politicians, although they never officially aligned with a political party.[70]

The most challenging aspect of women's mobilization in these decades was the fact that there were considerable discrepancies within the membership of these groups with respect to education and ideological engagement.[71] Devoting campaigns to women's general training, developing knowledge, insights and awareness, was important but time consuming and demanding. The limited success of many mobilization efforts was, to a large extent, the result of these internal challenges and of a permanent shortage of capacity.[72] Nonetheless, in the longer term, the movement could claim some legal successes. This can be attributed largely to a core of strong-minded and intellectually shrewd women who could set an agenda and—profiting from small-scale and

---

67 Interview Stella Pieters Kwiers, December 14, 2018.

68 ANK, Collection UMA, file 10. (Note: the numbering of the UMA collection was temporary at the time of this research and publication.)

69 Schields, "Closer Ties. The Dutch Caribbean and the Aftermath of Empire," 2017, p. 17.

70 Interview Stella Pieters-Kwiers, December 14, 2018.

71 Interviews Gladys do Rego-Kuster, December 7, 2018, and Stella Pieters Kwiers, December 14, 2018.

72 Ibid.

excellent networking—managed to be accepted as a valid interlocutor for the government.[73]

8 Conclusion

This study of the women's movement in Aruba and Curaçao from its 1940s beginnings to the early 1990s focused on the sources of strength of the women. These strengths were needed to invest and persevere in activities that differed substantially from what was expected from them in these small, traditional and religious island societies. The analysis of women's movements presented in this article sustains the view that women's successful strategies depended primarily on their adjustment to their particular environment. Throughout the twentieth century, civil society was very limited on the islands and, until the 1980s, only a small minority of islanders profited from higher education. The majority of the population suffered from a long history of repression, erasure and silencing, with no critical mass prepared to engage in radical protest. In this context, promoting women's rights required astute pragmatism and recognition of the difficulties of collective action. The women and women's organizations presented in this contribution all lived and breathed that reality. Although their successes can be attributed to strong intellectual forces and a keen understanding of political tides, in the end the strength of successful operations lay not primarily in knowledge, ideology or strategy but in the ability to find the right moment, to align and to cooperate and to ride the tidal waves of progress.

Acknowledgments

This contribution is an abridged and edited version of an article published in 2019 in French as Groenewoud, Margo. "Les mobilisations féminines dans les Antilles néerlandaises (Curaçao et Aruba, 1946–1993)." *Clio. Women, Gender, History* 50, no. 2 (2019): 63–85. https://www.cairn-int.info/journal-clio-women-gender-history-2019-2-page-63.htm. This was translated by Nicole G. Albert and the original version in English was published online as "Women's Mobilization in the Dutch Caribbean (Curaçao and Aruba, 1946–1993)." Reproduction of this text courtesy of *Clio*.

73 Rodriguez, *The Rise of Women's Rights in Curaçao*, 2015, pp. 103–4.

Bibliography

Abraham-Van der Mark, Eva. "Continuity and Change in the Afro-Caribbean Family in Curaçao in the Twentieth Century." *Community, Work & Family* 6, no. 1 (2003): 77–88.

Abraham-Van der Mark, Eva. "The Impact of Industrialization on Women: A Caribbean Case." In *Women, Men, and the International Division of Labor*, edited by June Nash and Maria Patricia Fernández-Kelly, 374–86. Albany: State University of New York Press, 1983.

Allen, Rose Mary. *Di ki manera? A Social History of Afro-Curaçaoans, 1863–1917*. Amsterdam: SWP Publishers, 2007.

Allen, Rose Mary. "Negotiating Gender, Citizenship and Nationhood through Universal Adult Suffrage in Curaçao." *Caribbean Review of Gender Studies* 12 (2018): 299–318.

Alofs, Luc. "Onderhorigheid en separatisme, koloniaal bestuur en lokale politiek op Aruba, 1816–1955" [Subordination and separatism, colonial governance and local politics on Aruba, 1816–1955]. PhD diss., Leiden University, 2011. https://openaccess.leidenuniv.nl/handle/1887/17992.

Ansano, Richenel, Jocelyn A. Clemencia, Jeanette Cook, and Eithel Martis, eds. *Mundu yama sinta mira: Womanhood in Curaçao* [The name of the world is sit and see: Womanhood in Curaçao]. Curaçao: Fundashon Publikashon, 1992.

Bailey, Barbara, and Elsa Leo-Rhynie, eds. *Gender in the 21st Century: Caribbean Perspectives, Visions and Possibilities*. Kingston, Jamaica: Ian Randle, 2004.

Bonilla, Yarimar. "Ordinary Sovereignty." *Small Axe: A Caribbean Journal of Criticism* 17, no. 3(42) (2013): 152–65.

Castello, June. "Where Have All the Feminists Gone? Learning the Lessons of a Long Time Passed in the Women's Movement in the Caribbean." *Caribbean Quarterly* 54, no. 1–2 (2008): 139–55.

Cijntje, Gilbert J, and Frank Quirindongo. "De participatie van vrouwen in de Curaçaose politiek in de jaren tachtig" [The participation of women in Curaçaoan politics in the 1980s]. In *Mundu yama sinta mira: Womanhood in Curaçao*, edited by Richenel Ansano, Joceline A. Clemencia, Jeanette Cook, and Eithel Martis, 129–41. Curaçao: Fundashon Publikashon, 1992.

Clemencia, Joceline A. "Introduction." In *Mundu yama sinta mira: Womanhood in Curaçao*, edited by Richenel Ansano, Joceline A. Clemencia, Jeanette Cook, and Eithel Martis, IX–XII. Curaçao: Fundashon Publikashon, 1992.

Cuales, Sonia M. "In Search of Our Memory: Gender in the Netherlands Antilles." *Feminist Review* 59, no. 1 (1998): 86–100.

Cuales, Sonia M. *Verslag van een candidaats-leeronderzoek naar de positie van de Curaçaose vrouw die bij Texas Instruments heeft gewerkt in de periode 1968–1976*

[Graduate research report on the position of Curaçaoan women working at Texas Instruments from 1968 to 1976]. Master's thesis, Leiden University, 1977.

"De staten van Curaçao, Minister Jonkman en het vrouwenkiesrecht" [The states of Curaçao, Minister Jonkman and women's voting rights]. *Amigoe di Curaçao*, April 10, 1948.

Ditzhuijzen, Jeanette van. *Anyway... Sergio Leon: Vrouwenarts en eilandskind* [Anyway... Sergio Leon: Gynecologist and island child]. Volendam: LM Publishers, 2015.

"Eindvergadering commissie ter uitbanning van discriminatie tegen vrouwen 1972" [Final meeting of the commission for the elimination of discrimination against women 1972]. *Amigoe di Curaçao*, April 5, 1972.

Groenewoud, Margo. "Les mobilisations féminines dans les Antilles Néerlandaises (Curaçao et Aruba, 1946–1993)." *Clio. Women, Gender, History* 50, no. 2 (2019): 63–85. https://www.cairn-int.info/journal-clio-women-gender-history-2019-2-page-63.htm.

Groenewoud, Margo. "'Nou koest, nou kalm.' De ontwikkeling van de Curaçaose samenleving, 1915–1973: Van koloniaal en kerkelijk gezag naar zelfbestuur en burgerschap" ["Hush now, calm down." The development of Curaçaoan society, 1915–1973: From colonial and church authority to self-government and citizenship]. PhD diss., Leiden University, 2017. https://openaccess.leidenuniv.nl/handle/1887/50108.

Groenewoud, Margo. "Social Exclusion and the Entanglement of State, Religion and Civil Society in Mid-Twentieth Century Curaçao." *Journal of Caribbean History* 56, no. 1 (2022): 81–95. https://doi.org/10.1353/jch.2022.0003.

Henriquez, Jeanne D., and Lucillle Berry-Haseth. *Kòrsou su muhénan pionero: Original na Papiamento* [Curaçao pioneering women: Original in Papiamentu]. Curaçao: Archivo Nashonal di Antia Hulandes, 2002.

"Het bestuur van Curaçao gedecentraliseerd" [Governing board of Curaçao decentralized]. *Amigoe di Curaçao*, April 21, 1944.

Horst, Els van der. "Oecumenische vrouwengroepen op Curaçao gericht op strategie of praktijk" [Ecumenical women's groups on Curaçao directed toward strategy or practice]. Master's thesis, VU Amsterdam, 1988.

Jong, Lammert de. "Extended Statehood in the Caribbean: Definition and Forces." In *Extended Statehood in the Caribbean: Paradoxes of Quasi Colonialism, Local Autonomy and Extended Statehood in the USA, French, Dutch and British Caribbean*, edited by Lammert de Jong and Dirk Kruijt, 3–24. Amsterdam: Rozenberg, 2006.

Kleijn, Mariëlle, and Marlou Schrover. "The Dutch State as a Pimp. Policies Regarding a Brothel on Curaçao (1945–1956)." *Tijdschrift voor Sociale en Economische Geschiedenis* 10, no. 3 (2013): 33–54.

Macpherson, Anne. "Toward Decolonization. Impulses, Processes, and Consequences since the 1930s." In *The Caribbean: A History of the Region and Its Peoples*, edited by Stephan Palmié and Francisco Antonio Scarano, 475–89. Chicago: University of Chicago Press, 2011.

Oostindie, Gert, ed. *Curaçao, 30 mei 1969. Verhalen over de Revolte* [Curaçao May 30, 1969. Stories about the Revolt]. Amsterdam: Amsterdam University Press, 1999.

Oostindie, Gert, ed. *Dromen en littekens: Dertig jaar na de Curaçaose Revolte, 30 Mei 1969* [Dreams and scars: Thirty years after the Curaçao Revolt of May 30, 1969]. Amsterdam: Amsterdam University Press, 1999.

Oostindie, Gert, and Inge Klinkers. *Decolonising the Caribbean: Dutch Policies in a Comparative Perspective*. Amsterdam: Amsterdam University Press, 2003.

Oostindie, Gert, and Inge Klinkers. *Knellende koninkrijksbanden: Het Nederlandse dekolonisatiebeleid in de Caraïben, 1940–2000* [Oppressive kingdom relations: Dutch decolonization policy in the Caribbean, 1940–2000]. Amsterdam: Amsterdam University Press, 2001.

Ramdas, Anil. *De papegaai, de stier en de klimmende bougainvillea: Essays* [The parrot, the bull and the climbing bougainvillea: Essays]. Amsterdam: De Bezige Bij, 2017.

Ramdas, Anil. *De strijd van de dansers: Biografische vertellingen* [The struggle of the dancers: Biographical tales]. Amsterdam: Muntinga, 1994.

Reinders, Alex. *Politieke geschiedenis van de Nederlandse Antillen en Aruba: 1950–1993* [Political history of the Dutch Antilles and Aruba: 1950–1993]. Zutphen: Walburg Press, 1993.

Robinson, Nancy. "Women's Political Participation in the Dominican Republic: The Case of the Mirabal Sisters." *Caribbean Quarterly* 52, no. 2–3 (2006): 172–83.

Rodriguez, Adaly. *The Rise of Women's Rights in Curaçao: The Potential of the Women's Convention to the Empowerment and Equal Rights of Women in Curaçao*. Amsterdam: Uitgeverij SWP, 2015.

Schields, Chelsea. "Closer Ties. The Dutch Caribbean and the Aftermath of Empire, 1942–2012." PhD diss., City University of New York, 2017. http://academicworks.cuny.edu/gc_etds/1993.

Schields, Chelsea. "'This Is the Soul of Aruba Speaking': The 1951 Campo Alegre Protest and Insular Identity on Aruba." *New West Indian Guide / Nieuwe West-Indische Gids* 90, no. 3–4 (2016): 195–224.

Try Ellis, W. Ch. de la. "Rapport van de commissie, bij gouvernements-beschikking van 10 october 1945 no.7981 ingesteld, tot onderzoek en bestudeering van de in het staatsdeel Curaçao levende politieke opvattingen en wenschen, ter voorbereiding van de rijksconferentie" [Report of the commission, established by governmental decision of 10 October 1945 no.7981, to research and study the political views and desires of those living in Curaçao, in preparation of the state conference]. The Hague: Algemeene Landsdrukkerij, 1946.

CHAPTER 11

Gender Policy and Institutionalization in Curaçao: Governmental and Civil Society Interactions since the 1930s

Jacqueline Martis

Abstract

This contribution examines relevant developments on governmental and nongovernmental levels pertaining to gender equality in the former Netherlands Antilles and present-day Curaçao from the late 1930s onwards. Women were organized in social clubs, political organizations and feminist groups for women's equality and rights. The contribution examines institutional shifts, policies and actions in dealing with women's equality and rights. A major area of focus was legal reform, which impacted women's rights and public position, but did not necessarily impact traditional social and cultural roles, nor, indeed, lessen their vulnerability to violence and poverty.

Keywords

gender policy – government of Curaçao – nongovernmental organizations – women's rights – legal reform

1 Introduction: the Road to Women's Equality in Curaçao

Emancipation Policy in the Netherlands Antilles: Still an Illusion? was the title of the first shadow report on the Convention on the Elimination of All Forms of Discrimination Against Women (CEDAW) presented to the CEDAW Committee in 2001 by the Caribbean Association for Feminist Research and Action (CAFRA Curaçao), a cross-Caribbean organization concerned with the plight of women, founded in 1985.[1] The shadow report, intended to supplement

1 Henriquez and Martis, *Emancipation Policy in the Netherlands Antilles: Still an Illusion*, 2001.

 | DOI:10.1163/9789004690882_013

government reports under international treaties, noted that the governments of the islands of the Netherlands Antilles, notwithstanding good intentions, lacked a comprehensive and holistic policy to address the continued unequal position of women. It viewed the measures taken to improve the position of women as ad hoc and lacking structure, follow-up measures, monitoring and evaluation mechanisms. Following the dissolution of the Netherlands Antilles in 2010, when Curaçao became an autonomous country within the Kingdom of the Netherlands, a second shadow report by SEDA (Women's Development Center) was submitted to the CEDAW Committee in 2015, also criticizing the government's gender equality policies or lack thereof.[2]

This critique is indicative of a constant struggle and critical relationship between the government's position and that of civil society and women's NGOs. The latter have always been critical of the government's policy formulations and the lived realities of women as documented by NGOs on the ground.

In this contribution, I examine some of the relevant developments pertaining to gender equality in Curaçao from the late 1930s to the present. I discuss social changes that influenced the women's movement, women's struggle for equality and the government's responses to them. The period in question covers three constitutional periods in what has come to be known as the Dutch Caribbean islands. The first period, from 1930 to 1960, marks a moment when the six islands were still under direct Dutch colonial rule and there were growing political demands for self-government and citizenship. In the second period, from 1960 to 2010, the islands achieved greater autonomy within the kingdom as the Netherlands Antilles (from 1954 to 2010). Finally, in the third period, from 2010 to the present, the contribution focuses on developments in Curaçao after it became a constituent country within the kingdom in October 2010.

2 From 1930 to 1960: Women's Quest for Political Participation

Until 1936, Afro-Curaçaoans had no say in administering the island and only white intellectual elites were in power.[3] This political inequality changed with the new Code of Governance, which came into force in 1937 and gave Afro-Curaçaoans some limited involvement in administrative matters. At that time, most middle-class members were descendants of the mixed or colored

2 SEDA, *Lighted Torches*, 2015. Editors' note: see contribution by Pieters Kwiers in this volume.

3 Römer, "Ethnicity and Social Change in Curaçao," 1998.

population, who had greater privileges, such as access to better schools, as compared to the black underclass living in large numbers outside the city.[4]

The first election for the new *Staten* or parliament in the Territory of Curaçao was held on December 20, 1937, but only a select group of land-owning, tax-paying men above twenty-five years of age, with at least a seventh-grade education, were allowed to vote.[5] This excluded all female and most male Afro-Curaçaoans. The literacy and education levels of the Afro-Curaçaoan population were low at the time, considering that it was only a generation or two after the abolition of slavery, when education was a privilege for the few white inhabitants.[6]

Women's political activism was instrumental in gaining universal suffrage. One of the fighters for the right to vote for women was Adèle Rigaud, born in Curaçao in 1924. After secondary school, she worked as an administrative assistant for the government. In 1948, she joined the then called Katholieke Partij Curaçao (KPC, Catholic Party Curaçao) and was the first woman to become a member of the executive committee of a political party. She believed that women should be involved in political decisions and that they should have the right to vote.[7] She joined other women who called themselves Luchadónan pa Derecho di Voto pa Hende Muhé (Champions of the Right to Vote for Women) and were involved in women's political education and awareness raising.

Another important group was the Damanan di Djárason, the so-called Wednesday Women. The PNP (Partido Nashonal di Pueblo [National People's Party]) formed a women's committee, led by Clarita da Costa Gomez, who was the aunt of the PNP's leader Frumencio da Costa Gomez, popularly known as "Dòktor."[8] Wednesday was considered to be the lightest day in their schedule of domestic duties, and they used this time for political and social activities.[9]

---

4 Ibid.

5 Rodriguez, *The Rise of Women's Rights in Curaçao*, 2015; and Rosaria, "70 Years Women's Voting Rights/70 aña derechi di voto hende muhé," 2018.

6 Groenewoud, "'Nou koest, nou kalm.' De ontwikkeling van de Curaçaose samenleving, 1915–1973: Van koloniaal en kerkelijk gezag naar zelfbestuur en burgerschap" ["Hush now, calm down." The development of Curaçaoan society, 1915–1973: From colonial and church authority to self-government and citizenship], 2017. Editors' note: see contribution by Groenewoud in this volume.

7 Henriquez, *Kòrsou su muhénan pionero: Original na Papiamento* [Curaçao pioneering women: Original in Papiamento], 2002; and personal archive of Adèle Rigaud 1948–1967, Willemstad, Curaçao, 1967. Editors' note: see contribution by Henriquez in this volume.

8 Henriquez, *Kòrsou su muhénan pionero*, 2002.

9 Pieters Kwiers, *Dòktor da Costa Gomez: Polítiko i estadista prominente di siglo XX* [Doctor da Costa Gomez: Politician and prominent statesman of the twentieth century], 2018; and Rosaria, "70 Years Women's Voting Rights," 2018.

They sensitized women to the fact that, as women, they had to fight for their rights, "buska nan derechi." They emphasized political participation and went door to door, talking to people about joining the PNP.

The women on the committee came from different socioeconomic and educational backgrounds and included small business owners.[10] The committee also provided social and financial assistance to people in need. At the end of each meeting, they raised money from merchants to help those in need. Until 1970, the government had no formal welfare program, although it provided some financial assistance to religious, social and political organizations that took on this responsibility.

Like the Luchadónan pa Derechi di Voto pa Hende Muhé, the Wednesday Women believed that women had rights and a responsibility to be politically active and informed. They were clear that laws and policies would have to change if they wanted more rights for women, which could only happen at the political level. Their main areas of concern were the alleviation of poverty, work and domestic violence.

Both groups took crucial steps for women's rights in the Netherlands Antilles and Curaçao. After mobilizing for and obtaining the right to vote, the two groups collected signatures and sent a letter to the Dutch parliament, thanking them for their support in obtaining universal suffrage.

On March 17, 1948, suffrage went into effect for all citizens of the island territories, and the first election for parliament was held in April 1949. The first woman elected to parliament was Angela Altagracia de Lannoy-Willems of the PNP. When she married Thomas Francis de Lannoy in 1942, she lost her government position and was sent home. Under the law at the time, married women were not allowed to work for the government. After the intervention of her Dutch boss, the government secretary, she was able to get her job back but on a contractual basis. Her situation shed light on one of the major issues facing women at the time: the loss of the right to work at marriage. Women had limited rights or no rights at all when they got married.

Another example of women's political participation and activism was the participation of Luisa van der Linde-Helmeijer in the elections of June 1951 of the Island Council.[11] She was the first woman to win a seat on the Island Council for the Partido Democraat (DP, Democratic Party) and served on the Island

10 Henriquez, *Kòrsou su muhénan pionero*, 2002.

11 In 1954, the Dutch colony Curaçao and its dependencies became the Netherlands Antilles after attaining autonomy for regulating their internal affairs and forming their own government. The Netherlands Antilles comprised a central government and local island governments, with a constitutional division of the duties and responsibilities of each level.

Council from 1951 to 1956, and, from 1954, she also served as the first female member of parliament for the Democratic Party. Luisa van der Linde-Helmeijer worked both positions for a few years and was the secretary of the leadership of the party. Her story illustrates that, although women became involved in governmental activities, their role as caretakers in society did not change. They were still expected to take care of the household, family and the community, including the political party, while working full-time. As the only woman in the DP, it was expected that she attended all meetings of her assigned zones, work office hours and take care of her family. She recounts that she once came home from a full day of campaigning, took her suitcase, went to the hospital and gave birth to her child the next day.[12]

As a member of parliament (1954–1967), Van der Linde-Helmeijer introduced a bill for a Volkskredietbank, a people's cooperative bank that would help the working class with loans at lower interest rates than local banks. She is also credited with drafting the bill to abolish women's legal incapacity, which was later pushed by Lucina da Costa Gomez and signed by Prime Minister J. Evertsz in 1975.

3 From 1960 to 2010: the Impact of the 1960s on Women's Liberation Movements in Curaçao

The 1960s was a time of much change internationally and regionally. The fight for independence in the region from colonial powers, the black power movement in the US, students returning to the island after studying abroad with socialist and anticolonial ideologies and the women's liberation movements: all these would have a lasting impact on the island of Curaçao and its development.

With the establishment of the Texas Instruments (TI) assembly factory in Curaçao in 1968, which employed approximately sixteen hundred women, many Afro-Curaçaoan women witnessed a major improvement of their socio-economic situation. This chance to work and earn their own money gave them financial independence and a degree of power over their own lives. At the same time, the working conditions that the government had negotiated with TI were far from ideal or fair and would impact women's health, among other issues. These included low wages, long working hours standing on an assembly

12 Henriquez, *Kòrsou su muhénan pionero*, 2002.

line, minimal (bathroom) breaks and inadequate on-site medical and reproductive health services.[13] The high unemployment, poverty, wage disparities between local workers and Dutch workers and other immigrant workers and anticolonial sentiments led to a volatile situation with strikes and, finally, to the workers' uprising on May 30, 1969, popularly called Trinta di Mei. Its impact on women's affairs needs to be studied more profoundly.

4 Women Moving and Organizing

During the 1960s and 1970s women increasingly organized themselves in professional, social and cultural associations and clubs, often referred to as Klup di Dama (Ladies' Club). The Klup di Dama provided a space for especially working-class and lower-middle-class women to socialize, educate themselves and discuss issues of importance to them while maintaining their traditional roles as housewives and mothers. Most of the clubs were influenced or intertwined with religious organizations.[14]

One salient point for some of these organizations was the fact that they were organized around "the married woman" and would include husbands in some of their events. The bylaws of some of these clubs did not allow single or divorced women to join or remain in the clubs after divorce.[15] My mother, who was a member of one of the prominent women's clubs, OSCULDA (Organizacion Social i Cultural di Damas Antiyanas [Antillean Sociocultural Women's Organization]), was forced to end her membership of the club at the time of her divorce in the 1970s.[16] Over time, they admitted women of all civil statuses as members; however, the bylaws have not yet been rectified.

Women's struggle for equality in Curaçao was cemented by the establishment of the Steering Committee Curaçao (SCC) in 1974, formed in preparation

13 Anil Ramdas, *De strijd van de dansers: Biografische vertellingen* [The fight of the dancers: Biographical tales], 1994; and Cuales, "Mujer, reproducción y capital extranjero: El caso de una empresa multinacional en Curazao" [Women, reproduction and foreign capital: The case of a multinational company in Curaçao], 1984. Editors' note: see contribution by Cuales in Section I in this volume.

14 Editors' note: see contributions by Groenewoud and Do Rego-Kuster in this volume.

15 Glenda Maduro, president of OSCULDA, in conversation with the author (Willemstad, October 2018).

16 OSCULDA continues to exist, albeit on a smaller scale. Glenda Maduro in conversation with the author (Willemstad, October 2018).

for the participation of the Netherlands Antilles in the first world conference on women in 1975 and the International Year of Women declared by the UN.[17] About sixty women's clubs would eventually become members of the SCC, which remains the umbrella organization for about thirty women's organizations and is an autonomous body partially subsidized by the government.

According to Glenda Maduro, president of the women's club OSCULDA, many women's clubs are no longer in existence as they have been unable to attract younger women in their membership.[18]

Another type of women's organization also gained a foothold in Antillean society in the 1970s and 1980s. These were formed by students returning to the island from their studies in the Netherlands, often politically influenced by feminism, Marxist or broadly leftist ideologies and anticolonial sentiments, who organized themselves and mobilized on women's issues on the island. Two such prominent feminist groups were the Union Muhénan Antiano (Union of Antillean Women, UMA), and later CAFRA. UMA was founded in 1975 with a clear anticolonial agenda alongside the emphasis on equal rights for women. It was instrumental in organizing protests and sit-ins on issues such as housing for women and violence against women. In addition, UMA was at the forefront in the fight for women's sexual and reproductive health and rights. They organized in cooperation with the other women's organizations and were involved in a series of local and regional activities dealing with different forms of violence against women and sex work. It ceased its activities in the mid-1980s. The feminist agenda was then carried forward in the 1990s by the Curaçao chapter of CAFRA, a regional network of feminists, independent researchers, activists and women's organizations who define feminist politics as a matter of both consciousness and action. Founded in 1985, CAFRA's vision statement expresses a commitment to understanding the relationship between the oppression of women and other forms of oppression in the society and working actively for change.

As NGOs became more vocal, politically aware and used mobilization, lobbying and advocacy as strategies to advance the rights of women and other disadvantaged groups, they exerted great pressure on governments for change and helped set the ground for the advancement of women's rights.

---

17 Editors' note: see contribution by Pieters Kwiers in this volume.

18 Glenda Maduro in conversation with the author (Willemstad, October 2018).

5 Changes at the Governmental Level

The Netherlands Antilles have had a total of five female prime ministers between 1969 and 2010.[19] This fact is often viewed as an indication of the emancipated position of Dutch Caribbean women as a whole. In 1969, Lucina da Costa Gomez, the widow of "Dòktor," became the first woman to lead a political party. She also held a seat in the central government until 1977, both as a member of parliament and as a minister. In 1977, she became the first female prime minister of the Netherlands Antilles, albeit for only ten days in a caretaker government.

In 1971, she set up a committee for the elimination of discrimination against women for the Netherlands Antilles (Commissie uitbanning discriminatie van de vrouw), tasked to advise the government on policy and implementation measures. The committee inventoried concerns relating to women's rights and emancipation and recommended the elimination of dozens of laws and regulations that discriminated against women. Furthermore, they also recommended a list of social and economic measures to advance the position of women in the Antillean society and the acceptance of women as equal citizens.[20] These recommendations served as the blueprint for the women and development work later undertaken by the government. Among the changes made in the 1970s were the admittance of women to uniformed services, such as the police and customs, and welfare measures, such as parental leave and social security.

As minister of social welfare, Lucina da Costa Gomez also appointed the first woman as head of the Department of Social Welfare in 1974. This department also launched a Bureau for Life and Family Problems, the first governmental agency offering services to female victims of abuse and rape and support with social, personal and family problems. The bureau was replaced by the Office of Women and Humanitarian Affairs (Women's Bureau) in 1989. This move was probably made in part in keeping with international obligations of setting up a national machinery for the advancement of women. An interministerial

---

19 Lucina da Costa Gomez-Matheeuws (October 4–14, 1977); Maria Liberia-Peters (September 18, 1984 – January 1, 1986; and May 7, 1988 – November 25, 1993); Suzanne Camelia-Römer (November 25, 1993 – December 28, 1993; and May 14, 1998 – November 8, 1999); Mirna Louisa-Godett (August 11, 2003 – June 3, 2004); Emily de Jongh-Elhage (March 26, 2006 – October 10, 2010).

20 *Eindverslag van de commissie 'Uitbanning discriminatie van de vrouw'* [Final report of the committee for the elimination of women's discrimination], unpublished report (Curaçao: Government of Curaçao, Bureau of Women's Affairs), 1972.

advisory group on women and development was also established to support the work of the Women's Bureau. This advisory group can be considered as the first official gender mainstreaming attempt in the government apparatus for the Netherlands Antilles.[21]

The closure of the Women's Bureau in 1995 created a change in the commitment of the central government and shifted some of the responsibilities for what was then called gender affairs to the island government level. In 1996, a new Department of Welfare, Family and Humanitarian Affairs was opened and shifted the main focus away from solely women's issues. In 1999, the government reduced the department's staff from eleven to three professionals, of whom one was the senior official for gender affairs. This reduction in staff had a negative impact on the results of gender policy affairs. Emancipation or gender policy, up to this point and thereafter, had mostly focused on legislative reforms and ad hoc programs and projects. In 2002, the Department of Welfare, Family and Humanitarian Affairs was again restructured and became the Directorate for Social Development. Gender issues remained one of the main areas of work, albeit more in theory than in practice as the budget was cut and the staff for this directorate was reduced to one person. At the end of 2002, I was appointed as senior official for gender affairs and worked mostly on human rights reporting, regional networking and gender awareness raising within the Netherlands Antilles until 2010.

The policies devised by the government and their implementation have been consistently critically appraised by civil society organizations. The shadow reports submitted by NGOs to the CEDAW Committee indicate lacunae at the structural level and hold governments to account.

In 2001, CAFRA submitted a shadow report to the committee of the CEDAW titled *Emancipation Policy in the Netherlands Antilles: Still an Illusion?* CAFRA was very critical of the government not structurally addressing the problems of inequality and discrimination against women at multiple levels. The CAFRA report highlighted several areas of particular concern such as women and poverty, labor, trafficking in women and prostitution, women's sexual and reproductive health, including HIV/AIDS, teenage pregnancy and violence against women. These concerns were echoed in large part by a second shadow report in 2015 by the women's center SEDA. Their shadow report also highlighted a continuing lack of awareness of the concepts of gender equality and women's rights in general among stakeholders and partners as well as overall noncompliance with the human rights conventions on women's rights.

21 Editors' note: for a critique of this bureau's approach to single and unmarried women in particular, see contribution by Do Rego-Kuster in this section.

In 2012, Aliansa, or the alliance of NGOs working with victims of domestic violence and child abuse, organized a national conference to develop a plan of action for combating gender-based violence and child abuse. This plan was to form the basis of a national action plan against domestic violence and child abuse. One of the first actions taken was to set up a permanent committee of government agencies and NGOs in 2015. However, working together proved to be difficult and the plan failed. In 2018, a new interministerial Working Group against Domestic Violence and Child Abuse and the Permanent Commission, consisting of the four ministries and four representatives of NGOs, were established under the coordination of the Family and Youth Division. The National Plan of Action has set up a cooperation with UNICEF for the development of a protection code for victims of child abuse and domestic violence, to be implemented in 2024.

6 From 2010 to the Present: Gender Policy and Gender Mainstreaming, Are We Backsliding?

As of 2010, there is no national machinery for gender policy in the government structure as required by numerous conventions and international obligations. The business plan for the new government of Curaçao from 2010 mentions gender issues, gender mainstreaming and regular reporting to the CEDAW as part of the Family and Youth Division of the Ministry of Social Development, Labor and Welfare.

However, since 2010, coalition agreements and subsequent government agreements have made no mention of women's or gender rights or gender mainstreaming as areas of priority. In the five-year coalition agreement and government agreement (2017–2021), only domestic violence and child abuse are mentioned as areas of focus. The noted areas of focus for the subsequent 2022–2026 government agreement are families, children and youth, community developments and rights of vulnerable groups.

The fact that the government no longer prioritizes women's and other human rights issues and needs also stems from the systemic lack of understanding and knowledge of what gender is and how to apply a gendered lens to the needs of all genders. It is further difficult to create policies without gender (disaggregated) data and research.

There does, however, seem to be some light at the end of the tunnel. The government of Curaçao has signed and committed itself to the United Nations Multicountry Sustainable Development Framework for the English and Dutch speaking Caribbean 2022 to 2026. This sustainable development framework is an instrument for planning and implementing UN developmental activities at a country level and has gender safety and gender equality as the central sine qua non targets. This commitment includes technical support and guidance for meeting the Sustainable Development Goals for 2030.

7 Conclusion: the Way Forward

"Women wanted to be valued like men."[22] This was the aspiration of women who joined the Wednesday Women in the late 1940s, seeking opportunities to make their own decisions, find gainful employment and lead a life free of violence.

They pressed for legal reform, as a result of which important changes were made through the decades that have given women civil, political, labor and employment rights as well as sexual and reproductive rights. Social and cultural ideas and expectations of women's and men's roles and places in society have evolved and continue to dynamically transform, although not all goals have been achieved.

Women are still overrepresented and underpaid in the service and care sectors; poverty and unemployment remain serious problems for women.

In the private sphere, violence against women, including domestic violence, sexual violence and femicide, remain tenacious problems. Critical NGOs are concerned and remain vocal about the lack of effective policy, policing and judicial and social intervention to stop violence against women.

It is clear that, throughout the three periods outlined in this contribution, gender was not always prioritized and effectively mainstreamed in policy in the Netherlands Antilles and has not been taken up as a major area of policy since the constitutional changes for Curaçao in 2010. The reality is that governmental organizations, NGOs and other stakeholders have to work together and prioritize a shared vision and strategy for gender equality and gender mainstreaming in all sectors of government and society to effectively achieve an equal and just society.

Bibliography

Cuales, Sonia M. "Mujer, reproducción y capital extranjero: El caso de una empresa multinacional en Curazao" [Women, reproduction and foreign capital: The case of

22 Quote by Thelma Römer (Damanan di Djárason), cited in Henriquez, *Muhénan pionero di kòrsou*, 2002, p. x.

a multinational company in Curaçao]. In *Mujer en el sector popular urbano: America Latina y el Caribe*, edited by UN Economic Commission for Latin America and the Caribbean, 165–71. Santiago de Chile: United Nations, 1984.

Eindverslag van de commissie "Uitbanning discriminatie van de vrouw" [Final report of the committee for the elimination of women's discrimination]. Unpublished report. Curaçao: Government of Curaçao and Bureau of Women's Affairs, 1972.

Groenewoud, Margo. "'Nou koest, nou kalm.' De ontwikkeling van de Curaçaose samenleving, 1915–1973: Van koloniaal en kerkelijk gezag naar zelfbestuur en burgerschap" ["Hush now, calm down." The development of Curaçaoan society, 1915–1973: From colonial and church authority to self-government and citizenship]. PhD diss., Leiden University, 2017. https://openaccess.leidenuniv.nl/handle/1887/50108.

Henriquez, Jeanne D. *Kòrsou su muhénan pionero* [Curaçao pioneering women]. Willemstad: Archivo Nashonal di Antia Hulandes, 2002.

Henriquez, Jeanne, and Jacqueline Martis. *Emancipation Policy in the Netherlands: Still an Illusion?* CEDAW Shadow Report of the Netherlands Antilles. Curaçao: Caribbean Association for Feminist Research and Action (CAFRA), 2001.

Pieters Kwiers, Stella. *Dòktor da Costa Gomez: Polítiko i estadista prominente di XX* [Dòktor da Costa Gomez: Politician and prominent statesman of the twentieth century]. Curaçao: printed by the author, 2018.

Ramdas, Anil. *De strijd van de dansers: Biografische vertellingen* [The struggle of the dancers: Biographical tales]. Amsterdam: Muntinga, 1994.

Rodriguez, Adaly. *The Rise of Women's Rights in Curaçao: The Potential of the Women's Convention to the Empowerment and Equal Rights of Women in Curaçao*. Amsterdam: Caribpublishing; Amsterdam: SWP Publishers, 2015.

Römer, René. "Ethnicity and Social Change in Curaçao." In *The White Minority in the Caribbean*, edited by Howard Johnson and Karl Watson, 159–67. Princeton, NJ: Markus Wiener Publishers, 1998.

Rosaria, Alex David. "70 Years Women's Voting Rights/70 aña derechi di voto hende muhé." *Alex David Rosaria* (blog). January 2, 2018. https://alexdavidrosaria.wordpress.com/2018/01/02/70-years-womens-voting-rights-70-ana-derechi-di-voto-hende-muhe.

SEDA. *Lighted Torches*. CEDAW Shadow Report of Curaçao. Curaçao: SEDA, 2015.

CHAPTER 12

The Dutch Caribbean Women's Movement and the Efforts of the Women's Development Center (SEDA) toward Societal Transformation

Stella Pieters Kwiers

Abstract

By tracing the trajectory the women's organization SEDA (Women's Development Center) over five decades, the contribution appraises the influential role they played in setting the agenda for governmental action on women's rights in the Dutch Caribbean as well as in transforming the public perception and understanding of women's issues.

Keywords

women's movement – Curaçao – Women's Development Center (SEDA) – nongovernmental organizations – United Nations – steering committee

The women's movement in the Dutch Caribbean islands began with the establishment of the umbrella association known as the Steering Committee Curaçao. Its objective was to organize women and build their capacity to steer societal transformations that nurtured gender equality. The steering committee conducted a survey in 1975 to identify and prioritize women's problems and issues and later organized a Caribbean Women's Congress in Curaçao, which brought together women and men from the Caribbean and Latin America.

The movement started at the grassroots level by raising consciousness about the benefits of education in achieving active leadership and participation, aiming at liberating women from and making them conscious of socially oppressive mechanisms and barriers. This was based on three strategies, namely: the elimination of all discriminatory laws as per the UN Convention on the Elimination of All Forms of Discrimination Against Women (CEDAW), the promotion of women's participation in electoral politics and the stimulation of education and financial independence for young women.

 | DOI:10.1163/9789004690882_014

Each of the six Dutch Caribbean islands formed a local steering committee, working closely together, sharing information and exchanging knowledge.[1] Preparatory conferences related to the UN International Women's Conferences were held in Curaçao in 1975, 1985 and 1995 respectively, attended by representatives of the steering committees of all six islands. The Women's Development Center (SEDA)[2] was created a few years after the establishment of the Steering Committee Curaçao in 1980 as a women's development bureau, following UN recommendations to set up local groups around the world for the social upliftment of women and families.

The present contribution is derived from my own involvement with the steering committee and SEDA since their inception. I designed and conducted surveys with representatives on all six islands. I was part of the team preparing the reports submitted to the UN International Women's Conferences in Nairobi (1985) and Beijing (1995). I was involved in the preconferences in Curaçao, attended by representatives from the steering committees from all the islands. As SEDA advisor on women in development issues, I also conducted workshops for NGO members in various developmental approaches and techniques and facilitated discussions with affiliated women's groups on the findings of the UN Conferences.

1 The Establishment and Different Levels of Engagement of SEDA

SEDA trained members of the Steering Committee Curaçao and affiliated NGOs in grassroots development approaches, discussion and meeting techniques as well as survey skills. From its outset, it focused on societal problems from a gender perspective. Board members raised funds to purchase their own building, which they called "[a] house for and by women." In the 1990s, both the steering committee and SEDA focused on youth, with a 1990 conference on young women and men in development serving as the starting point for inventorizing and planning priority areas. Young leaders were trained as peer leaders and problem solvers. A program for young people in development was written and carried out in the various neighborhoods of the island. The NGOs felt that

1 Editors' note: the contribution by Allen, De Geus and Brekelmans in this volume elaborates on the activities of the steering committee in Bonaire.

2 SEDA is an acronym for Sentro di Dama (Women's Center), which was re-named in the 1990s as Sentro di Desaroyo di Hende Muhé (Center for the Development of Women's Rights) and later expanded as Sentro pa Desaroyo di Dama i su Famia (Center for the Development of Women and Family).

men should also participate in this struggle for gender equality and that their participation was also necessary in bringing about changes in attitudes around gender relations. SEDA developed different programs, such as working with pregnant teenage girls on their self-esteem and dignity and providing them with sex education. They also worked together with young men and women to improve their economic conditions through income-generating projects.

At the political level, SEDA and the steering committee organized political fora and workshops during election campaigns dealing with questions of women's political emancipation process, gender equality, legal rights for women and women's leadership.[3] These activities emphasized the necessity to engage the public in recognizing women's roles in politics and educated male politicians and the public at large in acquiring insights into women's development. The political fora followed the philosophy of the Damanan di Djárason (Wednesday Women) of the 1940s, the women's wing of the National People's Party, which understood that women had to enter the political arena in order to fight for gender equality, political rights and the liberation of women from subordination and the confinement of their homes.[4]

It is not least due to the efforts of SEDA and the steering committee toward eliminating the gender gap in political representation that the Netherlands Antilles elected its first female prime minister in 1977. Since then, the Dutch Caribbean island governments have continued to have a high percentage of women in politics, including five female prime ministers, several female members of parliament and four female presidents of parliament. Notwithstanding these achievements, the political structures continue to be male dominated and more gender sensitization and politically trained female politicians are needed to represent the public in parliament and in the government, make laws that benefit women and ultimately transform society in a more gender-balanced way.

On the economic level, SEDA developed projects to combat poverty among families on welfare, young sex workers and single mothers dependent on financial assistance. It developed an income-generating project called "Keep your money in your pocket and become economically self-reliant."[5] The objective of the project was to raise awareness and educate women on improving the

3 SEDA, *Nos i nos forsa* [We and our power], 1997. See also "Sentro di Damas stimuleert discussie over vrouwenrecht" [SEDA stimulates discussion about women's rights], *Amigoe di Curaçao*, April 17, 1991, p. 6.

4 Rodriguez, "The Rise of Women's Rights in Curaçao," 2015. Editors' note: for more on the Wednesday Women, see contributions by Groenewoud, Martis and West-Davelaar in this section.

5 SEDA, *Nos i nos forsa*, 1997.

socioeconomic conditions of their families. In the first phase of the project, the women were trained in budgeting, horticulture, health, environmental protection and management. Women were trained to manage their finances more efficiently, eat a balanced meal, cultivate their own vegetables and recycle old wood and furniture as a form of income generation. In the second phase, they were trained to become microentrepreneurs and manage their expenses, become economically independent and less dependent on the welfare system and increase their confidence, self-esteem and dignity.

Due to the poor economic situation and the devastating socioeconomic consequences of the COVID-19 pandemic, SEDA increased its social services to assist people with material and immaterial aid. During the pandemic, the organization was approached by many immigrants who were in disadvantaged positions. The COVID-19 pandemic also impacted the labor market, forcing people into temporary work with a lack of a steady income. Many in search of work lack the necessary knowledge, capacity and experience and do not meet the necessary requirements to be included in the labor market. In most cases, older women seek assistance because they want to join the labor market again. However, this is difficult since there is a greater demand for young workers. SEDA also refers people to the relevant government departments that are equipped to offer help.

2 Violence against Women

Violence against women remains a serious problem and occupies a special place on the women's development agenda. Domestic and relational violence against women is increasing as gender roles change and women become more assertive and independent, leading to men feeling threatened and responding with violence. Studies have indicated that certain social mechanisms such as machismo, a traditional family upbringing, patriarchal gender politics, power inequalities and social media generate and provoke violence against women.[6] A working group called Violence against Women and Crisis Center for Battered Women was installed in 1994 by SEDA.[7] It aimed at reaching the necessary

6 Government of Curaçao, "Nationaal Plan van Curaçao bestrijding van geweld tegen kinderen/jongeren en huiselijk/relationeel geweld" [National plan of Curaçao to combat violence against children/young people and domestic/relational violence], 2018. Editors' note: on perceptions of partner violence, see also the contribution by Kristen Martina in this volume.

7 Jeanne Henriquez, "Crisisopvang centrum een must: SEDA biedt in 1994 hulp aan driehonderd mishandelde vrouwen" [Crisis support center is a must: SEDA offers support to three hundred abused women in 1994], *Amigoe di Curaçao*, December 24, 1994, p. 2.

legislative changes to address the problem effectively as the existing laws did not adequately protect victims of sexual violence. Following consultations with experts, discussions are currently ongoing about establishing a crisis center.[8] The group received representatives from the Netherlands to assist the local police in providing professional assistance to domestic and sexual violence victims. The service was geared toward helping the victims, educating offenders as well as offering specialized training for local police officers on handling situations of violence against women. During the pandemic years 2020 and 2021, the stay-at-home orders, together with anxiety and stress over pay cuts, job insecurity and the inability to make ends meet, led to an increase in domestic violence and sexual abuse against women and children. In addressing these structural problems and their impacts in families, SEDA worked together with the CAFRA (Caribbean Association for Feminist Research and Action), which serves as a resource in the Caribbean region.

3 SEDA at the International Level

SEDA has also remained active on the international level. Members of several NGOs attended the UN International Women's Conferences in Nairobi in 1985 and Beijing in 1995. Prior to the conferences, I conducted a survey on each island to analyze the achievements of the NGOs in the field of women and development as well as the obstacles they encountered. The findings were submitted in a report to the government and to the conference. The survey was a tool to inform the UN about the status of women in the distinctive islands of the Dutch Caribbean. The findings brought forward by all the Dutch islands demonstrated that, although the women's movement had made many advances, it still had a long way to go. It was ascertained that more knowledge, training and economic independence was needed to sustain the women's movement. The report also called for more involvement of men since it is a struggle concerning both men and women, demanding a change of mentality and relationships. In addition, representatives of the women's movement attended the annual UN Commission on the Status of Women (CSW) conference in New York to give an update on the progress made and results achieved in the movement's work.[9]

The 1995 UN Conference on Women in Beijing, attended by a delegation from all six islands of the Dutch Caribbean, resulted in the Beijing Declaration

---

8 Editors' note: for a policy perspective, see the contribution by Martis in this volume.

9 SEDA, *Lighted Torches. NGO Shadow Report of Curaçao*, 2015.

and Platform for Action, highlighting twelve critical areas of concern.[10] After the delegations returned from the Beijing conference, the SEDA president brought all the NGO leaders together and held several meetings to discuss the Beijing Platform for Action with them, a process I was closely involved in facilitating. The areas of concern remain relevant because they touched upon women's issues and problems in all the islands. SEDA organized talks and training sessions on these issues with the aim of broadening the women's movement with new knowledge and methods to address them. SEDA proposed projects around the twelve concerns on topics such as women and poverty, women and the economy and violence against women. A few NGOs currently collaborate on projects dealing with combating poverty. SEDA further conducts a project on entrepreneurship, empowering women to set up small enterprises, and training migrants to become economically self-reliant. Regarding women and health, talks are held on diet and nutritional habits, food security and the promotion of sustainable agriculture. Television programs and neighborhood talks on women and education seek to influence social norms and promote lifelong learning. Most of these projects are long-term efforts with an aim to foster gender equality.

SEDA regularly observes the annual International Women's Day on March 8 by discussing a UN-specific theme, such as the UN Sustainable Development Goals (SDGs). Talks and debates are held on issues relating to gender equality on an international level. These activities help and sustain the involvement of Caribbean women in the transnational women's movement, making women on the islands broaden their horizons, become eager to know what is going on worldwide, communicate their concerns in an international platform and make critical changes to their local approaches. Through an increased awareness of global issues, women leaders also learn to understand and take action on these issues on a small island scale.

At a lecture I gave in December 2022 on women and political participation, a few weeks before the first female prime minister of Curaçao, Maria Liberia-Peters, was awarded an honorary doctorate at the University of Curaçao, I was pleasantly surprised at the widespread acknowledgment of the role of the women's movement on the island in promoting women's participation in politics, occupying high offices and becoming ministers and presidents of parliament. There was a broad recognition on the part of the government and

10 These are: poverty; education; health; ending violence; war and armed conflicts; employment and economic access; decision-making and political participation; human rights; media; the girl child; environment and climate change; and institutional mechanisms in advancing gender equality. See "Beijing Declaration and Platform for Action," 1995.

politicians that women can no longer be left out of decision-making and governing processes.

In 2015, the president of SEDA attended the International Conference on the Convention on the Elimination of all Forms of Discrimination Against Women (CEDAW) in Geneva. In addition to the Dutch Kingdom report, she presented a recommendation to establish a national action plan for gender. In addition to that, her report addressed progress made by the NGOs in women's development and pointed out the differences between the Netherlands (Europe) and the Dutch Caribbean islands, with their specific cultures and developmental problems.

Since 2000, SEDA has changed from a locally rooted women's organization to a globally connected women's development agency. It is now part of the Netwerk VN-Vrouwenverdrag (Women's Network of the Netherlands). It has broadened its scope and methods of action, now also dealing with the situation of migrants to Curaçao. Due to decades of experience, expertise and knowledge about the Curaçaoan culture, SEDA is now subsidized by the government and authorized to carry out activities such as assistance to women and families, poverty alleviation, training and education, restorative practices, responsible parenthood, commemorating international remembrance days around women, information programs and cultural actions. SEDA also changed because the fruits of women's development from 1975 to 2000 were visible and demanded the integration of new methodologies. However, SEDA is not a government agency and thus remains autonomous.

4 Methods of SEDA: Restorative Practices and World Café

SEDA has broadened its scope of operation by introducing several new methods, such as the restorative practices model, in response to a wide range of situations that may arise in families, schools and the community. This model departs from the idea that decisions are best made and conflicts are best resolved by those most directly involved in them. It has been successfully applied in schools to resolve conflicts between pupils and to increase social cohesion. It creates a healthy environment that helps young people grow, make positive life changes and build a culture of community in schools.

The restorative practices model is derived from developments in the criminal justice field, where, instead of simply punishing offenders, restorative justice holds offenders accountable for their crimes by involving them in face-to-face encounters with the people they have harmed. Restoration can happen at all societal levels. Life in many families can be violent and unhealthy and needs to be restored on many levels. Due to violence in the family, some children grow up with traumas. There is a general belief that violence originates in our societies because of a culture of machismo and also as consequences of the Caribbean matrifocal family structure, where males are privileged within the family by their mothers.[11] The restorative model also seeks to revive and revitalize existing legacies and traditions, such as the community centers that played a prominent social role in the 1960s as institutions of information, education, family guidance and community development.[12]

SEDA also introduced in its work a method called the World Café, which focuses on "shaping our future through conversations that matter."[13] The World Café is a conversation-led technique developed in 1995 in Mill Valley, California. It is a simple tool for bringing people together around issues that matter to them using a set of conversational principles. The World Café process has been used in various contexts among many different age groups and for many purposes. It emphasizes the powerful role that conversations play in shaping our future. Several World Café sessions have taken place through SEDA, with a special one organized in cooperation with the Red Cross and PAN (Plataforma Agrario Nashonal [National Agrarian Platform]) on food security in Curaçao in 2009.

5 Conclusion

The women's movement, consisting of the steering committee, SEDA and affiliated women's organizations, has undeniably transformed Dutch Caribbean societies over the last six decades. Women have been involved in the emancipation process and have improved their social status and position. The movement has challenged traditions and enhanced the public visibility and presence of women. Women have improved their political and socioeconomic statuses by entering into parliamentary politics and through massive participation in the labor force and educational sector. They have repeatedly addressed male-dominated political structures and become more assertive and conscious of their strengths, capabilities, responsibilities and their legal and political rights. Since its inception in 1980, SEDA's participatory and transformative approach

11 Smith, *The Matrifocal Family*, 2014.

12 Pieters Kwiers, "Sentro di bario. Un pila pa desaroyo i re-konstrukshon di nos famianan" [The community center. A pillar for the development and reconstruction of our families], 2018.

13 Brown and Isaacs, *The World Café*, 2005.

has honed its ability to engage at the grassroots level and follow the pulse of the shifting environment with regard to gender relations, which has enabled it to stand firm until the present day.

Bibliography

"Beijing Declaration and Platform for Action." United Nations, September 15, 1995. https://www.un.org/womenwatch/daw/beijing/pdf/BDPfA%20E.pdf.

Brown, Juanita, and David Isaacs. *The World Café: Shaping Our Futures through Conversations That Matter*. San Francisco: Berrett-Koehler Publishers, 2005.

Government of Curaçao. "Nationaal plan van Curaçao bestrijding van geweld tegen kinderen/jongeren en huiselijk/relationeel geweld" [National plan of Curaçao to combat violence against children/young people and domestic/relational violence]. Curaçao: Ministerie van Sociale Ontwikkeling, Arbeid en Welzijn (SOAW), 2018. https://gobiernu.cw/wp-content/uploads/2019/06/nationaal_plan_tegen_geweld.pdf.

Henriquez, Jeanne. "Crisisopvang centrum een must: SEDA biedt in 1994 hulp aan driehonderd mishandelde vrouwen" [Crisis support center is a must: SEDA offers support to three hundred abused women in 1994], *Amigoe di Curaçao*, December 24, 1994, p. 2.

Pieters Kwiers, Stella. "Sentro di bario. Un pila pa desaroyo i re-konstrukshon di nos famianan" [The community center. A pillar for the development and reconstruction of our families]. Public talk on International Women's Day at Women's Development Center (SEDA), Curaçao, March 8, 2018.

Rodriguez, Adaly. "The Rise of Women's Rights in Curaçao: The Potential of the Women's Convention to the Empowerment and Equal Rights of Women in Curaçao." PhD diss., Utrecht University, 2015.

SEDA. *Lighted Torches: NGO Shadow Report of Curaçao*. Willemstad: Women's Development Center Curaçao, 2016.

SEDA. *Nos i nos forsa* [We and our power]. Willemstad: Women's Development Center Curaçao, 1997.

"Sentro di Damas stimuleert discussie over vrouwenrecht" [SEDA stimulates discussion about women's rights], *Amigoe di Curaçao*, April 17, 1991, p. 6.

Smith, Raymond T. *The Matrifocal Family*. New York: Routledge, 2014. https://doi.org/10.4324/9781315021911.

CHAPTER 13

In Search of Our Memory: Gender in the Netherlands Antilles

Sonia M. Cuales

Abstract

The history of class, race and gender relations remains largely underresearched for the islands of the former Netherlands Antilles. While there are archival sources for some of this history, much of it remains submerged in our memories due to our self-imposed silences on these social issues. In this contribution, I extract some of this memory from fragments of research already carried out, available statistical evidence and the struggles of the feminist movement regarding discriminatory legislations against women to provide a glimpse of this postcolonial variation that also constitutes part of the Caribbean.

Keywords

Netherlands Antilles – feminist movement – race and gender – memory – silence

1 Introduction

The Netherlands Antilles have a distinct character within the region. They are not always viewed as part of the Caribbean, possibly because of their long-standing links with Holland. The islands and peoples are considered Dutch in appearance, behavior and thinking, although we see ourselves as Antillean and Caribbean. If we are more Dutch than we acknowledge, it is not surprising: over three hundred years of such close association with Holland would make anyone a captive. But a captive plant grown from another seed, from another culture, escapes at times, and in these moments of escape its roots unfold. Our gender relations have grown and developed on Caribbean soil, even though the history of our settlement and governance has been affected by many other cultures. In this paper, I retrieve aspects of the

 | DOI:10.1163/9789004690882_015

society that are evolving as Antillean. The paper paints a picture of the woman of the Netherlands Antilles and attempts to explore the gender[1] relations of the society. The term "Antillean women" refers to the women of the Netherlands Antilles. This area comprises five islands scattered across the Caribbean Sea: Bonaire, Curaçao, Saba, St. Eustatius and St. Maarten. There are some references to Aruba and Suriname because of the historic ties and the resulting loyalty and closeness that exist among the present and former Dutch Colonies. [...]

2 Our Memory as Our History

During the past two decades, very little has been done to retrieve Antillean women's history and record it in books or official publications to make it widely accessible. Nor has the development and history of the women's movement in the Netherlands Antilles been systematically and analytically documented. Various explanations have been put forward to account for the scarcity of publications on the history of the Antillean woman, whether by male or female Antilleans. Joceline Clemencia, in her introduction to a collection of essays titled *Mundu yama sinta mira* (The name of the world is sit and see),[2] suggests that the people of Curaçao, as in other colonized countries, have been shaped by a culture of silence that manifests itself in a pervasive fear. She argues that when the people of Curaçao do express themselves, they do so in camouflaged ways.[3]

---

1 Author's note: my use of gender is derived from the ideas developed by a group of feminist academics based at the Institute of Development Studies of the University of Sussex in England in 1978. The leader of the Sussex group, Ann Whitehead, offered a definition of the concept in an IDS seminar, in which she based her terminology on the collective debates of her colleagues. The approach studies men and women and, more specifically, the relations between them. Likewise, sex is considered to be a biological term, while the category of gender is thought to be more appropriate for the social sciences since it refers to the structures that evolve in the course of the history of social relations and interactions. The concept was applied, refined and debated in the seminar "Social Production in the Caribbean," which took place in Rio Piedras, Puerto Rico, in 1980, with widespread participation from women in the subregion. I was one of the participants at this seminar.

2 Clemencia, "Introduction," 1992.

3 Clemencia, *Het grote camouflagespel van de OPI: Een thematische benadering van de poëzie van Elis Juliana* [The great camouflaging game of the OPI: A thematic approach to the poetry of Elis Juliana], 1989, p. 7.

It has also been suggested that the Netherlands Antilles possess a very limited capacity to undertake research and publication. There is no indigenous academic tradition and most of those who have had academic training live abroad. The small size of the islands has implications for professionals: either they are said to be overburdened, or, since they are in great demand, they may select more lucrative jobs. Research and publication do not fall into the category of lucrative employment.

There is no major body of work on the subjects of either history or gender relations. The fact is that the few reliable sources of information that do exist are often inaccessible. In addition, the existing publications have generally been written by foreigners. It is within this context that my article seeks to analyze the Antillean women from the vantage point of historical and contemporary gender relations. The dearth of documented sources also propels me toward oral history and memory for our history.

Before the United Nations women's decades, a Curaçaoan historian, Nolda Römer-Kenepa, did a study on the female straw hat makers at the beginning of the twentieth century.[4] These women produced the famous Panama hats, and it appears that they formed the first workers' organization, which can be considered a forerunner to a trade union. With the help of small studies such as this, we begin to explore some aspects of women's lives of the period. Another study on the free blacks and mulattoes confirms that black women were engaged in low-income, working-class jobs as washerwomen, seamstresses, weavers and domestic workers as early as the eighteenth century.[5]

Two more recent and important works are worthy of mention. One is the *opus magnum* by Emy Maduro, "Nos a bai Ulanda" [We went to Holland], in which she records meticulously, from primary sources, the special case of the slave Virginie, who went to Holland.[6] The other is the previously mentioned

4 Nolda Römer-Kenepa, "Vrouwenleven op Curaçao: Laat achttiende eeuw en vroeg negentiende eeuw" [Women's lives in Curaçao: Late eighteenth and early nineteenth centuries], 1980; see also Veen, *Hoedenvlechten als kostwinning: Een onderzoek naar de invloed van de hoedenvlechterij op de sociaal-economische positie van vrouwen op Curaçao en Bonaire in de eerste helft van de twintigste eeuw* [Hat-braiding as breadwinning: A study of the influence of hat-braiding on the socioeconomic position of women in Curaçao and Bonaire in the first half of the twentieth century], 1984. Editors' note: see also contribution by Römer-Kenepa in this section.

5 Klooster, "Curaçao's Free Blacks and Mulattoes in the Eighteenth Century," 1994, p. 285. Editor's note: see also Table 2 of original publication; Central Bureau of Statistics Curaçao, 1993.

6 Maduro, "Nos a bai Ulanda" [We went to Holland], 1986.

Mundu yama sinta mira. Here, the authors break the silence of the Antilleans, both male and female, by writing their own stories from a feminist perspective.[7]

Interestingly, feminists in Curaçao have relied on the oral tradition to videotape interviews with women. Gladys do Rego-Kuster of the Union of Antillean Women (UMA) produced a video about rape, titled *Mi sa kon bo ta sinti bo* [I know how you are feeling], that has been used extensively for seminars and workshops on sexuality.[8] In the video *Hidden Voices*, Rose Mary Allen and Jeanne Henriquez recorded interviews with four women between the ages of sixty and eighty on their daily lives, including their creative activities.[9] Jeanne Henriquez, with a team of researchers, collected artifacts, photographs and other material on the working lives of women to produce a mobile exhibition.[10] It is a continually expanding exhibition as it improves from comments and contributions from spectators as it travels around.

3 The Construction of Gender Relations in the Netherlands Antilles

Gender relations among the different classes and racial groupings are complex in their historical construction in the Netherlands Antilles as they are elsewhere in the region. The racial question, always a very sensitive aspect of Caribbean life, has been avoided throughout our history and is still being avoided in the present day. Racial factors have influenced life and reproduction in these islands to such an extent that a few relevant details must be indicated.[11]

The position of the different groups on the racial continuum of the Netherlands Antilles depends on the extent of intermarriage that had taken place with people of Latin blood, with the more light-skinned mixtures with Latin being placed in a higher social category of the continuum. Mixtures of Latin and black are referred to as mulatto or mestizo.

The particular way in which slavery was experienced in the Antilles has also played its part in constructing gender relations in the Netherlands Antilles.

7 Ansano et al., *Mundu yama sinta mira: Womanhood in Curaçao* [The name of the world is sit and see: Womanhood in Curaçao], 1992.

8 Corry van Heijningen, *Mi sa kon bo ta sinti bo* [I know how you are feeling] (Union di Muhé Antiano), 1982.

9 Allen and Henriquez, *Bosnan skondi* [Hidden voices], 1992.

10 Editors' note: see contribution by Henriquez in this volume.

11 Editors' note: a diagram in the original publication indicates a correlation between racial categorizations such as black, various "shades" of Latino and white on the one hand, and religious affiliations on the other. See Central Bureau of Statistics Curaçao, "Census 1992, Third Population and Housing Census Netherlands-Antilles," 1993; Cuales, 1998, p. 90.

The Netherlands Antilles were not part of the plantation mode of production, although they were part of Caribbean plantation society. On these islands there were no plantations. Curaçao was a slave market for the Western hemisphere. Income-generating activities took place in the city, and, from time to time, the better-off retired to houses in the countryside, usually built on the top of a hill from which the surrounding space could be controlled. On their country estates, where they reared small stock such as pigs and goats, planted beans, sorghum and fruits, the more affluent ones entertained friends from the city. They employed mainly black slaves to work on the agricultural property and in the family mansions.

The history of trade in the Netherlands Antilles has determined both the demographic development and the legal structures of the islands. This historical reality has left its mark on social relations and equally on gender relations. Before the advent of the petroleum industry, the economy of the Antilles was based on trade and business transactions. In Curaçao during the seventeenth and eighteenth centuries, an interesting phenomenon occurred. Toward the end of the seventeenth century, this society was rapidly developing as a center for commercial exchanges between the coastal area of what is now Venezuela and the rest of the region. This development was based primarily on the island's slave market: the commodity that was being bought and sold was labor—negroes[12] from the west coast of Africa and from Angola. Merchandise that was not sold remained in Curaçao where they were used for the trading company's work or in other businesses on the island. The slaves were able to go out to work as artisans or sailors. With the persistence of the slave trade, negroes came to account for the majority of the island's population, although whites continued to be the dominant social group.

A particular social and racial mix was forged as well as a distinct set of gender relations. Black people inspired either fear or indifference in the white minority. Even so, in Curaçao, there were many more manumissions (letters granting freedom), and, in this way, the metissage grew more rapidly than in the other countries in the region. Therefore, a large group of non-whites was formed whose artisan skills and commercial astuteness enabled them to compete with the less prosperous white business people. Their assertiveness alarmed the whites. White men had unions with mulatto women, but their relationships always reflected a combination of fear and indifference.

12 Editors' note: terms such as "slave," "negro" and "mulatto" that are now pejoratively connoted have not been altered to suit current usage as the author is deceased.

4 Sexuality

Primarily to preserve distance from other groups and classes, there were intra-familial sexual relations, sometimes incestuous, among the Catholic middle-class segment of the population. The men, who had children with two or more sisters, cousins, neighbors and perhaps also with the servants, continued to be spoiled, adored and granted privileges by all the women in the family.[13] Among members of the middle class, dances were organized in private homes or in Catholic clubs so that young men and women could meet regularly to converse and court. In the wealthy commercial Jewish community and the Protestant community, where top public officials were to be found—both groups considered white—undoubtedly gender relations were informed largely by religious tradition.

5 Migration, Slavery and Gender Relations: the Case of Virginie

The first waves of migration carried mostly young men to be educated in Holland. However, historical records offer ample proof that, ever since slavery, and even more so during the period of manumission, both slaves and freed slaves went to Europe, accompanying the families for whom they worked as domestic servants.

Historian and sociologist Emy Maduro highlights the case of Virginie, a slave born in Curaçao who waged an intense struggle for her freedom. Virginie argued that, once she had stepped on Dutch soil while traveling as a servant with her mistress, she was entitled to her freedom. Virginie took her campaign to the highest levels and included her children, who had accompanied her, in the same petition. Her mistress was the daughter of Baron [Lord] van Raders, the ex-governor of Suriname. The case was complicated by factors such as the abolition of the slave trade, bilateral treaties on the trade and personal and political interests. The treaty between Holland and England placed certain restrictions on Antilleans who had slaves and who wanted to transport them to another country. At one stage, it became illegal to transport slaves from one colony to another. Likewise, slaves could only remain in the country to which the owner had taken them for a limited period of time.

13 Author's note: in the eyes of the public, that is, as far as the town gossip was concerned, many of these families lived in total harmony, and the care and mutual affection shown endured into the final stage of sharing the afflictions and difficulties of old age.

When it was time for Virginie to be returned from Europe back to Curaçao, she was sent to Suriname because no ships were scheduled to leave for Curaçao. In Suriname, Virginie presented her petition to the highest authorities. Baron van Raders launched a tenacious administrative and legal battle to ensure that Virginie was not granted her freedom. He also claimed that Virginie was too lazy and insolent to deserve her freedom.[14]

The interesting and perhaps unique case of Virginie shows the fighting spirit of this woman even under such inhuman circumstances and her determination to realize her aspirations for her freedom and that of her children.

6 The Social Relations of Work

The slave or ex-slave/servant who provided personal services to the mistress of the house, to the daughter or to any other member of the family held a key position in the household. This woman may well have been a blood relative of that family. This black *aya*, or *yaya* in Papiamentu, was totally responsible for raising the children.[15] In a country where there were no real plantations and the slaves lived and worked in the home of the owner, as *yaya*, cook, housekeeper, coachman or gardener, the interaction between blacks and whites, including boys and girls, men and women, was very close. The *yaya* had an important role to play in gender socialization. Accepted by everyone in the society, these social relations delineated through work had an impact on the overall construction of gender in Antillean society as a whole.

In analyzing the complexity of such relations, one must take into consideration the differences within the privileged class, comprising the Sephardic Jewish community, the white Protestants, white Catholics and, finally, the mestizos. In the course of the socioeconomic history of the different groups within the islands, social structures and the power bases have also undergone change and have become more intricate.

There are many mestizo descendants of Jews and negroes, as well as some descendants of negroes and Latinos from the South American coast or Europe. In some cases, class cuts across racial intermarriage. It is also important to consider the erosion of the old power bases and the emergence of a racial and

14 Maduro, "Nos a bai Ulanda," 1986.

15 Römer, *La sociedad Curazoleña (una interpretación sociológica)* [Curaçaoan society (a sociological interpretation)], 1987.

class grouping that, before their access to education, had few opportunities for social mobility. The expanded access to higher education in the 1950s, followed by greater political and administrative participation, allowed the development of new power bases.

Social relations are characterized by an exploitative paternalism, which may be either subtle or open. Perhaps the most overt paternalism is found among a social group that operates small private businesses, the Ashkenazi Jews. This group did not seek to conceal the ways in which they exploited black people, the largest yet most disadvantaged group in the country in the twentieth century. They completely misunderstood the cultural values of poor, black people, treating them with contempt and disrespect. Black and mulatto women suffered the most terrible treatment. Although there have been changes in modern society, many women continue to suffer as a sex, although this must be differentiated by race and class.

7 The Antillean Family

Due to the intrinsic relationship between the family, sexuality and gender relations in the society, it is crucial that we understand the nature of the family in Antillean society. Although the concept of the family is defined in different ways in different societies and in different historical periods, it always refers to a social space in which both the private and public spheres intersect. Thus, it fulfills productive and reproductive functions, economic, political, social, cultural and leisure functions. The family exists within a context of global and national changes to which it responds. While taking into account class differences, it has to be acknowledged that, in general, the nuclear family model has never been either popular or predominant in any social class. If it existed de jure, it was certainly never there de facto.

I have mentioned some instances of gender relations that are peculiar to the middle and upper classes and differ according to racial grouping. In terms of the popular classes, Hoetink describes man as a migratory being who maintains sexual relations with a number of women, leaving a son here and another there and continuing calmly on his way.[16] Numerous single mothers are the results of these relationships, a phenomenon that, today, astonishes and disturbs many. Even though, in the contemporary period, the woman may have

16 Hoetink, *Het patroon van de oude Curaçaose samenleving: Een sociologische studie* [The pattern of the old Curaçao society: A sociological study], 1958.

some social space for her own escapades, the man has much more for his, and his have been accepted to a far greater degree. What emerges is a distribution of family typologies that includes a legitimate category defined by the statistical records as female-headed households. In 1991, of the total 2,889 households recorded for the island of Bonaire, twenty-seven percent were described as female-headed households. In Curaçao, of the 41,279 households, thirty-six percent were female headed and, in St. Maarten, of 12,164 households, thirty-one percent were female headed.[17]

In general, single mothers are heads of households. However, Antillean households are headed by a woman not simply because the man has abandoned the family. The woman may opt to raise a family on her own, or the female-headed home is often the result of migration. Some studies suggest that women choose this situation because of their experiences with irresponsible partners. In many cases as well, the female-headed household will contain single adult males who may have women and children in other homes while, generally, continuing to live in their mother's house. Some research, for example the work of Gladys do Rego-Kuster,[18] predicts a significant increase in the number of female-headed households in the future. It is not surprising to find that female-headed households are a recurring phenomenon. It must also be understood that the relations of gender with regard to female-headed households may not be pertinent to her emotional or sexual life but to the material conditions of life. The laws and social services have not been designed to consider the single mother or female household head as the norm but rather as the exception.

8 Overcoming the Subordination of Women

A significant factor maintaining women's subordination in Antillean society was women's legal status. For example, women's legal status as a minor meant that women could not sign contracts, transfer goods or have access to loans without the consent of their partners. Following the end of the turbulent 1960s in the Netherlands Antilles, by the 1970s, the government began to show concern about women's subordination. A number of legal and social mechanisms

17 Compiled from data in the unpublished *National Report of Aruba 1994*, 1995.

18 Do Rego-Kuster, "Het Afro-Caribisch gezinsweb en de emancipatie van de vrouw" [Afro-Caribbean family networks and the emancipation of women], 1990. Editors' note: see the English translation of Do Rego-Kuster's text in this section.

were reviewed, including inequalities in the salaries of married men and women.

Social services were always open to political manipulation. One example in Curaçao is the peculiar approach to administering low-income housing. Before a housing foundation was set up,[19] single mothers were not eligible for a house unless they had a guarantor who signed on their behalf. The requirements for this signatory implied that he had to be a man possessing adequate economic resources. A determined struggle by twenty-four mothers culminated in the removal of this requirement. They also succeeded in partly depoliticizing the procedures for distributing low-income housing projects. In 1978, the process of depoliticizing housing policies was accelerated.

9 Discriminatory Practices toward Married and Unmarried Women

A discriminatory law, which was abolished in 1983, concerned female public employees. It dealt with their appointment and their civil status. Clause 6.3 of this law stipulated that a married woman could not be given a permanent civil service appointment. Her temporary appointment to the civil service was possible only in cases where there were no men or unmarried women to fill the post. Under the same law as well, a woman had to leave the civil service when she got married or began to live with a male companion. Due to laws such as this, women had far more limited career opportunities in the public service than had men.

Differences between married and unmarried female public servants were legislated such that married women received twenty-five percent less salary than either her male or unmarried counterpart. This inequality created tensions among various sectors in society and led to a constant paralysis of the education service due to massive strikes dating back to the early 1980s and prolonged unrest in the trade unions. The Union of Educational Workers (SITEK, Sindikato di Trahadó den Edukashon na Kòrsou) waged a concerted campaign from the start of 1990. The process lasted until 1994, when the supreme court passed a law that brought about equal pay for all female public servants, whether married or unmarried. These changes were significant since they signaled an environment willing to bend and new attitudes toward gender relations in the country.

Meanwhile, the government, in an attempt to avoid a loss of revenue, formulated a new taxation scheme, which, both in principle and in practice,

19 In Papiamentu: Fundashon Kas Popular (FKP), 1978.

reintroduced gender discrimination as regards unmarried women. A large percentage of the female population are single mothers with children and heads of households who have to pay higher taxes than married women. This has yet to be dealt with by the feminist movement. Although it is clear that significant legal advances have been made in some cases with major struggles, in others there were necessary changes due to global developments in the status of women. Nonetheless, while, as in other countries, passing legislation is much easier to achieve than previously, putting such legislation into operation is another matter. Inevitably, there is usually a long delay between one stage and the next.

The kind of legislation and regulations existing as illustrated above, until recently, have led to the unfortunate situation of a very limited female representation in leadership posts and in public service managerial positions at the national level. In the middle to high-level posts in public administration, there are 19 women to 122 men as of April 1995 (Kompas, 1995). At the same time, however, in terms of political participation, the Netherlands Antilles do not measure up badly against other countries in the region. The first time that two women won seats in the Netherlands Antilles parliament was in 1949, shortly after the introduction of universal suffrage. The country has boasted a woman as prime minister for almost ten years and, between 1985 and 1995, has had four female parliamentarians, six female members of the Island Council, three female ministers and six female deputies. The prime minister came out of the ranks of the women's movement, as did some of the others. It is also interesting to note that the women who occupy positions of political power have generally been young.[20] Although there is still a long way to go, women are now occupying posts in areas where previously they were not represented at all.

Similarly, data for Aruba shows that, out of a total of twenty-one seats in the Aruban parliament, over the period 1986 to 1993, women held one or two seats, and this increased to three seats in the year 1993–1994.[21]

10 The Women's Movement

As in most Caribbean countries, the women's movement, which provided the initial impetus toward overcoming the structural forms of subordination of women, was preceded by another type of women's organization: clubs and

20 Editors' note: the gender distribution of political/administrative leadership for 1995 is shown in Table 3 in the original publication.

21 *National Report of Aruba, 1994*, 1995.

women's meetings. The challenges, campaigns and achievements of the women's movement in the 1970s, 1980s and in the current period cannot be analyzed without taking into account the existence of a tradition of women's meetings. This tradition has its own history.

Women pooled resources to organize activities with specific objectives, and, in this way, the women's organizations were formed. These organizations could be found at various social levels, and they provided women with an opportunity to develop their spiritual life, artistic creativity, cultural expression, cooperation and solidarity with the community. The organizations offered a refuge where women found understanding, affection and support. Some of them also reinforced paternalism. In most cases, the spiritual base of these groups was the Catholic Church.

Some of the women's organizations of the 1950s and 1960s survived and coexisted in the 1970s and 1980s with the new groupings, including the feminist organizations that were then emerging. During this period, the number of organizations increased greatly. On the island of Curaçao, there were some seventy groups. In 1974, coordinating committees were set up in all the islands to coordinate activities for the International Women's Year in 1975. Three have survived to the present time. At the island level, the coordinating committees are members of the Island Advisory Council for Women's Affairs.

In the same year, the Union of Antillean Women (UMA, Union Muhénan Antiano) was formed, the first organization with a clearly feminist vision and perspective. UMA fought against discrimination and subordination of women and worked dynamically to bring about structural changes in Antillean society. In addition to the tradition of organizing and the spirit of accomplishing goals, various traditional groups also continued some of the archaic rules. One of these stipulates that the membership should consist only of married women, obviously still influenced by the church. In most cases, single women, excluded from participating, are the ones who suffer more discrimination in society. Despite this rule, most women's organizations draw their membership from the working class. Even if these women are married, invariably their mothers were not.

The first UN Decade for Women (1976–1985) enabled women's groups to develop a common objective. Notwithstanding the diversity of their interests, the more these groups combined their efforts, the more they realized that there was a common struggle against the insubordination of women and that there was a single objective: to forge gender equality. Since that time, unfortunately, the social, economic and class contradictions among women have continued to divide various groups.

In 1980, the Women's Development Center (SEDA) was established. Its primary purpose is that of human resource development and training. SEDA seeks to serve men and women at the individual level or in their capacity as members of organizations. Its priority is to prepare women for self-reliance and self-defense. To this end, symposia, workshops and study and training seminars are organized at the organization's headquarters and in community centers. Recently, the organization has been actively involved in programs, including legal action, concerning the incidence of violence against women and on the issue of sexual harassment. SEDA's work has been positively received in the communities and recognized in governmental and nongovernmental quarters.

In July 1987, INFESE (Informashon, Formashon i Edukashon di Seksualidat i Embaraso [Sexual and Reproductive Health Education and Information]) began as a research and education project on sexuality. In 1994, INFESE began offering programs and services to young people and fathers-to-be on matters of sexuality, pregnancy and birth. The significance of this process of research and action lies in its feminist conceptualization of sexuality, reproductive health and reproductive rights. The process has not been easy and would not have been institutionalized without vigorous feminist struggles. The impact of INFESE has been growing on many levels and in many directions.

11 Conclusion

The women's movement in the Antillean islands and its feminist components have influenced the direction and the pace of the advance made by Antillean women. The residual effects of the history of slavery and continued migration in and out of the region is, however, still evident in the complexity of social and gender relations that exist today. A careful and systematic analysis needs to be carried out on the Netherlands Antilles as much of this history remains hidden in our archives and our memory.

The most important achievements during the last two decades have been legal advances. Some of these have taken a long time and, in some cases, have yet to come into effect. The greatest victory in the future would be genuine respect for women as individuals and as a social group, on all levels, irrespective of social class or racial grouping. Perhaps, at that point, one can start to build a society free of oppressive disequilibria.

Acknowledgments

The unabridged version of this text was originally published as Cuales, Sonia Magdalena. "In Search of Our Memory: Gender in the Netherlands Antilles." *Feminist Review* 59, no. 1 (1998): 86–100. https://doi.org/10.1080/014177898339479.

Reproduction courtesy of SAGE Publications. The text has been lightly edited for linguistic clarity.

Bibliography

Allsop, Richard. *A Dictionary of Caribbean English Usage*. New York: Oxford University Press, 1996.

Ansano, Richenel, Joceline Clemencia, Jeanette Cook, and Eithel Martis, eds. *Mundu yama sinta mira: Womanhood in Curaçao* [The name of the world is sit and see: Womanhood in Curaçao]. Curaçao: Fundashon Publikashon, 1992.

Bosnan Skondí [Hidden voices]. Rose Mary Allen and Jeanne Henriquez. Video. Institute of Archaeology and Anthropology of the Netherlands Antilles (AAINA) and Centre for the Development of Women (SEDA), Curaçao, July 1992.

Central Bureau of Statistics Curaçao. "Census 1992, Third Population and Housing Census Netherlands-Antilles." Curaçao: CBS, 1993.

Clemencia, Joceline. *Het grote camouflagespel van de OPI: Een thematische benadering van de poëzie van Elis Juliana* [The great camouflaging game of the OPI: A thematic approach to the poetry of Elis Juliana]. Antillean Working Papers 14. Leiden: KITLV; Leiden: Royal Netherlands Institute for Southeast Asian and Caribbean Studies, 1989.

Clemencia, Joceline. "Introduction." In *Mundu yama sinta mira: Womanhood in Curaçao*, edited by Richenel Ansano, Joceline Clemencia, Jeanette Cook, and Eithel Martis, IX–XII. Curaçao: Fundashon Publikashon, 1992.

Cuales, Sonia Magdalena. "In Search of Our Memory: Gender in the Netherlands Antilles." *Feminist Review* 59, no. 1 (1998): 86–100.

Do Rego-Kuster, Gladys. "Het Afro-Caribisch gezinsweb en de emancipatie van de vrouw" [Afro-Caribbean family networks and the emancipation of women]. *De Gids* 153, no. 7–8 (July–August 1990): 542–47.

Heijningen, Corry van. *Mi sa kon bo ta sinti bo* [I know how you are feeling]. Video. Union di Muhé Antiano, Curaçao, 1982.

Hoetink, Harry. *Het patroon van de oude Curaçaose samenleving: Een sociologische studie* [The pattern of the old Curaçaoan society: A sociological study]. Assen: Van Gorcum, 1958.

Klooster, Wim. "Curaçao's Free Blacks and Mulattoes in the Eighteenth Century." *New West Indian Guide* 68, no. 3–4 (1994): 283–300.

Maduro, Emy. "Nos a bai Ulanda" [We went to Holland]. In *In het land van de overheerser, deel II: Antillianen en Surinamers in Nederland 1634/1667–1954*, edited by Gert Oostindie and Emy Maduro, 135–225. Verhandelingen van het Koninklijk Instituut voor Taal-, Land- en Volkenkunde. Leiden: Brill, 1986.

National Report of Aruba 1994. In preparation for the Fourth World Conference on Women, to be held in Beijing. Unpublished report, 1995.

Römer, René A. *La sociedad Curazoleña (una interpretacion sociológica)* [Curaçaoan society: A sociological interpretation]. Caracas: Ministerio de Relaciones Exteriores de Venezuela, 1987.

Römer-Kenepa, Nolda. "Vrouwenleven op Curaçao: Laat achttiende eeuw en vroeg negentiende eeuw" [Women's lives in Curaçao: Late eighteenth and early nineteenth centuries]. Master's thesis, VU Amsterdam, 1980.

Veen, Annemiek van der. *Hoedenvlechten als kostwinning: Een onderzoek naar de invloed van de hoedenvlechterij op de sociaal-economische positie van vrouwen op Curaçao en Bonaire in de eerste helft van de twintigste eeuw* [Hat-braiding as breadwinning: A study of the influence of hat-braiding on the socioeconomic position of women in Curaçao and Bonaire in the first half of the twentieth century]. Leiden, 1984.

SECTION 2

Gender, Race, Class and Coloniality

CHAPTER 14

Former Slave Owner's House [Lanthùis]

Crisèn Schorea

How innocent you look Cradle of those who consciously contributed to the contamination of courageous souls	Esta parse inosente Kontribushon konsiente na kontaminashon di almanan balente
Mysterious empire Ingenious design Doors closed Windows open	Misterioso imperio Ingenioso diseño Porta será Bentana habrí
How innocent you look guarded by demented walls decayed (de)fence Faked security	Esta parse inosente Muraya demente Tranké dekaí Seguridat fingí

Acknowledgments

This poem was first published in Papiamentu as Schorea, Crisèn. "Lanthùis" [Former Slave Owner's House]. In *Sinti mi Sintí* [To feel my feelings and or thoughts], 18. Curaçao: printed by the author, 2016. Translation by the author.

 | DOI:10.1163/9789004690882_016

CHAPTER 15

Indigenous Identity, Gender and Colonialism in Bonaire

Oliver Antczak

Abstract

Bonaire's Indigenous presence stretches back millennia and continues being felt into the current day. A persistent narrative of "extinction" resulting from colonial history and cemented in history books maintains that the Indigenous peoples of Bonaire were entirely removed from the island five centuries ago. Despite this, Indigenous identity continues being felt and expressed in Bonaire. This contribution discusses data from interviews conducted in Bonaire, highlighting instances where gender, Indigenous identity, race and coloniality intersect. The concept of the *Sentimento Indjan* is introduced as a binding feeling that has maintained Indigenous identity through more than five hundred years of colonialism. Physical features, the history of Nort di Saliña and family structures are other areas where Indigeneity plays a key role in Bonairean society.

Keywords

Indigenous identity – heritage – Bonaire – *Sentimento Indjan* – race and gender

1 Introduction

In this contribution, I discuss several instances where contemporary Indigenous identity and gender intersect in the colonial context of Bonaire. To position myself, I am a Venezuelan and Polish anthropologist who is not specialized in gender studies, raised in Venezuela and educated in universities in the Netherlands and the UK. I am a cisgender white male and these identities and the privileges and biases they carry undeniably color my interpretations and discussion in this study. I invite readers to engage critically with my writing here, countering and developing the ideas discussed, to hopefully reach

 | DOI:10.1163/9789004690882_017

richer and more complete understandings of the complexities of identity formation and maintenance in this region of the world.

This discussion is shaped around data collected during fieldwork seasons between 2018–2022, part of a long-term project in the southeastern Caribbean that focuses on Bonaire alongside the sibling islands of Margarita (Venezuela) and Trinidad (Trinidad and Tobago). During these periods, I conducted interviews, heritage surveys and historical research, placing an emphasis on the relationship between heritage and present-day expressions of Indigenous identity. My focus has been on partnering with Indigenous peoples in the region to better understand how this key relationship has been impacted by the unique histories of colonialism on each island. It is out of this framework that I approach the topic of this volume—and I draw from interviews conducted for my master's thesis to identify important intersections between Indigeneity, gender and colonialism in Bonaire.[1] Although the focus here is Bonaire, I believe much of what is discussed here will resonate in Curaçao and Aruba as well as other islands of the Caribbean. I hope it can contribute to a more complete discussion about gender, race and coloniality in the region and encourages more research into this important part of Dutch Caribbean history and culture.

2 Indigeneity in the Present Day

As Europeans arrived to the Americas in the late fifteenth and early sixteenth century, Indigenous peoples were thrust into new socioeconomic systems. In the Caribbean, enslavement, encomiendas (an early colonial system of labor, where colonial settlers were granted native people's land and labor), conversions and violent incursions all contributed to a rapid process of transculturation where primordial attachments to identity—land, languages, physical appearance, practices, beliefs, etc.—were profoundly transformed.[2] Across the region, colonialism caused the dissolution of values, leading to new ways of doing things in a material and social sense, fundamentally changing

1 Interviews cited in this contribution are drawn from Antczak, "Unpicking a Feeling," 2018. Interviewees were kept anonymous and given codes that can be referenced in the cited work. Interviews were conducted mostly in Spanish, although also in English and, in one case, with an interpreter in Papiamentu. All translations are done by the author.

2 Anderson-Córdova, *Surviving Spanish Conquest*, 2017; Deagan, "Reconsidering Taino Social Dynamics after Spanish Conquest," 2004.

heritage and ways of identifying.[3] This context produced, for native inhabitants, "a sense of a past that has been somehow lost in long and eventful years of transformation."[4] As a Bonairean interviewee told me: "You get lost because somebody has to talk for an Indian who is not there, as nobody can trace it back, so then he can't talk."[5]

Archaeology reveals that, just before Bonaire was first visited by Europeans, it was inhabited by a few dozen families (likely a maximum of eight hundred individuals) who are today identified as bearers of the Dabajuroid culture.[6] In the ensuing early colonial period (1498–1550), these inhabitants would be referred to as the Caquetío.[7] This term arose concurrently with the categorization between *Arawak* and *Carib* native groups, two terms that were in effect proxies of "good" and "bad" capriciously imposed by the colonizing powers to groups based on their resistance—the latter categorization permitting arbitrary killings and enslavement of the denominated group.[8] These categorizations and the arising economic and social relationships forged new instrumental identities that persist till today—consequently, we cannot confidently say that the Caquetío of the colonial period overlapped neatly with any precolonial group. It was after 1513 that Bonaire, having been labeled an *isla inútil*, or useless island, was raided by *indieros* or slavers who are reported to have "virtually depopulated" the islands.[9]

This history, sketched with rough strokes and filled in with biased colonial accounts, is the most well-known version of events and obscures that Indigenous people have always been in Bonaire, through the sixteenth century, in the role of agriculturalists for the Spanish inhabitants and, eventually, mixing into broader society after emancipation.[10] Indigenous people maintained a distinct identity throughout these centuries and their precolonial traditions have persisted through to today in various ways. This is made clear through

3 Gosden, *Archaeology and Colonialism*, 2004, p. 25.

4 Waterton and Watson, "Reconnections," 2017, p. 47. Such a sense has been theorized as "Indianness," see, for example, Peroff, "Indian Identity," 1997.

5 KRM1 in Antczak, "Unpicking a Feeling," 2018, p. 56.

6 Haviser, *The First Bonaireans*, 1991, p. 68.

7 Rouse and Cruxent, *Venezuelan Archaeology*, 1963.

8 Sued-Badillo, "The Island Caribs," 1995; Whitehead, "Ethnic Plurality and Cultural Continuity in the Native Caribbean," 1995.

9 Castellanos, "Elegias de varones ilustres de Indias" [Elegies of illustrious men of the Indies], 1874; Hartog, *A Short History of Bonaire*, 1975; Goslinga, *A Short History of the Netherlands Antilles and Surinam*, 1979.

10 Antczak, "Unpicking a Feeling," 2018; Goslinga, *A Short History of the Netherlands Antilles and Surinam*, 1979; Hartog, *Bonaire: Van Indianen tot toeristen* [Bonaire: From Indians to tourists], 1957.

archaeological, historical and anthropological research.[11] And yet, persistent narratives purport that no Indigenous peoples of "pure-blood" have been found on the ABC islands since the early twentieth century.[12] As one interviewee told me, the "Indigenous are gone."[13]

This problematic "myth of extinction"[14] harkens to a lost "authentic" subject most often expected to look and live just as the ancestors who were met by the Europeans on the beaches of the ABC islands in 1499 would have. Academics have long perceived this colonial transformation as a gradual loss of an authentic precolonial condition and, ultimately, a rupture. Consequently, those who identify as Indigenous in the present-day Caribbean are often challenged by academics, popular narratives and themselves—their claims are perceived as inauthentic and/or romanticized.[15] To counter this, here, *Indigenous* refers to peoples who have a historical continuity with long-rooted precolonial societies that inhabited Bonaire and who maintain distinctness today.[16]

With such a definition of Indigeneity, a paradigm shift occurs and present-day Indigenous identity processes can be seen as the result of the identity's resistance through more than five hundred years of colonialism rather than its erasure. This kind of resistance can be termed *survivance*, a portmanteau of resistance and survival that highlights the fluid and generative ways in which Indigenous peoples have been agents in their own existence and not passive "survivors."[17] By changing our frame of analysis, we stop questioning the validity of identity (upheld against an impossible precolonial standard to encourage present-day erasure) and, instead, aim to understand present-day identities for what they are in an intersectional historical context. As Voss argues, we need to "de-naturalize and de-essentialize aspects of identity that are often experienced as fixed and stable."[18]

2.1 *Sentimento Indjan*

It is within this theoretical framing that the first element of discussion, the *Sentimento Indjan*, or Indian feeling, emerges. This is a "feeling" or "spark" that

11 Antczak, "Unpicking a Feeling," 2018; Haviser, *The First Bonaireans*, 1991; Haviser, "Towards Romanticized Amerindian Identities among Caribbean Peoples," 1995.

12 Goslinga, *A Short History of the Netherlands Antilles and Surinam*, 1979, p. 7; Van Heekeren, "A Survey of the Non-Ceramic Artifacts," 1960, p. 103.

13 KRM1 in Antczak, "Unpicking a Feeling," 2018, p. 55.

14 Castanha, *The Myth of Indigenous Caribbean Extinction*, 2011.

15 Haviser, "Towards Romanticized Amerindian Identities among Caribbean Peoples," 1995.

16 Cobo, "Study of the Problem of Discrimination against Indigenous Populations," 1987.

17 Vizenor, *Manifest Manners*, 1999.

18 Voss, *The Archaeology of Ethnogenesis*, 2015, p. 15.

tells an individual they are Indigenous, and it is passed down generationally. Importantly, it can be a rebellious and prideful sense that rejects colonial notions—for example, by countering Western notions of a nature/culture divide or a rigid gender binary.[19] This plasticity and mischievous character of the "feeling" is a key characteristic of Indigenous identity in the region, which has allowed it to survive intense transculturation and erasure attempts up until today.

For several informants, this feeling was conceptualized as "Indian blood," something that moved them to action. One interviewee claimed that his "Indian blood came up" and made him rise to fight for Bonaire, leaving his life as a successful banker and launching a political call for Bonaire's autonomy from the Netherlands in particular following 10/10/10.[20] Another informant felt Indigenous since his youth, when he noticed that he was more daring than his non-Indigenous peers, for example, by drinking iguana blood during hunts, claiming that it was "because I'm Indian."[21] In these cases, Indigeneity can manifest itself as more masculine expressions of daring feats and the breaking of societal norms. As one informant said: "There is an aspect that you can feel but that you cannot prove strongly, that the people say we are like Indians, free, brave, they want to fight, and with a lot of pride."[22]

Waterton and Watson describe a similar phenomenon and define it as "deracination," or the removal of roots effectively separating the present populations from their past.[23] In this case, the function of the "feeling" is to blanket over these transformations and maintain identity. As Gillman explains, "[i]t is not important that present communities practice past practices for that to be their heritage."[24] Indigenous identity can therefore be expressed as someone

---

19 Due to the vagueness of knowledge about precolonial beliefs and practices, it is an open field for attribution for those with a *Sentimento Indjan*. The precolonial period offers evidence of a variety of different approaches to gender, see, for example, Alberti, "Los cuerpos en prehistória: Más allá de la división entre sexo/género" [Bodies in prehistory: Beyond the sex/gender divide], 1999.

20 KRM1 in Antczak, "Unpicking a Feeling," 2018, p. 41. 10/10/10, denoting October 10, 2010, is the date when the Netherlands Antilles was officially dissolved. Under the new structure, Bonaire became a "special municipality" of the Netherlands. What this change has meant for Bonaire and the implementation of the new structure attracted criticism from the interviewee.

21 TCM1, ibid.

22 NSM1, ibid.

23 Waterton and Watson, "Reconnections," p. 47.

24 Gillman, *The Idea of Cultural Heritage*, 2010, p. 25.

declaring themselves as Indigenous on a census or an exam, singing a sports team anthem or feeling an affinity to a place.[25]

The *Sentimento Indjan* is an important element of Indigenous identity in Bonaire because it binds together many different expressions that can vary per community or individual. This "feeling" acts as a glue that holds together many identifying features, some of which are discussed below, even when members of the community may differ on their authenticity or legitimacy. Next, I discuss some of these elements that particularly engage with notions of gender.

3 Physical Features and Nort Di Saliña

The first of these features is physical appearance. Nort di Saliña (also known as Nort'i Saliña or Kunuku Bieu) is a *bario*, or neighborhood, known as the last bastion of Indigenous traits in Bonaire and it is often cited as the place where these features are most seen. Today, the neighborhood is set apart from the rest of the island's *barios* by its streets, which are all named after Indigenous groups from the Americas (Azteca, Maya, Carib, Arawak, etc.), murals that depict Indigenous peoples and plaques of an Indigenous person of the Great Plains that can be found decorating many of the houses.

As a result of these physical manifestations, Nort di Saliña today more easily maintains and promotes its fame as an Indigenous part of the island, but all these elements only arose in the last fifty years.[26] At the center of the claim to Indigeneity in Nort di Saliña is the relative proliferation of physical features in this *bario* as compared to others. Appearance was even the only distinguishing aspect for one of the informants who claimed that "everything was the same [as other Bonaireans] in my family apart from [our] appearance."[27]

The physical feature that is most mentioned in interviews is hair. It is described as long, straight and black, usually split into two braids that are

25 Chavers, "Correcting Untruths, Half-Truths and the Exaggeration of College Statistics," 1996; Nagel, *American Indian Ethnic Renewal*, 1997; Waterton and Watson, "Reconnections," 2017. Editors' note: see also contribution by Dresscher-Lambertus in this volume for a discussion of indigeneity and life writing practices in the Aruban context.

26 Another important source of Indigenous identity is potentially the notion that, around 1660, Peter Stuyvesant allegedly exiled eleven North American Indians from the Dutch dominion in North America to Bonaire (Menkman, *De Nederlanders in het Caraibische zeegebied* [The Dutch in the Caribbean Sea], 1942.) However, I found that this narrative is not known or was not mentioned in any of my interviews.

27 NSM2 in Antczak, "Unpicking a Feeling," 2018, p. 48.

tied.[28] Historical sources confirm this importance of hair in two *trenzas* or braids for the coastal Caquetío and link them to a sense of pride that can be lost if the hair is cut.[29] There are also other features, mostly facial, that are recognized and can, together, contribute to an Indigenous appearance. One informant claimed that an Indigenous person has a certain type of "eyes, black long hair, nose."[30] In my research, these features of Indigenous identity were mostly identified in women as they are the ones to most often grow out their hair to such a length. However, some men will let their hair grow out to show it as a proud marker of their identity—stepping out of gendered expectations in Bonaire to mark their Indigenous heritage.

A further point has to do with class and race, which are perceived to be drivers in why Indigenous features were maintained in this *bario* and not in others. One interviewee argued that, historically, the people of Nort di Saliña, who were mainly Dutch, did not mix with African descendants because they "didn't have property, while the Indians did have it."[31] This socioeconomic reason became racial as the interviewee continues that Nort di Saliña's inhabitants "were more beautiful, they didn't want that the race made itself, for example, thicker hair, it had to stay pretty and straight, in this way … they were very proud of their appearance, yes, yes. They didn't like dark men, the dark people."[32] Another informant offered that "the local people did not want to identify with the black people who were captives, that is why surely they identified with the Indians."[33]

After emancipation, this segregation of the *barios* continued. One interviewee claimed that it "used to be very difficult to mix with other *barios*," which meant that Nort di Saliña preserved its Indigenous traits. Another Bonairean with dark skin told me that, when he was young, he would get stones thrown at him if he got too close to Nort di Saliña as the inhabitants did not want him close to their daughters. As Bonaire opened to new industries in the late twentieth century—tourism, BOPEC, Cargill—the barriers between these neighborhoods became more permeable.

Today, Nort di Saliña prides itself in this Indigenous visual distinction that is central to the *barios* identity. One interviewee showed me a newspaper cutout picturing his family claiming that the last of the Caquetío lived in Nort di

---

28 Ibid.

29 Cey, *Viaje y descripción de las Indias, 1539–1553* [Voyage and description of the Indies, 1539–1553], 1995, pp. 106–8.

30 KRM1 in Antczak, "Unpicking a Feeling," 2018, p. 48.

31 KRM8, ibid., p. 49.

32 NSF1, ibid.

33 NSM1, ibid., p. 41.

Saliña. Another interviewee showed me a picture of her long black hair, which she felt expressed her Indigeneity, saying that "everyone wants to touch it to see if it's real because there are not many people like that."[34] These objects that promote Indigenous appearance became important pieces for identity formation. Despite Indigenous peoples living across the island, Nort di Saliña continues to be seen as an enclave of Indigenous identity in Bonaire and promotes this idea through tangible heritage.

4 Social Relationships and Matriarchy

Another prominent recurring feature of Bonairean (and Caribbean at large) culture that is brought up in interviews as Indigenous is matrifocality.[35] This refers to the fact that, while men are perceived as the leaders of the household and families are predominantly patrilocal,[36] in practice, it is often women who, by necessity, run affairs and have the most sway in decision-making. There is an enduring notion that the central role women, specifically mothers, play in the family structure is a legacy of the Indigenous inhabitants of Bonaire.

On the islands of the southeastern Caribbean, matrifocal family structures can be related to the practice of seasonal fisheries and rancherias, a form of campsite that is a tradition that is still maintained across the region.[37] This practice is marked by defined gender roles; men are expected to go out for long trips, living communally for extended periods abroad, while women raise the family and keep the land productive.[38] Evidence from my interviews suggests that this also persisted in Bonaire into the twentieth century and still goes on to a lesser extent, with week- or month-long trips to the Las Aves and Los Roques Archipelagos and, even further, to La Tortuga and Margarita for fish, wood, guano, salt, turtle and bird eggs and more.[39] Such expeditions continue

---

34 Group Interview 3, ibid., p. 50.

35 Ho, "Caribbean Transnationalism as a Gendered Process," 1999. Editors' note: on matrifocality in Aruba, see contribution by Yolanda Richardson in this volume.

36 Beek, "The Forming of a Community in the Heart of the Dutch Caribbean," 2013, p. 58.

37 Antczak et al., "Rancherías," 2019.

38 There is evidence for a similar gendered practice of seasonal camping from precolonial Cariban- and Arawakan-speaking Valencioid and Ocumaroid peoples of north central Venezuela, who traveled primarily to Los Roques and carried female figurines with them. See Antczak and Antczak, *Los ídolos de las Islas Prometidas: Arqueología prehispánica del archipiélago de los Roques* [The idols of the Promised Islands: Prehispanic archeology of the Roques archipelago], 2006.

39 Antczak, *Islands of Salt. Historical Archaeology of Seafarers and Things in the Venezuelan Caribbean, 1624–1880*, 2019; Antczak, "Unpicking a Feeling," 2018.

to play an important role in the Bonairean cultural imagination and identity, having surely been central in the celebrated tradition of sailors and sailboat manufacture that marked the turn of the twentieth century for Bonaire.

While the coastal Caquetío were purportedly patrilineal in their power succession,[40] matrilineal relations and women leaders, for example Cacica Isabel in Margarita,[41] are noted among many historical and contemporary Indigenous communities in the region, such as the Wayuu from the Guajira Peninsula in Venezuela and Colombia.[42] This phenomenon forms its own area of significant research and debate.[43] Some interesting case studies from the Caribbean can help us think about how colonialism would have impacted precolonial gender roles and social structures. Deagan's work about the Taíno suggests that nonspecialized gender roles may have helped Taíno cultural practices resist Spanish colonialism.[44] Other arguments from the eastern coast of Venezuela reveal that the colonial imposition of a patriarchal relation was fundamental to the development of a new system of labor. In this case, Cariban-speaking groups were broadly matrilocal and cultural knowledge was passed down through women—men would readily assimilate to new groups as part of a custom of the (violent and non-violent) exchange of members between groups.[45] Having been pressed into new forms of labor and into new systems of belief, and thrust into violent hierarchies of power, precolonial gender roles would have similarly resisted, changed and adapted in Bonaire. Today, with unique family structures and relationships and the continuing cultural tradition of seasonal fishing, Indigenous identity promotes itself through difference from traditional Western expectations.[46]

---

40 Oliver, "The Archaeological, Linguistic and Ethnohistorical Evidence," 1989.

41 Ayala Lafée-Wilbert, Rivas Gómez, and Wilbert, *Caballeros del mar: Los Guaiquerí, un pueblo con historia* [Knights of the sea: The Guaiquerí, a people with history], 2017; Gandica Silva, *Las mujeres de la región insular de la Costa de Las Perlas* [The women of the insular region of the Pearl Coast], 2013.

42 Velásquez, "Roles y relaciones de género en el pueblo Indígena Wayuu" [Roles and gender relations among the Wayuu Indigenous people], 2016.

43 Ochoa and Guengerich, *Cacicas*, 2021.

44 Deagan, "Reconsidering Taino Social Dynamics after Spanish Conquest," 2004.

45 Tiapa, "Sistemas interétnicos, matrilocalidad y construcción colonial" [Interethnic systems, matrilocality and colonial construction], 2016.

46 In this case, these countered expectations can be promoted by the beliefs of the Catholic Church, which holds great sway in Bonaire, although the cult of the Virgin Mary can be an interesting source that reaffirms Indigeneity. See Bondarenko, "Culto a la Virgen del Valle como creencia Autóctona Guaiquerí en las Islas Orientales Venezolanas" [Worship of the Virgin of the Valley as Guaiquerí Native belief], 2015.

Another related perceived unique feature of the Indigenous Bonairean family structure to come out of the interviews was the unproblematic inclusion of extramarital children into the family structure. According to several informants, the fact that families did not mistreat nonmarital children and did not privilege children born within wedlock was a feature of Bonairean society that derived from its Indigenous history.[47] More research should be done to better understand this feature of Bonairean culture and its link to Indigeneity.

5 Conclusions

Of course, matrifocality or female-headed families are not solely a legacy of Indigenous traditions; plenty has been written about this phenomenon in the Afro-Caribbean family structure and the two conversations should not be had separately.[48] The importance of Afro-Curaçaoan seafarers has been developed by Allen, for example, and is perhaps another example of the intersection of the Indigenous legacies and traditions with class, race and gender on the ABC islands.[49] In similar fashion, much of what has been discussed has been excised from the web of connections and influences that results from the diverse history of the Caribbean with its many influences, which are perhaps inseparable from—but still an essential part of—the maintenance and promotion of Indigeneity. While it may be heuristically useful to highlight Indigeneity in present-day Bonairean society (particularly due to its comparative invisibility resulting from the "narratives of extinction"), ultimately, it must be brought back into a broader discussion in the context of this larger volume.

Beyond the points discussed in this brief contribution, there are more intersections to be identified and the ones delineated need to be better understood. For example, a much more extensive discussion is due of the practice of *kuranderia*, or traditional herbal healing—a powerful undercurrent of Bonairean society. Notably, this practice is in great part undertaken by women.[50] The figure of the *kurandera* plays in parallel with the figure of the matron leader of the household and places women as brokers of traditional and natural knowledge. Women overseeing the realm of spirituality and healing is consistent with some of what we know ethnographically from adjacent Venezuela, and

47 Antczak, "Unpicking a Feeling," 2018.

48 See, for example, Stuart, "Female-Headed Families," 1996.

49 Allen, "'Learning to Be a Man,'" 2011.

50 Antoin, *Kuranderia popular: Natural i spiritual* [Popular *Kuranderia*: Natural and spiritual], 2018.

we have historical references to the roles of the *boratio* and/or *piache*, a priest/doctor who would have had extensive knowledge about the weather and medicine, using local plants such as tobacco and agave to treat ailments.[51]

I encourage further research into *kuranderia* practices and its links not only with Indigenous practices but also Afro-descended practices. I also urge research on cultural events in Bonaire such as *simadan* and *maskarada*, which have also been identified as having Indigenous elements in my interviews. Roles and expressions of gender as well as a deeper understanding of the music, dress and dances could yield further insights. As for my own research, I plan to involve gender more concretely into my analysis and interpretations and to reach a more diverse group of informants, which has thus far been mostly composed of men.

Looking toward the future, one interviewee considered that it was not too late to redefine identity for this generation but noted that it was elders who had to give indication to the young.[52] In contrast, interviewed elders expressed their inability to guide the younger generation as they felt like they did not have the adequate knowledge to pass down.[53] As researchers, heritage managers and academics, I encourage us to judiciously offer our resources to aid the *Sentimento Indjan* in its ebb and flow, with sensitive and collaborative bottom-up approaches always giving space to local voices and interpretations.

Bibliography

Alberti, Benjamin. "Los cuerpos en prehistória: Más allá de la división entre sexo/género" [Bodies in prehistory: Beyond the sex/gender divide]. *Revista Do Museu de Arqueologia e Etnologia. Suplemento*, no. 3 (November 1999), 57–67. https://doi.org/10.11606/issn.2594-5939.revmaesupl.1999.113459.

Allen, Rose Mary. "'Learning to Be a Man': Afro-Caribbean Seamen and Maritime Workers from Curaçao in the Beginning of the Twentieth Century." *Caribbean Studies* 39, no. 1 (2011): 43–64. https://doi.org/10.1353/crb.2011.0014.

Anderson-Córdova, Karen F. *Surviving Spanish Conquest: Indian Fight, Flight, and Cultural Transformation in Hispaniola and Puerto Rico*. Tuscaloosa: University of Alabama Press, 2017.

51 Cey, *Viaje y descripción de las Indias, 1539–1553*, 1995; Fernando de Oviedo, *Sumario de la natural historia de las Indias* [Summary of the natural history of the Indies], 1986.

52 KRM2 in Antczak, "Unpicking a Feeling," 2018, p. 56.

53 Group Interview 2, ibid., p. 43.

Antczak, Andrzej T., María Magdalena Antczak, Oliver Antczak, and Luis A. Lemoine Buffet. "Rancherías: Historical Archaeology of Early Colonial Campsites on Margarita and Coche Islands, Venezuela." In *Material Encounters and Indigenous Transformations in the Early Colonial Americas*, edited by Corinne L. Hofman and Floris W.M. Keehnen:146–74. The Early Americas: History and Culture 9. Leiden: Brill, 2019. https://doi.org/10.1163/9789004273689_008.

Antczak, Konrad A. *Islands of Salt. Historical Archaeology of Seafarers and Things in the Venezuelan Caribbean, 1624–1880*. Taboui 6. Leiden: Sidestone Press Academics, 2019.

Antczak, María Magdalena, and Andrzej T. Antczak. *Los ídolos de las Islas Prometidas: Arqueología prehispánica del archipiélago de los Roques* [The idols of the Promised Islands: Prehispanic archeology of the Roques archipelago]. Caracas: Editorial Equinoccio, 2006.

Antczak, Oliver. "Unpicking a Feeling: Interrogating the Role of Heritage in Indigenous Collective Identity Formation on the Caribbean Island of Bonaire." Master's thesis, University of Cambridge, 2018.

Antoin, Boi. *Kuranderia popular: Natural i spiritual* [Popular *Kuranderia*: Natural and spiritual]. Kralendijk: FuHiKuBo, 2018.

Ayala Lafée-Wilbert, C., Pedro Rivas Gómez, and Werner Wilbert. *Caballeros del mar: Los Guaiquerí, un pueblo con historia* [Knights of the sea: The Guaiquerí, a people with history]. Caracas: Fundación Salle de Ciencias Naturales, 2017.

Beek, Julisa van. "The Forming of a Community in the Heart of the Dutch Caribbean." Master's thesis, Erasmus University Rotterdam, 2013. https://thesis.eur.nl/pub/15062/Beek-J.-van.pdf.

Bondarenko, Natalia. "Culto a la Virgen del Valle como creencia Autóctona Guaiquerí en las Islas Orientales Venezolanas" [Worship of the Virgin of the Valley as Guaiquerí Native belief]. *Cultura y Religión* 9, no. 2 (2015): 16–38.

Castanha, Tony. *The Myth of Indigenous Caribbean Extinction: Continuity and Reclamation in Borikén (Puerto Rico*. New York: Palgrave Macmillan, 2011. https://doi.org/10.1057/9780230116405.

Castellanos, Juan de. "Elegias de varones ilustres de Indias" [Elegies of illustrious men of the Indies]. In *Biblioteca de autores Espanoles, IV*, 3rd ed. Madrid: Aribau y Compania, 1874.

Cey, G. *Viaje y descripción de las Indias, 1539–1553* [Voyage and description of the Indies, 1539–1553], Vol. 12. Colección V centenario de encuentro entre dos mundos 1492–1992, 1498–1998. Caracas: Fundación Banco Venezolano de Crédito, 1995.

Chavers, D. "Correcting Untruths, Half-Truths and the Exaggeration of College Statistics." *Indian Country Today* 16, no. 5 (1996): 5.

Cobo, José R. Martínez. *Study of the Problem of Discrimination against Indigenous Populations: Conclusions, Proposals, and Recommendations*. United Nations

Sub-Commission on Prevention of Discrimination and Protection of Minorities, 1987. https://digitallibrary.un.org/record/133666.

Deagan, Kathleen. "Reconsidering Taino Social Dynamics after Spanish Conquest: Gender and Class in Culture Contact Studies." *American Antiquity* 69, no. 4 (October 2004): 597–627.

Fernández de Oviedo, G. *Sumario de la natural historia de las Indias* [Summary of the natural history of the Indies]. Crónicas de América 21. Madrid: Historia 16, 1986.

Gandica Silva, Ana Luisa. *Las mujeres de la región insular de la Costa de Las Perlas* [The women of the insular region of the Pearl Coast]. La Asunción: Gobierno Bolivariano del Estado Nueva Esparta, 2013.

Gillman, Derek. *The Idea of Cultural Heritage*. Cambridge: Cambridge University Press, 2010.

Gosden, Chris. *Archaeology and Colonialism: Cultural Contact from 5000 BC to the Present*. London: Cambridge University Press, 2004.

Goslinga, Cornelis C. *A Short History of the Netherlands Antilles and Surinam*. The Hague: Martinus Nijhoff, 1979.

Hartog, Johan. *A Short History of Bonaire*. Translated by Victoria Gideon Oenes. 2nd ed. Bonaire: Island Territory of Bonaire, 1975.

Hartog, Johan. *Bonaire: Van Indianen tot toeristen* [Bonaire: From Indians to tourists]. Vol. 2. Oranjestad: Gebroeders de Wit, 1957.

Haviser, Jay B. *The First Bonaireans*. Vol. 10. Curaçao: Archaeological-Anthropological Institute of the Netherlands Antilles, 1991.

Haviser, Jay B. "Towards Romanticized Amerindian Identities among Caribbean Peoples: A Case Study from Bonaire, Netherlands Antilles." In *Wolves from the Sea*, edited by Neil L. Whitehead, 139–56. Caribbean Series 14. Leiden: KITLV Press, 1995.

Heekeren, H.R. "A Survey of the Non-Ceramic Artifacts of Aruba, Curacao and Bonaire." In *Studies on the Archaeology of the Netherlands Antilles: 1–2*. Vol. 40. The Hague: Martinus Nijhoff, 1960.

Ho, Christine G.T. "Caribbean Transnationalism as a Gendered Process." *Latin American Perspectives* 26, no. 5 (1999): 34–54.

Menkman, W. R. *De Nederlanders in het Caraibische zeegebied* [The Dutch in the Caribbean Sea]. Amsterdam: P. N. van Kampen & Zoon N.V, 1942.

Nagel, Joane. *American Indian Ethnic Renewal: Red Power and the Resurgence of Identity and Culture*. Oxford: Oxford University Press, 1997.

Ochoa, Margarita R., and Sara V. Guengerich. *Cacicas: The Indigenous Women Leaders of Spanish America, 1492–1825*. Norman: University of Oklahoma Press, 2021.

Oliver, J. R. "The Archaeological, Linguistic and Ethnohistorical Evidence for the Expansion of Arawakan into Northwestern Venezuela and Northeastern Colombia." PhD. diss., University of Illinois at Urbana-Champaign, 1989.

Peroff, N. C. "Indian Identity." *The Social Science Journal* 34, no. 4 (January 1997): 485–94. https://doi.org/10.1016/S0362-3319(97)90007-0.

Rouse, Irving, and José María Cruxent. *Venezuelan Archaeology*. New Haven: Yale University Press, 1963.

Stuart, Sheila. "Female-Headed Families: A Comparative Perspective of the Caribbean and the Developed World." *Gender and Development* 4, no. 2 (1996): 28–34.

Sued-Badillo, Jalil. "The Island Caribs: New Approaches to the Question of Ethnicity in the Early Colonial Caribbean." In *Wolves from the Sea*, edited by Neil L. Whitehead, 61–89. Leiden: KITLV Press, 1995.

Tiapa, Francisco. "Sistemas interétnicos, matrilocalidad y construcción colonial del patriarcado en el oriente de Venezuela, siglos XVII–XVIII" [Interethnic systems, matrilocality and colonial construction in Eastern Venezuela, 17th–18th centuries]. *Procesos históricos: Revista de historia, arte y ciencias sociales* 14, no. 29 (2016): 45–76.

Velásquez, Saida Luisa Guerra. "Roles y relaciones de género en el pueblo indígena Wayuu" [Roles and gender relations among the Wayuu Indigenous people]. *Praxis Investigativa ReDIE: Revista electrónica de la Red Durango de Investigadores Educativos* 8, no. 15 (2016): 79–92.

Vizenor, Gerald Robert. *Manifest Manners: Narratives on Postindian Survivance*. Lincoln: University of Nebraska Press, 1999.

Voss, Barbara L. *The Archaeology of Ethnogenesis: Race and Sexuality in Colonial San Francisco*. Gainesville: University Press of Florida, 2015.

Waterton, Emma, and Steve Watson. "Reconnections." In *Heritage in Action: Making the Past in the Present*, edited by Helaine Silverman, Emma Waterton and Steve Watson and, 47–60. Cham: Springer International Publishing, 2017.

Whitehead, Neil L. "Ethnic Plurality and Cultural Continuity in the Native Caribbean: Remarks and Uncertainties as to Data and Theory." In *Wolves from the Sea*, edited by Neil L. Whitehead, 91–112. Caribbean Series 14. Leiden: KITLV Press, 1995.

CHAPTER 16

Respectability and Resistance: Race, Gender and the Microdimensions of Power in the Colony

Angela E. Roe

Abstract

This contribution explores how the colonial power structure is passed on, solidified but also resisted in the realm of intimate relations. It examines these microdimensions of colonial oppression through an exploration of the stories of ancestors and their traces in family narratives, genealogies, colonial ledgers and old newspaper clippings. Who bedded who, who wed who and under what circumstances? What were the consequences of their choices? And what may have been their motives? This exploration intends to particularly illustrate how gendered race and the distribution of power are in the colony. It equally exposes that resistance to the familiar hegemonic structures was ample and multilayered.

Keywords

Curaçao – family narratives – race and gender – microdimensions of colonial oppression – intimate relations

My mother was raised in Curaçao but born in Suriname. Like her, many Curaçaoans have links to this large former colony on the South American mainland. My grandparents moved to Curaçao to benefit from the arrival of the Shell refinery after 1915, which brought along a great deal of social change. My grandfather set up an electronics shop in Otrobanda, and my grandmother had her own sewing atelier. They became much appreciated and well-integrated members of Curaçaoan society, but they brought along roots and experiences from a world that was both nearby and a distance away. Nearby in the sense that Suriname, too, was colonized by the Dutch and thus shared certain cultural particularities; far away as the distance between Curaçao and Suriname is 1,694 km, which, today, amounts to a three-hour flight. Due to its size

 | DOI:10.1163/9789004690882_018

and climate, plantations in Suriname were generally much larger than those in Curaçao or on the other islands of the Dutch Caribbean. Yet, there were similarities between both colonial sites as far as the mechanisms and power relations of race and gender in the intimate sphere were concerned.

The aim of this contribution is to explore how colonial hegemonic ideology and power structures were perpetuated and contested in nineteenth- and twentieth-century Suriname through the intersections of gender, race and nation. Through constructing an ethnographic family history, I explore how the ideology of race and nation that was active during this era shaped my grandmother's performances of self in relation to my mother and others in the world that she lived in.[1] Following Ann Stoler and Jean Rahier, I zoom in on the microdimensions of intimacy as the everyday life mechanizations of hegemony.[2] An inquiry into the lives of my grandmother, her ancestors and my mother as her firstborn child illustrates how ideological fragments of race and nation are quintessentially gendered and how they are both perpetuated and contested.

Ann Laura Stoler argues that intimacy is colonialism's handmaiden.[3] When reflecting about colonial power, people often think exclusively about the economic and political dimensions of colonialism, its rules and regulations about trade and economic profit, its division of labor and the issues of freedom, servitude, ownership and citizenship. However, Stoler contends that colonialism is always gendered, which becomes clearly visible on the most intimate levels of the colonials' lives; their interactions with the colonized were particularly a source of great preoccupation for colonial authorities. It is in the spoken and unspoken rules about who could bed and wed whom, who served whom and how and who raised whom and how that the dimensions of race and power were solidified in everyday practice. She illustrates how ideas about race and miscegenation, gender, sexuality, intimacy, power, identity and belonging are pliable, political constructs that were adaptable enough to keep both colonizers and colonized in line. In the end, colonial rules and regulations, and

1 The doctoral dissertation explores personal narratives of three figures in my family history, namely my grandmother, my mother and myself. The present contribution mainly focuses on my grandmother and her ancestors.

2 See Stoler, *Carnal Knowledge and Imperial Power*, 2002; Rahier, "The Ghost of Leopold II," 2003; Rahier, "Introduction: Mestizaje, Mulataje, Mestiçagem in Latin American Ideologies of National Identities," 2008; Rahier, "Soccer and the (Tri-) Color of the Ecuadorian Nation," 2008; Rahier, "The Microphysics of Colonial Power," 2010; and Rahier, *Black Social Movements in Latin America*, 2012.

3 Stoler, *Carnal Knowledge and Imperial Power*, 2002. Editors' note: see also contribution by Espersen in this volume for a discussion of the racialized aspects of colonialism in Saba.

the sanctions and prohibitions they entailed, established the seat of imperial power and dominance.[4]

Jean Rahier makes a similar argument: sex, race and power intersect, Rahier states, because "affective sentiments, emotions, joys and pains … marked the lives of both colonizers and colonized."[5] These constitute "the micro-dimensions of the practice of colonial power in the interactions between colonizers and colonized."[6] Following Michel Foucault's theorizing that power is always in circulation and in flux,[7] Rahier argues that, in order to comprehend the way power operates, one must zoom in on the processes of interpersonal interactions, on the realm of the intimate, as much as on the larger social, economic and political dimensions of the colonial order.[8]

I focus on the microdimensions of intimacy in the everyday mechanizations of hegemony. I specifically explore (a) what hegemonic messages were central to the worlds of my great-grandmothers and my grandmother; (b) how these instructed them to comply with the rules of the colony; and (c) how they both embraced and resisted these rules. Despite being one specific family narrative and perspective, the stories portrayed here reveal larger patterns and present a vivid example of the complex ways in which hegemony operates in a gendered context. The stories that I present here are a reflexive presentation of an intergenerational family history, which I collected over the course of several years, based on archival study and conversations with my mother, father, grandmother and my mother's siblings and cousins.

1 Silence, Hegemony, Censure and Resistance

Silence plays a pivotal role in the intimate dimensions within colonial and postcolonial discourses of white supremacy. Scholars such as Pierre Bourdieu have shown how silence can be a powerful means of implementing hegemony, with "social silences" that can be both "deliberately or involuntarily complicitous."[9]

Yet, as hegemony imposes and evokes censorship, silence can equally be a powerful means of protection from and resistance to hegemony's effects. James C. Scott argues that what he calls the "hidden transcript" is the offstage

4 Ibid., p. 45.

5 Rahier, "The Microphysics of Colonial Power," 2010, p. 41.

6 Ibid., p. 42.

7 Foucault, *Discipline and Punish*, 1995.

8 Rahier, "The Microphysics of Colonial Power," 2010, p. 42.

9 See Bourdieu, *Outline of a Theory of Practice*, 2019, p. 188; and Trouillot, *Silencing the Past*, 1995.

critique of and coping with the public transcript or the official discourse projected by the elites.[10] Anthropological linguist Robin Sheriff's ethnography yields ample examples of both the subjugation and the resistance silence involves in a racialized context.[11] Like Scott, Sheriff argues that silence should not necessarily be understood as the acceptance of dominant discourse.[12] Her study reveals that racism, racial prejudice and race-based discrimination are rarely discussed by the inhabitants of the shantytown or favela she studied. To talk openly and complain about racism would mean to acknowledge its power and thus "involve a kind of personal and collective surrender."[13] Complicitous silence offers a way to cope with these predicaments.

Both Scott and Sheriff claim that silence does more than simply perpetuate oppression. Euphemism, deception, avoidance and denial are necessary means to soften the internalized oppression, the shame and the wounds that one cannot adequately protect oneself from. But they are also ways to camouflage these negative impacts, making them invisible to the perpetrator, as well as to disobey. Silence is a multifaceted and multifunctional "space" in which oppression can thrive, but it is also a haven that offers the protection and shelter in which resistance grows.

Lastly, silence is a well-known response to trauma.[14] Dissociation or avoidance behavior is a common individual response to emotional shock sustained during a very distressing physical or emotional event. In addition to numbness, a condition where the capacity to feel pain is temporarily suspended, amnesia and repression are defenses of the mind against such a violent intrusion.[15] But trauma also exists on a cultural or societal level, when a group or social segment is collectively affected by a crisis.[16] The trauma that is experienced on the individual and collective level—a significant alteration or even loss of identity—becomes framed and expressed in a collectively shared narrative,

10 Scott, *Domination and the Art of Resistance*, 1992.
11 Sheriff, *Dreaming Equality: Color, Race and Racism in Urban Brazil*, 2001.
12 Ibid., p. 118.
13 Ibid., p. 75.
14 See Caruth, *Unclaimed Experience*, 1996; Eyerman, *Cultural Trauma*, 2001; and Eyerman, "Social Theory and Trauma," 2013.
15 Caruth, *Unclaimed Experience*, 1996, p. 4; and Eyerman, "Social Theory and Trauma," 2013, p. 42.
16 See Alexander, Entwisle, and Horsey, "From First Grade Forward," 1997; Connerton, *How Societies Remember*, 1989; Eyerman, *Cultural Trauma*, 2001; and Eyerman, "Social Theory and Trauma," 2013.

which, as Jeffrey Alexander's theoretical model for collective trauma suggests, may either be empowering or detrimental to the collective at hand.[17]

Silence is thus not an empty space, and it is never quiet but full of power struggles, conflicting allegiances and meanings, opposed codes of behavior, norms, values, hopes, dreams, rituals, fears and pains. Like any bit of cultural discourse, silences are passed on from one person to another, consciously or unconsciously, as part of people's socialization into dominant discourses, or of counter-hegemonic discourses of resistance and protection, as well as of a society's specific traumas. The present contribution thus uses my own family history as a site to investigate the place of silence in the social reality of my ancestors.

2 My Grandmother Sophie and Our Forgotten Ancestors

My grandmother Sophie was born in 1919 in Paramaribo, Suriname. She was a free-spirited, light-skinned girl, brimming with a creativity that only died when she did, at the age of ninety-two while sipping her morning coffee at her sewing table. Sophie's slender hands preferred the piano over typewriters and ledgers, her feet danced rather than carried her to run errands or sit still behind a desk. She wanted to sing, act and be on stage. But, in the 1930s, such things were not suitable for respectable, light-skinned girls from the lower-middle class. Her parents wanted her to become a decent and sensible woman, which meant that she had to act properly and her chastity and reputation had to be preserved so she could marry a man of good societal standing. Her father was a professional tailor who ran a successful business, sewing, among other things, the uniforms of Paramaribo's police officers. With a family of six children, he had the means to allow his daughters some education but nothing extravagant. They were lucky to even receive secondary education: many young women did not have that opportunity in those days. Sophie studied bookkeeping. She learned how to count her blessings, but the fiery passion for arts, creativity and excitement that she carried inside remained and suppressing it was a burden for her throughout her life.

Once she told me that she was so angry with her father that he would not let her join the theater. But she did sneak away once, when a big theater company came to town, and participated in a play. She giggled in her typical way and said to me: "*Ai baja* ("Oh God" or "Good heavens" in Sranan Tongo, the creole

17 Alexander, *Cultural Trauma and Collective Identity*, 2004. Editors' note: see also contribution by Henriquez in this volume.

language of Suriname), I just did it, and I had such fun! My parents never even knew …"

Sophie's silence was an act of resistance against the hegemonic, societal norm of respectability, which subscribed to white, European norms of proper conduct and shames those who do not adhere to them. It thus has a strong hegemonic component.[18] "Respectability politics," a notion keyed by Peter Wilson in 1969, entail a set of rules for the subjugated masses through which they can achieve social upward mobility through adhering to white, Eurocentric cultural standards.[19] Deborah A. Thomas, writing about twentieth-century Jamaica, describes respectability as: "a value complex emphasizing the cultivation of education, thrift, industry, self-sufficiency via land ownership, moderate Christian living, community uplift, the constitution of family through legal marriage and gender related experiences, and leadership by the educated middle classes."[20]

Sophie was one of the lightest skinned of her siblings. She had gray eyes, wavy, auburn hair and a light *café-au-lait* skin tone. Her features had a social currency that she was expected to protect throughout her life. My relatives often referred to her as white, and my family never self-identified as black, Afro-descendant. This always puzzled me as no one actually looks white. What, then, are we really? Thus, in my doctoral research, I decided to uncover the hidden stories on my grandmother's side.

Sophie's father, Rudolf Vervuurt, was a fourth-generation descendant of a Dutchman who had come to Suriname in 1795. Some of his relatives had been colonial officials, some had managed plantations and others, like him, were tradesmen and craftsmen. My mother remembers her grandfather as a tall, white man with piercing blue eyes, who dressed in the typical white colonial outfits that the Europeans wore. Other relatives also remember him as a white man of German descent. Yet, on the old black-and-white photographs, my

18 See Thomas, *Modern Blackness*, 2004; Besson, "Reputation & Respectability Reconsidered," 1993; and White, *Dark Continent of Our Bodies*, 2001, who also identify the emancipatory elements of these politics, in which it becomes a seat of resistance and counter-hegemony. Adopting these standards does not automatically equate hegemony: it can be a strategy in order to achieve greater social upward mobility and strengthen pro-black reform.

19 See Wilson, "Reputation and Respectability," 1969. Speech, appearance (dress, hairstyle and makeup) and control over one's emotions are also part of these politics of respectability; see Roe, "The Sound of Silence," 2016, p. 296. Editors' note: see also contribution by Allen in this volume.

20 Thomas, *Modern Blackness*, 2004, pp. 5–6.

great-grandfather's skin seemed to have a light brown hue and his slender face did not look European at all.

In the family's genealogical records, I traced Rudolf's grandparents and great-grandparents back to the first Vervuurt, who left the harbor of seventeenth-century Delfzijl, situated in the northernmost part of the Netherlands. In the digitized Surinamese ledgers, I found Rudolf's mother, Julia Emelina Zechiël.[21] Suriname's manumission records revealed that Julia had been born as an enslaved person on the sugar plantation De Drie Gebroeders (The Three Brothers) in upper Suriname. She had been what the ledgers termed a "house slave." The fact that Julia had worked in the house may have meant that she was a child of the man who owned the plantation or that she was his "housekeeper-concubine."[22] In both cases, it is likely that she was of lighter skin. Her mother, Bruinetta Dorothea Zechiël, had worked in the fields.

The ledgers showed that not only was Rudolph not of German but of Dutch origin, but he was also of African descent! Of all the tales I heard about my family, this certainly was not one of them. I remember that my mother proudly self-identified as part Javanese and Indigenous Surinamese, all of whom constitute large population segments in Suriname. But never did I hear anyone in my family acknowledge our African descendance.

During the colonial era, intimate relations between white men and women of color were common in Suriname. Yet, while such relations were encouraged in Curaçao,[23] the colonial government in Suriname strictly forbade white men from having sexual relations with their enslaved women.[24] If discovered, the men would be fined small amounts of money or sugar. For white women and enslaved men maintaining intimate relations, the punishments would be far worse. But due to the large surplus of white men compared to white women, these colonial rules were often bent and broken. It was common for white men to live in concubinage with enslaved women who would be employed as housekeepers, something that the colonial government condoned. The mixed-race children who would result from these relations, who came to be known in Suriname as "creole," often held a privileged position and might even be

21 I consulted the Dutch National Archive (Nationaal Archief), the Foundation for Surinameese Genealogy (Stiching voor Surinaamse Genealogie), Geneanet, Ancestry.com and MyHeritage. URLs are listed in the bibliography.

22 Helman, *Facetten van de Surinaamse samenleving* [Facets of Surinamese society], 1977, p. 245.

23 Hoetink, *Het patroon van de oude Curaçaose samenleving: Een sociologische studie* [The pattern of the old Curaçaoan society: A sociological study], 1958.

24 Ibid.

freed.[25] Thus, like in Curaçao, a mixed-race segment developed early on in colonial times in Suriname, which became a separate segment of the population existing in between white Europeans and enslaved Africans.

This group commonly adopted white norms, practices and culture, as argued by Surinamese writer Albert Helman.[26] In these explicit and implicit rules about interracial relations in Suriname, one can observe the same contradiction that Stoler finds in the twentieth-century Dutch Indies: there is an explicit rule that established white endogamy as the ideal, meaning that whiteness is not only superior to non-white but also that white men's allegiance should remain with the white Dutch colonial forces and the goals of dominance and economic gain they pursued. The flip side of this explicit decree is "the unspoken norm,"[27] which, in fact, supports the message of the explicit decree as it dictates that women of color are perfectly fine to perform the household tasks and to provide sexual, physical and emotional sustenance. Yet, women of color could never become the legitimate partner who represents European membership and access to privileges, property and prosperity.[28] Thus, argues Stoler, "it was in the disarray of unwanted, sought after, and troubled intimacies of domestic space that colonial relations were refurbished and their distinctions made."[29]

Recasting Rudolph as white and European thus placed him and his descendants in the realm of European membership. This may have opened up some of the privileges that came with it. Labeling him a man of color, on the other hand, would have denied him all that.

I suddenly remembered having seen an old photograph of Julia. The photo is dated 1917, shortly before Julia's death as an old woman and two years before Sophie's birth. There she was, a brown-skinned woman with an *anisa* (an intricately folded headscarf worn by Surinamese women of African descent) on, sitting amidst three generations of her offspring. The *anisa* is a clear indicator of her African descent; Javanese and Indigenous women dressed differently. It was a poor photocopy of an old black-and-white photograph, so I could not

25 Helman, *Facetten van de Surinaamse samenleving*, 1977.

26 Ibid., p. 245.

27 Stoler, *Carnal Knowledge and Imperial Power*, 2002, p. 1.

28 Ibid., p. 39. Stoler writes: "That prohibitions against interracial marriage were commonly late rather than early colonial inventions (in such diverse contexts as Mexico, Cuba, India, Indonesia, and the U.S. South) suggests that it was not interracial sexual contact that was seen as dangerous but its public legitimation in marriage. Similarly, it was not the progeny of such unions who were problematic but the possibility that they might be recognized as heirs to European inheritance."

29 Ibid., p. 6.

make out her face. But she was clearly not a very dark-skinned woman, nor were her offspring. It is highly likely that Julia was indeed the daughter of a white colonial, but whether her mother Bruinetta had sought after the intimacy or subjected involuntarily cannot be known.

Another archival entry showed me that Julia married the Dutch Carel Constantijn Vervuurt in 1868, six years after her manumission. It is worth noting that mixed-race marriages and marriages between people of color had by then only just become allowed in post-abolition Suriname as they had been strictly forbidden during slavery. I found their wedding announcement in the newspaper archive of the *Surinaamse Courant*, one of the big newspapers during colonial times. She must have left the plantation sometime after being freed, and she spent the rest of her life in Paramaribo as did many creoles after manumission.[30] The ledger only says that Julia and Carel had seven children, including my "white" great-grandfather Rudolf.

The racial label "white" that my family had attributed to Rudolph should be understood within the colorist context in both colonial Suriname and Curaçao. The elastic category of whiteness surfaces in my family history at a time when there was a significant change in marriage laws, which coincided with the onset of a new racial ideology of hybridity and creolization. My family narrative illustrates that, in the early twentieth-century Suriname of Sophie and her parents, the racial category "white" also included light-skinned people of mixed racial ancestry. This label of whiteness became even easier to reach when one had a higher socioeconomic standing or at least adopted the behaviors, norms and values of the lighter-skinned socioeconomic elites, which is where respectability politics comes into play again. I therefore argue that, in these Dutch Caribbean contexts, taking on a white identity is not only dependent upon showcasing light skin color. It also results from one's willingness or even eagerness to subscribe to the nation's hegemonic sociocultural and political order and to demonstrate this through appropriate behavior and allegiance or a performance of "racial passing." The rewards of passing for white are safety, protection and economic but also about "social and political entitlements, and psychological rewards," as American historian Allyson Hobbs has argued.[31]

Most of my uncles and aunts remembered Rudolf and his siblings as white. The aunt who had cared for my grandmother Sophie and lived with her when my grandmother was old did know that Julia was a woman of color and that she had been born into slavery. As my aunt had been closest to Sophie, she had

30 Helman, *Facetten van de Surinaamse samenleving*, 1977, p. 247.

31 Hobbs, *A Chosen Exile*, 2014, p. 12. Editors' note: see also a discussion of this in the contribution by Loewenthal in this volume.

heard many more of her stories than the rest of us. But this was not common knowledge among her siblings and cousins nor part of our family's publicly performed racial identity. In fact, I have never heard my uncles or aunts identify as creole, which, in Suriname, refers to Afro-descendants who live in the city and who have some white ancestry. Nor do I know them as self-identifying as Afro-descendant or black. Never did I hear anyone call my grandmother Sophie creole, Afro-descendant or black. To all of them, Sophie was white.

I had uncovered Rudolph's silenced African background, but what about his wife, my great-grandmother Laurina van Sprang? My mother told me that her grandmother Laurina, or "Madje," and her siblings were all light brown people. This was a story I knew: my mother had always described her grandmother as indigenous and took pride in this alleged non-black heritage. But I would soon discover that Laurina, too, had a silenced genealogy.

Laurina's mother, Maria Jansje Wolfina Murk, had been born into slavery in 1857, to Magdalena Adjoeba Murk (born in 1828), who had been a house slave. Adjoeba was manumitted with her two young daughters in 1862, a year before slavery ended officially. They had lived on the wood plantation La Prosperité. An old newspaper announcement showed that my great-great-grandmother Adjoeba Murk married Georgius van Sprang in Paramaribo. This is where Adjoeba, Laurina's grandmother, lived until her death. Georgius van Sprang appears to have been born in Amsterdam, but the sources vary on that. I wondered if he was a white Dutchman, or if he was a man of color as well, perhaps mixed with the indigenous Surinamese population or with one of the many other ethnic groups that started to arrive in the colony at the time. His name alone did not reveal enough. The marriage announcement only showed that Adjoeba had two more children, two boys, who were born after her manumission but before her marriage. Georgius recognized all four children, which indeed may all have been his own. With the marriage, they all took on his name. Laurina's mother, Wolfina Murk, thus became Wolfina van Sprang, and my family remembers her as a descendent of a well-known white family.

If Adjoeba had been born into slavery, to all likelihood she had African roots. But it is likely that racial mixing—unwanted or wanted—had already occurred before she came around. She probably married a white or light-skinned man, and so did Wolfina. Wolfina married Johan Jacob Willem Muntz, a man from what appears to have been a rather well-off Jewish lineage, who was born and raised in the city of Paramaribo. Wolfina and Jacob had five children together, among whom Sophie's mother Laurina. As Stoler indicates, selecting white partners, or deliberately seeking white intimacies, is a well-known gendered strategy for upward social mobility in a society where skin color used to determine if one was free or property. This strategy supports hegemony as it is premised on the assumption that white trumps black. But can this strategy also be seen as a form of resistance? Across the colonial world, we see that upward mobility did result in a shift in power for people of color, who, in turn, obtained increasing means to safeguard their own. I therefore argue that it is not sensible to try and capture the workings of hegemony and resistance in dichotomies; they present themselves in an intimate entanglement that is so telling for the human experience.

Neither my mother nor my aunts and uncles knew Wolfina's story. They knew that their great-grandmother was not white but had a brown skin, which they attributed to being Javanese or indigenous, labels in Suriname that tend to deflect potential blackness. None of my relatives had heard of Adjoeba or her other children. This reconnection to my forgotten great-great-grandmothers was painful. It hurt me deeply to discover how much of the narratives of my family are premised on silence, perpetuated through censorship, omission, denial and avoidance. A forgetting that was both deliberate and inherited, sustained through six generations. It is also striking, although not at all uncommon, that these silences were on the matrilateral side of our family. In the Vervuurt genealogy that I used as my point of departure, the Afro-descendant women had been left out. I found them in the manumission ledgers, which identify the mothers, who are of African descent, and their children. However, as is quite common to the colonial account, they often present inconclusive information about the fathers, who form yet another censored part of our past. But in this story, these silences also erase the various processes of whitening that our family underwent and the levels of violence that were part of it. Was it rape, a fleeting passionate exchange, forced or voluntary concubinage?

With regard to identity politics, it appears that, when my grandmother and her parents were alive, passing for white was not exceedingly difficult. Their accounts suggest that society encouraged this type of silencing of one's black roots to, instead, subscribe to ideologies that emulate miscegenation, creolization, *mulataje, mestizaje* and non-black racial identities. For both Rudolf and Laurina to respectively pass for white or light skinned with an indigenous (or at least non-black) background suggests that those around them condoned it.

Charles Hale states that "mestizaje has been a remarkably effective ideological tool in the hands of elites in many parts of Latin America, a unifying myth put to the service of state and nation building."[32] This became increasingly important as colonies decolonized, and nations now had to find a narrative that unified white and black, owner and owned, under the same nomenclature

32 Hale, "Introduction," 1996, p. 2.

of "citizen." National myths have had the ability to homogenize, harmonize, indoctrinate, include, exclude and silence. *Créolité*, Hintzen argues, was devised by white elites to obscure racial inequality, colonial exploitation and white privilege. In Hintzen's perspective, "the Creole," then, produces a "discursive space" characterized by the hybridization of specific ethnic, racial, cultural and national peoples and cultures within the colony. Through these discourses of hybridity, differences were "transformed in a regime of identific solidarity."[33] Racial passing neither subverts nor rejects these discourses of creolization, which confirm white supremacy. The colorist systems of Suriname thus encourage passing: the importance of phenotype over ancestry in these multiracial societies dominated by white, and light-skinned, elites allowed for an erasure of black heritage.

The negotiating of racial identity through proposing racial mixedness or even whiteness was—and is—a manifestation of hegemony. It brought certain possibilities for upward social mobility and improved social status while supporting rather than dissolving the racist ideologies and realities upon which these colonies were premised. The cases of my great-great-grandparents illustrate this quite well. Being white was the ideal, and hegemony rewards those who submit to it. However, Stoler argues, "[s]uch a shifting and arbitrary assignment of social membership makes clear that 'European' and 'colonizer' were not always synonymous categories."[34] The significance of whiteness or Europeanness could shift, but that did not automatically coincide with membership to white colonial ranks and with access to their privileges of domination and access to property. Mixed-race people could adopt a "European" lifestyle and adhere to "European" norms. As a consequence, they would enjoy certain possibilities for upward social mobility. Yet, many other privileges were still not available to them.[35]

3 Conclusion: a Complex Tangle of Silences

This contribution seeks to make visible how ideologies of white supremacy shape the most intimate dimensions of lives, often without us being consciously aware of it. These intergenerational family stories highlight the deliberate and unconscious choices people made in the quest to improve their lives, satisfy curiosities or keep themselves safe in the face of—often implicit—racist

33 Hintzen, "Race and Creole Ethnicity in the Caribbean," 2002, p. 92.

34 Stoler, *Carnal Knowledge and Imperial Power*, 2002, p. 39.

35 Ibid., pp. 39–40.

challenges and restrictions. They also illustrate how the colonial ideology of white supremacy shifted over the course of centuries from an explicit to a more covert form, adapting to new contestations by the masses. White supremacy remains a reality in Suriname and Curaçao, shaping people's lives and perceptions of self, even if it is usually not easy to identify it. The mechanisms of racialization meant that the pain of exclusion and oppression were, at times, acutely felt and, at other times, misidentified or normalized. Furthermore, the investigation of silences in my family history shows that hegemony is executed and protected but also challenged by a complex tangle of silences, which entail multiple dimensions of oppression and resistance: our stories are full of silences, generated by censorship, omission, denial, avoidance and resistance. And it is perpetuated through the realm of intimacy, one of the foundational elements in the colonial apparatus. The deeply racialized nature of intimate relationships in colonial and postcolonial spaces informs the place that both elites and the masses occupy in society.

Intimacy is but one of the gatekeeping mechanisms; the family narratives and self-perceptions reveal many more. My grandmother and her ancestors complied with these gatekeeping mechanisms but also sought to omit them and found ways to circumvent the marginalizations and exclusions that they composed.

The main silence is that of our family's black roots, of our black, female ancestors, and thus of the existence of Ajoeba, Wolfina, Bruinetta and Julia and the many others who remain unnamed. Our enslaved ancestors, Bruinetta and Adjoeba, had lived under the yoke of explicit race-based dominance and exploitation, which was wrought with violence and danger. The possibilities of moving away from this detrimental situation were restricted by various gatekeeping mechanisms. Mixed-race marriages were legalized in Suriname at the end of the nineteenth century. It is interesting to note that, once people of color were officially allowed to wed, Bruinetta's and Adjoeba's daughters Julia and Wolfina both married men that were, to all likelihood, white. This may again signal both the power of complying with the Eurocentric norms of respectability as well as a resistance to it. These young women had both been born into slavery and had intimately known the ramifications of the system. In all likelihood, they had been well aware of the fact that marriage to a white man would enhance the upward social mobility of their children and themselves. It will have been a way to find refuge from a system that is rife with legally justified trespassings.

Both my great-grandfather Rudolph and great-grandmother Laurina were born from a marriage between a black (though possibly partly white) and formerly enslaved mother and a white father. Compared to their darker-skinned mothers, the lighter phenotypes of my great-grandparents and of my grandmother allowed them a higher social status in Suriname and later Curaçao, where they moved to. Whether they did so consciously and purposefully or not, they shed their blackness and their connection to slavery over the course of their lifetimes. In the end, through the silence that my ancestors created, we forgot where we came from. But those who initiated this process sought refuge, safety and a better space for those who would come after. The hegemonic value of white-is-better coupled with resistance: still we stand. We are still here. And in the end, we did not forget; we remembered.

Acknowledgments

This contribution is based on research undertaken for my doctoral dissertation, see Roe, "The Sound of Silence: Ideology of National Identity and Racial Inequality in Contemporary Curaçao," PhD Diss., Florida International University, 2016. https://doi.org/10.25148/etd.FIDC000734.

Bibliography

Alexander, Jeffrey. *Cultural Trauma and Collective Identity*. Berkeley: University of California Press, 2004. https://doi.org/10.1525/california/9780520235946.001.0001.

Alexander, Karl L., Doris R. Entwisle, and Carrie S. Horsey. "From First Grade Forward: Early Foundations of High School Dropout." *Sociology of Education* 70, no. 2 (1997): 87–107. https://doi.org/10.2307/2673158.

Ancestry.com. Accessed August 12, 2022. https://www.ancestry.com.

Besson, Jean. "Reputation & Respectability Reconsidered: A New Perspective on Afro-Caribbean Peasant Women." In *Women & Change in the Caribbean: A Pan-Caribbean Perspective*, edited by Janet Henshall Momsen, 15–37. Kingston: Ian Randle; Bloomington: Indiana University Press; London: J. Currey, 1993.

Bourdieu, Pierre. *Outline of a Theory of Practice*. First published in 1977 and translated by Richard Nice. Cambridge: Cambridge University Press, 2019. https://doi.org/10.1017/CBO9780511812507.

Caruth, Cathy. *Unclaimed Experience: Trauma, Narrative, and History*. Baltimore: Johns Hopkins University Press, 1996.

Connerton, Paul. *How Societies Remember*. Cambridge: Cambridge University Press, 1989. https://doi.org/10.1017/CBO9780511628061.

Eyerman, Ron. *Cultural Trauma: Slavery and the Formation of African American Identity*. Cambridge: Cambridge University Press, 2001. https://doi.org/10.1017/CBO9780511488788.

Eyerman, Ron. “Social Theory and Trauma.” *Acta Sociologica* 56, no. 1 (2013): 41–53. https://doi.org/10.1177/0001699312461035.

Foucault, Michel. *Discipline and Punish: The Birth of the Prison*. 2nd ed. New York: Vintage Books, 1995.

Geneanet. Accessed August 12, 2022. https://nl.geneanet.org.

Hale, Charles R. “Introduction.” *Journal of Latin American Anthropology* 2, no. 1 (September 1996): 2–3. https://doi.org/10.1525/jlca.1996.2.1.2.

Helman, Albert. *Facetten van de Surinaamse samenleving* [Facets of Surinamese society]. Zutphen: Walburg Pers, 1977.

Hintzen, Percy. “Race and Creole Ethnicity in the Caribbean.” In *Questioning Creole: Creolisation Discourses in Caribbean Culture: In Honour of Kamau Brathwaite*, edited by Kamau Brathwaite, Verene Shepherd, and Glen L. Richards, 92–110. Kingston, Jamaica: Ian Randle Publishers; Oxford: James Currey Publishers, 2002.

Hobbs, Allyson. *A Chosen Exile: A History of Racial Passing in American Life*. Cambridge, MA: Harvard University Press, 2014. https://doi.org/10.4159/harvard.9780674735811.

Hoetink, Harry. *Het patroon van de oude Curaçaose samenleving: Een sociologische studie* [The pattern of the old Curaçaoan society: A sociological study]. Assen: Van Gorcum, 1958.

MyHeritage. Accessed August 12, 2022. https://www.myheritage.nl.

Rahier, Jean. “The Microphysics of Colonial Power: Violence, Intimacy, and Sexuality in Belgian Colonial Literature.” In *Présence africaine en Europe et au-delà*, edited by Kathleen Gyssels and Bénédicte Ledent, 41–64. Études africaines. Paris: l’Harmattan, 2010.

Rahier, Jean Muteba, ed. *Black Social Movements in Latin America: From Monocultural Mestizaje to Multiculturalism*. New York: Palgrave Macmillan, 2012.

Rahier, Jean Muteba. “Introduction: Mestizaje, Mulataje, Mestiçagem in Latin American Ideologies of National Identities.” *Journal of Latin American Anthropology* 8, no. 1 (June 2008): 40–50. https://doi.org/10.1525/jlca.2003.8.1.40.

Rahier, Jean Muteba. “Soccer and the (Tri-) Color of the Ecuadorian Nation: Visual and Ideological (Dis-) Continuities of Black Otherness from Monocultural Mestizaje to Multiculturalism.” *Visual Anthropology Review* 24, no. 2 (2008): 148–82. https://doi.org/10.1111/j.1548-7458.2008.00011.x.

Rahier, Jean Muteba. “The Ghost of Leopold II: The Belgian Royal Museum of Central Africa and Its Dusty Colonialist Exhibition.” *Research in African Literatures* 34, no. 1 (2003): 58–84. https://doi.org/10.2979/RAL.2003.34.1.58.

Roe, Angela E. “The Sound of Silence: Ideology of National Identity and Racial Inequality in Contemporary Curaçao.” PhD Diss., Florida International University, 2016. https://doi.org/10.25148/etd.FIDC000734.

Scott, James C. *Domination and the Arts of Resistance: Hidden Transcripts*. New Haven: Yale University Press, 1992.

Sheriff, Robin E. *Dreaming Equality: Color, Race, and Racism in Urban Brazil.* New Brunswick: Rutgers University Press, 2001.

Stoler, Ann Laura. *Carnal Knowledge and Imperial Power: Race and the Intimate in Colonial Rule.* Berkeley: University of California Press, 2002.

Thomas, Deborah A. *Modern Blackness: Nationalism, Globalization, and the Politics of Culture in Jamaica.* Latin America Otherwise. Durham, NC: Duke University Press, 2004.

Trouillot, Michel-Rolph. *Silencing the Past: Power and the Production of History.* Boston: Beacon Press, 1995.

White, E. Frances. *Dark Continent of Our Bodies: Black Feminism and the Politics of Respectability.* Mapping Racisms. Philadelphia: Temple University Press, 2001.

Wilson, Peter J. "Reputation and Respectability: A Suggestion for Caribbean Ethnology." *Man* 4, no. 1 (1969): 70–84. https://doi.org/10.2307/2799265.

CHAPTER 17

The Ivory Tower of Women's Studies

Troetje Loewenthal

Abstract

In this lecture originally delivered during the Winter School of Women's Studies at the then called Catholic University of Nijmegen in 1983, the premises of liberal, white, imperial feminism are radically challenged from the vantage point of black women in the Netherlands and the Dutch Caribbean. The text, which appears for the first time in English translation, offers a glimpse of the rifts and transformations in women's studies and in feminist movements in the Netherlands against the backdrop of the rise of right-wing political parties that explicitly embraced a racist and anti-immigrant ideology. In the preface, Loewenthal reflects on the times in which this lecture was written and to which it responded and delineates the nurturing of a feminist consciousness from the vantage point of growing up in both Curaçao as well as the Netherlands.

Keywords

women's studies – race and gender – right-wing political parties in the Netherlands – black women – imperial feminism

1 Preface

I gave the following lecture during the Winter School of Women's Studies at the then called Catholic University of Nijmegen in the Netherlands. The school ran from December 17–23, 1983, and attracted 4,000 participants.

Inspired by the women's movement, a number of universities established departments of women's studies. Like the 1981 summer school, the winter school was a gathering of a wide and varied audience of feminists from the wider women's movement, and its purpose was to present and test the different views of women's studies. There were lectures, workshops and a publication of conference proceedings.

 | DOI:10.1163/9789004690882_019

It was because I'd already spoken out against racism that I was invited to the winter school to give a lecture about feminism and antiracism. For the first time since the Second World War, an extremist right-wing party with a racist and anti-immigrant manifesto had been elected to the Dutch parliament in 1982. That was the moment when the taboo over racism was broken and it became acceptable to express racist views. The organizers of the winter school felt they couldn't allow that to be left uncommented.

My father was a National People's Party (Partido Nashonal di Pueblo, PNP) politician in Curaçao, where I lived until I was ten. The party's founder was Moises Frumencio da Costa Gomez, who, in 1954, was closely involved in developing the Charter for the Kingdom of the Netherlands, which set out terms for a more democratic government of Suriname and the Dutch Antilles and was to signal the formal end of the colonial period.

Politics was important in our home. I can remember the election campaigns, the motorcades in my father's green car (green being the party color), the election posters with photos of Da Costa Gomez, my father making speeches under the lights onstage in Bandabou, the gloom whenever an election failed to return the result we hoped for. And the overarching atmosphere of anticolonialism.

Because I often went with my father as he did his political work, I was very young when I saw Curaçao's social structure alongside the extent of Dutch colonial control. I saw how important class and skin color were among the native population and that blacks were poor. I can still remember being shocked to see a whole family having to live in just one room. The most shocking thing was that the *kunuku* huts didn't have wooden or brick floors, and the people living in them slept on the bare earth.

I remember my own first anticolonial act was to read aloud the line "The Rhine enters *our land* at Lobith …" from one of our school textbooks by substituting it with "The Rhine enters *the Netherlands* …" I recall, too, how upset one of our teachers was telling us about the 1953 Dutch floods. All I could think was, "quite right, too! You see? You're not as superior as you think!"

When I was a student in Amsterdam in the 1970s, I got deeply involved in left-wing politics and contemporary thinking about class-based repression. I was quite into the civil rights movement and had an Angela Davis poster on my wall for years. But I could never express my discomfiture at racism, neither in theory nor in the movement. Because, like a comrade who knew a lot about Marxism used to say, "exploitation is an economic category" and doesn't apply to racism. In those days, no one was making the connection between race and class.

I integrated, as well—or as badly—as I could. I even lost the Brabant accent I'd adopted from the nuns in the private school I'd been to in Roosendaal, replacing it with nicely enunciated proper Dutch. I closed my ears to racist and sexist remarks and laughed sheepishly at the jokes. Like the man I got talking to in a café once: he'd been involved in what used to then be called "police actions" in Indonesia—today widely recognized as war crimes—and who proudly told me how he'd fought "the blues"[1] and boasted of all the *ploppers*[2] he'd shot out of the trees. I let him talk. I said nothing about the racist colonial things he was saying. But it was too much. When I got home, I made a resolution that I'd never take racist talk for granted. My life as an antiracist activist had begun.

I was attracted to feminism not only because it offered a framework to research the unequal status and treatment of women. As a child, I always wondered why the hurricanes that wreaked havoc in the Caribbean all had female names. Were women really so awful and terrifying?

The feminist approach to analyzing the oppression of women also seemed much more promising in its analysis of racism in comparison to classical left-wing thought that focused mainly on class. With my lecture at the winter school, I wanted to highlight the dominance of underlying white perspectives in Dutch feminism and alert the audience to increasing racism in Dutch society.

The lecture during the winter school became part of a historic moment because the Moluccan student Julia da Lima got up and went on stage uninvited during the opening ceremony to denounce the whiteness of the conference agenda. Her action drew great praise from the black women present, who immediately resolved to hold a parallel conference focusing on the perspectives of black women.

Finally, it is worth mentioning that, for about a year after the conference, I continually received threatening phone calls, which I suspected as coming from members of the Centrumpartij (Centre Party]), although I could never prove it. To protect my young daughter and myself, I eventually acquired an unlisted phone number.

1 "*De blauwen*," a pejorative term used by white Dutch people toward people of Indonesian origin.

2 Author's note: "plopper," bastardization of *pelopor*, Indonesian for scout or explorer. In the Indonesian independence war against the Dutch, this term became a negatively connoted term for Indonesian people—another pejorative term synonymous to *de blauwen*.

2 The *White* Women's Movement in the Netherlands

If "the woman is the nigger of the world," what, then, is the black woman?[3]

The women's movement in the Netherlands is a *white* women's movement.[4] That means that, both in the women's movement and in women's studies, the frames of reference used systematically exclude black women.

The point is that it is important for the women's movement to position itself as antiracist because that is the choice now; an antiracist women's movement or a racist one, an antiracist women's studies or racist women's studies. There is no middle way. Racism is so firmly entrenched and such a normalized part of everyday life in general, and academic life in particular, that, in many cases, no one even notices it. Racism is so deeply rooted in Dutch society that every individual must make an active choice to develop sensitivity to racism and a strategy against it, unless one is black because then you've got no choice.

I'm presuming that most people here aren't actively racist and will recognize the most obvious forms of racism, so I shall concentrate on the more hidden forms of racism. I shall briefly sketch my own general experience of how racism has developed in the Netherlands, then I shall draw our attention to two forms of racism that I think are significant to the women's movement, namely the mechanism of exclusion and the so-called "new racism." But first I want to say something about the concept of "racism."

I'm not going to define racism. Racism has so many forms that any attempt to define it is bound to fail. A definition that seeks to cover all forms of racism tends to be too broad; the definition that is too narrow tends to exclude some forms of racism.

An example of too narrow a definition is to think of racism as race-based oppression. Now, the concise nature of that definition makes it seem extremely attractive, but problems emerge as soon as you try to define "race." Before you know it, you find yourself having to think like a racist. You have to say how many races there are and what they are, establish their distinguishing features and define when an individual is "full-blooded," a "half-blood" and so on. Which is precisely why the United Nations International Convention on the Elimination of All Forms of Racial Discrimination includes a wide definition of race, such that "racial discrimination" is understood to include "any

---

3 My question is a riff on the title of the song "The woman is the nigger of the world" (1972) by John Lennon/Plastic Ono Band.

4 I use the terms "white" and "black," although I find them problematic. The lack of nuance in the term "black" (after all, how many truly black-skinned people do you all know?) is at least matched by the fact that the term "white" has a similar problem (for, of course, "whites" are actually pinkish, reddish or yellowish).

distinction, exclusion, restriction or preference based on race, color, descent, or national or ethnic origin."[5]

Albert Memmi offers an even wider definition that seeks to encompass the general mechanisms enabling racism. Memmi believes racism is "a generalizing definition and valuation of differences, whether real or imaginary, to the advantage of the one defining and deploying them, and to the detriment of the one subjected to that act of definition, whose purpose is to justify (social or physical) hostility and assault."[6]

For Memmi, the key point is to expose the roots of *all* forms of discrimination, thus not just racism but also sexism. He is inclined to see it as an inherent trait of humankind, which is actually one of the problematic aspects of his analysis. According to Memmi, "each time one finds oneself in contact with an individual or group that is different and only poorly understood, one can react in a way that would signify a [*sic*] racism."[7]

Other scholars emphasize the distinct manifestations of racism rather than its universal features. Racism of the colonial era differed from racism of our own times, and, even within this period, Spanish colonial racism, for instance, differed from Dutch or British iterations. The racism of today's South Africa is not to be equated with the situation in North America or the Netherlands. Another common misconception is that racism occurs mainly or exclusively in extremist or fascist groups or nations.[8]

However, although there is no simple definition of racism that does justice to all its facets, I would like to emphasize the following: racism doesn't stay the same; its face changes to reflect the historical circumstances, and, even then, we can identify three distinct layers. There is cultural-ideological racism, institutional-structural racism and organizational racism.[9] At the cultural-ideological level, we can speak of ideas, opinions, theories, relationships and the behavior of individuals and groups in everyday situations. The institutional-structural level refers to the government and its branches such as the police and judiciary. At the organizational level, we find localized groupings that are

---

5 "International Convention on the Elimination of All Forms of Racial Discrimination," December 21, 1965, United Nations, Treaty Series 660, p. 195, Part 1, article 1.1., https://www.refworld.org/docid/3ae6b3940.html.

6 Memmi, *Racism*, 2000, p. 100.

7 Ibid., p. 23.

8 Editors' note: the contribution by Roe in this section addresses colorism in the Curaçaoan context.

9 See also: Ben-Tovim, Gideon, "The Struggle against Racism: Theoretical and Strategic Perspectives," 1978.

organized along racialized lines or are racist in practice. I intend to concentrate on the cultural-ideological level.

3 The Mechanism of Exclusion

A distinguishing feature of any ideology is that it determines which observable facts should be considered to be of importance. For example, in a *sexist* ideology, the biological difference, that is possession of female or male genitalia, is seen as one of the most significant pieces of information. Not only is a whole social arrangement based on it, but it actually serves to explain that social arrangement. A *racist* ideology declares another biological difference, skin color, to be the most significant difference between people.

By setting out which characteristics should be considered significant, an ideology ascribes certain values to those characteristics. One set of characteristics is then upheld as the norm, which is considered positive, or normal, or important to possess; other characteristics are then judged abnormal and therefore negative, strange or unimportant. The purpose of this mechanism is to justify a particular way of treating people. The group in possession of the characteristics elevated to norms is considered significant; those not in possession of these characteristics are wholly or partly excluded from the social process and are ignored.

We recognize many forms of sexist exclusion. We are all familiar with the following riddle: A young boy sits next to his father in the car. There is an accident that kills the father, but the boy, grievously injured, is taken to the nearest hospital and immediately rushed to the operating theater. The surgeon comes in, sees the boy and says, "I can't do this operation! That's my son!" So, how can that be?

I've been amazed at how many complicated solutions I've heard people try to come up with! All sorts of family relations, transsexualism, adoption, family break-up, baby mix-up; there's almost nothing too far-fetched for someone to have suggested it. But very few people give the correct and the obvious answer, which is that the surgeon is a woman and, of course, the boy's mother. And that, by the way, is why I'm in favor of feminine forms of names of professions. The exclusion of women from certain professions is so complete that it is deeply enough reflected in the language that, even when a perfectly ordinary usage such as "mother love" is so common, the possibility that a surgeon might be a woman hardly occurs to us.

Another example: consider this passage cited in one of the first issues of *Socialisties-feministiese teksten* (Socialist-feminist texts) and characterized as sexist garbage: "They lived in a commune and a maid did the cooking and looked after the rest of the domestic arrangements." It is worth noting that this passage was cited from the book *Bedrijven in eigen beheer* [Self-organized businesses], published in 1976 by a socialist publishing house.[10]

Examples of racist exclusion are far less known in comparison to cases of sexism. An example of racist garbage is given by Anton de Kom, who criticizes the well-known Dutch socialist historian, H. P. G. Quack. Quack described how, in 1684, the followers of Jean Labadie set up "La Providence" as a religious-socialist plantation colony in Suriname. De Kom pointed out that "Quack, however, failed to mention that these people considered their religious-socialist community compatible with owning and exploiting an army of slaves."[11]

Similarly, the renowned American feminist, Linda Gordon, claimed on Dutch television that American women went to work outside their homes in large numbers only after the second wave of feminism began, apparently not having noticed that, while that might have been true for middle-class white women, it certainly didn't apply to millions of black women. Five internationally reputed feminists took part in the TV debate, and not one of them corrected Gordon.[12]

It is clear from those examples that the enslaved domestic workers could not be counted as belonging to the seventeenth century commune of La Providence. Labadie's ideal of equality, with which Quack agreed, clearly did not apply to enslaved people. Similarly, in Linda Gordon's view, black women were somehow not part of the general category of women.

Exclusion can therefore be political as well as ideological. Thanks to years of actions and initiatives of the women's movement, people are now more aware that women in "democratic" Switzerland were granted the vote only in 1970,

---

10 Sevenhuijsen, Outshoorn, and Meulenbelt, *Socialisties-feministiese teksten* [Socialist-feminist texts], 1978, p. 124; The quote is taken from Frans Becker and Johan Frieswijk, *Bedrijven in eigen beheer. Kolonies en productieve associaties in Nederland 1901–1958* [Self-organized businesses. Workers' colonies and cooperatives in the Netherlands, 1901–1958] (Nijmegen: Socialist Publishers Nijmegen, 1976). The same issue of *Socialisties-feministiese teksten* (p. 206) cites another example of sexist garbage (and, one might also ask, why not racist garbage?): "youth wages, women's wages and 'guest worker' wages remain lower than those of adults, and exert downward pressure on them," which is taken from G. Harmsen and B. Reinalds, *Voor de bevrijding van de arbeid* [For the liberation of labour] (Nijmegen: Socialist Publishers Nijmegen, 1975), p. 406.

11 De Kom, Anton, *Wij slaven van Suriname* [We, the enslaved of Suriname], 1981, pp. 51–52. Translated from Dutch by Marcus Ferley.

12 Deux Pieces, "Deux Pieces (2)," aired February 10, 1983, on NOS.

and, in the Netherlands, this took place not in 1917 but in 1919.[13] But did you know that universal suffrage in the United States was introduced only around 1970? For only then were the "tests" that were mandatory for voter registration abolished in the southern states of the US, which had previously ensured that most Southern black people had, in practice, been denied their right to vote.

All these forms of exclusion based on the nonpossession of the required norms were legitimized by theories, some of which were simplistic remnants of outlived theories and others presented as new and scientific. Both are actually dangerous because neither can exist without the other and both supplement each other. The echoes of outdated theories remain alive as popular myths, and, conversely, new scientific theories derive their credibility from the fact that they appear to explain ideas and feelings that already existed in one form or the other.

Although one might say most women know all about exclusion in both theory and practice, the mechanism has still, here again, worked perfectly at this winter school: I mean; where are the black women?

The application form states: "In setting up the winter school, we've chosen themes emerging from and relevant to the wider society rather than from disciplinary perspectives." Those social themes are labor, image/language/sign, aid and relief efforts, motherhood, non-Western cultures, politics, religion, sexuality and science. And what about black women? Where are they? Years of experience makes me think, "Oh, yes; they're probably in 'Non-Western Cultures'—as usual," even though I don't think of myself as belonging to a non-Western culture. Like my father, I've had a Dutch passport from birth. I'm a confirmed Catholic; I speak Dutch, French, German, English, Spanish; I've read Homer. I even eat with a knife and fork! But ... I'm obviously black, not white, so ... am I not at least a *bit* non-Western ... ? But then I have to laugh because, under the thematic outline of "Non-Western Cultures," I see Kenya, Colombia, Peru, Ghana, Bangladesh, the West Bank, Southeast Asia and ... "Foreign Women in the Netherlands"!

But what kind of a social category is "black women"? And where, then, is the category "white women"? But you've guessed it! It can only be that they are included in all the categories: that must be it! Or am I thinking too dualistically?

13 Editors' note: this extension of suffrage did not, however, include the Dutch colonial territories. Even when the constitutional changes of 1948 were drafted, the extension of universal suffrage to the Dutch Caribbean islands only came to include women after much organized campaigning—as is detailed in the contribution by Groenewoud in this volume.

But it's even crazier than that because, under the heading "Foreign Women in the Netherlands" comes, "The Position of Turkish Women on the Employment Market." I can only conclude that this is a completely different topic from "labor," which includes interesting subtopics such as domestic work, unemployment, economic dependence; things I never knew were specifically "white" problems.

Let's have a look at what else the category of "white women" encompasses. I'll take a quick look through the program pamphlet and let you know what I think:

"Aid and Relief Efforts": well, yes; *we* don't see much of that. "Motherhood": that's just natural for us; it's not something you have to theorize over endlessly. Under "Non-Western Cultures," we find the more specific subject "Family Planning in Bangladesh." Ah! That's much more relevant to us![14] "Education": "Research into sex and class is a central theme." So emphatically not us. You can bet it's about those schools where the white kids all sit together because they're scared all those black kids will lower the standards. "Politics": aha! At last! The word *racism* appears! "Religion": what was that again about the role of church ideology in legitimizing anti-Semitism and Ham, Shem and Japhet? "Sexuality": all that sex-talk! We think it's "dirty"; we don't want anything to do with it, but we are kind of curious about what it says. "Science": come on! Everybody knows we're not scientists! But the science that devises racist theories? Shouldn't more attention be paid to that? "Housing": no research necessary there; we live in the Bijlmer neighborhood in Amsterdam or in old neighborhoods in the big cities, or we've got to be rehoused and our population spread out. Everyone knows that!

Enough sarcasm …

In any case, it's clear that, just by creating a category of "Non-Western Cultures," a total segregation between white and black women is created; and, via this detour around non-Western cultures, skin color reemerges as a significant distinguishing feature.

Turkish, Moluccan and other women in the Netherlands are not seen as having enough in common to justify belonging to the same category.

What is the ethnocentric theory here that is so ingrained that neither the organizers of this winter school—other than at the eleventh hour—nor the white women here noticed it? It's an unconscious frame of reference that

14 The confusion seems total; women in Sri Lanka suddenly appear as a subtopic of "Motherhood."

white culture is so superior to black culture that there's no real need to take black culture seriously.

Ideological exclusion is the first step on the slippery slope of racism for it determines which groups are to be considered worthwhile and which are not. It also determines which characteristics are to be taken as norms, strengthening the sense of "us" in the dominant group and defining everyone else as "them." But ideology is both word and deed; it is a way of speaking that prepares the way for exclusion, a way of treating people facilitated by a way of speaking.[15] Women of the section "Image, Language and Sign," are you still there?

4 Historical Experience

We know all about ethnocentric theorizing because every immigrant to the Netherlands is used to fairly quickly learning something that most Dutch people aren't aware of, namely, that their society is racist and discriminatory and that the much-celebrated Dutch tolerance is pretty disappointing in practice. A number of facts are known about anti-Semitism and the persecution of the Jews but not much about the role Dutch people played in it. Did you know, for example, that the Netherlands expelled 75 percent of its Jews? Did you know that this was a higher percentage than any other Nazi-occupied country? France expelled 25 percent of its Jewish population.

I learned about colonial racism in the Antilles, where we were forced to rinse our mouths if we were caught speaking Papiamentu, our native language, and where the white Dutch lived separately from us, had their own swimming pools and clubs and beaches out of reach to us blacks, with barriers to keep us out.[16]

Then when I was ten, I came to the Netherlands—and I was cat-called, insulted and laughed at in the streets. In those days, too, Surinamese and Antillean students were refused rooms, and, without good reason, the police used to stop and search Surinamese and Antillean men going about their business. Meanwhile, the old concentration camp at Vught was used as temporary accommodation for Moluccans.

All these experiences were talked about and shared within one's own communities, and, although there was little actual contact among these groups, we all assumed that the others, in the meantime officially titled as

---

15 See Memmi, *Racism*, 2000, p. 113.

16 Editors' note: on the issue of first language education, see contribution by Linda Richardson in this volume.

"allochthones"—oh! the blessings of civilization—all experienced much the same sort of thing.

That such experience of racism was kept behind closed doors had various reasons. On the one hand, we were ashamed to acknowledge what was going on. Perhaps it was possible that individuals were somehow doing something that was causing other people's racism? Perhaps people felt guilty that they had failed to integrate sufficiently and that was what had prompted the racism. (We all suffered from the "raped women" syndrome). On the other hand, however, people were all too keen to believe the official line that there was no racism in the Netherlands. They called their experiences isolated incidents, involving a few people who "didn't know any better," and felt they should rise above them. But perhaps the strongest motive for their silence was that everyone knew they would get no empathy from white Dutch people.

However, despite what was far from a pleasant situation, and however difficult it was to stomach this sort of daily racism, the Dutch would have nothing to do with it—officially at least—which led to the situation where racist articles in response to Indonesian immigration were not printed in Dutch newspapers.

If, until the 1970s, our view of Dutch society was that it had a racist mentality that was certainly present even if suppressed, during the 70s, we began to see that slowly change. The rationale that Dutch businesses had brought foreign workers to do the dirty work disappeared slowly but surely from the discourse to make way for the idea of the foreigner as a problem. "Guest workers" became an ethnic minority as did all non-whites along with them, and the Netherlands now had another problem.

The fact that the so-called guest workers were housed in overcrowded, flammable boarding houses or barracks on their employer's property with all kinds of restrictions that made the accommodation look like an internment camp had never been regarded as a problem. It was even less of a problem that landlords were asking extortionate rents for housing entire Surinamese families in single rooms. No, of course not. Problems arose only when these guest workers, who had, in the meantime, become "allochthones," brought over their wives and families—from whom many of them had been separated for years—and, after bidding farewell to the fellow sufferers they'd shared beds with in shifts, after having to deal with all sorts of bureaucratic red tape, were offered an apartment in some run-down neighborhood, only then were foreigners defined as a problem for, again, racist ideological thinking determined what mattered. Not the housing shortage, not the dilapidation, not the greedy landlords, not the crisis; no, the foreigners were the problem, and chiefly because there were "a large number" of them.

That is a racist way of presenting a problem. The transformation from exotic guest to resident had triggered an ideological transformation. It was not "the minority's" factual living circumstances but the dominant group's subjective sense of that minority that was elevated to the essential characteristic of "the minorities."

Such was the climate into which the Centrumpartij arrived. For the first time in the post-war history of the Netherlands, a political party with a program based on racism saw an opportunity to penetrate parliamentary politics as fully-fledged discussion partners. Drumming on the nonissue of the foreigner as a problem, the party fanned the flames of existing feelings of fear and repugnance at foreigners, offering as the "solution" to the "problem" a more or less coherent ideology amounting to "Foreigners Out!" Most importantly, the Centrumpartij adopted a two-pronged strategy. They espoused a façade of decent intellectualism in parliament that they both combined with and used as a cover for the violent gangs they were also organizing.

5 A New Racism

Organizationally then, we can locate racism in the Centrumpartij, but it is more complicated to see why the behavior of the party led to the presence of racist attitudes on the political agenda. But it did cause a shift in mainstream political thinking such that racist remarks and points of policy were no longer perceived as racist. We can sum up the Centrumpartij's more or less coherent ideology as being based on the notions that:

a. There is such a thing as a homogeneous indigenous Dutch culture, which is indissoluble from the Dutch state.
b. Foreigners are strange for they have a different culture.
c. Different cultures are by nature mutually exclusive.
d. Therefore, it is quite natural to feel hostile to a foreign culture that is threatening to one's own.

In 1982, the Centrumpartij began its election campaign with the following words: "The Dutch state derives its right to exist from the dynamic growth and sustenance of Dutch culture as it has unfolded throughout Europe's history in adherence with Christian and Humanist norms."[17]

17 "De nederlandse staat ontleent zijn voornaamste bestaansrecht aan het behoud en het dynamisch uitbouwen van de nederlandse kultuur, zoals die zich in de loop van de europese geschiedenis volgens christelijke en humanistische normen en waarden heeft ontwikkeld." See: Centrumpartij/Middenweg, "Partijprogramma samengevat in 10 punten" [Party program summarised in 10 points], 1982, p. 4. https://dnpprepo.ub.rug.nl/287/1/Partijprogramma%20CP%201982.pdf. Translation by Marcus Ferley.

According to Martin Barker, it is the idea that different cultures cannot tolerate each other and that a natural instinct demands a hostile reaction to the effects of other cultures on one's own that forms the kernel of this new racism.[18] In this worldview, nations do not come into existence based on political and economic developments but grow "organically" on a particular territory.

It is now becoming clear that the comprehensive lack of awareness of the racism fully woven into Dutch society is coming home to roost. When the first signs of virulent racism reared its ugly head, the rationale went as follows: the Dutch aren't racist people, so something must be misleading them, or they were simply poorly informed. The misinformed or poorly educated Dutch must be offered the right information, then matters would improve. The tensions in the older neighborhoods were explained as arising from people not being acquainted with the different cultural habits of the foreigners living there. Everyone ought to be educated about the particular characteristics of the different ethnic groups from Suriname, and everyone must have some knowledge of Islam. But never a word about racism.

If racism was ever mentioned, it was exclusively with reference to the Second World War. Nothing about immigration policy, nothing about everyday anti-Semitism. Nor was anything said about the Dutch ministry that refused to use the term "migrants" for black people because of the logic that "the Netherlands isn't a land of immigrants" and, instead, proposed the term "allochthonous minority."[19] The most significant thing about them, after all, was that they were "different" or "foreign."

The antiracism policy was thus designed to inform the Dutch about other cultures, cultures that were strange and not like theirs. The so-called "native" or "autochthonous" culture was clearly presumed to be a given and well-known. As a result, people who were, for instance, unaware that, unlike the Antilles, Suriname is located on the South American mainland, now felt able to explain the most minuscule differences between creoles and Hindustanis like fully qualified anthropologists. People were educated about Islam in a similar way. Those who had never had any interest in religion, who had never even made the effort to find out anything about Christianity, suddenly appeared to be experts after watching a TV program or looking through a few brochures. The particular interest in Islam and the immense fascination it seems to have aroused sometimes create the impression that we're at the brink of a religious

18 Barker, *The New Racism*, 1982.

19 Amersfoort, "Migratie-onderzoek, overheidsfinanciering en beleid. Aantekeningen van een participant" [Migration research, government funding and policy. Notes from a participant], 1983, p. 138.

war. A modern crusade, with Alfred Vierling from the Centrumpartij as our own Richard the Lionheart!

Feminists will have to be extremely wary of the attention Islam is getting, because anti-Islamic attitudes often appear under a feminist guise, like in the 1980 article in *Middenweg* (The middle way), the Centrumpartij's magazine, with the title proclaiming that "women's emancipation has regressed by four hundred years." The article claimed that Muslims have medieval views of women and that most Muslims are abusers and rapists, such that Dutch women would no longer dare to go out on the streets.

On the other hand, feminists themselves, in any interactions they have with Muslim women, appear to be most interested in how Muslim women's husbands repress them. A woman interviewing Turkish women in a filmed segment for the TV program *Kijk haar* (Look at her) declared out loud, "We know absolutely nothing about you except that you are oppressed by your husbands!"[20] It's no wonder that this was the only thing the interviewer knew about Turkish women, and she proceeded to ask nothing else but questions about their oppressive husbands. Even the fact that the residence permits of Turkish women brought to the Netherlands are dependent on those of their husbands was presented in such a way that the undoubtedly sexist Turkish husband was given the blame and not the obviously sexist Dutch legal system that had come up with the rule.

There are evident signs that xenophobia is assuming the form of an opposition to Islam under the pretext of standing up for women's rights. Women are being mobilized to the racist cause through arousing sentiments against supposed Islamic inclinations to polygamy and the social backwardness of women. As Wim Couwenberg from the Centrumpartij phrases it: "You can hardly expect us ... to accept the structural discrimination against women such as is seen in Islamic circles as being completely normal."[21]

---

20 *De Volkskrant*, October 16, 1982. Editors' note: we were unfortunately unable to locate this particular article, so the citation has been left as in the original publication. However, readers are assured that a quick glance at newspaper archives will show that many articles about Turkish women appeared to the same effect in the early 80s.

21 Ischa Meijer, "Rede der droom" [The reason for the dream], in *De Volkskrant*, November 26, 1983, p. 2. The paragraph from which the quote is taken is as follows: "Some aspects of feminism are general, others are specific. Incidentally, the great problem for women is currently not so much men, capitalism or communism but mainly Islam, which is on the rise around the world in an unbelievable manner, and of which we have a fifth column in our midst in the meantime. It would be horrific for women in Western Europe as well if we would give Islam the free rein." Translated from Dutch by the editors.

6 Conclusion

This is an ideology based on white norms that, at best, leads to blind spots in the questions asked and, at worst, to outright racism. My intention here is not to call upon women to interrogate their own racism in their social groups; rather, it's about exposing an ideology that legitimizes oppression. Beware of all forms of racism; intervene when you're confronted with racism, whether it's on the street, at the bakery or in academia.

As far as women's studies is concerned, it would be good if research could be done into the mechanisms of exclusion, which would contribute to our knowledge about the real differences that do exist between women.

The systematic exclusion of "non-white" women from women's studies produces not only limited knowledge, but, more importantly, it produces a racist knowledge where it is taken for granted that white women's positions can be generalized to all women and where the culture, identity and material circumstances of white women are left unchallenged.

Acknowledgments

I would like to express my gratitude to Meindert Fennema. This is a translation of a slightly amended version of a lecture held in Dutch on December 21, 1983, for the Winter School for Women's Studies at Nijmegen. It was originally published as Loewenthal, Troetje. "De witte toren van vrouwenstudies." *Tijdschrift Voor Vrouwenstudies* 5, no. 1 (1984): 5–17. The new preface was written for this volume. Translation by Marcus Ferley.

Bibliography

Amersfoort, Hans van. "Migratie-onderzoek, overheidsfinanciering en beleid: Aantekeningen van een participant" [Migration research, government funding and policy: Notes from a participant]. *Grafiet*, Autumn 1983.

Barker, Martin. *The New Racism*. London: Junction Book Ltd., 1982.

Ben-Tovim, Gideon. "The Struggle against Racism: Theoretical and Strategic Perspectives." *Marxism Today*, July 1978.

Deux Pieces. Episode 2, "Deux Pieces (2)." Directed by Don Rook, moderated by Annemarie Grewel. Aired February 10, 1983, on NOS.

"International Convention on the Elimination of All Forms of Racial Discrimination." International Treaty. United Nations Treaty Series. New York: United Nations

General Assembly, December 21, 1965. https://www.refworld.org/docid/3ae6b3940.html.

"Interview met Ischa Meijer" [Interview with Ischa Meijer]. *De Volkskrant*, October 26, 1983.

Kom, Anton de. *Wij slaven van Suriname* [We, the enslaved of Suriname]. Bussum: Wereldvenster, 1981.

Memmi, Albert. *Racism*. Minneapolis: University of Minnesota Press, 2000.

Sevenhuijsen, Selma, Joyce Outshoorn, and Anja Meulenbelt, eds. *Socialisties-feministiese teksten* [Socialist-feminist texts]. Amsterdam: Sara, 1978.

CHAPTER 18

Graduate Research Report on the Position of Curaçaoan Women Working at Texas Instruments from 1968 to 1976

Sonia M. Cuales

Abstract

How did the rise in women's employment in Curaçao affect their lives and social realities? This study was undertaken in 1977 and investigated the impact of labor opportunities on the lives of women employed by Texas Instruments (TI), an American electronics company established in 1968. Using in-depth interviews and participatory observation, the author sampled the position of forty-three women employed at TI for at least three years and triangulated the findings with data from government sources. During the 1960s, TI employed approximately 1,600 women as operators and shop stewards. The study examined how women's positions in the household were affected by their working conditions, considering aspects such as childbearing, caregiving and social networking as well as women's productivity, their consumer behavior and financial relationships with their husbands. The report also looked at their reading habits and relation to mass media.

Keywords

Curaçao – labor – women's working conditions – households – social networks

1 Introduction

When I was in Curaçao in August 1976, I noticed that the position of women employed at Texas Instruments (TI) were constant topics of conversation. I found myself thinking about a thematic interest: the social position of women and regional interest in the Caribbean. This combination of theme and region immediately made me think of the phenomenon of traditional household groups.

 | DOI:10.1163/9789004690882_020

If economic interests have always influenced the lives of Afro-American household groups, was it possible that a significant improvement in women's economic positions might have changed their positions in the household? And in the particular case of Curaçao, might Texas Instruments have influenced a situation of that sort? What, in fact, do we see happening there? A large number of women with virtually no prior education and/or work experience were deemed ready to offer their services as labor to Texas Instruments, which is especially keen on attracting women workers to whom it can offer low wages. About 1,600 uneducated women have been employed by Texas Instruments. It is the first time so many women in Curaçao have been hired for industrial work. It therefore seemed interesting to see whether participation in industrial labor has caused any change in the traditional position of women in the household group.

The research, carried out as a pilot study, was done on the island of Curaçao from January 3 through February 10, 1977. The specific question addressed by this study is participation in modern employment and how it affects the social and economic positions of working-class Curaçaoan women.

Taking the family group as a unit, we are going to examine the social and economic positions of women within it. Women in this group fulfill various kinds of functions: there is the biological function of procreation, the social and caregiving functions (social networks and information gained from mass media) and an economic or productive function.

2 Procreation

At the time of the research, the 43 women sampled had 106 children in total, of whom 21 were born while their mothers were employed by TI and 3 in the period after their mothers' employment. It appears that none of them used contraception before their employment by TI, but that changed to some extent when they began working there, with contraception becoming more commonplace as the years passed.

There is a discrepancy between stated preference and actual practice. Since beginning to work at TI, women have had fewer children, which strongly suggests that the TI women have deliberately chosen not to have children and taken care not to. [...]

Actually, regardless of the matter of contraception, we see that there has been a marked reduction in the number of births throughout the island over the last twenty years. Data from the Foundation for the Promotion of Responsible Parenthood (Famia Plania) reveal that in the year 1975, 130 TI women used the foundation's services through the suboffice within the TI factory—which amounted to 28.2 percent of the 457 women working at TI in 1975. In our sample, 23.3 percent of respondents indicated that they had actually taken steps to make sure they had no more children while working at TI, which differs a little from the percentage mentioned above.

Given that there were 37,724 women of childbearing age on the entire island in 1975, we can see that 2,026 of them (5.4 percent) made use of the services of Famia Plania. This is a smaller percentage than those who worked at TI. Bearing in mind the possibly doubtful usefulness of those statistics for such a comparison, we might well still conclude that a greater proportion of women working at TI sought assistance from Famia Plania than did the rest of Curaçao's women, perhaps because the TI women found it easier to do so thanks to the counseling office located within TI. All the women interviewed thought they should have at least two children, and all thought, according to their cultural values, that their children should be born within marriage and preferably all to the same father. The facts, however, revealed a completely different picture. Of the forty-three women, twelve were married and thirty-one unmarried; and of those thirty-one unmarried women, twenty-four had children and seven did not. Of the twenty-four unmarried women, eleven had children by different fathers. [...]

In almost all cases, the intervals of pregnancies and births were approximately the same: on average eighteen months to two years, give or take a few exceptions of four years and upwards, indicating that the woman concerned was not in any long-term relationship with one man and that the children were the result of casual relationships.

3 Caregiving

3.1 *The Household*

There were certain household tasks in and around a house that women had to do. Some of them were general housework such as shopping, cleaning, doing the laundry and ironing, while others were required only on smallholdings with a few animals or crops, such as in the districts of Bandariba and Bandabou. Whether a particular woman did most of those tasks in the three periods depended in the first place on her place in the household. If she was the senior person, then most of the work fell on her shoulders. In the time of TI, therefore, she took measures to ensure she herself did most of the organizing and left the bulk of the actual work to the other female members of the household and the older children. If she wasn't the senior figure, then things were different. In some households, both before and after TI, the work was divided randomly, being done in turn by her or by other members of the household, or they were shared. During the TI period, most women in this group gave up nearly all such caregiving functions as they simply didn't have the time.

Many women who were not the senior household figure actually did no housework, and that was true in all three periods. It was noticeable that it were mostly the unmarried young women without children who said that they never had to do any work. Their mothers, aunts or grandmothers did everything themselves. One respondent who married after leaving TI said, "I never had a chance to do anything at home. My mother did everything herself. In the kitchen, I couldn't even pick up a saucepan. If my mother was sick or had to go away, she'd have my grandmother or my aunt come around. But, now I'm married, I do everything myself. And I can do it perfectly well." During an interview with another young, unmarried, childless woman, her mother interrupted, saying: "no, ma'am; my daughter doesn't have to do any work, because we see her as our princess" (*ta nos prinsesa e ta*).

3.2 *Children*

The child-rearing function includes a number of tasks, activities and responsibilities, which were taken on and carried out by different members of the household.

Although in most cases the mother assumed most of the burden, it was never a matter of trial and error because—as convenience and necessity dictated—others in the household helped out. Sometimes, this led to enormous changes if the mother went to work at TI but not always. Some women organized the time more efficiently both before and after work. In that sense, no clear trend can be seen. However, we did notice that it closely matched the characters and physical capabilities of individual women. One might well suggest two categories: one who found working at TI so challenging and exhausting that they were in no condition to do anything else either before or after work; and another category who never found work too much, and who could still do a great deal outside of work.

It is possible that this might all have been connected to diet, commuting time and many other factors. We started by thinking shift patterns would be the determinant because we could imagine that someone working the 12 pm –8 pm shift would be more tired and able to do less during the day than someone on, say, 8 am – 4 pm or 4 pm – 12 am. It should be noted that people worked the same shifts year in, year out with no variations in working time. However, that presumption turned out to be wrong, because we found similar proportions in both categories of women in all three of the possible shifts. [...]

Where women had been solely responsible for domestic work before they went to work at TI and shared them while at work—with mothers, aunts, sisters and the woman next door, for example—the "help situation" with relatives has stayed the same for most of them. "Oh, the children are used to it by now!" was something we often heard said to explain actions that perhaps earlier might have indicated regression to and reinforcing of traditional patterns of behavior. Many women handed their children to mothers, sisters, aunts or godmothers, or the children were "snatched" by childless relatives, as one of our respondents put it. But the same thing went on before TI as well. And, in as much as it happened while women were employed there, while it might have been the easy solution for a mother, her job at TI wasn't the reason for it.

Only four women had always managed on their own and continued to do so. It appears, therefore, that there has been no great change in women's caring functions, although that isn't quite true for taking the children out and general upbringing, including discipline and social control. The majority had never taken the children out and that remained so. However, for those who had been accustomed to taking the children out alone (nine in our research group) or who took them out accompanied by their husbands (four in the group), this habit more or less completely ceased during TI. Trips used to include a bus ride to the airport, the Proeftuin (gardens with farm animals) or perhaps the Coney Island amusement park.

Going out completely stopped during their TI work for mothers who did everything alone because they simply couldn't manage it. "Sunday is your only day off, and even then only when you don't have to work a full shift. And then you've got to do so much: the laundry, ironing; you've got to do your hair and all that. There's just no time left and no energy to take the children out." Going out also ceased for those few husbands and wives who took the children out together during their time at TI, unless the husband had a car—in which case (there were two such cases) they still went for an occasional joyride with the children. In the time after TI, nothing at all happened any more in those two cases. The two cars concerned were old tubs and had broken down anyway, and there was no money to repair them. Those women who, directly or indirectly, hadn't been able to do so do not take their children out now, first of all because they're now old enough (they're talking about children of eight, nine and eleven years) to go out on their own with their friends. But they also feel they've become lazy with all the sitting around the house and don't find it so easy to go out any more. [...]

Raising the children was primarily a woman's task, and men had very little to do with it—unless a man lived with a woman and therefore, as father or partner, had the right to discipline the children. During employment at TI, children's upbringing was not supported by fathers or other men but was taken on by mothers, aunts, older sons or daughters and older sisters and brothers. Mothers, then, resumed the role after work hours at TI.

3.3 *Men*

As far as men who lived with women were concerned, whether legally married or not, all caregiving tasks were done by women, both before and after TI. Women working 8 am – 4 pm or 4 pm – 12 am made sure dinner was ready before they left the house, so all their husbands had to do was to heat it up and put it on a plate when they felt like eating and perhaps give some to the children. During the TI time, that was all a man had to do for himself. In all three periods, the majority of men did not live with their women and so the women did nothing for them.

The caregiving function with regard to men therefore remained unchanged during TI, as women worked even harder to "fulfill their duty" as fully as possible. If any woman did not manage to do so, her husband might forbid her from going to work! We interpreted this as a show of power, but, as one of the women remarked, in fact, men were all too happy that their wives were able to earn their own money.

4 Social Networks

Activities considered to be social network maintaining functions were: visiting friends and relations, parties, church attendance and visiting the sick and bereaved.

During the period when women worked at TI, there was a noticeable reduction in all such activities—which people explained by pointing out that they were no longer able to manage all that and go to work—although people did continue to try to find time for visiting the sick and offering condolences. And it was generally agreed to be regrettable that, during TI, most people found it impossible. [...]

Church attendance also declined. The relation between this and employment at TI is evident. However, it emerged that a few of the respondents had not only stopped going to church but had left the Catholic faith and became Jehovah's Witnesses or joined the Seventh-Day Adventists (a type of conversion that our informants indicated was growing in the general population). Where we found this to be the case in our research, respondents from those neighborhoods told us that it was very common. No connection with TI was found, however. This pointed to a partial explanation at least for this group's reduced participation in dance parties. Respondents and informants confirmed that, indeed, Jehovah's Witnesses and Seventh-Day Adventists do not go to dance parties. At first, we found the decline surprising, because we had always assumed that, in Curaçao, there would never be a shortage of people going dancing!

The picture we saw was actually rather more complex. Of the forty-three women, fourteen never or hardly ever went dancing even before they worked at TI—for reasons such as lack of contacts, their children being too young, their husband not liking dancing and so on. Such reasons were never mentioned for the TI period, when the usual response was, "Too tired!" And twenty-five of the forty-three did not go dancing during that time. After TI, even fewer went dancing: twenty-eight of the forty-three. They gave as reasons, "all the sitting at home makes you lazy and reluctant to go out. Plus, you need the right clothes and if you're out of work you can't afford to buy them."

During TI, a certain number of those who had been accustomed to going out stopped doing so because they became "too tired." Of the ones who never went out, a number now did go out, because they had got to know a lot of people and made friends who invited them out—something especially true of the women working the 4 pm – 12 am shift, most of whom took their party clothes with them and changed after work at midnight, ready to go out. All that stopped after TI, and people hardly see their former colleagues any more. Mostly, other activities were fully abandoned during TI, the reasons most commonly given being exhaustion and lack of time.

Although those reasons were no longer present after TI, we saw no significant increase. [...]

5 Productivity

Incomes in the sector were no more than fifty to sixty Antillean guilders per month for housemaids and ninety to hundred guilders per month for shop assistants. The rest earned far less. Prior to TI, working conditions were those of the informal sector.

During TI, a number of women attempted to earn extra money from other sources besides their steady jobs. There were two categories of such women. The first category tried to earn money in the informal sector and off the TI premises: working part-time as seamstresses or selling items of crochet work and embroidery they had made and doing ironing. The second category developed business activities in their workplace: such as running illegal lotteries, dealing in clothing and jewelry from Colombia and Venezuela and selling homemade cakes and pastries etc.[1] and selling frozen meat and chicken they had acquired wholesale (ham at Christmas, tinned vegetables, fruit juice and so on). There was certainly no lack of commercial instinct. Incidentally but significantly, four out of five of the research subjects were in the second category.

During TI, many people played *sam*, a group savings scheme. A settled group of, say, nine would each pay in an agreed sum for ten months. Taking turns, each of the members collected what all nine of the group had contributed minus one month, amounting to her own full contribution minus one month. The remaining tenth month's money paid in by everyone was then given to the organizer of the *sam*, who therefore was the one who made money while the others could benefit from the total contributed sum at a time that suited them. And on the subject of commercial instinct, it wasn't always the case that the women working at TI, who did business on the side, were doing it on their own accounts. They sometimes acted as intermediaries for their mothers, aunts, husbands or other acquaintances.

With the exception of one woman, who continued her crochet and gambling businesses, all other side activities done during TI have stopped.

1 Editor's note: the author lists the following local dishes: *repa, pastechi, johnny cake, adelicia, kokada, tentalaria.*

The woman who did ironing part-time stopped for health reasons. She suffered a collapse while at TI caused by her working two jobs and was told by her doctor to stop doing the ironing work, just at the moment when she had even greater need of it. The seamstress and the two women who sold their own work had seen their market disappear. "Our colleagues at TI were our customers and they were always there; but now you don't see them anymore, so there's no point."

The group that was commercially active, including those among the research subjects, told us they had stopped their commercial activity because "there's no market now, because we don't see each other anymore and anyway there's no money to buy stock." Our informants told us that this category of people was quite large at TI, and their activities were widespread. "No matter what crazy thing you could think of, there'd be somebody going round the factory selling it." And the research subjects themselves were quite happy to tell us about all this. [...]

The women therefore developed a great deal of commercial activity among themselves within TI, which, for the practical reasons mentioned, had not existed previously and could not be continued afterward. [...]

We see that, after TI, one woman went to work as a road sweeper. We had seen for ourselves in our observations of the island that there were women working as road sweepers in cities. Our informants had said that almost all of them were former TI employees, and when we found a woman street sweeper among our respondents, we tried to gain more information from her. She then introduced us to three other women who had also gone into the same work. We were therefore able to form a general picture of this new situation, which seemed strange to us, to say the least, for the following reasons. First of all, we knew that the question of "honor" played an important role in an individual's work situation. Second, we already knew that women in Curaçaoan society had never done this work. Third, we had the impression, from what we knew of the mentality of that section of society, that their sense of self-respect would lead them to eschew anything that would make them feel inferior, so that we should not see them doing anything of the sort.

It became clear to us from talking to these women that they had themselves found it less than easy to do it. It was their great need and necessity of finding a way to support themselves and their children that had induced them to take the step, an extremely important component of which had been their encouragement of each other and the positive attitude of those around them. The fact that they found, as they did their work, that they did not have to deal with the derogatory remarks from passersby, such as they had expected and feared, only made things easier for them. In fact, they told us proudly that the city's shopkeepers had given them a big thumbs-up and said they did the job better than the men! [...]

They and others were able to tell us that hundreds of women, including many former TI workers, had applied to the public cleaning department for street sweeping jobs. For these women, the pay was relatively good in comparison with other suitable work. According to word-of-mouth information we obtained from officials, on April 1, 1977, thirty-five women were working as street sweepers, of whom twelve were former TI employees. Those women were not replacing men who had left the job or been dismissed but had been taken on quite simply to bolster the ranks. They earned the same money as the men, although it was true that male sweepers tended to be transferred to the garbage truck service and were assigned to sweep on the late shifts. The women swept only during the day.

The unemployed group were doing nothing at all at the time of the research. A few of them had made various attempts to secure incomes, always in the informal sector, as babysitters, doing laundry work or working in a Chinese restaurant. They also sold items on commission for various businesses or sold illegal lottery tickets. None of these jobs lasted more than four weeks—they were either fired or found the work disagreeable. [...]

Most people were at home when I called on them. Quite often, at random times of day, the women would be in bed when I came. Yet, they were always prepared to talk to me. It seemed they saw it as a diversion from their idleness and wanted me to come back for a few more chats. They spoke almost nostalgically of their TI time, as a mixture of pleasant and unpleasant experiences.

It was a period of physical and mental exhaustion; some had trouble with their eyes after the years of staring down a microscope for hours on end, day after day. There was something paradoxical in nearly all of their remarks that they were glad to be able to take things easy but that, if a similar company were to set up in Curaçao again, they would immediately apply for a job there. [...] People seem to forget the tiredness and lack of sleep (many of the night shift workers had been unable to get enough sleep during the daytime), but they didn't forget that it had been a time when people could support themselves, and they remembered the possibilities that opened up for them all. Life got better for everyone; people could buy what they needed, the children could go to school regularly and people could save with the credit union. [...]

6 Consumer Habits

We saw a significant expansion of their consumption pattern during the TI period. People could afford much more in terms of food, clothing and extras than they could before TI. One thing that increased greatly during the TI time was the purchase of large items such as cars, fridges, washing machines and furniture. In the less built-up areas, people built houses—or completed the building of them—and began new building projects. One might think that the women were earning astronomical sums at TI to make all this possible—and, certainly, before TI such expenditure was scarcely possible if at all. However, nothing could have been further from the truth: people were earning 100–150 Antillean guilders per fortnight. In fact, it is the way people could afford such expenditure that leads to an understanding of the situation. Many people saved up with the credit union to be able to afford the first down payment, and a job at TI was sufficient guarantee for local businesses to deliver all the desired items on credit—which was widely used. People were less concerned about the duration of credit agreements, so that when TI disappeared, many people found themselves with articles that were far from being paid off and which they could hardly pay off now that they had lost their incomes.

A few had put money aside during the years they worked. Most of these people lived in the outer districts rather than in the city. But the majority had not done so. A good proportion of the fortnightly wages went to illegal gambling, food, snacks and the trinkets being sold in the factory by many of the workers. All of it on fortnightly installments that could not be avoided because the creditors were on the spot demanding their money on pay day. Payment of wages in fact was done on the premises, where the bank operated a dedicated branch. [...]

One informant told us that, for many of the women, this was the first time they had earned their own money and were unaccustomed to having regular access to so much of it. With so much money in their hands, and with so much being offered for sale both in the factory and outside of it, they had the greatest difficulty in establishing priorities and in realizing that certain payments, such as those for gas, electricity, water, rent and so forth, must take priority over new clothes, shoes, wigs and the like. As a result, many people found themselves in continual difficulties in spite of their earnings.

In comparison with the time before TI, people shopped for food in the same shops and supermarkets, although they found it easier to open accounts with them while they were employed by TI. During TI, some people started buying their clothes from boutiques, although they were the exceptions among the research subjects.

None of the research subjects had bought large items since losing their TI incomes, and, in fact, most had reduced their expenditure to the absolute minimum.

People traveled much more during their employment at TI. They went to Colombia, in the first place for medical assistance but sometimes combining these trips with a holiday. For normal holidays, most of the group went to other islands, like Aruba, Bonaire, St. Maarten and Santo Domingo. For just a short period, people went to Venezuela; the trip was usually intended as a "business trip."[2] [...]

7 Economic Relations with Men

We looked into the extent to which women were financially bound to men, and how those relationships worked in the different periods. Family and household costs were borne by the man who was married to a woman or lived with her—and, for those families, a woman's TI income bolstered the family budget. In this area, there was a small but noticeable difference between women in more urban areas and those in less urban areas such as Bandabou. The first group attached great value to the fact that they now had their own income and could do what they wanted with it without having to involve their men. For the other group, it was more about supporting their husband financially so that they could achieve more together, such as building a house. In cases where a man was not a member of a household, the woman concerned was not financially supported by him, which the women concerned considered to be of no matter, saying, "it wouldn't be right." Before TI, such women were completely dependent on mothers, brothers, sisters or other members of the household. A woman with children received money for them from the respective fathers. If fathers failed to fulfill financial obligations to their children, the mothers could apply to the child welfare board to compel them to. The child welfare board would not be called in if:

2 Editors' note: business trip here refers to the practice of buying cheap goods in Venezuela to resell at home.

a. the husband had no steady job. Some women were of the opinion that some men took care not to have a steady job, so that the child welfare board would not be able to approach them. That was quite commonly seen among professions such as bricklayers, carpenters, mechanics, cab drivers and the like, who were self-employed with no permanent customers;
b. if the husband happened to have won a larger amount of money (through illegal gambling, on the Venezuelan horse races or betting) and provided a sizable sum for the children. In such cases, a woman might prefer to have a one-off hundred guilders than a regular thirty guilders a month. Because, if she reported her man to the child welfare board, "I'd lose him altogether!";
c. if the woman was convinced the husband would contribute. She lived in complete uncertainty of how much he might give her and when, but she had faith because … "E ta juda si" (He does help out).

One informant compared such a relationship to the belief of "good Catholics" in a saint from whom they expect some favor or other. If people can only exercise patience and never lose faith, they'll get their favor one day, but they must be careful not to do anything to incur the saint's disfavor. Women in that category always stand by their husbands. They never call in the child welfare board and months might go by when they receive nothing at all. This remark by one of our respondents says it all: "He does help out … not regularly, because sometimes he is restrained … I mean, it's been nearly three months now since I received any money."[3]

Similar situations were obvious to us and confirmed again and again by our informants, and, in a way, they prove the weakness of women's positions, which follows on from their precarious economic situation and from considerations of social prestige.[4] […]

8 Mass Media

Almost everyone owned a radio; no-one listened to specific programs, it was just on all day. Most of those who owned a television tended to watch live shows and telenovellas that were shown four or five times per day. A lot of people read the papers but only the local news and ads.

3 "E ta juda si … , no vast, pasó e sa hanjele strobá … , aworaki mes ta mei' tres kuna ku mi no a hanja sens." Translated by editors from Papiamentu.
4 Henry and Wilson,"The Status of Women in Caribbean Societies," 1975.

There was little change in this pattern before and after TI—although, during TI, people rarely spent time at home and couldn't watch nearly as much. If people read anything other than the papers, it were graphic novels and things such as *True Story*, *Selina*, *Chicas*, *Joyas Romanticas*, *Idylle* and *Story*,[5] which, in certain remote parts of the island, were often peddled door-to-door. Some women read less while they were employed by TI than they had before, because they were too tired or didn't have time. Others actually read more, because they swapped magazines with their colleagues, had long bus journeys or read during down time—although such women were a very small minority. Most people were pretty indifferent to the possibility of being able to read, listen to the radio or watch TV. Everyone simply accepted that the possibilities for doing so were much fewer during TI. Absorbing information from the media privately within the household gave way during TI to verbal and more intellectual contact with colleagues.

The closure of TI came as a huge blow to most of our respondents. The overwhelming majority of them have not been able to find a source of income since and have fallen into deep poverty. Psychologically, it is impossible for them to deal with, and the women in rural districts, such as Bandabou, most of all feel their personal dignity has been greatly affected. The way they were put on the street shocked them to the core of their humanity and self-worth. In fact, when they turned up for work as usual, they had found the gates locked and were told they weren't even allowed in the facility; the business was permanently closed. Later, they received checks in the mail for their pay arrears.

Acknowledgments

This text consists of translated excerpts from a Dutch master's thesis originally published as Cuales, Sonia M. "Verslag van een candidaats-leeronderzoek naar de positie van de Curaçaose vrouw die bij Texas Instruments heeft gewerkt in de periode from 1968 to 1976" [Graduate research report into the position of Curaçaoan women working at Texas Instruments during 1968–1976]. Master's thesis, Leiden University, 1977. The text has been minimally edited and omissions have been marked with ellipses. Additional footnotes have been added by the editors for clarification. All numbers and data are cited directly from the original and so given without notes. Translation by Marcus Ferley.

5 Editors' note: magazines with serialized drama stories, popular in the 1970s.

Bibliography

Cuales, Sonia M. "Verslag van een candidaats-leeronderzoek naar de positie van de Curaçaose vrouw die bij Texas Instruments heeft gewerkt in de periode 1968–1976" [Graduate research report into the position of Curaçaoan women working at Texas Instruments during 1968–1976]. Master's thesis, Leiden University, 1977.

Henry, Frances, and Pamela Wilson. "The Status of Women in Caribbean Societies: An Overview of Their Social, Economic and Sexual Roles." *Social and Economic Studies* 24, no. 2 (1975): 165–99.

CHAPTER 19

From the Womb: Reflections on Single Motherhood in Curaçao

Jeanne Henriquez

Abstract

As part of a study originally conducted in 1990–1991, Henriquez interviewed forty working-class Curaçaoan women, mostly single mothers, and invited them to write letters and poems to their loved ones. An analysis of these writings reveals how coloniality, race, gender and class are experienced at a personal level. What are the values that shape and inform poor women's attitudes toward different forms of oppression? How do women construct their social identities and find self-esteem in the face of these hurdles? Based on a selection of writings on the mother–child relationship, Henriquez argues that the problem was not single motherhood in itself but the financial burdens of unsupported female-headed households and the increasing isolation they faced from the extended family network. The writings attest to the resilience and solidarity of the women interviewed and equally reveal an absence of awareness of the historical and structural reasons for oppression.

Keywords

Curaçao – oral history – working-class women – mother–child relationship – female-headed households

1 Researching with Working-Class Women in Curaçao

In 1990–1991, I conducted a study of how coloniality, race, gender and class are experienced and how the struggle for individuation is expressed in the daily lives of women of Curaçao. I was interested in the values that shape and inform women's attitudes toward different forms of oppression. I was eager to understand how women construct their social identities and find self-esteem in the face of these oppressions.

 | DOI:10.1163/9789004690882_021

Many books have been published on the problems of race, class and gender. Theorists such as Frantz Fanon, Aimé Césaire and Albert Memmi have elaborated on the consequences of colonialism on the mentality of the colonized. Fanon eloquently demonstrated how colonialism and racism feed each other. He argued that colonialism has created a milieu that fosters neuroses, alienation and inferiority complexes, creating in the psyche of the colonized an irresistible attraction toward the colonizer and his way of life. Fanon stated that the Antillean had lost his self-initiative and creativity, thus becoming alienated from himself and his culture.[1] This analysis of Fanon partly helps me understand the starting point of consciousness of colonized people, in my specific case the women of Curaçao. Fanon, however, focused only on one side of the dialectical process, namely the disfigurement and dehumanization of the colonized people by the "mother country." He failed to see that the relationship is one of love–hate. The love relationship creates self-denial, the alienation that Fanon described in such depth, ranging on a scale of emotions from shame to self-hate. Yet, the hate relationship creates contempt, repulsion and the mockery of the culture of the oppressor. This is a way for the oppressed to fight back, and this is what creates women's cultures of resistance.

In the study, I conducted interviews and group discussions with numerous working-class and middle-class women in Curaçao. I also invited them to write poems and letters to a loved one. The present contribution is a revised extract from one of the chapters of the dissertation, in which I interviewed forty working-class women in Curaçao, several of whom were single mothers living on social welfare.

Informed by theories of African-American feminists and thinkers such as Fanon and Paulo Freire, I used the materials generated in the process of research to name, describe and comprehend the reality of these women's lives. The theories were tested and grounded in the actual experiences of the women participants. Guided by feminist standpoint epistemologies, I interpreted the individual forms of exploitation exposed by the women as manifestations of oppressive social relations. This methodology also deployed as the starting point and a guiding principle my own subjective response to multifaceted discrimination and the rebellion against it.

The materials gathered reveal a constant tension between the contradictory aspects within the lives of the participants, which informs their self-image, reflecting both their strengths and weaknesses, the authentic and the imitative, the Antillean and the European and societal norms and the rejection

1 Fanon, *Black Skin, White Masks*, 1967.

of these norms. A second conclusion is that the uniqueness of each personal history must be taken into account in understanding women's experiences of oppression. No primary force of oppression can be identified. All the different forms of oppression intermingle within the person; the particular configuration of most felt forms of oppression differ even within the same social class.

It also became apparent that, although there are many similarities between women of the working classes and of the middle class within this society, there are also many differences. The voices of the women of the poorer classes were more direct, whereas the women of the middle class spoke with what is called a "golden tongue," often preferring indirect forms of speech.[2] On the other hand, there was more reflective thinking on the part of the women of the middle class on several themes, including a sense of historical transformation. This was generally absent within the speech of the women of the working classes. Their voices were more in the present and concrete.

By making these poems and letters public, women in our society acknowledge that their experiences have social origins, that, although their lives are unique, their problems are not. Most importantly, they will realize that they ought not to blame themselves and feel guilty about "mistakes" committed.

By showing the specific dynamics of our situation, old concepts will have to be reformulated to generate new insights into our social reality and to identify the differences and similarities of forms of oppression and survival mechanisms of women of Curaçao within a semicolonial society. The purpose of this analysis is to name and to make visible the differences of experiences and patterns of consciousness of women from different social classes within Curaçaoan society. It remains my conviction that examining our own experiences will allow us to not only empower ourselves but also share our knowledge with sisters from other countries of the transnational feminist movement.

2 Letters to a Dear One

As part of the research process, I asked all women to write a letter to a loved one, whoever that may be, including themselves. In this letter, they would open themselves up to this beloved person and tell them what worries them most and express what gives them joy. Most of the women were part of an educational program sponsored by a nongovernmental organization called Ayudo Social (Social Aid). Some of them were participants in a government-sponsored

2 Editors' note: see contribution by Römer in this volume on the significance of *forma di papia* (ways of speaking) in studying gender and sexuality.

cultural program for welfare recipients. Many, if not most of the women, were single mothers. They gathered once a week to educate themselves either at Ayudo Social or at the district community center Seroe Fortuna (Fortune Hill). Having worked as an instructor for several years with Ayudo Social, I learned to value these women's experiences and to derive strength from the testimonies of their lives. Although the monthly food packages distributed by the project offered a means to supplement their meager incomes, these gatherings were also socially significant to most women who attended—the discussions were always lively, therapeutic and forged a sense of community.

Of the forty letters I collected, nineteen were notably addressed to one or more of their children. Several letters also included a discussion with a mother, sister or female friend; five letters were addressed to "brother" and "friend" Jesus; two letters were addressed to the self and twelve letters were addressed to a male partner. This confirms what several studies have already shown, that even if women give sexual preference to a heterosexual relationship due to the prevalent heterosexual cultural norms, their emotional preference and bonding tend to be with other women and/or children, with whom they feel they can express themselves freely.

The process of research taught me to scrutinize my own middle-class cultural stereotyping of poor women. Being a single mother myself, there was a common ground of solidarity, but, as a middle-class woman with the privilege of a good education, I had to learn to understand the complex feelings attached to poverty. The problem of those labeled as "unwed mothers" was not in the mere fact of being unmarried but in the financial burdens of unsupported female-headed households and the increasing isolation they faced from the extended family network. They taught me the role of laughter and humor as survival mechanisms. I learned not to view them with pity, because being poor does not mean being miserable. I promised to write about their lives in a way that would do justice to their reality, that would not be belittling or ridiculing. The present study is an attempt at that endeavor.

Although these women did not have a writing tradition, all of them tried their best to open their hearts on paper, even if it meant writing only a few lines. The letters were not written in neat paragraphs, the structure was often not linear, featuring incomplete sentences and repetitions, and were written in the style of spoken language. This led me to the question of whether the letters might more aptly be approached as poetry. Reading Daphne Patai's *Brazilian Women Speak*, in which interviews with Brazilian women were transcribed in poetic structures, I developed the idea to present the letters as poetry, to arrange seemingly ordinary words in ways that call attention to their poetic and expressive dimensions.[3] The language of the letters was creatively approached to accentuate the images the woman wants to construct in her letter. Following Clifford Geertz, Daphne Patai argues that the task of understanding peoples' inner lives is akin to the interpretation of poetry or proverbs and fiction.[4] Such a view challenges the assumption that literary value resides in "high" cultural texts alone.

There were several recurring themes in the letters, with kinship, partnerships, spirituality and class relations being some of the outstanding ones. In the following, I highlight some of the letters that dealt with the mother–child relationship.

In *Of Woman Born*, Adrienne Rich emphasizes that, while motherhood is the experience of women, the institution of motherhood has historically remained under male control.[5] Rich thus distinguishes between the experience of motherhood in contrast to the institutional aspects of motherhood. This distinction allows for a discussion of what has been done to women as mothers under patriarchy as separate from what might be the experience of women as mothers when detached and freed from the bondage imposed by male domination. Motherhood involves suffering and deprivation for most women under patriarchy. Yet, even under these conditions, the experience of motherhood could suggest an alternative since it contains within itself the potential for great creativity and joy. It is not women's capacity to reproduce that led to women's enslavement but the fact that motherhood had become integrated into the system of male political and economic power over women. Among the elements of the institution enumerated by Rich are marriage as economic dependence; the concept of the "illegitimacy" of a child born out of wedlock; the laws regulating contraception and abortion; the inadequacy of childcare facilities in most part of the world; the nature of fatherhood, which gives a man rights and privileges over children toward whom he assumes minimal responsibility; and the burden of emotional work borne by women in the family. This list blends together the physical, or material, the legal, the economic and the psychosocial, including the attitudes of those considered as experts toward mothers as well as the attitudes internalized by mothers toward themselves. Rich marvels at the fact that, despite all the constraints of motherhood, women have retained and developed capacities of resistance to male power.

3 Patai, *Brazilian Women Speak: Contemporary Life Stories*, 1988, p. 18.

4 Ibid., pp. 32–33.

5 Rich, *Of Woman Born: Motherhood as Experience and Institution*, 1976, pp. 274–80.

Motherhood has great social significance in Curaçaoan society. A woman without children is widely seen as an incomplete woman. However, many childless women are and have been functional mothers in our society, playing the role of aunties or caregivers in the broadest sense. Literary images of motherhood in writings by men tend to revolve around the strength of the mother under stress. A good example is the poetry collection of the deceased Hubert Wanga with the title *Dolo di amor* (Pain of love).[6] The societal attitude toward mothers is one of both idealization and degradation. The mother's role in the family is symbolic of societal contradictions in attitudes toward women. We still need to describe the multidimensional character of motherhood within our culture, exposing the complexity of experiences and how motherhood is affected by class and colorism in our society. With their books *Je kunt maar beter bij je moeder blijven* (Better to stay with your mother) and *Mama soltera* (Single mother), Anke van Dijke, Linda Terpstra and Hans van Hulst have started a discussion departing from the standpoints of poor mothers in our society and not the Eurocentric viewpoint of many researchers before them.[7]

The reality of many mothers of Curaçao is that of being the heads of households, living in or close to poverty and rearing children who do not have the basic necessities of life. These mothers are clearly under attack, despite claims of the sanctity of motherhood.[8] The research analyzed nineteen letters written by single mothers and styled in poetry form. These not only reflect the love and tenderness of the mother toward her children and concern for their education but also speak of the dependency of the mother on the child, of how these young lives break the solitude of the mother and give her life meaning. The tension between mother and child in the child's search to establish their autonomous self is another recurring theme, and some letters expose the dire effects of poverty that impedes the education of their children.

It becomes clear from most of these letters that the crucial relationship in the lives of these women is with children, closely followed in intensity and importance with the relationship with their own mothers. One woman expresses her love for the child of her sister, whom she helps to educate and fears being separated from. Another speaks of the intensity of bringing up children:

> I love my children
> When they are there

6 Wanga and Monsanto, *Doló di amor* [Pain of love], 1984.

7 Dijke and Terpstra, *Je kunt maar beter bij je moeder blijven: Ongehuwde vrouwen met kinderen op Curaçao* [Better to stay with your mother: Unmarried women with children in Curaçao], 1987; Dijke, Hulst, and Terpstra, *Mama soltera* [Single mother], 1990.

8 Editors' note: see contribution by Do Rego-Kuster in this volume.

They satisfy me, yet they tire me somewhat
Do not be impudent,
Let's go to sleep
My loved ones.[9]

The mother is the embodiment of two tendencies: there is the urge to love and bring up a child or children of one's own, but there is also the need for children to fulfill the mother's own desire and pride:

Children,
I hope all the best for all
of you.
I want you to study well at school
Keep your attention in the classroom
Do your homework before you play.

Then you take a nap,
Calm your mind,
Afterward you can play,
but first you take a bath,
put on clean clothes
before you go to bed.[10]

The letter-poem continues with a list of daily instructions to the children. Since the mother has no understanding, no control and no participation in the education of her children, all she can offer is the framework of discipline to study. Helping the children perform better at school is presented as essential not only for the sake of the children but for the mother's own pride and self-esteem. Similarly, another letter speaks of the mother's own learning journey together with her children:

I walk with Lidia
to the animal park
we walk around the park
we see and learn about

---

9 Mi ta stima mi yunan / debi cu ora nan tei / nan ta teneimi contentu / nan ta cansami un poco / stop di hasi vrijposter / ban drumi / mi amornan. Editors' note: The women's writings do not conform to the standard orthography of Curaçaoan Papiamentu.

10 Mi yunan / muchanan mi ta desea / tur ko bon pa bosnan / sina bon na school. / Let op den klas / hasi boso huiswerknan / prome ku hunga. Kaba drumi un tiki / sosega e mente / despwes atardi / por bai hunga un ratoe / anto mester banja promo si.

different types of animals,
how each of them develops,
the name of each type
of animal of Kòrsou
or from another country
later we write a report about
everything we saw:
what the animals do
and how they develop.[11]

After the abolition of slavery, education was almost the only means for people of color to escape poverty and exploitation. All over the Caribbean, parents made enormous sacrifices to send their children to school and urged their children to seize all educational opportunities open to them as schooling became a sign of social mobility. At the same time, the combating of illiteracy and the need for possibilities for adult learning for women is still in its nascent stages.

Many times, the hope to create a better future for the children is thwarted because of poverty. In order to provide good schooling for her children, the mother must put her pride aside to try to get what is necessary for the children. The anguish of a mother, who, despite all her efforts, must seek help to pay for her child to get extra private lessons, resounds in the following letter:

I'm a woman who loves herself
Who likes to work
Herself into perspiration
To get what is needed,
Yet
It is a pity
That I need help now
...
After finishing paying the
Electricity bill,
The rent, water, telephone

11 Ma ta hasi un pasejo ku Lidia / bai na parke di bestia / haci un pasejo ront di e parke / conoce y mira tur / tipo di bestianan / con cada unu ta deseroya / con yama cada un tipo di bestia / cu ta di Korsou of otro pais / y despues traha un opstèl / di tur loke e ta mira / e bestianan ta haci / of con nan ta desaroya nan mes. Author's note: all names have been anonymized.

The money left over is not enough to eat

There is a school bill of f.95
I do not have the money to pay it
Love of one's neighbor does not exist for me.
That is all.[12]

The strength resounding in the first part of the letter is absent at the end of the letter. She is frustrated by the overwhelming powerlessness of her situation. The constant economic worries make it impossible for her to tolerate her child's supplementary needs. It is one thing to not have the money to pay for extra tuition for the child, it is another thing when it is difficult to get the money together to pay for daily expenses such as food or transportation to school. This existential concern is echoed by another mother in her letter:

Good day my loved ones,
I love my children
I love my cousins
I love my children,
But I do not have anything
For them to eat.[13]

What is expressed in several letters is that the problem of single motherhood lies not in the very fact of being a single mother but rather in the high demands placed on oneself, the difficulties of coping and the anxieties of not fulfilling the basic needs of life. The above short letter not only reveals that society does not value women but also that it inflicts violence on children by denying them their basic rights.

The letters reveal the importance of a strong kinship network that supports poor women in their daily survival and in raising their children. As Jane Price has argued in her book *Motherhood*, a number of studies have concluded that it is the quality of the interpersonal relationships, particularly with other women, that makes the difference in coping or not, particularly during the early childhood years.[14] The letters collected in the research depict women

12 Mi ta un muhé / cu ta stima mi mes / cu stima traha/ ku sodo di mi frente/ pa logra loke ta necesario/Tòg/lastimamente/mi mester di yudansa awor/Despues di paga elektrisidat,húr,awa,telefòn/kasi no a sobra sèn pa kome/Tin un debedi skol di fl 95,-/Mi no tin sèn pa pagé// Mi ta kere / ku amor pa otra a kaba pa mi / pwes asaki ta tur kos.

13 Bon dia amor nan / mi stima mi yunan / mi subrina i mi subrinonan / mi stima mi yunan / pero mi no tin nada di come pa nan.

14 Price, *Motherhood: What It Does to Your Mind*, 1988, p. 110.

being role models for their daughters. This model is of particular importance to these women as a way of gaining self-respect. They also illustrate the interdependence in the relation of women with their mothers and other women where it concerns the care of their children. Many have the assurance that their mother will always be there to support them. This strong tie between mother and daughter that emerges in these letters must also be viewed in the framework of the societal expectation for children to take care of their parents in their old age. Mothers often tend to nurture the secret hope that their daughters will mother them. The following letter-poem with the title "A lasting friendship between two women" can be interpreted in the context of this bond of love and mutual support between women.

> There is nothing so beautiful as
> Having someone who cherishes you
> And with whom you can share
> Your happiness and sadness
> There is nothing more
> Beautiful than to remember
> These moments with a person like you.[15]

Adrienne Rich characterizes these bonds between women, not necessarily materialized in sexual experience, as the lesbian continuum, arguing that the absence of male dominance and male power makes the relationship more egalitarian.[16] In the letter cited above, what is most praised in the friendship of these women is the sharing of pain and happiness. The following letter, which one of the women dictated to me, offers another example of the support and kinship shared by women:

> Dear Friend …
> I hope that you as an aunt
> can watch over my child
> when I go to Holland.
> When you do this, God will
> bless you, because you have

15 No tin algu mas bunita / di komparti momentonan di tristeza i di legria / koe un hende koe sa di apresia bo. / Pero no tin algo mas bunita di / recorda e momentonan ey koe un hende / bon manera abo.

16 Rich, "Compulsory Heterosexuality and Lesbian Existence," 1980.

helped him on the good road
I go "for the doctor"
but I hope to be back soon
depending on my health.
If the doctor says that I cannot come back
I will come and fetch my child.[17]

According to the social security system of the island, it is possible that if medical attention cannot be given to a specific illness there, a person can travel to the Netherlands to receive treatment. In this case, the woman asked her friend, who happened to be the sister of her child's father, to give her a helping hand by looking after her child. These letters are evidence of the crucial bonds and support networks between women that sustain the lives of single mothers.

3 Conclusions

The primary concern of these writing mothers is with survival. Their mode of thinking is contextual and narrative rather than abstract and formal. Their ways of knowing are oriented to the present, to the concrete, to the specific. There is a constant uncertainty of what the day will bring tomorrow. The letters, however, do not recognize or address the sources of conflict and distress. A lack of class consciousness and critical consciousness hinder the women from seeing the root causes of their problems. That is why, for instance, the woman who has to pay for extra lessons for her son does not criticize the school system that is supposed to be free but, instead, obliges her to pay if she wants to see her son stay in the race. The letters reveal the problems of the school system in terms of the individual difficulties faced by children but do not reveal how the school system is itself part of the problem. Yet, although class consciousness is absent in these letters, the women nevertheless challenge patriarchal norms and values. They do not express self-pity or regret for being single mothers. Rather, their problems are structural: not having access to the means of survival for

17 Estimada amiga … / Mi ta spera ku abo, komo tanta / por tuma un bista riba mi yu / ora mi bai Ulanda. / Ora bo hasje / dios lo bindisiona bo / pasombra ba yudé den bon kaminda. / Mi ta bai pa dokter / pero mi ta pensa di bin pronto bèk / dependé di e salut. / Si dokter bisa mi no por bini bèk / anto e ora e / mi ta bin buska mi yu.

sustaining their families, poor education, heavy dependency on others for the most basic needs and the emotional burden this brings them.

Although most of the letters reflect the frustration and emotional insecurity in their chaotic daily lives, not all women fall prey to a sense of powerlessness. The letters bear testimony to the brightness, joy and laughter in their lives as mothers. The letters radiate a tenderness toward their children, accompanied by a sense of responsibility guiding the mothers' decisions on the children's futures, a concern for raising children to become responsible citizens themselves. The maternal sentiment connects to the public task of developing life and a better society. The letters reflect hope for the future. At the same time, there is an undertone of fear concerning how the children will grow up. The language of instruction and discipline becomes the means of protecting children from the perils of the world. In the context of Curaçaoan society, where womanhood tends to be equated with motherhood, especially for working-class women, becoming a mother offers the only possibility to grow and develop the self through raising children. For many women, it is also the only place to receive and experience genuine love, thus the only arena where women can hope to not be confronted with oppressive situations.

The normative ideal of the self-sacrificing mother is also widely expressed in the letters; however, in the way this norm is experienced, the letters reveal a sense of disequilibrium between the responsibility toward children and the need to care for the self in order to make it possible to maintain a level of responsible caring. The grinding effect of poverty on the lives of several women stands out in the letters. Those who learn to cope and develop survival mechanisms succeed because of the social networks of family and friends surrounding them. These friendships have an emotional and material function of support. Those who miss these ties of support perceive themselves as highly vulnerable.

The letters also present motherhood as providing insight into the value of life, which is the cornerstone of freedom. Being a guardian to a child cannot be the sole responsibility of the mother. The norms of the individualistic society assume that a woman ought to look after children alone, even when there is a male partner, day after day without damaging her psyche. The satisfaction of a job and the access to other adults without the continuous presence of children, together with the possibility to develop her other potentials, make her capable of relating to her children in a healthy way.[18] Yet, a society that

18 Price, *Motherhood*, 1988, pp. 126–30.

does not value women likewise turns a deaf ear to its children. In other words, society casts off its own future by not valuing women.

That is why being feminist means recognizing that welfare is also a women's issue and raising a child is a societal issue. It is not enough for feminists to sit on our laurels and simply expect affirmative action to come from the government. It means demanding an end to the barriers of employment faced by women today. It means demanding that women's work and contributions to the nation and the world be honored. It means building a movement against women's poverty. It means rediscovering the communal spirit where the values underlying the work of motherhood are held in high esteem. It will be a society where people care for one another.

4 Reflections Three Decades On

In revisiting a study I conducted thirty-three years ago for the purpose of this publication, the first thought that came to mind was the current well-being of the women who participated in writing their letters, drawing their bodies and engaging in intense discussions about their own lives as part of my oral history research. How are they faring now? Has there been general progress for women who have to raise their children alone? Has the world become more just for women who face significant challenges surviving in a colonial society? To what extent would the context for a similar study today be different? Would I choose different research methods today? Has my perspective as a feminist changed? I close this contribution with a brief reflection on some of these questions.

After returning to Curaçao from the United States in 1991, I continued to stay in contact with two or three of the women who participated in the research, in particular one woman, now deceased, who proudly reminisced on her achievements as a mother and shared with me the career successes of her children despite the barriers of an unjust world, thus making her feel that her efforts were not in vain. However, most people I interviewed have not been able to escape the pool of poverty. Women who have to raise their children alone are overrepresented in the population groups living below and just above the poverty line.[19] On the other hand, the percentage of women in the labor market

19 The recent government statistics on subjective poverty levels in Curaçao indicate that the poorest section of the population continues to be female-headed single-parent households. Maduro-Jeandor, *Armoede: Een subjectieve benadering* [Poverty: A subjective approach], 2019, p. 12.

has significantly increased, including in higher positions.[20] Women form the majority of students in tertiary education institutions. Notwithstanding these developments, the economic structure of society remains one of injustice, with limited opportunities for upward mobility, especially for those without a diploma, without work and with limited resources to start their own businesses. Educational policies continue to be influenced by colonial paradigms. Some former decolonial leaders have grown weary and even chosen a different ideology; conflicts within the social movements in Curaçao abound. We can conclude that the situation has improved for women at large but not significantly changed for women who raise their children alone and live on welfare, especially in areas such as education, healthcare and housing. The woman who has to raise her children alone, often without the biological father fulfilling his obligations of child support, remains the most affected. The political vision and strategic plan to alleviate poverty and disadvantages for a large part of the population are still absent. The lack of decolonial political leadership needs to be addressed.

The context in which I would like to conduct future gender research in Curaçao has thus not significantly changed.

I remain committed to Black feminist perspectives and specifically the idea of "theory in the flesh." My own independent research practice of the last decades has convinced me of the importance of cultural heritage as part of a holistic research framework. What we want to analyze should be based on the knowledge we have gained from our daily practice. When setting up our research, we need to incorporate our cultural heritage into our methodologies as it helps us better understand the issues at hand. Rather than propose abstract solutions to problems, the emphasis should be on investigating the creative solutions that communities have devised themselves. Gender studies continues to have a Eurocentric bias and tends to implicitly foreground individualist explanatory frameworks. The relative neglect of the instruments of cultural heritage leads to a skewed picture of our research results. My experience is that the creative and unabashed use of our own cultural expressions helps us acquire knowledge about the needs and problems of the communities we research, especially in their gendered dimensions, thus supporting the quest for solutions for the sustainable development of our society. This means that our starting point is the people's own experiences based on their cultural heritage. Research methodologies must thus address questions related to the

20 See Central Bureau of Statistics Curaçao, "De ontwikkeling van de werkloosheid in de periode 2014–2022" [The development of unemployment in Curaçao in the period 2014–2022], 2023, p. 8.

creation of a humanistic and decolonized society and serve to construct new paths of justice.

In conclusion, thirty-three years after conducting the research on motherhood in Curaçao, I can state that my perspective as a Black feminist remains focused on contributing to the construction of a just world, promoting equality between humans and advocating for women in practice, with a focus on the youth who shape the future without neglecting the role of educators such as parents, grandparents and teachers. I am grateful to all the women who contributed to the development of my master's thesis. A better world remains possible with the efforts of international social movements, including those of Curaçao.

Acknowledgments

This contribution is based on research undertaken for the author's unpublished postgraduate dissertation. Henriquez, Jeanne D. "From the Womb: Curaçaoan Women Speak Out about Their Identity." Master's thesis, George Washington University, 1991.

Bibliography

Central Bureau of Statistics Curaçao. "De ontwikkeling van de werkloosheid in de periode 2014–2022" [The development of unemployment in the period 2014–2022]. Curaçao: Central Bureau of Statistics, 2023. https://cuatro.sim-cdn.nl/cbscuracao/uploads/de_ontwikkeling_van_de_werkloosheid_in_de_periode_2014-2022.pdf.

Fanon, Frantz. *Black Skin, White Masks.* New York: Grove Press, 1967.

Henriquez, Jeanne D. "From the Womb: Curaçaoan Women Speak Out about Their Identity." Master's thesis, George Washington University, 1991.

Maduro-Jeandor, Ellen. *Armoede: Een subjectieve benadering* [Poverty: A subjective approach]. Report on the results of the 2016 budget survey. Curaçao: Central Bureau of Statistics, 2019. https://cuatro.sim-cdn.nl/cbscuracao/uploads/231019-publicatie-armoede-een-subjectieve-benadering.pdf.

Patai, Daphne. *Brazilian Women Speak: Contemporary Life Stories.* New Brunswick, NJ; Rutgers University Press, 1988.

Price, Jane. *Motherhood: What It Does to Your Mind.* London: Pandora, 1988.

Rich, Adrienne. "Compulsory Heterosexuality and Lesbian Existence." *Signs* 5 (1980): 631–60.

Rich, Adrienne. *Of Woman Born: Motherhood as Experience and Institution.* New York: W.W. Norton, 1976.

Van Dijke, Anke, Hans van Hulst and Linda Terpstra. *Mama soltera* [Single mother]. The Hague: Warray, 1990.

Van Dijke, Anke, and Linda Terpstra. *Je kunt maar beter bij je moeder blijven: Ongehuwde vrouwen met kinderen op Curaçao* [You better stay with your mother: Unmarried women with children in Curaçao]. Leiden: KITLV, 1987.

Wanga, Hubert R., and Tony Monsanto. *Doló di amor* [Pain of love]. Willemstad: Editorial Kooperativo Antiyano "Kolibri," 1984.

CHAPTER 20

Cracks in the Glass Ceiling: Opportunities, Barriers and Strategies for Women in the Labor Market in Curaçao and Aruba

Paula Kibbelaar

Abstract

The contribution analyzes the underrepresentation of women in managerial jobs in business and government in Curaçao, using the conceptual tool of the glass ceiling from a financial-economic perspective. How does this underrepresentation come about and how does it affect women's participation and position within the labor market? It charts the factors that sustain and reinforce the glass ceiling in the context of Curaçao, namely ambitions, family support, broader social networks, organizational cultures and gender-sensitive institutional policies. It operationalizes the notion of the "thickness" of the glass ceiling to examine barriers in the upward mobility of women from middle to higher career levels. It concludes with reflections on recent developments in gender equality in Aruba, thereby marking substantive cracks in the glass ceiling in the last decades.

Keywords

Curaçao – Aruba – glass ceiling – managerial jobs – labor market – intersectionality

1 Introduction

The present contribution, building on the findings of a doctoral dissertation published in 2005, analyzes the underrepresentation of women in managerial jobs in business and government in Curaçao, using the conceptual tool of the glass ceiling from a financial-economic perspective. How does this

 | DOI:10.1163/9789004690882_022

underrepresentation come about and how does it affect the labor market development and women's participation and position within it?[1]

The contribution offers an overview of the limitations that women face at the microenvironmental level on the one hand, such as the division of labor and care tasks, and, on the other hand, the macroenvironmental concerns around women's participation in society, which affect the interpretation of women's participation in a broader context. It discusses five aspects that sustain, reinforce or help to break through the glass ceiling in the context of Curaçao, namely ambitions, family support, broader social networks, organizational cultures and gender-sensitive institutional policies. It operationalizes the notion of the "thickness" of the glass ceiling to examine barriers and imbalances in the upward mobility of women from middle to higher career levels. This research investigates both the case of women who succeeded in breaking through the glass ceiling as well as those who did not, analyzing their characteristics and the issues each of them faced. It concludes with reflections on recent developments in Aruba, marking substantive cracks in the glass ceiling in the last decades.

Quantitative data collection methods were used to study how educated women experienced opportunities and obstacles in their career in Curaçao's developing economy and what they perceive as the aspects that determine the glass ceiling. Data from the Central Bureau of Statistics Curaçao and relevant conference reports and policy papers were triangulated with an appraisal of economic literature on the glass ceiling concept and data collection using structured interviews, semi-structured questionnaires, face-to-face, duo and trio interviews and focus group sessions. The sample consisted of 50–125 Curaçaoan women between the age of twenty-five and fifty-five, living and working for at least five years on the island, all or most of whom had completed higher vocational or academic education and were employed in various functions in the public or private sector in the period 1997–2001. The snowball method was employed for selecting participants, using networks such as labor unions, chambers of commerce and professional associations. A distinction was made between women who have broken through the glass ceiling and

1 Kibbelaar, Paula M. E. "Barsten in het glazen plafond. Opgeleide vrouwen op de Curaçaose arbeidsmarkt; Mogelijkheden, barrières en strategieën" [Cracks in the glass ceiling: Tertiary educated women on the Curaçao labour market: Possibilities, barriers and strategies]. PhD diss., Utrecht University, 2005. The dissertation was published by SWP in 2005. The first draft translation of the contribution was provided by the author.

those who did not, based on the criteria of education level, income and/or job function or rank.

2 Definitions of the Glass Ceiling

The phenomenon of the glass ceiling is broadly understood as vertical gender segregation in labor organizations, leading to what has been described as an "unbalanced composition of the workforce."[2] In their studies of the phenomenon in the Netherlands, De Olde and Slinkman (1999) examine the extent to which the composition of the workforce in higher positions reflects that of middle positions. To achieve this, they developed an index to measure what is referred to as the "thickness" of the glass ceiling.[3]

Other scholars, such as Wirth, link the glass ceiling concept, which was first used in the US in the 1970s, to perceptions around gender roles, understanding it as a reflection of social and economic gender inequality. Wirth (2001) defines the phenomenon as "the invisible artificial barriers, created by attitudinal and organizational prejudices, which block women from senior executive positions [...]in the workplace or in politics."[4] Thus viewed, she suggests, the issue requires a global human development approach in policy formation, integrating indices such as the UN Gender Development Index (GDI) and the Gender Empowerment Measure (GEM), which take into account life expectancy, education and income levels in ascertaining measures to overcome gender disparity.

A third, related approach to the concept of the glass ceiling specifically emphasizes the barriers in women's advancement to managerial positions or top jobs. It is understood as a transparent barrier, in the sense that, although the possibilities of career advancement are theoretically available to women, they nevertheless face hurdles in practice.[5] This contribution combines

2 Olde and Slinkman, *Het glazen plafond: Een inventarisatie van cijfers, literatuur en onderzoek met betrekking tot de doorstroom van vrouwen naar de top* [The glass ceiling: An inventory of figures, literature and research regarding the advancement of women to the top], 1999; and Velenturf, "Wat vrouwen bindt: Een nieuwe kijk op arbeidsvoorwaarde" [What makes women stick: A new look at working conditions], 2001.

3 Olde and Slinkman, *Het glazen plafond*, 1999.

4 Wirth, *Breaking through the Glass Ceiling*, 2001, p. 1.

5 Scholarship adopting this approach is mentioned in a newsletter sent by the agency De Jong & Van Doorne-Huiskes and Partners in 1999, titled "Het glazen plafond. Een inventarisatie van cijfers, literatuur, onderzoek en aanbevelingen met betrekking tot de doorstroom van vrouwen naar de top" [The glass ceiling. An inventory of figures, literature, research and

insights from the above three conceptions of the glass ceiling, examining their relevance to Curaçao.

When the composition of the workforce is similar at different job levels, that is, the proportion of men and women in mid-level functions equals their representation in higher functions, it indicates what is referred to as an equilibrium. Conversely, there is an imbalance when the number of women in middle functions is high but the share of women in senior positions is low. This determination of balance is described by researchers as the "thickness of the glass ceiling." The glass ceiling thus represents the barrier or imbalance between middle and higher functions. The greater the imbalance between middle and higher positions, the thicker the glass ceiling.

The labor supply model, within which the concept of the glass ceiling is operationalized, assumes that every individual has specific background characteristics, which affect the values the individual places on different aspects of life and determines their economic activities and opportunities. These demographic characteristics influence the freedom of choice and the interpretation of an individual's lifestyle. Age, gender, educational level, ethnic background, income level and job level are some of the background variables used in this data analysis, which used a mixed-methods approach.[6] These so-called objective variables or indicators can have an impact on whether the glass ceiling is broken through. Subjective or qualitative variables or subaspects include ambitions, family support, social network, inclusion and exclusion mechanisms within organizational cultures and the local social context. The social context includes gender visions and gender policies relating to socioeconomic development within the community. It also includes factors such as upbringing, parental influence, role models, personality traits, familial arrangements, leisure activities and existing social networks. Migration histories and personal attitudes toward the local community and society are further relevant background characteristics. In studying the context of Curaçao, these characteristics are fed back to the labor supply model to understand how the glass ceiling operates.

The glass ceiling concept has been criticized as Eurocentric and being relevant primarily in the context of US-American and European gender disparity management.[7] However, it has increasingly become commonplace among

---

recommendations regarding the advancement of women to the top]; and Morrison, White, and Van Velsor, *Breaking the Glass Ceiling*, 1992.

6 Versantvoort and Laan, "Analyse en voorspelling van het regionale arbeidsaanbod in een leefstijl-perspectief" [Analysis and forecasting of the regional labor supply in a lifestyle perspective], 1998.

7 See, for example: Gasper and Van Staveren, "Development as Freedom," 2003; Sen, "Work and Rights," 2001.

policymakers globally and is a recognized indicator in gender mainstreaming programs worldwide.[8] That being said, it is important to consider developmental factors, wherein poverty reduction is central and migration and global transformations are considered.[9]

3 The Glass Ceiling in Curaçao

At first glance, there seems to be a tension between the concept of the "glass ceiling" and a gender perspective in developmental economics.[10] The former tends to emphasize senior positions in labor organizations in Europe and the United States, whereas the latter focuses on grassroots problems in developing countries, such as women's access to the labor market. The Dutch Caribbean fits in both these approaches: on the one hand, basic developmental issues need attention and governmental action, and, on the other hand, private and public sector organizations reveal characteristics that pertain to a Euro-American context. For instance, female college graduates may not advance as easily within the hierarchy of the government or bureaucratic system as they might do in the business world, even though they may experience struggles in both sectors. The percentage of women with a net income above Naf 5,000 or 6,000 (€2,500–€3,500) in the public sector is low, although women are well represented in the middle-income category. The small scale of the island society and its precarious economic situation implies that the government often lacks funds to introduce measures to address women's advancement in higher positions. Understanding household organization and women's participation rates in professional sectors on the Curaçaoan labor market therefore becomes central to addressing the gender income gap. On the other hand, certain professional sectors in Curaçao, such as politics, see many more women at higher

8 Adler and Izraeli, *Competitive Frontiers*, 1994; Olde and Slinkman, *Het glazen plafond*, 1999; Fischer and Vianen, "Sekseverschillen in voorkeuren voor een 'mannelijke' organisatiecultuur" [Sex differences in preferences for a "masculine" organizational culture], 1998; Morrison, White, and Van Velsor, *Breaking the Glass Ceiling*, 1992; and Powell, *Handbook of Gender & Work*, 1999.

9 Loutfi, *Women, Gender and Work*, 2001; Gasper and Van Staveren, "Development As Freedom – And as What Else?" 2003; Sen and Foster, *On Economic Inequality*, 1997.

10 Olde and Slinkman, *Het glazen plafond*, 1999; International Labour Office, *Breaking through the Glass Ceiling*, 1997; Lim, *More & Better Jobs for Women*, 1996; Loutfi, *Women, Gender and Work*, 2001; Velenturf, "Wat vrouwen bindt. Een nieuwe kijk op arbeidsvoorwaarde," 2001; Powell, *Handbook of Gender & Work*, 1999; Gasper and Van Staveren, "Development as Freedom," 2003; and Sen and Foster, *On Economic Inequality*, 1997.

levels than in Europe and the US, even though there remains an underrepresentation of women in leadership positions overall.[11] The scenario changes when looking at the offshore, consultancy and trust world in Curaçao, which has a global orientation, where the phenomenon of the glass ceiling is much more apparent.[12] The majority of senior account managers and company heads are men, mostly employed by contacts from the Netherlands or the US. Women employed in these sectors in Curaçao can thus experience gender and diversity barriers that correspond to the European and North American labor markets, such as conflicting work ethics, the diversity of work styles and the heterogeneity of organizational cultures.[13]

When studying women's underrepresentation in the Curaçaoan labor market, the specificities of the island need to be taken into consideration. Although the present contribution focuses on highly qualified women in Curaçao, there are plenty of women who have built successful careers with little prior education. Women employed in the labor market without higher education can be entrepreneurs with exceptional talents or abilities, often with jobs that carry a high level of responsibility. Some women become active in the labor market much later in life. Despite a significant level of teenage pregnancies and female school dropouts in Curaçao, girls in Curaçao are seeking higher levels of education and perform better in school exams, thereby exposing the so-called boy problem.[14] Curaçao also has a brain drain problem due to the economic downturn and a large emigrant population.

Another decisive factor is the influence of organizational cultures. Where incentives are offered to attract more women employees and make the workplace friendly to women's needs, there are clear indicators of more women entering the workforce at a higher level as well as not prematurely leaving the organization.[15] A checklist, scan or test indicating what a woman-friendly work

---

11 Central Bureau of Statistics Curaçao, *Statistical Orientation Curaçao 2020*, 2021; Narain, *The Boy Problem: Gender Differences in Education Participation on the Islands of the Netherlands Antilles*, 2010.

12 As of 2005, when this research was undertaken, Curaçao had one female consultant employed in the offshore business, indicating that this professional group operates in a highly male-dominated world.

13 Collinson and Hearn, *Men as Managers, Managers as Men*, 1996; Fischer, Rodriguez Mosquera, and Rojahn, *Masculiniteit met een feminien gezicht: Onderzoek naar de rol van organisatiecultuur in de doorstroming van vrouwen naar hogere functies* [Masculinity with a feminine face: Research into the role of organizational culture in the advancement of women to higher positions], 2000.

14 Kibbelaar and Haersma Buma, *Hoge hakken, wereldbaan! Vrouwen in sleutelposities op Curaçao* [High heels, world job! Women in key positions in Curaçao], 2003, p. 14.

15 Ibid., pp. 151–2.

organization looks like is one such good practice that has been introduced in many Curaçaoan public organizations.[16] Yet, notwithstanding these trends and good practices, there is still a need for targeted policy and legislation.[17]

4 Aspects Affecting the Thickness of the Glass Ceiling in Curaçao

In the following, I discuss principal factors that influence the "thickness" of the glass ceiling in Curaçao: ambition, family support, broader social networks, organization cultures and gender-sensitive institutional policies.

Whether a woman has the ambition to break through the glass ceiling and seek out high-level positions in her career is not simply a personal choice, but is influenced by upbringing, education levels, personality traits and the cultural value placed on ambition. Without a higher educational or tertiary qualification such as at MBO or, preferably, HBO or vocational level, it becomes difficult to qualify for a middle management or managerial position.[18] Personal traits and feminized social skills such as patience, friendliness, adaptability, perseverance, self-confidence, being informed about society, having a social network and openness to criticism are also experienced by women as qualities that are necessary for career advancement. Setting personal goals of overcoming mental, psychological or social barriers are further regarded as important prerequisites. Fischer, Rodriguez Mosquera and Rojahn claim that the process of self-selection, whereby masculine organizational cultures are replicated, is the main barrier for women within organizations.[19] Given the pressures of complying with gender norms, the difficulties of penetrating through masculine organizational cultures and the absence of social and professional networks, women tend to be excluded from chances to career advancement or assume these are not reachable. Socialization processes and patterns thus determine women's participation in the labor market and the realization of their ambitions.

Family support, motivation and networks are crucial not only for success at the workplace but also in making household arrangements and sharing family responsibilities. Being a tight-knit society, family support systems are often

---

16 Ibid., Appendix 9.

17 Ibid., p. 135.

18 MBO means community college or associate educational level and HBO means bachelor and or vocational level.

19 Fischer, Rodriguez Mosquera, and Rojahn, *Masculiniteit met een feminien gezicht*, 2000, p. 8.

essential for entry and participation in the Curaçaoan labor market. Yet, paradoxically, the same family support can also hinder women's careers due to traditional socialization norms or expectations relating to parenting or caring for the elderly. Women thus feel responsible for caregiving and household tasks and are willing to sacrifice their career ambitions for the sake of the family.[20]

In terms of the relevance of a broader social network, several factors can be identified, such as the influence of what is conventionally referred to as an old boys' network, which offers contacts, privileges and access to nodes of power through long-term acquaintances from the same socioeconomic milieu. As the term "old boys' network" indicates, formal and informal social and professional networks tend to structurally exclude women.[21] Cooperation and support among women and between women and men in workplaces is another factor. A social network means access to sources of information, gaining entry to organizations, institutions, companies and semigovernment services.[22] The entry points for a social network are memberships in networking organizations, clubs, unions, chambers of commerce, educational institutions and interest groups. They can also exist outside of the work context, as in sports clubs, political parties and school networks.

Organizational cultures are also crucial to understanding the glass ceiling. Organizations with a structural understanding of women's needs and requirements take steps to make the workplace friendly to women through arrangements, such as working in teams, home-based work, a horizontal organizational culture, flexible working hours, part-time work and childcare facilities. In the research undertaken for my dissertation, I found that caregiving responsibilities weigh heavily on women's careers in Curaçao. A lack of childcare facilities in the private sector, in small enterprises and government poses a major hurdle for women.[23] Many women I interviewed at that time spoke of the inadequacy of existing subsidized child care institutions and the need for after-school care and homework help.[24]

---

20 Greenhaus and Parasuraman, "Research on Work, Family, and Gender. Current Status and Future Directions," 1999; International Labour Office, *Breaking through the Glass Ceiling*, 1997; Lim, *More & Better Jobs for Women*, 1996.

21 Morrison, White, and Van Velsor, *Breaking the Glass Ceiling*, 1992.

22 Fischer, Rodriguez Mosquera, and Rojahn, *Masculiniteit met een feminien gezicht*, 2000; and Kibbelaar and Haersma Buma, *Hoge hakken, wereldbaan! Vrouwen in sleutelposities op Curaçao*, 2003.

23 This continues to be the case nearly two decades later, as indicated in the government of Curaçao's National Development Plan: United Nations Development Programme, "Building on Strengths: National Development Plan Curacao – 2015–2030," 2016, p. 44.

24 Bussemaker, *Struikelblokken en verbindingswegen. Nieuwe oriëntaties voor het emancipatiebeleid* [Stumbling blocks and connecting roads. New orientations for emancipation

Apart from these practical measures, one can also think of antidiscriminatory policies, which take racial and gender discrimination seriously. In the Curaçaoan context, one can think of the negative perceptions about Curaçaoans regarding culture and customs and work ethics, all of which implicitly carry norms about women's roles.[25] Training in tackling organizational issues can make the culture of an organization diverse, dynamic, accessible and pluralistic.[26] Gender differences cannot be separated from other variables, such as race, ethnicity, culture, religion and age, thus necessitating an intersectional approach. All of these can impact career advancement to senior leadership positions, as revealed by numerous studies.[27]

Gender awareness in organizations and companies refers to an institutional sensitivity regarding the provisions that facilitate female employees.[28] This involves not only creating concrete, practical measures but also setting in place mechanisms to address perceived and experienced exclusion and isolation, from the moment a female employee enters the organization to later stages in their career.[29]

The gender pay gap refers to the income differences between women and men. Research shows that women, by large, earn less than men.[30] Progression to managerial jobs is hindered by (lack of) work experience, networks,

---

policy], 1996; Kibbelaar and Haersma Buma, *Hoge hakken, wereldbaan! Vrouwen in sleutelposities op Curaçao*, 2003.

25 Davidson, *The Black and Ethnic Minority Woman Manager*, 1997; Fischer, Rodriguez Mosquera, and Rojahn, *Masculiniteit met een feminien gezicht*, 2000; Sokoloff, *Black Women and White Women in the Professions*, 1992; and Marcha and Verweel, *Management of Diversity in Antillean Organisations*, 1996.

26 Collinson and Hearn, *Men as Managers, Managers as Men*, 1996; Fischer, Rodriguez Mosquera, and Rojahn, *Masculiniteit met een feminien gezicht*, 2000; and Siebers, Verweel, and Ruijter, *Management van diversiteit in arbeidsorganisaties* [Management of diversity in labor organizations], 2002.

27 Essed and Graaff, *De actualiteit van diversiteit: Het gemeentelijk beleid onder de loep* [The actuality of diversity: A closer look at municipal policy], 2002; Fischer, Rodriguez Mosquera, and Rojahn, *Masculiniteit met een feminien gezicht*, 2000; and Wirth, *Breaking through the Glass Ceiling*, 2001.

28 Benschop and Doorewaard, "Organisaties en diversiteit: Naar een contextuele benadering van intercultureel management" [Organizations and diversity: Toward a contextual approach to intercultural management], 1999; Benschop, *De mantel der gelijkheid: Gender in organisaties* [The cloak of equality: Gender in organizations], 1996; Fischer, Rodriguez Mosquera, and Rojahn, *Masculiniteit met een feminien gezicht*, 2000; Wirth, *Breaking through the Glass Ceiling*, 2001; and Siebers, Verweel, and Ruijter, *Management van diversiteit in arbeidsorganisaties*, 2002.

29 Adler and Izraeli, *Competitive Frontiers*, 1994; World Bank, "Excellence through Equality: An Increased Role for Women in the World Bank," 1992; Lim, *More & Better Jobs for Women*, 1996; and Velenturf, "Wat vrouwen bindt. Een nieuwe kijk op arbeidsvoorwaarde," 2001.

30 See Kibbelaar, "Barsten in het glazen plafond," 2005, Chapter 2.

ambitions, family obligations, time, masculine organizational cultures and psychological obstacles.[31] Thus, women often tend to undertake responsibilities and perform tasks that ought to qualify them for a higher income scale, yet they tend to be denied the benefits of pay hikes or promotions.

All these factors must be considered against broader policy changes. Where there is a vision for addressing gender disparities in labor market participation at a policy level, significant changes can be observed in women's labor participation over an extended time.[32] The rise of women to positions of political power in Curaçao has brought gender questions to the forefront of public discussion. Governmental policies are, in turn, influenced by regional and international developments. The involvement of Curaçao in UN conferences and the establishment of a steering committee for gender action in 1980 has had a significant impact on women's self-perceptions and their ambitions in public life and in their careers.[33] As Curaçao has features of both an advanced as well as a developing economy, these determine government policy on emancipation issues, such as provisions regarding after-school care, pregnancy or parental leave, part-time work or telecommuting.[34]

5 Reflections from Aruba

Since the completion of the study in 2005, much has changed in the arena of gender equality. The societal relevance of gender has been placed firmly on the political agenda in the Kingdom of the Netherlands, even as a binary understanding of gender is being challenged, redefined and politically reframed as a spectrum. Having relocated to Aruba, I have had the opportunity to closely observe developments in gender policy in the Aruban context over the past decade. I thus conclude by sharing recent developments in Aruba, which indicate the extent of transformations in gender emancipation. Under the

31 Maassen van den Brink and Groot, *Obstakels: Vrouwen tussen arbeidsmarkt en gezin* [Obstacles: Women between the labor market and family], 1994; Olde and Slinkman, *Het glazen plafond*, 1999; Fischer, Rodriguez Mosquera, and Rojahn, *Masculiniteit met een feminien gezicht*, 2000; and Collinson and Hearn, *Men as Managers, Managers as Men*, 1996.

32 Amott and Matthaei, *Race, Gender, and Work*, 1996; Peterson and Runyan, *Global Gender Issues*, 1999; and Wirth, *Breaking through the Glass Ceiling*, 2001.

33 Editors' note: see contribution by Pieters Kwiers in this volume.

34 Maassen van den Brink and Groot, *Obstakels: Vrouwen tussen arbeidsmarkt en gezin*, 1994; *Contourennota nationale sociale ontwikkelings en welzijnsbeleid 1997–2002* [Plan of approach national social development and welfare policy 1997–2002], 1997; ECLAC, *ECLAC Programme Performance Report for the Biennium 2000–2001*, 2002.

leadership of its first female prime minister, Aruba installed a Gender Steering Committee in 2020 and a Gender Action Plan in May 2022, supervised by the UN Women Multi-Country Office - Caribbean and guided by the seventeen Sustainable Development Goals (SDGs) of the United Nations.[35] Shortly after the installation of the committee, the prime minister commissioned an investigation into the rise of domestic violence cases in Aruban households in the wake of the COVID-19 pandemic. The outcomes of this investigation were published in a 2021 report.[36]

Since the first female leadership conference in Aruba in 2011, there has been a spectacular rise of activities and initiatives on the island relating to women's emancipation. The national women's agency CEDHEM has recently embarked on an investigation of women's labor market participation, the opportunities and barriers that women and men face in Aruba and the influence of gender on these matters. In 2021, a dissertation was defended at the Faculty of Tourism, Hospitality and Management Studies at the University of Aruba, examining gender relations within the Aruban tourism sector, the first analysis of female CEOs, directors and managers within the hotel sector in Aruba.[37] In 2022, female students of science, technology, engineering and mathematics (STEM) from the Dutch Caribbean islands, studying in the Netherlands, the US and other countries, initiated a conference on the opportunities and barriers for migrant female students at Dutch and American universities and colleges to advance in STEM-related disciplines, studies and/or occupations. The students, self-organized under the name "STEM Embassy," called for an introduction of a STEM research agenda and gender mainstreaming in the curriculum, among other demands.

Deploying the concept of the glass ceiling, the present contribution seeks to identify the factors that negatively or positively impact the career advancement of highly educated women in Curaçao. Based on data from the Central Bureau of Statistics, it can be concluded that the glass ceiling has become thinner in the past three decades due to societal transformations, policy changes, organizational cultural shifts and a broader recognition of the need to address women's exclusion from high positions. Analyzing two groups of women, those who succeeded in breaking through the glass ceiling on the one hand and those who did not on the other, the research identified five aspects that

35 Editors' note: see contribution by Wever-Croes in this volume.

36 Steering Committee for the Development of a Gender Policy in Aruba, *Framing of the Feminization of Covid-19 in Aruba*, 2021.

37 Jadnanansing, "Female Leaders in the Aruban Lodging Industry: An Exploratory Study of Perceptions of Second-Generation Gender Bias," 2021.

influence the glass ceiling both objectively and subjectively: ambitions, family support, broader social networks, organizational cultures and gender-sensitive institutional policies. I argue that the unique situation of Curaçao and the other Dutch Caribbean islands, as Small Island Developing States (SIDS) and, at the same time, as part of the framework of the Kingdom of the Netherlands, places challenges in interpreting and analyzing both external constraints as well as subjective perceptions of the glass ceiling. The standards used to measure career advancement for highly qualified women in the labor market in Aruba and Curaçao thus need to be adapted to the dynamic local contexts.

Bibliography

Adler, Nancy J., and Dafna N. Izraeli, eds. *Competitive Frontiers: Women Managers in a Global Economy*. Cambridge, MA: Blackwell, 1994.

Amott, Teresa L., and Julie A. Matthaei. *Race, Gender, and Work: A Multi-Cultural Economic History of Women in the United States*. Rev. ed. Boston: South End Press, 1996.

Benschop, Y., and H. Doorewaard. "Organisaties en diversiteit: Naar een contextuele benadering van intercultureel management" [Organizations and diversity: Toward a contextual approach to intercultural management]. In *Organisaties en diversiteit: Naar een contextuele benadering van intercultureel management*, edited by Folke Glastra, 181–96. Utrecht: Lemma, 1999.

Benschop, Yvonne. *De mantel der gelijkheid: Gender in organisaties* [The cloak of equality: Gender in organizations]. Assen: Van Gorcum, 1996.

Bussemaker, M. *Struikelblokken en verbindingswegen. Nieuwe oriëntaties voor het emancipatiebeleid* [Stumbling blocks and connecting roads. New orientations for emancipation policy]. The Hague: VUGA; The Hague, Ministerie van Sociale Zaken en Werkgelegenheid, 1996.

Central Bureau of Statistics Curaçao. *Statistical Orientation Curaçao 2020*. Willemstad: Central Bureau of Statistics Curaçao, 2021. https://www.cbs.cw/statistical-orientation-curacao-2020.

Collinson, David, and Jeff Hearn. *Men as Managers, Managers as Men: Critical Perspectives on Men, Masculinities and Managements*. London: SAGE Publications Ltd, 1996.

Contourennota nationale sociale ontwikkelings en welzijnsbeleid 1997–2002 [Plan of approach national social development and welfare policy]. Curaçao: DWGHZ, 1997.

Davidson, Marilyn. *The Black and Ethnic Minority Woman Manager: Cracking the Concrete Ceiling*. London: Paul Chapman Pub. Ltd, 1997.

ECLAC. *ECLAC Programme Performance Report for the Biennium 2000–2001*. ECLAC, March 25, 2002. https://repositorio.cepal.org/bitstream/handle/11362/13004/S023215_en.pdf?sequence=1.

Essed, Philomena, and Maaike de Graaff. *De actualiteit van diversiteit: Het gemeentelijk beleid onder de loep* [The actuality of diversity: A closer look at municipal policy]. The Hague: E-Quality, Experts in gender en etniciteit; Utrecht: FORUM, Instituut voor Multiculturele Ontwikkeling, 2002.

Fischer, Agneta H., Patricia M. Rodriguez Mosquera, and Krystyna Rojahn. *Masculiniteit met een feminien gezicht: Onderzoek naar de rol van organisatiecultuur in de doorstroming van vrouwen naar hogere functies* [Masculinity with a feminine face: Research into the role of organizational culture in the advancement of women to higher positions]. The Hague: Elsevier, 2000.

Fischer, A. H., and A. Vianen. "Sekseverschillen in voorkeuren voor een 'mannelijke' organisatiecultuur" [Sex differences in preferences for a "masculine" organizational culture]. *Gedrag en organisatie: Tijdschrift voor sociale, economische, arbeids- en organisatiepsychologie* 11, no. 5 (1998): 264–79.

Gasper, Des, and Irene van Staveren. "Development as Freedom – And as What Else?" *Feminist Economics* 9, no. 2–3 (2003): 137–61. https://doi.org/10.1080/135457003200 0078663.

Government of Curaçao. "Building on Strengths: National Development Plan 2015–2030." Curaçao: UNDP, 2016. https://www.undp.org/trinidad-and-tobago/publica tions/national-development-plan-curacao-2015-2030.

Greenhaus, J. H., and S. Parasuraman. "Research on Work, Family, and Gender. Current Status and Future Directions." In *Handbook of Gender & Work*, edited by Gary N. Powell, 413–28. Thousand Oaks: Sage Publications, 1999.

International Labour Office, ed. *Breaking through the Glass Ceiling: Women in Management: Report for Discussion at the Tripartite Meeting on Breaking through the Glass Ceiling: Women in Management*. Geneva: International Labour Office, 1997.

Jadnanansing, Madhu. "Female Leaders in the Aruban Lodging Industry: An Exploratory Study of Perceptions of Second-Generation Gender Bias." PhD diss., University of Aruba, 2021.

Kibbelaar, Paula, and Clarisse van Haersma Buma. *Hoge hakken, wereldbaan! Vrouwen in sleutelposities op Curaçao* [High heels, world job! Women in key positions in Curaçao]. Zutphen: Walburg Pers, 2003.

Kibbelaar, Paula M. E. "Barsten in het glazen plafond. Opgeleide vrouwen op de Curaçaose arbeidsmarkt; mogelijkheden, barrières en strategieën" [Cracks in the glass ceiling: Tertiary educated women on the Curacao labour market: Possibilities, barriers and strategies]. PhD diss., University of Utrecht, 2005.

Lim, Lin Lean. *More & Better Jobs for Women: An Action Guide: An ILO Follow-up to the Fourth World Conference on Women and the World Summit for Social Development.* Geneva: International Labour Office, 1996.

Loutfi, Martha Fetherolf, ed. *Women, Gender and Work: What Is Equality and How Do We Get There?* Geneva: International Labour Office, 2001.

Maassen van den Brink, Henriëtte, and W. N. J. Groot. *Obstakels: Vrouwen tussen arbeidsmarkt en gezin* [*Obstacles: Women between the labor market and family*]. Amsterdam: Amsterdam University Press, 1994.

Marcha, V., and P. Verweel. *Management of Diversity in Antillean Organisations*. Utrecht: ISOR, Center for Policy and Management Studies, 1996.

Morrison, Ann M., Randall P. White, and Ellen Van Velsor. *Breaking the Glass Ceiling: Can Women Reach the Top of America's Largest Corporations?* Rev. ed. Reading, MA: Addison-Wesley, 1994.

Narain, Goretti. *The Boy Problem: Gender Differences in Education Participation on the Islands of the Netherlands Antilles*. Curaçao: National UNESCO Commission of the Netherlands Antilles, 2010.

Olde, Cora de, and Esther Slinkman. *Het glazen plafond: Een inventarisatie van cijfers, literatuur en onderzoek met betrekking tot de doorstroom van vrouwen naar de top* [The glass ceiling: An inventory of figures, literature and research regarding the advancement of women to the top]. The Hague: Ministerie van Sociale Zaken en Werkgelegenheid, 1999.

Peterson, V. Spike, and Anne Sisson Runyan. *Global Gender Issues*. 2nd ed. Boulder: Westview Press, 1999.

Powell, Gary N., ed. *Handbook of Gender & Work*. Thousand Oaks: Sage Publications, 1999.

Sen, Amartya, and James E. Foster. *On Economic Inequality*. Oxford: Oxford University Press, 1997.

Sen, Amartya. "Work and Rights." In *Women, Gender and Work: What Is Equality and How Do We Get There?* edited by Martha Fetherolf Loutfi, 33–44. Geneva: International Labour Office, 2001.

Siebers, Hans, Paul Verweel, and Arie de Ruijter. *Management van diversiteit in arbeidsorganisaties* [Management of diversity in labor organizations]. Utrecht: LEMMA, 2002.

Sokoloff, Natalie J. *Black Women and White Women in the Professions: Occupational Segregation by Race and Gender, 1960–1980*. New York: Routledge, 1992.

Steering Committee for the Development of a Gender Policy in Aruba. *Framing of the Feminization of Covid-19 in Aruba*. Report submitted to the Office of the Prime Minister of Aruba, 2021.

United Nations Development Programme. "Building on Strengths: National Development Plan Curacao – 2015–2030." UNDP, August 16, 2016. https://www.undp.org/trinidad-and-tobago/publications/national-development-plan-curacao-2015-2030.

Velenturf, M. "Wat vrouwen bindt. Een nieuwe kijk op arbeidsvoorwaarde" [What makes women stick. A new look at working conditions]. Amstelveen: Opportunity in bedrijf, 2001.

Versantvoort, M., and L. van der Laan. "Analyse en voorspelling van het regionale arbeidsaanbod in een leefstijl-perspectief" [Analysis and forecasting of the regional labor supply in a lifestyle perspective]. In *Innovatie in bedrijf en regio*, edited by J. van Dijk and Frans Boekema, 151–71. Assen: Van Gorcum, 1998.

Wirth, Linda. *Breaking through the Glass Ceiling: Women in Management*. Geneva: International Labour Office, 2001.

World Bank. *Excellence through Equality: An Increased Role for Women in the World Bank*. A report of the advisory group on higher-level women's issues. Washington, DC: World Bank Group, 1992.

CHAPTER 21

Nine Houses, Nine Families: Oral History in the Rancho Neighborhood

Yolanda Richardson

Abstract

Using oral historical research interviews with forty-two long-term residents of the Aruban neighborhood of Rancho, this contribution presents glimpses from the social history of a closely knit, enterprising, matrifocal community. The research formed the basis of an exhibition held in 2009 at the National Archaeological Museum in Aruba, located in Rancho. The exhibition sought to challenge hardwired stereotypes about the area being a derelict drug den by foregrounding the daily lives of its resilient and enterprising community members, the memories of people's involvements in political and labor struggles in the 1940s and 1950s as well as the unique relations of the community to the coastline. The contribution charts how the socioeconomic transformations during the twentieth century impacted the daily lives of Rancho residents.

Keywords

Aruba – Rancho – social history – fishing community – resilience

1 Introduction

In December 2008, I was approached by the Aruban Department of Culture about conducting a study of the Aruban neighborhood of Rancho, known as being dilapidated, ruled by drug addicts and largely avoided by those seeking to enter the main shopping area in Oranjestad, the Aruban capital. The research was commissioned by the National Archaeological Museum Aruba (NAMA), which hosted an exhibition on Rancho on the occasion of the museum's relocation to this neighborhood in July 2009. The aim of the department and NAMA was to challenge stereotypical narratives about Rancho with

 | DOI:10.1163/9789004690882_023

research that centered the experiences of the residents of the neighborhood.[1] The museum was concerned about its own sustainability and integration in a neighborhood largely neglected by both governmental and nongovernmental organizations, where residents seemed to be rendered hopeless as a consequence of the despair in the streets caused by the rise of drug addiction.

Given my own family origins in Rancho, my experience as an educator and having recently coorganized an exhibition on slavery at the Aruban National Archives in 2008, I viewed the study as an opportunity to contribute to the formation of knowledge about Rancho using intersectional feminist methods of oral history research, centering the perspective of inhabitants with a view to decolonizing existing views of Rancho.[2]

2 Background

Rancho is one of the first settlements close to Oranjestad, which officially became the capital of Aruba in 1824.[3] Fishing formed the livelihood for most residents of Rancho until the early twentieth century.[4] This changed with the establishment of two international oil companies, the Lago Oil & Transport Company in the southern part of the island in 1924 and the Arend Oil Company in the northwestern end of the island, which was in operation between 1929 and 1953.[5] Another critical historical moment was the erection of the harbor in Oranjestad in 1924, as well as its renovation shortly after World War II in 1947, facilitating the transport of materials to the southern part of the island, where the oil company was located. With rising unemployment in the wake of automation processes in the refinery in the 1960s, transformations in the international oil market and increasing political instability in Venezuela, the

1 Tuhiwai-Smith, *Decolonizing Methodologies*, 1999; CohenMiller and Boivin, "Uncovering the Spectrum of Insider-Outsiderness," 2022, pp. 73–95.

2 Hill-Collins, *Learning from the Outsider Within*, 1986; Duran and Jones, "Intersectionality as a Lens in Qualitative Research," 2023; Nakhid-Chatoor et al, "Exploring Liming and Ole Talk as a Culturally Relevant Methodology for Researching with Caribbean People," 2018.

3 Hartog, *Aruba zoals het was – zoals het werd: Van de tijd der Indianen tot op heden* [Aruba as it was – as it became: From the era of the Indians to the present], 1953.

4 According to the colonial historian Johan Hartog, the number of fishermen in Rancho ranged from 132 in 1910 to 189 in 1930 and 160 in 1952. As per the 2020 Census of Aruba, 68 people were registered as fishermen across the island. See Hartog, *Aruba zoals het was – zoals het werd*, 1953; Central Bureau of Statistics Aruba, "Population and Housing Census 2020, tables P. I-6;8," 2021.

5 Alofs and Merkies, *Ken ta Arubiano? Sociale integratie en natievorming op Aruba* [Who is the Aruban? Social integration and nation-building in Aruba], 1990.

Government of Aruba started promoting tourism as an alternative economic activity.[6] Since the construction of the first high-rise hotel in 1959, tourism has become one of the central economic pillars of the island. By the late 1960s, most residents of Rancho worked as laborers at the harbor, while merchants settled in the vicinity, securing Rancho's position as an important satellite neighborhood of Oranjestad. Rancho's period of economic prosperity was not long-lived, as the boom was disrupted after drug addicts were spotted in the area and Rancho was deemed the epicenter for drug trafficking. Interviewees speculated that drugs entered Rancho through trafficking and smuggling through the seas between South America and Aruba.

3 Research Design

The objective of the research was to dispel stereotypical narratives about Rancho by foregrounding the experiences of the residents and thereby igniting a sense of belonging, community spirit and responsibility toward the neighborhood. The management of the museum anticipated that this could foster community initiatives for restoration and self-empowerment and thus indirectly create the conditions for the sustainability of the museum's future.

Unstructured interviews were conducted with forty-two residents, focusing on their lives and experiences in Rancho between 1945 and 2005.[7] Three themes served as the organizing frames for the exhibition: (a) the history of the name, location and boundaries of Rancho; (b) architecture, monuments and legends of the neighborhood and (c) commercial life and livelihoods. A part of the research was published in Dutch and Papiamentu in a museum publication in 2010.[8]

6 Dresscher, "Aruba: An Island Navigating a Globalizing World," 2009, p. 22.

7 Of the forty-two individuals who were approached for an interview using a snowballing method, one person did not participate and two others ultimately did not give their consent for using the interviews in the research, although they candidly recounted their memories as residents of the neighborhood. Eighteen participants were female and twenty-one were male. The interviews were conducted from February to June 2009, mostly at the homes of the participants or at the NAMA or other businesses or offices in the neighborhood, and a small number were conducted on the street. Most interviews were individual conversations in Papiamentu, but it was not uncommon to have other persons present and listening.

8 Huygen, *Rancho, nos bario – nos museo, tira un bista*, 2010.

4 Life *bou baranca*

A vivid memory for many residents of Rancho is the demolition of nine houses between 1949 and 1950, known at the time as the *bou baranca* (under the rock) houses. These houses were located between the coastal depot, the salt pans that evaporated prior to 1945, Weststraat and today's Arendstraat, below a *calichi*[9] elevation. *Bou baranca* was the name given to an area adjacent to a low-cliff formation. Rancho is close to the shore and the sea line was probably much closer in the early twentieth century than it is today. Two paths with steps served as points of access to this *sabana* (savanna), one west of Weststraat and another south of Arendstraat, well-known streets in the area. In exchange for their property, the nine families were allotted government-built houses a couple of blocks further in the streets called Boliviastraat and Guatemalastraat. This move veritably ushered in the beginning of a new era as it meant the gradual end to some distinctive customs and the prevalent modest lifestyle on the *sabana*. It also meant that those who lived on the *sabana* had to leave what was home to them at a time when infrastructural developments at the harbor, types of employment available and patterns of communal living were rapidly changing.

5 Livelihoods

Families who lived *bou baranca* mainly earned their living from fishing, using either their own boats or sharing them. The residents of Rancho were remembered as walking around barefoot, a custom that led to the label *Ranchero pia plat* (barefooted Ranchero). Most women were caregivers who did the housekeeping, but they often also supplemented their household income by selling fish, mutton, goat meat, local pastries and homemade bread. A few enterprising women sold tobacco or kerosene from home or washed clothes for travelers. Participants remarked that housekeeping was no easy chore in the 1950s and often involved heavy physical labor.

The men would leave with their boats in the early evening hours and return to land in the morning, often leaving the catch of the day in the hands of their

9 *Calichi* (caliche) is a sedimentary rock composed of calcium carbonate, which commonly colors from white to light pink to reddish brown.

spouses,[10] who took responsibility for prizing and selling the catch. On those occasions when no fish were caught, shrimps, lobsters or *calcos*[11] (the Caribbean queen conch) were caught in the salt pan or in the rocks on the shore. Another local delicacy was the *webo di bubi* (tern eggs), which were collected on Monk's Islands[12] by Venezuelans or local fishermen from larger boats and delivered in full buckets. Other foods, such as milk and beans, were often obtained through a barter system with residents from outside Playa,[13] with Rancheros trading fish for agricultural produce.

6 Social Life

Rancheros were traditional families with many children and community life was characterized by conviviality, mutual support and kinship. Material amenities were not plentiful but there was enough food for all, with fresh fish arriving daily. Interviewees remarked that it was a common custom to cook a generous quantity of food to offer to anyone who spontaneously dropped by for dinner, indicating a closely knit community.

Parents, particularly mothers, who were mainly responsible for the children while the men were at sea, were described as strict, sincere and honest. Children were expected to be obedient and not challenge rules. While respect, orderliness and discipline were held high as social values, Rancheros were also known as people who neither buckled to injustice nor avoided direct confrontation. Interview participants described Rancheros as straightforward, proud and unapologetic people who knew how to stand up for themselves. A combination of these traits, compounded by small island community ties, were used to explain why Rancheros were often known to be involved in fist fights in and outside the neighborhood.

Most children attended school during the week, with a few completing the tenth grade. Once secondary education was introduced in Aruba, it was often difficult for parents to enroll children due to financial difficulties. While boys were taken to sea at a young age to learn the fishing profession, girls tended to be restricted to housekeeping and caring for younger siblings. In the afternoon

10 Note that this term is used here to refer to those united by civil matrimony, religious unions or who formed a household by mutual agreement.

11 Editors' note: see contribution by Dresscher-Lambertus in this section.

12 Los Monjes Islands is a federal dependency of Venezuela and located to the southwest of Aruba.

13 Playa is the local name for Oranjestad, derived from the Spanish term Playa Caballos (Horse Bay).

hours, people resided outdoors, with men drinking coffee, sharing jokes, having fiery conversations or telling children Compa Nanzi[14] stories. At sunset, the children would rinse themselves at a well in front of one of the nine houses after having played together all afternoon before returning home to finish any homework by kerosene light. On Sundays, children and youth went swimming at the Paardenbaai (Horse Bay) beach. After the harbor was dredged, swimming at Mambo Beach became the usual Sunday activity.

Interviewees recounted memories of growing up in a community that was religious and strict in observing rituals and services,[15] with children often instructed to attend mass twice on Sundays. At the same time, it was often mentioned in the interviews that men were reputed to drink heavily, a habit that was explained as a coping mechanism for handling the risks and pressures of a precarious life at sea.

7 Political Activities

Many of the interview participants proudly recounted their involvement with local politics, including the separatist movement (Separacion)[16] in Aruba in 1947–1948 as well as the labor union Union Portuario Arubano (UPA, Union of Aruban Dock Workers). The participants mentioned names of at least three presidents of the UPA who were from Rancho as well as various residents who signed the petition for Separacion, known as the petition of March 18, 1948.[17] While women did not have voting rights at the time and could thus not sign the petition, there is evidence that they were present and participated in protest activities from late 1947 to early 1948.[18]

14 Compa Nanzi stories are about a trickster spider named Anansi or Ananse. These tales originated in West Africa and were brought to the Caribbean through slavery.

15 Hartog, *Aruba zoals het was – zoals het werd*, 1953; Alofs, *Slaven zonder plantage* [Slaves without a plantation], 2013.

16 Alofs and Merkies, *Ken ta Arubiano?* 1990, p. 81.

17 Alofs, "Onderhorigheid en separatisme: Koloniaal bestuur en lokale politiek op Aruba 1816–1955" [Subordination and separatism: Colonial governance and local politics in Aruba 1816–1955], 2011, pp. 209–18.

18 This is indicated in a booklet in honor of the citizens who signed the petition for a new constitutional arrangement in favor of Aruba separating from the then called colony of Curaçao. See Croes, *18 maart 1948: Honor y reconocemento* [March 18, 1948: Honor and recognition], 2016. A list of petitioners held at Aruba National Archives further notes that there were five protest meetings between September 1947 and January 1948, held at a house in Rancho and at Gloria Theater, an open-air theater in Oranjestad, where both men and women participated.

The headquarters of two Aruban political parties have historically been in Rancho. The Christian Democratic Aruban People's Party (AVP, Arubaanse Volkspartij or Partido di Pueblo Arubano) has had its main office in Rancho for over forty years and the People's Electoral Movement (MEP, Electorale Volksbeweging or Movimiento Electoral di Pueblo) was stationed in the neighborhood for at least eight years. The choice of Rancho may be related to the location of the local administration only a few streets away. Yet, the presence of these parties in Rancho was also significant because it gave Rancheros a proximity to the political decision-making arenas and socialized them to actively participate in party politics. Prior to the Separacion movement, Rancheros also witnessed World War II and, after the war, the women were possibly involved in the protests against the erection of the brothel Campo Alegre[19] in the 1950s. Some years later, in the late 1970s and early 1980s, Rancheros also participated in the protests and strikes that reignited Aruban claims to acquire a separate status within the Kingdom of the Netherlands.[20]

The involvement in these political movements was expressed in the interviews with a sense of community pride and motivated by a desire to better their lives and seek social and economic improvement. Some interviewees alluded to the importance of social justice and equity as necessary preconditions for addressing issues such as drug addiction in the neighborhood. The underlying tone in the interview narratives was thus not of poverty, victimization or hopelessness but of pride, survival and resilience.

8 Concluding Reflections on the Gendered Dimensions of the History of Rancho

Although the research for the exhibition did not explicitly focus on questions relating to gender, it nevertheless offered the opportunity to delve into the differences in experiences of men and women in an Aruban neighborhood and contextualize it in the light of regional developments in the broader former Netherlands Antilles.[21]

19 Kelly, *Protesten van Arubaanse vrouwen tegen een Campo Alegre: 1950–1957* [Protests by Aruban women against Campo Alegre: 1950–1957], 2015. Editors' note: a translated extract of Kelly's text is included in this volume.

20 Alofs and Merkies, *Ken ta Arubiano?* 1990, pp. 155–8.

21 University of the Netherlands Antilles, ed., *Vrouwen van de Nederlandse Antillen en Aruba: Naar een betere toekomst. De positie van de Antilliaanse en Arubaanse vrouw in het heden, verleden en in de toekomst* [Women of the Netherlands Antilles and Aruba: Toward a

The reminiscences of the interviewed residents of Rancho shed light on the changing roles of women because of the socioeconomic transformations that the fishing village underwent in the course of the twentieth century. The possibility to gain employment as a consequence of the presence of the oil refinery, the proximity to the trade center at the harbor and growing tourism made women reimagine their traditional roles as child bearers and caregivers.[22]

The picture of life *bou baranca* as sketched in the narratives of its residents depicts women as adopting traditional roles within the household but also as being active in generating income through their own small enterprises as well as participating in public life.[23] The women of Rancho were entrepreneurial and formed the stable axis of the family and community, considering that men spent long periods at sea, with a real risk of dying in its waters, in addition to them being prone to excessive alcohol and drug consumption. Being cognizant of the perils of a livelihood dependent on the sea may also explain why women in Rancho were socialized to fulfill multiple roles in the household. Being a fisherman's spouse implied always being prepared to transition into the role of head of the household while simultaneously taking care of the family because a husband could be away at sea for days or tragically lose his life while on a fishing expedition. Rancho thus exhibits the characteristics of a fluid and relational matrifocal community: fluid to the extent of adopting traditional feminized roles of social reproduction without being defined by them and, at the same time, relational because the community was heavily dependent on whether the sea would *duna of tuma*[24] (give or take).

Acknowledgments

This contribution is based on an unpublished report submitted to the National Archaeological Museum Aruba (NAMA), parts of which were published in the exhibition catalogue. See Richardson, *Negen huizen, verschillende gezinnen en veel kinderen bou baranca* [Nine houses, different families and many children

better future. The position of the Antillean and Aruban woman in the present, past and future], 2010, pp. 36–37.

22 Powell, "The Role of Women in the Caribbean," 1984.

23 Cuales, "In Search of Our Memory: Gender in the Netherlands Antilles," 1998. Editors' note: this text is included in this volume.

24 The Papiamentu proverb *lama ta duna lama ta tuma* (the sea gives and the sea takes) is used in the wake of natural disasters or heavy rains or, in this case, when fishermen do not return from a fishing expedition.

under the rocks], 2009; Huygen, *Rancho, nos bario – nos museo, tira un bista* [Rancho, our neighborhood – our museum, take a look], 2010.

Bibliography

Alofs, Luc and Leontine Merkies. *Ken ta Arubiano? Sociale integratie en natievorming op Aruba* [Who is the Aruban? Social integration and nation-building in Aruba]. Leiden: KITLV, 1990.

Alofs, Luc. "Onderhorigheid en separatisme: Koloniaal bestuur en lokale politiek op Aruba 1816–1955" [Subordination and separatism: Colonial governance and local politics in Aruba 1816–1955]. PhD diss., Leiden University, 2011. https://hdl.handle.net/1887/17992.

Alofs, Luc. *Slaven zonder plantage* [Slaves without a plantation]. Aruba: Charuba, 2013.

Central Bureau of Statistics Aruba. "Population and Housing Census 2020, tables P. I-6;8." Oranjestad: Central Bureau of Statistics Aruba, 2021. https://cbs.aw/wp/index.php/2021/12/02/tables-dealing-with-the-economic-activity-of-the-populationi.

CohenMiller, Anna and Nettie Boivin. "Uncovering the Spectrum of Insider-Outsiderness." In *Questions in Qualitative Social Justice Research in Multicultural Contexts*, edited by Anna CohenMiller and Nettie Bovin, 73–95. Abingdon: Routledge, 2022.

Croes, Mito. *18 maart 1948: Honor y reconocemento* [March 18, 1948: Honor and recognition]. 2nd ed. Aruba: Interprint Aruba, 2016.

Cuales, Sonia M. "In Search of Our Memory: Gender in the Netherlands Antilles." *Feminist Review* 59, no. 1 (1998): 86–100.

Dresscher, Eduard. "Aruba: An Island Navigating a Globalizing World. A Brief History." *Ceque: Journal of the National Archaeological Museum Aruba*, no. 1 (2009): 22.

Duran, Antonio and Susan R. Jones. "Intersectionality as a Lens in Qualitative Research." In *Advancing Culturally Responsive Research and Researchers: Qualitative, Quantitative, and Mixed Methods*, edited by Penny Pasque and E. Alexander, 103–18. Abingdon: Routledge, 2023.

Kelly, Lucia. *Protesten van Arubaanse vrouwen tegen een Campo Alegre: 1950–1957* [Protests by Aruban women against Campo Alegre: 1950–1957]. Oranjestad: UNOCA, 2015.

Hartog, Johan. *Aruba zoals het was – zoals het werd: Van de tijd der Indianen tot op heden* [Aruba as it was – as it became: From the era of the Indians to the present]. Aruba: Gebroeders de Wit, 1953.

Hill-Collins, Patricia. "Learning from the Outsider Within: The Sociological Significance of Black Feminist Thought." *Social Problems* 33, no. 6 (December 1986): 14–32.

Huygen, Floor. *Rancho, nos bario – nos museo, tira un bista* [Rancho, our neighborhood – our museum, take a look]. Aruba: National Archaeological Museum of Aruba, 2010.

Nakhid-Chatoor, Margaret, Camille Nakhid, Shakeisha Wilson, and Anabel Fernandez Santana. "Exploring Liming and Ole Talk as a Culturally Relevant Methodology for Researching with Caribbean People." *International Journal of Qualitative Methods* 17, no. 1 (December 2018): 1–10. https://doi.org/10.1177/1609406918813772.

Powell, Dorian. "The Role of Women in the Caribbean." *Social and Economic Studies* 33, no. 2 (1984): 97–122. http://www.jstor.org/stable/27862073.

Richardson, Yolanda. *Negen huizen, verschillende gezinnen en veel kinderen bou baranca* [Nine houses, different families and many children under the rocks]. Unpublished exhibition research report. Oranjestad: National Archaeological Museum Aruba, July 2009.

Tuhiwai-Smith, Linda. *Decolonizing Methodologies: Research and Indigenous Peoples.* London: Zed Books, 1999.

University of the Netherlands Antilles, ed. *Vrouwen van de Nederlandse Antillen en Aruba: Naar een betere toekomst. De positie van de Antilliaanse en Arubaanse vrouw in het heden, verleden en in de toekomst* [Women of the Netherlands Antilles and Aruba: Toward a better future. The position of the Antillean and Aruban woman in the present, past and future]. Ministerie van Binnenlandse Zaken en Koninkrijksrelaties, 2010. https://open.overheid.nl/repository/ronl-archief-e9a8b4ec-aed9-4b4a-98b4-e5d79690a805/1/pdf/vrouwen-van-de-na-enaruba.pdf.

CHAPTER 22

"Sintimentunan Derá, Sla Ekspresá": How Curaçaoans in the Netherlands Perceive Partner Violence

Kristen Martina

Abstract

Partner violence is one of the most common forms of domestic violence in the Dutch Caribbean. In the literature on domestic violence in the Dutch Caribbean context, little attention has been paid to how the islanders themselves define and perceive domestic violence. The focus of this criminological study is on perceptions of physical violence between partners among Curaçaoans in the Netherlands and their views of the roles of gender and emotion regulation within it. The study is situated against the backdrop of legal developments regarding the Istanbul Convention. Critically employing the concepts of machismo and marianismo, the contribution assesses the relationship between gender and emotion regulation in partner violence and offers directions for further research and policy directions in the Dutch Caribbean context.

Keywords

domestic violence – perceptions of violence – diaspora – machismo – marianismo

1 Developments Regarding the Istanbul Convention

In the Caribbean part of the Kingdom of the Netherlands, partner violence is one of the most common forms of violence in the home.[1] In the literature on

1 The title of this contribution is a Papiamentu proverb that translates as "hidden emotions, expressed violence." In the Netherlands, domestic violence is defined as "violence committed by someone in the victim's immediate personal environment, where the victim is in a relationship of dependency and/or unfreedom with respect to the perpetrator and where, in a number of cases, inequalities between and stereotypical norms about women and men as a

 | DOI:10.1163/9789004690882_024

domestic violence in the Dutch Caribbean context, little attention has been paid to how the islanders themselves define and perceive domestic violence.[2] This contribution is a synopsis of a wider criminological research undertaken in 2017 on perceptions of physical violence between partners among Curaçaoans in the Netherlands and their views of the roles of gender and emotion regulation within it. First, it establishes a theoretical framework to approach the prevalence of partner violence. Then, it assesses the relationship between gender and emotion regulation in partner violence against the backdrop of current legal developments regarding the Istanbul Convention. The contribution ends with conclusions and suggestions for further research and policy directions in the Dutch Caribbean context.

In 2015, the Netherlands signed the Istanbul Convention on behalf of all its territories. It is a Council of Europe convention opposing and preventing violence against women and domestic violence. The convention's aim was to strengthen the approach to domestic violence with a view to reducing the number of victims. However, when it came into effect in 2016, it applied only to the European part of the Kingdom of the Netherlands, not its Caribbean territories.

A group of experts on action against violence against women and domestic violence (GREVIO), which monitors and promotes the convention, urged the Netherlands in a 2020 report to put together an action plan for the convention and to apply all possible means to encourage the islands, which are autonomous, to ratify the convention and implement it.[3] Meanwhile, the islands themselves have made a certain amount of progress in their efforts against domestic violence. In 2018, Curaçao instituted a multiyear plan to combat domestic violence and the BES islands have taken steps to implement

---

social group play a role" (Boom and Wittebrood, 2019). Partner violence can be understood as the totality of behaviors and actions by one person within a partner relationship with the intent to cause slight or severe harm to the other during conflict situations. Multiple forms of violence can be part of this, such as physical, psychological, sexual and/or economic violence. Sunday et al., "The Role of Adolescent Physical Abuse in Adult Intimate Partner Violence," 2011; Veen, "Secundaire analyses slachtofferdata landelijk onderzoek huiselijk geweld" [Secondary analyses of victim data national domestic violence research], 2011; and Akkersmans et al., "Prevalentiemonitor huiselijk geweld en seksueel geweld 2020" [Prevalence monitor for domestic violence and sexual violence 2020], 2020.

2 Janssen, "Caribbean Crime and Criminal Justice," 2018.

3 GREVIO, *GREVIO's evaluatierapport, Nederland* [GREVIO's evaluation report, Netherlands], 2020.

a government accord that came into effect in 2020.[4] This accord aims to strengthen efforts against domestic violence using a sustainable approach and features temporary restraining orders for perpetrators of domestic violence along with an education campaign.[5]

2 Prevalence

In figures from 2020, 1.2 million people in the Netherlands reported that they had been victims of domestic violence. Seventy percent had suffered chronic abuse (i.e., at least once a month) and it is estimated that 1.1 percent of the total population of women and 0.2 percent of men experience chronic domestic violence. Women suffered more serious physical effects from violence than men; between 2016 and 2020, 56 percent of murdered women had been killed by their partners or former partners. [6] By comparison, the same applies to 4 percent of murdered men.[7] Somewhat older research focusing on specific ethnic groups in the Netherlands shows that Dutch Caribbeans experience relatively more domestic violence than other minority groups: while 42 percent of Dutch Caribbeans report domestic violence, considerably fewer people from Suriname (33%) experience it, as do people from Turkey (23%) and Morocco (17%).[8]

---

4 Hendriksen, "Training voor daders huiselijk geweld: 'We moeten meer doen dan straffen'" [Training for perpetrators of domestic violence: "We must do more than punish"], 2021; Government of Curaçao, "Nationaal plan van Curaçao bestrijding van geweld tegen kinderen/jongeren en huiselijk/relationeel geweld" [National plan of Curaçao to combat violence against children/young people and domestic/relational violence], 2018; and Government of Curaçao, "Bestuursakkoord: Aanpak huiselijk geweld en kindermishandeling in Caribisch Nederland 2021–2024" [Administrative agreement: Approach to domestic violence and child abuse in the Caribbean Netherlands 2021–2024], n.d.

5 Bonaire.nu, "Schaamte centraal in campagne tegen huiselijk geweld en kindermishandeling" [Shame central to campaign against domestic violence and child abuse], 2022; Dossier Koninkrijksrelaties, "Verdrag tegen huiselijk geweld niet voor 2025 van kracht op BES-eilanden" [Convention against domestic violence not in force before 2025 on BES islands], 2022.

6 Boom and Wittebrood, "De prevalentie van huiselijk geweld en kindermishandeling in Nederland" [The prevalence of domestic violence and child abuse in the Netherlands], 2019.

7 CBS Statistics Netherlands, "Minder moorden in 2020, wel meer jongeren vermoord" [Fewer murders in 2020, but more young people murdered], 2021.

8 Dijk et al., *Huiselijk geweld onder Surinamers, Antillianen en Arubanen, Marokkanen en Turken in Nederland* [Domestic violence among Surinamese, Antilleans and Arubans, Moroccans and Turks in the Netherlands], 2002.

One of the few Dutch Caribbean studies of partner violence on the basis of self-reporting was conducted by Van Wijk and De Bruin in 2012 in Curaçao.[9] Recent government data offers further empirical evidence on cases reported to the police.[10] The current contribution focuses on perceptions of physical partner violence among the Dutch Caribbean (specifically Curaçaoan) diaspora in the Netherlands. It addresses what Van Wijk observes to be a research gap, thus offering much-needed insight into the nature and context of violence and the importance of Dutch Caribbean-specific factors such as socioeconomic gender relations, family structures and how they influence partner violence.[11]

3 The Relationship between Gender, Emotion Regulation and Physical Partner Violence

Gender describes the pattern of sociocultural roles and expectations of the sexes and is associated with the power differences they imply. Masculine and feminine gender roles exert important influences on partnerships.[12] Differences in expectations and power between men and women can lead to conflicts with varying physical, emotional, social and economic effects. This can be the case if one partner does not act in accordance with normative expectations of their gender or if such expectations are applied to a partner's disadvantage. An example is a father who loses his job and is unable to support his family financially, then takes to drinking out of shame and becomes aggressive. The man's behavior toward his wife could, in turn, make her respond aggressively. The friction created by such unfulfilled normative expectations can, in turn, lead to violence.[13] The literature on gender perceptions makes a distinction

9 Wijk, *Domestic Violence by and against Men and Women in Curaçao*, 2012. The study showed that 38 percent of women and 25 percent of men had experienced domestic violence as adults and, of these, 61 percent of the women and 5 percent of the men experienced that as partner violence. Of the women victims, 85 percent experienced serious physical violence, such as hitting and kicking.

10 Korps Politie Curaçao, *Veiligheidsontwikkeling* [Safety development], n.d. The report indicates 120 reported instances of domestic violence in 2019 and 190 cases in 2020 respectively. During those years, police made 156 arrests in total (110 men and 46 women).

11 Wijk, *Domestic Violence by and against Men and Women in Curaçao*, 2012.

12 People who do not identify as men or women, or who are in queer relationships, experience the effects of masculine and feminine gender roles as well. This article primarily addresses those gender roles.

13 Vaan, Harthoorn, and Martina, *Gendersensitiviteit in de Nederlandse aanpak van huiselijk geweld: Nadere concretisering van de GREVIO-aanbevelingen* [Gender sensitivity in the Dutch approach to domestic violence: Further concretization of the GREVIO

between machismo and marianismo as socially established gender roles in Caribbean society, whereby machismo is the hallmark of a man who never takes a step back and who has sexual relationships outside marriage. Men are seen as dominating marriage relations and machismo shapes men's relationships with both women and other men. The term marianismo describes the role of women as primary caregivers of children, as tolerant and subservient to their husbands and as behaving modestly and chastely with other men.[14] In fact, such gender norms are only partially true, for Caribbean women have traditionally been seen as highly independent and many have been heads of families and anything but submissive.[15] Some men have no problem accepting this, while others see women's independence as a threat to their dominant status and use violence and controlling behavior to reinforce their position.[16]

Earlier research has suggested that traditional ideas about gender-specific upbringing as well as about machismo and marianismo have had an important influence on partner violence, especially against women.[17] It is important to note that machismo and marianismo are disputed concepts that reinforce stereotyping and are reductive. For the purposes of this research, the terms are used in a specific way, that is, with reference to perceptions of domestic and partner violence by men and women. The terms are neither treated as established wisdom, nor do they describe the beliefs of the researcher or the respondents.[18]

The ability to properly experience and to control our emotions is learned in the parent–child relationship within the family. What is learned in that context is internalized and then later applied to other contexts and other relationships. A safe and positive relationship between parent and child can lead to healthy

---

recommendations], 2021; and Boom and Wittebrood, "De prevalentie van huiselijk geweld en kindermishandeling in Nederland," 2019.

14 Sanabria, *The Anthropology of Latin America and the Caribbean*, 2007; Chant and Craske, *Gender in Latin America*, 2003.

15 Marcha and Verweel, *De Curaçaose man: Vrouwen over de sociale identiteit van Curaçaose mannen* [The Curaçaoan man: Women on the social identity of Curaçaoan men], 2005; and Marcha, Verweel, and Werkman, *De Curaçaose jeugd: Over zichzelf en gezien door anderen* [The Curaçaoan youth: How they see themselves and are seen by others], 2010.

16 Gibbons, "Family Violence in the Caribbean," 2015.

17 Baugher and Gazmararian, "Masculine Gender Role Stress and Violence," 2015; Reyes et al., "Gender Role Attitudes and Male Adolescent Dating Violence Perpetration," 2016; Sanabria, *The Anthropology of Latin America and the Caribbean*, 2007.

18 Sanabria, *The Anthropology of Latin America and the Caribbean*, 2019.

emotion regulation in adult life, whereas a negative or unsafe relationship can lead to problems with emotion regulation.[19]

Failing to learn healthy emotional expression, for instance, learning to resolve conflict through peaceful discussion, can result in emotional, verbal and physical violence in partner relationships. In such cases, the use of violence is seen as a legitimate way of enforcing discipline on children and of resolving conflict in adulthood.[20] Earlier research has similarly shown that those prone to use physical domestic and partner violence are more likely to have difficulty controlling their emotions, which might, in turn, be related to the experience of domestic violence as children.[21]

4 Research Questions and Methodology

Departing from these conceptual and theoretical premises around the relationship between gender, emotion regulation and physical partner violence, the present research inquires into how Curaçaoans living in the Netherlands perceive the use of physical violence within partner relationships. This central question prompts a number of related sub-questions: How do Curaçaoans' opinions on physical partner violence differ from their views on use of violence in general? Do Curaçaoans consider partner violence a crime and what is the role of context, such as the length of a relationship or of the violence within it, the seriousness of the violence and the influence of drugs and alcohol? What do Curaçaoans think of the role of emotions and of emotion regulation in the use of partner violence? What are the effects of normative gender roles in the use of physical partner violence? What role is played by upbringing in the shaping of perceptions of the use of violence within relationships?

---

19 Dallos, *Attachment Narrative Therapy*, 2023; Spangler and Zimmermann, "Emotional and Adrenocortical Regulation in Early Adolescence," 2014. Positive disciplining encompasses offering children points of reference to learn how to change their behavior and understand why something is or is not allowed, combined with offering explanations and acknowledging and recognizing desirable behavior. Negative disciplining includes physical punishment, threats, control through show of power and nonreaction to undesirable behavior or negative feedback. Asscher, Deković, and Hermanns, "Home-Start: Effectieve opvoedingsondersteuning voor ouders van peuters en kleuters?" [Home-Start: Effective parenting support for parents of preschool children?], 2007.

20 Krug et al., "The World Report on Violence and Health," 2002; and San, *Stelen en steken: Delinquent gedrag van Curaçaose jongens in Nederland* [Stealing and stabbing: Delinquent behavior of boys from Curaçao in the Netherlands], 1998.

21 Veen and Bogaerts, "Huiselijk geweld in Nederland" [Domestic violence in the Netherlands], 2010.

The research, using data collected by way of qualitative interviews carried out in 2016, was qualitative and descriptive in nature and centered on understanding the lives of individuals, the meaning they ascribed to their surroundings and how they conducted themselves in turn.[22] The point of the research was not to achieve any supposedly objective accuracy; I rather was interested in individual feelings, experiences and observations.[23] The criteria for participants were that they had been born in Curaçao but were residing in the Netherlands as first-generation immigrants, that they were between the ages of twenty-one and forty-five and were currently or had previously at some point been in partner relationships. The particular type of relationship, whether temporary or long-term, heterosexual or not, married or not, was of no importance for our purposes, nor were socioeconomic standing, level of education, sexual orientation, physical disability and whether or not they had children or in fact any other such characteristics: none of that formed any criterion for taking part in the research. Personal experience of partner violence was not necessary either, and, indeed, most respondents had no experience of it. The snowball method[24] was adopted to attract participants for this research as well as respondents who took part in Joosen and Slotboom's 2017 Caribbean Women & Crime (CWC) research.[25] In the end, twenty-one Afro-Curaçaoan respondents took part, including eleven men and ten women, of whom fourteen belonged to the age group of twenty-one to thirty, and seven to the age group thirty-one to forty-five. Eleven respondents were students at the time at various levels of education, seven were employed while the economic status of the remaining three was unknown. All the respondents lived in the large

22 The master's thesis also pays attention to perceptions around reporting violence to the police and to victims receiving government aid and welfare support. See Martina, "Sintimentunan derá, sla ekspresá," 2017. On the methodological orientation of the interviews, see Boeije and Bleijenbergh, *Analyseren in kwalitatief onderzoek: Denken en doen* [Analysis in quantitative research: Thinking and doing], 2023; and Leun and Bijleveld, "Empirisch onderzoek in de Nederlandse criminologie. Een inventarisatie van 25 jaar methoden en technieken" [Empirical research in Dutch criminology. An inventory of 25 years of methods and techniques], 2009.

23 Here, I follow the insights offered in Baarda et al., *Basisboek kwalitatief onderzoek: handleiding voor het opzetten en uitvoeren van kwalitatief onderzoek* [Learning book on qualitative research: Manual for setting up and conducting qualitative research], 2021.

24 Kleemans, Korf, and Staring, "Mensen van vlees en bloed. Kwalitatief onderzoek in de criminologie" [People of flesh and blood. Qualitative research in criminology], 2008. In the snowball method, individual research respondents help to recruit more potential respondents.

25 Joosen and Slotboom, "Experienced Racism, Attachment and the Risk of Offending among Dutch Caribbean Women," 2021.

metropolitan areas of the Netherlands. A direct, qualitative approach was used, with selected individuals being interviewed one at a time and face-to-face, using a set list of question-subjects but with no multiple-choice answers. Literal transcriptions of the interviews were compiled, names were anonymized and the results were analyzed by hand using a labeling system to answer the main research question.[26]

5 Violence within and outside Partner Relationships and the Perception of Partner Violence as a Crime

None of the respondents were in favor of the use of physical violence whether within or outside partner relationships; in fact, all disapproved of violence in the strongest terms. All the respondents said that they would never want to initiate physical violence and would want to avoid it. However, opinions differed on the subject of whether there is a difference between partner violence and violence in general, with six of the respondents seeing no difference and seeing both sorts of violence as equally deplorable. Respondents said that, in many cases, non-partner violence relationships are of shorter duration, with bystanders often able to intervene to prevent the possibility of serious injury. Furthermore, with that sort of violence, there is less chance that the perpetrator and victim will encounter each other again. In cases of violence involving third parties (non-domestic, by strangers), it was perceived that people are more inclined to use violence to defend themselves, in which case the presence of others is named as a reinforcing factor to the use of violence, so as to avoid looking silly or cowardly in front of others. Respondents were less likely to use this reasoning in cases of partner violence as the point is to recover a certain amount of respect or dignity—from the bystanders or from the perpetrator or for one's own self-respect. Some see such violence as a matter of establishing rank, as just about the only way of earning respect in such circumstances, to save face and show oneself to be anyone's equal. Previous research, too, has established the important role of respect and dignity in resorting to violent behavior.[27]

---

26 Baarda et al., *Basisboek kwalitatief onderzoek*, 2021; Gibbs, *Analyzing Qualitative Data*, 2008.

27 Janssen and San, "In de leer over eer bij Curaçaose jongens: Mogelijkheden voor verdieping van het begrip 'eergerelateerd geweld'" [Learning about honor among Curaçaoan boys: Possibilities for deepening the concept of "honor-related violence"], 2014; Oldenboom, "De Antilliaans-Nederlandse subcultuur van geweld" [The Antillean-Dutch

Ten of the respondents considered partner violence to be more reprehensible than general violence. In cases of partner violence and the acceptance of partner violence, respondents were readier to cite factors such as love, emotional bonds and financial dependence. Respondents thought it important to give the perpetrator an effective signal, the ending of the relationship being seen as the primary means of escape. Respondents saw it as quite "natural" that the acceptance of even a single instance of physical violence would encourage a perpetrator to use more violence in the future. A number of respondents, while aware that violence might be used by either partner, still used masculine terms in reference to perpetrators, implying that most people expect that most perpetrators will be men. Agreeing with earlier research, respondents to this research, too, said that power, in the sense of wishing to exert control over others, is an important factor.[28] Respondents felt it was about one partner forcing the other to do what they wanted them to do, even against their will.[29]

Two respondents gave examples of the role of power. Juni (27), who, at the time of his interview, was in a non-violent relationship, had this to say about his former partner:

> She used to hit me, really hit me, and if we disagreed or anything or things didn't go as she wanted, we argued and had shouting matches and stuff.

Maritza (45), also in a non-violent relationship at the time of her interview, said this of her ex:

> No, it was just him who hit me. He kept yelling at you, and if you didn't react as he wanted you to, you got a slap. I couldn't do anything. Respect, that was his reason. And to make me the person he wanted me to be. I think it was wrong: I'm still not over it.

All the respondents in this research saw partner violence as a crime. Matters of context, such as the length of the relationship or the length of time violence had gone on, the severity of the violence and the influence of narcotics, played no significant part in perceptions of violence as criminal. The severity of the violence was of greater significance to a smaller proportion (five) of the respondents.

---

subculture of violence], 2010. Editors' note: see also contribution by Henriquez in this section, discussing the class dimensions of perceptions of violence.

28 Boonzaier and De La Rey, "Woman Abuse," 2004; DeShong, "Gender, Sexuality & Sexual Violence: A Feminist Analysis of Vincentian Women's Experiences in Violent Heterosexual Relationships," 2011; Hadeed and El-Bassel, "Social Support Among Afro-Trinidadian Women Experiencing Intimate Partner Violence," 2006.

29 Dobash and Dobash, "Women's Violence to Men in Intimate Relationships," 2004.

6 How Curaçaoans View Emotions in Connection with Partner Violence

Various respondents described themselves as being reticent about their negative feelings. The majority reported that, if they felt angry or disappointed or depressed, they tried to remain self-possessed and avoided saying or doing anything they might come to regret. Most respondents did say that, once they had calmed down, they would approach the person or partner concerned to discuss things and resolve the problem. A remarkable thing here was that none of the respondents gave details of exactly how they personally would do that; they all tended to answer in the abstract. Very rarely did they say anything about their deeper feelings, in particular negative experiences with their own partners. Most of the respondents thought emotions play a significant role in physical violence in relationships, believing that negative emotions arising in combination with inadequate communication could lead to physical violence as a means of release because of not adequately addressing the root cause of the conflict. The respondents also said that, for some sections of Curaçaoan society, the expression of negative feelings is seen as making oneself vulnerable, which is seen as a sign of weakness.

Respondents spoke of two more factors that have an effect on emotional expression within relationships. The first of those is upbringing. On the one hand, children in conflict with parents have little room to express negative feelings and talk through the conflict. On the other hand, children are less likely to see their parents expressing negative feelings toward each other in a healthy way. Children must be obedient above all and do as their parents tell them. One of the respondents, Mayron (22), who is a student, gave this example of how things go:

> In Curaçao, we're brought up being told, you mustn't contradict and stuff; so if a child wants to express an opinion, say, he's more likely to be told, 'you hold your tongue and go to your room!'

Some of the respondents saw their reticence about negative feelings as part of their nature rather than their upbringing. Neither girls nor boys are taught much about how to deal with negative feelings; they are not used to being asked about or sharing their thoughts about things. Having too much to say and unusual opinions can soon be seen as disrespectful. Some parents find it hard to talk to their children about sensitive subjects, such as sex or their general problems, or to talk openly about difficult things, such as sadness, anger and disappointment. A well-known saying describes this: "Ora florin ta papia, depchi ta keda afo" (when dollars [adults] talk, dimes [children] keep quiet).

Various respondents in this research reported that they want to raise their own children with more openness and two-way communication about both positive and negative feelings.

The second factor is how feelings are associated with masculine and feminine gender roles. On the one hand, they said that it is less acceptable for boys to cry and that men are more reluctant to show their feelings by crying or talking about their emotional needs in order not to seem weak, or "gay," for none of that matches the picture of men and macho behavior. Men, therefore, seek other ways of dealing with their feelings, such as shouting, using violence, leaving a relationship or being unfaithful. Both men and women explained away certain behavioral differences on the basis of sexual difference and as having nothing to do with gender norms attached to their upbringing. This is apparent in the answer given by Jeandrelica, a working mother of four children, who, when asked about the different ways boys and girls express their feelings, said:

> Women are always gentle. I can already see that I'm more protective of my daughter because I can see that my sons are able to deal with their own problems. They fight their corner straight away, they hit back immediately. But my daughter's more, like, you know, 'Whatever ... !'

On the other hand, women are raised to believe that men can not be trusted, that they will be unfaithful to their women or will leave them. Respondent Maritza (45), a working mother of two, who was in a relationship with a man at the time of the interview, stated:

> I've always got it in the back of my mind that men will walk away; in every one of my relationships, it was like: If you want to leave, then go ... Everyone always leaves. And so they all left, literally and figuratively.

Such expectations leave little room for people to make themselves emotionally available and create sustainable relationships.[30] Confirming earlier Curaçaoan research, various respondents acknowledged that cultures of communication in Curaçaoan relationships are generally inadequate or lacking in depth, which causes lack of mutual trust, negative expectations, unfaithfulness, tension in relationships and violence.[31]

---

30 Dijke, Hulst, and Terpstra, *Mama soltera: De positie van "alleenstaande" Curaçaose en Arubaanse moeders in Nederland* [Single mothers: The position of "single" Curaçaoan and Aruban mothers in the Netherlands], 1990.

31 Marcha and Verweel, *De Curaçaose man: Vrouwen over de sociale identiteit van Curaçaose mannen*, 2005; and Marcha, Verweel, and Werkman, *De Curaçaose jeugd: Over zichzelf en gezien door anderen*, 2010.

7 Masculine and Feminine Gender Roles in Relation to Physical Partner Violence

According to the respondents, certain aspects of machismo and marianismo can have their parts to play in partner violence, with many of them mentioning the authoritarian and aggressive element of machismo. The physical violence of men is seen as a way for them to maintain or reinforce their "honor" or their position of power. For example, if a man is insulted or humiliated in words or deeds, or if his wife fails to treat him as he wishes or expects, he might consider that behavior as provocative. DeShong suggests that violence against women is often rationalized and justified as a normal response to behavior that threatens traditional gender roles—such as women being unfaithful—because a man's honor depends on his wife's sexual integrity.[32] Other research has shown that men use violence to reinforce the predominance of their masculine identity and position of power and the attendant subordination of women.[33] A number of respondents said they often recognized this mindset in men. Along with it comes the subordinate and subservient aspect of marianismo and the particular levels of (in)dependence of Curaçaoan women that are seen as a factor in their acceptance of men's physical violence. However, the ability to look after themselves and the refusal to be submissive are also seen as risk factors for violence. All in all, the respondents do not ignore the role of machismo in partner violence. Respondent Jeandrelica had this to say about it:

> Most men think they can hit you. As I see it, they're allowed to do what they like, but as soon as a woman does what they do, for example, that's it. They go absolutely mad. I think that's strange. In other words, you're allowed to do things that women aren't.

Respondent Ramir, a thirty-seven-year-old police officer with experience of domestic violence cases in the community, confirms this view:

> Well, a certain value is ascribed to men in Curaçaoan society. That means men do what they like, they think they can lay hands on women with no consequence ... No woman wants to be a side chick. Women come

32 DeShong, "Gender, Sexuality & Sexual Violence: A Feminist Analysis of Vincentian Women's Experiences in Violent Heterosexual Relationships," 2011; Di Bella, "Name, Blood and Miracles: The Claims to Renown in Traditional Sicily," 1992; and Janssen and San, "In de leer over eer bij Curaçaose jongens: Mogelijkheden voor verdieping van het begrip 'eergerelateerd geweld,'" 2014.

33 Boonzaier and De La Rey, "Woman Abuse," 2004. Editors' note: for a discussion of machismo in relation to homosexuality, see contribution by Kleinmoedig in this volume.

> with their fancy talk to get in a relationship with a man and once they're in, they start applying pressure: "You've got no time for me!" ... and all this: "We never go out anymore, we don't do anything ..." And all this talk drives men mad. Especially if the man isn't so well off and that. Then he gets angry and puts his hands on the woman, you see?

When a relationship is to some degree unequal, a certain pattern of behavior is used to maintain the power of one partner over the other. Partners then play their assigned gender roles within the relationship and perpetuate each other's behavior.[34] In addition to recognizing the effect gender roles can have on partner violence, various respondents reported that gender roles alone are not the only determining factor but that the particular circumstances, individual character and the level of communication and understanding in any given relationship also have significant effects in cases of partner violence.

8 Upbringing and Partner Violence

The respondents felt that upbringing plays a significant role regarding the use of physical violence but is not the determining factor for either its perception or the use of it. The respondents recognize the presence of physical discipline in Curaçaoan upbringing—in the form of a light correctional slap—which more of the respondents (8) disapproved of than approved of (4) as a form of discipline. The student Mayron (22) approves of it, saying:

> In my case, if I got a slap, I deserved it, when I look back ... It wasn't as if they were going to beat me or anything, it was more to teach me a valuable lesson. It's just got its place in molding the child.

Jeandrick (32) disapproves of this view. He was subjected to domestic violence as a boy and sees things differently:

> If children grow up with it, they've all got it in them ... so it passes down the generations ... If you hit a child, parents have no idea how much aggression you're giving to that child.

It is worth noting that those in favor pointed out that they approved only if children were given multiple warnings, as a means of learning valuable lessons

34 Whisman and Jacobson, "Power, Marital Satisfaction, and Response to Marital Therapy," 1990.

and to give the child clear boundaries regarding childhood behavior. None of the respondents approved of serious violence as a form of correction. Ten of the respondents saw no clear relationship between physical discipline in upbringing and physical partner violence, although they agreed that seeing partner violence between one's own parents might play a big part in partner violence in adulthood. Six of the respondents reported that they thought physical discipline can lead to the belief that violence is a normal way of resolving conflict, and most of the respondents would not wish to use physical discipline as parents. Parent–child relationships in Curaçaoan culture are characterized by a clear hierarchy, characterized among other things by respect and obedience of children for their parents.[35] Respondents confirmed that some parents use physical discipline to maintain parents' power and authority. If children resist their authority, that is seen as disobedience and rudeness and physical discipline is usually administered in such cases. Four of the respondents saw that type of discipline as quite proper and a legitimate method of teaching children a lesson, for example, that they must not cross boundaries their parents have laid down. They distinguish between light smacking, which is seen as positive disciplining, and severe beating, which is seen as abuse. Previous research in the Dutch Caribbean by UNICEF in 2013 and by the Ombudsman for Children in 2021 confirms that image, and, in this research, too, respondents made distinctions in the degree of violence, seeing only severe violence against children as "domestic violence" or mistreatment.[36] A number of parents in the studies mentioned above acknowledged that they lacked information about how they could raise their children using alternatives to violence.

9 Conclusion

The research into perceptions of partner violence attempts to throw some light onto the deep-seated culturally and historically influenced assumptions underlying the acceptance of violence by both victim and perpetrator. The reasons for the violence described here must not be seen as the only reasons for

35 Behaviors that are seen as disrespectful include arguing with parents, being rude and refusing to do what they are told. Editors' note: see similar observations in relation to Aruba and St. Maarten in the contributions by Yolanda Richardson and Linda Richardson respectively.

36 De Kinderombudsman, *Rapport: Als je het ons vraagt – Onderzoek kinderen op de BES* [Report: If you ask us – Research children on the BES], 2021; Kloosterboer, *Kind op Bonaire, Sint Eustatius en Saba: Kinderrechten in Caribisch Nederland samenvatting* [Child on Bonaire, Sint Eustatius and Saba: Children's rights in the Caribbean Netherlands summary], 2013.

partner violence, for there are undoubtedly various significant factors in each individual case. Rather, the results give a picture of how the Curaçaoan community in the Netherlands perceives physical violence between partners.

What emerged from this research is that there is a double standard regarding physical violence. On the one hand, violence is seen as unacceptable and people are opposed to it; on the other hand, it is considered acceptable in certain situations requiring conflict resolution. On the one hand, parents teach their children that physical violence against others is not permissible, but, on the other hand, they tend to use physical punishment to teach their children obedience and respect for their parents.

Respondents think that power, personal respect and a sense of honor are important core principles in cases of physical partner violence. The reasoning behind the use of physical discipline in the upbringing of children, whether or not in the form of a correctional slap or as a way to instill obedience or to enforce power or respect, is consequently used to justify acceptance of the use of violence for such purposes in other relationships, including partner relationships. These results are supported by previous research.[37]

In addition, several paradoxes emerge, the first of which is that communication is seen as essential to relationships. Respondents who grew up with two parents and those who grew up with a single parent both agreed that they had learned from their parents that the giving of love, support and good communication between partners is crucial. All the same, they thought that communication between partners is superficial when it comes to talking about feelings and discussing unresolved conflicts, which can then cause more conflict. Second, people say that sharing negative feelings should not be seen as vulnerability or weakness and admit that this is one of the things that hinders the strengthening of relationships. However, many of the respondents told me that they themselves are reticent about such things in their own relationships and were more likely to see this as part of their nature. Women and men respondents were equally reluctant to share feelings that made them feel vulnerable. In the case of men, this behavior fits within the concept of machismo, in the sense of not showing vulnerability because they are supposed to be tough. For women, however, this does not fit within the concept of marianismo, which suggests they should be gentler and more emotional. Third, it became clear that, although a relationship based on equality between men

37 See, for instance, Althoff, "Multiple Identities and Crime," 2013; Janssen and San, "In de leer over eer bij Curaçaose jongens: Mogelijkheden voor verdieping van het begrip 'eergerelateerd geweld,'" 2014; Oldenboom, "De Antilliaans-Nederlandse subcultuur van geweld," 2010; Hadeed and El-Bassel, "Social Support Among Afro-Trinidadian Women Experiencing Intimate Partner Violence," 2006.

and women is the ideal, people do admit that they nevertheless experience some degree of inequality in their own relationships or see it in relationships around them in the Curaçaoan community. This does indeed fit in with the concepts of machismo and marianismo, which are predicated on inequality between men and women. Respondents did not perceive themselves as fitting the machismo/marianismo concepts, which they saw as no longer appropriate to a modern society. At the same time, they paradoxically recognized the prevalence of these attitudes in society, which continues to exert pressure on people to conform to gender roles. Some of the statements revealed the internalization of these norms.

This research has a number of implications. In practical terms, it suggests that a gender- and culture-sensitive approach is needed regarding partner violence. In view of the significantly gendered origin of domestic and partner violence, gender sensitivity is essential to ensure an effective way of addressing it.[38] Cultural sensitivity is necessary too: knowledge and understanding of its diversity leads to an open-minded attitude, better communication and more trust between social workers and clients and, most importantly, brings social services closer to clients.[39] It is also important to raise awareness of the effects and negative consequences of physical punishment in combination with harsh and authoritarian styles of childrearing. Researchers and educators alike must be more attentive to teaching alternative communication and childrearing skills that will work within Curaçaoan culture, especially on the matter of dealing with emotions in conflict resolution. Adequate support must also be given to those involved in domestic and partner violence, both in the whole of the judicial process and in the area of personal development, mental health and education. The subject of domestic violence must be discussed everywhere that exerts formative influence (at home, in schools, in churches, at clubs and in politics), and more information must be made available.

Also, gender roles and its consequences in conflict situations appear to remain a stubborn problem. Ever since the 1970s, women's organizations and

38 Gender sensitivity means taking gender into account and focusing on recognizing, acknowledging, tackling and removing causes of the emergence and persistence of partner violence that are related to gender. De Vaan, Harthoorn, and Martina, *Gendersensitiviteit in de Nederlandse aanpak van huiselijk geweld*, 2021. Cultural sensitivity means awareness of and taking into account the ways in which cultural aspects can play a role in people's perceptions and behavior. Hoffer, "Cultuursensitief werken in zorg en welzijn: Een kwestie van kennis én houding" [Culturally sensitive working in care and welfare: A matter of knowledge and attitude], 2016.

39 Bellaart and Pehlivan, *Met één hand kun je niet klappen!: Migrantenorganisaties en jeugdvoorzieningen werken samen aan toegankelijke hulp voor migrantengezinnen* [You can't clap with one hand!: Migrant organizations and youth services work together on accessible help for migrant families], 2011.

the women's movements in Curaçao, such as the Steering Committee Curaçao and the Women's Development Center (SEDA), have been fighting for more rights for women and prevention of violence against women in the community.[40] Even in those years, those organizations noted gender roles as key factors in the matter of women's rights and violence against women.[41] Sadly, domestic and partner violence persist; defeating them is a long process. Progress has been made over the years: there are awareness campaigns, professionals are trained in dealing with domestic violence, there is a national anti-violence plan and organizations such as Safe House, the Aliansa foundation and Skuchami are making strenuous and sustained efforts against domestic violence.[42]

Finally, it is important to state that domestic and partner violence do not exist in a vacuum. Systemic social problems such as poverty, unemployment, inequality, housing problems, addiction and mental as well as general health must all be improved as a means to prevent and address violence. For that, both the European and Caribbean parts of the Dutch Kingdom must focus on working together from an integrated approach in the fight against the root causes of domestic and partner violence.

Acknowledgments

The present contribution is based on my postgraduate research dissertation in Intervention Criminology at the Vrije Universiteit Amsterdam; Martina, Kristen, "Sintimentunan derá, sla ekspresá" [Hidden emotions, expressed violence], master's thesis, VU Amsterdam, 2017. This revised text based on the dissertation was originally written in Dutch and the first draft of the translation was prepared by Marcus Ferley.

Bibliography

Akkersmans, M., W. Gielen, R. Kloosterman, E. Moons, C. Reep, and M. Wingen. "Prevalentiemonitor huiselijk geweld en seksueel geweld 2020" [Prevalence monitor for domestic and sexual violence 2020]. WODC, December 2020. https://repository.wodc.nl/handle/20.500.12832/3019.

40 Editors' note: see the contributions by Groenewoud, Pieters Kwiers and Martis in this volume.

41 Rodriguez, "The Rise of Women's Rights in Curaçao," 2015.

42 Hendriksen, "Training voor daders huiselijk geweld," 2021.

Althoff, Martina. "Multiple Identities and Crime: A Study of Antillean Women and Girls in the Netherlands." *European Journal of Criminology* 10, no. 4 (2013): 394–407. https://doi.org/10.1177/1477370812468808.

Asscher, Jessica, Maja Deković, and Jo Hermanns. "Home-Start: Effectieve opvoedingsondersteuning voor ouders van peuters en kleuters?" [Home-Start: Effective parenting support for parents of preschool children?]. *Kind en Adolescent Praktijk* 6, no. 3 (2007): 91–98. https://doi.org/10.1007/BF03059649.

Baarda, Ben, Esther Bakker, Tom Fischer, Mark Julsing, Erik Kostelijk, and Therèse van der Velden. *Basisboek kwalitatief onderzoek: Handleiding voor het opzetten en uitvoeren van kwalitatief onderzoek* [Learning book on qualitative research: Manual for setting up and conducting qualitative research]. 4th ed. Groningen: Noordhoff, 2021.

Baugher, Amy R., and Julie A. Gazmararian. "Masculine Gender Role Stress and Violence: A Literature Review and Future Directions." *Aggression and Violent Behavior* 24 (Sep–Oct 2015): 107–12. https://doi.org/10.1016/j.avb.2015.04.002.

Bellaart, Hans, and Abdullah Pehlivan. *Met één hand kun je niet klappen!: Migrantenorganisaties en jeugdvoorzieningen werken samen aan toegankelijke hulp voor migrantengezinnen* [You can't clap with one hand!: Migrant organizations and youth services work together on accessible help for migrant families]. Utrecht: FORUM, 2011.

Boeije, Hennie, and Inge Bleijenbergh. *Analyseren in kwalitatief onderzoek: Denken en doen* [Analysis in quantitative research: Thinking and doing]. 4th ed. Amsterdam: Boom, 2023.

Bonaire.nu. "Schaamte centraal in campagne tegen huiselijk geweld en kindermishandeling" [Shame central to campaign against domestic violence and child abuse]. *Bonaire.nu* (blog), September 6, 2022. https://bonaire.nu/2022/09/06/grote-voorlichtingscampagne-van-start-huiselijk-geweld-en-kindermishandeling.

Boom, A. ten, and K. Wittebrood. "De prevalentie van huiselijk geweld en kindermishandeling in Nederland" [The prevalence of domestic violence and child abuse in the Netherlands]. WODC, 2019. https://repository.wodc.nl/handle/20.500.12832/219.

Boonzaier, Fioretta, and Cheryl De La Rey. "Woman Abuse: The Construction of Gender in Women and Men's Narratives of Violence." *South African Journal of Psychology* 34, no. 3 (2004): 443–63. https://doi.org/10.1177/008124630403400307.

CBS Statistics Netherlands. "Minder moorden in 2020, wel meer jongeren vermoord" [Fewer murders in 2020, but more young people murdered]. CBS Statistics Netherlands, September 26, 2021. https://www.cbs.nl/nl-nl/nieuws/2021/39/minder-moorden-in-2020-wel-meer-jongeren-vermoord.

Chant, Sylvia H., and Nikki Craske. *Gender in Latin America*. New Brunswick, NJ: Rutgers University Press, 2003.

Dallos, Rudi. *Attachment Narrative Therapy: Applications and Developments*. Cham: Springer International Publishing AG, 2023.

De Kinderombudsman. *Rapport: Als je het ons vraagt – Onderzoek kinderen op de BES* [Report: If you ask us – Research children on the BES]. The Hague: De Kinderombudsman, 2021. https://www.kinderombudsman.nl/publicaties/rapport-als-je-het-ons-vraagt-onderzoek-kinderen-op-de-bes.

DeShong, Halimah. "Gender, Sexuality & Sexual Violence: A Feminist Analysis of Vincentian Women's Experiences in Violent Heterosexual Relationships." *Journal of Eastern Caribbean Studies* 36, no. 2 (2011): 63–97.

Di Bella, M. P. "Name, Blood and Miracles: The Claims to Renown in Traditional Sicily." In *Honor and Grace in Anthropology*, edited by John G. Peristiany and Julian Alfred Pitt-Rivers, 151–65. Cambridge Studies in Social and Cultural Anthropology 76. Cambridge: Cambridge University Press, 1992.

Dijk, T. van, E. Oppenhuis, A. Abrahamse, and A. Meier. *Huiselijk geweld onder Surinamers, Antillianen en Arubanen, Marokkanen en Turken in Nederland* [Domestic violence among Surinamese, Antilleans and Arubans, Moroccans and Turks in the Netherlands]. Hilversum: Intomart Beleidsonderzoek, 2002. https://repository.wodc.nl/handle/20.500.12832/2742.

Dijke, Anke van, Hans van Hulst, and Linda Terpstra. *Mama soltera: De positie van "alleenstaande" Curacaose en Arubaanse moeders in Nederland* [Single mothers: The position of "single" Curaçaoan and Aruban mothers in the Netherlands]. The Hague: Warray, 1990.

Dobash, R. P., and R. E. Dobash. "Women's Violence to Men in Intimate Relationships: Working on a Puzzle." *British Journal of Criminology* 44, no. 3 (April 2004): 324–49. https://doi.org/10.1093/bjc/azh026.

Dossier Koninkrijksrelaties. "Verdrag tegen huiselijk geweld niet voor 2025 van kracht op BES-eilanden [Convention against domestic violence not in force before 2025 on BES islands]." Dossier Koninkrijksrelaties, February 25, 2022. https://dossierko·ninkrijksrelatie.nl/2022/02/25/verdrag-tegen-huiselijk-geweld-niet-voor-2025-van-kracht-op-bes-eilanden.

Gibbons, Allison Y. "Family Violence in the Caribbean." Paper presented at the Expert Group Meeting on Family Policy Development: Achievements and Challenges United Nations Headquarters, New York, May 2015. https://www.un.org/esa/socdev/family/docs/egm15/Gibbonspaper.pdf.

Gibbs, Graham. *Analyzing Qualitative Data*. Qualitative Research Kit 6. Los Angeles: SAGE, 2008.

Government of Curaçao. "Bestuursakkoord: Aanpak huiselijk geweld en kindermishandeling in Caribisch Nederland 2021–2024" [Administrative agreement: Approach to domestic violence and child abuse in the Caribbean Netherlands 2021–2024]. Ministry of Public Health, Welfare and Sports, n.d. https://www.rijksoverheid.nl/documenten/publicaties/2022/02/25/zjcn-1025034-b-bestuursakkoord-aanpak-huiselijk-geweld-en-kindermishandeling-cn-2021-2024-zonder-handtekeningen-1.

Government of Curaçao. "Nationaal plan van Curaçao bestrijding van geweld tegen kinderen/jongeren en huiselijk/relationeel geweld" [National plan of Curaçao to combat violence against children/young people and domestic/relational violence]. Curaçao: Ministerie van Sociale Ontwikkeling, Arbeid en Welzijn (SOAW), 2018. https://gobiernu.cw/wp-content/uploads/2019/06/nationaal_plan_tegen_geweld.pdf.

GREVIO. *GREVIO's evaluatierapport, Nederland* [GREVIO evaluation report, Netherlands]. Rijksoverheid, 2020. https://www.rijksoverheid.nl/documenten/rapporten/2020/01/20/grevios-evaluatierapport.

Hadeed, Linda F., and Nabila El-Bassel. "Social Support Among Afro-Trinidadian Women Experiencing Intimate Partner Violence." *Violence Against Women* 12, no. 8 (2006): 740–60. https://doi.org/10.1177/1077801206291562.

Hendriksen, Kim. "Training voor daders huiselijk geweld: 'We moeten meer doen dan straffen'" [Training for perpetrators of domestic violence: "We must do more than punish"]. Caribisch Netwerk, October 5, 2021. https://caribischnetwerk.ntr.nl/2021/10/05/training-voor-daders-huiselijk-geweld-we-moeten-meer-doen-dan-straffen.

Hoffer, Cor. "Cultuursensitief werken in zorg en welzijn: Een kwestie van kennis én houding" [Culturally sensitive working in care and welfare: A matter of knowledge and attitude]. *Epidemiologisch Bulletin* 51, no. 4 (2016). https://www.corhoffer.nl/wp-content/uploads/2019/05/Artikel-CorHoffer-Epidemiologisch-Bulletin-dec-2016.pdf.

Janssen, J. "Honour, Gender, and Violence in the Dutch Caribbean and Suriname." In *Caribbean Crime and Criminal Justice: Impacts of Post-Colonialism and Gender*, edited by Katharina J. Joosen and Corin A. Bailey, 33–49. Routledge Studies in Crime and Society 34. London: Routledge; New York: Taylor & Francis Group, 2018.

Janssen, Janine, and Marion van San. "In de leer over eer bij Curaçaose jongens: Mogelijkheden voor verdieping van het begrip 'eergerelateerd geweld'" [Learning about honor among Curaçaoan boys: Possibilities for deepening the concept of "honor-related violence"]. *PROCES* 93, no. 6 (2014).

Joosen, Katharina J., and Anne-Marie Slotboom. "Experienced Racism, Attachment and the Risk of Offending among Dutch Caribbean Women." *Journal of Ethnicity in Criminal Justice* 19, no. 1 (January 2021): 46–72. https://doi.org/10.1080/15377938.2021.1907826.

Kleemans, E. R., D. J. Korf, and R. Staring. "Mensen van vlees en bloed. Kwalitatief onderzoek in de criminologie" [People of flesh and blood. Qualitative research in criminology]. *Tijdschrift voor Criminologie* 50, no. 4 (2008): 323–36.

Kloosterboer, Karin. *Kind op Bonaire, Sint Eustatius en Saba: Kinderrechten in Caribisch Nederland samenvatting* [Child on Bonaire, Sint Eustatius and Saba: Children's rights in the Caribbean Netherlands summary]. Voorburg: UNICEF Nederland, 2013. https://www.unicef.nl/media/1402135/samenvatting_kind_op_bes.pdf.

Korps Politie Curaçao. *Veiligheidsontwikkeling* [Safety development]. Korps Politie Curaçao, n.d. https://www.polis.cw/wp-content/uploads/2021/01/Veiligheidsontwikkeling.pdf.

Krug, Etienne G., James A. Mercy, Linda L. Dahlberg, and Anthony B. Zwi. "The World Report on Violence and Health." *The Lancet* 360, no. 9339 (2002): 1083–8. https://doi.org/10.1016/S0140-6736(02)11133–0.

Leun, J. P. van der, and C. C. J. H. Bijleveld. "Empirisch onderzoek in de Nederlandse criminologie. Een inventarisatie van 25 jaar methoden en technieken" [Empirical research in Dutch criminology. An inventory of 25 years of methods and techniques]. *Tijdschrift voor Criminologie* 51, no. 2 (2009): 190–204.

Marcha, Valdemar, and Paul Verweel. *De Curaçaose man: Vrouwen over de sociale identiteit van Curaçaose mannen* [The Curaçaoan man: Women on the social identity of Curaçaoan men]. Amsterdam: SWP, 2005.

Marcha, Valdemar, Paul Verweel, and Jacqueline Werkman. *De Curaçaose jeugd: Over zichzelf en gezien door anderen* [The Curaçaoan youth: How they see themselves and are seen by others]. Amsterdam: Caribpublishing, 2010.

Martina, Kristen. "Sintimentunan derá, sla ekspresá" [Hidden emotions, expressed violence]. Master's thesis, VU Amsterdam, 2017. https://www.academia.edu/38985512/_Sintimentu_derá_sla_ekspresá_Begraven_emotie_geuit_geweld_Hidden_emotions_expressed_violence_.

Oldenboom, Johan F. W. "De Antilliaans-Nederlandse subcultuur van geweld" [The Antillean-Dutch subculture of violence]. Master's thesis, Erasmus University Rotterdam, 2010. https://thesis.eur.nl/pub/6790/Oldenboom.pdf.

Reyes, H. Luz McNaughton, Vangie A. Foshee, Phyllis Holditch Niolon, Dennis E. Reidy, and Jeffrey E. Hall. "Gender Role Attitudes and Male Adolescent Dating Violence Perpetration: Normative Beliefs as Moderators." *Journal of Youth and Adolescence* 45, no. 2 (2016): 350–60. https://doi.org/10.1007/s10964-015-0278-0.

Rodriguez, Adaly. "The Rise of Women's Rights in Curaçao: The Potential of the Women's Convention to the Empowerment and Equal Rights of Women in Curaçao." PhD diss., Utrecht University, 2015.

San, Marion van. *Stelen en steken: Delinquent gedrag van Curacaose jongens in Nederland* [Stealing and stabbing: Delinquent behavior of boys from Curaçao in the Netherlands]. Amsterdam: Het Spinhuis, 1998.

Sanabria, Harry. *The Anthropology of Latin America and the Caribbean.* Boston: Pearson Allyn and Bacon, 2007.

Sanabria, Harry. *The Anthropology of Latin America and the Caribbean.* 2nd ed. London: Routledge; New York: Taylor & Francis Group, 2019.

Spangler, Gottfried, and Peter Zimmermann. "Emotional and Adrenocortical Regulation in Early Adolescence: Prediction by Attachment Security and Disorganization in Infancy." *International Journal of Behavioral Development* 38, no. 2 (2014): 142–54. https://doi.org/10.1177/0165025414520808.

Sunday, Suzanne, Myriam Kline, Victor Labruna, David Pelcovitz, Suzanne Salzinger, and Sandra Kaplan. "The Role of Adolescent Physical Abuse in Adult Intimate Partner Violence." *Journal of Interpersonal Violence* 26, no. 18 (2011): 3773–89. https://doi.org/10.1177/0886260511403760.

Vaan, Katrien de, Hanna Harthoorn, and Kristen Martina. *Gendersensitiviteit in de Nederlandse aanpak van huiselijk geweld: Nadere concretisering van de GREVIO-aanbevelingen* [Gender sensitivity in the Dutch approach to domestic violence: Further concretization of the GREVIO recommendations]. Amsterdam: Regioplan, 2021.

Veen, H. C. J. van der. "Secundaire analyses slachtofferdata landelijk onderzoek huiselijk geweld" [Secondary analyses of victim data national domestic violence research]. WODC, 2011. https://repository.wodc.nl/handle/20.500.12832/351.

Veen, H. C. J. van der, and S. Bogaerts. "Huiselijk geweld in Nederland" [Domestic violence in the Netherlands]. International Victimology Institute Tilburg, 2010. https://repository.wodc.nl/handle/20.500.12832/1238.

Whisman, Mark A., and Neil S. Jacobson. "Power, Marital Satisfaction, and Response to Marital Therapy." *Journal of Family Psychology* 4, no. 2 (1990): 202–12. https://doi.org/10.1037/0893-3200.4.2.202.

Wijk, Nikil Ph L. van. *Domestic Violence by and against Men and Women in Curaçao: A Caribbean Study*. Amsterdam: VU Amsterdam, 2012.

CHAPTER 23

Venezuelan Sex Workers in Curaçao: Rethinking Human Trafficking and Migrant Smuggling in Curaçao's Refugee Crisis

Beatriz César Loureiro

Abstract

This contribution considers Venezuelan mass migration and its correlation with human trafficking and sex work in Curaçao. It examines Curaçao's position in the annual US Trafficking in Persons (TIP) reports of 2021 and 2022 and discusses the problems of definition and evidence in hegemonic discourses on trafficking. Building on these considerations, it argues that Venezuelan sex work in Curaçao cannot be reduced to a monolithic explanation of violence toward women. Drawing on the examples of Venezuelan sex workers in Curaçao, known as *trago meisjes*, the contribution calls for attention to the shortcomings of migration and refugee policies as well as the pitfalls of anti-trafficking discourses. It thereby reflects on the policy links between the framework of migration and refugee laws in the Kingdom of the Netherlands and their impact on the sex work industry and human trafficking in Curaçao.

Keywords

sex work – migration – refugee policies – human trafficking – Venezuela – Curaçao

1 Introduction

As of September 2022, 7.1 million Venezuelans have fled the country as a result of declining humanitarian and socioeconomic conditions in one of the biggest displacement crises in the world.[1] Approximately 80 percent travel to other

1 R4V, *Caribbean Situation Report May–June 2022*, 2022; Doocy, Page, and Broner, *Venezuela's Humanitarian Emergency*, 2019; UNHCR, "Refugees and Migrants from Venezuela Top 4 Million: UNHCR and IOM," 2019.

 | DOI:10.1163/9789004690882_025

countries in Latin America and the Caribbean in search of safety and better living conditions, and Curaçao is one of the Caribbean islands most impacted by the displacement of Venezuelans. Current projections by R4V, the interagency coordination platform for refugees and migrants from Venezuela, estimate that between 19,000 and 26,000 Venezuelans have migrated to Curaçao, with projected increases in the near future.[2]

The indefinite closure of borders in 2019 and the revision of Venezuela's diplomatic relations with Aruba, Bonaire and Curaçao limited inbound travel through regular ports of entry, prompting Venezuelans to resort to dangerous boat journeys in order to reach the Curaçaoan coast.[3] During these journeys, migrants are often transported in boats that smuggle weapons and drugs and are exposed to serious risks, such as drowning in capsized boats, human trafficking as well as other forms of abuse and exploitation. The reinforcement of border security measures and further visa restrictions in January 2021, aimed at mitigating the spread of COVID-19 and curbing illegal immigration, has disrupted preexisting irregular routes and led to the creation of even more dangerous routes.[4] Despite regular entry pathways being severely limited, these patterns of inbound travel notably increased in the latter part of 2021 and 2022. As of April 1, 2023, maritime and air borders have been reopened between Curaçao and Venezuela.[5]

Lured to Curaçao by promises of high-paying jobs in tourism, hospitality and domestic work, a percentage of the women that arrives on the island by informal means is recruited in Venezuela, transferred across the Caribbean Sea and put to work in local bars in Curaçao, called *snèks*. Because their income is dependent on the amount of *tragos* (drinks) patrons buy, they are nicknamed *trago meisjes*, or "drink girls."[6] Many of these women become sex workers,

---

2 Amnesty International, *Detained and Deported; Venezuelans Denied Protection in Curaçao*, 2018.

3 In 2019, the Venezuelan government justified the indefinite closure of borders with the Caribbean islands of Aruba, Bonaire and Curaçao, claiming that the islands supported US and European interventionist policies by serving as a collection center for humanitarian aid destined for Venezuela. "Venezuela Closes Sea Border with Dutch Islands," 2019; Cambero and Sequera, "Venezuela cierra frontera con Antillas, Guaidó anuncia movilización a cuarteles" [Venezuela closes border with Antilles, Guaidó announces mobilization to barracks], 2019.

4 R4V, *Caribbean Sub-regional Platform End of Year Report 2021*, 2021.

5 Sánchez, "Curaçao to reopen its borders with Venezuela," 2023.

6 Although the term *trago* girl is often used derogatorily, I do not intend to apply a specific negative or positive connotation to the term. For the purpose of this chapter, *trago* girl merely refers to women working in *snèks*. Nonetheless, note that not all women working in *snèks* are in fact working in the *trago* business.

some by choice, some through coercion, some in circumstances where consensual and coerced entry are blurred. Regardless of their consent, their illegal status relegates them to be seen as victims of human trafficking by local and international authorities. The identification of Venezuelan victims of trafficking by national institutions is estimated to be higher every year across Caribbean countries.[7]

2 Caught in Political Gray Zones

Despite the massive influx of Venezuelans in the last years, Curaçao is becoming rapidly known as one of the least welcoming countries for displaced Venezuelans, where migrants are met with asylum, deportation and detention policies that range from difficult to navigate to blatantly inhumane.[8] The dynamics of the precarity of the humanitarian situation of predominantly undocumented migrant sex workers in the Dutch Caribbean have been neglected. Any solutions to the problem often become lost in differing interpretations of the Charter for the Kingdom of the Netherlands.

The 2022 US *Trafficking in Persons* (TIP) report demoted Curaçao from Tier 2 to Tier 3 on the watchlist, stating that "the government did not convict any traffickers, it did not identify any victims, and it continued to condition foreign victims' assistance, including residency, on cooperation with law enforcement in cases against traffickers. Lack of funding remained a primary obstacle to robust anti-trafficking efforts. Officials conflated human trafficking with migrant smuggling, hindering the effectiveness of prosecution, prevention, and protection efforts."[9] In the Amnesty International report of 2018, these practices are referred to as an "active removal strategy" in response to the growing numbers of Venezuelans arriving and staying in Curaçao.[10] Although raids by

---

7 R4V, *Background Notes – Trafficking in Persons*, 2020.

8 Camilleri and Hampson, *No Strangers at the Gate; Collective Responsibility and a Region's Response to the Venezuelan Refugee and Migration Crisis*, 2018, p. 13; Leghtas and Thea, *Hidden and Afraid—Venezuelans without Status or Protection on the Dutch Caribbean Island of Curaçao*, 2019, p. 4; Neelen, "Ook op Curaçao schendt Nederland asielrecht" [The Netherlands also violates asylum law in Curaçao], 2023; Witteveen, "The Case of Venezuelan Refugees and Migrants in Curaçao," 2019.

9 U.S. State Department's Office to Monitor and Combat Trafficking in Persons, *Trafficking in Persons Report 2022*, 2022, pp. 194–5; Western Hemisphere Program, "IOM Presents Curaçao Needs Assessment on Migration Governance," 2022.

10 Amnesty International, *Detained and Deported*, 2018, p. 10. Being a signatory of the ECHR and a member of the Caribbean Migration Consultations (CMC) should mean that undocumented people can go against deportation, opting for non-refoulement by addressing

the Curaçao Police Force have reduced since 2021, paperless Venezuelans are detained and often immediately deported.[11] Since borders between Venezuela and Curaçao have been closed indefinitely since 2018, arrested Venezuelans are detained at the Sentro di Detenshon i Korekshon Kòrsou (SDKK, Center for Detention and Correction Curaçao) with no current indications of legal and logistical arrangements available to safely facilitate deportations to Venezuela.

As Curaçao is one of the four constituent countries in the Kingdom of the Netherlands, human rights organizations have urged the Netherlands to act responsibly and warned that it risks violating international obligations.[12] According to Article 43 of the Charter for the Kingdom of the Netherlands, all constituent countries—the Netherlands, Curaçao, Aruba and St. Maarten—are responsible for promoting the realization of fundamental human rights and freedoms, legal certainty and reliable and good governance since safeguarding these rights and freedoms is a kingdom affair, making the Netherlands directly responsible for the current treatment of Venezuelans in Curaçao.[13] The Netherlands continuously emphasizes that the Curaçaoan government is solely responsible for migration and asylum policies on its territory as outlined in the Curaçaoan national ordinance on entry and expulsion (Landsverordening toelating en uitzetting, LTU), ignoring calls for responsible action by members of the House of Representatives as well as by international human rights organizations.[14]

Article 3 Prohibition of torture of the ECHR. However, the nonexistence of protection and a rather negative attitude toward displaced Venezuelans have made policies of detention and deportation the center of attention instead of protection and prevention initiatives. Until July 2017, due to the lack of legislation governing refugee protection and asylum procedures, Refugee Status Determination (RSD) assessments were conducted by the UNHCR and a local branch of the International Committee of the Red Cross (ICRC). Camilleri and Hampson, *No Strangers at the Gate,* 2018, p. 10; and European Court of Human Rights, "European Convention on Human Rights 1950," n.d.; Amnesty International, *Detained and Deported,* 2018, p. 30.

11 U.S. State Department's Office to Monitor and Combat Trafficking in Persons, *Trafficking in Persons Report 2022*, 2022.

12 Vivanco, "The Netherlands should protect Venezuelan refugees. Fate of asylum seekers in Curaçao continues to cause concern," 2018; Amnesty International, "Naar Curaçao gevluchte Venezolanen moeten worden beschermd" [Curaçao and the Netherlands: Improve protection for Venezuelan refugees], 2023; Heintze, Hilhorst, and Dijkzeul, "Venezuelan Refugees on Curaçao: Human Right Violations in a Tropical Paradise," 2019.

13 Dutch Ministry of Foreign Affairs, "The Charter of the Kingdom of the Netherlands," 2002.

14 Vivanco, "The Netherlands should protect Venezuelan refugees," 2018; and Rogier and Biegelaar, *Het vreemdelingenrecht van Curaçao* [The immigration law of Curaçao], 2018, pp. 28–29, 51; Overheid.nl., "Landsverordeningen van de 24ste april 1962 houdende regeling van de toelating tot en de uitzetting uit de Nederlandse Antillen" [National ordinances

However, recent years have seen progress in the fields of prevention, identification, protection, prosecution and partnerships, such as the support of R4V partners.[15] In December 2019, the Dutch House of Representatives accepted a motion concerning the improvement of the reception and asylum procedures within the kingdom for Venezuelan refugees.[16] This motion requested the government to provide adequate assistance to the ministers of justice and to the secretaries of state for asylum and kingdom affairs in consultation with the Caribbean countries in the kingdom to ensure that asylum seekers can be received humanely and that a careful and appropriate procedure ensures that violations of human rights are prevented at all times.[17] The government of the Netherlands offered to provide technical assistance in setting up adequate procedures and processes concerning the immigration chain as well as training and supervision by the Ministry of Justice and Security. Although these measures feature in the annual budgetary and policy provisions since 2019, the so-called Landspakketten, the situation for Venezuelan asylum seekers in Curaçao has yet to show any tangible improvements.[18]

---

of April 24, 1962, regulating admission to and deportation from the Netherlands Antilles], n.d.; "Blok: Nederland gaat geen vluchtelingen uit Venezuela opnemen" [Blok: The Netherlands will not accept refugees from Venezuela], 2018; Dutch Ministry of Foreign Affairs, "The Charter of the Kingdom of The Netherlands," 2002; Eerste Kamer der Staten-Generaal, "Nederlands buitenlands beleid ten aanzien van Latijns-Amerika en de Cariben" [Dutch foreign policy toward Latin America and the Caribbean], n.d.

15 U.S. State Department's Office to Monitor and Combat Trafficking in Persons, *Trafficking in Persons Report 2021*, 2021, p. 194; U.S. State Department's Office to Monitor and Combat Trafficking in Persons, *Trafficking in Persons Report 2022*, 2022, p. 196; Mengerink, "The Precarious Drinking Game: How Do State and Non-State Institutions Create, Enhance and Influence the Precarity of Women Engaged in the Trago Business on Curaçao in 2019?," 2019, pp. 43–44; Human Rights Watch, "Addressing the Human Rights and Humanitarian Crisis in Venezuela," 2018; Human Rights Watch, "Letter to Curaçaoan and Dutch Authorities on Venezuelan Asylum Seekers," 2018.

16 Strik, "Motie-Strik (GroenLinks) c.s. over opvang en asielprocedures binnen het Koninkrijk voor Venezolaanse vluchtelingen" [Motion (GroenLinks) on reception and asylum procedures within the kingdom for Venezuelan refugees], 2018. See also House of Representatives, "Vaststelling van de begrotingsstaten van Koninkrijksrelaties (iv) en het BES-fonds (H) voor het jaar 2023" [Adoption of budget statements for kingdom relations (iv) and BES funds (H) for the year 2023], 2022.

17 An explanatory letter on this motion clarifies that, on the basis of Article 36 of the charter (mutual aid and assistance), the Netherlands has an obligation to provide the necessary aid for Curaçao to meet the international standards stated under Article 3 of the European Convention of Human Rights (ECHR). Ibid; United Nations, *National Report Submitted Pursuant to Human Rights Council Resolutions 5/1 and 16/21. Netherlands*, 2022.

18 Caribisch Orgaan voor Hervorming en Ontwikkeling, "Landspakket Curaçao 1 april – 30 juni 2022" [Curaçao country package April 1 – June 30, 2022], n.d.; Caribisch Orgaan voor

3 Human Trafficking vs. Migrant Smuggling

The continued focus on detention and deportation, instead of sustainable prevention and protection measures, is a symptom of what the TIP has pointed out as the conflation between human trafficking and migrant smuggling. Some authors have recognized the linkages between trafficking and migration: both originate in the pressing need to migrate in search of work, and both are at risk of exploitation by traffickers or other otherwise unscrupulous agents.[19] For the purpose of this contribution, I adopt a definition of traffic following the United Nations trafficking protocol, which sponsors a coercion-based definition of trafficking and excludes consensual migration for sex work.[20] This reinforces the distinction between migrant smuggling and human trafficking as smuggling happens with the a priori consent of the person involved.[21] Rejecting the conflation between trafficking and migration, Coomaraswamy states in a report of the UN Economic and Social Council (ECOSOC) that "the lack of informed consent must not be confused with the illegality of certain forms of migration. While all trafficking is, or should be, illegal, all illegal migration is not trafficking. It is important to refrain from collapsing the concepts of trafficking and illegal migration."[22] Consent, agency and free choice thus

Hervorming en Ontwikkeling, "Landspakket Curaçao 1 januari – 31 maart 2022" [Curaçao Country country package package January 1 – March 31, 2022], n.d; Caribisch Orgaan voor Hervorming en Ontwikkeling, "Landspakket Curaçao 1 oktober – 30 december 2022" [Curaçao country package October 1 – December 30, 2022], n.d.

19 George, Vindhya, and Ray, "Sex Trafficking and Sex Work," 2010.

20 Gallagher, "Human Rights and the New UN Protocols on Trafficking and Migrant Smuggling," 2001, p. 986; Chuang, "The United States as Global Sheriff," 2006, p. 437; and Simm, "Negotiating the United Nations Trafficking Protocol," 2004, p. 134; Reanda, "Prostitution as a Human Rights Question: Problems and Prospects of United Nations Action," 1991.

21 Only recently, international consensus was reached on a precise and unambiguous definition of trafficking. Article 3 of the United Nations Trafficking Protocol, or Palermo Protocol, defines trafficking as follows: "Trafficking in persons shall mean the recruitment, transportation, transfer, harboring or receipt of persons, by means of the threat or use of force or other forms of coercion, of abduction, of fraud, of deception, of the abuse of power or of a position of vulnerability or of the giving or receiving of payments or benefits to achieve the consent of a person having control over another person for the purposes of exploitation. Exploitation shall include, at a minimum, the exploitation of the prostitution of others or other forms of sexual exploitation, forced labor or services, slavery or practices similar to slavery, servitude or the removal of organs." For an overview of the definitions and discussion surrounding trafficking in persons, see: Lansink, "Human Rights Focus on Trafficked Women," 2006, pp. 48–52.

22 Coomaraswamy, *Integration of the Human Rights of Women and the Gender Perspective*, 2000, p. 8.

become the most important factors in distinctions between human trafficking and migrant smuggling.[23] Nonetheless, trafficking and migrant smuggling can become enmeshed since the migration process can range from highly coercive and exploitative to practices of informed consent and intentionality—there are instances when a journey contains elements of both smuggling and trafficking.[24]

This conflation between trafficking and migration has important implications in discussions regarding counter-migration policies that aim to prevent trafficking but end up being detrimental for the "victims." Without a paradigm shift that considers the different nature of migrancy and trafficking, not only will asylum seekers keep being detained alongside convicted criminals in inhumane conditions but efforts concerning the effectiveness of prosecution, prevention and protection of both victims of trafficking and asylum seekers will be considerably hindered. Moreover, because gendered perceptions often play a role in the categorization—men are usually treated as being smuggled, while women as being trafficked—such policies potentially lead to gender-based violence and discrimination.[25] Many women are dissuaded from moving entirely or from choosing other irregular and oftentimes more dangerous inbound routes in the name of protection and security, giving rise to gendered migration flows.[26] This conflation is particularly prejudicial to asylum seekers who willingly engage in sex work since the majority of women are migrants who have made a conscious decision to migrate, while only a small percentage of sex workers are trafficked.[27]

4 Human Trafficking vs. Sex Work: the Case of *Trago* Women

Intimately related to the rising number of women of Latin American descent in the global sex trade, this tendency has given rise to particularly complex

23 Bakewell, "Some Reflections on Structure and Agency in Migration Theory," 2010.

24 Gallagher, "Human Rights and the New UN Protocols on Trafficking and Migrant Smuggling," 2001, p. 1000.

25 It is acknowledged that trafficking is a form of violence against women. Both the Convention on Elimination of All Forms of Discrimination against Women in General Recommendation no. 19 on Violence against Women (CEDAW, 1993), the Vienna Declaration and the Beijing Platform for Action identify trafficking as a form of gender-based violence. Lansink, "Human Rights Focus on Trafficked Women," 2006, p. 47.

26 Ibid., p. 68; Segrave and Milivojevic, "Sex Trafficking: A New Agenda," 2005, pp. 11–16.

27 Kapur, "Tricks and the Law," 2001; and Lansink, "Human Rights Focus on Trafficked Women," 2006, p. 46.

and damaging situations for Venezuelan *trago* women in Curaçao.[28] *Trago* women often work under a system in which women working in bars locally known as *snèks* earn money by way of hosting clients. Through flirtation and other kinds of sexual services, these clients will then be more likely to purchase more drinks, increasing the hostess's nightly income according to the number of drinks purchased. In Curaçao, the number of Venezuelan hostesses has risen exponentially, parallel to the increase of Venezuelan asylum seekers on the island.[29] The *snèks* known for employing *trago* women are sometimes derogatorily referred to as *puta snèks* (whore bars), even if only a fraction of all *snèks* employ *trago* women.[30]

This phenomenon is directly connected to the humanitarian crisis in Venezuela and the outflow of Venezuelan refugees and migrants to the subregion since 2017, further exacerbated by the COVID-19 pandemic. Capitalizing on these crises, trafficking networks that often operate under the guise of migrant smuggling have increased numbers of potential victims within easy reach.[31] Searching for ways to financially survive, thousands of Venezuelans arrive on the shores of Curaçao through informal means every year. Once in the country of destination, job offers can turn into sexual exploitation or forced labor with the use of violence or intimidation or by more subtle means, such a debt bondage, retention of identity papers, limitation of movement and threats of exposure to immigration authorities.[32] In these situations, those who freely chose to resort to sex work as means of financial sustenance may see themselves forced to work under dangerous conditions and caught in the same coercive

28 This claim is difficult to substantiate with quantitative data and official reports given that sex work occurs for the most part in informal sectors. See Kempadoo, "Women of Color and the Global Sex Trade," 2001, p. 29; Mengerink, "The Precarious Drinking Game," 2019.

29 It is important to note, however, that both exact numbers of inbound asylum seekers and the percentage of those who end up working as *trago meisjes* are impossible to provide. The lack of a streamlined asylum-seeking system, the UNHCR's lack of personnel to process requests as well as the nature of the work *trago meisjes* engage in imply that many people end up as invisible residents on the island. Likewise, even if the TIP report of 2022 can be used as a tool to help with such estimates, the reported decrease in both trafficking prosecutions and in victim protection and identification can most likely be attributed to lack of funding, personnel shortages and sex work networks having been moved underground rather than any tangible decrease. Mengerink, "The Precarious Drinking Game," 2019; U.S. State Department's Office to Monitor and Combat Trafficking in Persons, *Trafficking in Persons Report 2022*, 2022, p. 196.

30 Mengerink, "The Precarious Drinking Game," 2019, p. 27.

31 R4V, *Caribbean Situation Report May–June 2022*, 2022; U.S. State Department's Office to Monitor and Combat Trafficking in Persons, *Trafficking in Persons Report 2022*, 2022.

32 Ibid, pp. 8–15.

dynamics of trafficking victims due to their irregular status as nonrecognized asylum seekers.

Despite being interconnected, differences need to be demarcated between those who are victims of trafficking and those deliberately choosing to work in *snèks* or otherwise turn to sex work as a means to reach financial security. The question of whether sex work is voluntary or forced is complex and open-ended since, in reality, the distinction between trafficking and consensual entry may be extremely blurred: the socioeconomic circumstances that drive women to choose sex work or to migrate and subsequently end up trafficked may be the same. The forced conditions of work and debt bondage may be the same as those of trafficking victims. Trafficking victims may, after some time, conclude that sex work is a reliable means of financial survival and choose to continue.[33] Recent scholarship therefore often critically approaches the distinction between "forced" and "voluntary" sex work, instead of focusing on anti-trafficking interventions that respect human rights, yet ignore women's agency in the migration process and choices that lead to sex work.[34]

Even though sex work in government-sanctioned brothels such as Campo Alegre is not illegal, most Venezuelan sex worker migrants do not possess any permits.[35] As a consequence, they do not enjoy any protection under the country's labor laws.[36] Due to their informal and exploitative work situation, a *trago meisje* who wishes to report her conditions of work to the authorities will be treated as a trafficking victim. If she is willing to cooperate with the authorities in building a case against traffickers, she can apply for a temporary residence permit valid for six months. Officials can then renew the permit if the criminal investigation is undergoing. However, authorities will cancel residence permits upon the conclusion or dismissal of these criminal proceedings. In

33 George, Vindhya and Ray, "Sex Trafficking and Sex Work," 2010, p. 67; Marx, "The System Made Me Do It: Strategies of Survival," 2018. Editors' note: see also contribution by Kleinmoedig in this volume.

34 Evans and Bhattarai, *Trafficking in Nepal: Intervention Modes*, 2000.

35 Campo Alegre (Happy Camp) in Curaçao closed down in June 2020. Editors' note: see contribution by Kelly in this volume on the history of protests against the establishment of a Campo Alegre in Aruba.

36 They are thus only legally considered under Articles 2:154 and 2:239 to 2:247 of Curaçao's penal code, which criminalizes sex trafficking. See Rodriguez, *The Rise of Women's Rights in Curaçao*, 2015, p. 294; and Allen, "Acceptatie of uitsluiting? Enkele belangrijke invalshoeken voor de discussie over beeldvorming over immigranten uit de regio en over de Curaçaoënaars" [Acceptance or exclusion? Some important perspectives for the discussion about the image of immigrants from the region and of the Curaçaoans], 2003, pp. 85–87; Sloot, "Identity construction of Latin American immigrants in Curaçao," 2011, p. 352–3; R4V, *Background Notes – Trafficking in Persons*, 2020.

practice, funding shortfalls delay permit applications and temporary residency permits are canceled prematurely since lack of resources and personnel leads to the dismissal of criminal investigations.[37] This situation complicates what is already an extremely precarious reality for *trago* women, making them particularly vulnerable to deportation or incarceration in the SDKK. Asylum seekers who do not participate in investigations against traffickers are not eligible for temporary residence permits and cannot legally remain in Curaçao. Due to the inconsistent application of victim identification protocols and conflation between trafficking and migrant smuggling, authorities are at risk of deporting some misidentified trafficking victims, including Venezuelan nationals.[38]

If the core issue in the misidentification between trafficking victims and sex workers who arrived in the country through migrant smuggling is their level of agency, this means that the fight against human trafficking is intimately connected with all global manifestations of sex work. Both abolitionist and protectionist feminist scholars, that is, those who oppose all forms of sex work and those who seek to protect rights of sex workers respectively, agree on the need to address the exploitative conditions inherent in the sex market and to protect the rights of women involved in sex work.[39] For this end, women's sexual agency is important for any account of global manifestations of sex work and sex trafficking and perhaps particularly important when the goal is to articulate a framework that highlights the various perspectives of sex workers. Because it fails to account for the complex matrix of gendered, racialized, sexualized and international relations of power, a prevention and protection strategy promotes a gender essentialism that fails to consider multiple and contradictory subject positions.[40] Such strategies do not empower women,

37 The 2022 TIP report states that: "Authorities initiated one investigation in 2021, compared with one in 2020 and one in 2019. The government did not report any ongoing investigations from previous years. The government prosecuted one alleged trafficker for sex and labor trafficking in 2021, compared with no prosecutions in 2020 and prosecuting four traffickers (in one case) in 2019. Judges did not convict any traffickers in 2021, compared with convicting five traffickers (three for sex trafficking and two for sex and labor trafficking) in 2020 and eight traffickers in 2019." U.S. State Department's Office to Monitor and Combat Trafficking in Persons, *Trafficking in Persons Report 2021*, 2021, p. 196.

38 "UNHCR Aruba and Curaçao Factsheet – May June 2022," 2022; Raad voor de rechtshandhaving, "Aanpak illegale migratie van Venezuelaneren" [Tackling illegal migration of Venezuelans], 2018; "Standard operating procedure: Identification, referral, assistance and protection of victims of human trafficking," 2021.

39 For an overview on abolitionist and protectionist discussion on feminist theory, see Lansink, "Human Rights Focus on Trafficked Women," 2006, pp. 50–54; and Evans and Bhattarai, *Trafficking in Nepal*, 2000.

40 Kempadoo, "Women of Color and the Global Sex Trade," 2001, p. 40.

instead controlling and further policing their bodies. In this case, because of the essentialization of sex workers solely as trafficking victims instead of smuggled migrants, prevention and protection do not present a solution but become just another technique of power, contributing to the reproduction of the helpless victim.

Furthermore, viewing sex trafficking merely as a criminal offense, without consideration for its gendered implications in free sex work, tends to relegate the issues of exploitable labor and dangerous working conditions to the foreground. This begs the question: what is the dominant anti-trafficking discourse and whose interests does it serve? Transnational feminist authors have pointed out that tourism in several parts of Asia is not only embraced by the government, but it adds to longstanding racist stereotypes of Asian women as exotic and erotic to attract tourists. Kamala Kempadoo highlighted this tendency in the Dutch Caribbean, where it is through the reliance on sexual labor that sex tourism, which involves sex trafficking, has become vital to the national economy and contributes to the stereotyping of Latin American and Caribbean women.[41] It is important to keep this thought in mind when speaking in defense of both free sex workers and sex trafficking victims so as to neither run the risk of obscuring state complicity nor of underestimating how anti-trafficking policies inform the law through their connection to the national economy.

5 Further Lines of Inquiry

The case of Venezuelan *trago meisjes* is thus central to discussions of sex worker rights and victims of sex trafficking in the Caribbean alike. To give voice to the individual experiences of *trago* women adds new dimensions of understanding to feminist theories by recognizing the agency, autonomy and resilience of (displaced) women. The importance of highlighting individual choices, agency and the freedom of choice of sex workers prevents research and theory from reinforcing what Ratna Kapur has referred to as the hegemonic discourse that reinforces the depiction of women "in the Third World as perpetually marginalized and underprivileged," which enforces gender and cultural stereotypes.[42] While such an expansive view on the interconnections between sex work, race and mobility is outside the scope of this article, recent progress has been made on this front with the analyses of Kamala Kempadoo, Ratna Kapur, Amalia

41 Kempadoo, "The War on Humans," 2016, p. 32.

42 Kapur, "Tricks and the Law," 2001, p. 6.

Cabezas, Catherine Benoît, Thanh-Đạm Trương and Joane Nagel, who move from established anti-trafficking discourse toward more complex explorations of sex worker agency and sexuality, both within migrant and native-born communities.[43] An explicit transnational feminist politics of articulation on the subject of sex work could advance this work, particularly when considering that sex work cannot be simply reduced to one monolithic explanation of violence to women and that not all women who migrate for sex work are trafficked victims, even though this might be difficult to determine.[44]

Furthermore, literature identifies a drastic need for explicit and progressive language on sexual rights, with respect to many aspects of sexuality and sexual health.[45] What Evelyn Hammonds has called the "politics of silence," as in the lack of research, lack of education and lack of knowledge about sexuality, is a major obstacle for any account of global manifestations of sex work that wishes to focus on women's agency.[46] Instead, to echo Hammonds, "there is a need to develop a politics of articulation that can build on the interrogation of what makes it possible for women of color to speak and act."[47] Indeed, more women of color need to be involved in the research and theorizing of sex work. Research needs to explore the histories and interrogate contemporary meanings of women's sexuality within networks of gendered relations of power, racism, colorism and colonialism as strategies of resistance to violence and control. Rather than using a reductive notion of sex work that victimizes women, a transnational feminist approach proposes that sex work is not gendered a priori, having been, and continuing to be, performed and organized in a variety of ways that call for gendered, individualized and culturally specific approaches.[48]

For the case of *trago meisjes*, there is an additional need to weave both transnational feminist and borderland approaches in the study of sex workers' experiences and movements in and toward receptor countries. Julia Zulver

---

43 Cabezas, "Pleasure and Its Pain: Sex Tourism in Sosua, the Dominican Republic," 1999; Kapur, "Tricks and the Law," 2001; Nagel, "States of Arousal/Fantasy Islands," 2000; Benoît, "Sex, AIDS, Migration, and Prostitution: Human Trafficking in the Caribbean," 1999, pp. 27–42; Trương, "Sex, Money, and Morality: Prostitution and Tourism in Southeast Asia," 1990.

44 Kempadoo, "The War on Humans," 2016, p. 38; George, Vindhya and Ray, "Sex Trafficking and Sex Work," 2010, p. 69.

45 Miller, "Sexual but Not Reproductive," 2000; Heidari, "Sexual Rights and Bodily Integrity as Human Rights," 2015, pp. 1–6.

46 Hammonds, "Toward a Genealogy of Black Female Sexuality," 1997, p. 180.

47 Ibid.

48 Kempadoo, "Women of Color and the Global Sex Trade," 2001, p. 38.

and Annette Idler's gendered border study on the Colombian–Venezuelan border calls for further research with a borderland approach, which considers how the four border effect mechanisms—as a facilitator, deterrent, magnet and/or disguise—reinforce gendered insecurities that help define migrants' agency.[49] By gendering the border effect, we are able to expand beyond a binary understanding of the nuanced ways in which migrants are exposed to gender-based violence, thus furthering transnational feminist understandings of migrant conflicts that *trago meisjes*—and sex workers in general—are exposed to.[50] In this sense, research concerning experiences of migrant sex workers should be more closely connected to social research by engaging transnational gendered, racial and historically and culturally specific perspectives to avoid the conflation of these categories of difference in migration processes within the Caribbean.[51]

Here, Dahinden's call to both "de-migranticize" migration studies and "migranticize" the social sciences ring true in as much as migration and integration focused research runs the risk of contributing to the perpetuation of the same migration apparatus it stems from.[52] One way to avoid the risk of reproducing categories of difference created by the nation-state, which are prevalent in a worldview where migration and ethnic differences are naturalized, is to bring migrants into the social sciences through the interconnection of race, ethnicity and gender studies alongside a transnational feminist approach. A call for the "migranticization" of studies on sex work implies the need to find a way around the confusion between human trafficking and migrant smuggling that relegates sex workers to the position of sex traffic victims and erases struggles particular to their situation as well as making invisible any distinction between conditions of labor and the nature of labor. Such an approach means spotlighting histories, legacies and transformations of sex work that are conditioned by, or are themselves sites of, resistance within the contemporary global political economy.

A more empowering research-based approach would thus be closer to Halimah DeShong's feminist reflexive interviews, which seek ways to talk about culturally specific constructions of sexuality and sex work, avoid conceptual

49 Zulver and Idler, "Gendering the Border Effect," 2020.

50 Robbers and Morgan, "Programme Potential for the Prevention of and Response to Sexual Violence among Female Refugees: A Literature Review," 2017, pp. 69–89.

51 Ho, "Caribbean Transnationalism as a Gendered Process," 1999, pp. 34–54.

52 Dahinden, "A Plea for the 'De-Migranticization' of Research on Migration and Integration," 2016.

generalizations, acknowledge consent and involve sex workers in the conversations surrounding the manifold implications that gendered and racialized relations of power, migration and labor laws have on global accounts of sex work.[53] The research presented in this article therefore points to the directions that research in the social sciences can take, the benefits of which are transversal to both migrant communities as well as native-born sex workers. In this sense, the social sciences can play a crucial role in fostering a political environment that is conducive to the implementation of policies, which are a key prerequisite for the realization of sexual rights, whereas a transnational feminist theory of sex work includes a rethinking of practical strategies that protect women's rights in the sex industry and reduce exploitative practices in the work environment.[54]

In essence, there is a need for networks of sex workers that challenge both the usefulness of the trafficking concept to describe the conditions of migrating sex workers as well as the distinction between free vs. forced labor. Sex worker collectives that deal with issues concerning rights, working conditions, decriminalization and legitimacy are inexistent in Curaçao. Despite several organizations having spoken negatively about how undocumented Venezuelans, including sex workers, are being treated in Curaçao—such as Human Rights Watch (HRW), Human Rights Defense Curaçao (HRDC), Amnesty International, Refugees International, the International Committee of the Red Cross (ICRC) and the United Nations High Commissioner for Refugees (UNHCR)—local organizations seem to have a more direct positive effect on the situation of *trago* women, whereas bigger international organizations seem more focused on influencing political policies, especially with regard to much-needed changes in legal status. In recent years, the HRDC and the UNHCR have supported the community-based organization Famia Plania (Foundation for the Promotion of Responsible Parenthood) in Curaçao, conducting several outreach activities for women engaged in sex work.[55] Famia Plania operates in the field of public health, addressing the sexual and reproductive rights of sex workers, providing programs on sexual health and education among the population and, inter alia, promoting practices of safe sex and the knowledge and use of contraceptives among (undocumented) sex workers. Alongside Famia Plania, Fundashon Salú Pa Tur (Foundation Healthcare for All), founded

53 DeShong, "Feminist Reflexive Interviewing: Researching Violence Against Women in St. Vincent and the Grenadines," 2013, pp. 1–24.

54 Meyers, "Feminism and Sex Trafficking," 2014, p. 435.

55 Rodriguez, *The Rise of Women's Rights in Curaçao*, 2015, p. 264.

in 2019 in response to the lack of health policies dedicated to migrants with irregular statuses, often reports lack of funding as one of the biggest obstacles for the realization of programs.[56] A number of NGOs in Curaçao engaged in the improvement of women's rights on the island, such as Famia Plania, Salú Pa Tur and Stichting Maatschappelijk Zorg en Herstel (Foundation Social Welfare and Rehabilitation), provide emergency shelter for undocumented gender-based violence survivors in Curaçao in collaboration with the HRDC and the UNHCR.

Likewise, echoing the recommendations of the UNHCR Curaçao, processes for asylum requests need to be developed and implemented in order to regulate questions of status for Venezuelan sex workers.[57] Recent research in the Caribbean has found that most issues sex workers face in their work environment are due to lack of policies and laws that fail to recognize their status either as legal sex workers or as legal migrants.[58] In Curaçao, lack of migrancy status gives way to practices that encourage police harassment and abuse and prevents lack of legal access to workers' rights, healthcare and social security benefits. Conversely, a regulated migrant status for Venezuelan sex workers could lead to funding and resources being more meaningfully allocated toward human trafficking prevention initiatives and support for the victims.

In closing, the first section of this contribution briefly touched on the tensions between the Netherlands and Curaçao regarding questions of governmental responsibility for the Venezuelans displaced in Curaçao. Considering the precarious humanitarian situation of predominantly undocumented migrant sex workers in the Dutch Caribbean, this contribution then focused on the policy links between the framework of migration and refugee laws in the Kingdom of the Netherlands as well as their impact on the sex work industry and human trafficking in Curaçao. Building on these considerations, this contribution looked at Venezuelan mass migration and its correlation with human trafficking and sex work in Curaçao. Here, it was argued that Venezuelan sex work in Curaçao can neither be reduced to a monolithic explanation of violence toward women nor should it conflate sex work with human trafficking experiences. Drawing on the examples of Venezuelan *trago meisjes*, this contribution championed that a better understanding of global manifestations of sex work requires placing sex workers' experiences in relation to the shortcomings

56 For an overview of a selection of these NGOs, their focus and a summary of their programs, see: ibid., pp. 16, 262–7; and R4V, *Caribbean Sub-regional Platform End of Year Report 2021*, 2021.

57 UNHCR, "Convention and Protocol Relating to the Status of Refugees 1951," n.d.

58 Kempadoo, "The War on Humans," 2016, p. 43.

of migration and refugee policies as well as the pitfalls of anti-trafficking discourses. In this regard, if impactful change is to happen, there is a need for a paradigm shift that addresses the core issue in the misidentification between trafficking victims and sex workers who arrived in the country through migrant smuggling. Engaging an explicit transnational feminist politics of articulation on the subject of sex work could advance this purpose in as much as it considers women's agency, all the while bringing together gendered, racial and historically and culturally specific perspectives within social research. Moving away from the risk of conflation between these categories of difference and, instead, considering the different nature of migrancy and trafficking is one of the many ways to bring together researchers and policymakers and further the progress in the fields of prevention, identification, protection, prosecution and partnerships.

Bibliography

Allen, R. M. "Acceptatie of uitsluiting? Enkele belangrijke invalshoeken voor de discussie over beeldvorming over immigranten uit de regio en over de Curaçaoënaars" [Acceptance or exclusion? Some important perspectives for the discussion about the image of immigrants from the region and of the Curaçaoans]. In *Emancipatie & acceptatie. Curacao en Curacaoënaars. Beeldvorming en identiteit honderdveertig jaar na de slavernij*, edited by C. P. A. Heijes, R. M. Allen, and V. Marcha, 72–90. Utrecht: SWP Uitgeverij, 2003.

Amnesty International. *Detained and Deported; Venezuelans Denied Protection in Curaçao*. London: Amnesty International Ltd., 2018. https://www.amnestyusa.org/wp-content/uploads/2018/09/AMN_18_45_rapport-Curacao.pdf.

Amnesty International. "Naar Curaçao gevluchte Venezolanen moeten worden beschermd" [Curaçao and the Netherlands: Improve protection for Venezuelan refugees]. Amnesty International, February 7, 2023. https://www.amnesty.nl/actueel/gevluchte-venezolanen-moeten-beter-worden-beschermd.

Bakewell, Oliver. "Some Reflections on Structure and Agency in Migration Theory." *Journal of Ethnic and Migration Studies* 36, no. 10 (2010): 1689–1708. https://doi.org/10.1080/1369183X.2010.489382.

Benoît, Catherine. "Sex, AIDS, Migration, and Prostitution: Human Trafficking in the Caribbean." *New West Indian Guide / Nieuwe West-Indische Gids* 73, no. 3–4 (January 1999): 27–42. https://doi.org/10.1163/13822373-90002576.

"Blok: Nederland gaat geen vluchtelingen uit Venezuela opnemen" [Blok: The Netherlands will not accept refugees from Venezuela]. *NOS*, May 22, 2018. https://nos.nl/artikel/2233100-blok-nederland-gaat-geen-vluchtelingen-uit-venezuela-opnemen.

Cabezas, A. "Pleasure and Its Pain: Sex Tourism in Sosua, the Dominican Republic." PhD diss., University of California, 1999.

Cambero, Fabián Andrés, and Vivian Sequera. "Venezuela cierra frontera con Antillas, Guaidó anuncia movilización a cuarteles" [Venezuela closes border with Antilles, Guaidó announces mobilization to barracks]. *Reuters*, February 20, 2019. https://www.reuters.com/article/politica-venezuela-frontera-idLTAKCN1Q923G.

Camilleri, Michael J., and Fen Osler Hampson. *No Strangers at the Gate: Collective Responsibility and a Region's Response to the Venezuelan Refugee and Migration Crisis*. Washington, DC: Centre for International Governance Innovation and Inter-American Dialogue, 2018. https://www.cigionline.org/static/documents/documents/CIGI_IAD_Venezuela_report-English-final.pdf.

Caribisch Orgaan voor Hervorming en Ontwikkeling. "Landspakket Curaçao 1 april – 30 juni 2022" [Curaçao country package April 1 – June 30, 2022]. Caribisch Orgaan voor Hervorming en Ontwikkeling, n.d. https://open.overheid.nl/documenten/ronl-17f7a7223657793f8b5015fdda48cceed900425d5/pdf.

Caribisch Orgaan voor Hervorming en Ontwikkeling. "Landspakket Curaçao 1 januari – 31 maart 2022" [Curaçao country package January 1 – March 31, 2022]. Caribisch Orgaan voor Hervorming en Ontwikkeling, n.d. https://www.eerstekamer.nl/overig/20211222/landspakket_curacao/document.

Caribisch Orgaan voor Hervorming en Ontwikkeling. "Landspakket Curaçao 1 oktober – 30 december 2022" [Curaçao country package October 1 – December 30, 2022]. Caribisch Orgaan voor Hervorming en Ontwikkeling, n.d. https://dossierkoninkrijksrelaties.nl/wp-content/uploads/2022/10/Uitvoeringsagenda-Curacao-2022-Q4-1-oktober-31-december-2022.pdf.

Chuang, Janie. "The United States as Global Sheriff: Using Unilateral Sanctions to Combat Human Trafficking." *Michigan Journal of International Law* 27, no. 2 (January 2006): 437–94. https://repository.law.umich.edu/mjil/vol27/iss2/2.

Coomaraswamy, Radhika. *Integration of the Human Rights of Women and the Gender Perspective: Violence against Women, Report of the Special Rapporteur on Violence against Women, Its Causes and Consequences*. UN Economic and Social Council, January 27, 2000. https://www.peacewomen.org/sites/default/files/vaw_un_2000_0.pdf.

Dahinden, Janine. "A Plea for the 'De-Migranticization' of Research on Migration and Integration." *Ethnic and Racial Studies* 39, no. 13 (October 2016): 2207–25. https://doi.org/10.1080/01419870.2015.1124129.

DeShong, Halimah A. F. "Feminist Reflexive Interviewing: Researching Violence Against Women in St. Vincent and the Grenadines." *CRGS*, no. 7 (2013): 1–24.

Doocy, Shannon, Kathleen Page, and Tamara Taraciuk Broner. *Venezuela's Humanitarian Emergency*. Human Rights Watch, April 4, 2019. https://www.hrw.org

/report/2019/04/04/venezuelas-humanitarian-emergency/large-scale-un-response-needed-address-health.

Dutch Ministry of Foreign Affairs. "The Charter of the Kingdom of The Netherlands." Dutch Ministry of Foreign Affairs, 2002.

Eerste Kamer der Staten-Generaal. "Nederlands buitenlands beleid ten aanzien van Latijns-Amerika en de Cariben" [Dutch foreign policy toward Latin America and the Caribbean]. Eerste Kamer der Staten-Generaal, n.d. https://www.eerstekamer.nl/kamerstukdossier/nederlands_buitenlands_beleid_ten.

European Court of Human Rights. "European Convention on Human Rights 1950." European Court of Human Rights, n.d. https://www.echr.coe.int/Documents/Convention_ENG.pdf.

Evans, Catrin, and Pankaja Bhattarai. *Trafficking in Nepal: Intervention Modes – A Comparative Analysis of Anti-Trafficking Intervention Approaches in Nepal.* Kathmandu: The Asia Foundation, 2000. https://knowledgecommons.popcouncil.org/cgi/viewcontent.cgi?article=2569&context=departments_sbsr-pgy.

Gallagher, Anne. "Human Rights and the New UN Protocols on Trafficking and Migrant Smuggling: A Preliminary Analysis." *Human Rights Quarterly* 23, no. 4 (2001): 975–1004. https://www.jstor.org/stable/4489368.

George, Annie, U. Vindhya, and Sawmya Ray. "Sex Trafficking and Sex Work: Definitions, Debates and Dynamics – A Review of Literature." *Economic and Political Weekly* 45, no. 17 (2010): 64–73. https://www.jstor.org/stable/25664387.

Hammonds, Evelyn. "Toward a Genealogy of Black Female Sexuality: The Problematic of Silence." In *Feminist Genealogies, Colonial Legacies, Democratic Futures*, edited by M. Jacqui Alexander and Chandra Talpade Mohanty, 212–24. New York: Routledge, 1997.

Heidari, Shirin. "Sexual Rights and Bodily Integrity as Human Rights." *Reproductive Health Matters* 23, no. 46 (2015): 1–6. https://doi.org/10.1016/j.rhm.2015.12.001.

Heintze, Peter, Dorothea Hilhorst, and Dennis Dijkzeul. "Venezuelan Refugees on Curaçao: Human Right Violations in a Tropical Paradise." Amnesty International Research Brief 10. Erasmus University Rotterdam: International Institute of Social Studies, 2019.

Ho, Christine G. T. "Caribbean Transnationalism as a Gendered Process." *Latin American Perspectives* 26, no. 5 (1999): 34–54. https://doi.org/10.1177/0094582X9902600503.

Human Rights Watch. "Addressing the Human Rights and Humanitarian Crisis in Venezuela." Human Rights Watch, September 24, 2018. https://www.hrw.org/news/2018/09/24/addressing-human-rights-and-humanitarian-crisis-venezuela.

Human Rights Watch. "Letter to Curaçaoan and Dutch Authorities on Venezuelan Asylum Seekers." Human Rights Watch, October 15, 2018. https://www.hrw.org

/news/2018/10/15/letter-curacaoan-and-dutch-authorities-venezuelan-asylum-seekers.

Kapur, Ratna. "Tricks and the Law: Legal Regulation of Trafficking, Sex Work and Migration," Paper presented for the Technical Consultative Meeting on Anti Trafficking Programs in South Asia, Kathmandu, 2001.

Kempadoo, Kamala. "The War on Humans: Anti-Trafficking in the Caribbean." *Social and Economic Studies* 65, no. 4 (2016): 5–32. https://www.jstor.org/stable/26380246.

Kempadoo, Kamala. "Women of Color and the Global Sex Trade: Transnational Feminist Perspectives." *Meridians: Feminism, Race, Transnationalism* 1, no. 2 (2001): 28–51. https://www.jstor.org/stable/40338451.

Lansink, Annette. "Human Rights Focus on Trafficked Women: An International Law and Feminist Perspective." *Agenda: Empowering Women for Gender Equity* 1–2, no. 70 (2006): 45–56. https://www.jstor.org/stable/4066725.

Leghtas, Izza, and Jessica Thea. *Hidden and Afraid—Venezuelans without Status or Protection on the Dutch Caribbean Island of Curaçao*. Refugees International, April 10, 2019. https://www.refugeesinternational.org/reports-briefs/hidden-and-afraid-venezuelans-without-status-or-protection-on-the-dutch-caribbean-island-of-curacao.

Marx, Colin. "The System Made Me Do It: Strategies of Survival." In *Global Encyclopaedia of Informality: Understanding Social and Cultural Complexity*, edited by Anna Bailey, Sheelagh Barron, Costanza Curro, Elizabeth Teague, and Alena Ledeneva, 7–180. London: UCL Press, 2018. https://doi.org/10.2307/j.ctt20krxgs.

Mengerink, A. "The Precarious Drinking Game: How Do State and Non-State Institutions Create, Enhance and Influence the Precarity of Women Engaged in the Trago Business on Curaçao in 2019?" Master's thesis, Utrecht University, 2019.

Meyers, Diana Tietjens. "Feminism and Sex Trafficking: Rethinking Some Aspects of Autonomy and Paternalism." *Ethical Theory and Moral Practice* 17, no. 3 (2014): 427–41. https://www.jstor.org/stable/24478658.

Miller, A. M. "Sexual but Not Reproductive: Exploring the Junction and Disjunction of Sexual and Reproductive Rights." *Health and Human Rights* 4, no. 2 (2000): 68–109.

Nagel, Joane. "States of Arousal/Fantasy Islands: Race, Sex, and Romance in the Global Economy of Desire." *American Studies* 41, no. 2–3 (2000): 159–81. https://www.jstor.org/stable/40643235.

Neelen, Mathieu. "Ook op Curaçao schendt Nederland asielrecht" [The Netherlands also violates asylum law in Curaçao]. OneWorld, January 31, 2023. https://www.oneworld.nl/lezen/discriminatie/sociaal-onrecht/hoe-nederland-ook-op-curacao-een-asielcrisis-in-stand-houdt.

Overheid.nl. "Landsverordeningen van de 24ste april 1962 houdende regeling van de toelating tot en de uitzetting uit de Nederlandse Antillen" [National ordinances of April 24, 1962 regulating admission to and deportation from the Netherlands Antilles]. Overheid.nl, n.d. https://lokaleregelgeving.overheid.nl/CVDR144218.

R4V. *Background Notes – Trafficking in Persons*. R4V, August 2020. https://www.r4v.info/sites/default/files/2021-06/Background%20Notes%20-%20Trafficking%20in%20Persons.pdf.

R4V. *Caribbean Situation Report May–June 2022*. R4V, September 16, 2022. https://reliefweb.int/report/dominican-republic/caribbean-situation-report-may-june-2022.

R4V. *Caribbean Subregional Platform End of Year Report 2021*. R4V, April 2022. https://www.r4v.info/en/document/caribbean-subregional-platform-end-year-report-2021.

Raad voor de rechtshandhaving. "Aanpak illegale migratie van Venezolanen" [Tackling illegal migration of Venezuelans]. Raad voor de rechtshandhaving, 2018. https://www.raadrechtshandhaving.com/wp-content/uploads/2018/11/Inspectierapport-aanpak-illegale-migratie-van-Venezolanen.pdf.

Reanda, Laura. "Prostitution as a Human Rights Question: Problems and Prospects of United Nations Action." *Human Rights Quarterly* 13, no. 2 (1991): 202–28. https://doi.org/10.2307/762660.

Robbers, Gianna Maxi Leila, and Alison Morgan. "Programme Potential for the Prevention of and Response to Sexual Violence among Female Refugees: A Literature Review." *Reproductive Health Matters* 25, no. 51 (November, 2017): 69–89. https://doi.org/10.1080/09688080.2017.1401893.

Rodriguez, Adaly. *The Rise of Women's Rights in Curaçao: The Potential of the Women's Convention to the Empowerment and Equal Rights of Women in Curaçao*. Amsterdam: Caribpublishing; Amsterdam: SWP Publishers, 2015.

Rogier, Lodewijk J. J., and M. C. P. A. Biegelaar. *Het vreemdelingenrecht van Curaçao* [The immigration law of Curaçao]. SNAAR 33. The Hague: Boom Juridisch, 2018.

Sánchez, Wilder Alejandro. "Curaçao to Reopen Its Borders with Venezuela." *International Policy Digest*, February 17, 2023. https://intpolicydigest.org/curacao-to-reopen-its-borders-with-venezuela.

Segrave, Marie Therese, and Sanja Milivojevic. "Sex Trafficking – A New Agenda." *Social Alternatives* 24, no. 2 (2005): 11–16. https://research.monash.edu/en/publications/sex-trafficking-a-new-agenda.

Simm, Gabrielle. "Negotiating the United Nations Trafficking Protocol: Feminist Debates." *Australian Year Book of International Law* 23 (2004). https://doi.org/10.22145/aybil.23.6.

Sloot, K. van de. "Identity Construction of Latin American Immigrants in Curaçao." Master's thesis, Utrecht University, 2011.

"Standard Operating Procedure: Identification, Referral, Assistance and Protection of Victims of Human Trafficking." Human Trafficking Prevention Curaçao, December 31, 2021. http://www.humantraffickingpreventioncuracao.com/wp-content/uploads/2022/02/SOP-on-human-trafficking_31-Dec-2020_Final-updated-15112021-14213.pdf.

Strik, M. H. A. "Motie-Strik (GroenLinks) c.s. over opvang en asielprocedures binnen het Koninkrijk voor Venezolaanse vluchtelingen" [Motion (GroenLinks) on reception and asylum procedures within the kingdom for Venezuelan refugees]. Eerste Kamer der Staten-Generaal, December 18, 2018. https://www.eerstekamer.nl/motie dossier/35000_vi_j_motie_strik_groenlinks#p1.

Trương, Thanh-Đạm. *Sex, Money, and Morality: Prostitution and Tourism in Southeast Asia*. London: Zed Books, 1990.

Tweede Kamer der Staten-Generaal. "Vaststelling van de begrotingsstaten van Koninkrijksrelaties (iv) en het BES-fonds (H) voor het jaar 2023" [Adoption of budget statements of kingdom relations (IV) and BES funds (H) for the year 2023]. Tweede Kamer der Staten-Generaal, October 14, 2022. https://www.tweedekamer.nl/down loads/document?id=2022D41883.

UNHCR. "Convention and Protocol Relating to the Status of Refugees 1951." UNHCR: The UN Refugee Agency, n.d. https://www.unhcr.org/media/28185.

UNHCR. "Refugees and Migrants from Venezuela Top 4 Million: UNHCR and IOM." UNHCR: The UN Refugee Agency, June 7, 2019. https://www.unhcr.org/news /news-releases/refugees-and-migrants-venezuela-top-4-million-unhcr-and-iom.

UNHCR Operational Data Portal (ODP). "UNHCR Aruba and Curaçao Factsheet – May June 2022." UNHCR Operational Data Portal, July 4, 2022. https://data.unhcr.org/en /documents/details/97132.

United Nations. *National Report Submitted Pursuant to Human Rights Council Resolutions 5/1 and 16/21. Netherlands*. Human Rights Council Working Group on the Universal Periodic Review, November 2022. https://undocs.org/en/A/HRC/WG.6/41 /NLD/1.

U.S. State Department's Office to Monitor and Combat Trafficking in Persons. *Trafficking in Persons Report 2021*. U.S. State Department's Office to Monitor and Combat Trafficking in Persons, Washington, 2021. https://www.state.gov/wp-content/ uploads/2021/09/TIPR-GPA-upload-07222021.pdf.

U.S. State Department's Office to Monitor and Combat Trafficking in Persons. *Trafficking in Persons Report 2022*. U.S. State Department's Office to Monitor and Combat Trafficking in Persons, Washington, 2022. https://www.state.gov/wp-content /uploads/2022/10/20221020-2022-TIP-Report.pdf.

"Venezuela Closes Sea Border with Dutch Islands." *NL Times*, February 20, 2019. https:// nltimes.nl/2019/02/20/venezuela-closes-sea-border-dutch-islands.

Vivanco, José Miguel. "The Netherlands Should Protect Venezuelan Refugees." Human Rights Watch, October 15, 2018. https://www.hrw.org/news/2018/10/15/nether lands-should-protect-venezuelan-refugees.

Western Hemisphere Program. "IOM Presents Curaçao Needs Assessment on Migration Governance." International Organization for Migration, January 21, 2022. https://programamesocaribe.iom.int/en/curacao-needs-assessment.

Witteveen, Ieteke. "The Case of Venezuelan Refugees and Migrants in Curaçao." Paper presented at the Conference Migration SER, Curaçao, May 9–10, 2019. https://ser.cw/wp-content/uploads/sites/280/2019/05/Ieteke-Witteveen-Human-Rights-Caribbean-Foundation.pdf.

Zulver, Julia, and Annette Idler. "Gendering the Border Effect: The Double Impact of Colombian Insecurity and the Venezuelan Refugee Crisis." *Third World Quarterly* 41, no. 7 (July 2020): 1122–40. https://doi.org/10.1080/01436597.2020.1744130.

CHAPTER 24

Women and Power

Maria Liberia-Peters

Abstract

This is a revised version of a motivational speech delivered by the former prime minister of the Netherlands Antilles at a conference organized by Bright Ideas & Services Inc. on March 1, 2007, in Curaçao.

Keywords

women – power – female leaders – women's representation

"Women and power"! This is such a broad field, as power has so many faces.

Why is it still important to keep emphasizing and focusing on the way women perform, behave or demand their rightful privilege to experience life to the fullest in a world created by the Almighty? The Almighty created man and woman in order to be happy and free to fully develop and exercise their potentials. From the beginning of time, man and woman were created to be happy together and to supplement one another, both having the power and capacity to do so, and, together, bring about change whenever necessary. Yet, as has traditionally been transmitted, obviously something went wrong. We now have to exert ourselves in overcoming all the negative forces and challenges that we encounter on our road to fulfillment.

Women are still not sufficiently connected with the terms power, intellect or strategic management or with being leaders. If at all, they are only regarded as leaders in what is seen as typically "women's territory," such as teaching, nursing or being a housewife: fields in which men feel or are made to feel uncomfortable and deficient. For men, it is a choice between being either strong or weak, and weak means being a "sissy," which no male wants to be called. In the case of women, we notice that she is capable of handling power while being conscious of her vulnerability.

Power just for the sake of power is useless and can be very destructive.

Power does not stand on its own.

 | DOI:10.1163/9789004690882_026

For example: we speak of power versus strength, or power versus authority. Can we think of the one without including the other?

The reality is that we all know that women possess the natural strength to deal with the most complicated problems, the strength to cope, persevere, endure even under the most difficult circumstances. The big question is therefore: do women get sufficient recognition for this? Usually not, and why not? The answer is simple. Because most people think that it is a natural propensity in women. We are recognized as being strong. It is the woman who conceives, gives birth and, in most cases, nurtures the newly born. Isn't this a major responsibility?

We all know examples of strong women in our lives, women who have determined the course of events and the forms of human culture. From ancient history, women originated, founded, governed, prophesied, created art and fought for our rights and for our peoples. Unfortunately, many of these women have been edited out of history despite the miracles they performed under often very difficult circumstances, their stories to be replaced with those of an endless litany of men. These women did not stop to think: "Can I do it?" They simply did it because they had to. The strength and belief came from within. Be aware that this continues to be our natural source of power.

As I said earlier, power has many faces. Let me illustrate:

In many indigenous societies, there has been a striking interplay between women's spiritual leadership and their political leadership. To give an example from a place not too far from us: in 1791, the old priestess Cecile Fatiman inaugurated the Haitian revolution against slavery in a vodou ceremony in the Bois Caiman.[1]

These female leaders do not rely on institutionalized authority but on recognized personal power. Natural exercise of power manifested itself through their acts of bravery and self-determination.

From history we know that women bravely assumed male identities as a way to achieve their goals. In classical Athens, Agnodice practiced medicine disguised as a man, risking the death penalty. Nearly two thousand years later, it was revealed that a high-ranking military surgeon for the British navy in the nineteenth century named Dr. James Barry was, allegedly, born female as Miranda Stuart.[2] In many societies, female boldness was required to simply

1 For a discussion of these events, see, for example: Eddins, *Rituals, Runaways, and the Haitian Revolution*, 2022.

2 Several posthumous biographies have been published in recent years. See, for example: Holmes, *The Secret Life of Dr James Barry*, 2020; or Du Preez and Dronfield, *Dr James Barry*, 2016.

defend personal liberty and self-determination, to be able to cope with patriarchal constraints. The Cherokee Beloved Woman possessed the authority of representing the women at the men's council and even had the formal power to veto the decision to go to war.[3]

It is hard for many people today to conceive of such broad female authority.

It is imperative that young people be told that we have come a long way; otherwise, they are likely to become cynical. Maya Angelou once said that a cynical young person is almost the saddest sight to see because it means that they have gone from knowing nothing to believing in nothing.[4] Young people must not get to the point of saying, "You mean to tell me we had a Rosa Parks, an Angela Davis, in Curaçao? An Altagracia De Lannoy-Willems, an Imelda Valerianus, a Maria Daal, a Maria Liberia-Peters?" and many more. We need a remedial history that reconstructs women's experiences and achievements as part of human history.

The urge for rightful recognition and global support has encouraged women all around the world to seek alliances with other women, proving that the whole is stronger than the sum of the individual parts. During the past century, in all the corners of the world, women have stood up to advocate against obstacles and constraints that challenge their opportunities. The young girls who attended the Crystal Palace Rally in 1909 demanded for Girl Guides and Girl Scouts in the World Organization of the Scout Movement and its member organizations the necessary attention for issues regarding girls and women.[5] These organizations have continued to advocate for girls and young women through education, leadership training, nutrition, peace and world citizenship. Other examples are initiatives such as the Million Women March[6] or the Council for Women World Leaders, of which I was a founding member in Stockholm in 1997.

In many cultures, women are not educated to be bold and take a stand. Decades after the United Nations proclaimed 1975 as the year for the advancement of women in all levels of social and economic life, women must still fight to prove themselves in many fields. The reason for this is because we, in thinking of power, automatically tend to turn to the way in which men usually see power, a way that is usually more self-centered! In many cultures, leadership is

3 For an example of one such influential Cherokee, see: Moore, Brooks, and Wigginton, "Nancy Ward/Nanye'hi (Nancy Ward/Nanye'hi (Cherokee; 1738?–1824) and Cherokee Women," 2012.

4 This was expressed during a TV conference on the subject of "facing evil." For the transcript, see: "Facing Evil," BillMoyers.com, 1988.

5 See, for example: Mills, "Scouting for Girls?" 2011.

6 See: Jaynes, "Million Woman March," 2005.

automatically expected from boys, and girls are expected to take up the role of caregivers. Even many mothers and educators fall into this trap. I think that's why women very often manifest a tendency to compromise to get things going and to keep things going. Compromising does not necessarily have to be seen as negative, but it is just that women must know when to stand firm in our beliefs.

Why should we fear representation by women when more than fifty percent of the world's population are women? Why is their power insufficiently recognized in the higher ranks?

Gradually, people have recognized that it is time for a change. According to studies on global leadership in business and societal dynamics, women in the high ranks in world business have proven to be more vision and mission driven than their male counterparts.[7] Such studies show that most women in political positions are guided by a vision, mission and cause. They are motivated by a compelling agenda that they want to achieve, not primarily by a desire for power per se. They see power as a means to achieve their mission, not as the mission itself. Women in powerful positions tend to see their way of exercising power as more diverse: more harmonious as opposed to waging war, arms reduction instead of arms increase and investing in housing, nutrition and genuine battles against poverty as opposed to an arms race.

It is my belief that our legacy must serve to enhance self-esteem and determination, thus strengthening the spirits of our young generations. It is with deep pride that I think of my parents, particularly my mother, a housewife, who stood tall in the neighborhood. She was very courageous and determined to reach the goals she had set for herself in life. When I read the publication *The Rebel Woman in the British West Indies during Slavery* by the Jamaican anthropologist Lucille Mathurin Mair,[8] dealing with the women who came to our countries in the seventeenth century from the African continent, I shivered but was simultaneously filled with a deep sense of pride to be a descendant of those strong women.

Our mothers and grandmothers belonged to a people who were stolen into subjugation, denied chastity and refused innocence. The strength of our ancestors inherited in my genes commits me to be a living testimony of respect for the lives of all those who lived through conditions of cruelties so horrible, so bizarre, that the women had to reinvent themselves.

7 Adler, "Global Leadership," 1997; and Adler, "Global Women Political Leaders," 1996.

8 Mair and Ranston, *The Rebel Woman in the British West Indies during Slavery*, 2007.

My mother used to repeat to us again and again, calling each one of us by name: "Iris, Maria, Louise and Doris, I want you to look up and be proud! Don't allow anybody to drag you down!"

In order to look up, you have to be conscious of the importance of building on your inner strength to safeguard your self-respect. This will strengthen your personality, which is an important part of your inner power that becomes visible in everything you represent.

My parents did not possess what is considered to be economic wealth and thus power. They were poor in material goods, rich in intellect and creative in finding means to manage their lives in a positive direction, not seeing themselves as inferior to anybody.

They showed respect to everybody, rich or poor, but demanded the same in return.

These are the values that served me well in taking up responsibilities and positions such as prime minister, member of parliament, commissioner, acting lieutenant governor as well as a volunteer member of youth groups or charity foundations.

Let us not make the mistake of associating power with formal education or academic titles. The most important thing is for the individual to ask oneself, in whatever position or situation that you may be: Who am I, what are my goals in life and what path do I set out to reach my goal? What are the constraints I have to face as a woman, mother and wife? What are my weaknesses and what are my strengths? And how can I turn liability into opportunity so that I, too, can be part of a remedial history tomorrow?

A remedial history that will reconstruct women's experiences and achievements so as to empower our future generation of women, fill their hearts with pride, and, as was always meant to be, walk side by side with our male brothers, taking care of God's creation while ruling this beautiful planet earth.

Bibliography

Adler, Nancy J. "Global Leadership: Women Leaders." *Management International Review* 37, no. 1 (1997): 171–97.

Adler, Nancy J. "Global Women Political Leaders: An Invisible History, an Increasingly Important Future." *The Leadership Quarterly* 7, no. 1 (1996): 133–61. https://doi.org/10.1016/S1048-9843(96)90038-7.

Du Preez, Michael, and Jeremy Dronfield. *Dr James Barry: A Woman Ahead of Her Time.* London: Oneworld, 2016.

Eddins, Crystal Nicole. *Rituals, Runaways, and the Haitian Revolution: Collective Action in the African Diaspora*. Cambridge Studies on the African Diaspora. Cambridge: Cambridge University Press, 2022.

"Facing Evil." BillMoyers.com, March 28, 1988. https://billmoyers.com/content/facing-evil.

Holmes, Rachel. *The Secret Life of Dr James Barry: Victorian England's Most Eminent Surgeon*. London: Bloomsbury Publishing, 2020.

Jaynes, Gerald. "Million Woman March." In *Encyclopedia of African American Society*, edited by Gerald Jaynes, 544–45. Thousand Oaks: SAGE Publications, Inc., 2005. https://doi.org/10.4135/9781412952507.

Mair, Lucille Mathurin, and Dennis Ranston. *The Rebel Woman in the British West Indies during Slavery*. Kingston, Jamaica: UWI Press, 2007.

Mills, Sarah. "Scouting for Girls? Gender and the Scout Movement in Britain." *Gender, Place & Culture* 18, no. 4 (2011): 537–56. https://doi.org/10.1080/0966369X.2011.583342.

Moore, Lisa L., Joanna Brooks, and Caroline Wigginton, eds. "Nancy Ward/Nanye'hi (Cherokee; 1738?–1824) and Cherokee Women." In *Transatlantic Feminisms in the Age of Revolutions*, edited by Lisa L. Moore, Joanna Brooks, and Caroline Wigginton, 178–82. Oxford: Oxford University Press, 2012. https://doi.org/10.1093/acprof:osobl/9780199743483.003.0034.

CHAPTER 25

Gender Equality and Justice in Aruba: Policies and Practices

Evelyn Wever-Croes

Abstract

The text outlines the recently adopted national gender policy in Aruba, the strategic priority areas identified in this policy and the specific challenges that Aruba faces in terms of gender equality, in particular the ways that gender is related to other social categories such as race and class in Aruba. The text also includes an abridged version of the speech delivered by the prime minister at the United Nations on the occasion of International Women's Day 2023. It concludes with insights into the prime minister's personal journey and her views on being the first female leader of the island state.

Keywords

Aruba – national gender policy – race, class and gender – International Women's Day – steering committee

1 Introduction

Under the Constitution of Aruba, following the ratification of the Convention on the Elimination of All Forms of Discrimination Against Women (CEDAW), the Government of Aruba (GOA) recognizes gender equality as a right to be upheld and protected. However, despite notable strides in the advancement of gender equality and women's empowerment nationally, there are critical gaps that perpetuate inequalities and impede the achievement of sustainable development. A targeted gender policy and an action plan are therefore needed to ensure both focused and mainstreamed efforts toward the sustainable achievement of gender equality.

On March 8, 2019, International Women's Day, I installed a steering committee for the development of a national gender policy, which is overseen by the

 | DOI:10.1163/9789004690882_027

offices of the prime minister and the minister of labor and social affairs. Under the guidance of the steering committee and through key stakeholder consultations, the Aruba National Gender Policy was developed with the technical support of the United Nations Women Multi-Country Office Caribbean.

To operationalize the gender policy and guarantee its sustained, effective and appropriate implementation, the Gender Equality Action Plan was also developed, which includes a comprehensive Monitoring and Evaluation Framework. The action plan provides an integrated, multisectoral and structured approach to the key issues and challenges with respect to gender equality and women's empowerment in Aruba. The Gender Equality Action Plan acknowledges the need to incorporate a socially inclusive, human rights-centered and diverse approach to progressing gender equality and women's empowerment. This action plan leverages linkages and synergies with national policies and programs and between government ministries, agencies and departments, the private sector and civil society.

The Aruba National Gender Policy was developed through a comprehensive situational analysis on the gendered dimensions of the status of women and men, using a participatory and consultative process and considering the international legal framework and national legislative framework. This led to the identification of four priority areas:

a. Strengthening systems and removing structural barriers that impede gender equality and transforming gender relations at all levels, including by countering gender stereotyping.
b. Increasing decent work opportunities and strengthening capacities to entrepreneurship and employment.
c. Enhancing access to justice and quality services regarding gender-based discrimination and violence.
d. Strengthening quality gender-sensitive health and nutrition services and education to women and girls, including the protection of sexual and reproductive health and rights.

2 Identifying Priorities for Gender Equity in Aruba

Given that many women in Aruba do well in terms of holding high profile and key positions, there has not been much initiative from policy and governance till date to address different kinds of gender inequalities that still exist on the island. This is accentuated by the fact that it is hardly an issue at the center of public debates, except for a few journalists writing on the subject.

On the contrary, the language used in the media is often discriminatory and the way that women are portrayed perpetuates a certain stereotype of women. However, the situation of single women as well as women in the labor market and in trade unions, and, on a different scale, at the university or at the teachers' training colleges, demonstrates that inequalities exist and need to be addressed.

The Gender Steering Committee sought to address these lacunae by conducting a situation analysis that ascertained the forms of discrimination that still exist in Aruba and put forward recommendations for the strategic priority areas. The analysis found, for instance, that discriminatory practices continue to exist in the service sector, even though the legislation and the constitution preclude unequal pay for women. The challenge thus lies in addressing the barriers in the implementation of this legislation. Civil society organizations campaigning and working against domestic violence also play a role in raising awareness and stimulating both government and civic organizations to speak about men's responsibility and stronger involvement in gender equality and equal and shared responsibility at work, at home and in all spheres of life.

Aruba has many similarities with other islands in the region, as well as with Europe and North America, when it comes to the challenges around gender equality and justice. However, gender equality has its specific historical and cultural contexts in Aruba.

Gender-based violence, abuse and unequal treatment at work and home are some of the main challenges that are not unique to Aruba. The societal attitudes toward women in relation to certain areas of learning, such as science, technology, engineering and mathematics, also negatively influence the opportunities available to women and their access to education and employment in these fields.

Specific to Aruba as a strong, multicultural society is that you have vast differences in terms of how women and men and LGBTQI+ communities are perceived. The societal perception of women is often skewed as it neither corresponds to the actual tasks of leadership they perform nor to their actual earnings. On the one hand, Aruba is shaped by secular European cultural influences, and, on the other hand, there is a prominent presence of immigrant communities from Latin America and the Caribbean, who largely, though not entirely, uphold neoconservative Christian values. These churches and their networks play a role in integrating newly arrived migrants into society and thus have a significant influence on their attitudes to a range of social issues, including gender and sexuality.

Having said that, my strong belief is in the human-centered approach. We need to navigate these different movements in society, upholding the principles and practices of justice premised on human rights and equality between and among genders. At the same time, I am committed to shaping policy in a way that ensures that the most vulnerable groups receive the governmental support they need. It is crucial to make sure that public interventions don't achieve the opposite of their set objectives because different sections of society have contrasting views on certain issues.

3 Gender and the Social Categories of Race and Class in Aruba

Aruba is a multicultural society with over eighty different nationalities living on a small island. This makes it complex to offer any generalizations about social categories such as race, class and sexuality.

In terms of gender and class, women from a certain middle and upper class have been able to advance in comparison to more economically marginalized women. Pervasive discrimination in terms of opportunities and access to the labor market as well as bearing the sole responsibility for the household remain impediments in gender equity. Class and race divides are complicated in Aruba because of the long-standing history of migration to the island, with many different nationalities and differently racialized groups living here. This is an area in which further, detailed research is needed.

A noticeable feature in Aruba is the strong sense of cultural identity maintained especially by more recent migrant communities. This can have both negative and positive consequences. Given the strong alliances with churches in many of these communities, conservative, and sometimes more neoconservative, Christian norms find their way into the island's sociocultural life. It also influences the way women and men are perceived in society and within the communities.

In a small island community such as ours, there is a degree of social mobility for women of all classes and racial categories. But there's clearly more difficulty for women from the lower strata of society as we have a disproportionately high number of women employed in the care and service industry as well as the informal sectors. And these are not only women from the working classes but also lower middle classes. It's usually women of the lower middle class who bear the greatest burden of care work.

The gender policy is thus based on a human-centered and intersectoral approach, which looks at what facilities can be created for women to ascend to the next level and participate more fully in society. The gender policy has further demonstrated the need for more research on these complex issues and how they manifest themselves in our society and how they impede women's social advancement and the breaking of glass ceilings in their different societal roles.

4 Abridged Statement at the United Nations on International Women's Day, March 8, 2023

Digital transformations in recent decades have profoundly impacted our daily lives. They have come with great opportunities for gender equality but also risks and pitfalls. New technologies are proliferating that perpetuate and amplify existing inequalities and stereotypes. Online gender-based violence, gender bias and algorithms and persisting gender gaps in access to digital knowledge and skills are but a few examples of the latter. It is up to us to enable women and girls to seize the opportunities that digital innovation has to offer in terms of social inclusion and economic perspective and to mitigate the dangers posed. Crucial herein is the equal representation of women and girls in STEM (science, technology, engineering and mathematics), ICT (information and communication technology) and R&D (research and development) sectors, which are currently still male dominated. Let us not make the mistake of thinking that the underrepresentation of women and girls in STEM, ICT and R&D is detrimental only to them. Above all, it is a huge missed opportunity for all our communities. With the world being confronted with multiple challenges, from inflation and effects of climate change, it has become clear that we need everyone's contributions in order to address the challenges at hand. Women and girls' potentials must be utilized to the fullest. Their voices, their experience and their knowledge still too frequently go unheard. Women and girls have enormous potential for contributing to a green and digital future that leaves no one behind. Their full, equal and meaningful participation is thus necessary. And that is why Aruba, through workshops and immersive experiences led by our national innovation lab Futura, aims to ignite the interest of young girls to pursue careers in science, technology, engineering or mathematics. Furthermore, the University of Aruba established a bachelor, master and PhD program with a focus on sustainable development in small island developing states called SISTEM (Sustainable Island Solutions through Science, Technology, Engineering and Mathematics). We are proud to say that fifty-six percent of the SISTEM faculty and teaching team are women, and we have also seen an increasing participation of female students. It is my hope that, through initiatives such as these, we motivate everyone to close the gender gaps both online and offline. To do so, we need to apply a gender transformative and intersectional lens to digital innovation. This means putting women and girls in all their diversity at the center of the digital transformation agenda. Let us not forget it is only through the engagement of all stakeholders that we can make this happen. It is therefore essential that civil society, including women human rights defenders, are provided with the space, means and protection to play their vital role both online and offline. Only then will we be able to capitalize on the largest reservoir of untapped talent in the world, that of women and girls. And only then can we ensure an equitable digital future for all.

5 Personal and Political Visions

As the first female prime minister of Aruba, I hope to be able to inspire girls and women to strive to achieve their maximum potential. Gender equality is very important to me, and I want to leverage my position to make a difference in gender equality in Aruba.

I am convinced that women bring different qualities to the table of politics. We are more empathetic, we tend to be better listeners and we are able to make difficult decisions faster. These characteristics also form the basis of my political vision. I am also aware that being the first woman in this position brings with it extra pressure not to fail.

I never felt discriminated against based on my gender and grew up with the sense that this was never an issue for me. My parents raised me the same way they raised my late brother. My role models were my grandmother, who worked as a teacher well into her seventies, and my mother, who also worked as a teacher. The idea that men had more rights or opportunities never crossed my mind. I have come to realize that this is, unfortunately, not the case for all women in Aruba or around the world. That is also why I want to make my leadership as a woman count.

In my professional career in the public and private sector, it sometimes indeed seemed that women needed to work twice as hard as men, only to be recognized half as much. Yet, that never bothered me: it challenged me to become a better version of myself. And I was happy with this.

When I entered into politics, I chose to follow in the footsteps of Nel Oduber, the second prime minister of Aruba, which was very challenging. Mr. Oduber had been in politics for forty years and served four terms as prime minister. These were very big shoes to fill, not because I am a woman but because of his legacy! Our supporters loved him dearly, and I was compared to him for the longest time. I continue to receive the support of my constituency, despite the differences in our leadership style.

I entered politics because I wanted to make a difference in the lives of the less fortunate in our community. The late Betico Croes, one of the most famous politicians in Aruban history, was my uncle and godfather and an enormous source of inspiration for me. I am aware that I am privileged to not feel discriminated against in my environment and to have opportunities to break through the glass ceiling. I am proud of having broken through a very important glass ceiling as the first female prime minister of Aruba. However, I am equally aware that I am not the only one.

The challenges I have faced were more on a personal level. Being a politician means no private life whatsoever, neither for me nor for the members of my family. It took some time for me to get used to this idea. The sacrifices this position brings with it in my family life are enormous. However, being a woman in this position also has its advantages. The main advantage is that I am able to strive for gender equality and address gender-based violence with more authority and credibility. The support I receive makes the sacrifices more bearable. Aruban society has shown great support for female leadership.

I am in politics to make a difference and my hope is that when I leave politics, my legacy will speak for itself and inspire young girls in particular.

SECTION 3

Gender and Sexuality

CHAPTER 26

Contesting Respectability and Sexual Politics in Post-Emancipation Curaçao

Rose Mary Allen

Abstract

This contribution explores the historically specific manifestations of sexuality that have culturally defined or challenged popular conceptions of gender in Curaçao. It attempts to find out in which ways colonial cultural institutional policies helped to shape the gender attitudes and behaviors of black working-class men and women in Curaçao after the abolition of slavery in 1863. It also looks at how this specific group replicated and contested these impositions on their lives. Central to this contribution is the concept of respectability, expressed in Papiamento as *hende drechi* (respectable people). Abiding to the norm of respectability meant a better chance of socioeconomic progress when compared to that of people who challenged it.

Keywords

sexuality – respectability – Curaçao – *tambú* – *kambrada* – Roman Catholic church

1 Introduction

In this contribution, I explore the historically specific manifestations of sexuality that have culturally defined or challenged popular conceptions of gender in Curaçao. I look at the cultural politics deployed during colonial times, aimed at shaping ideal male and female Curaçaoan behaviors in the post-emancipation period. I also look at how this was replicated and contested by those to whom it was directed. I use 1863 as a turning point in the history of Curaçao, when slavery was abolished and about 35 percent of the population became freed citizens.[1] I apply the term "respectability"—which is expressed in the local

1 Oostindie, *Fifty Years Later*, 1996, p. 56.

 | DOI:10.1163/9789004690882_028

creole language of Papiamento through terms such as *hende drechi* (respectable people)—to address both the colonial cultural politics of gender relationships and its social implications for the Curaçaoan working class.

It is important to look at how respectability was defined in the colonial policy of westernization as it was implemented within the power dynamics of the state and the Roman Catholic Church after abolition in 1863. Principally during the nineteenth century, this church became a social institution that increasingly played a very important part in the dynamic cultural encounter between enslaved, freed and free people. After abolition, while the African-descendant working class struggled to define the meaning of freedom, the Catholic Church, much more than the colonial state, grew to become an important primary institution exercising authority and control over the lives of this segment of the population.

The purpose of this contribution is to give insight into the ways in which institutions with power in Curaçao approached respectability in the post-emancipation period not only as a class and race ideology but on gendered lines. The paper also aims to illustrate how the popular classes dealt with respectability by replicating and/or resisting it.

2 Respectable Behavior: *Hende Drechi* and More

In Papiamento, the term *hende drechi* (a respectable person) has been and is still used to denote someone who behaves according to certain moral values and norms, such as good manners, piousness and chastity as well as other Roman Catholic virtues. The adjective *drechi* also appears as a verb, *drecha*, in the expression *drecha bida*, which literally means reforming or bettering one's life, in this case specifically as part of the process of becoming a *hende drechi*. The Roman Catholic Church came to use the expression *drecha bida* to promote having a "proper" family relationship by regulating one's sexual life through (monogamous) heterosexual marriage. An informant born in 1903 explained it explicitly to me during an interview I conducted with her in 1983: "In the past, the Roman Catholic Church would visit your home and when the priest came to your home and [noticed that] you were living together as man and woman without being married, he would advise you to get married, to *drecha bida*, that is, to better your life."[2]

2 Interview with Severina Valks, born in Kenepa in 1903, by Rose Mary Allen, September 8, 1983.

After the abolition of slavery, a certain notion of marriage was used to urge cohabiting black working-class men and women toward a legal and religious union and, in that way, become properly married spouses, living monogamously in a nuclear family household.[3] In his letter, read at the emancipation of the enslaved in the Dutch Caribbean in 1863, the vicar apostolic J. F. A. Kistemaker explicitly emphasized this notion and stated that the formerly enslaved should adhere to the norms of sexual morality and monogamy instead of the less secure and unstable family lives that they had presumably lived during slavery.[4]

So, especially in the post-emancipation period, the term *drecha bida* came to hold more meaning than just that of its two constituent words. The term represented an ideology with certain attitudes toward sexuality for the African-descended working class and stood for specific patriarchal notions of gender roles and behavior for men and women. *Drecha bida* became central in the life of the African-descended working class, who used the term to refer to the ideal family. During conversations with me, elderly people would often say about a couple that had lived a long, married life: "*Nan a biba drechi*" or "*nan a biba un bida drechi*," both meaning that the couple had lived a respectable life.[5]

Individual members of the working class who adhered to the ideology of *drecha bida* tended to experience advancement in their status in society. Consequently, a *bida drechi* (respectable life) became an aspiration for social mobility for some as well as a way to contest the socially inferior position that society imposed upon them. In this sense, *drecha bida* as a process and *bida drechi* as the result of that process contain elements similar to the politics of respectability—a concept that has become central in African American gender history. Scholars such as Evelyn Brooks Higginbotham[6] and Victoria Wolcott[7] have applied the term respectability to refer to a certain way of life of African Americans, in which they adopt the manners and morality of the dominant European-descended culture in an attempt to counter the negative image attached to the behavior patterns associated with their own racialized

---

3 Allen, *Di ki manera: A Social History of Afro-Curaçaoans*, 2007.

4 Kistemaker, "Aan de slaven van Curaçao: Brief van Mgr. Kistemaker, voor te lezen op de dag van hun bevrijding, 1-7-1863" [To the enslaved of Curaçao: Letter from Mr. Kistemaker, to be read out on the day of their emancipation, 1-7-1863], 1963.

5 The concept continues to be used: in 2016, a fifty-five-year-old lady who had cohabited with her partner for over twenty-five years told me that she had "bettered her life" (*drecha bida*) through formal marriage.

6 Higginbotham, *Righteous Discontent*, 1994.

7 Wolcott, *Remaking Respectability*, 2001.

communities. Respectability is seen here to be a coping strategy adopted by African Americans in their efforts aimed at social advancement and at destigmatizing themselves from the prevailing status notions in American society. Higginbotham and Wolcott have applied the term to the attitude of middle-class and working-class African American women who, lacking the phenotypically European physical features preferred by society, may attempt to enhance their status by displaying certain practices (e.g., in terms of clothing and hairstyle), conduct and lifestyles similar to those of the European-descended upper classes.

Peter Wilson has also used respectability in his book *Crab Antics*, which is based on ethnographic research on the English and English lexifier creole-speaking Colombian island of Providencia, near the east coast of Nicaragua. Wilson defines respectability as a value system acted out (e.g., through language and lifestyle) by the middle class and by women of all social classes on the island in an attempt to attain a certain level of social advancement. Wilson considers the Christian church to be a principal agent in the formulation and propagation of respectability, being the foremost actor in the public domain of sociability for the middle class and especially for women, who are notably more devout than their male counterparts.[8]

Wilson coins the counter-concept of "reputation" with reference to men, which points to autochthonous behavior—the adaptation by men to local conditions, especially by spending time on the street and, by extension, in the rum shop where an all-male crew gathers at every opportunity to drink, play games and, above all, talk. Qualities that are important for creating male "reputation" are fathering children and supporting them economically but not necessarily raising them. According to Wilson, reputation also involves a readiness to fight in defense of one's honor and a proficiency in the use of language, notably sweet talk, word games, riddles, storytelling, boasting, puns, insults and cursing. Musical ability and knowledge of local lore, fishing, carpentry and mechanical skills are also essential parts of a man's reputation and of the ideal masculinity.[9] Wilson has been criticized for reducing a complex set of behaviors to a binary opposition since, in Caribbean societies, both men and women adhere to the principle of respectability,[10] as the case of Curaçao also shows.

8 Wilson, *Crab Antics*, 1973, p. 102.

9 Ibid., pp. 149–50.

10 Boucher, "Respectability and Reputation," 2011.

3 The Culture of Dissemblance as a Methodological Challenge

My feminist approach entails looking at how institutions constructed colonial-based power in the daily lives of marginalized groups. This approach also requires looking at how these groups contested these power constructs and articulated resistance. Consequently, in this contribution, I deal not only with the way in which the Roman Catholic Church promoted the post-emancipation politics of respectability, which I have been able to deduce from archival material such as newspapers and letters and other documents written by the religious leaders, but also listen to the voices of the people who experienced and responded to the politics of respectability, using oral history research.

The voices of those historically silenced can be heard through their narratives. What has struck me is that, during oral history interviews, women especially were at first less likely to cooperate.

Scholars of African American social life have called this phenomenon the "culture of dissemblance," which is visible particularly among African American women who have, in the course of time, learned to hide and mask their feelings, secrets and private lives from the prying and judgmental eyes of the dominant classes.[11] Darlene Clark Hine sees dissemblance as a kind of protective shield adopted in particular by African-descended women, who, while creating an appearance of openness and disclosure, actually shield the truth of their inner selves from the oppressor. According to her, one of the characteristics of the culture of dissemblance is that African American women remain silent about much of what they endure in their lives. They would rather not tell the whole story of their experience so as not to be judged according to the demeaning stereotypes to which they have long been subjected.[12] According to Francis White, this behavior became a habit transmitted intergenerationally: painful narratives would not be talked about or would be presented as mere fragments of stories that show more heroism and are less painful.[13]

Attention to body language becomes important when silence is exhibited in relation to inner experiences. An informant born in 1888, while recollecting how she had become pregnant by the overseer of the plantation where she lived and worked, did not use the term pregnancy but moved her eyes and hands to describe her situation. She said: "The overseer had many children by different women. Once he [here, the informant rapidly closed and opened her

---

11 Simmons, "'To Lay Aside All Morals,'" 2012, p. 433. Editors' note: see also contribution by Roe in this volume.

12 Hine, "Rape and the Inner Lives of Black Women in the Middle West," 1989, p. 915.

13 White cited in Malhotra and Rowe, *Silence, Feminism, Power*, 2013, p. 178.

eyes several times, while hitting her right fist in the palm of her left hand] me. After the child was born, I continued to work on the plantation." Informants could also use humor to camouflage certain feelings. Humor can function as a coping mechanism to release frustration and stress. It provides a sense of power and control over those who view them unquestionably as inferior.[14]

Oral narratives have enabled me to submerge myself into the deeper waters of the lives of informants and to bring forward meaningful insights that usually do not get mentioned, perhaps not even in conversation with their own relatives. Once trust has been gained, the oral history interviews give women in particular a space to comment upon issues in their lives that are relevant to them, to pinpoint values and to condemn what they see as wrong. Their narratives explain how women have understood, negotiated and sometimes challenged dominant societal ideals. It is their oral histories that have allowed them to redefine themselves by voicing their life testimonials and (in that way) construct their selfhood. They also initiated me, as a local researcher, in the ways in which ethnicity, race, gender, class and, in this case, also religion intersect and influence people's lives.

4 Creating a *Bida Drechi* as a Way of Life

As mentioned above, the years following abolition provided the paradigmatic context for *bida drechi* due to the fact that both the predominantly Protestant government and the Roman Catholic Church feared that emancipated Afro-Curaçaoans would slide back into what they called "an uncivilized state," believed to be the consequence of their African heritage and the destabilizing influences of slavery. The Catholic Church assumed that Afro-Curaçaoans ought to be uplifted especially from their "out of control" behavior consisting of sexual relationships outside the institution of marriage. The abovementioned letter of the vicar apostolic Kistemaker, read aloud on Emancipation Day, placed heavy emphasis on marriage and monogamy in association with moral behavior to temper the so-called hypersexuality of Afro-Curaçaoans.[15]

In Curaçao, the Catholic Church was significantly involved in the politics of respectability and attempted to instill values and respectable behavior in Afro-Curaçaoans. This does not exempt other powerful institutions from their part in this project. For example, in 1883, and again in 1885, the colonial government

14 Mason, "The Dynamics of Black Humor," 2008.

15 Kistemaker, "Aan de slaven van Curaçao," 1963.

passed a decree stating that unmarried women (even those with children) were not to be given a piece of land upon their request. For many formerly enslaved, a piece of land was a much-desired means to seek personal autonomy and escape the dominant power of the plantation owners. This escape was frequently called *Sali for di pia di shon* (coming out from under the feet [control/dominance] of the plantation owner). Married women, too, were denied a piece of land as such a request could only be made by their husband. In that period, the working class exerted growing pressure upon the government to make land accessible for the purpose of agriculture and home construction, and the government indeed increasingly distributed land.[16] In making decisions about land ownership, the colonial government applied a gender-biased policy and, in essence, institutionalized the husband as the head of the nuclear family in conformity with the teachings of the church.

Although the colonial state, the local upper classes and the Dutch Reformed Church all benefited from the politics of respectability upheld by the Catholic Church and had a vested interest in maintaining and promoting it, their involvement was less significant than that of the Catholic Church. The teachings of the Catholic Church—known popularly as *lei di pastor* (the law of the priests)—were embodied in many rules and measures that were used to exercise strong supervision over the moral lives of the faithful. Conversion to Catholicism was supposed to go along with a transformation of culture. To spread the gospel among the population, a weekly series of life stories was published in Papiamento newspapers; moral values were integrated into these stories that dealt with people's life situations.

Sexuality was viewed in sharply gendered terms and, therefore, sexual culture was structured around a heavily polarized understanding of gender. As part of the religious condemnation of premarital sex, single mothers and their children were especially stigmatized and shamed. For example, in baptism, the church made a distinction between children born in and out of wedlock, casting shame on the latter. Until far into the twentieth century, people born out of wedlock could not be ordained as priests or be trained to work as school teachers.[17] The following interview fragment gives some idea of how the church could apply humiliation very directly and personally: "My first children were twins. I was not married. I went to ask the priest to baptize them. When I

16 Allen, *Di ki manera: A Social History of Afro-Curaçaoans*, 2007.

17 Paula, *The Cry of My Life: Bitterzoete herinneringen aan een levensweg vol kronkels* [The cry of my life: Bittersweet memories of a life's twists and turns], 2005.

requested this of the priest, he walked away and every time I asked, he would slam the door in my face. I got many blows with the door from him ..."[18]

Around the end of the nineteenth and the beginning of the twentieth century, young working-class people experienced significant changes in their lives, which threatened the respectability and moral conduct endorsed by the church as a regulating and sanctioning institution.[19] Young men and women would migrate in large numbers from the countryside to town in search of work. Young men were also on the move to work elsewhere in the Caribbean region or as sailors on ships. Migration as a survival mechanism was condemned by the church as it was deemed to throw these young black men back into a state of "uncivilized rough behavior," which the church had tried hard to get rid of during their time in school. Priests frequently wrote about the perils that both sexes, but young women in particular, encountered in town, which impeded them from leading a moral and decent life. In town, young women were easily at risk of being sexually approached. Church archives are replete with letters about young women who were harassed by their employers. Some of these documents are based on complaints by these women or by their families, who acted as plaintiffs and presented harassment claims to church or even state officials.

The church made great efforts to educate young women and men in its attempt to create respectable citizens. For women, the church preached domesticity and purity, which it attempted to instill from an early age through the educational system. Women's respectability was defined in terms of their location within the domestic sphere as mothers and wives subordinate to their husband, who was the provider and the head of the family. In this way, the church worked toward ingraining the subordinate position of women within the patriarchal structure of the family and society in the popular consciousness. The church would also react whenever these values were at risk.

Respectability could mean becoming excluded from (segments of) society. For example, young women who joined the Maria Legioen (Legion of Saint Mary) or Kongregashi (Congregation) were placed under tight supervision and stringent constraints.[20] They had to display high moral conduct in terms of dress and action and were kept apart from their age group. They were not

18 Interview with Adeleida Matrona (born 1888) by R. M. Allen, January 15, 1980 (*NatAr*).

19 Broek, "The Rise of a Caribbean Island's Literature," 1990; Allen, *Di ki manera: A Social History of Afro-Curaçaoans*, 2007; and Allen, "Learning to Be a Man," 2011.

20 Some were chosen by the nuns, while others volunteered. The girls were called *kongrenis*.

allowed to participate in any popular events and could only attend mandatory church activities.

Respectability meant different things for men and women. The church approached boys and girls in very different ways. Boys were socialized to become responsible and dedicated husbands, providers and fathers who maintained a disciplined sexuality. The church often complained about having less control over working-class Afro-Curaçaoan males after they left school. It seemed less successful at disciplining males according to Catholic values.[21] However, deviation from the dominant codes of respectability was less damaging for men than for women. This position of relative privilege became expressed in the Papiamento proverb: "A man may fall in the mud, but he can stand up, shake off the mud, and still be considered a man."[22]

The church created opportunities for both local women and men who abided by the politics of respectability. They were able to get a "respectable job," for example in the teaching profession—although sometimes as non-qualified schoolteachers at certain primary schools—and they often obtained work upon the recommendation of a priest. People who lived such a respectable life could also make better use of the social facilities that the church had developed, such as hospital care[23] and social welfare, while their children could attend the best schools (*skol di plaka*).

Becoming respectable also required downplaying or rejecting one's own ethnicity as well as Afro-Curaçaoan customs. The expression *no hasi kos di bo koló* (don't behave like a typical black person) explicitly articulates the idea that being a respectable citizen means behaving and thinking differently than the rest of your racial or class category. One could argue that respectability meant that people had to engage in a type of mimicry and become what Frantz Fanon would have called people with "black skin, white masks."

In these ways, the ideology of respectability created a specific class of families that lived according to its rules and who enjoyed the social and sometimes economic advancement associated with it. Consequently, the drive for respectability, powered by a struggle for social advancement, widened the status differences between members of the working class. By linking status (worthiness of respect) to sexual propriety, behavioral decorum and neatness,

21 Allen, *Di ki manera: A Social History of Afro-Curaçaoans*, 2007.

22 "Un hòmber ta kai den lodo, lanta sagudí su kurpa, e ta keda hòmber." Author's own translation.

23 Abraham-Van der Mark, "Verlossing onder een religieus regiem: Ontwikkelingen in de zorg voor moeder en kind op Curaçao" [Deliverance under a religious regime: Developments in mother and child care in Curaçao], 1999.

respectability had a gatekeeping function. Respectability established the right to respect and to full citizenship.

5 Women Deviating from Norms of Femininity

Although men seemed to have more freedom to deviate from the principles of respectability than women, there were certainly women who did not feel compelled to live up to the standards of femininity dictated by respectability. In my research, I have encountered women who resisted and contradicted the dominant ideal of respectable behavior. In town, there existed what was known as the *kambrada*: an erotic relationship between two women. The *kambrada* can be compared to the *mati* relationship between Afro-Surinamese working-class women, studied by Gloria Wekker.[24] The *kambrada* relationship in Curaçao is highlighted in the book *E no por kasa* (She cannot get married) by Willem Kroon, published in 1923.[25] The author, a devout Catholic, wrote the book to condemn the erotic *kambrada* relationship. Oral history contains many memories of women who maintained same-sex relations, either out of preference or because their male partner had migrated or sailed out to sea. *Kambrada* relationships were not secretive but quite public—which means that they were, to some extent, accepted or tolerated. Still, while some of these women even adopted children from couples who had many offspring and were not able to take proper care of all of them, they were generally not considered respectable.

Another example of women openly flouting the norms of respectability is provided by *tambú*—a social event in which drumming accompanied singers who performed *kantika di tambú*: *tambú* songs.[26] *Tambú* was the most persecuted of all African-derived customs in Curaçao. During slavery, slave owners feared *tambú* as it offered opportunities for the enslaved to gather and to express disgust about their situation through song. Catholic clergy also heavily condemned the *tambú* songs and dance, which they saw as lascivious and sexually immoral. After emancipation, state and church continued to heavily condemn and criminalize *tambú*, seeing it as a repository of unruly, debased and unmanageable practices and behavior.

Women often served as *kantadó di tambú*: singers of *tambú* songs, which they themselves sometimes composed. The lyrics of the songs would comment

24 Wekker, *The Politics of Passion*, 2006.

25 Editors' note: see also contributions by Broek, Clemencia and Isenia in this section.

26 Editors' note: see also contribution by De Jong in this volume.

upon current events and had been the object of popular disapproval. They could refer to individuals from one's in-group or out-group, who had misbehaved. A characteristic of *tambú* songs is the use of cunning word play and double entendre.[27] The composition of the lyrics received much attention; the words were carefully chosen to trigger a response from the chorus singers, drummers, dancers and onlookers. These women composers/singers had the ability to conceive of sharp lyrics that really gave the people to whom the song referred a (verbal) whipping. The women often went beyond the boundaries set by society and showed assertiveness and courage in the composition and presentation of the *tambú* songs. In that way, they created a certain space for themselves in a patriarchal society. They would, for example, publicly complain about a misbehaving husband or another male in their household who had taken advantage of the privileges that males enjoyed in Curaçao's society.

These women *kantadó di tambú* and the women who participated as dancers and onlookers did not fit the prevailing notions of feminine respectability. No respectable woman could be found participating in *tambú* events, which were labeled as *ko'i bochincha* (disorderly events) or even *ko'i diabel* (gatherings of the devil). By transgressing the ideological norms of respectability, these women could not be viewed as *hende drechi*.

I would like to elaborate on one of these *tambú* singers, Petronilia Coco, better known as Petoi, whom I interviewed several times in 1992 together with the linguist Ini Statia. In that year, she received an award for her contribution to oral history during the third conference of the Association of Caribbean Women Writers, now known as the Association of Caribbean Women Writers and Scholars. The award was a conscious decision of the local organizing committee.[28] The committee defied many local prejudices by considering *tambú* as literature, by recognizing Petoi as an author and by giving her a prize for her major role in *tambú*. In her acceptance speech, Petoi expressed enormous gratitude and said that she would never in her life had expected to receive such an award. Her life had been full of challenges since the day she was born in 1915. As the eldest daughter in her family, she bore the socioeconomic burden of caring for the family. Whenever her mother became pregnant, she, as a young girl, had to maintain her mother's work, and, after her mother began to work again, she had to care for the young baby. Hence, she could not attend school for very long. She got introduced to *tambú* at a young age as it was a popular

27 Editors' note: see contributions by Römer and Clemencia in this section for a discussion of double-bottomed language, also referred to as *forma di papia*.

28 The president of the local organizing committee at that time was the late Joceline Clemencia.

cultural expression in her neighborhood. In one of her interviews, she related that when she sang, she would sometimes cry, because the lyrics of the songs were a replica of her own life.

Her looks did not meet the racialized somatic norm; she was often called ugly because of her dark skin color and wide nose. This did not prevent her from expressing herself in public, and, whenever she was reminded of her physiognomy during public events, she would reply to the person in question: "Looks do not determine who a person is but their behavior does." She never got married and had no children of her own, and, in this way, too, she challenged the norms of female respectability that dictated that women should be wives and mothers.

The dominant discourse described her, like all other female *tambú* singers, as unruly, disorderly and vulgar. These were women who behaved autonomously and defied the submissive "feminine" role imposed by patriarchy. Petoi expressed her autonomous behavior, saying: "I am my own keeper, I write my own name, and nobody can sign anything for me."[29]

Petoi's whole life was burdened by the societal expectations attached to being a "good" woman and her life story gives us some idea of how hard it was to live outside the bounds of gendered respectability. Despite her outstanding role in *tambú* and even her international recognition, Petoi continued to face many difficulties; until her death in 2001, she depended on a modest government pension and some assistance from people who valued her contribution to traditional culture.

6 Conclusion

The politics of respectability, for which I have used the local terms *bida drechi* and *drecha bida*, focuses our attention on how, in the post-emancipation period, ideology and power influenced unequal social relations in terms of gender, color, religion and class. It also brings to the fore hegemonic notions about sexualities and "proper" gender identities for men and women of Curaçao's African-descended working class in relation to social advancement. Some members of this group appropriated the politics of respectability for their own social advancement and adjusted their identities and self-perception accordingly. However, the notion of respectability was also contested, as people expressed oppositional views and intentionally displayed non-sanctioned behavior.

29 "Ami mes ta doño di mi mes, ta mi mes ta skibi mi nòmber, niun hende no por firma nada pa mi." Author's own translation.

Respectability resulted in a process of inclusion for those who were willing to adopt this ideology for their social advancement and exclusion for those who challenged this cultural constraint on their behavior. Those who challenged respectability were principally women who chose not to live up to the standards of femininity dictated upon them by the ideology of respectability.

By examining the traditionally unheard voices of counter-hegemonic discourse, I have sought to highlight the opposition and even resistance to the dominant ideals of respectable behavior that have had an impact especially on women in Curaçao's patriarchal society. By looking at it in this way, I have tried to discover how historically specific manifestations of discourses on sexuality have defined our conceptions of gender in Curaçao. The fact that *kambrada* relationships, the participation of women in *tambú* and even *tambú* itself continue to not be accepted as fully "respectable" by all sectors of society, that women resisting domesticity are still deemed unruly and seen as unfit to be mothers and that "respectable women" are still judged primarily by their somatic appearance and phenotypical characteristics instead of their intellect or other capabilities suggests that the old politics of respectability is still alive and plays an important role in present-day Curaçaoan society. This is important to take into consideration when trying to bring about changes in attitudes and beliefs regarding gender in society.

Acknowledgments

This is an adapted version of a public lecture titled "Contesting Respectability: Sexual Politics in Post-Emancipation Colonial Curaçao," delivered at Atria – Institute on Gender Equality and Women's History in Amsterdam on March 27, 2017.

Bibliography

Abraham-Van der Mark, Eva. "Verlossing onder een religieus regiem: Ontwikkelingen in de zorg voor moeder en kind op Curaçao" [Deliverance under a religious regime: Developments in mother and child care in Curaçao]. In *Gezond en wel: Vrouwen en de zorg voor gezondheid in de twintigste eeuw*, edited by Rineke van Daalen and Marijke Gijswijt-Hofstra, 213–31. Amsterdam: Amsterdam University Press, 2009.

Allen, Rose Mary. *Di ki manera: A Social History of Afro-Curaçaoans, 1863–1917*. Amsterdam: SWP Publishers, 2007.

Allen, Rose Mary. "'Learning to Be a Man': Afro-Caribbean Seamen and Maritime Workers from Curaçao in the Beginning of the Twentieth Century." *Institute of Caribbean Studies* 39, no. 1–2 (2011): 43–64. https://doi.org/10.1353/crb.2011.0014.

Boucher, Lisa. “Respectability and Reputation: A Balancing Act.” *Totem: The University of Western Ontario Journal of Anthropology* 11, no. 1 (June 2011). https://ir.lib.uwo.ca/totem/vol11/iss1/12.

Broek, Aart G. “The Rise of a Caribbean Island’s Literature: The Case of Curaçao and Its Writing in Papiamentu.” PhD diss., VU Amsterdam, 1990.

Higginbotham, Evelyn Brooks. *Righteous Discontent: The Women’s Movement in the Black Baptist Church, 1880–1920*. Cambridge, MA: Harvard University Press, 1994.

Hine, Darlene Clark. “Rape and the Inner Lives of Black Women in the Middle West.” *Signs: Journal of Women in Culture and Society* 14, no. 4 (July 1989): 912–20. https://doi.org/10.1086/494552.

Kistemaker, J. F. A. “Aan de slaven van Curaçao: Brief van Mgr. Kistemaker, voor te lezen op de dag van hun bevrijding, 1-7-1863” [To the enslaved of Curaçao: Letter from Mr. Kistemaker, to be read out on the day of their emancipation, 1-7-1863], *Indisch Missietijdschrift*, 46 (1963): 9–13.

Malhotra, Sheena, and Aimee Carrillo Rowe, eds. *Silence, Feminism, Power: Reflections at the Edges of Sound*. New York: Palgrave Macmillan, 2013.

Mason, Cheryl Banks. “The Dynamics of Black Humor from Africa to America and the Transformation from Slavery to the Twentieth Century, 2008.” Master’s thesis, Clark Atlanta University, 2008. https://radar.auctr.edu/islandora/object/cau.td%3A2008_mason_cheryl_b.

Oostindie, Gert, ed. *Fifty Years Later: Antislavery, Capitalism, and Modernity in the Dutch Orbit*. Pittsburgh: University of Pittsburgh Press, 1996.

Paula, Alejandro Felipe. *The Cry of My Life: Bitterzoete herinneringen aan een levensweg vol kronkels* [The cry of my life: Bittersweet memories of a life’s twists and turns]. Willemstad: Curaçaosche Courant, 2005.

Simmons, LaKisha Michelle. “‘To Lay Aside All Morals’: Respectability, Sexuality and Black College Students in the United States in the 1930s.” *Gender & History* 24, no. 2 (August 2012): 431–55. https://doi.org/10.1111/j.1468-0424.2012.01690.x.

Wekker, Gloria. *The Politics of Passion: Women’s Sexual Culture in the Afro-Surinamese Diaspora*. Between Men – between Women. New York: Columbia University Press, 2006.

Wilson, Peter J. *Crab Antics: The Social Anthropology of English-Speaking Negro Societies of the Caribbean*. Caribbean Series 14. New Haven: Yale University Press, 1973.

Wolcott, Victoria W. *Remaking Respectability: African American Women in Interwar Detroit*. Gender and American Culture. Chapel Hill: University of North Carolina Press, 2001.

CHAPTER 27

A Paragraph in the Unwritten History of Lesbian Love in the Caribbean: *Amor Di Kambrada*

Aart G. Broek

Abstract

This contribution examines the depiction of same-sex desire among women in the literary production (in Papiamentu) of the Dutch Caribbean in the first half of the twentieth century. The text analyzes several serial novels in the *roman à thèse* style. These can be understood to testify to the cultural contestations taking place in a rapidly industrializing society as an attempt by the Roman Catholic press to promote certain moral values. This corpus includes one of the few pieces of evidence of non-conforming forms of relationships practiced on the islands at the time, even if they appear only in a distorted form as examples of the corrupting influences of modernity.

Keywords

kambrada – same-sex desire – Papiamentu serial novel – Roman Catholic press – Willem Kroon

> Hari, muhé, hari tira garganta 'tras
>
> —Imelda Valerianus-Fermina[1]

∴

Although an integral part of Caribbean human relationships, lesbian love has been allotted relatively little attention in both scholarly and literary works in

1 "Laugh, woman, rock with laughter." Author's translation. From her poem "Muhé" (Woman), which was first published in Valerianus-Fermina, *Mi pensamentunan* [My thoughts], 1985, p. 9. Editors' note: this poem, along with an English translation, is included in this volume.

 | DOI:10.1163/9789004690882_029

the twentieth century; Van Lier's study of lesbian love relations in Suriname is an exception.[2] It is relatively hard to find a handful of well-known and widely read Caribbean authors who stand up for the acceptance of lesbianism or who discuss relationships and activities by homosexual women as something just as natural as the mango trees in the yards. The novel *Over de gekte van een vrouw* (About the madness of a woman), published in 1982 by the Surinamese Astrid Roemer, is a rare example of a literary publication in which lesbianism plays an essential role that has sold well, become a point of reference in criticism and found its way onto student reading lists.

Unfortunately, few lesbians from the Caribbean are as yet able to assert themselves as Audre Lorde did when she called herself a "black woman, poet, essayist, lesbian, feminist, mother, activist"[3] or as Leleti Tamu does when she describes herself as "a dyke, mother, poet, doing the left thing in a right-minded society."[4]

Judging from the dearth of scholarly attention and scarcity of literary references in present-day writing in Curaçao, lesbian relationships are still enveloped in a well-hidden, seemingly impenetrable cocoon. However many phenomena may have been foregrounded and highlighted in the literary output on the island, lesbianism is not one of these. Only once, as far as I have been able to establish, has a lesbian woman been granted an essential role in a written narrative text by an author from Curaçao: the role of a despicable woman who is bound to lead others and oneself to bottomless perdition in Willem Kroon's novel in Papiamentu, *E no por casa*,[5] serialized in the weekly *La Cruz* (The Cross, 1923).

As both the rosy and the thorny sides of lesbian relationships in Caribbean literary history deserve our attention, the following short exposition may be an apposite contribution to the process of gaining insight into the acceptance of lesbianism in Caribbean society. The novel concerned forms an integral part of a particular body of texts in Papiamentu; therefore, the context within which this literary production functioned and the major characteristics of these texts are sketched first.

---

2 Lier, *Tropische tribaden: Een verhandeling over homoseksualiteit en homoseksuele vrouwen in Suriname* [Tropical tribades: A treatise on homosexuality and homosexual women in Suriname], 1986.

3 Espinet and CAFRA, *Creation Fire*, 1990, p. 355.

4 Ibid., p. 363. Editors' note: see also contribution by Isenia in this volume.

5 A somewhat ambiguous title that can be read as both "she was not allowed to marry" and "she could not marry".

1 Roman a Thèse

In the two decades before the Second World War, Curaçao saw the publication of about a dozen novels in Papiamentu, the vernacular of the majority of the island's population.[6] This literary production was formed in a matrix of numerous economic, social and cultural changes, which were, if not triggered, greatly intensified by the decision by an international oil company to construct a refinery on the former plantations bordering the natural inland harbor in Willemstad, Curaçao.

The arrival of the oil refinery between 1915 and 1918 fundamentally changed the Curaçaoan society within two to three decades. The remaining years before the Second World War saw Curaçao evolve from a nineteenth-century agrarian-mercantile society into a twentieth-century industrialized and capitalist society. Gradually expanding and ultimately turning into the pivot of Curaçaoan economy, the refinery drew thousands of Caribbean workers and hundreds of well-educated, Dutch white-collar workers to the island of Curaçao.

With the rapid increase of the population, the existing limited set of ideas, ideals, moral standards, lifestyles and opinions diversified. Meanwhile, the social structure, which dated back to the days of slavery, saw a rapid change in the position of various groups in order to make room for newcomers and rising groups.

The Afro-Curaçaoan population, generally thought to be members of the local Roman Catholic Church, were "exposed" (to use a word the Roman Catholic mission would) to new, Western, primarily nonreligious or anti-Roman Catholic lifestyles and concomitant moral standards. This "exposure" was considered to be a serious threat and was to be one of the major concerns of the Roman Catholic mission in the 1920s as well as of the Curaçaoan male authors writing in Papiamentu: Willem E. Kroon, Manuel A. Fray, S. Miguel Suriel, Emilio Davelaar, Ernesto Petronia and, from Bonaire, Jozef S. Sint Jago.

Before the days of the oil refinery, a non-Roman Catholic lifestyle, set of moral standards and principles were almost exclusively the sociocultural attainment or inheritance of the white creole elite and, as such, unattainable for the Afro-Curaçaoan population. The Roman Catholic mission found their followers primarily among the Afro-Curaçaoan people, largely because the

6 For a detailed discussion of the pre-war Papiamentu literature, see Broek, "The Rise of a Caribbean Island's Literature: The Case of Curaçao and Its Writing in Papiamentu," 1990. It is also succinctly discussed in Broek, "Early Prose Writing in Papiamento: Educando un pueblo," 1989.

mission was the only powerful group to care for the general welfare of these people: their health, education, living conditions, work and financial problems. This care went hand-in-hand with the imposition of a Western, Roman Catholic lifestyle and way of thinking.[7] The mission held a relatively firm grip on the Afro-Curaçaoan people, although this does not imply that they have ever been fully successful in their attempts to Westernize Curaçaoan society according to the Roman Catholic view of the world.

This influence was threatened by the oil company: a young, powerful institution that provided work and an income that, although low, was higher than ever before without asking its workers to live up to the principles of a demanding doctrine for twenty-four hours a day. The Afro-Curaçaoan people's dependence on the mission to satisfy their material needs virtually came to an end. This undermined their dependence on the mission for spiritual comfort as well, not least because the numerous immigrants—especially those who came from other Caribbean islands—demonstrated alternative lifestyles. These Caribbean newcomers were more or less of the same social and ethnic group as the Curaçaoans but had a non-Roman Catholic background with different norms, values and moral standards. The Roman Catholic mission and their writers sought to oppose this threat to their influence on the Afro-Curaçaoan people's patterns of thinking and behaving by means of fictional texts.

Using fictional texts as a weapon against undesirable changes in the social and religious behavior of the Afro-Curaçaoan church members implies a strong belief in the effects of such texts. In the years before the Second World War, the Roman Catholic mission quite regularly aired their poetics (i.e., their ideas and ideals about the nature and function of fictional texts) in *La Union* (Unity) and the other two Roman Catholic weeklies in Curaçao, *La Cruz* (also in Papiamentu) and *Amigoe di Curaçao* (Friend of Curaçao, in Dutch).

Their poetics are first of all characterized by the conviction that literature, by definition, is a "perlocutionary" speech act: although it may not have been the intention of the writer, a fictional text persuades, convinces and makes someone act according to the "moral" propagated in the text. A short quotation from one of the many texts available illustrates this conviction: "When considering the increase in crime and the number of (especially young) criminals, when so many young people in desperation put an end to their lives, when many a degenerated son and sinful daughter are a disgrace to their parental

7 Editors' note: for discussions of the influence of the church, see contributions by Allen and Kleinmoedig in this volume.

home: one of the main causes of all this evil is to be found in the reading of immoral novels."[8]

The propagation of exclusively reading and writing "virtuous" novels is the logical, concomitant consequence as is the room given in the Roman Catholic weeklies *La Cruz* and *La Union* to serialized "virtuous" novels with a particularly strong didactic function. Because Dutch, the official language, was little understood by the Afro-Curaçaoan population, such novels were to be written in Papiamentu. Kroon, Fray and Suriel basically shared these Roman Catholic poetics. Writing novels meant writing "virtuous" novels in Papiamentu in which the Roman Catholic lifestyle, set of beliefs, ideals, principles and moral standards, as well as a Western (Dutch) cultural pattern, was defended and propagated. In the 1920s and 1930s, when the Roman Catholic "flock" drifted away from the mission's "pen," this task was realized by Kroon and his literary compatriots by writing *romans à thèse*.

Since the publication of Suleiman's well-documented and convincing study of *Authoritarian Fictions: The Ideological Novel as Literary Genre* (1983), the literary term *roman à thèse* is no longer a vague concept liable to be interpreted in divergent ways. While the application of her methodological analysis is to be left aside, the working definition of the *roman à thèse* has to suffice to describe the kind of novels that were produced in Curaçao in the 1920s and early 1930s: "a novel written in the realistic mode (that is, based on a aesthetic of verisimilitude and representation) which signals itself to the reader as primarily didactic in intent, seeking to demonstrate the validity of a political, philosophical or religious doctrine."[9]

2 Amor Di Kambrada

In the Papiamentu thesis novels, the characters learn to accept a particular "ideology" (in the general sense in which Suleiman also uses this concept) as the only beacon in their lives. With the characters, the readers are thought to be persuaded of the correctness of this particular way of interpreting the world. Against the mistakes that are being made and the potentially disastrous

8 "Wanneer wij het aantal misdaden en misdadigers, jeugdige vooral, met den dag zien toenemen; indien zoo menig jongeling in vertwijfeling de hand slaat aan zijn eigen leven; indien zoo menig ontaarde zoon en diep gevallen dochter verdriet en schande brengt over het ouderlijke huis: dan is een der hoofdoorzaken van al dat kwaad te vinden in het lezen van slechte romans." See "Een bisschoppelijk woord over lectuur" [An episcopal word on reading], 1910, p. 2. Author's translation.

9 Suleiman, *Authoritarian Fictions*, 1983, p. 7.

consequences these entail, the characters, and the readers, are offered the helping hand of Roman Catholicism. Living up to Roman Catholic "ideology" will ward off the dangers of the charming new lifestyles encroaching on the lives of Afro-Curaçaoan people and will reveal shallowness where life, despite its inevitable sad experiences, used to be full of meaning.

The dangers of "modern life" were numerous: gambling, dancing, carousing, the excessive use of alcohol, entertainment in theaters and cinemas, beach parties and picnics; in short, any behavior directed at improving or indulging in physical material well-being. Such life was qualified by cupidity, jealousy, unreliable friendships, cheating, fear, egoism, gossip, vanity and extramarital and premarital relationships; these, in their turn, would lead to alcoholism, poverty, unmarried motherhood, chronic illness, extreme psychological tensions, prostitution, death and murder. Two alleged aberrations, indissolubly tied to the adherence to a non-Roman Catholic way of life, were incest and lesbian love.

The former was a serious problem for various characters—especially for the man who had children with two women and the boy and girl from these unions who happened to fall in love with each other, as in Kroon's *Castigo di un abuso* (Punishment of an abuse)[10] and *Mientrastanto anochi n'sera, careda n'caba* (The race will not end before nightfall).[11] Ernesto Petronia's *Venganza di un amigo* (Revenge of a friend)[12] also took incest as its central issue.

Lesbian love is discredited in William Kroon's first *roman à thèse, E no por casa*. This is a remarkably early and inevitably unfavorable discussion of the consequences of lesbian love in written Caribbean literature. In his novel, Kroon speaks about it in terms of "a mad and impossible love," "unnatural love," "a ridiculous and impure love," "the forbidden and damned friendship" and "lesbian love" (*amor di kambrada*).[13]

Between January 10 and March 14, 1923, *La Cruz* serialized Kroon's *E no por casa*. This narrative text, like most others from these years, is set in Otrobanda, the quarter of Willemstad where *La Cruz* and *La Union* found a substantial number of their readers. The storyline is as follows:

Guillermo, a young shoemaker whose parents had died, declares his love to Cecilia, a young woman whose parents have also died. Josefa, an elderly lady

10 Kroon, *Castigo di un abuso*, 1929–1930.

11 Kroon, *Mientrastanto anochi n'sera, careda n'caba*, 1925–1926.

12 Petronia, *Venganza di un amigo*, 1932.

13 "Un amor loco e imposible," "amor inatural," "un amor ridículo e impuro" and "maldita amistad prohibé." All taken from Kroon, *E no por casa*, 1923. Author's translation.

and relatively well-off, has taken care of Cecilia and her elder brother Henry ever since their parents' death. She has used her influence and money to secure Henry a promising position in commercial business while Cecilia attends to their benefactor daily—a light job made easier by Josefa letting a lower floor of her house to Henry and Cecilia.

Cecilia, in love with Guillermo, is only too willing to accept his declaration and subsequent proposal. Josefa, however, appears to be anything but pleased with Guillermo. He is, Josefa states more than once, but an *artesano* (artisan), while Cecilia and Henry, because of her interest and concern, have been drawn away from this *categoría di hende* (social group) to a higher social position. Partly because he is afraid to lose his position and Josefa's protection, and partly because he doubts Guillermo's sincerity, Henry, too, disapproves.

In an attempt to put an end to the love relation between Guillermo and Cecilia, Josefa tries to convince Cecilia that Guillermo has stolen a sum of money belonging to her. Josefa finds an accomplice in Adela, a young woman who lives in extreme poverty and bears a grudge against Guillermo for having refused to answer her love for him favorably. Guillermo is invited to the house to meet Cecilia's brother and her benefactor. With a little pecuniary help from Josefa, Adela drops the envelope containing Josefa's money through Guillermo's open window the very same night after the visit. The following day it is found by Guillermo and Henry, who, informed about the "theft" and Josefa's suspicion of Guillermo, pays Guillermo a visit and asks to search his house "to take away the suspicion." Despite the fact that Cecilia is convinced of Guillermo's innocence, she is now forced to forget about a marriage with Guillermo (at least for the time being). Guillermo is given the choice by Josefa either to be handed over to the police or to leave the island. "For the sake of Cecilia's honor," Josefa (and Henry) urge him to leave for Venezuela, which he does.

In the meantime, Adela pays Josefa another visit asking for more money. This attempt at blackmail is answered by Josefa with an attempt to poison Adela. Very sick, Adela is found in the yard by Cecilia who saves Adela by acting instantly. The next step is taken by Adela, who, in the presence of Cecilia and Henry, accuses Josefa of attempted murder and of calumny, confessing her own contribution to the latter. Thereupon, Josefa is struck by a heart attack. However, before she dies, she is able to plead forgiveness for all her sinful deeds. One of these is her *amor di kambrada*, which appears to have formed the actual basis of her strong opposition to Cecilia's pending marriage. Cecilia, strong in character and moral standards, never succumbed to Josefa as Adela appears to have done. The latter's predicament should therefore not come as a surprise. Cecilia withstood "hard times" and finally does marry her Guillermo.

Kroon's *E no por casa* does not give us any insights into the way a lesbian woman experienced her life in pre-war Curaçaoan society. Strictly speaking, it is even hazardous to state that the serialized publication of the novel in a widely read weekly in Papiamentu is indicative of the open manifestation of lesbian love relationships among Afro-Curaçaoan women. However, as all the other "problems" discussed in the pre-war Papiamentu thesis novels are known to have been in existence at the time of writing, lesbianism will not have been enveloped in a well-hidden and seemingly impenetrable cocoon in everyday life. Lesbian love may well have been just as manifest as other "rocks of offense," such as unmarried motherhood, the rise of dance houses and cinemas or the indulgence in *paranda* (carousing). It seems justified to state that lesbian relationships manifested themselves quite openly and at least to such an extent that lesbianism was experienced by the Roman Catholic missionaries and by the local authors they guided as undermining the ideology, influence and power of the Roman Catholic mission or, as they phrased it themselves, undermining the social and moral well-being of the Afro-Curaçaoan population.[14] To what extent readers actually agreed with the authors is not known. We are, however, familiar with the process of secularization of Curaçaoan society and its literature in Papiamentu, which set in at the end of the 1930s.[15] This resulted in open and generally more favorable discussion in literary texts of most of the phenomena the pre-war Afro-Curaçaoan authors and their religious guides had abhorred: dancing, feasting, physical love (of the hetero kind), going to movies and theaters, unmarried motherhood, premarital sex, etc.

14 In the years preceding the publication of Kroon's novel, thousands of men had left for Cuba to work in the cane fields. See Paula, *Problemen rondom de emigratie van arbeiders uit de kolonie Curaçao naar Cuba, 1917–1937* [Problems surrounding the emigration of workers from the colony of Curaçao to Cuba, 1917–1937], 1973; and Allen, "Ta Cuba mi ke bai; Curaçaose mannen op zoek naar een beter leven in Cuba aan het begin van de 20e eeuw" [Ta Cuba mi ke bai; Curaçaoan men seeking a better life in Cuba at the beginning of the 20th century], 1990. It is tempting to attribute *amor di kambrada* to the relative shortage of men on the island at the beginning of the 1920s. In my eyes, such an explanation—not quite absent from the studies in lesbianism in the Caribbean—has but a limited validity as it suggests too much that, if only enough men had been "available," lesbianism would actually have been nonexistent.

15 For more details about the process of secularization in Papiamentu literature, see Broek, "De deugd wordt gestraft en de zonde beloond. De secularisering van de Papiamentstalige poëzie" [Virtue is punished and sin rewarded. The secularization of Papiamentu poetry], 1990.

Lesbianism was not to be among the phenomena that were openly drawn away from the grip of Roman Catholicism.[16] In Curaçao, the cocoon, however much present, has still not opened up.

Acknowledgments

I am grateful to Lucille Berry-Haseth, Ithel Brute, Joceline Clemencia, Carel de Haseth, Gladys do Rego and Marijke Schweitz for advice in various ways. They are, of course, not to be held responsible for any of the statements in this essay.

This text first appeared as Broek, Aart G. "A paragraph in the unwritten history of lesbian love in the love in the Caribbean: *Amor di kambrada.*" In *Mundu yama sinta mira: Womanhood in Curaçao* [The name of the world is sit and see: Womanhood in Curaçao], edited by Richenel Ansano, Joceline A. Clemencia, Jeanette Cook, and Eithel Martis, 51–57. Curaçao: Fundashon Publikashon, 1992. Reproduction of this text courtesy of the author and Fundashon Publikashon.

Bibliography

Allen, Rose Mary. "Ta Cuba mi ke bai; Curaçaose mannen op zoek naar een beter leven in Cuba aan het begin van de 20e eeuw" [Ta Cuba mi ke bai; Curaçaoan men seeking a better life in Cuba at the beginning of the 20th century]. In *Op de bres voor eigenheid: Afhankelijkheid en dominantie in de Antillen,* edited by Rose Mary Allen and Paul van Gelder, 15–43. Amsterdam: Caraïbische Werkgroep AWIC, 1990.

Broek, Aart G. "De deugd wordt gestraft en de zonde beloond. De secularisering van de Papiamentstalige poëzie" [Virtue is punished and sin rewarded. The secularization of Papiamentu poetry]. In *Op de bres voor eigenheid: Afhankelijkheid en dominantie in de Antillen,* edited by Rose Mary Allen and Paul van Gelder, 190–208. Amsterdam: Caraïbische Werkgroep AWIC, 1990.

Broek, Aart G. "Early Prose Writing in Papiamento: Educando un pueblo." *Caribbean Studies* 22, no. 1–2 (1989): 37–51.

Broek, Aart G. "The Rise of a Caribbean Island's Literature: The Case of Curaçao and Its Writing in Papiamentu." PhD diss., VU Amsterdam, 1990.

"Een bisschoppelijk woord over lectuur" [An episcopal word on reading], *Amigoe di Curaçao: Weekblad voor de Curacaosche eilanden,* March 19, 1910, 1–3.

16 For obvious reasons, incest has not been given a more liberal treatment either.

Espinet, Ramabai, and CAFRA, eds. *Creation Fire: A CAFRA Anthology of Caribbean Women's Poetry*. Toronto, Ontario: Tunapuna; Trinidad and Tobago: Sister Vision; Trinidad and Tobago: CAFRA, 1990.

Kroon, Willem. *Castigo di un abuso* [Punishment of an abuse]. Curaçao: La Cruz, 1929–1930.

Kroon, Willem. *E no por casa* [She could not marry]. Curaçao: La Cruz, 1923.

Kroon, Willem. *Mientrastanto anochi n'sera, careda n'caba* [The race will not end before nightfall]. Curaçao: La Cruz, 1925–1926.

Petronia, Ernesto. *Venganza di un amigo* [Revenge of a friend]. Curaçao: La Cruz, 1932.

Lier, Rudolf Asveer Jacob van. *Tropische tribaden: Een verhandeling over homoseksualiteit en homoseksuele vrouwen in Suriname* [Tropical tribades: A treatise on homosexuality and homosexual women in Suriname]. Caribbean Series 4. Dordrecht: Foris Publications, 1986.

Paula, A. F. *Problemen rondom de emigratie van arbeiders uit de kolonie Curaçao naar Cuba, 1917–1937* [Problems surrounding the emigration of workers from the colony of Curaçao to Cuba, 1917–1937]. Curaçao: Centraal Historisch Archief, 1973.

Roemer, Astrid. *Over de gekte van een vrouw: Een fragmentarische biographie* [On a woman's madness: A fragmentary biography]. Amsterdam: In de Knipscheer, 1982.

Suleiman, Susan Rubin. *Authoritarian Fictions: The Ideological Novel as a Literary Genre*. New York: Columbia University Press, 1983.

Valerianus-Fermina, Imelda. *Mi pensamentunan* [My thoughts]. Willemstad: Cultureel Centrum Curaçao, 1985.

CHAPTER 28

No Rhythm (You)

Lysanne Charles

No rhythm moves me, like you move me
Your fingers on my hip sets it swaying
Forcing the sounds of dancehall to the recesses of my mind
And under the heavy pulse of lights; there is only you
You pulling me closer so that my breasts rest on your breasts
So that my legs brush against your legs
So that my stomach presses against your stomach
And all there is, is the madness of the next breath
The madness of the next moment and you whyning ever closer
There is only you:
A figure of dips and curves moving
Moving against me just right
Hands reaching out touching me in all the right places
There, right there,
Inching up my thigh, caressing my waist
Until above the music, beyond the rhythm; there is only you
You swinging to the beat of the music
Arms forming circles around me
Here, then here
Engulfing me in the sensuousness that is your movement
The rocking of your pelvis
The flow of your spine
Your dangerously smooth skin
All drawing moisture, sweat beading on my forehead
Your fingers run skillfully down my back
Making wet areas that long for you
Until there is, only you; a figure of arcs and bends moving
Moving between my legs
While the hard wood of the speaker presses me up and forward
Until we touch
Halting sound!
The music ends, the rhythm changes

 | DOI:10.1163/9789004690882_030

And still
Nothing moves me like you

Acknowledgments

This poem originally appeared as Charles, Lysanne. "No Rhythm (You)." *Journal of Lesbian Studies* 15, no. 1 (January 18, 2011): 73–74. https://doi.org/10.1080/10894160.2010.508422. Reproduction courtesy of Lysanne Charles.

CHAPTER 29

Women Who Love Women in Curaçao: from "Cachapera" to Open Throats: a Commentary in Collage

Joceline Clemencia

Abstract

The words used to describe same-sex loving people and nonheteronormative relationships are not universal, and even if terms such as gay and lesbian might appear to be neutral descriptions of sexual identities and life forms, they are not always experienced as such. This contribution explores the specific practices of naming different forms of relationships between women and self-identifying concepts in the context of Papiamentu. It brings together words from well-known writers, journalistic articles as well as from three women who attended a presentation given by the author at the Twentieth Annual Caribbean Studies Association Conference held in May 1995 in Curaçao to give as broad a picture as possible.

Keywords

same-sex relationships – naming practices – sexual identities – Papiamentu language – kinship

In my work as head of the National Language Institute Sede di Papiamentu, my colleagues and I have been engaged in considering the many disclosures still to be made in our society. At the institute, we regard Papiamentu, the national language of Curaçao, Aruba and Bonaire, as the source for a truly national development despite the marginal position official policy gives it.[1] I am particularly interested in the unheard voices of Curaçao, voices that include those of women who share their lives with other women as partners.

1 Editors' note: for a further discussion of language policy in the Netherlands Antilles, see contribution by Linda Richardson in this volume.

 | DOI:10.1163/9789004690882_031

This collage of voices, drawn from a presentation given at the Twentieth Annual Caribbean Studies Association Conference held May 1995 in Curaçao, is based on the few print sources and on audiotaped conversations with three young women, Mu, Zaza and Ana (the names are fictitious because, after the conference, life continues on a very small island). Together, we have explored and challenged our culture's layered emotional, physical, affectional, reproductive, historical and social "standards." I speak here as neither a distanced observer nor as an expert but as a participant in the historical process of the freeing of self. I speak of women who love other women instead of using the—in my view—patriarchal and stigmatizing term "lesbians." In exploring questions of naming and revelation, I recall these words from Adrienne Rich: "Where language and naming are power, silence is oppression and violence."[2]

1 Namegiving

Seventy-eight-year-old writer, poet and activist Guillermo Rosario explains that, in Curaçao, women who love women have been called in Papiamentu *cachapera*. Venezuelan Spanish speaks of *cachapa* as a bread roll, bun or dough made of maize.[3] *Repera* (pancake maker), *machoro* (dyke) and *marimachu* (mannish woman or butch) are other negative denotations for women who love women. *Kambrada*, which can denote friendship between women, has also become a common word in Papiamentu for women who love women; in Tip Marugg's *Un prinsipio pa un dikshonario erótiko Papiamentu* [A beginning of an erotic Papiamentu dictionary], *kambrada* is "said of two women who have a homosexual relationship with each other."[4] Surinamese immigrants referred to these women as *platte borden*, flat dishes.

Astrid Roemer: In the community from which I come, there is not so much talk about the phenomenon of women having relations with other women. There are, after all, things that aren't to be given names—giving them names kills them. But we do have age-old rituals originating from Africa by which women

2 Adrienne Rich, "Conditions for Work: The Common World of Women," 1977, p. 23.

3 Editors' note: see also contribution by Sleebe in this section.

4 "Bisa di dos muhe ku tin un relashon homoseksual ku otro." Author's translation. Marugg, *Un prinsipio pa un dikshonario erótiko Papiamentu* [A beginning of an erotic Papiamentu dictionary], 1992, p. 46.

can make quite clear that special relations exist between them. For instance, birthday rituals can be recognized by anyone and are quite obvious. Also, when two women are at a party and one hands another a glass or a plate of food, from which she has first tasted herself, it is clear to everybody and their mother what that means. Why then is it necessary to declare oneself a lesbian? It is usual there. Surinamese women claim the right to do what they want to do. They can love women, go to bed with men, have children.[5]

Guillermo Rosario: Things have changed for the homosexual or the lesbian here in Curaçao. Many years ago, two women who had something going would wear the same clothes and you could know at once from the twin clothing that they were *trahadónan di repa* (pancake makers) as they were called. In the old times you could hear people say: Talitha and Malita are *kambradas*. Petra and Senofia sleep with each other, etc. There were a lot in our society, out in the open and hidden. But at the Misa di Aurora (mass held at six a.m. in the week before Christmas), at the *tambú* dances, at the San Antoni mass, at the *belorio* (night watch before a burial), at parties you would recognize them at once because of the twin clothing. We used to talk about Dalia here, the name for a forbidden homosexual lover. That explains the popular song from which we often forget the origin: "If Dalia ain't my Dalia, how come her mother is my mother-in-law? If Dalia ain't my Dalia, what is she doing at my door?"[6]

These ritual moments of revelation—at parties and masses—were public and sometimes sacred even, perhaps suggesting acceptance or approval. So why a verbal naming? Journalist Elisabeth de Montsouris spoke with several women

5 Wekker, "Mati-ism and Black Lesbianism," 1993, p. 150.

6 "Si Dalia n'ta mi Dalia kon su mama ta mi suegra? Si Dalia n'ta mi Dalia ki mishiele na mi porta?" Author's translation. Rosario, *E tronkon heridá o máchu a skarsa* [The wounded trunk or the scarcity of men], n.d.

and men in Curaçao who have partners of the same sex: "Reina and Koko have been living together for some years now. They share a house and told everybody they did so to cover the high rent. Reina proposed to go to Curaçao to live where her lover was born. They both regret they came here, despite their good jobs. They can't stand the sneaky way."[7]

2 Why Don't We Use Our Real Names?

Mu: Frankly spoken, I don't have a problem using my name, but maybe later, they can make trouble for me. I don't really know if they're gonna make trouble, I think so. That is why, to avoid problems, don't you think so? That is why … Of "they," I mean people who perhaps know me and who have power.

Zaza: I told my mother you invited me for this interview and she said: Why do you have to be in this again? I replied: Well, I consider it important. It has been put aside for so long. This should be added to the history of women in Curaçao. This is part of the history and I want to give my cooperation. And when I told her it was anonymous, she became calm again. But at first it was *bllll*! Why you? And I thought: But you did tell it to the people who are important to you.

Mu: The social control is extra on me because I'm in the field of education. But at parties I say to hell, I dance and soft and merengue with her. I saw my students looking, but I didn't care. But kissing in the street, I don't do that in Curaçao.

3 Double Standards

Michael lost his best friends, male and female, when he started living with his boyfriend. Everybody knew he was homosexual but only when it became visible did the world react. With disdain and rejection.

Zaza: *Dat is dubbel doen.* That is being doublesided. Because when I told my mother about how I felt, she got in her car and went to tell or later phoned everybody she knew.

---

7 Montsouris, "Homosexualiteit bestaat niet: Curaçao houdt oren en ogen dicht" [Homosexuality does not exist: Curaçao keeps ears shut and eyes closed], 1993.

The double standard allows men to be heterosexual during the day and have sex with men when darkness falls. Many men think a man can have sex with another man and still not be a homosexual as long as the man has the leading role in intercourse. You are a queen only if you are passive. The terms *mariku kuedó* (gay who penetrates) and *mariku wantadó* (gay who is penetrated) distinguish between a real man and a queen.

La Pop: I go to snack bars very often. Till two o'clock at night, all men are machos. After that, all of a sudden, they all become fags.

Igor: It is quite easy to establish sexual contact here. But what does it really mean? You go to a bar. A hetero guy picks you up. You go to bed with each other and with sunrise they kick you out because you're a submissive *mariku* (fag).[8]

4 Open Throats

We have allowed the men in our society to be shut off from their feelings and to engage in wars and annihilation. We have allowed the women in our society to be shut off from their throats. Only yesterday I learned that one of the earlier mentioned women lost her job at a local industry because the management did not think it appropriate to have a lesbian working in the place.

Ana: Experience taught me that my feelings for women are deeper … With men, I tried on several occasions to see if I could get closer to them. But mostly, communication or getting close to a man is not as close as to a woman. From that discovery on I took the one decision in my life, let me put it that way, that gives me more satisfaction.

Mu: When you are with a man in the beginning, you are good friends. We talk about everything, but later on the pretending starts: I don't owe you no explanation. And you know what, it makes no difference whether they are educated men or not, or if they wear a tie around their neck. I simply don't get it. I'm serious. I like people to be real. If you're from out of the bushes, be bushy. Don't pretend and beat around the bush.

Ana: I still sometimes feel attracted to men. I admit that and I have those feelings. But after a month or two you discover that for

8 Ibid. Editors' note: see also contribution by Kleinmoedig in this section.

them it all has to do with sex. I don't say lesbians don't focus on sex, but I find it typical in relationships with men.

Mu: Sometimes you spot the same problems in a lesbian relationship as in a heterosexual one. Because you see, at least I do, relationships where the woman treats the other woman real bad. I don't understand how they deal in such a way with each other. But then I realize I'm evaluating them and that's wrong too. Because if that's ok with them ...

Ana: When I made the decision to start a relationship with a woman, I started analyzing things. I looked back at my youth. How it was. Everybody I was very close with was a woman.

Zaza: I heard from my mom ... that in their day, when they were young, that it wasn't a taboo at all. Everyone spoke of an aunt of my mom's who lived with a woman. She would cook at my mom's or at my grandma's and when leaving she would say: "*Mi ta bai serka mi kambrada*" [I'll go now to my love]. That's what she would say and everybody knew it, at least my grandma did, maybe my mom didn't because she was a child. But they lived together just like that. And there were these other women too. But I said to my mother, everybody knew it, but everybody remained silent about it too. Naming yourself lesbian is a political deed; that is why I think it's important to call myself lesbian.

Mu: Everybody gets their *golpi di bida*, their blows in life. I got them too, but I was looking more for someone who could understand me, you know. The person understands me and I am sharing with the person. And that's what Neno offered me. At first it was more a friendship ... Neno is younger than I am. But sometimes I think she is much more mature than I am, meaning she knows what she wants. And for me it is the friendship that comes first, later the other things. I don't know if I feel attracted to women. If I love a woman, it is not the woman that I see. It is the person that I love. And the person happens to be a woman. The person could have been a man too. In this case the person is a woman. And for the person she is, I love her.

At first sight, it looks like in Curaçao, too, the love between two women has been regarded for a long time as an illness and an offense to nature; that is, when we listen only to the sound of voices uttered by many. However, if we stop listening with only ears—strongly conditioned by religion, morality and society—and register the utterances with also the heart, we would notice that many women—and men—accepted and lived with intimate female love from a long time ago. They knew that it was more than just a matter of sex. It was about the respect and real human love people are truly able to give to each other. In this respect, women in Curaçao were ahead of the men in their time. They dared to break the silence, convinced that others would follow and that a new language would grow. Arnela Ten Meer expressed this feeling in "For a Woman Friend."

Pa un amiga
Arnela Ten Meer[17]

Nos pensamentunan
ta meskla ku otro
manera awa di riu
ku awa di laman.
Nos ta kompaai otro
sin niun palabra.
Mi sintimentu p'e ta profundo
manera e blou di laman.
Mi amistat p'e ta sinsero.
Tin bes mi tin gana
di mishi kune.
No! No pa nada no,
pero djis pa sinti kalor
di su kurpa,
pa sintimi mas serka,
si, mas serka di dje.
Pa sinti union total
ora mi ta huntu kune.
Si, mi ta stim'e,
manera por stima
un amiga.
Pero mi tin miedu.
Mi tin miedu di bras'e,
pa mustr'e kuantu
mi stim'e.

For a Woman Friend
Arnela Ten Meer

Our thoughts
mix together
like the water of the river
with the water of the sea.
We share moments with each other
without saying one word.
My feelings for her are deep
like the blue of the sea.
My friendship for her is sincere.
Sometimes I want
to touch her.
No! For no particular reason,
just to feel the warmth
of her body,
to feel her closer
yes, much closer to me.
To be fully one
when I'm with her.
Yes, I love her
the way you love
a woman friend.
But I'm scared.
I'm scared to embrace her
and show her how much
I love her.

9 This poem was originally published as ten Meer, Arnela, *Un* krenchi di mi mes [A small bit of myself] (Curaçao: Instituto Nashonal di Idioma, 1993), p. 17. Translation from Papiamentu by Joceline Clemencia.

Acknowledgments

This text was first published as Clemencia, Joceline. "Women Who Love Women in Curaçao: From 'Cachapera' to Open Throats: A Commentary in Collage." *Feminist Studies* 22, no. 1 (Spring, 1996): 81–88. Reproduction courtesy of *Feminist Studies*. The text has been lightly edited for linguistic clarity.

Bibliography

Marugg, Tip. *Un prinsipio pa un dikshonario erótiko Papiamentu* [A beginning of an erotic Papiamentu dictionary]. Willemstad: Drukkerij Scherpenheuvel, 1992.

Meer, Amela Ten. *Un krenchi di mi mes* [A small bit of myself]. Curaçao: Instituto Nashonal di Idioma, 1993.

Montsouris, Elisabeth de. "Homosexualiteit bestaat niet: Curaçao houdt oren en ogen dicht" [Homosexuality does not exist: Curaçao keeps ears shut and eyes closed]. *Amigoe Napa*. June 12, 1993.

Rich, Adrienne. "Conditions for Work: The Common World of Women." In *Working It Out: 23 Women Writers, Artists, Scientists, and Scholars Talk about Their Lives and Work*, edited by Sara Ruddick and Pamela Daniels, XIII–XXIV. New York: Pantheon Books, 1977.

Rosario, Guillermo. *E tronkon heridá o máchu a skarsa* [The wounded trunk or the scarcity of men]. Curaçao: printed by author, n.d.

Wekker, Gloria. "Mati-ism and Black Lesbianism: Two Idealtypical Expressions of Female Homosexuality in Black Communities of the Diaspora." *Journal of Homosexuality* 24, no. 3–4 (April 1993): 145–58. https://doi.org/10.1300/J082v24n03_11.

CHAPTER 30

Forma Di Papia (Ways of Speaking) in the Dutch Caribbean and Their Relevance for the Study of Gender and Sexuality

Louis Philippe M. Römer

Abstract

The concept of *forma di papia* (ways of speaking), developed by Elis Juliana and Joceline Clemencia, remains essential for scholarship that pushes back against the silences of the colonial archive. Engaging thoughtfully with *forma di papia* and the questions they raise about transparency, truth-telling, publicity, directness and the agency of marginalized speakers can guide scholars of gender and sexuality to rethink how to approach signs of feminist and queer life that exist outside of the archive and may otherwise evade documentation.

Keywords

sexuality – silence – language – *forma di papia* – Elis Juliana – Joceline Clemencia

Research on gender and sexuality in the Dutch Caribbean must contend with the "silences" within the colonial archive.[1] Elis Juliana's scholarship is significant in this context for how it opens up various forms of life that exist at the margins and interstices of Dutch Caribbean society.[2] This chapter will focus on the signature theoretical and methodological contributions of Elis Juliana and Joceline Clemencia to the study of gender and sexuality in the Dutch Caribbean. Elis Juliana (1927–2013) was an anthropologist, folklorist, public intellectual and poet. Juliana's work as an ethnographer of Curaçao and Bonaire

1 Trouillot, *Silencing the Past*, 1995.

2 Allen, "Di ki manera? A Social History of Afro-Curaçaoans, 1863–1917," 2007; Allen, "'See How I Talk about the Slavemaster': Searching for 'We' in Afro-Curaçaoan Oral Histories," 2016, pp. 164–82.

 | DOI:10.1163/9789004690882_032

over multiple decades created an archive of folklore, oral history, material culture and ethnographic descriptions of ritual that provides a rare window into Afro-Caribbean worldviews and everyday life.[3] Joceline Clemencia (1952–2011) was an eminent literary critic, cultural critic, Black feminist and activist for the independence of Curaçao who made important interventions in the study of oral literature, gender and sexuality in the Dutch Caribbean. Much of her scholarship as a literary critic has centered on *Organisashon planifikashon independensia* (Organization, planning, independence), a collection of Elis Juliana's poetry published over several volumes in the 1980s.[4] Clemencia has also written a comprehensive description and analysis of Juliana's ethnographic work in *Elis Juliana inbestigadó: Piedra di mulina* (Elis Juliana, investigator: The millstone), published in Papiamento by the National Anthropological and Archaeological Museum of Curaçao.[5] In *Piedra di mulina*, Clemencia analyzes her interviews with Elis Juliana to identify the theoretical and methodological approaches that characterize Juliana's ethnographic and literary works.

At the center of these contributions is *forma di papia* (ways of speaking), the preferred forms, norms and sensibilities that inform the organization of everyday discourse and the stylistic choices made in verbal art.[6] This concept was vital to how Juliana approached fieldwork and ethnographic analysis. Clemencia then draws upon *forma di papia* to reveal hidden forms of protest among Dutch Caribbean women who oppose heteronormativity and patriarchy.[7] This chapter traces the development of *forma di papia* through the works of Elis Juliana and Joceline Clemencia while drawing from theory and conceptual vocabulary from linguistic anthropology. With their interest in words with implications that go beyond the content of the words themselves and their

3 The ethnographic collections of Elis Juliana are housed at the National Anthropological and Archaeological Memory Management (NAAM) in Willemstad, Curaçao. They cover many areas of interest to gender and sexuality studies, from ethnographic descriptions of marriage, birth and death rituals to numerous stories, oral histories and songs that provide commentary and critique on gender roles and sexual practices.

4 Clemencia, *Het grote camouflagespel van de OPI: Een thematische benadering van de poëzie van Elis Juliana* [The OPI's great game of camouflage: A thematic approach to the poetry of Elis Juliana], 1989.

5 Clemencia, *Elis Juliana inbestigadó: Piedra di mulina*, 2004.

6 Much of Elis Juliana's thoughts on *forma di papia* has appeared in interviews between Elis Juliana and Joceline Clemencia that were published in Clemencia, *Elis Juliana inbestigadó: Piedra di mulina*, 2004 and Clemencia, *Het grote camouflagespel van de OPI*, 1989. This author has also conducted interviews in 2006 with Elis Juliana and Joceline Clemencia on the topic of *forma di papia*.

7 Clemencia, "Katibu ta galiña: From Hidden to Open Protest on Curaçao," 2001.

attentiveness to the multifunctionality of language, Juliana and Clemencia share much common ground with linguistic anthropology.[8]

Three factors explain the relevance of *forma di papia* for studying gender and sexuality in the Dutch Caribbean and beyond. First, *forma di papia* provides a guide for interpreting discourses emanating from the marginalized sectors of society. Second, it provides a framework for methodological interventions, such as ethnographic interviews or oral history research, which document perspectives that otherwise remain off the written record. Finally, and most importantly for this contribution, the concept of *forma di papia* generates creative, productive questions about agency and pathways toward liberation available to those subject to racial, gendered and heteronormative vectors of oppression.

1 *Forma Di Papia* as a Poetics of Concealment and Revelation

Central to Elis Juliana's methodology is what he termed *forma di papia*, a theorization of Curaçaoan linguistic practice that encompasses formal, structural features of language (*forma*) with patterns of language use in practice (*papia*).[9] When discussing *forma di papia*, Juliana seems less interested in distinguishing literature from everyday talk and more interested in excavating the underlying aesthetic preferences, poetic structures and discursive norms that explain common formal characteristics of artistic language, political oratory and everyday speech. With this concept, Elis Juliana is concerned with what linguistic anthropologists call language ideologies, discourses, attitudes and embodied sensibilities that speakers have about language and its appropriate use.[10] Implicit knowledge about what constitutes pleasant, compelling and appropriate communication is what linguistic anthropologists call "communicative competence."[11] Communicative competence is learned, habitual and thus acquired through ongoing social interaction.[12] Access to the frames of reference required to understand *forma di papia* is thus limited to those who have immersed themselves over an extended period, whether through socialization

8 "Palabra ku hopi mas implikashon ku e palabranan mes." Author's translation. Clemencia, *Elis Juliana inbestigadó*, 2004, p. 33.

9 Clemencia, *Elis Juliana inbestigadó*, 2004, pp. 32–38, 74.

10 Schieffelin, Woolard, and Kroskrity, *Language Ideologies: Practice and Theory*, 1998; and Rosa and Burdick, "Language Ideologies," 2016.

11 Hymes, "On Communicative Competence," 1972; Briggs, "Learning How to Ask: Native Metacommunicative Competence and the Incompetence of Fieldworkers," 1984.

12 Kulick and Schieffelin, "Language Socialization," 2004.

from infancy or intentional, long-term study. Elis Juliana emphasized that only due to extended interaction with Curaçaoan elders could he acquire the communicative competence to comprehend *forma di papia.*[13] In an interview between this author and Juliana in 2006, he reiterated the importance of competence in using *forma di papia* for ethnographic research.[14]

According to Juliana, a vital characteristic of *forma di papia* is a preference for opacity, concealment and euphemism in oratory, song, narrative and verbal art. To use *forma di papia* is to craft utterances "that do not say what they appear to be saying."[15] With allegories, metaphors and symbols invoking common local knowledge, Papiamento speakers fashion utterances that are at once opaque to interlopers and overhearers but perfectly transparent to their intended recipient. Occasionally, Juliana referred to *forma di papia* as *eufemismo afrikano* (African euphemism) because he believed these linguistic practices, poetics and stylistic preferences to be of African origin.[16] However, he held that *forma di papia* were incorporated into the repertoire of Curaçaoans who are not exclusively of African descent through processes of creolization. Access to *forma di papia* was determined by social proximity or distance from the everyday interactions that would enable a person to acquire skills in comprehending and using them.[17]

Joceline Clemencia, who drew from Elis Juliana's work in her studies of Curaçaoan verbal art and literature, expanded the framework for studying *forma di papia* with the concept of "double-bottomed" language.[18] Using the metaphor of a double-bottomed box, Clemencia clarifies a crucial aspect of *forma di papia* epitomized by the Papiamento idiom "those who know, know."[19] The double-bottomed box has one bottom that can be seen at first when anyone opens it. Yet, there is another, secret compartment underneath that first bottom that only those who know the box is double-bottomed will know to look for.[20] Using asymmetries of knowledge and information between cultural insiders, outsiders, novices and experts, double-bottomed language consists of utterances formed so that only insiders and cultural experts can fully comprehend their meaning. Thus, double-bottomed language entails a

13 Clemencia, *Elis Juliana inbestigadó*, 2004; and Allen, "Di ki manera?" 2007.

14 Elis Juliana, personal communication with the author, 2006.

15 "Ku no ta bisa loke nan ta parse di bisa." Author's translation. Clemencia, *Elis Juliana inbestigadó*, 2004, p. 33.

16 Ibid., pp. 32, 34.

17 Ibid., pp. 33, 38.

18 Clemencia, "Katibu ta galiña," 2001.

19 "Es ku sá, sá." Author's translation.

20 Clemencia, *Elis Juliana inbestigadó*, 2004; and Clemencia, "Katibu ta galiña," 2001, p. 148.

strategic deployment of recipient design, tailoring messages for a target audience based on the speaker's knowledge of that target audience's presuppositions and expectations. While recipient design is a factor in all communicative exchanges, double-bottomed language makes recipient design an art form that instrumentalizes the asymmetries of communicative competence between cultural insiders and outsiders.[21] For Clemencia, the song lyrics that belong to the musical genre of *tambú* exhibit this double-bottomed characteristic of appearing opaque to outsiders and direct to insiders.[22] As a genre of music often used for social commentary, the sharp edge of criticism is readily perceptible to the intended audiences that the *tambú* lyricist wishes to address. The same lyrics appear opaque and oblique to those without that insider knowledge. *Forma di papia* gave the marginalized the capacity to respond to the exclusion from elite-curated publics by creating a counter-public wherein information circulates while evading elite scrutiny.[23]

Clemencia has described double-bottomed language as indirectness.[24] However, Clemencia and Juliana, by their own accounts, present *forma di papia* as a concept that confounds the distinction between direct and indirect speech. Moreover, linguistic anthropologists have repeatedly found that "direct language" and "transparent language" are far more loaded than would seem at first glance. Much of this ideological baggage associated with "directness," "transparency" and "sincerity" traces to projects attempting to civilize or convert colonized subjects by changing their linguistic practices.[25] Furthermore, classifying discourse as either "direct" or "indirect" is not merely descriptive of a self-evident feature of that discourse. Instead, such determinations depend on the frames of reference, presuppositions and ideologies of those perceiving and classifying.[26] The case of *forma di papia* and double-bottomed language, where the same utterance can appear to be direct to one speaker and indirect to another, supports the case for paying attention to underlying factors that shape speakers' perceptions of language as transparent or indirect.

---

21 Hutchby, "Aspects of Recipient Design in Expert Advice-Giving on Call-in Radio," 1995.

22 Clemencia, "The Semiotics of Dark Clouds in Songs and Poems of Elia Isenia: Art as Female Therapy," 1992. Editors' note: this text by Clemencia is included in this volume. See also contribution by Allen in this section on the use of coded language in *tambú* songs.

23 Warner, "Publics and Counterpublics," 2002.

24 Clemencia, "The Semiotics of Dark Clouds," 1992, p. 210.

25 Keane, "Sincerity, 'Modernity,' and the Protestants," 2002; Kunreuther, "Transparent Media: Radio, Voice, and Ideologies of Directness in Postdemocratic Nepal," 2010.

26 Silverstein, "'Direct' and 'Indirect' Communicative Acts in Semiotic Perspective," 2010.

While important for understanding the politics of using *forma di papia*, the frameworks of resistance and refusal are incomplete.[27] Even under oppression, *forma di papia* remain expressions of agency and aesthetic sensibilities for what constitutes harmonious, persuasive and tasteful discourse. Juliana and Clemencia traced the origin of *forma di papia* not to slavery but precolonial West African discursive practices.[28] While attesting precolonial African origins remains a task for future research, available evidence suggests that discourse genres such as *forma di papia*, which employ metaphors, euphemisms and in-group references deemed indirect by Western standards, are not exclusive to the post-chattel slavery societies of the Americas.[29] Future research would benefit from situating *forma di papia* in conversation with the study of similar discursive practices worldwide, such as strategic bivalency, double-voicing, loud-talking and signifying.[30]

Nevertheless, Elis Juliana saw *forma di papia* as a defense against slavery, colonization and forms of domination.[31] He held that ontological violence was a key strategy of control. This ontological violence entailed classifying enslaved people as human flesh over which enslavers exercised property rights. At the same time, enslaved people were also denied permission to have their own ontology, their sense of what exists in the world and how they, as people, exist within it. With his emphasis on the political and legal ontology of slavery, Juliana contributes to an ongoing debate on how these legal and political fictions continue to impact racialization and socioeconomic dispossession faced by descendants of enslaved Africans in the Americas.[32] His significant contribution to this broader conversation was to think through the impact of

---

27 For a more detailed discussion of refusal, see Simpson, "On Ethnographic Refusal: Indigeneity, 'Voice' and Colonial Citizenship," 2007; McGranahan, "Theorizing Refusal: An Introduction," 2016; and Simpson, "Consent's Revenge," 2016.

28 Clemencia, *Het grote camouflagespel van de OPI*, 1989, pp. 42–43.

29 Silverstein, "'Direct' and 'Indirect' Communicative Acts in Semiotic Perspective," 2010; Obeng, "Verbal Indirection in Akan Informal Discourse," 1994.

30 Mitchell-Kernan, "Signifying and Marking: Two Afro-American Speech Acts," 1972; Abrahams, *The Man-of-Words in the West Indies: Performance and the Emergence of Creole Culture*, 1983; Morgan, "Conversational Signifying: Grammar and Indirectness among African American Women," 1996; Woolard, "Simultaneity and Bivalency as Strategies in Bilingualism," 1998; Spears, "Directness in the Use of African American English," 2001.

31 Clemencia, *Elis Juliana inbestigadó*, 2004, p. 74.

32 Fanon, *Black Skin, White Masks*, 2008; Paula, *From Objective to Subjective Social Barriers*, 1967; Wynter, "Unsettling the Coloniality of Being/Power/Truth/Freedom: Towards the Human, After Man, Its Overrepresentation – An Argument," 2003; Maldonado-Torres, "On the Coloniality of Being," 2007; Patterson, *Slavery and Social Death: A Comparative Study, With a New Preface*, 2018; and Gordon, *Fear of Black Consciousness*, 2022.

the ontological violence of slavery on language, poetics and the pragmatics of truth-telling.[33] His great insight was that silencing enslaved people went far beyond intimidation and retaliation. Instead, enslaved people were structurally excluded from the practice of truth-telling on an ontological basis. As human property, enslaved people did not enjoy full personhood, and it was thus impossible to recognize enslaved people as capable of truth-telling.[34] For Juliana, it is the ontological violence and structural disregard of slavery and post-slavery racism that explains the meaning behind the Papiamento idiom "truth usually finds no chair to sit on."[35] The enslaved quickly learned that, for them, acts of parrhesia, speaking truth to power, were doomed to fail. At worst, speaking the truth would reveal information that slaveholders could use against the enslaved. At best, anything enslaved people said—critique, complaint or lament—would be disregarded as meaningless, unimportant noise. Instead, enslaved people took to *forma di papia* to defend themselves. These *forma di papia* enabled the enslaved to create a world of ideas, sentiments and values that would remain opaque, inaccessible and thus ungovernable to the enslaver. Through proficiency in using *forma di papia*, enslaved people cultivated a sense of self-worth that did not depend on what enslavers thought of them.

Elis Juliana did not uncritically celebrate *forma di papia* and held that Curaçaoans often wielded them self-destructively.[36] At the same time, he urged researchers to adopt a stance of humility and appreciation for the artfulness and wisdom expressed through them.[37] Framing *forma di papia* as mere pathological adaptations to slavery and colonial racism risks overlooking the therapeutic effects that they can have.[38] Joceline Clemencia makes a case that Juliana applied concepts he developed from ethnographic fieldwork—such as *forma di papia* and *eufemismo afrikano*—to his literary production to tell

33 Juliana, "Katibu ta galiña" [Slaves are chickens], 1983; Juliana, "Nanzi, su origen, i su influensia riba desaroyo di nos komunidat" [Nanzi, his origin, and his influence on the development of our community], 1980; Juliana, "Algun pensamentu tokante política di religion den pasado i su desaroyo den nos komunidat di awe" [Some thoughts about the politics of religion in the past and its impact on the development of our community], 1976.

34 Elis Juliana, personal communication with the author, 2006.

35 "Bèrdat no sa haña stul pa sinta." Author's translation. Clemencia, *Elis Juliana inbestigadó*, 2004, p. 34; Clemencia, *Het grote camouflagespel van de OPI*, 1989, p. 44.

36 Juliana, "Nanzi, su origen, i su influensia riba desaroyo di nos komunidat," 1980; Clemencia, *Elis Juliana inbestigadó*, 2004.

37 Elis Juliana, personal communication with the author, 2006.

38 Clemencia, "The Semiotics of Dark Clouds," 1992. Editors' note: A shortened version of this text is included in this volume.

painful truths the Curaçaoan public would otherwise refuse to receive.[39] Juliana himself reaffirmed the importance of *forma di papia* as an ethnographic reality and an essential strategy for disseminating critical insights from ethnographic research to the Curaçaoan public.[40] A history of *forma di papia* would have to trace this fascinating paradoxical turn: a poetics of concealment becomes, for those who lived in a world that denied them the possibility of truth-telling, a resource that enables them to speak their truth.

2 The Implications of *Forma Di Papia* for the Study of Gender and Sexuality

Joceline Clemencia is arguably the most influential voice to bring Elis Juliana's approach and methodology to the study of gender and sexuality in the Dutch Caribbean. A grounding principle of *Julianismo* (Julianism), the methodological and theoretical approach Elis Juliana developed, is a respect for *grandinan* (elders) that places them on an equal epistemic and interpretive footing with the scholar.[41] Juliana was concerned that the pressure academic institutions put on researchers to perform their expertise, in his words, *hunga interesante* (acting interesting), would come at the expense of careful study of *forma di papia* and close readings of oral traditions.[42] *Grandinan* and other research participants are not to be treated as mere informants but as experts whose knowledge about the production and interpretation of oral tradition should be taken seriously, on their own terms.[43] The goal is not simply extracting texts from the elders so they can be examined or validated using academic theories. Instead, the scholar must attend to the underlying frameworks Curaçaoan elders employ to analyze language in verbal art and everyday life.

Clemencia demonstrates the value of a Julianist approach to studying gender and sexuality in the Dutch Caribbean by developing the concept of *forma di papia* into a framework for analyzing latent and tacit feminist and queer perspectives within Curaçaoan verbal art, oral history and oratory.[44] These

---

39 Clemencia, *Het grote camouflagespel van de OPI*, 1989, pp. 92, 103.

40 Elis Juliana, personal communication, 2006.

41 Clemencia, *Elis Juliana inbestigadó*, 2004, pp. 35–36, 74–77.

42 Juliana expressed this concern to Joceline Clemencia and reiterated it in an interview I had with him in 2006.

43 Clemencia, *Elis Juliana inbestigadó*, 2004, pp. 35–36.

44 Clemencia, "Katibu ta galiña," 2001; Clemencia, "Katalina beleku. A View on Curaçaoan Feminine Folklore," 1996; Clemencia, "The Semiotics of Dark Clouds," 1992; and Clemencia,

feminist and queer perspectives remain tacit either because of the necessity of survival in a patriarchal and heteronormative social order or because they go without saying—*tur hende sá* (everyone knows)—and no longer need overt explication.[45] In addition to these conceptual contributions, Juliana's ethnographic collections remain valuable for those interested in the Dutch Caribbean perspectives on gender and sexuality marginalized by the colonial archive and the literary production of elites.[46]

Forma di papia are a central component of the analytic lens that Joceline Clemencia directs at ritual practices of "naming and revelation" that form part of the lives of women whose identities and relationships defy heteronormativity.[47] By juxtaposing testimonies from Curaçaoan women who love women with written texts from Guillermo Rosario, Tip Marugg, Astrid Roemer and Arnela ten Meer, Clemencia reveals practices that paradoxically conceal and expose the presence of nonheteronormative relationships at the same time.[48] Clemencia mentions "ritual moments of revelation," such as wearing the same clothes when visiting public events to signal same-sex relationship status, sharing the same dishes when eating at parties and using codewords such as "Dalia" to refer to same-sex relationships in songs. These ritual moments of revelations were "public and sometimes sacred even."[49] These Curaçaoan rituals of revelation and concealment are reminiscent of situations elsewhere in the Caribbean, analyzed by scholars such as Gloria Wekker, Carlos Decena and Rosamond King, in which nonheteronormative ways of loving, desiring and relating with others are public secrets that hide in plain sight, tacit knowledge that everybody knows and goes without saying.[50]

"Women Who Love Women in Curaçao: From 'Cachapera' to Open Throats: A Commentary in Collage," 1996.

45 Decena, "Tacit Subjects," 2008.

46 In addition to an extensive ethnographic archive of oral histories, songs and artifacts that address gender and sexuality, Elis Juliana also has published ethnographic texts of interest to gender and sexuality studies. See Juliana, *Wazo riba ròndu I* [Wazo makes the rounds I], 1967; Juliana, *Curaçaose pinda's. Volkskunde van Curaçao: Hekserij, religie, sexologie, huwelijk, politiek* [Curaçaoan peanuts. Folklore of Curaçao: Witchcraft, religion, sexology, marriage, politics], 1969; Juliana, *Echa cuenta* [Casting stories], 1970; Juliana, *Guia etnologiko II: Kulto di morto* [Ethnological guide II: Death rituals], 1977; Juliana, *Wazo riba ròndu II* [Wazo makes the rounds II], 1981; Juliana, *Matrimonio i parto* [Marriage and childbirth], 1988; Juliana, *Wazo riba ròndu III* [Wazo makes the rounds III], 1988.

47 Clemencia, "Women Who Love Women in Curaçao," 1996.

48 Ibid.

49 Ibid., pp. 82–83.

50 Wekker, *The Politics of Passion: Women's Sexual Culture in the Afro-Surinamese Diaspora*, 2006; Decena, "Tacit Subjects," 2008; King, *Island Bodies: Transgressive Sexualities in the*

In her text, Clemencia makes several interventions that resonate with Juliana's overall methodology. First, it follows Juliana in choosing oral histories and testimonies as the initial entry point for investigating and challenging sexual and gender heteronormativity in Curaçaoan society. Second, it engages these testimonies not as information to be extracted and analyzed by a detached observer. Instead, the text positions the scholar and the testimonies provided by women who love women on equal footing as members of an epistemic and political community participating in the "historical process of freeing the self."[51] Third, the analysis of the rituals of revelation and concealment among women who love women builds on language ideologies, poetic sensibilities, aesthetic preferences and discursive practices discussed under the rubrics of *forma di papia* and double-bottomed language. Finally, Clemencia takes up one of the most critical challenges that Juliana posed for devising a politics of liberation through his analysis of *forma di papia*: the question of truth-telling from a position that is denied access to this possibility. Given that enslavement and colonization have placed Curaçaoans in a position where "the truth can never find a place to sit," Clemencia shifts her focus away from a politics of confessing or revealing the truth in public—rendered moot when the speaker is deemed incapable of truth-telling—and toward a politics of self-naming and self-definition.[52]

In contrast to the "epistemology of the closet" and the metaphor of "coming out" that entail a unidirectional progression from hiding in private to revealing and confessing in public, these rituals of revelation and concealment created a gossamer veil, both transparent and opaque at the same time.[53] Queer life is visible, public and hidden simultaneously, depending on who is familiar enough with the repertoire of signs, metaphors and figures of speech to see through the veil. Persons in same-sex relationships can draw from *forma di papia* and double-bottomed language to afford themselves the freedom to decide whom they will "come out" to and under what conditions. These rituals of revelation and the use of *forma di papia* destabilize the distinctions between private and public, in and out, transparent and opaque, hiding and revealing.

Publicity itself—the process of making things public—is complicated by *forma di papia*, which create transparent messages for one audience that

---

Caribbean Imagination, 2014; and La Fountain-Stokes, *Queer Ricans: Cultures and Sexualities in the Diaspora*, 2009.

51 Clemencia, "Women Who Love Women in Curaçao," 1996, p. 81.

52 Clemencia, "Women Who Love Women in Curaçao," 1996; cf. Hill Collins, *Black Feminist Thought: Knowledge, Consciousness, and the Politics of Empowerment*, 2000.

53 Sedgwick, *Epistemology of the Closet*, 2008; Butler, "Imitation and Gender Insubordination," 2013.

remain opaque to others. The teleology of "coming out of the closet" is further disrupted because using *forma di papia* preempts the formation of a unified public sphere wherein one could unambiguously come out. Instead, *forma di papia* generate multiple, unevenly accessible public spheres that are recursively embedded within each other like nested dolls. What is "public" discourse for one audience of insiders can simultaneously be "private" for those outsiders who lack the communicative competence to access and participate in that discourse.[54] The shifting, situational and recursive character of the public–private distinction further complicates the act of coming out and making one's sexual identity public. Narratives about the path toward queer liberation that center on notions of transparency, coming out, confession and publicity must be adjusted accordingly.

Bringing the rituals of revelation and concealment among women who love women into conversation with the theorization of *forma di papia* surfaces the strategic subtleties of exercising agency and freedom in the face of repression. The refusal to capitulate to fear and repression can be demonstrated, in some contexts, by revealing and naming, while, in other contexts, by a refusal to allow oneself to be transparent, legible and classifiable to everyone. Far from a simple expression of shame and fear, refusing transparency allows those whose relationships defy heteronormativity to choose which public they wish to out themselves to and under what terms. This perspective echoes the rhetorical question posed by Judith Butler: "so we are out of the closet, but into what?"[55] Refusing to be transparent and legible can be an act of insubordination in a situation where the demand to give an account of oneself is being imposed or where the very act of providing an account of the self can open up that person to surveillance and control. Refusing to make the self transparent and legible to a heteronormative public is another assertion of what Edouard Glissant calls "the right to opacity."[56]

Instead of publicity, transparency, revelation and the confessional genre of coming out, Joceline Clemencia focused her analysis on "naming" as the practice through which a liberatory struggle against patriarchy and heteronormativity can be waged. Clemencia suggests that the move that more profoundly unsettled heteronormativity in Curaçao was not the publicity of same-sex relations but their explicit naming. Clemencia provides the example of a couple whose same-sex relationship was tolerated when it was a public secret but

54 Gal, "A Semiotics of the Public/Private Distinction," 2002.
55 Butler, "Imitation and Gender Insubordination," 2013, p. 16.
56 Glissant, *Poetics of Relation*, 1997.

became ostracized when they publicly named themselves as a couple.[57] This example shows that it is naming and not publicity per se that provoked retaliatory action. With the shift in focus from making things public to naming, Clemencia seems to take from Elis Juliana the argument about how the ontological violence of slavery and its racialized constructs of humanity still constrain the possibilities for parrhesia, the speaking of truth to power, in post-slavery Curaçao. The exclusion from being a legitimate truth-telling subject, itself a legacy of slavery and its forms of governance, is further compounded by intersectional oppressions of racialization, patriarchy and heteronormativity. Attempted acts of confession or truth-telling will never be received or believed if the public denies the very existence of the one attempting to perform these speech acts. In this condition, making oneself intelligible and recognizable to an audience that structurally denies one's existence is not a viable first move in a struggle for liberation. Instead, the move is to name one's experience for oneself and enact that way of being before others. As one of Clemencia's interlocutors states: "naming oneself lesbian is a political deed."[58] The focus on the politics of naming brings Clemencia and her interlocutors into conversation with Patricia Hill Collins, who theorizes Black feminist politics of liberation as one of self-definition and the "power to name one's own reality."[59] Clemencia also expresses concern with naming as an act of self-determination through her use of periphrasis, such as "women who love women," and her avoidance of purportedly Euro-American, patriarchal labels such as "lesbian."[60] With this, Clemencia preempts imposing unintentional and unnecessary restrictions on the freedom to name oneself.[61] Clemencia's concern on the practice and politics of naming resonates with Gloria Wekker's writings on *mati*-work in Suriname, which, likewise, avoids imposing Eurocentric categories to interpret how Afro-Surinamese exercise sexual and romantic agency and challenge patriarchal frameworks.[62]

By no means does Clemencia seek to romanticize *forma di papia* and the ritual acts of naming and concealment among women who love women in Curaçao. These poetics make space for agency and refusal under oppression but do not represent the limit or end horizon for liberation. The women who love women whom Joceline Clemencia interviews state that they cannot stand

57 Clemencia, "Women Who Love Women in Curaçao," 1996, pp. 83–85.
58 Ibid., p. 85.
59 Hill Collins, *Black Feminist Thought*, 2000, p. 300.
60 Clemencia, "Women Who Love Women in Curaçao," 1996, p. 81.
61 Ibid.; see also Isenia, "Looking for Kambrada," 2019, p. 126.
62 Wekker, *The Politics of Passion*, 2006.

"the sneaky way" and condemn the "double standard" that tolerates homosexual relationships only as long as they remain public secrets.[63] At the same time, taking these ritual acts of naming and concealment along with *forma di papia* as expressions of agency allows us to chart pathways toward a *futura cuir* (queer future) of liberation beyond the terms and conditions set by dominant Euro-American frameworks and experiences.[64] An overly absolutist understanding of liberation, where anything that appears to deviate from the one true path must be jettisoned along the way, would miss the mark. Naming as an act of self-determination and liberation is contiguous with *forma di papia* and harbors the potential to unsettle heteronormative and patriarchal traditions. Discarding double-bottomed language and *forma di papia* would leave people with fewer strategies for expression in ways that disrupt heteronormativity.

3 Conclusion: *Julianismo* (Julianism) as a Guide for Future Research

Wigbertson Julian Isenia, in his analysis of archival sources on *kambrada*, confronted the limitations of the archive as a site for the recovery of queer subjectivity in the Dutch Caribbean.[65] Isenia concluded with a call to turn to oral history, performance and verbal art as necessary complements to methodologies that hinge upon what has been committed to the written record.[66] Thoughtfully engaging *forma di papia* and the questions they raise about transparency, publicity and the linguistic agency of marginalized speakers can guide scholars in approaching signs of feminist and queer life outside the archive that otherwise cunningly elude documentation.

As indicated at the beginning of this contribution, *forma di papia* provides a guide for interpreting and interacting with discourses emanating from those whose genders and sexualities positioned them at the margins. *Forma di papia* and their critical perspectives on ideologies of directness, transparency and publicity can help scholars revisit both the archive and the oral repertoire to read signs of feminist and queer subjectivity beyond categories such as

63 Clemencia, "Women Who Love Women in Curaçao," 1996, p. 83.

64 Bonilla, "Postdisaster Futures: Hopeful Pessimism, Imperial Ruination, and la futura cuir," 2020; Schields, "Eros against Empire," 2019.

65 *Kambrada* is a type of same-sex relationship between women in the Papiamento-speaking regions of the Dutch Caribbean. Most written accounts of *kambrada* were provided by elite or middle-class men who disapproved of such relationships and saw them as a threat to the patriarchal, race-and-class stratified order of Curaçaoan society; see Isenia, "Looking for Kambrada," 2019.

66 Ibid. Editors' note: see contribution by Isenia in this volume.

kambrada, which colonial archives and patriarchal literary texts have already enregistered. *Forma di papia* can guide researchers in documenting spoken language that remains off the record otherwise. When conducting ethnographic or oral history studies with the marginalized in the Dutch Caribbean, researchers will need proficiency in *forma di papia* to elicit commentary about sensitive topics, such as love, relationships, sexuality and gender identity.

Forma di papia shed critical light on "epistemologies of the closet" that shape research agendas.[67] Wrestling with *forma di papia* means recognizing that people may refuse transparency and make their subjectivities opaque and elusive to heal and liberate themselves. Should "coming out" into the written record be the desirable intervention for queer subjectivities who want to stay out of the archive and thus elude its forms of governance? Thinking through the ethics of revealing what was meant to remain hidden is another way the framework of *forma di papia* can guide future research. Sometimes, one should consider "refusing research" and imagine more appropriate interventions.[68] Joceline Clemencia's work on women who love women provides future research with a model through which the nuances in this ethical discussion about naming, revelation and concealment can be navigated.

Finally, by reading Joceline Clemencia's work on women who love women alongside the works that develop the concept of *forma di papia*, the present contribution seeks to demonstrate the value of this conceptual framework for theorizing how women, queers and other marginalized subjectivities engage in processes of "liberating the self."[69] Through engagement with the way *forma di papia* complicate distinctions between privacy, publicity, hiddenness and revelation, one can encounter theoretical resources to critique the binaries that underpin the "epistemology of the closet" while creating space for appreciating the theoretical potential of Dutch Caribbean scholarship on gender and sexuality.[70] For Joceline Clemencia, a "new language" for intimacy and relationships constituted the emancipatory horizon.[71] *Forma di papia* form part of the effort of creating this new language that would move beyond making queer relations and subjectivities intelligible to a heteronormative world. Instead, this effort would shift the ground upon which people of all sexualities and genders conceive of the possibilities of human intimacy and love.

67 Sedgwick, *Epistemology of the Closet*, 2008.

68 Tuck and Yang, "R-Words: Refusing Research," 2014; Simpson, "On Ethnographic Refusal: Indigeneity," 2007.

69 Clemencia, "Women Who Love Women in Curaçao," 1996, p. 81.

70 Sedgwick, *Epistemology of the Closet*, 2008.

71 Clemencia, "Women Who Love Women in Curaçao," 1996, p. 85.

Bibliography

Abrahams, Roger D. *The Man-of-Words in the West Indies: Performance and the Emergence of Creole Culture*. Johns Hopkins Studies in Atlantic History and Culture. Baltimore: Johns Hopkins University Press, 1983.

Allen, Rose Mary. "Di ki manera? A Social History of Afro-Curaçaoans, 1863–1917." PhD diss., Utrecht University, 2007. https://dspace.library.uu.nl/handle/1874/20718.

Allen, Rose Mary. "'See How I Talk about the Slavemaster': Searching for 'We' in Afro-Curaçaoan Oral Histories." In *Auto/Biography across the Americas: Transnational Themes in Life Writing*, edited by Ricia Anne Chansky, 164–82. Routledge Interdisciplinary Perspectives on Literature 68. New York: Routledge, 2016.

Bonilla, Yarimar. "Postdisaster Futures: Hopeful Pessimism, Imperial Ruination, and la futura cuir." *Small Axe: A Caribbean Journal of Criticism* 24, no. 2 (July 2020): 147–62. https://doi.org/10.1215/07990537-8604562.

Briggs, Charles L. "Learning How to Ask: Native Metacommunicative Competence and the Incompetence of Fieldworkers." *Language in Society* 13, no. 1 (1984): 1–28. https://www.jstor.org/stable/4167483.

Butler, Judith. "Imitation and Gender Insubordination." In *Inside/Out Lesbian Theories, Gay Theories*, edited by Diana Fuss, 13–31. London: Routledge, 2013.

Clemencia, Joceline. *Elis Juliana inbestigadó: Piedra di mulina*. Curaçao: NAAM, 2004.

Clemencia, Joceline. *Het grote camouflagespel van de OPI: Een thematische benadering van de poëzie van Elis Juliana* [The OPI's great game of camouflage: A thematic approach to the poetry of Elis Juliana]. Leiden: KITLV, 1989.

Clemencia, Joceline. "Katalina Beleku: A View on Curaçaoan Feminine Folklore." In *Papers of the Third Seminar on Latin-American and Caribbean Folklore*, edited by E. N. Ayubi, 83–93. Reports of the Archaeological-Anthropological Institute of the Netherlands Antilles 12. Curaçao: Archaeological-Anthropological Institute of the Netherlands Antilles, 1996.

Clemencia, Joceline. "Katibu ta galiña: From Hidden to Open Protest on Curaçao." In *A History of Literature in the Caribbean*, edited by A. James Arnold, Julio Rodríguez-Luis, and J. Michael Dash, 433–42. A Comparative History of Literatures in European Languages = Histoire Comparée Des Littératures de Langues Européennes 2: English-and Dutch-speaking Regions. Amsterdam: John Benjamins Publishing Company, 2001.

Clemencia, Joceline. "The Semiotics of Dark Clouds in Songs and Poems of Elia Isenia: Art as Female Therapy." In *Mundu yama sinta mira: Womanhood in Curaçao*, edited by Richenel Ansano, Joceline A. Clemencia, Jeanette Cook, and Eithel Martis, 207–31. Curaçao: Fundashon Publikashon, 1992.

Clemencia, Joceline. "Women Who Love Women in Curaçao: From 'Cachapera' to Open Throats: A Commentary in Collage." *Feminist Studies* 22, no. 1 (1996): 81. https://doi.org/10.2307/3178247.

Decena, Carlos Ulises. "Tacit Subjects." *GLQ: A Journal of Lesbian and Gay Studies* 14, no. 2–3 (June 2008): 339–59. https://doi.org/10.1215/10642684-2007-036.

Fanon, Frantz. *Black Skin, White Masks*. New York: Grove Press, 2008.

Gal, Susan. "A Semiotics of the Public/Private Distinction." *Differences: A Journal of Feminist Cultural Studies* 13, no. 1 (February 2002): 77–95. https://muse.jhu.edu/pub/4/article/9632.

Glissant, Edouard. *Poetics of Relation*. Translated by Betsy Wing. Ann Arbor: University of Michigan Press, 1997.

Gordon, Lewis R. *Fear of Black Consciousness*. New York: Farrar, Straus and Giroux, 2022.

Hill Collins, Patricia. *Black Feminist Thought: Knowledge, Consciousness, and the Politics of Empowerment*. Rev. 10th anniversary ed. London: Psychology Press, 2000.

Hutchby, Ian. "Aspects of Recipient Design in Expert Advice-Giving on Call-in Radio." *Discourse Processes* 19, no. 2 (1995): 219–38. https://doi.org/10.1080/01638539509544915.

Hymes, Dell H. "On Communicative Competence." In *Sociolinguistics*, edited by John B. Pride, 269–85. Harmondsworth: Penguin Books, 1972.

Isenia, Wigbertson Julian. "Looking for Kambrada: Sexuality and Social Anxieties in the Dutch Colonial Archive, 1882–1923." *Tijdschrift Voor Genderstudies* 22, no. 2 (June 2019): 125–43. https://doi.org/10.5117/TVGN2019.2.002.ISEN.

Juliana, Elis. "Algun pensamentu tokante polítika di religion den pasado i su desaroyo den nos komunidat di awe" [Some thoughts about the politics of religion in the past and its impact on the development of our community]. In *Week-end di estudio organisá pa Centraal Historisch Archief: Curaçao Hilton Hotel, 8–10 di oktober 1976*, edited by A. F. Paula, 51–55. Curaçao: Centraal Historisch Archief van de Nederlandse Antillen, 1976.

Juliana, Elis. *Curaçaose pinda's. Volkskunde van Curaçao: Hekserij, religie, sexologie, huwelijk, politiek* [Curaçaoan peanuts. Folklore of Curaçao: Witchcraft, religion, sexology, marriage, politics]. Curaçao: Scherpenheuvel, 1969.

Juliana, Elis. *Echa cuenta* [Casting stories]. Amsterdam: Bezige Bij, 1970.

Juliana, Elis. *Guia etnologiko II: Kulto di morto* [Ethnological guide II: Death rituals]. Curaçao: Scherpenheuvel, 1977.

Juliana, Elis. "Katibu ta galiña" [Slaves are chickens]. *Kristòf* 6, no. 4 (1983): 25–29.

Juliana, Elis. *Matrimonio i parto* [Marriage and childbirth]. Reports of the Archaeological-Anthropological Institute of the Netherlands Antilles 5. Curaçao: Archaeological-Anthropological Institute of the Netherlands Antilles, 1988.

Juliana, Elis. "Nanzi, su origen, i su influensia riba desaroyo di nos komunidat" [Nanzi, his origin, and his influence on the development of our community]. *Kristòf* 5, no. 5 (1980): 4–17.

Juliana, Elis. *Wazo riba ròndu I* [Wazo makes the rounds I]. Curaçao: Scherpenheuvel, 1967.

Juliana, Elis. *Wazo riba ròndu II* [Wazo makes the rounds II]. Curaçao: Scherpenheuvel, 1981.

Juliana, Elis. *Wazo riba ròndu III* [Wazo makes the rounds III]. Curaçao: Scherpenheuvel, 1988.

Keane, Webb. "Sincerity, 'Modernity,' and the Protestants." *Cultural Anthropology* 17, no. 1 (2002): 65–92. https://doi.org/10.1525/can.2002.17.1.65.

King, Rosamond S. *Island Bodies: Transgressive Sexualities in the Caribbean Imagination*. Gainesville: University Press of Florida, 2014.

Kulick, Don, and Bambi B. Schieffelin. "Language Socialization." In *A Companion to Linguistic Anthropology*, edited by Alessandro Duranti, 349–68. Blackwell Companions to Anthropology 1. Malden, MA: Blackwell, 2004.

Kunreuther, Laura. "Transparent Media: Radio, Voice, and Ideologies of Directness in Postdemocratic Nepal." *Journal of Linguistic Anthropology* 20, no. 2 (2010): 334–51. https://doi.org/10.1111/j.1548-1395.2010.01073.x.

La Fountain-Stokes, Lawrence M. *Queer Ricans: Cultures and Sexualities in the Diaspora*. Cultural Studies of the Americas 23. Minneapolis: University of Minnesota Press, 2009.

Maldonado-Torres, Nelson. "On The Coloniality of Being: Contributions to the Development of a Concept." *Cultural Studies* 21, no. 2–3 (2007): 240–70. https://doi.org/10.1080/09502380601162548.

McGranahan, Carole. "Theorizing Refusal: An Introduction." *Cultural Anthropology* 31, no. 3 (August 2016): 319–25. https://doi.org/10.14506/ca31.3.01.

Mitchell-Kernan, Claudia. "Signifying and Marking: Two Afro-American Speech Acts." In *Directions in Sociolinguistics: The Ethnography of Communication*, edited by John J. Gumperz and Dell H. Hymes, 161–79. New York: Holt, Rinehart and Winston, 1972.

Morgan, Marcyliena. "Conversational Signifying: Grammar and Indirectness among African American Women." *Studies in Interactional Sociolinguistics* 13 (1996): 405–34.

Obeng, Samuel Gyasi. "Verbal Indirection in Akan Informal Discourse." *Journal of Pragmatics* 21, no. 1 (1994): 37–65. https://doi.org/10.1016/0378-2166(94)90046-9.

Patterson, Orlando. *Slavery and Social Death: A Comparative Study, With a New Preface*. First Harvard University Press paperback edition. Cambridge, MA: Harvard University Press, 2018.

Paula, A. F. *From Objective to Subjective Social Barriers. A Historico-Philosophical Analysis of Certain Negative Attitudes among the Negroid Population of Curaçao*. Curaçao: Curaçaose Courant, 1967.

Rosa, Jonathan, and Christa Burdick. "Language Ideologies." In *The Oxford Handbook of Language and Society*, edited by Ofelia García, Nelson Flores, and Massimiliano Spotti, 103–24. New York: Oxford University Press, 2016. https://doi.org/10.1093/oxfordhb/9780190212896.013.15.

Schieffelin, Bambi B., Kathryn Ann Woolard, and Paul V. Kroskrity, eds. *Language Ideologies: Practice and Theory*. New York: Oxford University Press, 1998.

Schields, Chelsea. "Eros against Empire: Visions of Erotic Freedom in Archives of Decolonisation." *Tijdschrift Voor Genderstudies* 22, no. 2 (June 2019): 145–61. https://doi.org/10.5117/TVGN2019.2.003.SCHI.

Sedgwick, Eve Kosofsky. *Epistemology of the Closet. Updated with a new preface*. Berkeley: University of California Press, 2008.

Silverstein, Michael. "'Direct' and 'Indirect' Communicative Acts in Semiotic Perspective." *Journal of Pragmatics* 42, no. 2 (2010): 337–53. https://doi.org/10.1016/j.pragma.2009.06.003.

Simpson, Audra. "Consent's Revenge." *Cultural Anthropology* 31, no. 3 (August 2016): 326–33. https://doi.org/10.14506/ca31.3.02.

Simpson, Audra. "On Ethnographic Refusal: Indigeneity, 'Voice' and Colonial Citizenship." *Junctures: The Journal for Thematic Dialogue*, no. 9 (2007). https://junctures.org/index.php/junctures/article/view/66.

Spears, Arthur K. "Directness in the Use of African American English." In *Sociocultural and Historical Contexts of African American English*, edited by Sonja L. Lanehart, 257–78. Varieties of English around the World General Series 27. Amsterdam: John Benjamins Publishing Company, 2001.

Trouillot, Michel-Rolph. *Silencing the Past: Power and the Production of History*. Boston: Beacon Press, 1995.

Tuck, Eve, and K. Wayne Yang Yang. "R-Words: Refusing Research." In *Humanizing Research: Decolonizing Qualitative Inquiry with Youth and Communities*, edited by Django Paris and Maisha T. Winn, 223–48. London: SAGE Publications, 2014. https://doi.org/10.4135/9781544329611.

Warner, Michael. "Publics and Counterpublics." *Public Culture* 14, no. 1 (January 2002): 49–90. https://doi.org/10.1215/08992363-14-1-49.

Wekker, Gloria. *The Politics of Passion: Women's Sexual Culture in the Afro-Surinamese Diaspora*. Between Men~between Women. New York: Columbia University Press, 2006.

Woolard, Kathryn A. "Simultaneity and Bivalency as Strategies in Bilingualism." *Journal of Linguistic Anthropology* 8, no. 1 (1998): 3–29. https://doi.org/10.1525/jlin.1998.8.1.3.

Wynter, Sylvia. "Unsettling the Coloniality of Being/Power/Truth/Freedom: Towards the Human, After Man, Its Overrepresentation--An Argument." *CR: The New Centennial Review* 3, no. 3 (2003): 257–337. https://doi.org/10.1353/ncr.2004.0015.

CHAPTER 31

I Have to Come Out [Mi Tin Ku Sali]

Gilbert Bacilio

1 Introduction

The following poem was first published in 1994 in the Papiamentu magazine *Maribomba*.[1] It was inspired by the bitter fact that many gay men and boys in the Netherlands Antilles in the 1980s and 90s were kicked out of their homes by their parents if they had the courage to openly declare their gay identity.

In 1980, the civil rights group Grupo Homofilia Antiyano (GHA, Group of Antillean Homophiles) approached me as a writer and director of the theater group Teatro Foro [Forum Theater] to create a street theater performance in response to this. The performance was one of several activities that were planned by GHA in the period June 28 to July 5, 1980, as part of a campaign to raise public awareness relating to the widespread prejudices held against homosexuals. These activities included a radio program on Korsow-FM, an open public discussion evening and the publication of a special information brochure, which was to be made available at the bookstores of Van Dorp-Eddine on the island.

Teatro Foro, which used the forum theater method popularized by the Brazilian theater innovator, Augusto Boal, devised a scene in which a boy comes out to his family as gay. Spectators were meant to respond to the situation by stepping on stage themselves, thereby creating a public dialogue on the discrimination faced by gay people on the island. The play was planned to be staged on Wilhelminaplein, a busy public square in Willemstad, Curaçao.

The lieutenant governor refused to grant a permit for the presentation of the performance, arguing that "it would be objectionable and offend public sentiment for gay people to perform their views in public and a street theater performance would thus not be suitable for the public moral order."[2] Similarly, the local head of culture washed his hands off in innocence. In a letter to the editor, the GHA publicly objected to the lieutenant governor's actions, pointing

1 Bacilio, "Mi Tin Ku Sali", *Maribomba* 1, 1994, p. 13. Translated into English by Wernher Suares.

2 Grupo Homofilia Antiyano, "Ingezonden: Homofilie" [Letter to the editor: Homophilia], *Amigoe di Curaçao*, June 28, 1980, p. 6.

 | DOI:10.1163/9789004690882_033

out how they contradicted his own earlier public statements that society ought to show more openness to homosexuality.[3]

This was my reason for writing "Mi tin ku sali": to protest against the decision by the lieutenant governor and the lack of the support from the head of cultural affairs, as well as to show solidarity with and offer encouragement to these outcast youths.

∴

I Have to Come Out	**Mi Tin Ku Sali**
I want to get out of this musty closet,	Mi ke sali fo'i kashi mùf,
dead roaches, camphor.	kakalaka morto, kanfer.
I'm suffocating!	Mi ta stek!
I'm sick of wearing old bourgeois suits,	M'a kansa di bisti flus bieu burgues,
and strangling ties.	ku dashi te den korokoro choká.
I opened the closet doors …	M'a habri e port'i kashi …
fresh air,	airu fresku,
movement of bodies,	moveshon di kurpa,
human warmth,	kalor humano,
my skin comes alive	mi porionan ta reis
shaking my pale body.	sakudí mi kurpa dòf.
I'm coming out.	Mi ta sali.
I have to come out!	Mi tin ku sali!
A thousand pairs of eyes	Diesmil par di wowo
are penetrating my darkness,	ta penetrá mi skuridat,
piercing me,	ta wak skèrpi,
becoming water,	ta bira awa,
sparking fire,	ta spat kandela,
pushing me back.	ta pusha mi manda patras.
A thousand long fingers are aiming.	Diesmil dede largu ta mek.
Blunt nails chewed out of anger	Huña bòt komé pa rabia
are scratching on the closet doors	ta rask'e port'i kashi
pushing me to the back.	pusha mi manda patras.

3 The reference to the lieutenant governor's earlier statement is cited in this letter from *Amigoe di Curaçao*, March 20, 1980.

I Have to Come Out	**Mi Tin Ku Sali**
I want to get out.	Mi ke sali.
I have to get out!	Mi mester sali!
A thousand red lips	Diesmil lep kòrá
showing fake laughter,	ta hari fis,
shifting into growling teeth,	ta kambia bira djente,
grumbling nasty words,	gruña palabra insolente,
sending me to the back.	manda mi patras.
I'm definitely getting out now!	Awor sí mi ta sali!
I slammed the closet door shut.	M'a dal e port'i kashi sera.
Fiery eyes.	Wowo na kandela.
Injured fingers.	Dede heridá.
Frozen mouths.	Boka kongelá.
A storm of curses	Torment'i maldishon
is shaking heaven and earth.	ta tembla tera i shelu.
I locked the door,	M'a lòk e porta,
putting on old bourgeois suits once again.	bolbe bisti flus bieu burgues.
With a lump in my stomach	Ku un klòmpi den mi stoma
I hung myself	m'a kologá mi mes
on a rusty perch.	na un percha frus.
I want to get out	Mi ke sali
I have to get out ... !	Mi tin ku sali ... !
Who's knocking on the door?	Ta ken ta bati na porta?

Bibliography

Bacilio, Gilbert. "Mi Tin Ku Sali" [I have to come out]. *Maribomba* 1, 1994, 13.

Grupo Homofilia Antiyano. "Ingezonden: Homofilie" [Letter to the editor: Homophilia]. *Amigoe* 97, no. 139, June 28, 1980, 6.

"TV-programma ketst af op travestie-wet" [TV program falters over transvestism law]. *Amigoe* 97, no. 67, March 20, 1980, 3.

CHAPTER 32

You Think Too Much like a Dutch Woman [Bo Ta Pensa Muchu Manera Makamba]

Frida Domacassé

You think too much like a Dutch woman!
Antillean friends look at me severely,
their fingers pointing like rifles
to my heart.

I lean back.
I don't understand.

Am I a Dutch woman
if I say:
that I'm in love with a woman?

Am I a Dutch woman
if I hug her?

Am I a Dutch woman
if I kiss her
in the middle of the street?

What is so "Dutch"
about coming out?

Bo ta pensa muchu manera Makamba!
Amiganan Antiano ta mirami severo,
nan dede puntá manera skòpèt
riba mi kurason.

Mi ta lèn patras.
Mi no ta komprondé.

Makamba mi ta
si mi bisa:
mi ta namorá di un muhé?

Makamba mi ta
si mi ser'e den mi brasa?

Makamba mi ta
si mi dun'e un sunchi
mèimèi di kaya?

Kiko ta ,Makamba'
na coming out?

Acknowledgments

This poem was first published in Papiamentu and Dutch as Domacassé, Frida. "Bo ta pensa muchu manera Makamba/ Je denkt helemaal als een Hollandse!" [You think too much like a Dutch woman]. In *Ta ken mi ta/ Wie ik ben,* edited by Simia Literario, 38–39. Translated from Papiamentu into English by Wernher José Suares. Reproduction courtesy of Frida Domacassé.

 | DOI:10.1163/9789004690882_034

CHAPTER 33

Intimacy and Integration: the Ambivalent Achievement of Marriage Equality in the Dutch Caribbean, 2007–2012

Chelsea Schields

Abstract

This contribution reflects on the alliances and fissures created in the run-up to the first same-sex marriage officially performed in the Caribbean on the island of Saba in 2012. The international press celebrated this as a sign of progress under Saba's new status as a Dutch municipality. But the imposition of Dutch law polarized politicians, residents and activists on both sides of the Atlantic. On the one hand, island leaders who criticized marriage law as an infraction of self-determination found unlikely allies in the Dutch Christian right, who leveraged their rejection of gay rights as a defense against neocolonialism. On the other hand, a coalition of Dutch populist, leftist and liberal parties converged in their support for marriage equality. Yet, as these politicians improvised the terms of integration to include sexual rights, they circumvented crucial economic rights and marginalized Caribbean-based LGBTQ+ activists, retrenching inequality at the moment of integration.

Keywords

same-sex marriage – Saba – Dutch populism – LGBTQ+ activism – inequality

In 2012, Saba became the site of the first legally recognized same-sex marriage performed in the Caribbean. The legalization of same-sex marriage in Saba factored into a process of constitutional restructuring within the Kingdom of the Netherlands. Two years prior, in 2010, the Dutch Caribbean islands of Bonaire, St. Eustatius and Saba—the so-called BES islands—became special municipalities of the Netherlands. This change in the constitutional status of the BES islands and their impending integration into the Dutch state prompted a fraught debate on whether the islands would need to adopt Dutch marriage

 | DOI:10.1163/9789004690882_035

law. This chapter considers the role that sexual politics played in the integration of the BES islands into the Netherlands. From the run-up to integration in 2007 until the ultimate enforcement of Dutch marriage law in the Caribbean municipalities in 2012, same-sex marriage became a flash point issue on both sides of the Atlantic—one that ultimately factored into the uneven integration of the BES islands into the European Dutch state. European Dutch politicians insisted on full legal harmonization between the Netherlands and the BES islands in some areas but not others, demanding equivalence in marriage law while circumventing equal social welfare spending. A curious range of alliances mobilized in support of and in opposition to the legalization of same-sex marriage, with the revanchist right wing allying with liberal and progressive European Dutch parties to hasten the introduction of same-sex marriage and the European Dutch Christian right and island leaders indicting the move as a manifestation of neo-imperialism. Within this context, LGBTQ+ activists in the BES and other Dutch Caribbean islands struggled to frame the advancement of freedoms for same-sex couples as a homegrown achievement.

The debate over same-sex marriage represents at once troubling continuities and vexed novelties in the Caribbean or what Tracy Robinson in another context has called the formation of the "new-old."[1] At the turn of the twenty-first century, European Dutch assertions that acceptance of sexual minorities constitutes a cherished and timeless aspect of Dutchness itself (despite the recency of this position) helped to initiate a discursive reversal. Long fashioned as a site of sexual excess, the Caribbean islands were now remade in the European imaginary into a place of obstinate conservatism. This "new" portrayal retrenched other "old" inequities, with European fantasies of the Caribbean once again driving a top-down integration process that institutionalized an unequal rights regime.[2] At the same time, and as Vanessa Agard-Jones has observed of Martinique, queer and same-sex desiring individuals in the Dutch Caribbean became locally subjected to a "culturalist agenda that rationalize[d] homophobia as an expression of cultural sovereignty" to defend against European Dutch incursion.[3] It was within and against this fraught dynamic that Dutch Caribbean LGBTQ+ activists negotiated, in the words of Wigbertson Julian Isenia, "a historical and contemporary postcolonial framework to rethink sovereignty writ large through strategic alliances and intimacies."[4] This

1 Robinson, "New-Old Law in the Postcolony," 2022.

2 Tinsley, *Thiefing Sugar*, 2010, p. 30.

3 Agard-Jones, "What the Sands Remember," 2012, pp. 327–8.

4 Isenia, "Queer Sovereignties," 2022, p. 258.

chapter thus argues that attention to debates on sexual politics are vital for understanding how the boundaries of integration and autonomy are drawn—as well as how they are also being reimagined—in this transatlantic state.

1 Dissolving the Netherlands Antilles

Following decades of growing disenchantment with the political structure of the five-island Netherlands Antilles, at the turn of the twenty-first century, residents participated in consultative referenda to envision a new political status. Sharing broad support for the country's dissolution, constituents of Curaçao and St. Maarten elected to pursue autonomous statehood within the Kingdom of the Netherlands, while Bonaire, Saba and St. Eustatius chose to develop "direct ties" with the Netherlands. When island governments initially issued status referenda in 2004 and 2005, it was unclear what precisely "direct ties" with the Netherlands might look like beyond the transfer of some governing responsibilities from Curaçao, former seat of the Netherlands Antilles government, to the Netherlands. On November 2, 2006, European Dutch officials and elected representatives from the BES islands decided to forge "direct ties" with the Netherlands based on Article 134 of the Dutch Constitution.[5] The BES islands would thus be integrated as "special municipalities" of the Netherlands, forming administrative divisions of the European Dutch state that did not belong to a province. Ambiguity surrounding this new status, however, led to protracted debate in the Dutch parliament about the extent to which the BES islands would be legally assimilated into the Netherlands—a debate that played out in large measure on the terrain of sexual politics.

Since becoming the first country in the world to legalize same-sex marriage in 2001, the Netherlands has been widely recognized for its acceptance of sexual minorities. Yet, a mainstream anti-homophobic politics had only begun to develop in the 1990s, with populist parties such as Lijst Pim Fortuyn (LPF, List Pim Fortuyn) and later Partij voor de Vrijheid (PVV, Party for Freedom) successfully promoting a pro-gay marriage, anti-immigrant political platform. These parties have touted the acceptance of gay rights and women's rights as celebrated markers of Dutch identity that clash with the alleged conservatism

5 Oostindie and Klinkers, *Gedeeld koninkrijk: De ontmanteling van de Nederlandse Antillen en de vernieuwing van de trans-Atlantische relaties* [Shared kingdom: The dissolution of the Netherlands Antilles and the renewal of trans-Atlantic relations], 2012, p. 167.

of the Netherland's large Muslim population.[6] In recent decades, these same parties have also sought (so far unsuccessfully) to restrict the freedom of movement of Dutch citizens from the Caribbean islands to the European Netherlands.[7] Despite calls by some prominent European Dutch politicians to abandon the kingdom entirely,[8] European intervention in Caribbean affairs has increased in the past several decades owing to the perception that local governments cannot adequately handle matters related to good governance, crime, economics and civil rights.[9] Reflective of this impulse, in the nonsovereign Dutch, British and French Caribbean, LGBTQ+ rights and gender equality have drawn increased attention and intervention from European states, reigniting debates about the scope of metropolitan intervention.[10]

2 Debating Integration in The Hague

The expansion of LGBTQ+ rights throughout the kingdom emerged as a goal for European Dutch politicians in 2007. That year, a supreme court case in Aruba galvanized members of parliament (MPs) to make the advancement of gay rights a goal of constitutional restructuring.[11] The catalyst was a lawsuit filed in 2004 by European Dutch and Aruban couple Charlene and Esther Oduber-Lamers in Aruba. After the public registry in Aruba refused to recognize

6 Mepschen, Duyvendak, and Tonkens, "Sexual Politics, Orientalism and Multicultural Citizenship in the Netherlands," 2010. Editors' note: see also contribution by Loewenthal in this volume.

7 Notable examples to restrict freedom of movement from the Dutch Caribbean territories to the Netherlands include the 2010 Rijkswet Personenverkeer (movement of people act)—which was supported in parliament but ultimately rejected by the council of state during the dismantling process—and the 2014 Bosman Wet (Bosman bill). See Sharpe, "Extending Postcolonial Sovereignty Games," 2022, pp. 311–2.

8 In 2012, the PVV supported as part of its platform the dissolution of the Kingdom of the Netherlands and the total independence of its Caribbean territories; see "Hún Brussel, óns Nederland, verkiezingsprogramma, 2012–2017" [Their Brussels, our Netherlands, electoral program, 2012–2017], n.d., p. 47.

9 Jong, *De werkvloer van het koninkrijk: Over de samenwerking tussen Nederland met de Nederlandse Antillen en Aruba* [The workplace of the kingdom: The cooperation between the Netherlands and the Netherlands Antilles and Aruba], 2002; Jong, "The Implosion of the Netherlands Antilles," 2009; Giacalone, "The Political Status of Curaçao," 2001; Lampe, "The Recolonisation of Aruba," 2001.

10 Agard-Jones, "What the Sands Remember," 2012; Clegg, Dunwoodie-Stirton, and Cole, "Human Rights in the Overseas Territories," 2016.

11 I use the term "gay rights" to reflect the language of parliamentary sources, which refer predominantly to *homohuwelijk* (gay marriage) and *homoemancipatie* (gay emancipation).

the couple's marriage, performed in the Netherlands in 2001, the Oduber-Lamerses filed a lawsuit for discrimination, which made its way to the supreme court of the kingdom in 2007.

A month before the supreme court was set to rule on the Oduber-Lamers case, and amid ongoing discussion over the legal assimilation of the BES islands, a representative of the leftist Democraten 66 (D66, Democrats 66) requested clarification on the future of marriage law given the ambiguity surrounding the status of the Caribbean municipalities. Boris van der Ham implored: "If Bonaire becomes a new municipality of the Netherlands, I assume that Dutch same-sex marriage laws will also be in force … In the coming time surely there will be a lot of compromises made with Bonaire. We request that the government not compromise over the equal treatment of people."[12] Other leaders in the Netherlands, however, were hesitant to guarantee marriage equality, insisting that the gradual implementation of Dutch law and consultation with local leaders would prove critical to the long-term success of the restructured kingdom. The Dutch minister of justice, Hirsch Ballin, reasoned that European parliamentarians were "bound to address this in consultation [with the islands]."[13]

Despite Ballin's plea, support for the immediate legalization of same-sex marriage in the BES islands unified a broad coalition, including leftist parties D66 and GroenLinks (GreenLeft) and populist and centrist parties such as the PVV and the Volkspartij voor Vrijheid en Democratie (VVD, People's Party for Freedom and Democracy). At the close of the parliamentary year in December 2009, Ineke van Gent (GroenLinks) and Johan Remkes (VVD) jointly sponsored the first in a series of amendments, which urged the government to guarantee marriage equality after the implementation of the new constitutional status.[14] Parliament approved the Van Gent and Remkes amendment by a wide margin early in 2010. Hero Brinkman (PVV), who once controversially proposed selling the Dutch Caribbean islands on a popular e-commerce site, echoed the opinion of the majority of parliamentarians: "If the BES islands indicate that they would like to be part of the Netherlands, then some things go with this. In negotiations it should then be very simple and one-dimensional: if you want that, that is fine, but then you must also accept gay marriage."[15]

12 Netherlands, House of Representatives, *Question Hour*, vol. 47 (March 20, 2007), pp. 2813–6.

13 Ibid. Translated by author.

14 Netherlands, House of Representatives, *Proceedings*, vol. 32 213 (R1903), no. 45 (December 10, 2009). Translated by author.

15 Netherlands, House of Representatives, *Proceedings*, vol. 31 954, no. 13 (January 20, 2010), p. 35. Translated by author. Rijlaarsdam, "PVV – Vreemdelingenbeleid en de Antillen" [PVV – Immigration policy and the Antilles], 2009.

The majority of parliamentarians overlooked the disturbing irony that the former colonial authority was now, in the name of sexual progressivism, proposing to educate former colonies about the protection of human rights and civic freedoms. Writing on British aid conditionality and LGBTQ+ rights in Africa, political theorist Rahul Rao warns that such "a contemporary rerun of the civilizing mission ... is not one that is likely to engender the sort of change that its proponents wish for."[16] Following a similarly contradictory logic, parliamentarians refashioned "special municipality" status as undifferentiatingly European vis-à-vis sexual rights but unequal in the realm of economic rights.

Members of the Christian right attempted to draw attention to the inconsistencies in this logic to obstruct the legalization of same-sex marriage. Opposition to marriage equality unified the Staatkundig Gereformeerde Partij (SGP, Reformed Political Party), the Christen-Democratisch Appèl (CDA, Christian Democratic Appeal) and the ChristenUnie (CU, Christian Union). Although typically the intellectual preserve of the left, the Christian right appropriated the language of anticolonial critique in parliament and again in 2012, when the BES islands voted in their first Dutch national election. When D66 insisted on the swift implementation of marriage equality in Bonaire, the SGP immediately indicted the left, claiming: "My faction takes issue with the spirit of neocolonial patronizing from the left, who, with a raised finger, think they can help the whole world achieve gay marriage."[17] During one debate in January 2010, Curaçao-born CU representative Cynthia Ortega-Martijn called attention to discrepancies in the VVD's campaign for "equal" treatment, arguing, "we have just debated social security and insurance. In that instance, Remkes was a supporter of structurally unequal treatment. I just don't understand that."[18]

Although Remkes retorted that the cost of living in the BES islands was cheaper than in the Netherlands, he did not discuss how changes after 2010—including the introduction of the US dollar on the BES islands—might raise the cost of living to unprecedented levels. Ultimately, the Dutch parliament upheld this paradoxical vision of equality. In 2010, when Dutch law on old-age and retirement pensions was introduced in the Caribbean municipalities, qualifying residents could receive up to US $524 per month, while pensioners in the mainland Netherlands were entitled to a maximum of €1,064 per

16 Rao, "On 'Gay Conditionality,'" 2012.

17 Netherlands, House of Representatives, *Question Hour*, vol. 47 (March 20, 2007), pp. 2813–6. Translated by author.

18 Netherlands, House of Representatives, *Proceedings*, vol. 31 954, no. 13 (January 20, 2010), p. 39.

month.[19] Child benefits were not issued on the BES islands until 2016, with a maximum payment of US $38 per month, per child. That same year, parents in the mainland Netherlands were entitled to receive €63–€91 per month, per child, depending on the age of the child.[20] This differential allocation of social welfare undermined the purported equality of the Netherlands' European and Caribbean municipalities.

Parliament resolved the same-sex marriage question against the advice of leading government officials and Christian right opposition in both chambers of parliament. Among proponents of the law, a fundamental assumption emerged that the islands exercised their right to popular sovereignty and will to become "fully" juridically European in the 2004–2005 referenda, hence rationalizing European leadership in the transition process. After Van Gent and Remkes introduced yet another amendment to hasten the introduction of same-sex unions from 2015 to 2012, the senate approved these and other plans on May 12, 2010.[21] Although MPs who supported the implementation of marriage law insisted that the islands had chosen to integrate fully into the Dutch state, they held fast to the distinction between overseas and European Dutch municipalities in the realm of social welfare spending. It was therefore up to members of the Christian right, the only group who could risk unambiguity in their position on sexual freedoms, to question the incoherence of their opponent's rationale.

3 Opposition and Support in the BES Islands

Citing undemocratic deliberations and cultural differences between the European Netherlands and overseas entities, political and religious leaders in Bonaire and St. Eustatius attempted to halt the legalization of same-sex marriage and even threatened to abandon integration efforts entirely. While the international press and European Dutch politicians frequently cast this opposition as an extension of conservative social mores, surfacing in insular discussions were also anxieties over the loss of local autonomy and attempts to reconfigure the meaning of sovereignty in an integrated state. Also

19 Rijksoverheid, "Sociale voorzieningen op de BES eilanden aangepast" [Social services adjusted on the BES islands], 2010; "Court Rejects Claims for Higher Pensions on the BES Islands," 2014.

20 Hofmann, "VVD: Waarop is kinderbijslag BES gebaseerd?" [VVD: What is the BES child allowance based on?], 2015.

21 Eerste Kamer der Staten-Generaal, "Eerste Kamer stemt in met nieuwe staatkundige positie BES-eilanden" [Senate approves new constitutional position for BES islands], 2010.

overshadowed was the significant support for marriage equality on the islands. Leadership in Saba, for example, embraced marriage equality and an LGBTQ+ activist network across the Dutch islands also mobilized in support. These actors, however, operated within a narrowed discursive space in which enthusiasm for same-sex marriage could simultaneously be understood as support for neocolonial hegemony. As a result, many supporters of marriage equality advanced creative arguments that grounded sexual rights in visions of Caribbean freedom.

In the run-up to 2010, island representatives from Bonaire and St. Eustatius challenged parliament's interpretation of the new constitutional status. In meetings in The Hague, representatives from Bonaire and St. Eustatius drew attention to how the transition process strayed from the aims of the 2005 referenda and the decision to integrate the BES islands as "special" rather than traditional municipalities. Statian representative Reginald Zaandam averred that the people of St. Eustatius were "sitting in a constitutional train racing toward an endpoint they did not choose."[22] Ramoncito Booi, leader of the second largest political party in Bonaire, argued: "I find it unethical that suddenly [the implementation of the law] has been shortened from five to two years and that we need to swallow that."[23] These politicians opposed the legalization of same-sex marriage on the grounds that island leadership had been excluded in the restructuring process and, in this instance, avoided framing the issue as one of moral opposition. In this way, politicians hoped to expose how The Hague disavowed the terms of integration established during the 2006 Slotakkoord (final declaration), when European and island leadership agreed to integrate the BES islands as "special municipalities" and committed to a close working relationship throughout the transition process.

With the press as mouthpiece, Statian politicians continued the campaign to prevent the legalization of same-sex marriage at home. Although ultimately unsuccessful, the island council of St. Eustatius unanimously accepted an amendment to halt the introduction of same-sex marriage, abortion and euthanasia on the island and threatened to invoke the United Nations if the Netherlands did not comply with the request. One official argued: "During the process, the Netherlands indicated that they would take into account the fundamental human rights of the residents of the islands. Gay marriage, euthanasia and abortion are here morally rejected and are diametrically opposed to

22 Netherlands, House of Representatives. *Proceedings*, Vol. 32 213 (R1903), no. 45, p. 42. April 19, 2010. Translated by author.

23 Ibid., p. 39.

our community and culture."[24] Statian politicians defended their opposition to gay marriage in the language of human rights centered on principles of self-determination and democratic inclusion. However, it was precisely because St. Eustatius sought the right to self-determination within an integrated kingdom that some European observers dismissed the amendment as a "losing battle."[25] Such conflicts reveal the limited means for arbitrating conflicts in political spaces that do not conform to normative models of decolonization premised on the territorially bound nation-state.

For others on the BES islands who contested the legalization of same-sex marriage, fear of European political incursion and moral opposition to same-sex marriage were not discrete. Like the Dutch Christian right, some politicians pointed out the ambivalent interpretation of full European integration. Even in Saba, where political and popular support for marriage equality ran high, a leading deputy from the island insisted: "In our island council, we have a member who is openly gay. There are other same-sex couples on the island, too. But this does not take away from the fact that the people would like to have a say in the way we shape legislation."[26] A resident of St. Eustatius summed up the blurred boundaries between fear of renewed European hegemony and moral opposition: "These are issues that affect our culture, customs and religious sensibilities. You cannot just one day change the rules. This requires first a public debate."[27]

In debates over same-sex marriage, commentators often framed Caribbean "culture" as an impediment to sexual progressivism. For many European commentators, the region's Christian religiosity explained the ostensible cultural estrangement between the European Netherlands and the Caribbean. While Caribbean feminist scholars have rejected the idea that Christian respectability alone informs sexual mores in the region, they have nevertheless taken seriously sexual conservatism as a response to European labeling of the region as sexually aberrant and atavistic—perceptions that rationalized pervasive colonial efforts to "reform" the sexual and reproductive practices of people of African descent in the Caribbean.[28] In a sudden reversal, today it is the region's

24 Kooistra and Muddle, "BES-verzet tegen homohuwelijk" [BES opposition to gay marriage], 2010. Translated by author.

25 Groot, "St. Eustatius voert verloren strijd tegen homohuwelijk" [St. Eustatius wages losing battle against gay marriage], 2010. Translated by author.

26 Ibid.

27 Ibid.

28 Alexander, "Not Just Any (Body) Can Be a Citizen," 1994; Allen, "Contesting Respectability and Sexual Politics in Post-Emancipation Curaçao," 2017, pp. 107–8; Wekker, *The Politics of Passion*, 2006, pp. 45–46.

perceived *conservatism* that rationalizes European Dutch interference. This leaves the vexed question to what extent opposition to "ethical laws" stemmed from fear over the loss of political and cultural autonomy or from moral conservatism.

On October 10, 2012, same-sex marriage became legal in Bonaire, Saba and St. Eustatius. Shortly after the first couple wed in Saba in December 2012, numerous articles appeared in the international LGBTQ+ press with headlines such as "Legalization of Gay Marriage Sends [Saba's] Popularity Soaring"[29] and "Tiny Island Becomes Same-Sex Marriage Refuge."[30] The director of Saba's tourist bureau, a self-identifying gay man, announced that he would use gay marriage in promotional materials for the island's tourism and reported that inquiries had poured in from around the Caribbean after an Aruban and Venezuelan couple wed that year.[31]

Likewise, a group of LGBTQ+ activists across the former Netherlands Antilles supported the legalization of same-sex marriage and pushed for the social acceptance of sexual minorities broadly. In 2008, the LGBTQ+ organization FOKO Curaçao appealed to the Dutch parliament and urged its members not to allow any of the BES islands to integrate without first agreeing to uphold legislation on same-sex marriage. Moreover, they asserted, "[t]he excuse that Antillean politicians offer, that … same-sex marriage would not fit with Antillean culture is incorrect, and … if it were true, then it would nevertheless be unacceptable that Antillean leaders' misguided vision of their own culture takes precedence over the civil rights and international treaties arising from legal principles of equality."[32] Mario Kleinmoedig, a leading figure in FOKO Curaçao, nevertheless found the reliance on European Dutch leadership to be a frustrating legacy of unequal relations between Europe and the Caribbean. Although disputing the labeling of the ethical laws as "neocolonial," Kleinmoedig stated: "It is a big scandal that … in the fifteen years that the Antillean gay rights movement has existed, [politicians] never addressed our calls for a homegrown Antillean gay emancipation movement … As an autonomous but nonindependent country, we have little access to international arbitrators, which leaves nothing left for us to do than follow along with the kingdom government and the kingdom parliament."[33]

---

29 "Legalization of Gay Marriage Sends Tiny Island's Popularity Soaring," 2012.

30 Broverman, "Tiny Island Becomes Same-Sex Marriage Refuge," 2012.

31 "Legalization of Gay Marriage Sends Tiny Island's Popularity Soaring," 2012.

32 Gomez, "Karta di Foko parlamentarionan Hulandes" [Letter from FOKO to Dutch parliamentarians], 2008. Translated by author.

33 "Column Kleinmoedig in Gay Krant" [Kleinmoedig column in *Gay Krant*], *Antilliaans Dagblad*, 2010. Editors' note: see also contribution by Kleinmoedig in this section.

These comments illustrate how the legacy of colonialism and the configuration of nonsovereignty obstructed certain avenues for advancing sexual freedoms and marginalized the contributions and practices of self-fashioning among Caribbean people. Yet, activists also seized upon the historic moment of integration to advance sexual freedoms, a struggle they viewed as Caribbean in origin and yet compatible with—indeed, made in some ways possible by—closer ties with the Netherlands. In this instance, the condition of nonsovereignty provided for the radical extension of certain freedoms at the same time that it foreclosed others.

4 Conclusion

The controversy over same-sex marriage in the Dutch Caribbean played a formative role in shaping the uneven political relationship between the European Netherlands and the BES islands from 2007 to 2012. The integration of the BES islands followed an improvised course and the implementation of legislation on same-sex marriage did not originate from a prescribed policy of total legal assimilation. Rather, the accelerated enforcement of these laws deviated from established plans and mandates to include Caribbean public entities in negotiations concerning their political futures, raising the specter of "recolonization" in the Caribbean territories. This situation, in turn, produced a predicament for proponents of marriage equality in the Caribbean, who viewed the struggle for sexual rights as a homegrown program of Caribbean and human freedom.

While the so-called ethical laws have taken a back seat to concerns within the newly integrated territories, after 2010, the economic inequities ensconced at this moment of integration have become ever more apparent, with skyrocketing prices and the growing migration of European "pensioners" to the Caribbean territories driving up the cost of living.[34] At the same time, European officials replaced the locally-elected island council in St. Eustatius with a European government commission in 2018 in the name of rooting out corruption and straightening out financial affairs, a usurpation of representative governance that did not alter the fact that over half of Dutch citizens in the BES islands reside below the poverty line.[35] This chapter has contended that, in order to understand the contours of these structural and juridical

34 Follow the Money, "For Twelve Years, the Netherlands Has Kept Its Caribbean Citizens Poor," 2022.

35 Samson, "The Dutch Cabinet Takes Over Sint-Eustatius," 2018.

inequities, we must take into account the mobilizing debates on sexual politics that helped to define the uneven boundaries of autonomy and integration.

In the four years since marriage equality was implemented in the overseas municipalities of the Netherlands, activist demands in the Caribbean and its diaspora have propelled other important changes. After an international campaign, civil unions for same-sex couples in Aruba were successfully enshrined in the civil code in 2021. Alhough a judge in Curaçao ruled that the exclusion of same-sex couples from legal marriage was unconstitutional in 2021, same-sex marriage is not legally protected in the autonomous countries of the kingdom. Those countries are, however, compelled to recognize same-sex marriages performed in the Netherlands and its overseas municipalities.[36] Such legal pluralities, as Isenia maintains, illustrate the "odd or queer sovereignty of the islands"[37]—a lived condition that, as activist Mario Kleinmoedig's comments illustrate, at once foreclosed and opened paths for redefining rights in a transnational kingdom.

Acknowledgments

An earlier version of this contribution appeared as Schields, Chelsea. "Intimacy and Integration: The Ambivalent Achievement of Marriage Equality in the Dutch Caribbean, 2007–12." In *Euro-Caribbean Societies in the 21st Century: Offshore Finance, Local*, edited by Sébastien Chauvin, Peter Clegg, and Bruno Cousin, 176–89. Europa Regional Perspectives. Abingdon: Routledge, 2018. It has been slightly condensed and its introduction and conclusion updated to reflect political changes and recent publications. The reproduction of this text is courtesy of Routledge.

Bibliography

Agard-Jones, Vanessa. "What the Sands Remember." *GLQ: A Journal of Lesbian and Gay Studies* 18, no. 2–3 (June 2012): 325–46. https://doi.org/10.1215/10642684-1472917.

Alexander, M. Jacqui. "Not Just (Any) Body Can Be a Citizen: The Politics of Law, Sexuality and Postcoloniality in Trinidad and Tobago and the Bahamas." *Feminist Review*, no. 48 (Autumn 1994): 5–23. https://doi.org/10.2307/1395166.

36 Isenia, "Queer Sovereignties," 2022, p. 31. Editors' note: see also contribution by Isenia in this section.

37 Ibid.

Allen, Rose Mary. "Contesting Respectability and Sexual Politics in Post-Emancipation Curaçao." In *Archaeologies of Erasures and Silences: Recovering Othered Languages, Literatures and Cultures in the Dutch Caribbean and Beyond*, edited by Nicholas Faraclas, Ronald Severing, Christa Weijer, Elisabeth Echteld, Wim Rutgers, and Robert Dupey, 99–112. Curaçao: University of Curaçao; Puerto Rico: Universidad de Puerto Rico, 2017.

Broverman, Neal. "Tiny Island Becomes Same-Sex Marriage Refuge." *The Advocate*, December 14, 2012. http://www.advocate.com/news/world-news/2012/12/14/tiny-caribbean-island-becomes-same-sex-marriage-refuge.

Clegg, Peter, Fred Dunwoodie-Stirton, and Phillip Cole. "Human Rights in the Overseas Territories: In Policy but Not in Practice?" *Commonwealth & Comparative Politics* 54, no. 1 (January 2016): 46–68. https://doi.org/10.1080/14662043.2015.1126886.

"Column Kleinmoedig in Gay Krant" [Kleinmoedig column in Gay Krant], *Antilliaans Dagblad*, May 22, 2010. http://antilliaansdagblad.com/nieuws-menu/1237-column-kleinmoedig-in-gay-krant.

"Court Rejects Claims for Higher Pensions on the BES Islands." *Daily Herald*, March 14, 2014.

Eerste Kamer der Staten-Generaal. "Eerste Kamer stemt in met nieuwe staatkundige positie BES-eilanden" [Senate approves new constitutional position for BES islands]. Eerste Kamer der Staten-Generaal, May 12, 2010. http://www.eerstekamer.nl/nieuws/20100512/eerste_kamer_stemt_in_met_nieuwe.

Follow the Money. "For Twelve Years, the Netherlands Has Kept Its Caribbean Citizens Poor." Follow the Money, August 30, 2022. https://www.ftm.eu/articles/the-netherlands-kept-itscaribbean-citiziens-poor.

Giacalone, Rita. "The Political Status of Curaçao at the End of the Twentieth Century." In *Islands at the Crossroads: Politics in the Non-Independent Caribbean*, edited by Aarón Gamaliel Ramos and Ángel Israel Rivera Ortiz, 95–105. Boulder: Lynne Rienner Publishers; Kingston, Jamaica: Ian Randle Publishers, 2001.

Gomez, Suzanne. "Karta di Foko parlamentarionan Hulandes" [Letter from FOKO to Dutch parliamentarians]. FOKO Curaçao, September 2, 2008. http://curafoko.blogspot.com.

Groot, Willemien. "St. Eustatius voert verloren strijd tegen homohuwelijk" [St. Eustatius wages losing battle against gay marriage]. *RNW Media*, April 22, 2010. http://www.rnw.nl/nederlands/article/sint-eustatius-voert-verloren-strijd-tegen-homohuwelijk.

Hofmann, Pieter. "VVD: Waarop is kinderbijslag BES gebaseerd?" [VVD: What is the BES child allowance based on?]. Caribisch Netwerk, November 25, 2015. http://caribischnetwerk.ntr.nl/2015/11/25/vvd-waarop-is-kinderbijslag-bes-gebaseerd.

Isenia, Wigbertson Julian. "Queer Sovereignties: Cultural Practices of Sexual Citizenship in the Dutch Caribbean." PhD diss., University of Amsterdam, 2022.

Jong, Lammert de. *De werkvloer van het koninkrijk: Over de samenwerking van Nederland met de Nederlandse Antillen en Aruba* [The workplace of the kingdom: The cooperation of the Netherlands with the Netherlands Antilles and Aruba]. Amsterdam: Rozenberg, 2002.

Jong, Lammert de. "The Implosion of the Netherlands Antilles." In *Governance in the Non-Independent Caribbean: Challenges and Opportunities in the Twenty-First Century*, edited by Peter Clegg and Emilio Pantojas-García, 24–44. Kingston, Jamaica: Ian Randle, 2009.

Kooistra, Simon, and Leo Muddle. "BES-verzet tegen homohuwelijk" [BES opposition to gay marriage]. *VNG Magazine*, April 30, 2010. http://www.vngmagazine.nl/archief/111/bes-verzet-tegen-homohuwelijk.

Lampe, Armando. "The Recolonisation of Aruba." In *Islands at the Crossroads: Politics in the Non-Independent Caribbean*, edited by Aarón Gamaliel Ramos and Ángel Israel Rivera Ortiz, 106–14. Boulder: Lynne Rienner Publishers; Kingston, Jamaica: Ian Randle Publishers, 2001.

"Legalization of Gay Marriage Sends Tiny Island's Popularity Soaring." *Caribbean 360*, December 19, 2012. http://www.caribbean360.com/news/645699.html#axzz2K2ey50Ea.

Mepschen, Paul, Jan Willem Duyvendak, and Evelien H. Tonkens. "Sexual Politics, Orientalism and Multicultural Citizenship in the Netherlands." *Sociology* 44, no. 5 (October 2010): 962–79. https://doi.org/10.1177/0038038510375740.

Oostindie, Gert, and Inge Klinkers. *Gedeeld koninkrijk: De ontmanteling van de Nederlandse Antillen en de vernieuwing van de trans-Atlantische relaties* [Shared kingdom: The dissolution of the Netherlands Antilles and the renewal of trans-Atlantic relations]. Amsterdam: Amsterdam University Press, 2012.

Partij voor de Vrijheid. "Hún Brussel, óns Nederland, verkiezingsprogramma, 2012–2017" [Their Brussels, our Netherlands, electoral program, 2012–2017], n.d. http://www.pvv.nl/images/stories/verkiezingen2012/VerkiezingsProgramma-PVV-2012-final-web.pdf.

Rao, Rahul. "On 'Gay Conditionality': Imperial Power and Queer Liberation." *Kafila* (blog), January 1, 2012. http://kafila.org/2012/01/01/on-gay-conditionality-imperial-power-and-queer-liberation-rahul-rao.

Rijksoverheid. "Sociale voorzieningen op BES eilanden aangepast" [Social services adjusted on the BES Islands]. Rijksoverheid, April 19, 2010. https://www.rijksoverheid.nl/actueel/nieuws/2010/04/19/sociale-voorzieningen-op-bes-eilanden-aangepast.

Rijlaarsdam, Barbara. "PVV – Vreemdelingenbeleid en de Antillen" [PVV – Immigration policy and the Antilles]. *NRC*, June 12, 2009. http://vorige.nrc.nl/article2269987.ece.

Robinson, Tracy. "New-Old Law in the Postcolony: Regulating Sex in the Anglophone Caribbean." In *Citizenship on the Edge: Sex/Gender/Race*, edited by Nancy J.

Hirschmann and Deborah A. Thomas, 68–96. Democracy, Citizenship, and Constitutionalism. Philadelphia: University of Pennsylvania Press, 2022.

Samson, John. "The Dutch Cabinet Takes Over Sint Eustatius." Caribbean Network, February 5, 2018. https://caribbeannetwork.ntr.nl/2018/02/05/the-dutch-cabinet-takes-over-sint-eustatius.

Sharpe, Michael Orlando. "Extending Postcolonial Sovereignty Games: The Multilevel Negotiation of Autonomy and Integration in the 2010 Dissolution of the Netherlands Antilles and Dutch Kingdom Relations." *Ethnopolitics* 21, no. 3 (May 2022): 299–324. https://doi.org/10.1080/17449057.2020.1726031.

Tinsley, Omise'eke Natasha. *Thiefing Sugar: Eroticism between Women in Caribbean Literature*. Durham, NC: Duke University Press, 2010.

Wekker, Gloria. *The Politics of Passion: Women's Sexual Culture in the Afro-Surinamese Diaspora*. Between Men~between Women. New York: Columbia University Press, 2006.

CHAPTER 34

Sissies and Pancake Makers in Curaçao: Homosexuality as Shock Therapy

Vincent Sleebe

Abstract

This contribution was originally published in 1997 in Dutch in the magazine of the COC, the oldest organization for LGBTQ+ rights in the Netherlands, founded in Amsterdam in 1946. It charts the emergence of an organized voice for the rights of homosexuals in Curaçao and reflects on cultural and linguistic peculiarities surrounding the place of gays, lesbians and trans* persons on the island. It examines how community members navigate societal norms and establish a critical attitude to both Curaçao and the Netherlands. The article also references the beginnings of exchanges between LGBTQ+ initiatives in different regions of the Caribbean.

Keywords

LGBTQ+ rights – COC – Curaçao – Orguyo – Papiamentu terms for sexual minorities

Pantile roofs like the Netherlands, cobbled streets like the Netherlands, a Van der Valk hotel with its distinctive toucan symbol looking down on Willemstad. On the largest island of the Netherlands Antilles, the colonial past hasn't quite been erased. Although the population primarily speaks Papiamentu, a creole language with influences from Spanish, Portuguese, English, Dutch and African languages, the Dutch language remains honored as a second language. No wonder it is packed with Dutch tourists, who frequent cafés with names reminiscent of those in European metropoles, such as Het Bruin Café (The Brown Café) or Het Keizershof (The Imperial Court).

All the same, Curaçaoan society is not as Dutchified as it may seem. It is a society steeped in machismo, where women have long been disadvantaged compared to men. Men come and go as they like and make no secret of their various "sideline" families—and children—so much so that "possession" of

 | DOI:10.1163/9789004690882_036

more than one "girlfriend" has always counted as a token of manhood. In fact, no one thinks it the slightest bit strange if men "exercise their manhood" with other men—just as long as they are the "active" partner.

For that reason, then, just as throughout the Caribbean, households in Curaçao traditionally revolve around mothers and their children who, partly due to the absence of the fathers of their children, have to fend for themselves. Over recent years, women have been showing ever more independence, too, in that if men aren't prepared to take responsibility for their children, women are now saying: "Well, I'm not going to look after him. He can look after himself from now on!" The emancipation of women also means that they are taking more important roles in business and politics and allowing themselves more sexual freedom.

In a world that has had such fixed roles for men and women for such a long time, it is difficult for those of either sex with homosexual inclinations to find their place for, just as in most of the rest of the Caribbean, homosexuality in Curaçao has had to be hidden as much as possible.

Homosexual men are still referred to using the derogatory Papiamentu word *mariku* or *marikitu*, which more or less means sissy. The origin of the word is contested, in contrast to the Papiamentu slang for homosexual women, *kachaperas*, which literally means pancake makers, a name that is derived from the idea that it is impossible for sexual activity to occur in the absence of a "male member." Pancakes are flat, aren't they ... ?[1]

Marikus were ranked in third place in the traditional hierarchy after "real" men and women, and known homosexual men were looked down upon. Active male homosexuality drew less objections, but men who allowed themselves to be penetrated by another man were not seen as manly. They were expected to behave as women and wear women's clothes. And often men complied with this stereotype. If you were homosexual, then you had to put on a dress and wear your high heels, as simple as that! How integral this image of the homosexual as feminine is in the Antilles we can see from the Amsterdam group Marival, who seem to be most concerned with drag and who celebrate carnival dressed as women.[2]

1 Editors' note: see contributions by Clemencia, Isenia and Broek in this section, which elaborate on the concept of *kambrada*, which does not have the pejorative connotations of *kachapera*.

2 Editors' note: Felix de Rooy's 1996 documentary film and theater production offers a rather different interpretation of *Marival*, portraying the connections between carnival drag pageants and the day-to-day material struggles of five people whose lives extend across the

People not only look down on *marikus* but are a little afraid of them too, for they have a reputation as vodou experts. If you fall foul of a *mariku* on New Year's Eve, then you'll be looking over your shoulder for the rest of the year! Bad luck will follow you everywhere. And everyone's wary of what is perceived as the *mariku*'s sharp tongue.

Homosexual relationships for women are rather easier as it's not considered strange for women—with or without children—to live together. And, unlike homosexual men who feel obliged to behave like women, lesbians don't behave like men.

People who are unable or unwilling to live openly as homosexuals lead a difficult double life. Men are considered constitutionally incapable of managing without women; so, even if only to uphold the family honor, they must marry. But there will be an enormous scandal for the whole family if a man's wife discovers that he is indulging in homosexual activity. Married homosexual men therefore prefer to call themselves "bisexual."

For a few years now, there has been talk of a "gay movement" in Curaçao, and one woman who laid the foundation for that is "La Pop," a sort of "fairy godmother" who threw her house open to homosexual men for them to party, giving them a chance to meet other similar men and simply to be themselves. There were other organizations, but none of them lasted, most petering out as their members quickly retired from them.

Since November 1995, however, there has been an organization of homosexuals in Curaçao calling itself Orguyo (Proud), formed around a group of well-educated young people. Orguyo was originally something of an underground organization; the media knew of its existence thanks to a few press releases, but the club's committee and individual members kept their identities hidden. Then, according to current chair Dudley Ferdinandus, there came a day in early 1996 when that changed radically: "On Labor Day, May 1, we suddenly got huge publicity. What prompted it was that, in the Netherlands, people had started talking about registering homosexual relationships. We weren't thinking along those lines at all at that time; it might have seemed like a good idea to the Dutch, but here, in Curaçao, we had much more important things to think about. But because the media asked us what we thought of it, we suddenly saw an opportunity to interest people in the general subject of homosexuality."

As a result, Mario Kleinmoedig, Orguyo's spokesman, was never off the television. It was the first time anyone had publicly declared himself homosexual

---

spectrum of homosexuality and transgenderism. See Rooy, *Ego documenta: The Testament of My Ego in the Museum of My Mind*, 2012, pp. 122–4.

and long and open discussions went on for a good ten weeks. Orguyo's members found themselves in the news; they appeared on talk shows and in the papers. An influential business magazine even devoted a whole edition to the subject of sexuality in general and homosexuality in particular.[3]

As a result, homosexuality came out of the shadows for the first time in Curaçao. It became clear that not all homosexual men were in the habit of behaving like women, and not all homosexual women pretended to be men. "So your neighbor, the local schoolmistress, a police officer might be gay." Homosexuals were no longer the marginal groups of *marikus* and *kachaperas* they'd been until then. Dudley Ferdinandus believes that the mass publicity has led to an enormous increase in tolerance:

> People now knew that homosexuality was a reality in Curaçao and they had to get used to it. It was really important for our group. A lot of people felt as if a wall had come down; it was the first time homosexuality had been openly talked about. I could see that people recognized me on the street. They would look at me, start whispering to each other or they just turned around. Of course, not everybody reacted favorably, but in my own circles I had very few negative reactions. My boyfriend and I always got on well with the people in our neighborhood and nothing has changed there.

But none of this is to say that discrimination and violence against homosexual men and women has stopped happening. And the Curaçao press still occasionally mentions reports of violence against gays and lesbians.

There are currently 65 contributing members and 250 associate members of Orguyo.[4] It's a diverse club, but Dudley Ferdinandus admits that women tend to stay in the background. He says they seem to feel a greater need to get together among themselves and aren't so keen to come out. There's a new youth group, too, called Apex. The group is officially separate from Orguyo. "To avoid difficulties," Dudley explains with a chuckle, "parents might otherwise accuse us of teaching their sons or daughters to be gay!"

Orguyo has completely distanced itself from the traditional self-image of homosexuality. "Orguyo wants to confront society with men who feel

3 Editors' note: see contribution by Kleinmoedig in this section.

4 Editors' note: according to Mario Kleinmoedig, the membership started dropping after the wave of migration that started in 2003. In 2008, Orguyo was registered as a foundation with a more open system of association rather than membership. As of 2023, there are approximately twenty to forty associates of the organization.

masculine but who still might be attracted to other men. We're keen to make it clear that a gay man doesn't have to wear a dress and high heels and be boisterous and extravagant. Even gay men who did always dress as women because they thought they ought to now realize that's not necessary and are casting off those clothes again."

Orguyo has had very little government support; in fact, only the Dutch minister of foreign affairs has said she warmly welcomes the organization's work. Little has been heard from other departments and there has been absolutely no question of financial assistance. Orguyo offers a laconic response to this unforthcoming attitude: "We're more concerned with influencing the community. Individual attitudes are much more important to us."

Although there are certainly "gay friendly" cafés, there is no gay nor lesbian nightlife in Curaçao, but Dudley Ferdinandus thinks that's more of an advantage than a disadvantage. "We're all for integration, and if you go and sit in your little place with all the other gay folk, people are going to say, 'See? They don't want to integrate!'" For a while, Orguyo organized monthly get-togethers in one of the beautiful plantation houses on the island that are now repurposed as cafés, but, eventually, they stopped for lack of interest. "We consider our policy-oriented and lobby activities to be more important. The other organizations shot themselves in the foot precisely because they were only interested in partying. They just weren't serious about it. But now we organize just a few parties a year because our members ask us to." The parties are held at one of the many beautiful bays and have been a great success up to now, with the 'Mr. Gay' competitions especially turning plenty of heads!

The Curaçaoan homosexual community has developed its own idiom and slang. Homosexuals who are out of the closet refer to themselves not as *mariku* but *maré*, while lesbians call themselves *chimaré* and bisexuals prefer to be called *bimaré*. A rude term for bisexuals is *chuchubi*, which is actually the name of a bird native to Curaçao that, in popular belief, is known as the bringer of bad news and is therefore always chased away. Heterosexuals are "birds of prey" although some who are sympathetic to homosexuals are *orioles*, named after another native bird.

Without a doubt, one of Orguyo's most important activities is education at the school level, not least on the subject of AIDS, which is as much a health time bomb for heterosexuals in Curaçao as it is for homosexual men. Of course, young people are sexually active, but they know little of the risks involved, and men think that condom use is "unmanly." It's a worrying situation and the government and volunteer organizations are doing their best to explain why safe sex is so necessary. And that was why TV viewers were recently treated to the spectacle of Sister Kapel, head of the Dutch Antillean AIDS Foundation, getting busy with a dildo and condom on the 8 o'clock news![5]

Often too, Orguyo finds itself obliged to include sex education in its information presentations to secondary schools because pupils know absolutely nothing. The problem is not homosexuality in particular but ignorance around sexuality in general. Dudley Ferdinandus says that parents appreciate the information just as much as the pupils do: "Because of the enormous interest last year, lots of youngsters have come to us realizing they're gay or lesbian. Most of them can't wait to come out, but we always advise them to wait. You've got to remember that families here are really close-knit and it's awful to be excluded. So we always say to them, 'Wait before you hit your parents with your homosexuality until you've got yourself set up at least a bit, say with an educational qualification or a job. Because you never know how they're going to react.'" They also organize workshops for parents of homosexual children.

Orguyo has tried to get similar organizations going elsewhere in the Dutch Antilles. There appears to be little enthusiasm so far in Aruba or Bonaire, but in Saba—easily the smallest island with no more than a thousand inhabitants—nine people recently set up Orguyo II. Although it's a tiny island where everyone knows everyone else, something like homosexuality is treated with great openness. Orguyo has therefore quickly become the most successful homosexual organization in the Caribbean, and now they're working with other organizations from Jamaica, Trinidad and Suriname under the umbrella-name C-Flag (Caribbean Forum for Lesbians and Gays) for which they're hoping to gain formal status.[6] Last year (1996), C-Flag held a conference in Jamaica and, this spring, Orguyo is organizing the Caribbean conference; they're expecting to host between fifty and sixty participants.[7]

---

5 Editors' note: Zuster (Sister) Monica Kapel was a head nurse in Curaçao who used her professional position and expertise to raise awareness about HIV/AIDS. She passed away on March 10, 2015.

6 Editors' note: in 2008, C-Flag was renamed Cariflags (Caribbean Forum for the Liberation of All Genders and Sexualities) and eventually included the involvement of all islands in the Netherlands Antilles except for St. Eustatius in what was called the Pink Orange Alliance. In 2009, the COC took over the Pink Orange Alliance, a move regarded as controversial as some members felt the Dutch should be allies rather than members of the alliance. We thank Mario Kleinmoedig for these details.

7 Editors' note: the Caribbean Conference on Gay, Lesbian and Bisexual Issues, financed by the Dutch government, was hosted in Curaçao in 1997 and was attended by eighty delegates from twenty-one Caribbean islands and countries. We thank Wigbertson Julian Isenia for background research on this.

Acknowledgments

This is a translation from Dutch of an article that first appeared as Sleebe, Vincent. "Mariku's en kachapera's op Curaçao: Homoseksualiteit als shocktherapie." *XL: COC Magazine* 6, no. 2 (1997): 20–22. Translation by Marcus Ferley.

Bibliography

Rooy, Felix de. *Ego documenta: The Testament of My Ego in the Museum of My Mind.* Amsterdam: KIT Publishers, 2012.

Sleebe, Vincent. "Mariku's en kachapera's op Curaçao: Homoseksualiteit als shocktherapie" [Sissies and pancake makers in Curaçao: Homosexuality as shock therapy]. *XL: COC Magazine* 6, no. 2 (1997): 20–22.

CHAPTER 35

A Queer Cultural Perspective from Curaçao

Mario Kleinmoedig

Abstract

Reflecting on three decades of activism for the emancipation of LGBTQ+ communities in Curaçao and in the Netherlands Antilles more broadly, this contribution analyzes the achievements and the dangers of the course of institutionalization following the Euro-American model of queer identity. The contribution argues that queer emancipation has been understood by local activists to be about personal emancipation and self-identification and not enough about societal, communal and intersectional emancipation of the collective self. By entirely rejecting Curaçao's traditional cultural model of three genders and viewing practices of nondisclosure and male promiscuity as merely being grounded in patriarchy, the movement effectively created a form of segregation along class and colorist lines, which is visible today in Curaçao's dating and entertainment culture. The contribution pleads for support for sexually and genderfluid communities and for taking macho-identifying queer-behaving men seriously. This will entail a resexualizing and desanitizing of Caribbean and Curaçaoan queerness.

Keywords

LGBTQ+ activism – Curaçao – three genders – male promiscuity – colorism and class – collective self

1 A Culture of Shame and Fear

This contribution is an attempt at putting into words where I think our activism for queer emancipation in Curaçao and the Dutch Caribbean has been successful and where we made the wrong choices. Truth be told, Curaçaoan queer advocacy and activism has been quite successful in creating more acceptance and understanding of sexual diversity and queerness to the extent that a major aim, the legal recognition of queer relationships, including marriage

 | DOI:10.1163/9789004690882_037

rights, now seems to be within reach. Wrong choices were made when we adopted the seemingly ready-to-go definitions of queer identities and genders from the Global North without checking their applicability in or relevance to our local cultures.

Valdemar Marcha, one of Curaçao's leading social scientists, has described the island as a society governed by shame for disclosure of nonnormative behavior and fear of perceived sanctioning of that nonnormativity. But the greatest fear that can be identified is the fear of social exclusion. It should not be unexpected when we say that the main aim of queer activism in Curaçao has been social inclusion. My main claim in the present contribution is that, while emphasizing inclusion, less energy has been put into the actual emancipation of patriarchal and colonial structures in our society and culture, including within queer communities themselves. These structures heighten existing exclusions, create new ones and offer only shallow forms of inclusion to the most favored groups within our queer communities, leaving the large majority at the wayside. Hence, queer emancipation and identification have been mostly understood by our activists to be about personal and individual emancipation and identification and less about communal intersectional emancipation and identification with society—or the other self.

2 Sè Sua! (Yeah, Bro!)

To show how important this notion is, I will start with a story from my own youth. As a queer Caribbean man, I remember that first touch of the other that becomes the self in the act of touching. That hand-holding of each other's genitals, grabbing, rubbing, moving up and down. Then the very moment that they became me, I became them and we became us. The blissful recognition of sameness in our gaze locked into each other's eyes, ending in an ecstatic explosion of pure joy shattering our boundaries of self, albeit for a moment. A moment that felt like an eternity between the mangrove trees bordering the hidden remains of an old salt pan. Yet, I also remember the next moment of eyes retracting, averting. The return of the mold of proper distance between young men. The shrouding of emotions and joy, while still lingering on a fast-receding horizon of pleasure and joy, finishing in a whispered: "Sè sua" (Yeah, bro). Wiping our soiled hands on our thighs as if to rub away the seed of a growing feeling of shame. Then walking behind him on the narrow bush trail, watching the droplets of sweat on his back glitter in the sunlight. The yearning to clutch his shoulders and taste the glistening salty wetness, fighting with the fear of breaking the code of what is allowed between two horny men in a situation like that and what would be a transgression of the norm of manliness. Two young homeboys helping each other out, secluded from the eyes of society, in this case by the shade of mangrove and mansaliña (*Hippomane mancinella*) trees: that was allowed. Later, I learned that much more would have been allowed in the shadows of those trees that would not be a threat to my masculinity, so long as it was secluded from the eyes, ears and, ultimately, the tongues of society.

I remember how, on reaching the little *kunuku* country house where I had been camping with my teammates, both he and I were again wearing that mask of indifference and aloofness required of men in the company of others. By then, the memory of each other's hardness, then stickiness, confined to the tactile memory of the palms of our hands, was getting distant. Though I knew little about sex at the age of thirteen, the gendered roles that our Catholic Caribbean society imposed on everybody were already amply clear. If somebody would have witnessed our act and talked about it to others, the rumors would start that both of us were *mariku, boolers, battiman*. And that was not a good thing, because *mariku* meant "not being a man." And being a man meant being free. Free to act and free to choose, a freedom that, traditionally, in the patriarchal Curaçaoan ways, was not reserved for women and *mariku*.

3 Three Genders

In traditional Curaçao, if two guys were rumored to be *mariku*, the way back to manliness was only reserved for the one able to convince society that the other was the one who had propositioned him and provided the subservient sexual service. In traditional Caribbean society, both women and *mariku* serve to give sexual pleasure and validation to men. Women validate men in basically two ways: by birthing them children and by being perceived to be the subservient partner in sex. *Mariku*, not fathering children, can only validate men by being perceived to be the subservient partner in sex, making him a lower being on the ladder of sexual status, below women. Traditional manliness, labeled "macho," is validated by the number of children a male is deemed to have fathered and the amount and variety of sexual relations in which he is deemed to have played a sexually dominant role.[1]

What I had learned in my teenage years in Curaçao was that it was possible to have intimate experiences with other guys without having to publicly identify

1 Anderson, "Measuring Masculinity in an Afro-Caribbean Context," 2012, p. 55.

as anything. That evening in the *kunuku* house, after that first bush experience with a teammate, most of the team, including my buddy and I, slept on straw mats on the floor of the living quarters of the house. Other guys and our trainers slept on the balcony in the open air. But there was also a group of older teammates who had retreated to the smaller sleeping quarter of the house. The whole night, we could hear giggling and other sounds from that quarter. At midnight, I saw one of my teammates get up from his mat in the living room and silently enter the bedroom with the older guys. The next morning, he told me that he had let the other guys sexually penetrate him as an initiation into their inner circle. He was never labeled as *mariku* though, because, apart from him telling me, his confidant, nobody ever got to know what happened. Twelve years later in Holland, another teammate, who, like me, in the meantime self-identified as gay, revealed that sex was a regular occurrence in one of the separate changing rooms at our sports venue. He himself confessed to having had sex there with one of the trainers when we were training.

It was also in the Netherlands, while studying social science at Utrecht University, that I met the Curaçao-born social work student Nelson Debrot in the early 1980s, who explained the Curaçaoan gender perspective to me. He was studying at the Sociale Academie (Social Academy) in Driebergen and one of the first openly gay Curaçaoan men I met in the Netherlands. At age twenty-one, besides studying, I was working at the Dutch National Broadcasting Network as a reporter for the Dutch Caribbean radio talk show "Tambú," and I wanted to interview him for the program. We met in a café in Utrecht and Debrot explained his way of looking at the Curaçaoan traditional perspective on gender, sexual roles and hierarchy. Any person born male, who is not validated as macho, is suspected to be *mariku*, he stressed. Men were supposed to seek macho validation at any cost as being *mariku* means being the object of active cultural shaming and self-perceived shame by the person who identifies as such. However, the macho receiving, or even actively seeking, sexual subservience by other men deemed to be *mariku* is not perceived as an object of shaming. On the contrary, in conventional male circles, like over a game of dominos or a gathering of young men *bo'i palu* (in the shade of a big tree), men could even boast about having fucked one or more *mariku*. Or guys could safely share their experiences with a known *mariku di bario* (neighborhood *mariku*) given the right setting and audience. These are the *machu kuedó*, or *kuedó'i mariku* (*mariku* catchers, where *kue*/catching is a synonym for penetrative sexual intercourse). The term roughly covers what, in North America in the 1990s, became known as DL-men or men on the down-low.[2]

2 Boykin, *Beyond the Down-Low*, 2005.

I was mesmerized. For the first time, I got an impression of how different the culture I had left behind (temporarily) would deal with my queerness than the Dutch society in which I was slowly coming out of my closet. Sadly, the interview never happened and Debrot never expanded his perspective elsewhere in writing. As I explored my newfound gay self in Utrecht and Amsterdam, Nelson Debrot moved to Rotterdam and became an icon in the Rotterdam Caribbean Carnival scene, one of the niches where queerness is accepted and respected.

4 Queerer Than Imagined

Why is this important? Apparently, traditional sexual culture was much queerer in practice than the image that society presented of its sexual culture. I use the word "traditional" in contrast to the newer perspectives on sex and gender acquired by Curaçaoan students, like myself, returning from the Netherlands after years of soaking up elements of Dutch culture, and in contrast to the recent advent of global queer culture coming to younger Curaçaoans through the internet. Patriarchy is omnipresent in traditional Curaçaoan sexual culture because sexual and gendered roles are defined around the concepts of dominance and subservience. However, they nevertheless reserve niches for queerness. *Mariku* traditionally could be out (or outed) as long as they occupied the accepted traditional roles that society reserved for this group. It was accepted that *mariku* had sex with men as long as this happened along the lines of dominance and subservience prescribed by traditional patriarchal culture. Even so, shaming of *mariku* remained culturally imperative, more as an instrument to shame queerness in men than to punish already outed *mariku*. So although it remained imperative for queer men to cling to their status and the freedoms it entailed, it did not imply a total exclusion of male queerness. The key factor in determining a person's status was and still is "disclosure." Men remain free to adopt free sexual roles as long as these are not socially disclosed. Till today, most queer men thus still choose nondisclosure of sexual behavior or identity as a way of life. This turns out to be particularly true for the *machu kuedó*. His public persona is all about being perceived to be the penetrative partner in sexual encounters with *mariku*. Based on years of counseling services with Curaçaoan queer communities, those of us who have served as counselors know that, in practice, the so-called *machu kuedó*, often under the veil of privacy, also becomes the penetrated partner. So, again, it is perceived and projected sexual behavior, and not the actual behavior, that counts.

There is, however, one group in society that, by default, needs disclosure of sexuality and, by default, falls between the cracks: male-to-female transgender individuals. Nondisclosure is mostly not an option for trans women. It was this group that originally carved out the status of *mariku* in society as a shamed, but nearly socially accepted, third gender. As sexual relations were only considered within the parameters of dominance and subservience, and as sexual subservience toward women was either a nontopic or taboo in Curaçaoan traditional culture, transgender *mariku* were assumed to have a heterosexual orientation, as in being attracted to the other sex: men. This created an intersection of sexuality and gender in this category as convention makes no distinction between trans women and gay men, and this conjoined identity was traditionally internalized by out(ed) men who liked men. Even if they did not personally identify as transgender, it was considered "normal" for them to identify as *mariku*. This produced another reason for non-transgender men-who-like-men to maintain their nondisclosure: to avoid being classified as *mariku* and to behave in keeping with the *mariku* subculture. This further creates the impression that Curaçaoan patriarchal culture did not recognize or emphasize sexual orientations but rather two sexes (women and men) and three genders (male, female and *mariku*). This sadly implisd that female-to-male transgender individuals were still considered women and no separate gender was carved out for them.

An interesting cultural terrain, where queer men and women play an essential and respected role, is Afro-Curaçaoan music, both in the traditions of *tambú* and *seú*. Queer women and men have been heavily represented among the *tambú* singers (*kantadó di tambú*) of old as well as the *seú* singers (*kantadó mayó*).[3] This also goes for the organizers of the Marcha di Seú (Harvest Festival Parade) and the Curaçao Carnival Parades. Equally interesting is the presence of queer men as formal practitioners of Afro-Caribbean religiosity and spirituality and more formal Afro-Caribbean Santería in Curaçao. Reportedly, most Santería leaders in Curaçao are queer men and women. These remarks are based on common knowledge within the Curaçaoan queer communities and require further research. But it does indicate that cultural practices such as *tambú* and *seú* or Santería and *montamentu* (talking to spirits) accommodate and offer "safe spaces" for nonheteronormative sexual communities and practices.

Here, patriarchy meets coloniality in Curaçao's sexual culture. Whereas traditional Curaçaoan culture does recognize a third gender, the colonial legal superstructure and formal colonial culture, informed as they are by both a Roman Catholic and a Protestant Calvinist supraculture, did not. Likewise, whereas traditional Curaçaoan culture not only tolerates but actively rewards male nonmonogamy and promiscuity, the colonial and Roman Catholic/

3 Editors' note: see also contributions by Allen and De Jong in this volume.

Calvinist Protestant supraculture condemned it. Also, whereas traditional Curaçaoan culture has a niche for Afro-Caribbean spirituality and religiosity and its queer enclaves, colonial and Roman Catholic/Calvinist Protestant supraculture condemned and even tried to outlaw it. So colonial patriarchy added a supracultural norm to heteronormativity and cisgender normativity with a strong tendency to exclude visibly queer people from Curaçao's institutions. This reinforced the general culture of nondisclosure not only of queerness but also of male nonmonogamy and sexual promiscuity, which, in traditional Curaçaoan culture, was actively promoted among men. All this strengthened the cultural foundation of shaming and fear.

5 Amnesia of a Colonial Past and Present

I did not actively seek sexual encounters in my teenage years, and, in Curaçao, that one experience next to the salt pan was only one of very few. My real sexual awakening happened while studying at the university in the Netherlands, and it was a homosexual/gay awakening in a completely different society, one that actually emphasized sexual identity and disclosure. Self-identifying as a gay young man provided me with an identity that was not considered inferior in the progressive environment of a Dutch university and a city such as Amsterdam. Identifying as *mariku* in the traditional Curaçaoan connotation of the word was therefore not an option, nor did I want to identify as transgender, feminine or effeminate. I felt attracted by maleness and by men acting as men, sexually speaking, so calling it an orientation and not a separate gender worked for me. I remember mentioning to my parents in my eight-page coming out letter to them that the way Curaçaoan culture thought about people like me would make it very difficult for me to ever live in Curaçao again. I nevertheless moved back to Curaçao a few years later.

What I didn't realize at that time living in the Netherlands, and later back in Curaçao, was that accepting an orientation as sexual identity was not as essential or necessary as it seemed to me at the time. Nor was the emphasis on the disclosure of identity a prerequisite for emancipation. And I wasn't the only one who was led to believe that. This happened to most queer young people who returned to Curaçao after studying in the metropolis. We adopted the Western model of multiple orientations and genders as a means of emancipating and liberating ourselves from the traditional role patriarchy had carved out, at least for queer men. Queer women were, of course, invisible by design in traditional society—there was no identity for them to assume. For them, too, nondisclosure seemed more beneficial. The identification of women in a relationship or culture of *kambrada* (queer womanhood), as described by linguist Jocelyn Clemencia, was mostly an internal self-identification within the subculture but not by society as a whole.[4]

When I returned to Curaçao in the second half of the 1980s, an existing queer emancipation group, Grupo Homofilia Antiyano (Antillean Homophile Group, GHA), had become less active and gradually disappeared from the public scene. It would take until 1995 for a new group to form: Orguyo, cofounded by my then-partner Rymold Hose, who became the first chairperson, wherein I quickly became involved as media coordinator. When, in 1995, the Dutch parliament voted to prepare for opening civil marriage for same-sex couples in the Netherlands, a general homophobic uproar arose in Curaçao with month-long public debates, which forced our board to publicly come out in the media as queer citizens of Curaçao. From that period till the present day, for more than a quarter of a century, I have remained one of the principal proponents of queer emancipation and queer rights in Curaçao. I thus feel personally responsible for the choices we made in our work around queer awareness in our country. The common thread underlying these choices was that we rejected Curaçao's traditional cultural model of three genders, nondisclosure and male promiscuity because they were founded in patriarchy. We actively started promoting coming out into one of the many available orientations and genders of the growing LGBTQ+ spectrum as an act of personal liberation in an attempt to tear down the culture of nondisclosure. But this was also the era of the height of the AIDS epidemic, followed by the age of distribution of extremely expensive HIV medication and the promotion of universal use of condoms and nonpromiscuity among men. The effect was that our campaigns could indirectly, sometimes unintentionally but sometimes very intentionally, be seen as a criticism of the large majority of queer men, the *machu kuedó*. Till today, these men, who cherish nondisclosure, do not identify as having any sexual orientation. Gender-wise, they still identify as macho and live a life of nonmonogamous, promiscuous sexuality. The consequence of all these choices is that the great majority of queer men and women in Curaçao are still off the radar and do not participate in the activities of the more vocal and visible 10 percent. This is also true for an iconic success story such as the celebration of Curaçao Pride.

The mere fact that Curaçaoan queer activism has stayed in the public eye for a quarter of a century has contributed to greater visibility and acceptance of queerness, has made it possible for us to be consulted by governments on policy issues and has energized an ongoing campaign for recognition of queer

4 Editors' note: see contribution by Clemencia in this section of the volume.

relationships and allowing queer couples to marry. All this sounds like a success story. Add to that more than ten years of a successful Curaçao Pride celebration, known all over the Caribbean region, and one could ask, what has gone wrong? I would say that what has gone wrong is our blindness to the colonial and patriarchal nature of the indiscriminate adoption of a Western model of queerness and deafness for the message that traditional sexual culture conveys about what Curaçao-born scholar Wigbertson Julian Isenia calls "queer sovereignties" in contrast to queer identities. Isenia questions the extent of that sovereignty, among other reasons, because of that adoption of the Western model of queerness.[5] What has also gone wrong, I believe, if not only blindness, is a mixture of rejection and feelings of powerlessness to deal with the intersectionalities of race, color and class that segregate Curaçaoan queer communities. This powerlessness in Curaçao often becomes a stubborn unwillingness to recognize that this segregation of our community stems from our colonial past and our not-yet postcolonial present. Our own version of "amnesia concerning the colonial past," as queer Afro-Surinamese Dutch scholar Prof. Gloria Wekker describes it in her pathbreaking study *White Innocence: Paradoxes of Colonialism and Race*.[6]

The latter two factors, segregation based on color and class, can clearly be seen in Curaçao's queer entertainment culture and Curaçao Pride. Parties are successful when they are mainly attended by white and lighter-colored men from upwardly mobile middle-class backgrounds. Expats form a large part (30%–40%) of the attendance and the pricing at the events has made parties virtually off-limits to queer Curaçaoans. Some Curaçao Pride activities are attended by over 80 percent of expats and tourists. While there isn't necessarily that much active racial discrimination happening at the level of organizers of events, the actual discriminating factor is the financial accessibility of such events. As economic status is tied up with color and class, colorism still plays a role, which is directly reflected in the sexual politics of dating. Again, focusing, for the purpose of this contribution, only on men, parties may often end in dating and the search for casual sex. Where, in the initial years of Orguyo, which later became FOKO (Fundashon Orguyo Kòrsou [Curaçao Pride Foundation]), dating occurred during and at queer spaces or events, in a later phase, queer men of lighter skin color with more money to spend would attend higher-end venues and later pass by the less classy venues attended more by queer men of darker color for "last-minute pick-ups." All this is steeped in sexual fantasies

5 Isenia, "Queer Sovereignties," 2022. Editors' note: see also the contribution by Isenia in this section.

6 Wekker, *White Innocence*, 2016.

and myths around the sexual endowment or prowess of darker-skinned men. In the meantime, with the transition to online dating apps, venues for people with modest incomes have completely disappeared. Colorism, however, keeps playing a role in online dating with specifications such as "blacks need not apply," or either "light" or "dark skin preferred." The consequence of this is that spaces for richer queer people are not the same as the generally less safe spaces that more marginalized queer people visit, which involve them having to use much more covert language and signaling to avoid homophobic slurs and verbal confrontations. Physical violence against queer people in public spaces is not common. More than two decades of counseling practice show that it happens more often in the domestic spheres and in close family circles.

Something similar happened concerning the negotiation of sexual encounters, whether free or for money, and other forms of transactional sex between men. From the 1970s onward at least, this happened in temporarily created queer spaces, either in dilapidated old buildings on the narrow alleys of downtown Willemstad or in rented houses or apartments in the suburbs or countryside. One such tradition was a regular event where queer men, self-identifying as homosexual, would rent one or more vacation homes in Westpoint Village at the western tip of Curaçao for male queer partying and cruising. They would invite queer people from the east for an evening party to which they would also invite local fishermen and young guys (presumed *kuedó*) while advertising free beer and music, Westpoint being a traditional fishing village. The approach sought to facilitate sexual encounters between the invited men from the city and the local men of the village. Here, too, the uneasy intersections mentioned earlier would come into play. The men from the city were generally lighter-skinned, wealthier and mostly self-identifying as homosexual (*mariku*), and the local men were generally darker-skinned, financially marginalized and self-identifying as macho (*machu kuedó*). This tradition has now been completely replaced by private parties at homes, where both invitations and sexual encounters have been negotiated online before arrival. The intersections of colorism, classism and macho-normativity versus *mariku* deviance are still present. The wealthier organizers provide the drinks, drugs, condoms and blue[7] and other pills but also pay for the transport and other costs of the less wealthy visitors, with the encounters often having strong characteristics of transactional sex.

All this happens outside of the official attention of queer activist groups, or, at least, it is not openly talked about. Meanwhile, queer activism has

7 Viagra, Kamagra and other sexual performance-enhancing drugs.

successfully embraced the struggle for marriage and relational equality, achieving acceptance by a large section of society regarding sexual and gender variance and the different corresponding identities. The silent consensus among most queer activists in Curaçao tends to be that this identity-focused approach toward queerness, linking up with queer rights organizations in the Netherlands, "queer tourism" and the global queer movement and its identity-focused perspective, is their best chance to reach broad acceptance by society, creating new dependencies instead of focusing on emancipation and liberation of traditional categories, such as *mariku* and *machu kuedó*.[8] Another silent consensus seems to be a tendency to desexualize queerness in keeping with Curaçao's double standards on sexuality and sexual promiscuity, coming from its patriarchal, colonial, Christian and even Calvinist historical cultural roots. Queerness thus becomes respectable, about people liking each other, devoid of the "sleaziness" of lust and promiscuity and the "scandal" of drag, and wanting nothing more than to live perfectly normal lives within the new supracultural homonormative mold based on the same values as the heteronormative supraculture.

This recreates the same divide between supraculture and subculture within queer communities as exists in the heterosexual cisgender supraculture. Queer activists, who may lustily and happily participate in the queer sexual subculture in their private lives still dominated by the interplay between the three perceived genders of macho men, women and *mariku*, will still openly stress that queer people in Curaçao aim to live decent homonormative lives fashioned on heteronormative values. So what they purportedly want is a recognition of their varied identities and equal treatment by the law, that's all. The existing contradictions, inequalities and plain injustices produced by the intersectional reign of patriarchy and colonial and capitalist structures, inequalities and discriminatory relations and practices are never recognized, or they are neatly swept under the rug of aspirational queer normativity.

6 A Communal Decolonization of Queerness

Yet, traditional Afro-Caribbean notions of sex and gender have not gone away. Patriarchal relations, full of the prejudices of heteronormativity, cisgenderism, racism, colonialism, classist inequality, deprivation and exploitation are still rampant, and strongly so, within queer communities. It is time that we, as queer

8 Isenia, "Queer sovereignties," 2022, pp. 255–64.

activists who are conscious of this, recognize our own responsibility in creating and preserving this situation. What would be a more just way forward and, eventually, a break with this development? I strongly believe that the answer is to be found for a large part within the traditional sexual and gendered subcultures of Curaçao. The dilemma is clear. That subculture is as patriarchal, colonial, colorist and classist as its hypocritical supracultural counterpart. The difference is that the subcultures are based on actual human traditions, behaviors and beliefs and not on the unrealistic, hypocritical self-image proposed by the postcolonial, quasi-Christian-based supraculture. The great error of queer activism in Curaçao is that the emancipation it proposes is an emancipation from the inherent inequalities of the suprastructure while perfectly remaining within a new extended homonormative supraculture. This is a quasi-emancipation that rejects merely the sharp edges of patriarchy in the relationship between society and queer women and men while still maintaining the patriarchal, colorist and colonial prejudices and inequalities within our communities. The fact that the average skin color of Curaçao Pride participants, their average wallet size and their average educational preparation are clearly not the same as the corresponding averages of the general Curaçaoan population (a superficial coincidence and not a structural deficiency of our activism) should be seen as unacceptable. We should put our lip service to terms such as intersectionality and emancipation aside and, instead, start practicing intersectionality and emancipation for real.

In conclusion, I strongly believe that an important departure point for the required change of heart lies in real support for the transgender and upcoming sexually fluid and genderfluid communities and currents and the revindication of the *machu kuedó*. This last group has been incorrectly vilified as spreaders of HIV to the heterosexual majority because of the veil of secrecy and nondisclosure under which they operate sexually. It is a fact that the group plays a role in the spread of HIV, but there are several other high-risk groups and spreaders in this regard. It could also be argued that a much more open society and culture with regard to queerness would lift the perceived sanctions on disclosure and would allow this group and their sexual partners to negotiate prevention measures more openly. Revindication entails truth-telling, at least within the communities, about our practices and culture. Without that, there is no beating the patriarchy.

This will also entail a resexualizing and desanitizing of our notion of Caribbean and Curaçaoan queerness, a departure from an identity-oriented model of queerness to a queerness based on attitude and behavior and liberty to engage in queer sexual and social relationships. It would also mean a definitive departure from certain supracultural heteronormativities, such as monogamy and prudism, false puritanism and the rejection of promiscuity. Promiscuity, too, can become, if not an instrument, at least a pathway toward emancipation. It entails the realization that many of the norms that we silently, and sometimes even loudly, promote within our queer communities are born from the same heteronormative patriarchal qualities that we claim to reject. And in rejecting our real-time selves as Afro-Caribbean queer communities and individuals, we thereby reject the majority of queer individuals in our communities.

It also means that we need to emancipate the queer theory and underlying feminism of our incomplete emancipatory efforts. One slogan ought to be: more community and less individualism, and more communal realization of queer selfhood instead of an isolated clinging to queer identities predefined in the Global North. Why? Because that will help us stop demonizing and excluding large swaths of queer communities such as the down-low *machu kuedó*, sometimes medicalized with the reductive term MSM (Men having Sex with Men), introduced by the AIDS prevention campaigns in the region. It also means the inclusion of the informal queer spaces and events of these communities within the common culture and self-image of queer activists and activism. It would also help us steer the emphasis in transgender communities away from the need for medical transitions to the need for acceptance and inclusion of people in the bodies that they presently have and own, as long as and independent of whether an actual and full transition remains out of their reach.

I propose that we try to root our queer activism in the propositions of recent practices of Caribbean and Latin-American feminism. One such idea is "decolonial feminism," proposed by the Afro-Caribbean Dominican-Colombian anthropologist Uchy Curiel, who stresses the importance of dealing with the permanence of coloniality and colonial attitudes in our own communities, including racism and colorism.[9] There is also the practice of "communitarian feminism," proposed, among others, by the Bolivian feminist writer and activist Julieta Paredes.[10] For a male nonnormative perspective on countering the desexualization of queer experience, the work of Brazilian queer cultural theorist João Florêncio on "porous masculinities" could be a good point of departure to marry feminist insights with new nonhomonormative nonpatriarchal male experiences.[11]

---

9 Curiel, "Hacia la construcción de un feminismo descolonizado. A propósito de la realización del encuentro feminista autónomo: Haciendo comunidad en la casa de las diferencias" [Toward the construction of a decolonized feminism. Reflections on the realization of the autonomous feminist encounter: Making a community in the house of differences], 2010. Editors' note: see also contribution by Roe in this volume.

10 Paredes, "The Neocolonial Queer," 2015.

11 Florêncio, *Bareback Porn, Porous Masculinities, Queer Futures*, 2020.

In closing, that notion brings me back to my younger self and that early experience next to the lagoon. What a beautiful experience it would have been if, returning to our team at the country house, we could have told one or two friends about our adventure. If later, singing around the campfire and barbecue, we could have put an arm around each other's shoulder, allowing the new feelings of earlier hours to linger, simmer and deepen. What a beautiful experience it would have been if we could have told our parents and siblings or, at least, not have to dread an accidental disclosure. How beautiful it would have been if we had other models of being at our disposal as queer men other than the heteronormative, cisgender, monogamous frames we were formally brought up with while informally being pushed toward the prevailing opposite mold of promiscuous macho men, that was, and is, as unfitting to young queer men like us. What if … What if … ?

Bibliography

Anderson, Patricia. "Measuring Masculinity in an Afro-Caribbean Context." *Social and Economic Studies* 61, no. 1 (2012): 49–93.

Boykin, Keith. *Beyond the Down-Low: Sex, Lies and Denial in Black America*. New York: Carroll & Graf, 2005.

Curiel, Ochy. "Hacia la construcción de un feminismo descolonizado. A propósito de la realización del encuentro feminista autónomo: Haciendo comunidad en la casa de las diferencias" [Toward the construction of a decolonized feminism. Reflections on the realization of the autonomous feminist encounter: Making a community in the house of differences]. In *Emancipaciones feministas del siglo XXI*, edited by Gleidys Martínez Alonso and Yanet Martínez Toledo, 189–200. Havana: Editorial de Ciencias Sociales, 2010.

Florêncio, João. *Bareback Porn, Porous Masculinities, Queer Futures: The Ethics of Becoming-Pig*. New York: Routledge, 2020.

Isenia, Wigbertson Julian. "Queer Sovereignties: Cultural Practices of Sexual Citizenship in the Dutch Caribbean." PhD diss., University of Amsterdam, 2022.

Paredes, Julieta. "The Neocolonial Queer." In *The Global Trajectories of Queerness: Re-thinking Same-Sex Politics in the Global South*, edited by Ashley Tellis and Sruti Bala, 229–39. Thamyris/Intersecting: Place, Sex and Race 30. Leiden: Brill, 2015. https://doi.org/10.1163/9789004217942_016.

Wekker, Gloria. *White Innocence: Paradoxes of Colonialism and Race*. Durham, NC: Duke University Press, 2016.

CHAPTER 36

Studies on Trans* and Same-Sex Loving People in Curaçao: a Review Essay

Wigbertson Julian Isenia

Abstract

This contribution reviews available research on trans* and same-sex loving people in the Dutch Caribbean, focusing on five areas: female same-sex sexuality as a research focus that emerged in Dutch Caribbean studies in the 1950s; cultural practices such as academic works discussing novels, performances, clothing and religious practices; medical research on STDs, HIV and AIDS; sexual minority rights and activist movements from the 1970s onward; and the social and legal developments around trans* and same-sex cultures after the 2010 constitutional reforms. It aims to show how we can use a decolonial contextualizing approach to gain insight into sources marred by their colonial and heteronormative biases and to identify areas in need of further research.

Keywords

sexuality studies – constitutional reforms – social movements – medical research – performances – religion

When researching trans* and same-sex cultures in the Caribbean islands, researchers often point out that little or no research has been done on the Dutch Caribbean islands. This is partly true because, although there are some sporadic references to trans* and same-sex loving people in academic research, there are hardly any comprehensive studies on these topics. However, we can draw on several foundational texts on Curaçao, which I discuss in the present contribution.[1] It is important to note that the island of Curaçao dominates these studies in the Dutch Caribbean islands and that the studies were mainly

1 For a detailed engagement with these texts, see my doctoral dissertation: Isenia, "Queer Sovereignties: Cultural Practices of Sexual Citizenship in the Dutch Caribbean," 2022.

 | DOI:10.1163/9789004690882_038

conducted in lesbian, gay and bisexual communities. More studies need to be conducted on the other five islands of the kingdom and trans* communities.

This present contribution discusses five research foci in the existing literature. First, it examines how female same-sex sexuality emerged as a research category in the 1950s in Dutch Caribbean studies, and how colonial archives might be read against the grain. The second area of interest is research on cultural practices, such as novels, clothing and religious practices. Third, I will examine medical research on sexually transmitted diseases (STDs), HIV and AIDS. Fourth, I will focus on sexual minority rights activist movements from the 1970s onward. Finally, I look at the social and legal developments around trans* and same-sex cultures after the constitutional reforms of 2010.

1 From Sociological Attention to Sexual "Deviance" to Reading Colonial Archives against the Grain

Sociologists such as Harry Hoetink, Arnaud Marks and René Römer explain the emergence of female *kambrada* relations as a product of social and economic development.[2] *Kambrada*, a term that denotes friendship and companionship as well as a female homoerotic relationship suggests an understanding of sexuality as relational practice rather than fixed identity.[3] Hoetink, Marks and Römer view *kambrada* relationships as a result of the social mixing of women from different social classes and the isolation of Protestant female elites from their peers.[4] The social isolation of these Protestant women and the contacts the women sought with black personnel, Hoetink explains, did not always have a positive impact on Protestant women.[5] One such impact, according to him, was the *kambrada* relationship. Hoetink's understanding of *kambrada* relationships implies that they were a practice of the lower social classes that became adopted by upper-class women resulting from interracial

2 Hoetink, *Het patroon van de oude Curaçaosche samenleving: Een sociologische studie* [The pattern of old Curaçaoan society: A sociological study], 1958, pp. 54–55; Marks, *Male and Female in the Afro-Curaçaoan Household*, 1976, pp. 92, 332; Römer, *De Curaçaose samenleving* [The Curaçaoan society], 1998.

3 Isenia, "Looking for Kambrada: Sexuality and Social Anxieties in the Dutch Colonial Archive, 1882–1923," 2019, pp. 125–43; Isenia, "Queer Sovereignties," 2022.

4 Hoetink, *Het patroon van de oude Curaçaosche samenleving*, 1958; Marks, *Male and Female in the Afro-Curaçaoan Household*, 1976; Römer, *Un pueblo na kaminda: Een sociologisch historische studie van de Curaçaose samenleving* [A people on the move: A sociological and historical study of Curaçaoan society], 1979.

5 Hoetink, *Het patroon van de oude Curaçaosche samenleving*, 1958, p. 54.

and interclass relationships. These descriptions suggest that cross-race and cross-class relationships between the (formerly) enslaved and their descendants and Protestants were, in fact, commonplace in the domestic sphere in Curaçao.

These sociologists also explain the existence of *kambrada* relations as ensuing from the gender imbalance that resulted from the mass emigration of men to neighboring countries in search of work in the early twentieth century.[6] They concluded that female same-sex relationships on the islands flourished because of the absence of men. These early sociological accounts of female same-sex sexuality thus often adopted a patriarchal and heteronormative point of view, regarding it as a deviation from the "normal" due to socioeconomic reasons. This view is clear in the claim that the lack of men causes supposedly "unfavorable" social and sexual practices.[7] It is a conceptualization of female same-sex relationships that effectively centers men. These sociologists fail to recognize how *kambrada* relationships were not opposed to but existed in continuum with heterosexual relationships.[8] Critiquing the unspoken assumptions underlying these interpretations of women's sexuality is helpful in thinking about how, on the one hand, women entered into relationships with each other without the intervention of men, and how, on the other hand, the demand for male labor elsewhere facilitated and catapulted the emergence of creative and radical modes and networks of interdependence. Poor economic conditions enabled the development of practices that lay outside the normative framework. In this sense, we can include a material analysis without reducing the conditions to male absence.[9]

In my doctoral research, I examined a travelog, an ethnography and a novel from the 1880s to the 1920s, the first known sources to mention *kambrada* relations in the Dutch Caribbean.[10] Besides the negatively connoted

---

6 Marks, *Male and Female in the Afro-Curaçaoan Household*, 1976; Römer, *De Curaçaose samenleving*, 1998; Lier, *Tropische tribaden. Een verhandeling over homosexualiteit en homosexuele vrouwen in Suriname* [Tropical tribulations. A treatise on homosexuality and homosexual women in Suriname], 1986.

7 Marks, *Male and Female in the Afro-Curaçaoan Household*, 1976, p. 92; Lier, *Tropische tribaden*, 1986, pp. 23–24.

8 Few scholarly works criticize the assumed linkage between *kambrada* relationships and the migration-related shortage of men. However, see Broek, "A Paragraph in the Unwritten History of Lesbian Love in the Caribbean: Amor di kambrada," 1992, p. 56. Or, for the Surinamese context, see, Wekker, "What's Identity Got to Do with It?: Rethinking Identity in Light of the Mati Work in Suriname," 2009, p. 437. Editors' note: see contribution by Broek in this section.

9 Isenia, "Queer Sovereignties," 2022, pp. 84–89.

10 Isenia, "Looking for Kambrada," 2019.

colonial accounts of *kambrada* relations, some of which are mentioned in the sociological texts above, I was interested in knowing how to encounter historical subjects who cannot speak back from the colonial archives given the latter's predominantly racist and sexist modes of organization. These sources articulate patriarchal and racist domination and anxiety. Rather than concrete truths, we might find traces, nuances and representations of power relations in these accounts. *Kambrada* relations can be hierarchical, asymmetrical, both class- and race-based and even explicitly transactional.[11] Analyzing these historical works shows how important it was for women to not name a feeling or relationship and to see sexuality not as an identity but as belonging to the realm of social practice.[12]

2 Language, Cultural Practices and *Montamentu*

The second area of research in the existing scholarship on sexualities in Curaçao is that of literary and cultural practice. Literary scholar Aart Broek analyzed Willem Kroon's serial novel from 1923, *E no por casa* (She cannot marry), in which the protagonist, an older woman, wants to enter into a *kambrada* relationship with a younger woman who refuses her advances.[13] The Papiamentu-language novel, which appeared in weekly installments in the Roman Catholic *La Cruz* magazine, is part of a body of work from the 1920s and 1930s that accompanied the significant social changes after the introduction of the Shell oil refinery in Curaçao.[14] The transformation from a small agricultural and trading society during the slavery era to a capitalist and industrial country improved the island's socioeconomic conditions and social mobility. According to Broek, these novels, written exclusively by male authors close to the Roman Catholic Church, served to warn its readers, mainly formerly enslaved Afro-Curaçaoans, of the "dangers of modern life," stemming from the influx of immigrants of other faiths from other Caribbean islands, and to educate them about their religious duties.[15] In my doctoral research, I propose that the

11 This reading enabled me to contrast *kambrada* and Surinamese *mati* to identify the similarities and differences between these practices. See, for example, Wekker, *The Politics of Passion: Women's Sexual Culture in the Afro-Surinamese Diaspora*, 2006.

12 Isenia, "Queer Sovereignties," 2021, pp. 274–82.

13 Broek, "A Paragraph in the Unwritten History of Lesbian Love in the Caribbean: Amor di kambrada," 1992.

14 The novel was later published as a book in 1927.

15 Ibid., p. 54.

novel can be read as psychologizing and pathologizing nonnormative sexual practices.[16]

Language is another central question in Dutch Caribbean scholarship on sexuality. In discussions of Kroon's novel, it has been noted how the term *kambrada* is used in an elastic manner, as a slur, as a reference to a nonsexual relationship between women and as an expression of unfulfilled female same-sex desire. Joceline Clemencia questions the verbal naming of female same-sex relations in terms of sexual identities.[17] Clemencia proposes that language pertaining to sexuality ought to enable fluidity, not define and pigeonhole anyone and bring about transformation and liberation. Rejecting the term "lesbian" as patriarchal and stigmatizing, she speaks of "women who love other women."[18] She also criticizes Spanish-derived words in Papiamentu such as *kachapera, kambrada, machoro* and *repera* because these words are pejorative and refer to female same-sex love relationships as a disease and an insult to nature.[19] Clemencia uses oral histories to show various facets of female same-sex loving traditions, which have often been met with acceptance and approval, such as the cohabitation of women, the wearing of twin or matching clothing at parties and on special occasions, such as at *tambú* drum dances, the Misa di Aurora,[20] the San Antoni mass,[21] and the *belorio* funeral vigils. Clemencia asks: why would we want to name that verbally? It is important to note that, despite her criticism of existing words that refer to female same-sex relationships, she believes that language can still have a crucial function in sexual emancipation. She concludes by saying that if same-sex desiring women were to shed the terms smudged with negative connotations, to "break the silence" and shatter the taboo of same-sex desire, in time "a new language would grow."[22] This is also reflected in the subtitle of her article, "from 'cachapera' to open throats," implying that new and more appealing terminology will emanate from these open throats. Clemencia calls for a new vocabulary that does not necessarily reclaim pejorative words nor is tainted with guilt and shame that prevent

16 Isenia, "Queer Sovereignties," 2022, p. 75.

17 Clemencia, "Women Who Love Women in Curaçao: From 'Cachapera' to Open Throats: A Commentary in Collage," 1996. Editors' note: this text by Clemencia has been included in this section. See also contribution by Römer on the politics of language around sexual practices.

18 Ibid., p. 81.

19 Ibid., p. 85.

20 Aurora masses are the Catholic masses held at dawn for the course of nine days before Christmas.

21 A celebration of the syncretic religious practice of *montamentu*.

22 Ibid.

someone from expressing themselves but allows them to speak openly and publicly about same-sex sexuality.

Frieda Bernadina's dissertation is a third study in this area, which examines the syncretic Afro-religious practice of *montamentu*, wherein women and effeminate queer men from a lower social class play a prominent role. Bernardina's study investigates how the status and prestige these communities enjoy in the sphere of *montamentu* contrasts with the day-to-day discrimination they face.[23]

This work has begun to understand and theorize the cultural practices of same-sex loving cultures in Curaçao. Although many areas need further research and others need to be reexamined, these studies show how sexuality is practiced in different ways. This analysis can then allow for comparisons beyond the island.

3 Medical Research on STDs, HIV and AIDS

In the 1970s and 1990s, two major medical health studies took place in Curaçao. Although they focused mainly on advancing medical policy, they offer insights into sociocultural elements that are important to the humanities and social sciences.

Between May 1965 and May 1966, a survey was conducted among gay men and mainly female sex workers for Tjeerd de Reus's dissertation on the prevalence of STDs in Curaçao. De Reus identified sex work and homosexuality as the leading causes of STDs in Curaçao. He found the male subjects among 2,087 recruits tested for military service. Eighty-nine young men were found to have STDs due to homosexual contact.

The high incidence of STDs in young men was explained in the study by the fact that "marriage is associated with the virginity complex (the man is expected to marry a virgin), while great sexual freedom is granted to the man before marriage, who depends on a sex worker in this mindset and social structure."[24] The broader understanding of sexuality as a practice rather than an identity, as previously discussed in the female *kambrada* relationships

23 Bernadina, "Montamentoe, een beschrijvende en analyserenne studie van een Afro-Amerikaanse godsdienst op Curaçao" [Montamentu, a descriptive and analytical study of an Afro-American religion in Curaçao], 1981, pp. 109–10.

24 Reus, *Geslachtsziekten op Curaçao: Een onderzoek naar het voorkomen en de verspreiding van geslachtsziekten op Curaçao door middel van een enquête onder artsen, met daarop aansluitend contactonderzoek in de periode tussen 1 mei 1965 en 1 mei 1966* [Venereal diseases in Curaçao: An investigation into the occurrence and spread of venereal diseases in

of the late nineteenth and early twentieth centuries, was also considered in the spread of STDs among so-called heterosexual men. De Reus explains that self-proclaimed heterosexual men did not mind having sex with other men as long as they took the "active" role and penetrated the other man. In this way, their penetrative masculine role remains intact, and the gender of their sexual partner does not matter. De Reus recommends men who have sex with men to test their blood regularly for syphilis (two to three times a year) as they have an increased risk of contracting an STD due to frequently changing sexual contacts.[25] This study is important for the humanities and social sciences because it represents an archive of comprehensive descriptions and various quotes from men who had sex with men in the 1970s that has not been archived in other ways.

In her 1992 study, Tineke Alberts distinguishes between homosexual behavior and homosexual identity and lifestyle.[26] Six years after the first cases of HIV and AIDS were discovered in Curaçao in 1986, a large-scale study took place on the island based on a survey of 432 men and women and 18 interviews with 18 people. Previously, a study on HIV and AIDS was conducted in 1987 and 1991.[27]

This study was necessary to obtain better information about AIDS prevention measures. The rationale behind the study was that an effective HIV and AIDS prevention campaign must fit the population's norms, values and culture. According to Alberts, these cultural characteristics include that non-monogamy is widespread on the island, and heterosexual transmission plays a significant role in the region.[28] The ratio of men to women in the Dutch Caribbean in 1991 was 1.6:1, while, in the Netherlands and the United States in the same year, it was 13.1:1 and 8:1, respectively.[29]

Alberts concludes that homosexual risk behavior does not seem to play as prominent a role in the number of AIDS patients in the Netherlands and the

Curaçao by means of a survey among doctors, with subsequent contact research in the period between May 1, 1965 and May 1, 1966], 1970, p. 5. Author's translation.

25 Ibid., p. 134.

26 Alberts, *Je lust en je leven: Een inventariserend onderzoek naar relatievorming, sexueel gedrag en de preventie van aids op Curaçao* [Your lust and your life: An inventory study of relationship formation, sexual behaviour and the prevention of AIDS in Curaçao], 1992, p. 21.

27 Central Bureau of Statistics Curaçao, *Rapportage resultaten AIDS-enquête Curaçao* [Report results AIDS survey Curaçao], 1987; Alberts, "Evaluatie aidsvoorlichting Curaçao: Evaluatie-onderzoek naar de effectiviteit van de voorlichting rondom aids op Curaçao" [Evaluation AIDS information Curaçao. Evaluation research on the effectiveness of information on AIDS in Curaçao], 1991.

28 Alberts, "Evaluatie aidsvoorlichting Curaçao," 1991; Alberts, *Je lust en je leven*, 1992.

29 Alberts, *Je lust en je leven*, 1992, p. 5.

United States. Apart from the fact that women also predominate in infection rates on the islands, the men who are prevalent in the rates do not identify as homosexual. However, these "heterosexual" men have had sex with men. Alberts argues that male identity derives from fulfilling an active, dominant role, not from the gender of the partner. This is reflected in the Papiamentu terminology, where active and passive male partners are called *mariku kwedo* and *mariku wantadó* respectively. The "man" thus always takes an active role.[30] This *mariku kwedo* has relationships with women and sometimes long-term and occasional relationships with men but does not identify with a homosexual or bisexual identity and lifestyle.[31]

Since then, no large-scale research on HIV and AIDS has been conducted in Curaçao. Future research could focus on government and NGO campaigns to combat HIV and AIDS since the 1980s, including the use of visuals and ways to combat stigma. It should also examine how HIV- and AIDS-infected people are cared for in informal ways, such as by family and friends, and how the many who have died are remembered.

4 Activist Movements from the 1970s Onward

After the May 30, 1969, workers' strike, conversations about decolonization and a positive reevaluation of Dutch Caribbean culture and recognition of the Papiamentu language also led to groups advocating for sexual liberation especially for same-sex loving communities. Chelsea Schields analyzed how leftist groups in the Antilles, both in Curaçao and in the Dutch diaspora, viewed sexual liberation as an essential rather than an auxiliary endeavor to achieve self-determination.[32] *Vitó*, a newspaper published in 1966 by a group of recent graduates in Curaçao, wrote about reproductive politics, women's rights and, in 1969, the integration and emancipation of homosexual men in the community.[33] The group commented on the social isolation and victimization of same-sex desiring men.[34] *Kontakto Antiyano*, a newspaper of a left-wing Antillean group in the Netherlands, also reported on the founding of Sociedad homosexual Antillano Biba larga biba (Society for Antillean homosexuals

30 Ibid., p. 22.

31 Ibid., p. 55.

32 Schields, "Insurgent Intimacies: Sex, Socialism, and Black Power in the Dutch Atlantic," 2020.

33 Ibid., p. 105.

34 Schields, "Eros against Empire: Visions of Erotic Freedom in Archives of Decolonisation," 2019.

live and let live, SHA) in 1971 and questioned how a homosexual organization could change the outdated colonial and capitalist structures in the Dutch Caribbean.[35]

In my dissertation, I analyze SHA and the Grupo Homofilia Antiyano (Antillean Homophile Group, GHA) in Curaçao, founded in 1979.[36] I discuss two aspects of these groups' attitudes toward the *mariku* and the global and Dutch gay movements. Through their letters to the editor in the newspaper, I analyze the respectability politics of the SHA and the GHA, and how they portrayed themselves in newspaper articles as "proper" in contrast to the "messy queens" or the *marikunan* (a slur for trans* women, drag queens and effeminate men) who appeared in public in "women's clothes and wigs." SHA's and GHA's politics were groundbreaking but exclusive. Their politics against the so-called queens, femmes and trans* persons is evident in their newspaper articles. In both groups, a particular respectability politics can be observed, often at the expense of the *mariku*. These discussions reflect the current tensions between trans* politics and broader sexual minority politics, which puts pressure on coalition building and raises questions about the role of language in LGBTQ+ politics. The groups maintained relations with the press and with governmental and international groups in different ways: from literally copying texts of Dutch gay magazines for national magazines, as GHA has done, to receiving support from the Dutch House of Representatives in disputes with the government of Curaçao or getting government-allotted spaces for community activities.

The challenge is not to downplay the benefits these groups derive from these collaborations but to see these relationships as worth analyzing and how these actors claim self-determination through and despite these restricted spaces within the postcolonial situation of the Dutch Caribbean. In addition, this analysis can be used to further draw parallels with LGBTQ+ groups with Dutch Caribbean members in the Dutch diaspora to see what different or similar strategies they had, how they financed themselves and their relationship with the white LGBTQ+ community.[37]

35 Schields, "Insurgent Intimacies," 2020, p. 106.

36 Isenia, "Queer Sovereignties," 2022, pp. 181–218.

37 El-Tayeb, *European Others: Queering Ethnicity in Postnational Europe*, 2011; Colpani and Isenia, "Strange Fruits: The Intellectual Labor of Queers of Color in the Netherlands in the 1980s and 1990s," 2018; Colpani, Isenia, and Pieter, "Archiving Queer of Colour Politics in the Netherlands: A Roundtable Discussion," 2019.

5 LGBTQ+ Activism after the Post-2010 Constitutional Changes

Schields also examined how the Dutch legalized same-sex marriage in 2012 in the special municipalities (Bonaire, St. Eustatius and Saba) in the Dutch Caribbean.[38] Like the French overseas departments in the Caribbean, these islands occupy a unique position in the region in terms of sexual rights.[39] Their postcolonial, non-sovereign status means that they operate under a European legal system that promotes the protection of LGBTQ+ rights while simultaneously being subject to certain legal exceptions under Dutch jurisdiction. For example, as Schields argues, the Dutch government has introduced same-sex marriage on these islands, along with laws on abortion and euthanasia, while circumventing similar "European" laws such as social benefits.[40]

Some activists in Bonaire hoped for a further improvement in the situation of LGBTQ+ people on the BES islands as the islands would now be further integrated into the Netherlands.[41] Other activists, such as Mario Kleinmoedig in Curaçao, did not perceive the unilateral introduction of same-sex marriage as neocolonial, as Schields describes in her dissertation, but felt that the colonial history and nonindependent structure of the Dutch Caribbean forced activists to rely on Dutch metropolitan leadership and legislation to advance sexual rights.[42]

Other legal advances are gradually taking place. For example, the autonomous islands within the kingdom—Aruba, Curaçao and St. Maarten—continue to fight for same-sex marriage, registered partnership and adoption of children by gay couples as well as trans* people's rights, such as the right to officially change birth names and gender, the right to medical care and the possibility of gender-affirming surgery. However, most antidiscrimination laws (such as antidiscrimination laws in the workplace) were aligned with the laws in the Netherlands in 2011.

38 Schields, "Intimacy and Integration: The Ambivalent Achievement of Marriage Equality in the Dutch Caribbean, 2007–2012," 2018. Editors' note: an edited version of this text by Schields is included in this volume.

39 For the French departments, see Agard-Jones, "Le jeu de qui? Sexual Politics at Play in the French Caribbean," 2009.

40 Schields, "Intimacy and Integration: The Ambivalent Achievement of Marriage Equality in the Dutch Caribbean, 2007–2012," 2018.

41 Schields, "Closer Ties: The Dutch Caribbean and the Aftermath of Empire, 1942–2012," 2017, p. 186.

42 Ibid., pp. 186–7. Editors' note: see contributions by Kleinmoedig and Sleebe in this section.

6 Conclusion

Although this review summarizes existing research on trans* and same-sex loving people in the Dutch Caribbean, there are many gaps that can be filled by future research. Future research could look more closely at the role of religion and religious practices, including those outside Christianity, on the island. An important contribution to knowledge would be to explore the changing views on LGBTQ+ issues among youth and how new technology platforms such as social media influence discussions on sexuality.[43] The role of social media would also be crucial for a comprehensive study of contemporary ideas in general and arguments about LGBTQ+ issues. Although my dissertation began with how trans* and same-sex desiring people are represented in performances,[44] a broad study of how sexual and gender minorities are represented in different art forms and how artists who identify as LGBTQ+ incorporate specific issues of same-sex sexuality, trans* rights, oppression or agency into their work is needed. More research should be done on trans* communities, especially on the provision of care and gender-affirming surgery. In addition, research on HIV and AIDS should go beyond the medical perspective to explore the social and economic barriers, and research should take a historical perspective by looking at HIV and AIDS initiatives over the years since the 1970s. More research could be done on masculinity, butch and lesbian subcultures and, finally, the history of queer places (such as queer bars) since the 1970s.

Bibliography

Agard-Jones, Vanessa. "Le jeu de qui? Sexual Politics at Play in the French Caribbean." In *Sex and the Citizen. Interrogating the Caribbean*, edited by Faith Smith, 181–200. Charlottesville: University of Virginia Press, 2009.

Alberts, J. F. "Evaluatie aidsvoorlichting Curaçao: Evaluatie-onderzoek naar de effectiviteit van de voorlichting rondom aids op Curaçao" [Evaluation AIDS information Curaçao. Evaluation research on the effectiveness of information on AIDS in Curaçao]. Willemstad: Medical and Health Services of the Island Territory of Curaçao, Department of Epidemiology & Research, 1991.

Alberts, Tineke. *Je lust en je leven: Een inventariserend onderzoek naar relatievorming, sexueel gedrag en de preventie van AIDS op Curaçao* [Your lust and your life: An inventory study of relationship formation, sexual behaviour and the prevention of

43 Isenia, "Queer Sovereignties," 2022, pp. 255–8.

44 Ibid., pp. 238–53.

AIDS in Curaçao]. Willemstad: National AIDS Committee of the Netherlands Antilles; Willemstad: Medical and Health Services of the Island Territory of Curaçao, 1992.

Bernadina, Frieda. "Montamentoe, een beschrijvende en analyserende studie van een Afro-Amerikaanse godsdienst op Curaçao" [Montamentu, a descriptive and analytical study of an Afro-American religion in Curaçao]. PhD diss., University of Amsterdam, 1981.

Broek, Aart G. "A Paragraph in the Unwritten History of Lesbian Love in the Caribbean: Amor di kambrada." In *Mundu yama sinta mira: Womanhood in Curaçao*, edited by Richenel Ansano, Joceline Clemencia, Jeanette Cook, and Martis Eithel, 51–57. Curaçao: Fundashon Publikashon, 1992.

Central Bureau of Statistics Curaçao. *Rapportage resultaten AIDS-enquête Curaçao* [Report results AIDS survey Curaçao]. Willemstad: Central Bureau of Statistics Curaçao, 1987.

Clemencia, Joceline. "Women Who Love Women in Curaçao: From 'Cachapera' to Open Throats: A Commentary in Collage." *Feminist Studies* 22, no. 1 (1996): 81–88.

Colpani, Gianmaria, and Wigbertson Julian Isenia. "Strange Fruits: The Intellectual Labor of Queers of Color in the Netherlands in the 1980s and 1990s." In *Postcolonial Intellectuals in Europe: Portraits, Networks and Connections*, edited by Sandra Ponzanesi and Adriano José Habed, 213–30. Lanham: Rowman & Littlefield Publishers, 2018.

Colpani, Gianmaria, Wigbertson Julian Isenia, and Naomie Pieter. "Archiving Queer of Colour Politics in the Netherlands: A Roundtable Discussion." *Tijdschrift Voor Genderstudies* 22, no. 2 (2019): 163–82.

El-Tayeb, Fatima. *European Others: Queering Ethnicity in Postnational Europe*. Minneapolis: University of Minnesota Press, 2011.

Hoetink, Harry. *Het patroon van de oude Curaçaosche samenleving: Een sociologische studie* [The pattern of the old Curaçaoan society: A sociological study]. Assen: Van Gorcum & Co N.V, 1958.

Isenia, Wigbertson Julian. "Looking for Kambrada: Sexuality and Social Anxieties in the Dutch Colonial Archive, 1882–1923." *Tijdschrift Voor Genderstudies* 22, no. 2 (2019): 125–43.

Isenia, Wigbertson Julian. "Queer Sovereignties: Cultural Practices of Sexual Citizenship in the Dutch Caribbean." PhD Diss., University of Amsterdam, 2022.

Isenia, Wigbertson Julian. "Queer Sovereignties: Re-Imagining Sexual Citizenship from the Dutch Caribbean." In *The Routledge Companion to Sexuality and Colonialism*, edited by Chelsea Schields and Dagmar Herzog, 274–82. Abingdon: Routledge, 2021.

Lier, Rudolf van. *Tropische tribaden. Een verhandeling over homosexualiteit en homosexuele vrouwen in Suriname* [Tropical tribulations. A treatise on homosexuality and homosexual women in Suriname]. Dordrecht: Foris Publications, 1986.

Marks, Arnaud. *Male and Female in the Afro-Curaçaoan Household.* The Hague: KITLV, 1976.

Reus, Tjeerd de. *Geslachtsziekten op Curaçao: Een onderzoek naar het voorkomen en de verspreiding van geslachtsziekten op curaçao door middel van een enquête onder artsen, met daarop aansluitend contactonderzoek in de periode tussen 1 mei 1965 en 1 mei 1966* [Venereal diseases in Curaçao: An investigation into the occurrence and spread of venereal diseases in Curaçao by means of a survey among doctors, with subsequent contact research in the period between May 1, 1965, and May 1, 1966]. Assen: Van Gorcum, 1970.

Römer, René A. *De Curaçaose samenleving* [The Curaçaoan society]. Willemstad: Amigoe N.V, 1998.

Römer, René A. *Un pueblo na kaminda: Een sociologisch historische studie van de Curaçaose samenleving* [A people on the move: A sociological and historical study of Curaçaoan society]. Zutphen: De Walburg Pers, 1979.

Schields, Chelsea. "Closer Ties: The Dutch Caribbean and the Aftermath of Empire, 1942–2012." PhD diss., The City University of New York, 2017. https://academicworks.cuny.edu/gc_etds/1993.

Schields, Chelsea. "Eros against Empire: Visions of Erotic Freedom in Archives of Decolonisation." *Tijdschrift Voor Genderstudies* 22, no. 2 (2019): 145–61.

Schields, Chelsea. "Insurgent Intimacies: Sex, Socialism, and Black Power in the Dutch Atlantic." *Radical History Review* 2020, no. 136 (2020): 98–110.

Schields, Chelsea. "Intimacy and Integration: The Ambivalent Achievement of Marriage Equality in the Dutch Caribbean, 2007–2012." In *Euro-Caribbean Societies in the 21st Century: Offshore Europe and Its Discontents*, edited by Sébastien Chauvin, Peter Clegg, and Bruno Cousin, 176–89. Abingdon: Routledge, 2018.

Wekker, Gloria. *The Politics of Passion: Women's Sexual Culture in the Afro-Surinamese Diaspora.* New York: Columbia University Press, 2006.

Wekker, Gloria. "What's Identity Got to Do with It?: Rethinking Identity in Light of the Mati Work in Suriname." In *Female Desires: Same-Sex Relations and Transgender Practices across Cultures*, edited by Evelyn Blackwood and Saskia Wieringa, 119–38. New York: Columbia University Press, 2009.

CHAPTER 37

My Truth [Mi Bèrdat]

Crisèn Schorea

Some don't want to believe it
and some don't want to know
I've suddenly become
a not fully accepted human being

"You were not like that", they say
without realizing
how much of a heterosexual parody
the me they've known has been

Some consider me a masochist
for coming out and telling my truth
But ironically, I've finally discovered
what real freedom is all about

Tin ku no ke mira
tin ku no ke sa
Segun nan di ripiente m'a bira
un ser humano no kompletamente
aseptá

'Bo no tabata asina,' tur ta bisa
sin realisá
ku esun ku nan a konosé
ta parodia di hétero e tabata

Tin ta haña mi masokista
pasó m'a sali bisa mi bèrdat
Pero porfin, aunke ta parse ironia
m'a deskubrí e sintimentu di libertat

Acknowledgments

This poem was first published in Papiamentu as Schorea, Crisèn. "Mi bèrdat" [My truth]. In *Sinti mi Sintí* [To feel my feelings and or thoughts], 42. Curaçao: printed by the author, 2016. Translation by the author.

 | DOI:10.1163/9789004690882_039

SECTION 4

Gender, the Arts and Popular Culture

CHAPTER 38

Women's Literary Production in the Dutch Caribbean

Elisabeth Echteld and Wim Rutgers

Abstract

This contribution offers an inventory and historical contextualization of women's literary production in the Leeward and Windward Islands of the Dutch Caribbean. Besides highlighting key studies and anthologies, the article outlines some of the recurring concerns, stylistic features and genres of women's writing, such as memoirs, autobiographical novels, poetry and commentaries on societal problems. The contribution seeks to serve as a point of departure for further research and points to gaps in the study of the reception and distribution of women's writing and their public participation in literary activities.

Keywords

literary production – Leeward and Windward islands – genres of women's writing – stylistic features – Dutch Caribbean literary history

1 Preliminary Remarks

In her introduction to the 2002 compilation Kòrsou su muhénan pionero (Curaçao's female pioneers), Jeanne D. Henriquez describes the life, work and public influence of seventy-five Curaçaoan women who were trailblazers or role models in educational, cultural, political and socioeconomic terrains, remarking that "women's histories in Curaçao remain relatively unknown. Gender analysis is certainly in an embryonal stage."[1] In *Ansestro preokupá*

1 "Aki na Kòrsou ainda historia di hende muhé, no ta asina konosí. Por sierto análisis di género mes ta den un fase embrional." Authors' translation. Henriquez and Berry-Haseth, *Kòrsou su muhénan pionero* [Curaçao's women pioneers], 2002, p. 9.

 | DOI:10.1163/9789004690882_040

sosegá (Worried ancestor, rest in peace), Hemayel Martina similarly references thirteen historical figures who served as his inspiration, lamenting that many female "ancestors, who sweat for the Curaçao we enjoy today, do not have their rightful place yet in the history books."[2] Els Kloek's compilation *1001 vrouwen in de 20ste eeuw* (1001 women in the 20th century) includes ten women from the Dutch Caribbean "whose accomplishments or lives captured the attention of contemporaries or historians."[3] All these publications justify the attention to women's writing in terms of a rectification of a historical omission and an injustice that must be healed. The present contribution on the diversity of women's writing in the Dutch Caribbean is similarly motivated by the idea of a necessary restoration. While not claiming to be comprehensive, it nonetheless presupposes representativeness as an eye-opener and a plea for balance in the viewing of a hitherto largely male-dominated literary landscape.

Following Multatuli's famous lines—"what is fiction in particular, becomes truth in general"[4]—the underlying question of this investigation is whether and to what extent literature can contribute to knowledge acquisition on gender issues. Rather than being a mirror of reality, we argue that fiction is a searchlight employed by writers to shed light on and assert, following Multatuli, a "truth in general." Literature has a referential function, pointing to an extralingual reality or context. Literary works would not be readable without reference to the real or conceivable world that we are familiar with or that we are able to imagine based on our experience. On the wings of imagination, literary texts evoke a reality to the reader, offering a dimension radically different from texts of a scientific nature. Literature can thus be understood as a specific form of artistic communication between author and reader, between text and context.

In the following, we offer an overview of women's literary production from the islands of the Dutch Caribbean, combining an empirical and hermeneutic approach. On the one hand, we localize and contextualize the writers as well as the sociocultural environments from which their writings emerged. On the other hand, we elaborate on the different genres, recurring thematic concerns and some common characteristics of the writing. We explore the representation of women's lives and experiences in the writing of the twentieth century. Finally, we point to avenues for further research into the reception

2 Martina, *Ansestro preokupá sosegá* [Worried ancestor, rest in peace], 2010, p. 11.

3 Kloek, *1001 vrouwen in de 20ste eeuw* [1001 women in the 20th century], 2018, p. 9.

4 "Wat verdichtsel is in 't byzonder, waarheid wordt in 't algemeen." Editors' translation. In Multatuli, *Volledige werken. Deel 1* [Complete works. Part 1], 1973, p. 220.

and recognition of the writers. The overview covers women's writing in Papiamentu, Dutch, Spanish and English, the languages most widely spoken on the islands.

2 Historicizing Women's Literary Production

Papiamentu is the language of orature on the ABC islands, just as English remains lingua franca on the SSS islands. The first locally written literature in English dates from the end of the eighteenth century on St. Eustatius, with the English-language *Curaçao Gazette* (1812–1816) and the multilingual *Curaçaosche Courant* (1816–) following in the nineteenth century. As in many parts of the world, the earliest preserved literature of the islands was written by men. Women were, at best, the subject of their inspiration. This remains the case until the end of the nineteenth century. However, if we broaden our view to cover the extended literary landscape and not only consider published single-author works, it can be observed that women played an active role in generating and sustaining literary society toward the late nineteenth and early twentieth century. Members of the colonial elite such as Lelia Capriles, belonging to the Curaçaoan Jewish community, became famous for organizing literary salons in the French style of *soirée littéraire et musicale*, which came to be known as Salon Vredewijk, with a reference to the name of her home, where these literary gatherings took place. The Entre Nous Club, with numerous sociocultural activities, was another example of women's involvement in literary activity, cultivating sensibilities for the appreciation of literature on the islands, albeit among a colonial elite.[5] The popular genre of "poetry albums" of that era are another instance of women's involvement in literary culture. These albums were filled with literary expressions such as poetry and prose on the occasion of various memorable moments for the owner of the album. While detailed research on this literary activity is not available, a study of the phenomenon of poetry albums could offer valuable insights into the development of the literary traditions of female writing.[6]

---

5 Rutgers, "Schrijven is zilver, spreken is goud; oratuur, auratuur en literatuur van de Nederlandse Antillen en Aruba" [Writing is silver; speaking is gold; orature, aurature and literature of the Netherlands Antilles and Aruba], 1994, p. 108.

6 Hints of the popularity of this literary activity are to be found in Pool, *Del Curaçao que se va. Páginas arrancadas de "El libro de mis recuerdos"* [Old time curaçao. Pages torn from "The book of my memories"], 1935, pp. 100–102. See also forthcoming publication by Echteld, "Los recuerdos de Curazao: El legado del polifacético John de Pool" [Memories of Curaçao: The legacy of the multifaceted John de Pool], 2023.

With the influence of regional Catholic missionary institutions in the realms of proselytization, education, media and religious organizations, the Papiamentu language gained prominence on stage and in local newspapers such as *Amigoe di Curaçao*, *La Cruz* and *La Union*. While women were largely absent in missionary literary activities, notable exceptions in the early part of the twentieth century were the nuns in the Aruban parish of Savaneta, who formed a theater group called Las Violetas in the 1930s, which staged popular religious and humorous moral plays.[7] An early reference to literary production on the Windward Islands is found in the work of the poet Susan A. van Romondt, possibly the first poet from St. Maarten, who wrote three nationalistic poems in 1900 and 1901 about the Boer War in South Africa, with titles such as "An Appeal for the Boer," "Welcome to Oom Paul," and "To Her Gracious Majesty Queen Wilhelmina on Her Wedding-Day." The modern English-language theater in the Windward Islands similarly also arose from ecclesiastical circles, with various groupings of the Methodist Church and the Roman Catholic Church active in their parishes with their own theater groups.[8]

The *generashon binti*, or the generation born in the 1920s, witnessed a large number of writers from the islands emerging on the literary scene, especially in Aruba and Curaçao. Most of the women writers made their debut in the years after the Second World War and with the arrival of territorial autonomy in the 1950s. It was only after the mid-twentieth century that women started to make themselves heard and their voices became louder. Three of the most prominent writers of this period are Nydia Ecury, May Henriquez and Nilda Pinto, each of whom deserve a study in their own right. While Ecury and Henriquez have published poetry and prose, Nilda Pinto's contributions are in the realm of orality in the literature of the islands. The works of Oda Blinder, Alette Beaujon and Carla van Leeuwen were written in the 1960s and 1970s, although all of their works were published posthumously, the reasons for which are as yet unknown.

It is only after the uprisings of May 30, 1969, that female writers, particularly in Curaçao, began to emerge in a prominent manner and acquire a place in the literary landscape. The particular dynamics of this is a subject for further research. The canonical anthology of literary history of the Papiamentu language, *Pa saka kara* (To look good), lists more than a hundred writers from the

7 Rutgers, *Honderd jaar Arubaans toneel* [One hundred years of Aruban theater], 2021.

8 Some names mentioned in the *Amigoe di Curaçao* newspaper are Browlia Maillard of the Methodist Church, the Roman Catholic Carty ladies and the parish priests Hendriks and Spekle in the 1920s and 1930s, the reverend sisters of the Dominican Order, Sister Borgia, principal of the St Jozef Mulo in the 1950s and 1960s, as well as the Methodist Women's League: see *Amigoe di Curaçao*, Christmas edition, 1986; and Rutgers, "Schrijven is zilver, spreken is goud," 1994.

twentieth century, of whom no more than sixteen are women—mostly from Curaçao.[9] In the literary study *Kadans, literatuurgeschiedenis* (Kadans, a literary history), an annotated history of writing from the Dutch Caribbean, Nydia Ecury, Diana Lebacs and Philomena Wong are featured with dedicated lemmas, and numerous other female writers are referenced with shorter portraits.[10] The 1970s and 1980s also witnessed the growing popularity of children's literature, books for young adults and poetry, spearheaded by female writers and illustrators.[11] In the context of Aruba and Curaçao, these are writers who published both in Papiamentu as well as in Dutch.[12]

On the Windward Islands, women's writing in English has been published in anthologies, such as in the 2007 volume edited by Rhoda Arrindell, titled *Brother Rich, Nana Sweetie: Creative Writing in St. Martin*. Since the founding of the publisher House of Nehesi in 1982, literary culture in St. Maarten has flourished, with authors such as Cynthia Sharpe, Marian Juo-Finn and many others finding a broader readership.[13]

---

9 The 1998 literary anthology *Pa saka kara: Historia di literatura Papiamentu* [To look good: A history of Papiamentu literature], edited by Aart Broek, Lucille Berry-Haseth and Sidney Joubert, includes lemmas on the following female writers: Nena Bennett (1935) and Lydia Marchena-Geerman (1949) from Aruba; Belén Marchena (1942) and Lupe Reyes (1954) from Bonaire; Nydia Ecury (1926), Renée Hendrikse-Rigaud (1926), Ilse Winkel-Risseeuw (1930), Micky Hart (1930), Mila Palm (1936), Lucille Berry-Haseth (1937), Maria Diwan (1939), Marie-Céline Hendrikse (1942), Heske Levisson (1944) and Gladys do Rego (1948) from Curaçao. The poems of these writers, differing in language and tone, touch on universal themes that cannot be captured under one category.

10 Apart from the names mentioned above, other notable writers featured in the study are Alette Beaujon, Oda Blinder, May Henriquez, Deborah Jack and Myra Römer. See Severing, Rutgers, and Echteld, *Kadans, literatuurgeschiedenis* [Kadans, a literary history], 2006, pp. 171, 214.

11 Curaçaoan writers of books for children and young adults in Papiamentu and Dutch include Nydia Ecury, Sonia Garmers and Diana Lebacs; popular writers in Aruba in the same genre are Desirée Correa, Josette Daal and Frances Kelly. In terms of writing nourished by oral traditions, several works articulate women's perspectives on their traditional social and economic position and self-reflexively advocate change, such as writings by Yolanda Croes, Frida Domacassé, Giselle Ecury, Giolina Henriquez, Carmen Herrera, Rosabelle Illes, Caresse Isings, Alida Kock, Belén Kock-Marchena, Joan Leslie, Munye Oduber-Winklaar, Olga Orman, Belinda de Veer and Olga Buckley.

12 Characteristic of this generation of female writers is the versatility of subject matter in critical descriptions of their position in relation to their environment and kinship ties, as evidenced in the writings of Igma van Putte-de Windt, Els Langenfeld, Henriette de Mezquita and Bernadette Heiligers.

13 Other female writers published by House of Nehesi in St. Maarten include Molicia Egen, Stella Simmons, Yolanda Carter, Wynette Alexander-Greene and Yoslin "Tjai" Morton. See also Gracita Arrindell, *Looking Back to Move Forward*, 2006.

Women's involvement in theater groups in the Windward Islands is a noteworthy part of literary production. There was a burst of theater activities in the 1980s, mostly in St. Maarten, but there were also some active theater groups in St. Eustatius and Saba. The Methodist youth group's Cole Bay Theater Company is one such example from St. Maarten, with Ann Meyers being a driving force. The company participated several times in the Aruba International Theater Festival and became well-known outside St. Maarten. An interinsular theater festival (Festival di teatro interinsular) in Aruba was held in 1979, with, among others, the Saba Cultural Group performing *A Broken Dream*, written by Carmen Simmons and Wycliffe Smith. The all-female theater group The Oualichi Players in St. Maarten was founded by Linda Richardson.[14] The group bore the Carib name for the island, Oualichi or Qualichi, meaning "land of women." She performed for the first time in 1982 at the St. Maarten's Festival of Arts & Culture (SMAFESTAC) with her own texts for the stage. Millicent de Weever founded the group The Teenage Acting Company (TAC) in 1985, with theater productions for children, coming out of her work with the Methodist Agogic Centre School.[15]

Literary anthologies and studies of writing from the SSS islands serve as important repositories of information on women's literary production. Crucial reference points are Wycliffe S. Smith's *Windward Island Verse: A Survey of Poetry in the Dutch Windward Islands* (1981) and *Winds above the Hills* (1982), which references prose, drama and especially poetry by women in St. Maarten.[16] M. P. Sypkens-Smit's *Beyond the Tourist Trap: A Study of St. Maarten Culture* (1995) highlights storytelling traditions and oral literature on the island, although it does not specifically investigate gender perspectives in these practices.[17] Fabian Adekunle Badejo's *Salted Tongues: Modern Literature in St. Martin* (2003) includes brief appraisals of the literary works of women from the

14 Editors' note: see contribution by Linda Richardson in this section.

15 See "Schuchtere start Kunst-Academie op St. Maarten" [Modest start of art academy in St. Maarten], *Beurs- en Nieuwsberichten* (Curaçao), July 5, 1988, p. 4.

16 In this anthology, Wycliffe Smith speaks of various genres of poetry such as society oriented, patriotic and national verse as well as thematic clusters such as nature, religion, love or identity poetry. The study references nine female writers who published prior to 1980.

17 See especially chapter 7, "St. Maarten Culture Today," emphasizing literary cultures on the island.

island.[18] Finally, the publications of the House of Nehesi are an indispensable resource for studies of women's writing in the Windward Islands.[19]

Apart from historicizing women's writing, it is equally relevant to take into account women's reading habits. The serial novels published by the Catholic press in Papiamentu were a hugely popular genre in the first half of the twentieth century. More than twenty serial novels by male writers such as W. E. Kroon, M. A. Fraai, S. M. Suriel and J. S. Sint Iago were consumed by a wide readership, most certainly including women.[20] These serial novels often discussed marital and extramarital relationships, the morality of female characters and their pivotal roles in nuclear family relationships, including relations between parents and children as well as between extended families. From the perspective of the historicization of women's literary production, it is important to consider their role as readers and discussants of these serial novels. A point of departure for future research could be readers' letters to the editor on the serial novels, which might offer a glimpse of possible public debates at the time.

The following paragraphs will attempt to describe and delineate different genres of women's writing.

3 Biographies and Memoirs

The vast societal changes that the islands underwent following the end of the First World War, and their impact on women's lives, are recorded in several memoirs and biographies. The 1944 memoir by the educational reformer, writer and politician Laura Wernet-Paskel on her life in Aruba, *Ons eilandje Aruba* (Our little island Aruba), was characterized by a critical approach to the island and its people.[21] As a historical document, it is now considered as a part

18 Among the works annotated in Adekunle Badejo's study are: Drisana Deborah Jack, *The Rainy Season*, 1997; Ruby Bute, *Golden Voices of S'maatin*, 1989; Ruby Bute, *Floral Bouquets*, 1996; as well as Linda Richardson's *Pregnant Women*, a play that was staged in St. Maarten in the early 1980s.

19 Noteworthy recent publications include Rhoda Arrindell, *Language, Culture, and Identity in St. Martin*, 2014; Patricia G. Turnbull, *Ti Koko and Kush Kush*, 2018; and Yvonne Weekes, *Nomad*, 2019.

20 These novels are discussed in Broek, "The Rise of a Caribbean Island's Literature: The Case of Curaçao and Its Writing in Papiamentu," 1990. Editors' note: see also contribution by Broek in this volume.

21 Wernet-Paskel, *Ons eilandje Aruba* [Our little island Aruba], 1992.

of the educational canon.[22] The former prime minister of Curaçao, Maria Liberia-Peters, published a memoir about her experience as the first female head of state.[23] Biographies such as Josette Capriles Goldish's *Shon May: Renaissance Woman of Curacao* (2011) offer an entry point into the lives and experiences of Jewish women on the island.

4 Autobiographical Writing and Coming-of-Age Novels

There are several examples of strongly autobiographical novels in Dutch Caribbean women's writing by authors such as Diana Lebacs, Echi Cijntje and Bernadette Heiligers.[24] Characteristic of these works are the perspectives of women who are, as it were, doubly colonized as young women of color. As women who grow up into self-awareness and self-reliance, their experiences speak to the social group of women in general as well as to the specific political situation of the main character's country. The grandmother often appears as the personification of the oral tradition, a strong figure who passes on culture and womanhood to the granddaughter. The themes discussed in these works center around race, class and the role of gender in cultural identification. With the opportunities that education offers, women develop into independent individuals.

These coming-of-age novels can be seen as a counterpart to the male-dominated genre of childhood novels or the traditionally masculine bildungsroman in the ways female sexuality, kinship and selfhood are portrayed. They can be distinguished from autobiographical novels to the extent that the focus is primarily on the struggles of a young female protagonist. Diana Lebacs's 1971 debut novel *Sherry* presents a psychological portrait of a young Antillean woman and simultaneously comments on the sociopolitical transformations on the island following the May 1969 uprisings through her eyes. Her novels describe the awareness of the dissonance between the protagonist's carefree childhood experiences and her gradual alienation from the colonial reality, in

22 Editors' note: see contribution by Dresscher-Lambertus in this volume for a critical feminist reading of Wernet-Paskel.

23 Wal, Tromp, and Wal, *Politiek heeft een prijs: Leven en werk van Maria Liberia-Peters* [Politics has a price: The life and work of Maria Liberia-Peters], 2009. Editors' note: see contribution by Liberia-Peters in this volume.

24 Echi Cijntje, *Gacha: E mucha di Sabaneta* [Gacha, the child of Sabaneta], 2010; Bernadette Heiligers, *Van zo ver gekomen* [Come thus far], 2021; Diana Lebacs, *Sherry: Het begin van het begin* [Sherry: The beginning of the beginning], 1971.

which safety, unity, integration and an existence free of worry appear to no longer be possible.

In the coming-of-age novel, it is often an adult main character who looks back on her own childhood, becoming aware of the fact that this idealized childhood will never return and recognizing with irony the bittersweet experience of aging. Education plays an important role in this maturing process, as colonial and postcolonial education often meant alienation from the self-evident nature of the home environment of the "creole world," which is replaced by a cultural world bearing no connection whatsoever with the world at home. It is through education that the alienation process from child to adult is initiated and continued because the growing child cannot integrate these two different worlds into their life. Typically, the daughter blames the mother for this, and the mother, who personifies and defends the home environment, becomes an obstacle for the daughter to embrace the world of education. The strong emergence and maturing of the young female protagonist form key motifs of the coming-of-age novel.

5 Social Realism

It is striking that the works of contemporary novelists from Aruba, Bonaire and Curaçao address local issues with great critical attention, accentuating appalling living and social conditions and imagining a way out that offers hope for a better future for their island.[25] Instances of this are novels such as Giselle Ecury's *Erfdeel. Zoektocht naar een vader* (Inheritance. In search of a father), published in 2006, which addresses the consequences of growing up without a father, thereby touching on broader questions of migration and its attendant societal transformations. *Het geheim van Gracia* (The secret of Gracia, 2008) by Myra Römer delves into the lifelong impact of the rape of a sixteen-year-old schoolgirl at the hands of a substitute European Dutch teacher and her attempt to reclaim selfhood and identity against the backdrop of the sociopolitical changes on the island.[26] *Schutkleur* (Camouflage), a novel published in 2015 by Bernadette Heiligers, addresses racial and social sensitivities in Curaçao. *De lichtkamer* (The light room, 2015) by Henriette de Mezquita focuses on issues of failing healthcare in Curaçao.

25 This is the case in the writings of Giselle Ecury, Bernadette Heiligers, Els Langenfeld, Diana Lebacs, Henriette de Mezquita and Myra Römer, to name a few prominent examples.

26 For a detailed study of this book, see Cornet, "21st Century Curaçaoan Women Writers: Revisiting, Destabilizing and (Re)imagining the 'Kurasoleña,'" 2013.

In recent decades, writers such as Philomena Wong and Diana Lebacs have spoken out and warned against drug abuse on the islands, lamenting the presence of *chollers* (the generic name given to drug addicts) on the streets, who lead to people feeling unsafe but who are nevertheless also victims of their addiction, fed by ruthless local dealers and their international criminal contacts. The social realism of their writing is characterized by a subgenre that has been called "narco-realism" in the Latin American context.[27] These texts feature an intertwining of the underworld and the elite world, in which poor, underprivileged young people often become the victim of criminal drug gangs. In 1992, the Aruban poet Philomena Wong published a Papiamentu poem, "Sin titulo" (Untitled), in which she addressed the alarming rise of drug abuse on the island: "Cristina becomes Christ / hallucinating / temporary madness / convulsions seize the soul / possess the body."[28] In Diana Lebacs's *De langste maand* (The longest month) from 1994, one of the main motives is the drug addiction of the character Evy, an attentive and well-mannered young man who does not succeed in finding a job on the island of Curaçao after graduation, succumbs to the drug mafia and is eventually rescued by a good friend.

All these novels highlight an urgent sense of responsibility toward personal life and social behavior and plead for literature as a means of shaping a sensitive attitude toward societal challenges. They appeal to basic moral principles, an ethical attitude to life and personal and social integrity. Rather than being psychological investigations of their main characters, these novels cast a critical eye on a range of socioeconomic and sociopolitical issues. They are optimistic in tone, despite being fiercely critical, holding up a magnifying glass to the readers in which their social visions are reflected, but they ultimately offer perspectives and solutions to the problems charted and a better future for those who make the right choices and take responsibility for their actions. It would be worthwhile investigating the impact of the women's movements and transnational civil rights movements on literary production by women in the islands.

27 Rutgers, "Literair ethos: Schrijvers met de urgentie van een moreel kompas" [Literary ethos; Writers with an urgency of a moral compass], 2020.

28 "Cristina ta bira cristo / halucina, / locura momentaneo / ta podera un alma, / domina un curpa." Authors' translation. This poem appeared in 1993 in *Crusando frontera / Crossing borders*.

6 Poetry

Poetry, just like the local prose of the Leeward Islands, is multilingual, with a common preference for the Papiamentu language. Thematically, women's lyrical writings range from personal reflections to socially critical poetry. The form of published poetry remains close to the oral tradition: it is poetry that is intended to be recited and is therefore often performed to a live audience. Contemporary poets seek out a language and form that distances itself from inherited European genres and styles. Apart from this, there are poets whose works have a hermetic character and demand intensive analysis and interpretation. The role of women in cultures of orature on the islands is another subject worthy of further research.[29]

It is a popular practice to write poetry for various occasions, with verses in praise of flags and anthems and marking national holidays, Mother's Day and carnival. Initiatives such as Arte di Palabra organize poetry competitions for school pupils and across the ABC islands. The abundance of poetry/creative writing courses and their popularity among women further attests to the significance of poetry for women's self-expression. Due to the smaller editions and lower costs, poetry volumes outnumber prose and drama publications and have thus been a relatively accessible form for many women writers.

7 Writing for the Theater

In contrast to the multilingualism of prose and poetry writing, play texts are almost exclusively written in Papiamentu in the ABC islands and in English in the SSS islands, although relatively little is published. Stage theater came to Curaçao in the early nineteenth century and to Aruba in the early twentieth century, while the other islands also had their own theater groups around the turn of the twentieth century. A specific mode of orally disseminating literary texts takes place in theatrical performances and the broader activities of theater associations and companies, such as in Thalia, established in Curaçao in 1967, and Mascaruba, established in Aruba in 1961. The histories and repertoires of these companies attest to the prominent presence of women as authors of original works, translations and adaptations and in the roles of directors and actors. Noteworthy playwrights, directors and performers in Curaçao were May

29 For an exploration of women's role in orature, see Allen, "Tur hende a papia un ko. African-Curaçaoan Women Conveying Messages in Traditional Folk Songs at the Beginning of the XXth Century," 2002.

Henriquez and Nydia Ecury, who also brought international dramatic works to the stage through Papiamentu translations and theatrical adaptations. Laura Quast and Diana Lebacs are the representatives of a younger generation of theater makers in Curaçao. In Aruba, Burny Every and Carmen Herrera are well-known theater practitioners.[30]

8 Contexts

In the inventory of women's literary practices charted above, we have sought to present an initial overview of a range of works and writers. This inventory is an initial step and must be followed by further detailed analysis, interpretation and investigation. We conclude this overview with two areas that require further attention that have not yet been adequately researched. One of these concerns the position and role of women in the material contexts of the literary field, their participation in the literary landscape of production, distribution and reception as publishers, editors, bookstore owners, reviewers and broadcasters. Another area concerns the extent of recognition of women's literary activities: for instance, in their representation in anthologies and biographies; as literary award recipients; or, indeed, in other forms of symbolic recognition, such as literary prizes or streets or schools named after a woman. All these efforts are necessary to bring about a much-needed restoration and visibility of women's writing as well as a more just and balanced view of the literary landscapes of the Dutch Caribbean.

Acknowledgments

The first draft of this contribution was translated from Dutch by Hein van Maarschalkerwaart. Subsequent revisions and translations have been handled by the editors.

Bibliography

Adekunle Badejo, Fabian. *Salted Tongues: Modern Literature in St. Martin*. Philipsburg: House of Nehesi Publishers, 2003.

30 See Rutgers, *Honderd jaar Arubaans toneel*, 2021.

Allen, Rose Mary. "Tur hende a papia un ko'. African-Curaçaoan Women Conveying Messages in Traditional Folk Songs at the Beginning of the XXth Century." *Calabash: A Journal of Caribbean Arts and Letters* 2, no. 1 (2002): 157–73. https://doi.org/10.33682/41xr-0qcy.

Arrindell, Gracita R. *Looking Back to Move Forward: Speeches from the Forum of Former Prime Ministers of the Netherlands Antilles*. Philipsburg: House of Nehesi Publishers, 2006.

Arrindell, Rhoda. *Brother Rich, Nana Sweetie: Creative Writing in St. Martin*. Philipsburg: House of Nehesi Publishers, 2007.

Arrindell, Rhoda. *Language, Culture, and Identity in St. Martin*. Philipsburg: House of Nehesi Publishers, 2014.

Broek, Aart G., Lucille Berry-Haseth, and Sidney M. Joubert, eds. *Pa saka kara: Antologia di literatura Papiamentu* [To look good: A history of Papiamentu literature]. 3 vols. Willemstad: Fundashon Pierre Lauffer, 1998.

Broek, Aart G. "The Rise of a Caribbean Island's Literature: The Case of Curaçao and Its Writing in Papiamentu." PhD Diss., VU Amsterdam, 1990.

Bute, Ruby. *Floral Bouquets: To the Daughters of Eve*. San Francisco: Columbia Publishers, 1996.

Bute, Ruby. *Golden Voices of S'maatin*. Philipsburg: House of Nehesi Publishers, 1989.

Cijntje, Echi. *Gacha: E mucha di Sabaneta* [Gacha, the child of Sabaneta]. Willemstad: Prins Bernard Cultuurfonds, 2010.

Cornet, Florencia V. "21st Century Curaçaoan Women Writers: Revisiting, Destabilizing and (Re)Imagining the 'Kurasoleña.'" *Dutch Crossing* 37, no. 1 (March 2013): 93–108. https://doi.org/10.1179/0309656412Z.00000000027.

Echteld, Elisabeth. "Los recuerdos de Curazao: El legado del polifacético John de Pool" [Memories of Curaçao: The legacy of the multi-faceted John de Pool]. In *Caribbean Convivialities and Caribbean Sciences: Inclusive Approaches to the Study of the Languages, Literatures and Cultures of the Dutch Caribbean and Beyond*, edited by N. Faraclas, R. Severing, E. Echteld, and S. Delgado, 13–22. Curaçao: University of Curaçao; Puerto Rico: Universidad de Río Piedras, 2023.

Ecury, Giselle. *Erfdeel. Zoektocht naar een vader* [Inheritance. In search of a father]. Amsterdam: Uitgeverij Conserve, 2006.

Goldish Capriles, Josette. *Shon May: Renaissance Woman of Curaçao*. Curaçao: Port'i Heru Publications, 2011.

Heiligers, Bernadette. *Schutkleur*. Haarlem: In de Knipscheer, 2015.

Heiligers, Bernadette. *Van zo ver gekomen* [Come thus far]. Haarlem: In de Knipscheer, 2021.

Henriquez, Jeanne D, and Lucille Berry-Haseth. *Kòrsou su muhénan pionero* [Curaçao's women pioneers]. Willemstad: Archivo Nashonal di Antia Hulandes, 2002.

Jack, Drisana Deborah. *The Rainy Season.* Philipsburg: House of Nehesi Publishers, 1997.

Kloek, Els, ed. *1001 vrouwen in de 20ste eeuw* [1001 women in the 20th century]. Nijmegen: Uitgeverij Vantilt, 2018.

Lebacs, Diana. *Sherry: Het begin van een begin* [Sherry: The beginning of a beginning]. The Hague: Leopold, 1971.

Lebacs, Diana Melinda. *De langste maand* [The longest month]. Haarlem: In de Knipscheer, 2005.

Martina, Hemayel. *Ansestro preokupá sosegá* [Worried ancestor, rest in peace]. Curaçao: Curaçaosche Courant N.V., 2010.

Mezquita, Henriette de. *De lichtkamer* [The light room]. Haarlem: In de Knipscheer, 2015.

Multatuli. *Volledige werken. Deel 1* [Complete works. Part 1]. Edited by Garmt Stuiveling. Amsterdam: G.A. van Oorschot, 1950.

Pool, John de. *Del Curaçao que se va. Páginas arrancadas de "El libro de mis recuerdos"* [Old time curaçao. Pages torn from "The book of my memories"]. Santiago: Ed. Ercilla, 1935.

Römer, Myra. *Het geheim van Gracia* [The secret of Gracia]. Amsterdam: Atlas, 2008.

Romondt, Susan A. "An Appeal for the Boer. St. Martin Dutch West-Indies." *Curaçaosche Courant*, April 12, 1900.

Romondt, Susan A. "To Her Gracious Majesty Queen Wilhelmina on Her Wedding-Day. St. Martin Dutch West-Indies." De *Curaçaosche Courant*, February 8, 1901.

Romondt, Susan A. "Welcome to Oom Paul. St. Martin, October 1900." De *Curaçaosche Courant*, November 16, 1900.

Rutgers, Wim. *Het nulde hoofdstuk van de Antilliaanse literatuur: Koloniale poëzie in de Curaçaosche Courant* [Chapter zero of the Antillean literature: Colonial poetry in the *Curaçaosche Courant*]. Oranjestad: Charuba, 1988.

Rutgers, Wim. *Honderd jaar Arubaans toneel* [One hundred years of Aruban theater]. Aruba: Werkgroep Caraïbische Letteren, 2021. https://docplayer.nl/212124667-Honderd-jaar-arubaans-toneel.html.

Rutgers, Wim. "Schrijven is zilver, spreken is goud; oratuur, auratuur en literatuur van de Nederlandse Antillen en Aruba" [Writing is silver; speaking is gold; orature, aurature and literature of the Netherlands Antilles and Aruba]. PhD diss., Universiteit Utrecht, 1994.

Rutgers, Wim. "Literair ethos: Schrijvers met de urgentie van een moreel kompas" [Literary ethos: Writers with an urgency of a moral compass]. In *Navigating Crosscurrents. Trans-Linguality, Trans-Culturality and Trans-Identification in the Dutch Caribbean and Beyond*, edited by Nicholas Faraclas, Ronald Esperano Severing, Christa Weijer, Elisabeth Agnes Maria Echteld, and Wim Rutgers, 87–105. Willemstad: University of Curaçao, 2020.

"Schuchtere start Kunst-Academie op St. Maarten" [Modest start of art academy in St. Maarten]. *Beurs- en Nieuwsberichten* (Curaçao), July 5, 1988, p. 4.

Severing, Ronald, Wim Rutgers, and Elisabeth Agnes Maria Echteld. *Kadans, literatuurgeschiedenis* [Kadans, a literary history]. Curaçao: Fundashon pa Planifikashon di Idioma, 2006.

Severing, Ronnie, Wim Rutgers, and Elisabeth Agnes Maria Echteld. *Kadans: Literaire ontwikkeling en literaire begrippen.* Curaçao: Fundashon pa Planifikashon di Idioma, 2002.

Smith, Wycliffe S., ed. *Winds above the Hills: A Collection of Poems from St. Maarten, Netherlands Antilles.* St. Maarten: St. Maarten Council on the Arts, 1982.

Smith, Wycliffe S., ed. *Windward Islands Verse: A Survey of Poetry in the Dutch Windward Islands.* St. Maarten: printed by the author, 1981.

Sypkens Smit, M. P. *Beyond the Tourist Trap: A Study of Sint Maarten Culture.* Publication of the Foundation for Scientific Research in the Caribbean Region 136. Amsterdam: Natuurwetenschappelijke Studiekring voor het Caraïbisch Gebied, 1995.

Turnbull, Patricia G. *Ti Koko and Kush Kush.* St. Maarten: House of Nehesi Publishers, 2017.

Wal, Hellen A. van der, Emsley D. Tromp, and Nancy S. van der Wal. *Politiek heeft een prijs: Leven en werk van Maria Liberia-Peters* [Politics has a price: The life and work of Maria Liberia-Peters]. Amsterdam: SWP, 2009.

Weekes, Yvonne Mary Selina. *Nomad.* Philipsburg: House of Nehesi Publishers, 2019.

Wernet-Paskel, Laura. *Ons eilandje Aruba [1941]* [Our little island Aruba (1941)]. Zutphen: Walburg, 1992.

CHAPTER 39

The Semiotics of Dark Clouds in Songs and Poems of Elia Isenia: Art as Female Therapy

Joceline Clemencia

Abstract

This contribution explores the life and work of the singer and poet Elia Isenia, the first woman to win the tumba music contest in Curaçao. It discusses the challenges she faced in a male-dominated cultural field, her motivations for creating and sharing her art and the changes that her work, in turn, brought to the gender dynamics of the Curaçaoan traditional music scene. The author also reflects on the importance of narrating and sharing the stories of women for the construction of a Caribbean cultural tradition/history in relation to African heritage and colonial legacies and the methods one might use to uncover cultural traditions, such as live music performances, that do not rely on extensive written records.

Keywords

tambú – Elia Isenia – tumba music – semiotics – Curaçao

> For women … poetry is not a luxury
> It is a vital necessity of our existence[1]
>
> —Audre Lorde

Her songs made her famous in Curaçao. Her strong lyrics are about the every-day struggle she has waged. Elia Isenia is especially known as a singer of *tambú*

1 See Lorde, *Sister Outsider: Essays and Speeches*, 1984, p. 37.

 | DOI:10.1163/9789004690882_041

songs.[2] She also sings *tumba*[3] and mariachi[4] songs. Her popularity took a big leap forward early in 1991 when she made history by becoming the first woman to win the twenty-year old Curaçaoan *tumba* contest,[5] which provides the road march for each year's carnival parade. As the first *tumba* queen in the male-dominated contest, Elia Isenia drew the public's attention to her songs. Very few people, however, know that Elia Isenia has been writing poetry ever since she was a child.

In this essay, I will explore some texts of multitalented singer and poet Elia Isenia. I will look at the messages they convey and at the symbols used to communicate the messages. In her journey toward awareness, Isenia made her own otherness, her own standards of survival, and proved to other women that self-realization is within their reach too. She is a source of inspiration for other women looking for self-development. Writing about women such as Isenia thus becomes a political act. A political act of subversion because it challenges the patriarchal standards of art, beauty and female behavior. Marjorie Thorpe expressed it as follows: "It is the business of the feminist critic ... to deconstruct male patterns of thought and social practice, and to reconstruct female experience previously hidden or overlooked."[6]

Elaine Savory Fido considered that

> each paper and book completed takes us closer not only to understanding our woman-authored literature but to also encouraging it to grow.... If we put together many single texts by different women writers, our patchwork quilt of their creative vision becomes a communal one, and we build a special kind of literary tradition, different from the great individual writer school which has ended to dominate literary traditions in the past.[7]

2 The *tambú* was formerly sung by women. Elia Isenia is one of the few women who still sing *tambú*. Nowadays, *tambú* singers are mostly men.

3 Although both the *tumba* and the *tambú* are of African origin (according to ethnomusicologist Eric La Croes, the *tumba* developed from the *tambú*), the former is played with modern instruments, whereas the latter is played with the original instruments (hoe and little drum). Editors' note: see also contribution by De Jong in this section.

4 Mariachi: orchestral Mexican music. Elia Isenia showed courage to integrate in a mariachi group, which is usually formed by only men.

5 This occurrence marked a very important turn in the musical traditions on the island. Isenia became famous, drew the attention of everybody and contributed with her victory to the upgrading of women, of performing women of working-class origin and also of the *tambú*, because now it was a queen, although black, singing the *tambú*.

6 Thorpe, "Feminism and the Female Authored West Indian Novel," 1988, p. 319.

7 Savory Fido, "Where Do We Go from Here?" 1988, pp. 337–8.

Focusing on the female experience as expressed in Elia Isenia's songs, whether as singer or composer, we notice the dominant motifs of envy, harassment and survival carrying the following messages: the envy of people will not break me; I am aware of my talents, abilities and victories.

The recurring topics of her poetry—such as the woman, the mother, religion and the countryside—appear imbedded in messages like: a woman's life, a woman's struggle; Bandabou,[8] a vast oasis; and society, or look at the life we live.

Although the issues and the situations depicted in Isenia's work have a strong realistic value, and, in her style, simplicity prevails, it would be a denial of her artistry to look at her work exclusively in terms of its mimetic value. Therefore, this essay will consider both perspectives: the evocation of reality and the artistic devices used.

1 "My Name Is Sit and See"

One of the main songs in Elia's repertoire that contributed in a significant way to her popularity is the *tambú* "Sinta Mira" (Sit 'n See). [...]

I have chosen this song as the opening one because it holds a whole gamut of elements, strongly rooted in Curaçao's traditions. The totality of these elements forms a solid base from which Isenia operates. In the first place, we have the title "Mi yama sinta mira" (My name is sit and see), based on the old expression "mundu yama sinta mira," which holds a conception of wisdom, of standing aside and observing the greatness of the universe. The universe has in it everything a person needs, including justice. That is why we do not need to proceed in a hasty manner. Everything has its right moment in the universe.

From history we learn that *sinta mira* also conceptualized a form of resistance of black people during slavery. Black people used it to express their mental superiority over the white man, although the latter had all the power. The concept is generally linked with men, white and rich men, representing power. It speaks of the fact that the world changes all the time. The ones who are up today can be down tomorrow. The *mundu yama sinta mira* conception departs from factors such as patriarchy, power and seniority.

It is usually used with reference to older men (in former times mostly to rich men). Elia Isenia revolutionizes the conception by applying it to a woman (herself) and to the working class. While she revolutionizes the concept of this old popular wisdom, she applies it at the same time to the traditional *tambú*.

8 Bandabou is the name for Curaçao's countryside.

So, for Isenia, tradition and change can be perfectly matched. She does not break with or violate traditions by applying them to a woman; on the contrary, she makes use of them. Thus, her contribution is that of making traditions richer by adding dimensions to them. By doing so, her contribution becomes a revolutionary one.

As we deconstruct the text, we see that she starts establishing the powerful context within which she acts: "everything I do is legal according to the laws of ancestry, because parenthood or legacy has determined my condition. Hence, I speak with the authority that the inheritance from my ancestors provides. My performance must be accepted as any other would. Her wisdom speaks too: take good notice of the fact that I will sit back and, as a quiet observer, watch how the ones lacking the social and racial awareness I possess (*lembelansa*/bootlickers; sons of white niggers) can go on forever without being able to change my attitude because I know life." So trying to make her go back and change her luck (i.e., her progress) won't work. This is not a frustrated woman speaking but a self-assured woman who noticed that, whenever she had luck in one way or another, people would start nagging at her. In fact, the song reveals the result of the process she went through. What we can also notice in this song is a sense of communality in Isenia for she likes to help.

And, finally, there is the fact that she has changed her name so it will fit the person she really is better. Do not misunderstand: my name is no longer X (a woman people can harass), no, it is Sit and See (the survivor). She adopts the identity she pleases because she considers it to be correct. This is a very powerful stance where she decides to determine her own life by taking her identity into her own hands. In fact, we can consider the messages of "Mi yama sinta mira" as symbolic of Elia Isenia's work. We detect determination, struggle and the triumph that will come in the end. Thorpe quotes feminist critic Mary Ellman's list of eleven major stereotypes of femininity presented by male writers and critics. These include formlessness, passivity, instability, confinement, piety, materiality, spirituality, irrationality, compliancy and, finally, "the two incorrigible figures" of witch and shrew.[9] Elia Isenia opposes the stereotypes with assertiveness, wisdom and strength. A misogynist interpretation of "Mi yama sinta mira" would depict a woman who fears what other people think of her. Even the witch-shrew approach could be applied if we interpret her words as potential threats uttered by a witch eager to eliminate the people surrounding her. Isenia as a witch might get back the people who envy her. However, a reconstructed interpretation of "Mi yama sinta mira" shows us a woman who

9 Thorpe, "Feminism and the Female Authored West Indian Novel," 1988, p. 321.

has encountered problems on her path and has sought and found solutions for them. Despite the adversities she has met, for example, the dislike and criticism of people, she not only survived but even grew. This obviously does not fit the image of a woman who has to suffer in silence according to the stereotypes of passivity and irrationality. That is why she had to change her name. I am not who you want me to be. I am Sit and See, not Suffer and Cry. […]

2 Double-Bottomed Language

Elia Isenia reveals that she likes *tambú* for its rich dimensions of indirectness. […]

Metaphorical speech, a device used in *tambú* as well as a form of speech practiced as art by the elderly and influenced by the reality of slavery, has maintained its vitality and attraction despite modernization. This trait has been pointed out as a vital one for the interpretation of Curaçaoan oral literature.[10] Elia Isenia restores in her songs the worldwide old tradition that Vargas calls *lo no dicho* (the unspoken), that is, that which does not manifest itself at the surface of the expression but lies underneath.[11] When decoding, we must look for the following feature: "it may also happen that poetry uses the same words and the same grammar as everyday language, but … poetry expresses concepts and things by indirection. To put simply, a poem says one thing and means another."[12] As a true heiress of her ancestors' tradition, Elia Isenia recognizes

10 In my study of the Curaçaoan author and ethnologist Elis Juliana, I arrived, with Juliana, at the conclusion that, in the euphemism culture, rooted in slavery, the people developed an indirect way of speaking, which they even practiced as an art form. It was, however, an art of life or death, and those who did not know how to practice it could not survive, because the oppression of slavery did not allow the slaves to speak out freely. This camouflage or art of euphemism meant that interpreters of *tambú* songs arrived at entirely the wrong conclusions in their strictly literal interpretations. The hidden meaning—which, in Clemencia, *Het grote camouflagespel van de OPI: Een thematische benadering van de poëzie van Elis Juliana* [The OPI's great game of camouflage: A thematic approach to the poetry of Elis Juliana], 1989, I called double-bottomed language because it is like a box with two bottoms, one visible, the other hidden—was unreachable for the *shon* or slave owner. This is also the reason why such lyrics appear foolish at first sight to superficial outsiders. Editors' note: On double-bottomed language, see contribution by Louis Römer in this volume.

11 Vargas, *Una semiología del texto poético* [A semiology of poetic texts], 1989, p. 91.

12 Rifaterre cited in Cocco-de Filippis, *Estudios semióticos de poesía Dominicana* [Semiotic studies of Dominican poetry], 1984, p. 15.

the strength that lies in this discourse, which allows a blade-sharp approach covered with the subtlety of poetic language. […]

The envy of people, described earlier by Isenia as dark clouds, which we can also interpret here as being her female opponents, are represented in this song by the verbs: bother/underestimate/insult/slander and drain blood/humbug/bother/tire/make mad.

A closer look at these categories reveals three levels: level one refers to a process she went through and is expressed by verbs such as: bother; drain blood; underestimate. Level two represents a yet stronger process: insult; slander; humbug. At level three, she underwent both processes and this had the following growing effect: bother; tire; make mad.

At the opposite, we find her resistance modes: "I'll get angry and start revealing things," that is, compromising facts about wealthy people or people who want to appear wealthy (wearing jewelry). This we notice in the contrast: "I have neither gold nor silver." Her message is that she has put up with it for a long time. She was able to wait intelligently for the right moment to go public. But when she thinks it appropriate, she will get hmm [*sic*], abandon diplomacy and become as sharp as necessary. Her strongest weapon is obviously that of revealing secrets. […]

Elia Isenia discovered, like other *tambú* singers, that her art could be her defense mechanism. From that moment on, she effectively made use of this weapon. We also notice that Isenia searches for a link with the old traditions of her island. She "sings" an opponent at the drum. As a woman, she employs *tambú* as her resistance. […]

3 The Motif of Dark Clouds

The dark clouds that appear here are: "Making your hints" whenever I pass by; there are things of my life being discussed behind my back. People talk about me. "You make me suffer. You slander me." Slander occupies a very important place in the songs of Isenia. Slander is a manifestation of envy.

The opposing resistance is implied: "If their tongues were wounds, today my skin would be all torn." But her skin is not open, so their behavior obviously did not affect her. In fact, her real resistance is the singing. The slander is as effective on her as water on grease. […]

Consequently, her songs are about her own liberation because she freed herself from fear. Fear of what people might say about her, of their envy. When younger, she would keep quiet if attacked. She had no choice as a country girl, as a young mother. But she developed her awareness. Now she opens her mouth, sings back, talks back. She pictures the kind of woman people, herself included, despise and pictures at the same time the woman she has become. This dichotomy shows us that Elia Isenia's songs are the songs of freedom. She freed herself through her life story. The following songs complete the picture of a woman determined to keep on growing. She sang "Baha for di mi lomba" (Get off my back) and "Viktoria" after she won the *tumba* contest and some people questioned her victory.[13] [...]

A look at Elia Isenia's poetry reveals an interesting pattern when contrasted with the *tambú* songs. Her collection of poems deals for the most part with the relationship between women and men.[14] Also in the poems about the relationship between men and women we notice the presence of darkness caused by clouds, that is, problems. But her attitude toward them here is quite different from that in her songs. Notice that she states: I am scared to let you know. She never expressed fear in her songs. She considers in this poem that there is nothing left for her than to step back. The militancy we experienced in her songs is absent in her poetry. Here, she is vulnerable. [...]

It seems that Isenia reserves her poetry to express her most intimate feelings. This could be one of the reasons why she has not published her poetry. Her poetry is of past times; her *tambú* is of the present. Her poetry would show her weakness, her pain, her suffering. In her songs, she does not sing of problems anymore, she sings of how she defeated them.

The interpretation of Elia Isenia's poetry and songs would benefit from reference to her biography. Both gender and the human experience are fundamental categories of literary as well as social analysis. And Elia Isenia herself confirms that she often sings and writes about her own life: "Everytime I sing, even when I picture another woman, I do sing about my own life. My songs are about life's harshness, like my life was. A hard life and a life of joy." [...]

---

13 Editors' note: see Anita, *Baha for di mi lomba, dediká na Nicolaas Susana (Shon Colá)*. Fundashon Pincho y su grupo, 1991, LP record.

14 Her substantial collection of poems has been reduced by a ferocious fire that destroyed her house some years ago. On that occasion, she wrote an acrostic forming, from top to bottom, the sentence: My house got burned at Jan Kok. Her present collection consists of poems she managed to save from the fire and the ones of recent date. Frequent topics—such as her home country Bandabou, religion, nature's beauty and women—confirm her commitment to life and society. The collection also includes some rhythmical poems, such as "Elia den yobida" (Elia in the rain).

4 Poetry as Vital Material and Spiritual Necessity

Isenia's poems even speak about sacrifice, which she definitely did not intend to make, according to her songs. She could not afford the luxury of writing abstract poetry or composing abstract songs. When she wrote it was to soothe her pain. When she sang it was to defend herself. The art she created had a practical and direct goal.[15] As the statement quoted from Audre Lorde at the beginning of this paper says, poetry is not a luxury for women but a vital necessity in their existence. It was a vital spiritual and material necessity for Isenia.

Therefore, for many women, writing poetry is the only way to express, in secrecy and in intimacy, only with the paper they write upon, their sorrow, beliefs and joys. As their socialization imposes limitations on their spiritual, intellectual, psychological, artistic and thus human development, they use poetry as therapy. A lot of women do not write art in the first place, although they write beautiful poetry. They write life, they write healing. It is through the writing that they explore themselves, their feelings, their own selves in order to know themselves, their mother, their children, their partner, their friends, their work and society and gain self-confidence as well as strength.[16] That is why discouraging judgments of cultural elites, structural underestimation and ridicule of women's poetry does not affect primarily the artistic development of women. No, it has a far more devastating effect: it harms the psyche of women. To bring down their poetry is equal to tearing them down. Savory Fido states that "[w]omen often write as personal therapy, as a way of controlling their world. It is possible, then, that the encouragement of creative writing in women can have an important developmental effect."[17] Considering this, it should not surprise us that a lot of women, like Elia Isenia, have been writing

15 If she had a debt to pay, or one of the children had to take their first holy communion, Elia would participate in a *tumba* festival in order to earn some money. She has faced unemployment for quite some time in her life, does not like to ask for help and has developed for that reason a very practical view of her art, although she works with dedication on the artistry of her creations.

16 Women's studies graduate and historian Jeanne Henriquez made clear in her study: "How this knowledge affects our lives should be a start of discussion, in our consciousness raising, as a basis for therapeutic discussions, and towards our empowerment to emancipation of ourselves and towards the humanization of society." Henriquez, "From the Womb: Curaçaoan Women Speak Out about Their Identity," 1991, p. 259. Editors' note: see contribution by Henriquez in this section.

17 Savory Fido, "Where Do We Go from Here?" 1988, p. 330.

poetry for a very long time but have never dared to bring it out to the public by reading it aloud or publishing it because they were afraid of the ridicule they would suffer. Other reasons, such as the intimate character of the poetry, financial limitations and a lack of knowledge about publication matters, can also play a role, but the fear of ridicule often returns as the primary reason for not publishing. Specific life conditions such as poverty, lesbianism and racial oppression were entrusted to a piece of paper, this being one of the few ways to deal with problems. And it is exactly because of the fact that, for Elia Isenia, art has been her way of defeating adversities (first by suffering in silence and later by defying with assertiveness) that a look at her life circumstances will shed light on her art. We can understand Isenia's poetry and her journey to self-discovery through her biography. [...]

5 Isenia's Early Life and Biography

Thirty-four-year-old Elia Isenia has been performing ever since she was a child.[18] She grew up in the village of Jan Kok in Bandabou, Curaçao's countryside, as the first child of a happy, humble and music-loving family. Her father taught her at the age of ten to play the guitar. Her mother, a church choir singer with a beautiful voice, used to sing with this family of seven children, practically all of whom could play one instrument or another.[19] At the age of seventeen, Elia participated for the first time in a *tumba* contest.

Elia Isenia started her career as a singer of the traditionally prescribed repertoire: Latin American songs. Later, she developed her own style and began exploring *tambú* and *tumba,* two of Curaçao's most popular rhythms characterized by a strong metaphoric dimension. The fact that she is from the countryside undoubtedly played a role in this choice. Even though she has been living for quite some time now in the city, she has maintained a deep affection

18 From her personal file, we learn: "From the time I was eight I dreamed of becoming a poet."

19 Her father's grandmother was one of the two organ players of Bandabou. One grandfather played the accordion, the other grandfather played the guitar. And, in her family, there were players of the *muzik di zumbi,* music played with ancient instruments in the still of the night in former times when there was no electricity. The mysterious sounds in the darkness made people wonder where it came from and explains the name *muzik di zumbi,* ghost music.

for her place of birth. Elia states with pride: "I am a child of Bandabou.[20] I still miss the quietness of the place; the city is so noisy."

Why did this mother of three daughters choose to start singing? At the age of fifteen, juvenile ignorance led her into pregnancy. In the small, tradition-respecting village of Jan Kok, this caused deep sorrow and a profound feeling of shame. "It was like a member of the family had died, a complete mourning, because I had betrayed my people."

Elia does not agree with the people who advised her not to mention these facts of her life in her interviews after she was crowned queen of the *tumba* festival. She refuses to behave according to established stereotypes about "respectability" of women. […]

Earlier in life, she had faced all sorts of discrimination as a country girl. At the city school she attended, city children used to call country children all kinds of names, such as *kabritu di Bandabou* (country goats) or *muchanan di trùk di palu* (wooden truck children).[21] "I used to fight back with my sharp tongue,"[22] she says.

Isenia had from her youth the sharp tongue that she would use so frequently later in her *tambú* songs. Add to these circumstances the facts of early motherhood, her blackness and her so-called ugliness and we have the basis for her struggle and her motivation to start singing. […]

In 1975, the internationally proclaimed year of the woman, she participated at the age of seventeen in the *tumba* festival. Although nobody knew her at the time and she did not qualify for the prizes, her picture appeared in the newspapers: a woman singing in the festival. She was on the right track! From that moment on, she decided to continue so people would get to know her.

Her participation in more cultural events[23] was always inspired by a very strong desire and motivation to grow out of the dark cloud (this being the shame of early motherhood, racial discrimination and discrimination for

20 "Mi ta mucha di Bandabou." Translated from Papiamentu by the author.

21 The country children were transported to city schools in large trucks with a wooden body. They were laughed at for this and avoided conversation about their means of transportation.

22 Later in her life, she discovered she could strangle people with her tongue. "But I do not strangle for nothing. Only if you tickle me, I'll laugh." Or, when she could not strike back immediately, she would wait till the end of the year for the *tambú* season and strangle at the drum. Editors' note: see also contribution by Allen in this volume, discussing the *tambú* performer Petoi.

23 For example, the troubadours festival and the directing of cultural groups for the youth: Flornandi Kibrahacha.

being "ugly") that surrounded her. Her critical attitude toward life made her take, a few years after marriage, the decision to divorce. Ever since, she has been mother and father to her three daughters, who are as culturally gifted as herself.

Filomena Isenia, as her real name is,[24] possesses the characteristics of a "Big Mama" (*la mamá grande*, to use Gabriel García Márquez's words) in spite of her young age. This multidimensional woman (artist, mother, worker, leader of a historic winning team and cultural inspirer) is a mother with many talents. She comes from a family of *kurandero* and *kurioso*[25] and people consult her for a variety of things, such as the use of healing herbs. [...]

6 Attention to Cultural Heritage

Elia Isenia has a strong feeling and respect for the cultural traditions of Curaçao. Her songs always reflected the metaphorical speech of the elders. From ninety-two-year-old Martili Pieter, one of the few elders left on the island who know the African Guene language,[26] Elia has learned some Guene, which she often inserts in her songs. "I go to Pai Tili [Daddy Tili, nickname for Martili] to take words[27] that is, to get inspired by his words."

She is convinced that we should give more attention to our cultural heritage. For her, the elders possess wisdom we should cherish because it is a precious inheritance from our ancestors. Isenia revives African mythology with Guene. Her winning song in the 1991 *tumba* festival focused on the *tranvia*, the city train Curaçao had at the turn of the century. About this aspect, Cocco-De Filippis establishes that

> the use of archaisms and neologisms can increase the semic actualization of the poetic sign in a text ... The presence of an archaism ... a "marked" element in a "not marked" context, draws attention to itself and

24 After participating in 1975 in the *tumba* contest, she decided that if she wanted people to know her, she could not go along under the name of Filomena and changed her name into the, according to her, more suitable Elia.

25 People used to go to a *kurandero* or a *kurioso* for the healing of a broken arm or leg or whatever disease. The *kurandero* was a person of great respect and even medical doctors used to consult these healers in matters they could not handle themselves.

26 Guene. Set of African-derived languages spoken by the enslaved Africans and their descendants in Curaçao. See: Arion, "Guene. The Connection between Papiamentu and Africa," 1988.

27 To take words: "Tuma palabra." Translated from Papiamentu by the author.

> consequently actualizes and saturates that what follows with its semic potentials.[28]

This proved true in the case of Isenia where everybody hearing her lyrics would wonder about the meaning of certain words or expressions. In this way, she contributes with her songs to the diffusion of Guene and of archaisms of Papiamentu.

Not only the elders attract Elia Isenia. She believes in the youth. She has directed youth folkloric groups in which her own daughters also perform. But even the directing of cultural youth groups she did hoping to undo the false step she had taken at the age of fifteen. "I tried everything to make the dark cloud go away," she says.

Elia Isenia gives assistance to adults, especially women, who are competing in cultural events, and writes occasion-poetry for those who approach her for help.

As a black woman, Isenia has a strong racial consciousness. "We have in us the African culture. Although a lot of people deny this, for me it is an established fact."

This aspect of her life, her blackness, contributed also in her struggle to erase the dark cloud. Isenia remembers participating in a mariachi contest on the neighboring island of Aruba a long time ago. When she appeared on stage, the crowd started laughing and pointing at her, and yelled: "Look at a monkey from Curaçao. Go away, monkey!" She wished the floor would open and swallow her. Nevertheless, she stayed, sang and was one of the finalists. The poem from those early years lacks any form of the resistance we know from her *tambús*. We can even observe here that she tries to flee. [...]

The dark clouds above the head of Elia Isenia are rooted in the following: the bourgeois and Christian ideology of matrimonial decency—that is, marrying to cover pregnancy shame. Colonialism: blackness is a negative condition; inferiority complex creating beauty norms ("ugliness"). Metropolism: country people are stupid. Traditional gender models: decent women do not go around performing in men's groups.

In fact, Elia Isenia started with three strikes against her: black, working class and colonized. [...] She has been engaged in a long-lasting effort to prove to the world she had nothing to be ashamed of or pitied for. She used her own strategy (*tambú*) to grow out of a shame society had imposed on her. Has the dark cloud disappeared by now? [...]

---

28 Cocco-de Filippis, *Estudios semióticos de poesía dominicana*, 1984, p. 18.

What did the cloud become when it was transcended? What is the real meaning of the cloud? Because it was not with her early motherhood that the cloud appeared for the first time. Before that, there were the negative remarks about her being a country child as well as the remarks at home that the other daughters were pretty and she ugly. The drive to excel may have been fortified by her early motherhood, but at the basis of the drive lay other influential experiences from her childhood that determined her growth to excellence.

7 Conclusions

The firefly says: the darker the night, the stronger my light[29]

The choice of my object of study, songs and poetry of a working-class female artist, was based on the opinion that, for our society to fully develop, we need to include in the arsenal of changing agents at our disposal all those contributing elements that have so far not received the attention they deserve. Against middle-class and often foreign norms and values, which have determined in a decisive way our thinking and knowledge, we can place the rich variety of people's creativity. Considering this, the inclusion of the female contribution in order to achieve a more balanced society should not be regarded as a privilege conceded to women but as a necessity. This essay has dealt with Elia Isenia as a legitimate voice of female experience. The choice of Isenia makes it clear that intellectualism is not the sole source of knowledge, that the popular segments are actors of important experiences in Curaçao's society. In order to obtain a more complete panorama of ourselves, the general public as well as the female voices should be included.

This article was written with the awareness that this first exploration of Elia Isenia's songs and poetry must be further researched in order to open other dimensions not included here. I have tried to be faithful to Isenia's texts and life story. The decoding of Isenia's texts will hopefully contribute to the canonization of this division of Curaçao's literature, the people's division, which has been denied space by standards imposed by cultural elites. Accepting her story and her development, we, at the same time, accept all the female voices involved in self-exploration and growing. And by growing, these women make space for their children, partners and society to grow. Their art becomes an emancipatory catalyst in society's growth. That is why the process of documenting Curaçao's reality should rely more and more upon the voices, utterances

29 "Bich'i kandela di: mas nochi, mas ñéñé" Translated from Papiamentu by the author.

and discourses that have been denied space so far. Using the subjectivity of Isenia's life story as a source of knowledge makes her work more accessible to us because literature holds more richness than sociology or history when it comes to understanding a society, a personality or a social process. Her biography also made it possible to understand the therapeutic effect her art had in her life.

This essay has dealt with the disclosure of a piece of female subculture in Curaçao. In the reconstruction of the female experience expressed by Elia Isenia and the deciphering of myths, the different stages of development Isenia went through were revealed. At first, she adopted and internalized the stereotypes with which society shapes women and felt shame for her condition. In this stage of imitating the prevailing modes of the dominant tradition, she reproduced the standards of art and the social roles expected from her. Then she protested against these values and, finally, turned inward to search for her identity and free herself. The recognition of Isenia's complexity emphasizes her wisdom and her mythological features, traditionally attributed to men.

Just as in the British West Indies, the calypso became the vehicle for narratives about the everyday lives of ordinary Trinidadians.[30] Isenia's *tambú* songs tell the life stories of the many black working-class women who refused to be the "comforting, chattering Household Pearl."[31] The authentic popular expression of *tambú*, characterized by its protest, was a perfect means for the searching and defying Isenia. She used it to voice her development.

Both her poetry and songs shed light on her development toward self-realization. Her poetry is intimate, docile. Her songs can, on the contrary, be validly categorized as freedom songs. They show the result of her process. I thought it necessary to avoid a superficial judgment through which Isenia could be depicted as an insane, ever-quarreling woman, despite her statements such as "I will shake them up at the end of the year." In this context, the following quotation seems to explain Isenia's fury. In *Sexual/Textual Politics*, in the chapter titled "The Madwoman in the Attic," Toril Moi affirms that, often, the madwoman in literature is the author herself. The madwoman is the literary/literal answer to the question: How can she venture to take up the pen at all? It is the only chance for female writers to get rid of their own withheld fury.[32] Moi further states: "The fundamental problem of feminine literary criticism:

30 Rohlehr, "Images of Men and Women in the 1930s Calypsoes," 1988, p. 234.

31 Thorpe, "Feminism and the Female Authored West Indian Novel," 1988, p. 326.

32 "But behind the angel lurks the monster: the obverse of the male idealization of woman is the male fear of femininity. The monster woman is the woman who refuses to be selfless, acts on her own initiative, who has a story to tell—in short—a woman who rejects

'Since his is the chief voice she hears, does the Queen try to sound like the king, imitating his tone, his inflections, his phrasing, his point of view? Or does she talk back to him in her own vocabulary, her own timbre, insisting on her own viewpoint?'"[33] Isenia definitely did talk back. In a convincing way, she stood up, threw her head back and told in not misunderstandable words the story she demanded everybody to listen to. Because, she said, if we want a better life, we'd better accept this voice, the voice of women.

Acknowledgments

This text is an edited excerpt from a chapter originally published as Clemencia, Jocelyn. "The Semiotics of Dark Clouds in Songs and Poems of Elia Isenia: Art as Female Therapy." In *Mundu yama sinta mira: Womanhood in Curaçao* [The name of the world is sit and see: Womanhood in Curaçao], edited by Richenel Ansano, Joceline A. Clemencia, Jeanette Cook, and Eithel Martis, 207–31. Curaçao: Fundashon Publikashon, 1992. Reproduction is courtesy of Fundashon Publikashon. Omitted parts of the original text have been marked with ellipses and headings have been added for better overview.

Acknowledgments (from the original text): I am very indebted to Ms. Elia Isenia for sharing her life story with me, for allowing me to write about it and thus learn about women's strength. I am also grateful to Dr. Aart Broek.

Bibliography

Anita, Sherwin. *Baha for di mi lomba, dediká na Nicolaas Susana (Shon Colá)* [Get off my back, dedicated to Nicolaas Susana (Shon Colá)]. Fundashon Pincho y su grupo, 1991, LP record.

Ansano, Richenel, Jocelyn A. Clemencia, Jeanette Cook, and Eithel Martis, eds. *Mundu yama sinta mira: Womanhood in Curaçao* [The name of the world is sit and see: Womanhood in Curaçao]. Curaçao: Fundashon Publikashon, 1992.

Arion, Frank Martinus. "Guene. The Connection between Papiamentu and Africa." Presentation at Round Table on Africanisms in Afro-American language varieties, University of Georgia, Athens, 1988.

---

the submissive role patriarchy has reserved for her." Moi, *Sexual/Textual Politics: Feminist Literary Theory*, 1985, p. 58.

33 Gilbert and Guba cited in Moi, *Sexual/Textual Politics: Feminist Literary Theory*, 1985, p. 59.

Clemencia, Joceline. *Het grote camouflagespel van de OPI: Een thematische benadering van de poëzie van Elis Juliana* [The OPI's great game of camouflage: A thematic approach to the poetry of Elis Juliana]. Leiden: KITLV, 1989.

Cocco-DeFilippis, Daisy. *Estudios semióticos de poesía Dominicana* [Semiotic studies of Dominican poetry]. Santo Domingo: Editora Taller, 1984.

Henriquez, Jeanne D. "From the Womb: Curacaoan Women Speak Out about Their Identity." PhD diss., The George Washington University, 1991.

Isenia, Elia. *Mi gayo. Dediká na Petronilia Coco (Petoi).* [My rooster. Dedicated to Petronilia Coco]. Fundashon Pincho y su grupo, 1991, LP record.

Lorde, Audre. *Sister Outsider: Essays and Speeches.* Trumansburg: Crossing Press, 1984.

Moi, Toril. *Sexual/Textual Politics: Feminist Literary Theory.* New Accents. London: Routledge, 1985.

Rohlehr, Gordon. "Images of Men and Women in the 1930s Calypsoes: The Sociology of Food Acquisition in a Context of Survivalism." In *Gender in Caribbean Development: Papers Presented at the Inaugural Seminar of the University of the West Indies Women and Development Studies Project*, edited by Patricia Mohammed, 223–89. Kingston: Canoe Press, 1988.

Savory Fido, Elaine. "Where Do We Go from Here? Literature in English and the Women's Studies Programme at UWI." In *Gender in Caribbean Development: Papers Presented at the Inaugural Seminar of the University of the West Indies Women and Development Studies Project*, edited by Patricia Mohammed, 314–23. Kingston: Canoe Press, 1988.

Thorpe, Marjorie. "Feminism and the Female Authored West Indian Novel: Paule Marshall's Brown Girl, Brownstones." In *Gender in Caribbean Development: Papers Presented at the Inaugural Seminar of the University of the West Indies Women and Development Studies Project*, edited by Patricia Mohammed, 303–13. Kingston: Canoe Press, 1988.

Vargas, Vilma. *Una semiología del texto poético* [A semiology of poetic texts]. Colección monografías 20. Caracas: Universidad Central de Venezuela, Consejo de Desarrollo Científico y Humanístico, 1989.

CHAPTER 40

Tambú and the Arawak Princess Diyani: the Performance of History, Myth and Ritual

Nanette de Jong

Abstract

Tambú is a music and dance ritual that emerged during slavery on the Dutch island of Curaçao. Weaving together African cultural retentions and new-world realities, *Tambú* serves as a powerful site through which to reinterpret the past to meet present—and future—needs, creating instant mythologies that rewrite who the Curaçaoans were and are. The following contribution uses the *Tambú* and the ritual's deity, Princess Diyani, to investigate the multifaceted relationship between history and myth. As we shall see, Diyani represents not only a heroine and symbol of that complex history-myth partnership, she is also a gateway for women followers to destabilize the masculine narratives surrounding *Tambú*, thereby enabling opportunities to assume divine places within Curaçao's slave and colonial history.

Keywords

Tambú – spirituality – African cultures – colonial history – mythology

Tambú denotes an African-inspired music and dance ritual that developed during slavery on the island of Curaçao. Like other Afro-syncretized rituals in the Caribbean, *Tambú* became a refuge for displaced African and Caribbean deities and ancestral spirits, committed to supporting devotees as they traversed the unknown complexities and paradoxes of the New World. They brought meaning and coherence to the lives of ritual followers, positing important meanings and versions about historical events that lent value and coherence to the present-day.

Able to bridge the past with the present, these ancestors and deities shaped the collective memories of *Tambú* devotees in terms of how history was to be interpreted and remembered. Yet, what was presented as truth was usually

 | DOI:10.1163/9789004690882_042

entangled with imagined details from local legends and myths, thus blurring distinctions between fact and fiction. In fact, when *Tambú* devotees aligned particularly closely to the powerful historical narratives presented by these deities and spirits, it was not necessarily because the narratives they were presented were clear replicas of the past. Rather, it was because these sanctified interpretations essentially armored devotees with powerful and meaningful routes for understanding and surviving their New World.

This contribution inquires into the multifaceted relationship between history and myth in the Caribbean. With Curaçao's *Tambú* serving as a case study, it investigates how myths are made and to what extent they may lead us back to history.[1] As we shall see, through mythology, *Tambú* followers reconstructed Curaçao's colonial narrative by making themselves integral in it. The intricacies involved with that process point to many of the complexities surrounding the Caribbean experience, from a complicated quest for belonging to the collective longing for spiritual returns to homeland.

The discussion is focused on Diyani, a Curaçaoan-born Arawakan princess who was identified as the distant ancestor by *Tambú* devotee Haidee (her name has been changed to ensure anonymity). A bank teller by trade, Haidee, aged thirty-one at the time, kept her involvement in *Tambú* a guarded secret from coworkers and even some friends: the sacred *Tambú* was classified as immoral and low class by both the church and the state, and those who dared open participation faced possible social and religious retribution.

It was 1995 when I first was introduced to Diyani, at a *Tambú* ritual held in honor of the West African trickster deity Eshu and his Catholic saint counterpart, St. Anthony. Diyani appeared that night by manifesting herself through the possession of Haidee. Diyani symbolized a significant figure in *Tambú*: she was a powerful indigenous woman who boldly assumed her place in the ritual's pantheon alongside the West African deities Shango, the god of thunder, and Ogun, the god of iron. As Haidee explained it, Diyani had successfully escaped slavery under Dutch colonial rule by traveling through a network of underground caves that served as tunnels connecting Curaçao to Venezuela (Venezuela is located some seventy kilometers from Curaçao). Instead of basking in the sanctuary Venezuela provided, however, Diyani returned to Curaçao on numerous occasions to assist other Arawaks in traversing the underground caves to attain liberty in Venezuela.

To examine Diyani and her place in the *Tambú* ritual is to situate Curaçao's slave narratives into the allegorical realm, wherein the past assumed meaning

1 Fowler, *The Past in Contemporary Society: Then, Now*, 1992, p. 50.

in as much as it is framed by local beliefs and myths. The Arawaks, for example, had been raised to mythological status in Curaçao, revered around the understanding that they successfully fought off Dutch enslavement. As symbols of courage and strength, the Arawaks became recognized as leading figures in the Curaçaoans' own struggles for freedom and equality.

Diyani's life as an Arawak woman magnified that account. It therefore filled a void left by the island's "official" slave history, enabling a version of history that not only included the Arawak people but also the women of colonial Curaçao. The agency by which Diyani assumed her position of respect in *Tambú* emphasized not only how history might become "intertwined with mythic discourse"[2] but also how "questions of origin" manifest our myths and histories.[3] Rather than submitting Diyani and her life to objective scrutiny, the present contribution investigates what her inclusion in *Tambú*'s pantheon says about notions of identity and belonging, history and myth and displacement and dislocation.

The majority of literature on *Tambú* has concentrated on the ritual practices of male gods and ancestors commonly sought by *Tambú* devotees for leadership and advice.[4] Likewise, Curaçao's slavery history has been dominated by the heroic actions of the male descendants, with Tula, Louis Mercier, Bastiaan Karpata and Pedro Wakao governing the island's slave narratives. Little has been written on the women deities and ancestors, and accounts of the island's enslaved women have remained sparse. By bringing Diyani into the study of *Tambú*, the current study also fills this research gap.

The Arawaks are recognized as Curaçao's original inhabitants. A peaceful tribe, known for their accomplished fishery skills, they were believed to have taken residence in small groups across the island, settling notably in Ascension, near Curaçao's rocky north coast; in Sint Anna Bay, the channel located between what is today Punda and Otrobanda; and in Santa Barbara, the island's southeasternmost coast. The first documented contact between Curaçao's Arawaks and the Europeans was in 1492, during a Spanish expedition led by Amerigo Vespucci and Alonso de Ojeda. That expedition led to Curaçao being claimed by the Spanish crown.

Curaçao, unlike many other islands, never attained true plantation status due to its dry, arid weather and poor soil conditions. Because of these presumed

2 Françoise, *Rewriting the Return to Africa: Voices of Francophone Caribbean Women Writers*, 2011, p. XXVIII.

3 Barbara Webb, cited in Françoise, ibid.

4 De Jong, *Tambú: Curaçao's African-Caribbean Ritual and the Politics of Memory*, 2012; and Rosalia, "Represhon di kultura: E lucha di Tambú" [Repression of culture: The struggle of *Tambú*], 1997.

shortcomings, the island was ascribed the epithet *inutile* (useless) by the Spanish and fundamentally forgotten. When gold was discovered in Spain's other colonies, notably Venezuela, Colombia and Hispaniola, attempts were made to enslave and forcibly relocate Curaçao's indigenous Arawaks to those settlements to work the gold mines. One thousand two hundred Arawaks from Curaçao were believed to have been shipped across, but few survived the transfer.[5] As documented by Bartolomé de las Casas, the sixteenth-century Spanish missionary living in Hispaniola, Curaçao's Arawak peoples were "unable to withstand hard work or suffering and render them liable to succumb to almost any illness."[6]

The island of Curaçao went largely ignored until the Dutch took it over in 1634.[7] Under the auspices of the West Indies Company (WIC), the Dutch, in an attempt to broaden their role in the slave trade, took advantage of Curaçao's natural harbors and promptly transformed it into a lucrative slave port.[8] At the time of the Dutch occupation, the island's population comprised only thirty-two Spaniards and about five hundred Arawaks. Through mutual agreement, four hundred Arawaks, along with all the Spaniards, were transferred to Venezuela. Attempts were made by the Dutch to enslave the remaining one hundred or so Arawaks, but these were unsuccessful. Legend has it that the Arawaks resisted enslavement by fleeing to Venezuela via Curaçao's alleged labyrinth of underground caves. Whatever the actual circumstances of the Arawaks' disappearance, they became idolized on the island for their perceived resilience in withstanding Dutch colonial oppression. It is through this legend that Diyani stepped into, and found acceptance in, *Tambú*.

Diyani first visited Haidee through the medium of dreams, an important facet of *Tambú* that allowed ancestral spirits to communicate with the living. Haidee's dreams about Diyani were rich with information, providing intimate insights into key moments from the princess's life. As a result of these dreams, Haidee learned that Diyani was born into royalty but, despite her high status, remained humble and unpretentious. When the Dutch assumed control over Curaçao, Diyani was held captive, "physically and emotionally tortured," in Haidee's words.[9] Remarkably, Diyani managed to escape by traveling through the island's network of caves. She could have lived out her life in Venezuela untroubled, Haidee clarified, "but she was brave and she was noble.

5 Goslinga, *A Short History of the Netherlands Antilles and Surinam*, 1979.

6 Las Casas, *A Short Account of the Destruction of the Indies*, 1992, p. 10.

7 Goslinga, *The Dutch in the Caribbean and on the Wild Coast*, 1971, p. 264.

8 Postma, *The Dutch in the Atlantic Slave Trade*, 1990, p. 237.

9 Interview with author, Curaçao, 1995.

She escaped slavery, and just turned around and returned right back to it":[10] during her lifetime, Diyani made several return trips to Curaçao to assist other Arawaks in navigating the caves to attain their freedom. "I am proud to be her descendant," Haidee added.[11]

Haidee spoke with noticeable passion and pride when recalling her dreams of Diyani. Perhaps most poignant, however, was Haidee's reliance on the present progressive tense when repeating information from those dreams. Doing so enabled Haidee to speak about Diyani's lived experiences as if they were occurring in that very instant, as if she was right there, living out the experience alongside Diyani. Through this storytelling technique, boundaries between time and space buckled, and, albeit momentarily, the past and present intimately intertwined. Haidee's dreaming and waking life, her conscious and unconscious selves, had overlapped and intersected when she shared her dream stories with me.

Dreams are an important resource of ancestral knowledge in numerous Afro-Caribbean rituals. For example, among Cubans practicing Santería, as Diana Maitland Dean argues, dreams feature prominently in how devotees make and maintain contact with the spirit world.[12] Dreaming is not only the primary vehicle of communication between the living and the dead, she argues,[13] but is also the choice medium through which Afro-Cuban identity is explored and expressed. "Afro-Cuban dreams and rituals, therefore, must be approached not only as personal phenomena, but as social and political events," Dean concludes.[14]

Adam M. McGee defines dreaming in Haitian vodou as "guides" that assist "the dreamer through the complicated terrain of the living world."[15] In vodou, he writes, "[t]he dream cannot be said to originate or reside purely in the mind of the dreamer. Rather, the dream is a site of intersection—between the dreamer and disembodied entities, and between our physical world and a broader field of spiritual action."[16]

McGee points out how the "recitation of a dream narrative" by adherents of vodou can further amplify that juncture. When the dreamer in vodou uses the

10 Ibid.

11 Ibid.

12 Dean, *Dreaming the Dead: The Social Impact of Dreams in an Afro-Cuban Community*, 1993. Editors' note: see discussion of the significance of dream-talking in the context of Aruba in the contribution by Dresscher-Lambertus in this volume.

13 Ibid., p. 111.

14 Ibid.

15 McGee, "Dreaming in Haitian Vodou," 2012, p. 2.

16 Ibid., p. 3.

present progressive tense when recounting the dream, he argues, the dreams are no longer separate from "normal life" but, instead, extensions of it.[17]

Haidee's style of narration supported McGee's findings since she, too, relied on the present progressive tense when sharing her dreams. Doing so, to borrow from McGee, assigned "an immediacy and unmediated quality to [her] encounter" with Diyani, with Diyani's stories "enacted as though [they] were happening in that moment." Through the act of narration, then, Haidee was privileged with an opportunity to experience Diyani's life in real-time. For all intents and purposes, at the moment of recitation, Haidee joined Diyani in her gallant escape from Dutch tyranny and experienced the trepidation of navigating the unfamiliar, darkened caves to freedom. Again, echoing McGee's research, "the space of dreaming" for Haidee "[was] not simply an extension of waking life, but a porous territory suffused with spiritual powers and entities."[18]

Crucially, dreaming enabled Haidee to engage with the spirit world without the intercession of a *Tambú* priest. This meant that her relationship with Diyani could have remained a private affair. Yet, Diyani had made it markedly clear during her dreams that Haidee must invite her to *Tambú* so that she could address the wider ritual community. Adhering to this request, Haidee regularly attended the ritual with the purpose of "dancing for Diyani," hoping her movements and handclaps might convince Diyani to appear. Possession is the customary vehicle through which contact with the spiritual world is made in *Tambú*, and it was through possession that Diyani, now in control over Haidee's body and voice, could communicate with other *Tambú* devotees.

To become possessed, in the words of Robert Farris Thompson, is to "make the god."[19] From that perspective, Diyani was performed into existence at *Tambú*, evoking the meanings and memories of slavery for the wider ritual community. Her stories also invited devotees to consider alternative slave narratives, ones that celebrated Arawakan bravery and inserted women into the colonial experience. The spiritual and physical worlds intersected at the moment of possession, and divisions between past and present, visible and invisible, collapsed, albeit momentarily.

Diyani's arrival to *Tambú* was noticeable by the immediate changes it brought to Haidee's behavior, attitude and movements at the ritual. The dancing, for example, turned more flatfooted, her torso bent forward, repetitively twisting at the hips, and her open palms were held upwards above her head as if lobbying *Tambú* followers to come forward. These physical changes in Haidee

17 Ibid., pp. 2, 5.
18 Ibid., p. 5.
19 Thompson, *Flash of the Spirit: African and Afro-American Art and Philosophy*, 1983, p. 9

seemed to awaken a sense of community and purpose among the others in attendance, with several devotees, aware Diyani had arrived, quickly running up to ask particular questions or to pay homage. Diyani freely and amenably shared the stories from her past, privileging all in attendance the opportunity to hear about slavery and liberty from a woman's perspective.

That Diyani was welcomed at a ritual organized for Eshu speaks to a tradition of unity that has always defined *Tambú*. The *Tambú* ritual was born as a result of a multitude of African cultures and traditions coming together. As a lucrative slave trading port, Curaçao had become the interim stop for many different African nation groups. Half a million Africans are believed to have passed through the island during the years of slavery. Only some 2,300, however, were to remain permanently, either pressed into service as domestic servants to the Dutch families living there or left behind for any number of reasons that made them "unsaleable."[20] Two African communities, therefore, developed in Curaçao: the *negotie slaven* (enslaved people for trade), those detained on the island, usually for three to six months before being sold into slavery elsewhere in the New World; and *manquerons* (unsaleable ones), those who stayed. *Tambú* emerged in the throes of these two communities, absorbing the needs of and influences from both.

Those from Angola comprised the largest group of Africans arriving in Curaçao during the earliest years of slavery. This was due to the fact that Angola had come under Dutch rule. The initial roots of *Tambú*, therefore, are generally traced to the wider Angolan traditions, including stick fighting.[21] The Curaçaoan variant of this stick fight assumed the title of *kokomakaku*, its name taken from the island shrub *coco maque*, from whose trunks the combat fighting sticks were traditionally constructed. *Kokomakaku* was set in a binary form. It opened with a lead vocalist singing tributes to the stick fighters, sung to the accompaniment of a single drum, called *tambú*. Once the vocalist finished, the second section would commence, with stick fighters jumping into the prescribed ritual circle, ready for battle. The lead vocalist would continue in song but now members of the audience joined in as well.

A sacred form emerged that, based on the *kokomakaku*, relied on the stick fight's binary structure to connect with the ancestral realms. The first section was performed in tribute to the ancestors, presented as a vehicle to join the

20 Goslinga, *The Dutch in the Caribbean and on the Wild Coast*, 1971, p. 362; and Postma, *The Dutch in the Atlantic Slave Trade*, 1990, p. 237.

21 Dominguez, *Vivencia de un rito luango en el Tambú* [Experience of a luango ritual in *Tambú*], 1988; and De Jong and Williams, "Narratives of Return: Carricou and the Big Drum Ritual," 2022.

spiritual and physical worlds. Just as *kokomakaku* saved its second section for ritual action, this sacred form, too, reserved its second part for welcoming the ancestors to the ritual ring. It was in this section that ancestors would assume possession of the devotees, their human bodies temporarily transformed into spiritual vehicles through which these ancestors could communicate with the human world.[22] This sacred ritual assumed the title of *Tambú*, taking the name from its ritual drum.

This sacred *Tambú* was continually altered by its users to fit their changing needs. Thus, when the WIC shifted its trading focus from Angola to West Africa, *Tambú* transformed. One change was its accommodation of iron instruments, which held positions of significant ritual status among the West African nation groups. One of the most popular iron instruments to develop in Curaçao was the *chapi*, an indigenous instrument made from the metal end of a common garden hoe that was struck with an iron bar, creating a loud, high-pitched tone. It has since become a central accompaniment in contemporary *Tambú*. A second modification to the ritual was the inclusion of the West African gods, who were now regularly sought alongside the ancestral spirits for communal guidance and protection.

The next substantial change to *Tambú* came during the late eighteenth century, when WIC, in efforts to expand its role in the New World, established incarceration facilities in Curaçao. While such facilities held prisoners of Spanish, Portuguese, English and French descent, most were Blacks from colonies in South America and other parts of the Caribbean, countries where local politics and plantation economies established unique and divergent creole cultures and traditions. When these Black prisoners came to Curaçao, they brought with them the assorted creole cultures of their local New World regions.[23] The result had an even further broadening effect on *Tambú*: the ritual now also absorbed the creolized deities worshiped by these prisoners, with vodou laws and Santería orishas joining its sacred pantheon.

Tambú's ability to adapt and change according to the cultural and spiritual realities of its enslaved community has been central to its survival. It marked a flexibility that assured *Tambú* would remain relevant to devotees. Its binary structure, in particular, has been pinpointed as to why the ritual could accommodate an ever-changing spiritual world.[24] It allowed Angolan ancestors to

---

22 Honwana, "Spiritual Agency and Self-Renewal in Southern Mozambique," 1996; and Honwana, "Healing for Peace: Traditional Healers and Post-War Reconstruction in Southern Mozambique," 1997.

23 Postma, *The Dutch in the Atlantic Slave Trade*, 1990, pp. 33–34.

24 De Jong and Williams, "Narratives of Return: Carricou and the Big Drum Ritual," 2022.

be summoned alongside West African gods, Haitian *lwa* and Trinidadian orisha. Unlike many other Afro-syncretized rituals across the Caribbean, where rhythm might secure communication with the spirit world, it was *Tambú*'s binary structure that assured spiritual interaction. Although a particular song may have been sung at the *Tambú* ritual for purposes of honoring one specific deity or ancestral spirit, all were welcome to join the event. With its binary structure, *Tambú* comprised an "open door policy," which promised participants near limitless access to the supernatural.

Briefly, the first section of *Tambú* is called the *habrí* (translated as: open). It is where communication with the spiritual world is unlocked or opened. The lead singer (called *pregon*) communicates the performance-specific invitation to the accompaniment of the *tambú* drum and at least one *chapi* iron instrument. While only one drum can be used during the ritual, numerous *chapi* are allowed: it is not uncommon for eight or nine *chapi* musicians to crowd around the lone drummer at *Tambú*. The *Tambú* followers in attendance are expected to stay quiet during the *habrí* so as to give their undivided attention to the *pregon* and the text being shared. No dancing or hand clapping is allowed. The *tambú* and *chapi* must also follow specific performance etiquette during the *habrí*: the *chapi* is expected to serve as timekeeper, freeing the single *tambú* drummer to improvise.

The second section is called the *será* (translated as: closed). It commences with a wave or vocal call from the *pregon*, which lets audiences know that they are now free to dance and let the deities or ancestors know that they are now welcome to join the event. Like Haidee, the *Tambú* followers in attendance usually have an established relationship with one particular deity or ancestor, with possession manifested by that chosen deity or ancestor only. On the other hand, *Tambú* religious leaders (purporting to know each deity and ancestor intimately) may enter possession by whichever deity or ancestor is most needed at the time of the event.

In the *será*, the musical roles of the *chapi* and drummer are reversed: the drummer is now expected to maintain the downbeat, while the *chapi* provides quick, respective triplet phrases, interspersed with episodes of improvisation. During the *será*, the *pregon* is joined by the *coro* (chorus), who responds to the solo singer in a standard call-and-response manner. The dancing, done with one heel grounded in place while the toes of the free foot rhythmically stomp the ground, adds its own complex rhythm. Audiences and *coro* are also free to clap hands during the *será*, adding yet another rhythmic dimension to its already dense texture.

This binary form connotes a specific structural symmetry. The two sections can be repeated as often as the *pregon* desires, but the *habrí* and *será* must always be presented as a pair—never singly and never out of order. The traditional *tambú* and *chapi* rhythms from both the *habrí* and *será* sections are transcribed below as are the hand clapping and dancing rhythms from the *será*.

As argued, *Tambú*'s binary structure allowed for a variety of deities and ancestors to be invited into its ritual fold. Although the role of history in determining which deities and ancestors would become part of *Tambú*'s pantheon was pervasive, it were the mythologies enfolding these deities and ancestors that procured their relevance with devotees. Diyani, for example,

FIGURE 40.1 Musical transcription of the standard rhythm performed by the *tambú* during the *habrí* section

FIGURE 40.2 Musical transcription of the standard rhythm performed by the *chapi* during the *habrí* section

FIGURE 40.3 Musical transcription of the standard rhythm performed by the *tambú* during the *será* section

FIGURE 40.4 Musical transcription of the standard rhythm performed by the *chapi* during the *será* section

FIGURE 40.5 Musical transcription of the standard dance rhythm from the *será* section

FIGURE 40.6 Musical transcription of the standard hand clapping rhythm from the *será* section

became revered not necessarily as a result of historical fact but rather from the collective self-questioning of the *Tambú* community searching for a "firm foundation on which to base a shared sense of its social self."[25] The position and importance that Diyani acquired in the ritual provides an opportunity to explore *Tambú*'s allegorical power. Diyani was an icon, an archetype of strongly held, yet "imperfectly understood, beliefs."[26] She became a "construction of reality,"[27] one "carried on in a spirit of sentimental appreciation rather than of critical analysis."[28]

"[E]very nation needs a mythic explanation of its own creation," Michael Kammen argues,[29] a way to explain origins, create self-identities and establish collective belonging. That Curaçaoans would rely on myths surrounding the Arawaks to fulfill that goal is therefore not so unusual, Kammen reminds. Most societies "in fact reconstruct their pasts rather than faithfully record them" and do so "with the needs of contemporary culture clearly in mind."[30] Although the past is often regarded as something objective or eternal, in reality, it is malleable, with individuals and groups purposefully molding it to fit their own needs and wants. Curaçao's official colonial history had been largely a "one-sided portrayal," accuses historian Rosemarijn Hoefte, one that has dealt nearly exclusively with Dutch achievements and viewpoints.[31] With the Arawaks and with Diyani, then, an opportunity emerged to rewrite that past and to privilege alternative understandings of a lived historical remembrance.

Reverence for the Amerindians is evident in the rituals from other island nations as well. Among them is St. Lucia, home to the Kélé religion. During the Kélé ritual, a set of smooth stones are displayed in honor of the African ancestors. Yet, the origin of these stones is with the Amerindians, who are believed

25 Kammen, *Mystic Chords of Memory*, 2011, p. 65.
26 Shumate, "Full Circle: Juvenal's Egyptians and the Return of the 'Angry White Man' in Satire 15," 2021, p. 88.
27 Gillis, *Commemorations: The Politics of National Identity*, 1994, p. 3.
28 Hofstadter, *The American Political Tradition and the Men Who Made It*, 1948, p. v.
29 Kammen, *Mystic Chords of Memory*, 2011, p. 27.
30 Ibid., p. 3.
31 Hoefte, "The Dutch in the Caribbean and the Guianans, 1680–1791: Book Review," 1988, p. 125.

to have used them in precolonial St. Lucia as agricultural implements.[32] In Puerto Rico, Espiritismo utilizes healing methods borrowed from Taíno belief systems, specifically the prescription of plants and herbs to treat physical, emotional and spiritual ailments.[33] In the Dominican Republic, the Taínos are honored in vodou rituals with a separate altar, which, located on the ground near containers of water, is meant to honor the symbolic and multifunctional role nature has served in Taíno culture.[34]

In further tribute to the Arawaks, Curaçao's caves have acquired particular mythological importance. As supported by archaeological research, the Arawaks used these caves from 500 AD to bury their dead and hold ceremonial rites necessary to ensure deceased relatives would reach eternal realms.[35] This spiritual connection to the Arawaks, along with their assumed function as a route to freedom, helped elevate the island's caves to the rank of holy sites in *Tambú*. Today, the caves, which now sit above ground, are prime locations for practicing *Tambú* rites. Given the reverence *Tambú* followers hold for the island's caves, it is not surprising that Diyani's capable command of the caves also helped to raise her prestige among devotees, with her stories again validating versions of a perceived history that many Curaçaoans already held close.

Just as the island's caves had gained mythological prominence among *Tambú* followers, so, too, did Venezuela. In fact, it emerged as a sort of Mt. Olympus among devotees, revered not only as a site of freedom and liberty but also as a mythical invention of homeland. It was where ritual gods and ancestors were believed to reside when not participating in *Tambú*, and it was where *Tambú* followers, upon death, were believed to spend eternity.

Returning to ancestral homelands is a common quest across the globe. Yet, for the Afro-Caribbean, exact ancestral origins are impossible to realize—slavery and centuries of colonization have made that pursuit unattainable. "The 'original Africa' is no longer there," reminds Stuart Hall. "It too has been transformed. History is, in that sense, irreversible."[36] Any returns, therefore, must be accomplished "by another route,"[37] such as through ritual and remembrance. The Big Drum ritual of Carriacou is one such "narrative of return."[38] In Big Drum, participants employ rhythmic dance as a mechanism for taking

32 Simpson, "The Kele (Chango) Cult in St. Lucia," 1973.

33 Molina, "Community Healing among Puerto Ricans," 2001.

34 Davis, Guzmán, and Martínez, "Vodú of the Dominican Republic," 2007.

35 Haviser, "Perforated Prehistoric Ornaments of Curaçao and Bonaire, Netherlands Antilles," 1990.

36 Hall, *Selected Writings on Race and Difference*, 1990, p. 231.

37 Ibid., p. 232.

38 De Jong and Williams, "Narratives of Return: Carricou and the Big Drum Ritual," 2022.

spiritual "flights" home to Africa.[39] Igbo Landing provides yet another account of return: on an island off the coast of Georgia (United States), a community of enslaved Igbos is said to have escaped by flying across the waters back to Africa. Although documented as the largest mass suicide of enslaved peoples to have occurred in the Americas, it has been reclaimed in mythology not as "death" but as a return to the ancestors, not as a tragedy but as a celebration of resilience, rebellion and strength: the Igbos had refused to live in slavery, choosing instead to rejoin their African ancestors through this final, defiant act of rebellion.[40]

In *Tambú*, the ritual patterns of reverence and remembrance that transformed Venezuela into a spiritual site in Curaçao left Venezuela "less a geographical ideal than a cultural principle that celebrate[d] the connection between living and ancestral systems."[41] It transcended the confines of prescribed cultural and national difference to serve as medium through which *Tambú* devotees could build revised senses of belonging.

Diyani's stories validated Venezuela's mythologic status and reconfirmed Venezuela's promise of ancestral return. Her stories also stood as reminders that, in the Caribbean, connections to "homeland" cannot necessarily be reached via straight, unbroken lines. Rather, they must be "made and remade, undermined and transformed",[42] "realistically combed and plaited into unified strands of collective human experiences."[43] The motivation behind *Tambú* followers claiming Venezuela as a spiritual homeland, to paraphrase Paul Gilroy,[44] was not about trying to "fix" an "absolute" history but to foster a creative process that enabled devotees to establish a needed solidarity and collective belonging.

In the broadest sense, the mythologies around the Arawaks, the Curaçao caves and Venezuela are about a Caribbean community controlling its own past and myths. With Diyani, *Tambú* devotees had a mechanism not only for securing perceived ancestral lineages but also for retelling that history in ways that secured "national cohesiveness, spiritual outreach and the retention of ancestral communication."[45] Devotees who accepted Diyani as part of their *Tambú* pantheon did so through the collective optimism that the past could be

39 McDaniel, *The Big Drum Ritual of Carriacou: Praisesongs in Rememory of Flight*, 1998.

40 De Jong and Williams, "Narratives of Return: Carricou and the Big Drum Ritual," 2022, p. 209.

41 McDaniel, "Concept of Nation," 1993, p. 409.

42 Clarke and Thomas, *Globalization and Race*, 2006, p. 19.

43 McDaniel, "Musical Thoughts on Unresolved Questions and Recent Findings in Big Drum Research," 2002, p. 409.

44 Gilroy, *The Black Atlantic*, 1993, p. 223.

45 Ibid., p. 138.

imagined differently, reshaped so as to "make it more exemplary."[46] As David Lowenthal has written, "[w]e manipulate the legacy given us to secure it as heritage, hyped improvements sanctifying it in our eyes and distinguishing it from others."[47]

Diyani provided the perfect icon for that Curaçaoan optimism: she was an Arawak royal who sacrificed her own safety to ensure the freedom of others. She was cloaked in Curaçaoan legend and her life represented the strength and sovereignty Curaçaoans imagined—or wished—their past to be. She was bold and adventurous, brave and resourceful, availing a history that countered the legitimacy of Dutch domination. Importantly, Diyani also brought forward a woman's perspective, which had been sorely neglected. Genise Vertus argues that the enslaved women from the Caribbean have "too often disappeared from historical accounts of slavery ... receiv[ing] little or no credit for taking an active role in resistance to slavery."[48] With Diyani, that omission begins to be filled, with her stories reminding us that the women of Curaçao also serve as keepers of memories and history.

Standing at the intersection of myth, history and ritual, Diyani also enabled a means by which *Tambú* followers could embark on their quest for meaning and resolution. As Haidee so poignantly explained it, "Diyani is speaking. She tells us how to get on in life ... Diyani brings us answers if we listen."[49]

Bibliography

Clarke, Kamari Maxine, and Deborah A. Thomas, eds. *Globalization and Race: Transformations in the Cultural Production of Blackness*. Durham, NC: Duke University Press, 2006.

Davis, Martha Ellen, Jovanny Guzmán, and Norma Urraca Martínez. "Vodú of the Dominican Republic: Devotion to 'La veintiuna división.'" *Afro-Hispanic Review* 26, no. 1 (2007): 75–90.

Dean, Diana Maitland. *Dreaming the Dead: The Social Impact of Dreams in an Afro-Cuban Community*. Minneapolis: University of Minnesota, 1993.

De Jong, Nanette. *Tambú: Curaçao's African-Caribbean Ritual and the Politics of Memory*. Bloomington: Indiana University Press, 2012.

46 Lowenthal, *The Past Is a Foreign Country – Revisited*, 2015, p. 21.

47 Ibid.

48 Vertus, "An Even Stronger Woman: The Enslaved Black Caribbean Woman," n.d. Editors' note: see also contributions by Allen and Clemencia in this volume.

49 Interview with author, Curaçao, 1995.

De Jong, Nanette, and Linda Williams. "Narratives of Return: Carricou and the Big Drum Ritual." In *The Cambridge Companion to Caribbean Music*, edited by Nanette de Jong, 209–26. Cambridge: Cambridge University Press, 2022.

Dominguez, Luis Arturo. *Vivencia de un rito luango en el Tambú* [Experience of a luango ritual in *Tambú*]. Caracas, Venezuela: Ediciones Co-Bo, 1988.

Fowler, Peter. *The Past in Contemporary Society: Then, Now*. London: Routledge, 1992.

François, Anne M. *Rewriting the Return to Africa: Voices of Francophone Caribbean Women Writers*. Lanham: MD, 2011.

Gillis, John R., ed. *Commemorations: The Politics of National Identity*. Princeton, NJ: Princeton University Press, 1994.

Goslinga, Cornelis Charles. *A Short History of the Netherlands Antilles and Surinam*. Dordrecht: Springer Netherlands, 1979.

Goslinga, Cornelis Charles. *The Dutch in the Caribbean and on the Wild Coast 1580–1680*. Gainesville: University of Florida Press, 1971.

Hall, Stuart. *Selected Writings on Race and Difference*. Edited by Paul Gilroy and Ruth Wilson Gilmore. Durham, NC: Duke University Press, 2021. https://doi.org/10.1215/9781478021223.

Haviser, Jay B. "Perforated Prehistoric Ornaments of Curaçao and Bonaire, Netherlands Antilles." *BEADS: Journal of the Society of Bead Researchers* 2, no. 1 (1990): 85–92.

Hoefte, Rosemarijn. "The Dutch in the Caribbean and the Guianans, 1680–1791: Book Review." *Hispanic American Historical Review* 68, no. 1 (1986): 125–6.

Hofstadter, Richard. *The American Political Tradition and the Men Who Made It*. New York: Alfred A. Knopf, 1948.

Honwana, Alcinda. "Spiritual Agency and Self-Renewal in Southern Mozambique." PhD. diss., University of London, 1996.

Honwana, Alcinda. "Healing for Peace: Traditional Healers and Post-War Reconstruction in Southern Mozambique." *Peace and Conflict: Journal of Peace Psychology* 3 (1997): 293–305.

Kammen, Michael. *Mystic Chords of Memory: The Transformation of Tradition in American Culture*. New York: Vintage Books, 2011.

Las Casas, Bartolomé de. *A Short Account of the Destruction of the Indies*. London: Penguin Books, 1992.

Lowenthal, David. *The Past Is a Foreign Country – Revisited*. Cambridge: Cambridge University Press, 2015.

McDaniel, Lorna. "Musical Thoughts on Unresolved Questions and Recent Findings in Big Drum Research." *Black Music Research Journal* 22, no. 1 (2002): 127–39.

McDaniel, Lorna. *The Big Drum Ritual of Carriacou: Praisesongs in Rememory of Flight*. Gainesville: University of Florida Press, 1998.

McDaniel, Lorna. "Concept of Nation." In *Repercussions of the 1492 Encounter*, edited by Carol Robertson, pp. 395–410. Washington, DC: Smithsonian Institution Press, 1993.

McGee, Adam M. "Dreaming in Haitian Vodou: Vouchsafe, Guide, and Source of Liturgical Novelty." *Dreaming* 22, no. 2 (2012): 83–100.

Molina, M. A. N. "Community Healing among Puerto Ricans: Espiritismo As a Therapy for the Soul." In *Healing Cultures: Art and Religion As Curative Practices in the Caribbean and Its Diaspora*, edited by Margarite Fernández Olmos and Lizabeth Paravisini-Gebert, 115–29. New York: Palgrave, 2001.

Postma, Johannes. *The Dutch in the Atlantic Slave Trade, 1600–1815*. Cambridge: Cambridge University Press, 1990.

Rosalia, Rene. "Represhon di kultura: E lucha di Tambú" [Repression of culture: The struggle of *Tambú*]. PhD. diss., University of Amsterdam, 1997.

Shumate, Nancy. "Full Circle: Juvenal's Egyptians and the Return of the 'Angry White Man' in Satire 15." *New England Classical Journal* 48, no. 1 (2021): 81–96.

Simpson, George Eaton. "The Kele (Chango) Cult in St. Lucia." *Caribbean Studies* 13, no. 3 (1973): 110–16.

Thompson, Robert Farris. *Flash of the Spirit: African and Afro-American Art and Philosophy*. London: Random House, 1983.

Vertus, Genise. "An Even Stronger Woman: The Enslaved Black Caribbean Woman." Slave Resistance: A Caribbean Study, 2000. https://scholar.library.miami.edu/slaves/womens_resistance/individual_essays/genise.html.

CHAPTER 41

Sex, Spirit and the Artist in the Films of Felix de Rooy

Jean Antoine-Dunne

Abstract

The contribution analyzes three films of Felix de Rooy, *Desiree* (1981), *Almacita di desolato* (1985) and *Ava and Gabriel: A Love Story* (1990), arguing that sexuality and spirituality are the means through which de Rooy negotiates his own identity as an artist from the Dutch Caribbean and as a postcolonial subject. The films have in common a female protagonist who is suppressed, repressed or who is attempting to surface from under sexual repression. This is in itself significant given that the Caribbean has long privileged the male as the primary mover in the destiny of the region. De Rooy and his then partner and collaborator Norman de Palm seek to disturb easy categorization and demonstrate in the films that dominant ideas of masculinity are in need of interrogation and reimagining.

Keywords

Felix de Rooy – films – masculinity – spirituality – postcolonial identity

It may appear somewhat sensationalist to discuss the work of Curaçaoan filmmaker Felix de Rooy under a title such as "Sex and Spirit," but his trilogy suggests that these are the two perspectives through which de Rooy interrogates the nature of his own identity as an artist from the Dutch Caribbean and as a postcolonial subject.

The three films, *Desiree* (1981), *Almacita di desolato* (1985) and *Ava and Gabriel: A Love Story* (1990), have in common a female protagonist who is suppressed, repressed or who is attempting to surface from under sexual repression. That the primary subjects are female is in itself significant given that the Caribbean has long privileged the male as the primary mover in the destiny of the region. The fact that de Rooy is openly gay and that Norman de Palm, his partner at the time, is the coproducer and screenwriter of the second and

 | DOI:10.1163/9789004690882_043

third films of the trilogy suggests immediately that both artists are seeking to move beyond categorization and that they see dominant ideas of masculinity as something in need of interrogation and rethinking. It is also significant that de Palm is a clinical psychologist, and his influence is evident in all three films.[1]

There is no doubt that religion plays an important role in the repressive structures that cause Desiree, in the film of that name, to become "cracked up." In *Almacita di desolato*, religious bigotry also pushes a community (obviously reluctant to do so) to exert punitive measures on the priestess Solem when she becomes pregnant, thus causing her to go into exile. In *Ava and Gabriel*, religious bigotry conspires with racism and homophobia to destroy the painter Gabriel, to ostracize Ava and to bring their homosexual friend to the point of near death. But both *Almacita di desolato* and *Ava and Gabriel* also situate their narratives in a time past and, through story structures, provide insight into what the filmmakers seem to perceive to be the deep cause of the thread of madness that runs through all three films.

Almacita has its original focus on what appears at the onset to be a runaway from a place called San Christophe, a name that resonates with Haiti. The film, throughout its discourse, references a rich land, external markets, trade with foreign lands and the exploitation of the land's resources and also suggests that the riches of the soil have led to insurrection and internal strife. This, combined with costuming, hints that the film is loosely set at the time of the Haitian revolution.

The story also weaves a mythic tapestry and sets itself up as a dialogue between the past and the physical effects on the present through the repetition of the line "history is engraved in skin." But the film is also a mythic retelling since it speaks of the intercourse between gods (or the devil) and humans, through which the gift of fertility is given to both woman and land, and also involves the promise of a savior, the child Almacita (the little soul), who, as the product of the Alma Sola (force of evil) and the priestess and protector Solem (force of goodness), will unify the conflicting elements of good and evil[2] after Solem has defeated the devil to redeem her child and, by extension, her land.

There is, then, prophecy, trial and fulfillment, and this mythic story structure binds the society together. Through unified belief, it both heals and enables the community to move beyond the confines of its insularity.

What accomplishes this, and, indeed, the project is similar in *Ava and Gabriel*, is an interrogation of the force that spirit exerts on the communal

1 Felix de Rooy, email interview by author, September 30, 2012.
2 Martin, *Cinemas of the Black Diaspora*, 1995.

psyche and of the way in which the force field of spirit survives in memory and through lineage and is passed down from one generation to the next. Ideas of procreation and generational transmission are linked to ideas of spirit and spirituality from the earliest film, *Desiree*, which de Rooy produced as a student at New York University.[3]

The idea of children as a force for change and continuity is further delineated at the very beginning of *Ava and Gabriel*, where the young girl child from *Almacita* reappears. In *Almacita*, the mother and young boy had been portrayed as the individuals who had kept faith with a prophecy and had the strength to continue the journey to bring the baby Almacita to the chosen land. Almacita reappears at the onset of *Ava and Gabriel*. This dovetailing of individuals is a mechanism for bringing the three films into conversation with each other, but the opening sequence of *Ava and Gabriel*, in its tracking of the young girl's movement across the landscape, also solidifies the notion that new generations cement the bond between land, individual and community.

But de Rooy and de Palm seem to be arguing that sexual repression or narrowness destroys the spirit and leads to a madness that can only be seen as destructive. The capacity for change and communal and psychic wholeness is not simply a matter of regeneration but rather of the exertion of the will to reverse or resist the forces that seek power over the land and the community. Sexual repression is one of a number of factors that can lead to the abortion and death of communal life and vitality. One can read this in Desiree's final descent into the madness that causes her to throw her child into the furnace and in the present, where she carries an empty box as if it were a cradle. There is a blurring of events when she destroys her child that contribute to the viewer's sense that there are tangled motivations for her actions, but the film points to her male partner's frustration at Desiree's neurotic obsession with religion, her sense of sex as sin and the real poverty into which she descends once she loses her job because of her pregnancy. Economic deprivation, unfair social practices and racial stereotyping operate alongside and intensify an inherited belief that sex is opposed to sanctification and the body must be cleansed from sexual desire.

There is a clear line between the potency of the destructive force of religious zeal that demands total denial of the body and its desires and the madness that threatens Desiree's mother and that finally envelops Desiree as she becomes a desiring woman. It is no accident, I imagine, that the first film in this trilogy is called *Desiree*.

3 Felix de Rooy, interview by author, Curaçao, June 2011; email interview by author, September 28, 2012.

As the trilogy progresses in its arguments and ideas, de Rooy increasingly interrogates the problem of sexual desire and the role of the Christian church in repressing this. He links this repression to the lust for power and dominance that is located in institutions such as the Catholic Church, the police force and systems of governance that privilege white skin over black in Curaçao of the time. The use of a black woman by black artist Gabriel Goedbloed as model for the Virgin Mary transgresses these norms and systemic abuses and ends in his murder.

This discourse on skin color is codified in the meeting between Bishop Hildebrandt and other clergy, the governor and his wife and the artist Gabriel, which signals the intertwining of racist attitudes with Curaçao's power structures. The love between Ava and Gabriel then signifies a breach of law, primarily because it is a thwarting of the desires of those who hold and maintain power and these structures of power. The love story between two gay men is also viewed from the perspective of social standing and class since it is the mulatto, Maurice, who is beaten, while his white gay partner is left unscathed. In colonial Curaçao, black bodies and homosexual bodies must be kept in check by words and blows when they refuse to submit to their role as subordinate to bodies that are white and to heterosexually desiring flesh. De Rooy connects power to desire by making Ava the jealously guarded fiancée of the white police captain Zarius and Gabriel the sought-after object of the white governor's white wife. But the film is not simply about racism and homophobia. The mise-en-scène guides us to this conclusion in the key scene where Zarius seizes Gabriel and beats him in front of the battered Maurice on the left and the painting of the half-naked Ava on the right.

Racism and homophobia are signs of a power struggle between forces that seek to maintain control of the state and the minds of the people. Thus, Ava's and Gabriel's desires are to be controlled because, in their artistic creativity, they come to symbolize the gift of creation and the rights of humanity to express, desire and create and to proclaim their equality. The battle is seen as a battle of spirit against the backdrop of the Orisha belief structure that pervades the film narrative. The iguana seen at the beginning of this film then becomes the sign of the power of the land itself and of the people who inhabit it. De Rooy has pointed out that the iguana is not simply an iconic presence but is also a unifying link that binds Solem and her savior child Almacita to Desiree, whose child has mysteriously died although her presence remains a spiritual one, and integrates these two films into the narrative of Ava and Gabriel.[4]

4 De Rooy, email interview, September 28, 2012.

The iguana is a forbidding presence in *Ava and Gabriel* and is a mark of spiritual force and of the terror inherent in the reclamation of native creativity. In *Almacita*, Solem is confronted by an iguana when she emerges from the cave after hearing the prophecy that her child will save her people. The iguana is symbolically linked to the sublime force of the Santera, herself an enigmatic and terrifying presence. This force, throughout all three films, hovers near the surface of consciousness for the community and the viewer and suggests an always-threatening possibility that its potency will shatter the historic chains of repressive structures, whether these are the result of colonialism, Christianity or any other power structure, black or white, that has taken away freedom from the individual.

Ava and Gabriel is specifically located in colonial Curaçao of the 1950s, and the Dutch state, its governance, its policing mechanisms and the Christian church operate hand in hand. This suggests that de Rooy sees colonialism and its residual presence as significant factors in the destruction of human freedom. The languages spoken in the film, however, are predominantly those of Curaçao, and, in fact, there are several dialects used in the dialogue. Colonial power is seen to exist alongside a vibrant linguistic and cultural field, clearly evoked in the use of color symbolism and in the near-mythical presence of the Santera, who becomes a unifying thread for the whole work. Language as words and as myth becomes a visible sign of retained diversity and individual freedom, perhaps more clearly and persuasively demarcated in the use of the female griot and several mythic strands in *Almacita.*

But religious ritual is also a sign of such freedom. Such manifestations of spiritual belief are also resilient presences and these are carried both in the interaction with Santería and in the sense perceptions of the community, their choice of color, song, dance and even repartee. These are generational in that they are carried through the ages in bodily acts and memories, as is made apparent in the film *Almacita* when Solem's feet remember the ritual dance for water and wind, and when the ancestors rise to give new breath to her dead child.

As de Rooy has indicated, it is not possible to read *Ava and Gabriel* without placing it in the context of *Desiree* and *Almacita.*[5] Each woman is a development, one may even say a spiritual descendant, of the other, although, chronologically speaking, *Desiree* is set in the latter part of twentieth century, *Almacita* in the late nineteenth century[6] and *Ava and Gabriel* in the mid-twentieth century. Yet, speaking in terms of myth, *Desiree*, in particular, in its fluid

5 Ibid.

6 Ibid.

movement between present and past time, sets up a structure that suggests that her story is the one that motivates the narrative flow of the others.

In *Desiree*, the portrait of Desiree's mother hangs over the room that Desiree occupies as an adult and this figure forms the apex of her relationship with her lover, so that, even when she is dead, this mother dominates the mind and the life of her daughter. The film uses both framing and shallow filmic space to suggest this claustrophobic legacy. Desiree has been left with a neurotic obsession with her mother's body and sexuality and her mind reverts to these images in seamless fashion. The mother's ambivalent attitude to sexuality as both sin and pleasure is intensified in the young Desiree, who falls and is rescued by a preacher from the black Christian congregation. He preaches that only those who are in true communion can cohabit and all else is damnation. Set in the USA, the film opens with Desiree carrying an empty box and talking to an invisible presence. It flows into her early childhood, and, in fact, the dark color of the screen in the present suggests that the past is far more real and alive than the present moment. The camera plays with images: the cracked ceiling as she cracks mentally when she loses her job; the bleeding heart of the Sacred Heart when she wallows in her pain. There is no room to see Desiree, then, as anything other than a woman deeply marked and broken by a past that has left her literally divided into two irreconcilable selves: harlot and church mother.

No real evidence is given of the baby's death. But the unfeeling medical bureaucrat who threatens her with Social Services opens the door for a montage sequence that shows her living on herbs and carrying a pillow as if it were a child. The state, society and church are coconspirators in this film. The later films of this trilogy develop the psychological causes of Desiree's self-division and madness. We can also reason that the dead child signifies a dead end and a consequence of guilty sexual desire and economic powerlessness.

The films develop these themes of repression but use aesthetic means to question their power and their source. One such is the camera's evocative lingering on the bodies of Desiree and her lover in their room in New York. It is a luxuriant tracking of the body in ecstasy, and, as the shot moves to the face and figure of the Christ, it evokes a similar pleasure in the sight of the body of Christ, lingering on muscles and skin. There is the same voyeuristic approach to texture, and the filmmaker thus presents the ecstasy of the redeemer in his divinity and lovemaking as equal acts of sanctity. This kind of cinematography acts to assuage the guilt felt and projected by Desiree and to provide a counterpoint to psychological repression.

The films use color as a symbolic and ideological statement, adding to their complex visual language. The color blue is used in *Desiree* as an expression of both freedom and potent anger when her partner leaves home after a violent explosion of rage. This color is imbued with multiple meanings and is also deeply connected on several levels to motherhood and the transmission of generational beliefs. In *Ava and Gabriel*, it is associated with the Santera and with the Christian belief in the Virgin Mother (Ava and Mary can, without too much effort, be read as the Catholic prayer, Ave Maria). In *Ava and Gabriel*, blue has both Orisha and Christian signification, both of which are linked to the idea and the significance of motherhood.[7] This duality suggests that de Rooy has moved to an idea of what we might call hybrid religions or, more accurately, a state of play where the artist, through his palette, can point to the similarities and the equivalences between the dominant and the repressed religions and their role in cultural transmission.

Tolerance is, of course, one of the key messages of this film—since it highlights the result of intolerance in the killing of Gabriel and the brutalization of his gay friend. But the deeper idea, heralded in the film's opening, is that there are human forces that give agency and these have a deep spiritual basis. As in *Almacita* and *Desiree*, these are twinned: sexual desire has its climax in ecstasy but so does spiritual desire, and this spiritual focus is closely aligned to the creative and procreative urges within the human. The cinematographer caresses the body of Ava with his camera both to show the swelling lust in Gabriel's body and to point to the creative surge as he holds a paintbrush. The camera dwells in *Almacita* on the moving body of the priestess as she dominates the landscape to call the rain and save her child. The dance is, as it has been in so many Caribbean literary and cultural projects, an image/idea of power, syncretism and a link between the ancestral past and the present.

The artist takes as his task the marking of things, performing a kind of naming that draws various responses from the viewer as we begin to understand the function both of the camera and of artistic endeavor. The camera in *Almacita* and *Ava and Gabriel* draws forth deeper insights into the nature of human existence by the very concentration on the surface of things. "Ask our ancestors if their history isn't engraved in their skin," the film *Almacita* demands at its beginning. History is in the skin of the film, *Ava and Gabriel, Almacita* and *Desiree* suggest.[8]

What emerges out of de Rooy's attempts to bring these various elements together is a burgeoning idea that the human body is marked by its past but that this past is both complex and shaped by contradictory forces. As with montage itself, it is through the conflicts of these dissonant forces that something

7 Author's note: thanks to Rhoda Bharath for this information.

8 This observation is directly influenced by Laura Marks's *The Skin of the Film*, 2000.

creative emerges, and, in *Ava and Gabriel* as in *Almacita*, death precedes such transformation.

Neither film postulates an easy solution to the inherited problems of a colonial past or human frailty. In fact, colonialism itself is seen as resulting from an all too human desire for power and dominance. The films propose instead the wisdom of art and creativity not as weak, ineffective rationalizations of inaction but as possible vehicles of thought through which humankind might develop agency and true love. The films are in themselves vehicles of such thought, in particular in the use of symbolism and innovative camera angles and mise-en-scène, which all add density to the ideas unfolding on screen.

Ava and Gabriel begins with a close-up of the artist Gabriel drawing the landscape with the camera resting on fossils. The focus on such sketching is to ensure that the viewer understands that this love story is also a love story of the artist and his material. The mise-en-scène of this opening sequence links the iguana held by the boy to both fossils and land so that a cluster of ideas emerges. These ideas are already embedded in the story of *Almacita*, which also brought land, boy, art and the past as fossil together as a potent mix for changing the future.

Gabriel's entry into Curaçao is deliberately explosive. He "erupts" into the town on his motorbike during religious festivities and thus draws the attention of the schoolteacher, Ava, and her lover, Zarius, with whom he comes into conflict. In a manner not unlike the opening of that other iconic Caribbean film, Perry Henzell's *The Harder They Come* (1972), the film privileges a clash of cultures and the importance of conflict to change. Gabriel's confrontation with the policeman Zarius is a portent of what is to emerge as the story unwinds. But we also note from the onset that the Amsterdam-born Gabriel, who has studied art in The Hague, has brought with him a festering resentment against white superiority. At this initial confrontation, there is also a clash of religions, although the film is at pains to show that, for black Curaçaoan natives, even the most bourgeois, there is a seamless belief flowing between Christianity, with its ideas of discipline and its curtailment of sexual freedom, and the Orisha pantheon (Ava's mother, for example, while paying homage to the Catholic Church, also prays to Yemayá). The Santera sees with blazing eyes the noisy arrival of Gabriel. She holds a blue scarf—and this, too, signifies the fluid transitions between belief systems. But, here, the Santera is a witness to what she knows is a battle to the death.

This use of color and the choice of an artist figure as hero underline the value that the filmmakers place on art as a vehicle for seeing, synthesizing cultures and breaking with the dead traditions of the past. As Gabriel notes in speaking to Bishop Hildebrandt, "time defies tradition." His function as artist is to combine "Antillean elements with Dutch." This role makes him also a prophet and in league with the Santera, who has stated at a key moment that blue is the color of both sky and sea and has linked this color to the Orisha god of the sea and motherhood and made connections, in combining it with the color white, to the state of innocence of a soul. Both Gabriel and the Santera have access to divine knowledge and intuit through soul knowledge.

The shot of Gabriel, wearing blue, looking down at the children and Ava (also wearing blue) in the schoolyard at an early stage in the film makes this quite obvious. He is wearing blue as the symbolic color of divinity. His figure is shot from below, making him tower above the land and its institutions. But, set against the blue sky, Gabriel appears to be at one with the heavens—and truly a guardian angel.

But blue is also used in the two truly climactic moments when the action turns. The screen becomes almost completely blue when Zarius goes in search of Gabriel and begins to beat him before bearing him off in a police van to the governor and his wife. Blue is then associated not simply with divinity but with those moments when the main figures endure the effects of conflict. This conflictual action leads to a change in the perception of reality: in the second significant use of the color blue, the previously bigoted landlady turns after seeing the brutality enacted on Gabriel. The action here shifts between the destruction of Gabriel's painting, his arrest and battery and the action of the landlady as she offers her handkerchief to Maurice's lover, who is holding the battered Maurice in his arms. The scenes that are in conflict are bathed in blue light. The use of the color here unites the actions. The two acts, one the beating of a homosexual and the other the beating of a black painter who has dared to love the object of Zarius's desire (and who has also painted the governor's wife as she is, with an ugly facial blemish), suggest both the problem and a possible resolution through the incipient goodness at the heart of a community. This further signifies that film has the potential to bring issues into focus and that if the root causes of senseless violence are shown for what they are, then this visibility can lead to real change in society.

One of the interesting features of Gabriel's discourse is his discussion of black skin. Gabriel tells Ava that he wishes to paint the "light upon her skin." And, of course, the story revolves around skin color and inflections of color since it is the color of the Virgin Mary's skin that causes the problem; a concern with skin color is, in fact, threaded throughout the work as a fact of Curaçao's culture. When Gabriel is killed, the mural is whitewashed, again obviously a reference to the triumph of whiteness. But de Rooy makes no bones about the fact that he is not privileging black over white. Part of the argument of the film and one of the reasons that its main protagonist must be an artist is that

Curaçao is a rainbow nation—in the sense that all colors are represented and also because de Rooy and de Palm are gay, so that inclusiveness is the key idea. As an artist, Gabriel makes possible the use of the multifaceted nature of light as metaphor. The moment when the young priest Fr. Fidelius, accompanied by women from the town, sees the mural lit up as a rainbow points to the beauty and even mystic significance of the complex of differences in the societal makeup of Curaçao.

During the festival day in honor of the Dutch monarchy, both Gabriel and Ava wear red. This red becomes a sign of the approaching rise in passion as Ava poses naked for Gabriel and is a visual signifier of the political message of the film, since Zarius's attack is contextualized within several sequences that point directly to the suppression and marginalization of the black population.

These ideas are given greater symbolic value by the appearance of the iguana, as a sign of indigenous potential and power, when Ava runs to her home after seeing Maurice's beaten body. The iguana also appears when the governor's wife tears the portrait done by Gabriel, and it had also been a sign of obvious warning when she and Gabriel entered the elevator as she began to seduce him. Its image at the film's end suggests that, as in the film's beginning and in the film *Almacita*, it is a symbol not only of violent disruption but also of continuity and humanity's connection to the divine—as are the color blue and the figure of the Santera. The iguana, therefore, brings to full circle the filmmaker's understanding of art as a connecting force between generations and as vehicle for renewal and transformation because the artist is a conduit and perhaps a representative of divine ways of seeing.

Acknowledgments

This text was first published as Antoine-Dunne, Jean. "Sex, Spirit and the Artist in the Films of Felix de Rooy." *Caribbean Quarterly* 61, no. 2–3 (2015): 66–76. Reproduction is courtesy of *Caribbean Quarterly*.

Bibliography

Marks, Laura U. *The Skin of the Film: Intercultural Cinema, Embodiment, and the Senses*. Durham, NC: Duke University Press, 2000.

Martin, Michael T., ed. *Cinemas of the Black Diaspora: Diversity, Dependence, and Oppositionality*. Contemporary Film and Television Series. Detroit: Wayne State University Press, 1995.

CHAPTER 42

St. Maarten Is Like My Lover

Lysanne Charles

St. Martin is like my lover
The sight of her slopes
Brings comfort to my heart
And a hitch to my breath

The knowledge of her
Settles a restless chest
While being in her presence
Can stir the soul

She is a beauty
All curves and waters
Feminine by virtue
Of existence

She has birthed from her womb
Children she does not always
Understand
yet loves
Hoping only that they do not
Destroy too much of her
And leave some of her
For her

There are those
Who will challenge this fascination
With hills and curves
Not understanding her pull
And still
I am drawn
To parts of her geography
I know better than others
Those that I can name

 | DOI:10.1163/9789004690882_044

Off the top of my head
And yet
There are still parts I want to know
But maybe never will
She has regions that are yet to be explored
But perhaps will become known
To someone other than me
Who will look at her
And fall in love

With scents and salt

I may only remember
Like passing memory

Sweet Sweet St. Martin
Like my lover
Is beautiful in her vulnerability
Strong because of her history
And yet because of it
Fragile too

I leave her reluctantly
For I love her
More perhaps than she will ever know
And I yet I go to grow
Longing to stay
I am driven to leave
To expand horizons
Scale new heights
And weave
A life of my own
But the price to pay is heavy
I forfeit home

There is the uncertainty
Of return
And will she be the same
Unchanged
Or will time develop her

Somehow beyond my reach
Or more difficult yet
Turn my heart away

And what of our great love affair
Can it survive distance and time
New loves and lovers passing by

Can it change
So I too can change
And live and love without
Sense of betrayal

St. Martin
so like … My lover

Ours is a complicated matter

Acknowledgments

This poem was first published as Charles, Lysanne. "St. Maarten is like my lover." *Journal of Lesbian Studies* 15, no. 1 (January 18, 2011): 95–97. https://doi.org/10.1080/10894160.2010.508426. Reproduction courtesy of Lysanne Charles.

CHAPTER 43

Muhé Di Rancho, Be(com)ing with *Calco*: a Caribbean Feminist Practice for Decolonial Life Writing

Nadia Dresscher-Lambertus

Abstract

The queen conch—locally known as *calco*—is a vibrant assemblage of decolonial life force: creative inspiration, layered onto-epistemological symbol, ancestral carrier of stories and indigenous abundance and historical aquatic witness of the transatlantic Middle Passage. Combining autoethnography, decolonial Caribbean epistemologies and feminist posthumanisms, *calco* inspires a Caribbean feminist life writing practice emerging from a space of a slower ontology; it is creative, reparative, nonlinear, polyvocal and intergenerational in its movements and temporalities; it is an embodied practice expressing fleshy becomings; it is ecological, connected to the depths, fluidity and tidal waves of the Caribbean Sea, linked to situated shorelines. An ecotone space metaphorical for the liminal spaces of transformations and the numinous dimensions of everyday life. Writing ourselves into being from this space is a process of actively worlding our decolonial becomings.

Keywords

calco – hydrofeminism – Rancho – Aruba – Caribbean sea – decolonial life writing

Watery substance
full of ancestral sediments
of my aquatic beginnings.
The inner side
of my hearing
spiral-shelled like
a mollusk
so I can listen

 | DOI:10.1163/9789004690882_045

to the language
of waves

Revisiting histories
Each turning
whorl
bringing me closer
to worlding
the pluriverse
… home[1]

∵

Accompanying me in writing this essay are the remains of the shell of a *calco* on my writing desk. *Calco* is the Aruban local name for the *Strombus gigas*, popularly known as the Caribbean queen conch. I pick up the shell and put it against my ear. I make "kin" to her in an interspecies symbiosis.[2] I can hear the sounds of *lama di Caribe* (Caribbean Sea). The *calco* connects me to the sea and her waters.

In her magical embodiments, as a mollusk when alive or as a seashell in her afterlife form, the *calco* is a vibrant assemblage[3] of life force. *Calco* is creative inspiration, layered onto-epistemological symbol, an ancestral carrier of stories in differing times, temporalities and registers, a source of indigenous abundance and sustenance and, as a kin species, intimate knower of the Caribbean Sea, a historical aquatic witness of crossings, such as the transatlantic Middle Passage.

The *calco* is an important recurring theme in the history of Rancho, a small, historically resilient community at the outskirts of Paardenbaai in Oranjestad, Aruba, first mentioned in historical colonial archives in 1855 and topographically located on the Werbata maps in 1912.[4] Popular historical images of Rancho come to mind through Johan Hartog's classic *Aruba in de oude ansichten* (Aruba in old postcards).[5] Iconic examples are the images of

1 Dresscher-Lambertus, "Between Shores," forthcoming.
2 Haraway, *Staying with the Trouble*, 2016.
3 Bennett, *Vibrant Matter*, 2010.
4 Huygen, *Rancho, nos bario-nos museo, tira un bista* [Rancho, our neighbourhood–our museum, take a look], 2010.
5 Hartog, *Aruba in oude ansichten* [Aruba in old postcards], 1996.

barefooted small children in front of humble mud huts or boats of fishermen navigating the shores of Paardenbaai. Rancheros often figure in historical texts as signifiers of wildness and as violent people with peculiar ways of living. Laura Wernet-Paskel (1992) describes Rancho in *Ons eilandje Aruba* (Our little island Aruba) as a "carefree, primitive fisherfolk community who lived outdoors, were barely clothed, used foul language and loved to dance and have street brawls."[6] In a passage laced with sarcasm, the neighborhood is described as dangerous to visitors for "a queen conch *calico* [*sic*] well-aimed at one's head may not be that uncommon a gesture of friendliness."[7]

Wernet-Paskel's description reveals a stereotyped and sensationalizing portrayal of Rancheros. This discursive othering and class distinction becomes more obvious when she juxtaposes this to what she describes as the "other Playa-inhabitants who were also fishermen of a *different* kind. These were the grandfathers of our contemporary honorable shopkeepers."[8]

Another reference to Rancho and the *calco* is found in an older text from the colonial period. In *Nos potret* (Our portrait), Luc Alofs[9] recounts the visit of the Dutch member of parliament Henri van Kol to Rancho in 1903 and the impression the lives of impoverished fishermen in Aruba left on him. "Where battles with *karkos*, large *calico* [*sic*] shells deployed as weapons, used to be a common sight once upon a time," Henri van Kol notes, "they (the shells) were no longer to be seen, and everyone seemed to be preoccupied with eking out a living."[10] A specific comment in van Kol's travelog struck a chord within me: "Many came to listen to our conversations, not least women with long braids and of the finely crafted Native type; yet they did not complain, they spoke of their griefs only when asked; they meekly accepted their fate for it was beyond their comprehension that there were people in distant lands able and willing to give them help in their distress; they wanted to bear the hard fate without even daring to hope for improvement."[11]

The presence of the *calco* in numerous historical accounts serves as a reminder of the resilient community I come from, the women of Rancho and their vital role in the daily life of the small fisher community of Aruba.

---

6 Wernet-Paskel, *Ons eilandje Aruba* [Our little island Aruba], 1992, p. 60–61. Although *Ons eilandje Aruba* was published in 1992, Laura Wernet-Paskel wrote the text in 1941.

7 Ibid. Translation by editors.

8 Ibid., p. 61, emphasis mine. Translation by editors.

9 Alofs, "Stad van Oranje" [City of Oranje], 2006. Author's translation.

10 Translation by editors.

11 Alofs, "Stad van Oranje," 2006, pp. 16–17.

1 *Calco* Is a Numinous Signifier of Life Force, a Container and Archive of Situated Knowledges

It is problematic to rely solely on colonial archives, the written accounts of experts or internalized colonial social discourses to understand what it means to be a Ranchera. Here, one encounters stigmas and stereotypes that continue to reverberate in the present. As Saidiya Hartman cautions us: "Every historian of the multitude, the dispossessed, the subaltern, and the enslaved is forced to grapple with the power and authority of the archive, and the limits it sets on what can be known, whose perspective matters and who is endowed with the gravity and authority of historical actor."[12] Similarly, according to Maria Tamboukou, archives are: "Sites of fragments … there is always something missing since not everything found a place in an archive, due to chance, purposeful choices, and deselections, as well as certain principles of taxonomy and categorization that allow some documentation of life to be kept while others become obscure and marginalized."[13]

With a decolonial feminist archival sensitivity, I am interested in the documentation of lives that did not make it to the historical archives and in the opportunities emerging from the writing of lives. We are archives of stories that circulate in us and in the ecologies we are part of. In this contribution, I rework the understanding of *calco* from being a signifier of violence, supposedly peculiar to the ways of Rancheros, to a generative signifier and archive of situated knowledges. With *calco* as my writing companion and as an element of the situated ecology I am part of, I view life writing as a decolonial Caribbean feminist practice, which makes space to break away from genre-specific rules of forms, language, discipline and tone, to narrate our own stories and to speak back and catalyze processes of what Tuck and Yang describe as "unbecoming claims."[14] I follow Anna Poletti, who defines life writing as "writing and other forms of cultural production that draws on the lived experience of a historical (real) person, or group of people."[15] The self-inscription of our lived experiences as the process is core to the practice. As we assemble our life stories, we narrate our becomings.[16]

---

12 Hartman, *Wayward Lives, Beautiful Experiments*, 2019, p. XIII.

13 Moore et al., *The Archive Project*, 2016.

14 Tuck and Yang, "Unbecoming Claims," 2014.

15 StudiumGenerale UU, "Are Social Media Changing the Way We Document Our Lives?" 2022. Recording of a lecture given by Anna Poletti at Utrecht University, March 9, 2022.

16 Barad, *Meeting the Universe Halfway*, 2007.

Aruba is known as the "Island of Shells."[17] The creatures that produce marine shells and the shells themselves were considered important sources of food for Aruba's initial inhabitants. As in many Caribbean cultures, *calco* was and continues to be a highly valued economic resource for Aruba's people.

On the island, the *calco* predominates the remains of shells recovered from important archaeological sites such as Tanki Flip, which helped piece together Aruba's prehistoric data through radiocarbon readings. Dijkhoff and Linville emphasize the cultural value of marine mollusks as preservers of history. Shell fragments make up a significant component of the ecofacts and artifacts discovered during excavations.[18]

Hence, as a "knower," the *calco* is much older than Aruba's colonial period and the colonial epistemes it brought. *Calco* is a witness of precolonial times, which can be considered an archive of "situated knowledges."[19] However, *calco* is also literally an artifact with the capacity to carry stories, as Ursula K. Le Guin writes in *The Carrier Bag Theory of Fiction*: "A leaf a gourd *a shell* a net a bag a sling a sack a bottle a pot a box a container. A holder. A recipient."[20]

2 Life Writing as Decolonial Practice of Liberation

Feminists have advocated life writing as a practice and genre for liberation. Writing with the body, critiquing patriarchal epistemic systems, making space for one's emerging voice, taking your unique standpoint of intersectional experiences and stepping into a sovereignty of content, form, epistemology and even ontology is a lifelong process of liberation. Life writing offers a space for transformation.

In *Dreams of Archives Unfolded: Absence and Caribbean Life Writing*, Jocelyn Fenton Stitt positions life writing as essential to Caribbean historiographical knowledge production.[21] Life writing, according to her, is a "genre that both provides interiority for the subaltern and enables the writing of absent narratives."[22] In her close reading of how contemporary women's life writing in the Pan-Caribbean grapples with archival *absences* in their life stories, she sheds light on the generative ways in which life writing as a decolonial feminist

17 Dijkhoff and Linville, "Island of Shells," 2004.
18 Ibid.
19 Haraway, "Situated Knowledges," 1988.
20 Le Guin, Yi, and Haraway, *The Carrier Bag Theory of Fiction*, 2019, emphasis mine.
21 Stitt, *Dreams of Archives Unfolded*, 2021.
22 Ibid., p. 16.

practice "creates alternative ways of understanding the relationship of the past to the present."[23] Stitt's approach is inspired by María Lugones, focusing on how contemporary Caribbean life writing "traces colonial processes of gendering, and racialization in order to destabilize and resist these epistemologies."[24] For a historical overview of works by women in Aruba, I refer to Maureen Luidens's study "Desaroyo di scritura feminino durante tempo" (Development of women's writing during time).[25] Luidens argues that poetry in Papiamento was the most popular literary form of women's writing in Aruba, pointing to the possibilities poetry offers for life writing.

3 *Calco* as a Feminist Decolonial Practice of Life Writing

Calco emerges in this essay as an affective assemblage[26] of matter and meaning for the lifelong journey of decolonization through life writing. I engage with the Caribbean queen conch in its material form as wise, nonhuman, kin species and as a metaphorical figuration older-than-colonial invention and epistemes. Weaving posthumanist feminist phenomenology and feminist new materialisms with Caribbean thinkers, I engage with *calco* and other related concepts of water, the Caribbean Sea and geological ecotone spaces to inspire, summon, localize, vocalize and expand the repertoires of life writing.

Calco as a metaphor inspires a particular kind of feminist decolonial practice of life writing, a creative practice offering a generative repository for telling our stories. Telling stories of *calco* is thus autoethnographic[27] in that the self intersects with identities, cultures and lived experiences. It is phenomenological[28] to the extent that our lived experiences and how we become subjects is an embodied process. It is ecological and relational for we are entangled within the uniquely situated ecology we are part of, thus making it posthuman,[29] and it is decolonial, a practice that reclaims our oral historiographies, disrupting imposed cultural interpretations, social categories and colonial subjections,

23 Ibid., p. 3.

24 Lugones, "Toward a Decolonial Feminism," 2010; and Stitt, *Dreams of Archives Unfolded*, 2021, p. 3.

25 Molina-Luidens, "Desaroyo di scritura feminino durante tempo" [Development of women's writing during time], 2017.

26 Deleuze and Guattari, *A Thousand Plateaus*, 1987.

27 Ellis and Bochner, "Autoethnography, Personal Narrative, Reflexivity," 2000.

28 Merleau-Ponty and Smith, *Phenomenology of Perception*, 2006.

29 Neimanis, *Bodies of Water*, 2017; Bennett, *Vibrant Matter*, 2010; Alaimo, *Bodily Natures*, 2010; and Braidotti, *Posthuman Feminism*, 2022.

filling the absences of voices, weaving ancestral memories and lived experiences and worlding the decolonial imaginaries and futures we desire.

Calco as Caribbean feminist life writing[30] happens at the intersection of *intra-acting*[31] agential forces in an assemblage of lived experiences, events, social structures, intergenerational memories, microhistories, bodies and embodiment, movements, crossings, traumas, voices, resiliencies, affects, fragmented archives, ruptures, ordinary rhythms of everyday life, situated knowledges, intersecting identities, gender, sexuality, racialization, class, ethnicity, dis/ability, artifacts, dreams, desires, devotional and numinous life dimensions, intrapersonal shifts, metaphors, stories and poetic imagination, human and nonhuman entanglements and, notably, the situated unique natural ecology one is part of and so much more.

In what follows, I will continue to describe the key traits of *calco* as a Caribbean feminist life writing practice.

4 Slower Ontology and Creativity as Life Force

When women held me as I was growing up in Rancho, dressed in their *bata* (housecoats), they also rocked me in the ways of a *stoel di soya* (rocking chair) with their life stories and their wisdom. The movement of the rocking chair

---

30 *Calco* opens the space for combining different forms, sources and registers attempting to vocalize the immanence and situatedness of Caribbean realities. It is emergent, evocative and continuously improvised according to its natural environment. Forms of cultural production narrating self-representation and lived experiences can manifest in different forms, from the more complex first-person narratives, archival research, art pieces, (auto) biographies, autoethnography and poetry to the more fleeting everyday "documents of life" (e.g., letters, diaries, oral stories, recipes) but also the more popular cultural forms such as songs, social media posts and digital storytelling; Plummer, *Documents of Life 2*, 2001. Form becomes an open-end of possibilities: the point is not to stick to one form but to embrace what form the story and voice(s) need as a carrier, combining, remaking and remixing registers and media.

31 Throughout this contribution, I use the concept of *intra-action* coined by Karen Barad, a neologism alternative to interaction in which we assume that entities are prior or independent of one another and then participate in action with each other. Other than interaction, intra-action emphasizes relationality and dynamism of forces. Intra-action is closely related to the concept of agency. Intra-action understands agency not as an inherent property of an individual or human to be manifested but as a dynamic assemblage of forces in which all things are constantly exchanging and diffracting, influencing and working inseparably. Agency emerges from these intra-actions; agency is co-constituted and enfolded through the movements and vibrancy and flows in the assemblage. See Barad, *Meeting the Universe Halfway*, 2007, p. 141.

invites crossing over into a slow ontology. A slow ontology that is needed to slowly embody a more expansive way of being where we cross into the other spheres of knowing, being and feeling, to delve deeper into our bodies, psyches and the threads connecting us to an ecological web of beings. *Calco* invites a slower temporality. A slower temporality approaches the site of writing-creating, as a site of creative intervention.[32] *Calco* whispers: creativity is yours, ours, it is nature's cyclical life force to regenerate oneself, you are constantly in the process of becoming.

A slower ontology makes it possible to attend to "the creativity and generativity of emergent cultural things," which Kathleen Stewart calls *cultural poesis*.[33] Cultural poesis brings us into a gestational space of wonder. When time slows down, we start paying attention in porous and sensorial ways to "textures, and rhythms, trajectories and modes of attunement, attachment, and composition … and wonder where [these] might go and what potential modes of knowing, relating, and attending to things are already present in them."[34] Life writing as a practice as *calco* invites entering a space of thinking-feeling in a slower ontology.

5 Whorls in Tides: Nonlinearity and Different Temporalities

But where to start with the summoning of our life stories? The queen conch teaches us that narratives are not linear; they are formed as the spiraling whorls she produces as part of her shell navigating the tidal movements of the sea. *Calco* invites gestations through the use of verbs such as "spiraling, whirling, and coiling."[35] Spiral temporalities are not fixed; they are ever-changing and make space for the spaces in-between amid becomings, as Jane Alison explains about spiraling narrative: "a spiral begins at a point and moves onward, not extravagant or lackadaisical like a meander, but smooth and steady, spinning around and around that central point or a single axis."[36]

Unlearning nonlinearity is a practice of liberation. It is a way of decolonizing imposed ontologies stemming from colonial and patriarchal epistemes and embodying the sovereignty of my own epistemic agency to tell my story, the stories of my ancestors, and *to world* (emphasis on the verb *worlding*) by

32 Ulmer, "Writing Slow Ontology," 2017.
33 Stewart, "Cultural Poesis: The Generativity of Emergent Things," 2005, p. 1015.
34 Stewart, "Weak Theory in an Unfinished World," 2008.
35 Alison, *Meander, Spiral, Explode*, 2019.
36 Ibid., p. 143.

vocalizing and creating the decolonial, pluriverse[37] and ecologically-ethical futures I desire and envision. And, here, *calco* is just one of the many patterns in nature that can inspire us to transgress the constraints of seeing linearity as the only way; it is just one—often overrated—form out of the many.

Stories, whose voices have been muffled by suffocating colonial, racial and patriarchal systems of knowledge, are movements. They are alive, ecological beings that breathe, shapeshift, die, only to resurface again in new forms. Just as the spiraling whorls of *calco* keep track of the *tidalectical*[38] movements of the waves on its shell and of the histories of the Caribbean region, each whorl brings a new voice, a new layer of stretching, deepening and turning of stories, shifting in intergenerational temporalities and interpretations, intra-acting with collective memories, presents and futures. The spiral as form points us to the open-endedness of becomings. The movements of the stories invite others in and other stories to branch out and to merge with. *Calco* has the capacity to hold the symphony of polyvocality, diffracting,[39] holding differences and similarities. With our life stories, we become assemblages of voices, lived experiences and ecologies. The story itself, and *storying* is what Katherine McKittrick describes as an "interdisciplinary methodology, the story – theoretical, creative, groovy, skilled, action-based, *secreted*, shared – is a *verb-activity* that invites engagement, curiosity, and collaboration."[40]

6 A Bodily Practice: Let the Body Guide the Stories

Calco reminds us that we are bodies. Becoming (with) *calco* as a feminist practice of writing and creating starts with the body. We start listening to the stories in our bones, in our guts, the memories of our flesh. Our bodies keep traces of what it means to have kin, to love, to feel pain, to feel safe and unsafe, to heal, to dance, to cry, to desire, to explore our fluid sexualities, to feel joyous, to

37 Mignolo, *The Darker Side of Western Modernity*, 2011.

38 Tidalectics is a term coined by Caribbean writer and poet Kamau Brathwaite. It is breaking away from the Western principle of dialectics. Tidalectics refers to the movements of the Caribbean Sea and is a historical reference to the transatlantic Middle Passage, which infuses the present and future of Caribbean realities and experiences. Caribbean histories are embodied, according to Kamau Brathwaite, in "the movement of the water backwards and forwards as a kind of cyclic ... motion, rather than linear." In Brathwaite and Mackey, *Conversations with Nathaniel Mackey*, 1999, p. 34.

39 Barad, *Meeting the Universe Halfway*, 2007.

40 McKittrick, *Dear Science and Other Stories*, 2021, p. 9, emphasis mine.

feel hope, anguish, hopelessness, to feel sickness. Narratives emerge prompted by the movements and immobilities of our bodies.

Our bodies are archives with deep intergenerational memories and affective potentials. Feminist life writing-creating are bodily gestures. Writing as a body, with the body, is descending in bodily awareness. This is the type of creating, and writing, that is affected by "the capacity of the body to affect and be affected" by the world.[41]

The *calco* reminds me that my colored skin carries multiple stories, my heartbeat and hormones modulate agency, the different states my nervous system shifts into attune me to how I relate to the world and alters how I perceive and experience phenomena. That my voice, foremost, is a strong vibration resonating from my body.

7 Grief Work Connected to the Caribbean Sea

I grew up playing on the veranda while my grandmother "Nai," my great aunt "Tante Ties" and my great uncle "Kinchi" sat in their rocking chairs, conversing about daily life, recounting stories of older times on and on and on, just like the movements of their rocking chairs. Stories of what it means to live *bou di baranca*[42] (under the rock), of how Rancho was when they were growing up and how they experienced the shocking accelerations of modernity. Stories of how my great-grandfather and his father were fishermen and what that meant. How the craft of fishing and navigating the sailboats opened the men to the

41 Gregg & Seigworth, "An Inventory of Shimmers," 2011, p. 2.

42 Using archival research and interviews with elders in the community, Yolanda Richardson traced oral stories about the ways of living *bou baranca* (under rocks). According to Richardson, for infrastructural development purposes, "several houses were demolished around 1950, which at the time were known as the houses *bou baranca*. This physical change also meant a change in the character of the neighborhood. The demolition of the houses was a characteristic and unparalleled event for the community at the time. People had to leave their homes to move into more modern homes, most of them government-built. This move heralded the beginning of a new era. Nevertheless, the move also meant that the inhabitants had to renounce many characteristic customs, rituals, and modest lifestyles characteristic to that part of *sabana*" (p. 1). Bou Baranca was located beneath the shoreline depot (Oranjestad, Paardenbaai), next to the salt pans and the streets called Westraat and Arendstraat. With two staircases—one west of Westraat and another south of Arendstraat—the *sabana* with the houses *bou baranca* could be reached. In Richardson, *Negen huizen, verschillende gezinnen en veel kinderen bou baranca* [Nine houses, different families and many children under the rocks], 2009. Editors' note: see contribution by Yolanda Richardson in this volume.

ways of the sea, to intimately know and embody the Caribbean Sea's changing tides, subtleties and impulsiveness, to the many lives that were sacrificed at sea. My grandmother used to say, "the sea gives and takes away."[43] The men brought the fish, and the women negotiated and sold the catch. When the fishermen did not find fish, they always came back with *calcos.*[44] Reverence for the magnificence of the sea and "being in awe" of this immense body of water was a core lesson in my family, a source of surrealism and magic, inspiring regeneration through her shapeshifting hydrologic cycles.

The Caribbean Sea is ancestral water; it bears life, and it takes life away. A family story goes that my own great-grandfather, Santiago, was the only survivor of a fishing trip consisting of many Rancheros during his twenties. This story of the trauma of witnessing his intimate fishermen friends and his own father-in-law drown before his eyes was a recurring theme in the family.

The sea is holder of untold stories and, as such, one of the most powerful counter archives containing stories that sunk to its depths, never to be yet told or recorded or forgotten with time. These same shores of Paardenbaai are also holders of stories of migrations, crossings[45] and dislocations, stories that sunk deep in the bottom of the oceans but are still in the "wake"[46] of histories, waiting to be told, intra-acting with the changing weather patterns.

The women of Rancho knew deep down in their bodies that their men might not return from fishing, and this attuned them with their own mortality and that of their loved ones. Death, loss, poverty and grief was a constant companion for the families of the fisher community in Rancho. I suspect that seeing the suffering eye in eye, and doing the grief work, made them also feel light afterward.

8 We Are Water, and We Transform in Spaces of Ecotones

Living so near the sea and living from what the Caribbean Sea gives, and takes away, makes you aware of how the water touches the shores and the personal lives of Rancheras. The shore is the meeting point where the sand and the sea's waters touch each other. *Pia plat*[47] (barefooted) as a Ranchera, you can feel the

43 "Lama ta duna y lama ta kita." Author's translation.

44 Richardson, *Negen huizen, verschillende gezinnen en veel kinderen bou baranca*, 2009.

45 Alexander, *Pedagogies of Crossing*, 2005.

46 Sharpe, *In the Wake*, 2016.

47 According to Yolanda Richardson, Rancheros, and then the fishermen and other residents of the *sabana*, walked barefoot. This custom contributed to the calling of Rancheros as *Ranchero pia plat* (barefooted Ranchero). Walking barefooted signified poverty and hum-

aliveness, the slippery ways that are characteristic of these shores: the fluid and moveable ground, the changing wind summoning the swelling waves and the inherent fishy smell of the wet sand, a sign of fecundity. My ancestors have lived near these shores, *bou baranca*, as Rancheros say, as women of fishermen, as hat weavers, as *pikido di salo* (salt pickers).

Weaving posthumanist feminist phenomenology with Caribbean feminisms, I reflect on what these shores, the Caribbean Sea and *calco* can teach us. It draws me to feminists working with water, ecotones and the embodiment of these fluid spaces as ontologies of becomings and spaces of possibilities. As such, it helps me advance my invitation to attune to the generative ways of be(com)ing that our kin species and aquatic ancestor, *calco*, teaches us.

Hydrofeminist Astrida Neimanis reminds us that we are all bodies of water: "blood, bile, intracellular fluid, a small ocean swallowed, a wild wetland in our gut; rivulets forsaken making their way from our insides to out, from watery womb to watery world: *we are bodies of water.*"[48] Re-*membering* that we are bodies of water expands our capacities to know, embody and be connected to and *through* other bodies of water too: "as watery, we experience ourselves less as isolated entities, and more as oceanic eddies: *I'm singular, dynamic whorl dissolving in a complex, fluid circulation.*"[49] Thinking through water—in particular here, the Caribbean Sea—not only metaphorically but as matter and corporeally opens ontological possibilities of becoming, providing me with an ecological, relational, fluid and embodied experience.

Where the Caribbean Sea touches the sand at the shoreline is a space of ecotone. Neimanis describes ecotones as "transition areas between two adjacent but different ecosystems, ecotones appear as both gradual shifts, and abrupt demarcations ... 'separation' ... [and] 'connection.'"[50]

Life writing acts as an ecotone space where "something happens," a vibrant zone that Neimanis eloquently describes as full of "fecundity, creativity, transformation; of becoming, assembling, multiplying; of diverging, differentiating, relinquishing."[51] When we create, and write, ourselves into being, temporality becomes nonlinear, fluid and plural: pasts, presents and futures simultaneously

---

bleness but was foremost a way of being associated with freedom and contact with the ground, waters and shores. Richardson, *Negen huizen, verschillende gezinnen en veel kinderen bou baranca*, 2009. The writer, teacher and poet Digna Lacle-Herrera, a Ranchera, described *pia plat* as a way of being in her poem titled "Chito." See Lacle-Herrera, "Chito," 2008, pp. 34–35.

48 Neimanis, *Bodies of Water*, 2017, p. 1.

49 Neimanis, "Hydrofeminism: Or on Becoming a Body of Water," 2012, p. 85.

50 Ibid., p. 93.

51 Ibid.

come together, intra-acting to narrate our stories in whorls. In that sense, an ecotone acts as "a sort of membrane, too: a pause, or even an increase in velocity, where/when/how matter comes to matter differently."[52] *Calco*, as a life writing practice, offers that space of transformation.

Ecotones are spaces of becomings and intra-actions. Ecotones are spaces that hold tension;[53] this is characteristic for being in the in-between. Processes of thinking-feeling-being-becoming with water and in spaces of ecotones transform us. *Calco* as an aquatic species itself embodies a space of material ecotone where the soft body is attached to the outer protective hard shell. Life writing is a space of possibilities, each shore is a unique shifting space of stories, cultural practices and histories.

Working with water and in spaces of ecotone is a form of being in the world that is embodied, ecological and *transcorporeal*.[54] We expand the range of actors (both human and nonhuman) we intra-act with, making kin with other species.[55] Reimagining the embodied self in relation helps us experience how we are entangled in a larger ecology where agency is shared in an assemblage of intra-acting forces.[56]

Calco is an invitation to narrate your life and how it is entangled within all these forces. A slower ontology attunes us to the ecotone as a space of possibility, of wonder, not only as a space of becoming but also of unbecomings. Your interior and exterior are also a space of ecotone: pasts, presents and futures are constantly intra-acting. You intra-act with misrepresentations, silences and the gaps stemming from the colonial archive. With the dream and desire of unbecoming these but also with your shores, the unique ecology you are part of, and the stories these propel in you. *Calco*, as a decolonial feminist creative practice, provides an ecotone space for becoming and unbecoming subjectivities.[57]

---

52 Ibid.

53 Neimanis, "Hydrofeminism: Or on Becoming a Body of Water," 2012.

54 Alaimo, *Bodily Natures*, 2010.

55 Haraway, *Staying with the Trouble*, 2016.

56 Barad, *Meeting the Universe Halfway*, 2007.

57 Different spaces of ecotones have inspired other decolonial writers as spaces for ontological transformation. Examples in the Caribbean are Agard-Jones, "What the Sands Remember," 2012, where the sand is approached as an affective repository of "feeling, and of experience, affect and history in the Caribbean region" (p. 3) and, in particular, for queerness, connection and loss. Odile Ferly's symbol of the mangrove in Ferly, *A Poetics of Relation*, 2012, is a reworking of Edouard Glissant's *Poetics of Relation*, where the masculine rhizome is changed for the mangrove, making it possible to include the lens of gender; Glissant and Wing, *Poetics of Relation*, 1997. The mangrove has also been an ecotone of transformation, a symbol of feminist community archive of untold stories for Indo-Caribbean women in: Ro(u)ted by Our Stories Collective, "Stories the Mangroves

9 The Numinous as Ecotone Space

As a life writing practice, *calco* invites opening to the liminal, excavating deeper and becoming receptive to the numinous to explore those in-between spaces to find raw material that makes life stories. An example of such a numinous practice is *conta soño* (dream-talking). *Conta soño* is a microcultural practice stemming from my matriarchal line, the practice of telling each other the dreams we had the previous night. Dreams were taken seriously as a way of knowing. This practice of *conta soño* brings the imaginal, its symbolism and the feelings the dreams triggered in the dreamer as conversation material to coffee time to discuss and decipher together.[58]

Conta soño formed part of a more complex affective assemblage of numinous cultural elements making up the spiritual cosmologies of my grandmothers from Oranjestad, infusing all other dimensions of their daily lives. A patchwork of sacred epistemes consisting of folkloric practices, superstitious beliefs, local myths, cultural practices and rituals for venerating saints, the telling of ghost stories and afterlife stories, divination practices (such as *lesa carta`y lesa copi cofi*, reading cards and coffee grounds) and animistic worldviews of the medicinal power of plants and the mysterious forces of the sea—"Go wash yourself in the sea, it will heal you"[59]—and reverence for the natural landscape.

Although my patchwork cosmology deviates from how my grandmothers and their ancestors experienced the numinous dimensions of their lives, these sacred liminal spaces still reverberate in my childhood memories, imbuing my becomings with the vibrational experience of what it means to be a Caribbean woman. These are oral stories you do not read in texts but linger in your intergenerational psyche and at the level of the cellular body memory and inform cultural poesis. Other Caribbean writers have explored these rich numinous spaces before as portals in their journey of decolonization, as generative liminal spaces of knowing, guidance and where restoration takes place.[60]

Hold," 2021. We also encounter spaces of ecotone in Black intellectual thinkers in other regions who have also worked with spaces of ecotones for the expansion of ontological possibilities for bringing Indigenous ontologies and Black life ontologies closer. Think of King, *The Black Shoals*, 2019 or Butler, "Disruptions at the Edges," 2022.

58 Editors' note: see the contribution by De Jong in this section for a discussion of dream-talking.

59 "Bai baña den lama, e ta cura bo." Author's translation.

60 Examples of other writers in the Caribbean and Latin America who engage with the numinous are Brathwaite, "Note(s) on Caribbean Cosmology," 1996; Alexander, *Pedagogies of Crossing*, 2005, in particular the section on pedagogies of the sacred, in which she delves into the sacred dimensions of queer women's lives and works with ancestors as a

10 The Time Is Now to Self-Inscribe Oneself into Pasts, Presents and Futures

Once in abundance, the queen conch is now a vulnerable marine species[61] surrounded by bleached corals, running the risk of extinction. The queen conch faces extinction due to commercial and illegal overfishing practices, rising temperatures, acidification of the oceans, the toxic plastic soup at the bottom of our oceans and the continuing exoticization and commodification of Caribbean tourism[62] but also the unsatisfied hunger of capitalism and the fact that we do not see ourselves entangled with nature and as nature. The split between nature and human is a colonial invention[63] still toxifying our existence and planet. *Calco* teaches us that we are nature and kin species, and returning to our watery origins can help us realize that.

Hydrofeminism teaches us that "we find ourselves tangled in intricate choreographies of bodies and flows of all kinds—not only human bodies, but also other animal, vegetable, geophysical, meteorological, and technological ones; not only watery flows, but also flows of power, culture, politics, and economics."[64] There is, therefore, an urgent existential need to realize that we are part of an ecology. The *calco*, the Caribbean Sea, the dry and cacti landscape, the ecotones of the shores of Oranjestad and the ecotone spaces inside of me from which I write are all part of me. As kin species, they are my ancestors, carriers of stories, teaching me how to decolonize myself and who I am, where I belong and how I become within the Caribbean ecology I am part of and embody.

---

methodology of inquiry; and, Suzanne Césaire's (1941–1945) poetics and surrealism as acts of resistance to colonial powers and inspiring decolonial reimaginings, see Césaire and Maximin, *The Great Camouflage*, 2012. The work of Chicana feminist writer Gloria Anzaldúa resonates strongly with how I approach the liminal here, see Anzaldúa and Keating, *Light in the Dark*, 2015. Anzaldúa describes this liminal space where transformations occur as *nepantla*: "In nepantla you sense more keenly the overlap between the material and spiritual worlds; you are in both places simultaneously – you glimpse el espíritu – see the body as inspirited. Nepantla is the point of contact where the 'mundane' and the 'numinous' converge, where you are in full awareness of the present moment" (p. 128). Anzaldúa warns us of awkwardness, uncomfortableness and frustration that will arise in this liminal space. This is because we are amid transformation: "to be healed, we must be dismembered, pulled apart" (p. 29). In a way, *nepantla* is an ecotone space for transformation.

61 Boekhoudt and Linville, "Aruba's Seashell Producers: Biology, Ecology, and Contributions to Archaeological Research," 2004.

62 Sheller, *Consuming the Caribbean*, 2003; and Sheller, *Island Futures*, 2020.

63 Wynter, "Unsettling the Coloniality of Being/Power/Truth/Freedom," 2003.

64 Neimanis, "Hydrofeminism: Or on Becoming a Body of Water," 2012, p. 96.

Calco is also known for the strength of her shell. Her home, the hard calcium carbonate shell secreted by the soft mantle covering her body, has self-healing capacities, bringing bio-mineralogists, materials scientists, molecular biologists and engineers in awe and wonder. Material engineers find bioinspiration in the self-healing capacities of the queen conch to cure the wounds of her shell, trying to learn and mimic these capacities in their engineering of sustainable material.[65] It is this same capacity to self-regenerate that *calco*, as a practice of life writing, makes possible in providing us with an ecotone space where, in fecund opacity, we dive deeper into the layers of ourselves moving in spiral movements of becomings and unbecomings, carried by the tidalectical rhythms of the Caribbean Sea and her histories. Here, our histories, presents and futures are constantly intra-acting.

The queen conch keeps a record of these tides on her shell. Each *calco*, in its afterlife form, has a unique imprint of how the Caribbean Sea intra-acted with, and thus touched, her, during her lifetime. In a way, just as cave drawings tell the stories of Aruba's Indigenous origins,[66] the shell as a memory keeper kept record of other stories in the language of the tides of the Caribbean Sea.

Bibliography

Agard-Jones, Vanessa. "What the Sands Remember." *GLQ: A Journal of Lesbian and Gay Studies* 18, no. 2–3 (June 2012): 325–46. https://doi.org/10.1215/10642684-1472917.

Alaimo, Stacy. *Bodily Natures: Science, Environment, and the Material Self.* Bloomington: Indiana University Press, 2010.

Alexander, M. Jacqui. *Pedagogies of Crossing: Meditations on Feminism, Sexual Politics, Memory, and the Sacred.* Perverse Modernities. Durham, NC: Duke University Press, 2005.

Alison, Jane. *Meander, Spiral, Explode: Design and Pattern in Narrative.* New York: Catapult, 2019.

Alofs, Luc. "Stad van Oranje" [City of Orange]. In *Nos potret. Een beeld van Aruba in verleden, heden en toekomst*, edited by Renwick Heronimo et al., 12–21. Oranjestad: Committee for the Royal Visit of Her Majesty Queen Beatrix to Aruba, 2006.

Anzaldúa, Gloria, and AnaLouise Keating. *Light in the Dark: Luz en lo oscuro: Rewriting Identity, Spirituality, Reality.* Latin America Otherwise: Languages, Empires, Nations. Durham, NC: Duke University Press, 2015.

65 Ballarini and Heuer, "Secrets in the Shell," 2007.

66 Dijkhoff et al., *The Archaeology of Aruba*, 2004. Editors' note: see contribution by Antczak in this volume on indigeneity in the context of Bonaire.

Ballarini, Roberto, and Arthur H. Heuer. "Secrets in the Shell." *American Scientist* 95, no. 5 (2007): 422. https://www.americanscientist.org/article/secrets-in-the-shell.

Barad, Karen Michelle. *Meeting the Universe Halfway: Quantum Physics and the Entanglement of Matter and Meaning*. Durham, NC: Duke University Press, 2007.

Bennett, Jane. *Vibrant Matter: A Political Ecology of Things*. Durham, NC: Duke University Press, 2010.

Boekhoudt, B. G., and M. S. Linville. "Aruba's Seashell Producers: Biology, Ecology, and Contributions to Archaeological Research." In *The Archaeology of Aruba: The Marine Shell Heritage*, edited by Raymundo A. C. F. Dijkhoff and Marlene S. Linville, 17–33. Oranjestad: Archaeological Museum of Aruba, 2004.

Braidotti, Rosi. *Posthuman Feminism*. Cambridge: Polity, 2022.

Brathwaite, Kamau. "Note(s) on Caribbean Cosmology." *River City: A Journal of Contemporary Culture* 16, no. 2 (1996): 1–17.

Brathwaite, Kamau, and Nathaniel Mackey. *Conversations with Nathaniel Mackey: An Evening with Nate Mackey & Kamau Brathwaite 18 Nov. 1993*. Staten Island: We Press, 1999.

Butler, Tamara T. "Disruptions at the Edges: Ecotone Crossing with Black and Indigenous Creative Pedagogues." *Curriculum Inquiry* 52, no. 2 (March 2022): 205–17. https://doi.org/10.1080/03626784.2022.2041979.

Césaire, Suzanne, and Daniel Maximin. *The Great Camouflage: Writings of Dissent (1941–1945)*. 1st Wesleyan ed. Middletown, CT: Wesleyan University Press, 2012.

Deleuze, Gilles, and Félix Guattari. *A Thousand Plateaus: Capitalism and Schizophrenia*. Minneapolis: University of Minnesota Press, 1987.

Dijkhoff, Raymundo A. C. F., Marlene Linville, Arminda C. Ruiz, and Ramón Dacal Moure. *The Archaeology of Aruba: The Marine Shell Heritage*. Oranjestad: Archaeological Museum of Aruba, 2004.

Dijkhoff, R. A. C. F. and M. S. Linville. "Island of Shells." In *The Archaeology of Aruba: The Marine Shell Heritage*, edited by Raymundo A. C. F. Dijkhoff and Marlene S. Linville, 3–7. Oranjestad: Archaeological Museum of Aruba, 2004.

Dresscher-Lambertus, Nadia. "Between Shores." In *Aquatic Encounters: Art and Hydrofeminisms*, edited by Anastasia Khodyreva and Elina Suoyrjö. Helsinki: Rooftop Press, forthcoming.

Ellis, C., and A. P. Bochner. "Autoethnography, Personal Narrative, Reflexivity: Researcher as Subject." In *Handbook of Qualitative Research*, edited by Norman K. Denzin and Yvonna S. Lincoln, 2nd ed., 733–68. Thousand Oaks: Sage Publications, 2000.

Ferly, Odile. *A Poetics of Relation: Caribbean Women Writing at the Millennium*. New York: Palgrave Macmillan, 2012.

Glissant, Édouard, and Betsy Wing. *Poetics of Relation*. Ann Arbor: University of Michigan Press, 1997.

Gregg, Melissa, and Gregory Seigworth, "An Inventory of Shimmers," In *The Affect Theory Reader*, edited by Gregory J. Seigworth and Melissa Gregg, 1–25. Durham, NC: Duke University Press, 2010.

Haraway, Donna. "Situated Knowledges: The Science Question in Feminism and the Privilege of Partial Perspective." *Feminist Studies* 14, no. 3 (1988): 575–99. https://doi.org/10.2307/3178066.

Haraway, Donna Jeanne. *Staying with the Trouble: Making Kin in the Chthulucene*. Experimental Futures: Technological Lives, Scientific Arts, Anthropological Voices. Durham, NC: Duke University Press, 2016.

Hartman, Saidiya V. *Wayward Lives, Beautiful Experiments: Intimate Histories of Social Upheaval*. London: Serpent's Tail, 2019.

Hartog, Johan. *Aruba in oude ansichten* [Aruba in old postcards]. 3rd. rev. ed. Toen Boekje. Zaltbommel: Europese Bibliotheek, 1996.

Huygen, Floor. *Rancho, nos bario–nos museo, tira un bista* [Rancho, our neighbourhood–our museum, take a look]. Aruba: Nationaal Archeologisch Museum Aruba, 2010.

King, Tiffany Lethabo. *The Black Shoals: Offshore Formations of Black and Native Studies*. Durham, NC: Duke University Press, 2019.

Lacle-Herrera, Digná. "Chito." In *Mi Aruba bunita*, edited by Frank Williams, 34–35. Oranjestad: UNOCA, 2008.

Le Guin, Ursula K., Pul Yi, and Donna Jeanne Haraway. *The Carrier Bag Theory of Fiction*. London: Ignota, 2019.

Lugones, Marìa. "Toward a Decolonial Feminism." *Hypatia* 25, no. 4 (2010): 742–59. https://doi.org/10.1111/j.1527-2001.2010.01137.x.

McKittrick, Katherine. *Dear Science and Other Stories*. Errantries. Durham, NC: Duke University Press, 2021.

Merleau-Ponty, Maurice, and Colin Smith. *Phenomenology of Perception: An Introduction*. Repr. Routledge Classics. London: Routledge, 2006.

Mignolo, Walter. *The Darker Side of Western Modernity: Global Futures, Decolonial Options*. Latin America Otherwise: Languages, Empires, Nations. Durham, NC: Duke University Press, 2011.

Molina-Luidens, Maureen M. "Desaroyo di scritura feminino durante tempo" [Development of women's writing during time]. In *Archaeologies of Erasures and Silences: Recovering Othered Languages, Literatures and Cultures in the Dutch Caribbean and Beyond*, edited by Nicholas Faraclas, Ronald Severing, Christa Weijer, Elisabeth Agnes Maria Echteld, Wim Rutgers, and Robert Duprey, 269–76. Curaçao: FPI, Fundashon pa Planifikashon di Idioma; Curaçao, University of Curaçao, 2017.

Moore, Niamh, Andrea Salter, Liz Stanley, and Maria Tamboukou. *The Archive Project*. London: Routledge, 2016. https://doi.org/10.4324/9781315612577.

Neimanis, Astrida. *Bodies of Water: Posthuman Feminist Phenomenology*. Environmental Cultures Series. London: Bloomsbury Academic, 2017.

Neimanis, Astrida. "Hydrofeminism: Or on Becoming a Body of Water." In *Undutiful Daughters: New Directions in Feminist Thought and Practice*, edited by Henriette Gunkel, Chrysanthi Nigianni, and Fanny Söderbäck. Breaking Feminist Waves. New York: Palgrave Macmillan, 2012.

Plummer, Kenneth. *Documents of Life 2: An Invitation to a Critical Humanism*. London: Sage Publications, 2001.

Richardson, Yolanda. *Negen huizen, verschillende gezinnen en veel kinderen bou baranca* [Nine houses, different families and many children under the rocks]. Unpublished exhibition research report. Oranjestad: National Archaeological Museum Aruba, July 2009.

Ro(u)ted by Our Stories Collective. "Stories the Mangroves Hold: Reflections on Indo-Caribbean Feminist Community Archiving." *Journal of Indentureship and Its Legacies* 1, no. 1 (September 2021). https://doi.org/10.13169/jofstudindentleg.1.1.0063.

Sharpe, Christina Elizabeth. *In the Wake: On Blackness and Being*. Durham, NC: Duke University Press, 2016.

Sheller, Mimi. *Consuming the Caribbean: From Arawaks to Zombies*. London: Routledge, 2003.

Sheller, Mimi. *Island Futures: Caribbean Survival in the Anthropocene*. Durham, NC: Duke University Press, 2020.

Stewart, Kathleen. "Cultural Poesis: The Generativity of Emergent Things." In *The SAGE Handbook of Qualitative Research*, edited by Norman K. Denzin and Yvonna S. Lincoln, 3rd ed., 1015–30. Thousand Oaks: Sage Publications, 2005.

Stewart, Kathleen. "Weak Theory in an Unfinished World." *Journal of Folklore Research: An International Journal of Folklore and Ethnomusicology* 45, no. 1 (January 2008): 71–82. https://doi.org/10.2979/JFR.2008.45.1.71.

Stitt, Jocelyn Fenton. *Dreams of Archives Unfolded: Absence and Caribbean Life Writing*. Critical Caribbean Studies. New Brunswick: Rutgers University Press, 2021.

StudiumGeneraleUU. "Are Social Media Changing the Way We Document Our Lives?" Streamed live on March 9, 2022. YouTube video. https://www.youtube.com/live/eHO4BeliTek.

Tuck, Eve, and K. Wayne Yang. "Unbecoming Claims: Pedagogies of Refusal in Qualitative Research." *Qualitative Inquiry* 20, no. 6 (July 2014): 811–8. https://doi.org/10.1177/1077800414530265.

Ulmer, Jasmine B. "Writing Slow Ontology." *Qualitative Inquiry* 23, no. 3 (March 2017): 201–11. https://doi.org/10.1177/1077800416643994.

Wernet-Paskel, Laura. *Ons eilandje Aruba [1941]* [Our little island Aruba (1941)]. Zutphen: Walburg Pers, 1992.

Wynter, Sylvia. "Unsettling the Coloniality of Being/Power/Truth/Freedom: Towards the Human, After Man, Its Overrepresentation–An Argument." *CR: The New Centennial Review* 3, no. 3 (2003): 257–337. https://doi.org/10.1353/ncr.2004.0015.

CHAPTER 44

Saba Lace: History, Culture and Art

Eric A. Eliason

Abstract

This contribution traces the history of Saba lace—also known as Spanish work, fancy work and drawn thread work—an emblematic cultural product of the island of Saba, which also served as an important source of income for islanders through the changing colonial and social contexts of the late nineteenth and twentieth centuries. Through presenting the conditions that influenced the development of this craft, the text discusses the social hierarchies in Saba and the gendered divisions of labor as well as the way Saban women oriented themselves toward North America for the purpose of selling their work. It finally reflects on the transformation of Saba lace into a cultural rather than commercial object of interest as a result of the economic and political developments of the last fifty years.

Keywords

Saba – lace – craft – gendered labor – colonial society

1 Introduction

No single creative activity has shaped the lives of so many Saban women in the last 130 years as has the practice of drawn thread work, also known as Spanish work, fancy work, lacework and Saba lace. Certainly, no other activity has made Saban women and their island so renowned. In tourist literature and history books, the island of Saba has two common nicknames: Island of Women and Island of Lace. While many places are known for a particular handicraft, few places' identities are so linked with one art form as is Saba's. Sabans themselves use drawn thread work to symbolize the uniqueness of their island. To them, the symbol's meaning is clear: lacework expresses the ingenuity, diligence, bold inventiveness, pride in workmanship, love of beauty and respect for tradition that define the Saban spirit. The present contribution tells the story of lacework's central role in Saba's culture, economy and history.

 | DOI:10.1163/9789004690882_046

2 What Is Saban Lacework?

Saba lace is a folk art that makes functional cloth items more beautiful. Saba lace is made the opposite way of "proper" lace. With normal lace, such as the famous variety made in Belgium, one starts with nothing. Lace is made by tying numerous free threads together, sometimes with bobbins, sometimes around pins stuck on a solid surface for guidance. Drawn thread work, on the other hand, although it often resembles lace in its patterns, is made by starting with a solid bolt of linen. At the place on the fabric where the artist wishes to make a pattern, parallel threads are snipped and pulled out. The artist is then left with a section of cloth with parallel threads perpendicular to the ones pulled out. These remaining parallel threads are then meticulously counted, tied off and worked into various designs with a needle and several pieces of free thread. Traditionally, the linen and thread have been white, but artists now often use colored linen and colored threads. This is the basic process. Variation in design comes mainly from the way artists count, tie and embellish the undrawn threads in the linen.

Saba lace can be used on almost anything the lace worker cares to decorate. In the early history of Saba lace, long strips of finished lacework borders were sewn onto slips, pillowcases and the square necklines of women's nightgowns. Saban women once called this older style of lacework "Spanish work" to distinguish it from the now pervasive technique of working designs directly into the fabric of items.

For their own use, Sabans have worked lace onto almost every cloth item imaginable. Examples include dresses, blouses—a style of shirt once popular and still occasionally worn by Saban men—children's play suits, scarves, hats, diaper covers, handkerchiefs, table napkins, placemats, tablecloths, covers for kitchen appliances, sheets, pillowcases, towel edges and bookmarks. Sabans commonly use their lace to decorate religious places and celebrate important life events. Some of the most elaborate and careful designs are worked into altar cloths, christening dresses, first communion dresses, wedding dresses, wedding handkerchiefs and burial veils. Some christening dresses have been worn by several generations of infants in a family, are still used today and will likely continue to be used for many generations to come.

Among island visitors and overseas buyers, traditionally popular items have included handkerchiefs, napkins, runners and tablecloths. In recent years, lace workers have begun selling samplers showing several examples of border, corner and pattern stitches. These samplers serve no functional purpose; they are made for beauty's sake and hang framed on the walls of many Saban homes as well as many homes of former visitors to Saba. Samplers are especially attractive for people who want a variety of lacework patterns but do not want their Saba lace used in any way that might damage it.

3 Drawn Thread Work Comes to Saba

Sabans know the story of how Mary Gertrude Hassell (1854–1939) introduced drawn thread work to Saba. Today, she is perhaps the most honored person in island history; in fact, in August 1996, the Netherlands Antilles postal service released a stamp in her honor. Gertrude was born in Saba to prominent Sabans Ester Lovel Johnson (1832–1914) and Peter Hassell (1828–1930). In the early 1870s, young Gertrude's parents sent her to Caracas, Venezuela, to study with Spanish nuns, presumably in a convent.[1] Saba's resident Dutch priest, Father Josephus Phillip Thomas Kock, who hoped Gertrude would return to serve as a much-needed teacher for Saba's children, encouraged and assisted in this endeavor. Island tradition holds that the nuns taught her not only how to read and write but also how to work intricate, airy patterns into sections of linen. Learning to do "Spanish work," as she later called it, would prove to be Gertrude Hassell's most valuable lesson.

On her return to Saba, Gertrude Hassell married James Benjamin Johnson (1854–1919) and taught children in Saba's Roman Catholic schools as planned. Initially, she taught lacework to nearby friends and relatives, but lacework as a pastime spread quickly from her home in Windwardside to the other villages on the island.

In 1884, regular mail service came to Saba for the first time. Enterprising women seized this opportunity to turn their pastime into a mail-order cottage industry. The 1917 edition of the Encyclopedia of the Dutch West Indies states that, by the beginning of the First World War, about 250 of the island's fewer than 2,500 inhabitants made their living working lace. Within a few decades, most able-bodied women on the island were making lacework and selling it to clients abroad—mostly in the United States. The emerging mail-order lacework industry greatly stimulated both the development of Saba's postal service

1 In recent years, Will Johnson, native Saban historian and former senator to the Netherlands Antilles government, has speculated that young Gertrude actually went to Curaçao rather than Caracas to learn lacework as many Sabans with enough means sent their children there to be educated. In Curaçao, young Gertrude may have learned Spanish work from Venezuelan nuns or fellow students. Johnson, *Saban Lore*, 1989; and Johnson, "'Saba Lace' – A Time-Honored Craft," n.d. Editors' note: see also contribution by Espersen in this volume.

and the advancement of literacy on the island as women learned the skills necessary to sell their lacework abroad.

4 The Conditions for Growth

Saba did not become the Island of Lace only because mail service was established. Many factors on the island made a mail-order cottage industry the only real option Saba residents had if they wanted to participate in offshore economies that could bring new goods to Saba. As any visitor soon notices, Saba juts up from the sea, looking just as tall as it is across: a giant green gumdrop. The island has no natural harbors, so becoming any sort of shipping or trade center was always out of the question. Saba's terrain is so treacherous that this island, barely three miles across, has four separate villages and several distinct regional accents. Until recently, the terrain made life in Saba one of extreme village seclusion. As late as 1945, a woman in the neighborhood of Hell's Gate told a Dutch historian she had never been to The Bottom, Saba's largest town, which was most in contact with the outside world at the time, because "wicked people" lived there. While beautiful, Saba's mountainous terrain made it impossible for the islanders to develop a large-scale system of export agriculture or come together in large-scale manufacturing enterprises. Plots of land were too small and travel was too difficult. In 1902, Saba's non-lacework export for 2,265 people amounted to only 3,583 guilders—2,150 guilders of livestock, 750 of potatoes, 578 of onions and 105 of bay leaves—a guilder being approximately equal to fifty cents at the time. Of course, every family had prodigious fruit and vegetable gardens that flourished in Saba's warm climate. But to benefit from the world economy, the island had to look beyond its natural resources.

The answer to Sabans' needs had long been small-scale home industry for items of daily living as well as export items for the world economy. Before becoming the Island of Lace, Saba was the Island of Shoes. Through much of the seventeenth and eighteenth centuries, shoemaking dominated Saba's export economy. In the eighteenth century, stockings and gloves made from local cotton replaced the shoe industry. Through the course of the nineteenth century, the increasing availability of mass-produced clothing in the Caribbean caused the gradual decline of Saban cotton gloves and socks. The home manufacture of straw hats made from Cuban and Puerto Rican sugar cane limped along into the twentieth century, but this industry ultimately also fell victim to cheap machine-produced goods.

Through much of the seventeenth and eighteenth century, Sabans went about their business unmolested by the various colonial powers that lay claim to their island. However, life was mostly hard subsistence farming. English privateers captured the island in 1665, probably using Saba as a base for some time. In 1772, the island secretary of St. Eustatius and Saba called the latter "an island of poor people."

Unfortunately, the closing decades of the century saw raids by privateers and colonial navies, a particularly devastating hurricane in 1772, which led to increased emigration to Statia, and a brief capture by England in 1781. During the nineteenth century, numerous rotations between French, English and Dutch control disrupted the island as it struggled to hold on to its steadily evaporating home industries. Throughout the nineteenth century, the Dutch Windward Islands of Saba, St. Maarten and St. Eustatius together showed yearly deficiencies of up to 700,000 guilders. Saba was in decline. As political conditions stabilized, what Sabans needed for renewed prosperity was an export staple that could not be duplicated by machine.

5 Becoming the Island of Women

The one exportable resource Saba has always had is people. Island lore has it that much of Saba's population is descended from escaped indentured servants who fled to the safety of the island's impenetrable seclusion. But people with enough gumption to escape servitude rarely stay put. Saban men took to the sea in a male tradition as strong as is the lacework for island women. Family oral histories suggest that Saba served as a base for pirate raiders during its early history. Later, Saban men found work in the navies and shipping fleets of many lands, but mostly North America's, and earned a reputation as first-rate seamen and harbormasters. Beginning in the 1920s, many Saban men left for oil refinery work in Aruba and Curaçao. Between 1923 and 1960, the island population plummeted by one-third, from 1,655 people to 980. The persistent necessity for men to work elsewhere left their island home predominantly female—thus, the nickname Island of Women.[2]

With few men to care for, and stuck on a secluded island with little agricultural or industrial potential, Saban women worked fabric while their men were at sea. They took control of their own financial affairs and offered high-quality homemade handicrafts to the world through the dependable Dutch mail. Soon, lacework was a booming business. Saban women truly made Gertrude

2 Editors' note: the nickname is also used with reference to St. Maarten and other islands. See contribution by Linda Richardson in this section.

Hassell's imported tradition their own by creating new patterns and perfecting their skills. With the whole island culture focused on one product, Saba soon produced first-rate artists. In 1898, Miss Florence Every went to the Netherlands to show her lacework at a women's handicraft exhibition in The Hague and won an honorable mention. Six years later, a Saban woman won first prize at a handicrafts competition in Copenhagen. Members of the Danish government were so impressed that they invited her to stay for four months. The rise of Saba lace may have contributed to the decline of other Saba handicrafts, such as hat making and basket weaving. Because lacework allowed women to purchase manufactured items from abroad, it began to consume the time of Saban women.

As drawn thread work became the definitive island art, Sabans began a tradition of presenting gifts of Saba lace to visiting dignitaries. Some of the most elaborate pieces of Saba lace ever made were in honor of special occasions in the lives of members of the Dutch royal family, such as the birth of a child. Although Sabans sometimes find their relationship with the Dutch government frustrating, many feel a special attachment to the royal family, no doubt in part because of the royal family's gracious reception of Sabans' painstakingly exquisite lacework.

At its peak, lacework was the island's only meaningful export and accounted for probably 30–40 percent of the island's gross "national" product, including remittances from seamen and refinery workers abroad. If only work done in Saba is counted in figuring the GNP, then lacework had become the defining pillar of the island economy, accounting for about 75 percent of all economic activity on the island. Exact figures are hard to come by because statisticians tended to overlook women's work, much of the lace workers' income was in the form of bartered goods and taxation provided an incentive to underreport this source of income. Oral tradition clearly affords lacework the central role in Saban economic activity during the first third of the twentieth century and a major role into the 1950s.

6 Getting Linen

Because lacework required no land, no group effort and no men, it was an art and economic venture perfectly suited for conditions in Saba. All that Saban women needed was a steady supply of raw bolts of linen and eager customers. At the time of the rise of lacework in Saba, the island functioned on a barter and credit economy and very little currency changed hands, making it difficult to get linen from suppliers in England, Ireland and Belgium. Saban men at sea, especially schooner captain Ben Hassell, were helpful in this regard; during their travels, they kept an eye out for raw linen at good prices. Eleanor Durner (sometimes remembered as Duna), the wife of a Saban seaman living on the economically active island of St. Thomas, sent reasonably priced linen and lacework supplies to women in Saba. A skilled lace worker herself, Mrs. Durner incorporated patterns from St. Thomas's lacework tradition into the Saban tradition and marketed her own and others' Saba lace in St. Thomas. Her influence in the early growth and establishment of Saba's drawn thread work tradition is so significant that oral history occasionally incorrectly credits her with introducing the craft to Sabans.

7 Getting Customers

A few gift shops in St. Thomas and Curaçao sold lacework from time to time with the help of Saban expatriates such as Eleanor Durner, but most lace workers began to conduct their business directly with North Americans and, to a lesser extent, Canadians. Sabans bypassed their Dutch colonial rulers as seemingly obvious customers because North America shares the English language with Saba and is geographically much closer than the Netherlands.

The way Saban women went about getting customers in the United States without advertising and sophisticated market analysis would inspire any entrepreneur. They chose a bold, direct, person-to-person technique—indeed, it was the only option available to them. A woman seeking to sell her wares abroad copied company addresses off shipping crates or merchandise sent to the island from North America. She then wrote letters to these companies, explaining that she was willing to take orders for drawn thread work, enclosing a sample of her work and asking whoever received the letter to post it on the company bulletin board or in the company newsletter.

Later, Saban women used the same technique with addresses from magazine advertisements, newspapers, mail-order catalogs and even the publishing houses of the romance novels the women read—basically, any address they could lay their hands on. In 1947, when the government brought the first motorized vehicle to the island, a US Army surplus jeep, Saban women immediately wrote to the president of Willys-Overland Motors, explaining their craft. Many women working in the Willys office became lacework customers for years to come. Many lace workers remember that the possibility of buying goods from flashy North American catalogs inspired them to work hard at their art to bring new items to their isolated island.

The lace workers' bold soliciting was surprisingly effective. Many of the first transactions were trades for items that the North American companies made. The women then exchanged their surplus items for other goods and services on the island. Later, cash transactions with mail-order clients became more common. Lace workers played a major role in moving Saba from a barter and credit system to a cash economy.

Often, company officials wrote to the Saban government, inquiring into the legitimacy and financial status of the women soliciting business from their companies' employees. In their duty as promoters of island economic development, island officials often replied that the women were excellent artists who could "use some help," even though lacework solicitors were sometimes among the island's most affluent residents. In so doing, Saban officials wisely made use of North Americans' traditional willingness to help those who help themselves.

8 Cooperation and Competition among Lace Workers

Saban lace workers closely guarded the identity and addresses of good North American buyers they found. Any slip in secrecy could lead to a client being poached by a neighbor. Postal workers received strict instructions to give mail from the United States to only the addressee and only when the addressee personally came to the post office to get it. Gossip and feuds, sometimes lasting for years, swirled around questions of who stole whose addresses and who wrote bad things about a competitor in a letter to prospective clients. Such quarrels may seem trivial now, but then they were serious matters of independence versus dependence that influenced one's status within the community and, sometimes, where a family's next meal was coming from.

Women who accumulated more buyers than they could handle hired additional workers to work for them. Often, perhaps unbeknown to clients, thread work items coming from a single address in Saba might have been produced by half a dozen pairs of hands. They were the ones most likely to have other women working for them. Those who were literate had an enormous advantage in dealing with customers by mail. Those who already had money were better able to risk mailing expenses and the purchase costs of linen and other materials. Less affluent Sabans often worked for others on a payment-per-item basis. Often, women who were better artists remained subordinate to women who were better at self-promotion, had more money to put at risk or were simply luckier. Some women spent decades working for someone else before finding a single customer of their own.

9 Demographics, Geography and Lacework

Saba's topography, so unsuited for the plantation agriculture that dominated the rest of the Caribbean, made the island relatively inhospitable to slavery. Still, until abolition in 1863, one-third to one-half of Saba's population was enslaved. In the eighteenth century, there were four sugar plantations and some coffee plantations. Except for the elfin forest at the very top of Mount Scenery, the bejungled look of Saba today does not match the topography of the past. Virtually every patch of arable land, including steep and precarious mountain slopes buttressed by rock walls, was cultivated.

In the 1920s, two-thirds of the island was white. Around this time, Saban men, often with their families, began to leave the island for work. Racist policies at Standard Oil and Lago refineries, as well as racial immigration quotas in the United States, made it easier for white Sabans to find a place abroad to work. Saba became and has remained, in the perception of most islanders I encountered over the years, about 50 percent black and 50 percent white.[3] Many white-looking Sabans will freely acknowledge having a black grandparent and vice versa. Some Sabans, on the other hand, choose not to bring up this topic.

The history of lacework in Saba has involved Sabans of all lineages, but, occasionally, one hears lacework referred to as a "white thing." White Sabans have generally been more likely than black Sabans to make a living working lace. Before the worldwide civil rights movement in the latter half of the twentieth century, white Sabans were more likely to have access to education and resources, placing them in a better position to manage the marketing aspects of lacework and employ others to work for them.

Geography also played a role in determining who was likely to work lace. In expatriate Saban communities in Curaçao, Bermuda and North America's "little Saba" of Richmond Hill in New York City, Saban women continued to make and sell lacework but, as they were acculturated, not nearly to the extent as back in Saba. Gertrude Hassell first introduced her craft in her own village of Windwardside, but it caught on the strongest in Hell's Gate, Saba's most isolated village before the completion of the island's airstrip nearby. Hell's Gate

3 Author's note: this is not based on my own observation but rather the perceptions of islanders themselves as they expressed them to me regarding Saban demographics. I also remember them talking about how St. Barts is "almost completely white," while the historical population of St. Maarten, although having a few white families, consisted mostly of black people. Now, the island has many, maybe mostly, expatriates. And Sabans' perception of Statia is that it is almost entirely black.

women had very few options for work and recreation to while away their hours of solitude. Until the mid-1990s, some would still say the best lacework was done there. At the other end of the island, The Bottom was closer to where ships landed and lies on relatively flat terrain. It provided more, although still limited, opportunities for agricultural work, recreation and contact with other Sabans and outsiders. In recent times, as lacework has become more of an optional activity than a necessity, it has hung on the strongest in Hell's Gate, less so in Windwardside and even less so in The Bottom.

As a legacy of the agricultural slavery in Saba, the island's black population is concentrated in The Bottom, with fewer black families in Windwardside and even fewer in Hell's Gate. This geographic distribution also partly explains why drawn thread work has more commonly been associated with white Saban women. But since the turn of the twenty-first century, Windwardside has emerged as Saba's lace-working center: it is more tourist oriented, home to many of the women returning to lacework and the site of the Saba Lace Ladies' Foundation at the Eugenius Johnson Center.

10 What Was It Like to Be a Lace-Working Woman?

Remembering their mothers working late was overwhelmingly the most common lacework-related memory Sabans shared with me during my research. Island philosopher George Seaman calls lace-working women the "true heroes of Saba, a story that needs to be told."[4] Through long hours of tedious work, they kept the island afloat financially. For much of the island's history, being female meant working lace, not principally for love of the art form but out of economic necessity. While many today may romanticize the lace working of the past, many women remember hating it as children. For most of her life, lace-working legend Pearl Zagers of Hell's Gate has worked over eight hours a day producing lacework after tending the garden and doing other household chores. "I must have done three or four steamer loads of lace," she said. Adelle Hassell, who now works drawn thread work as a hobby, remembers loathing it as a child and running away when her mother called her to come work lace.

Children, mostly girls but boys as well, crocheted hemstitching as soon as they could, at around age five or six. Enterprising kids could finish up to eight napkins a day for one Antillean cent each. Girls graduated to making patterns

4 Telephone conversation with George Seaman, July 2009.

as soon as possible when the demand for lacework was high and when they showed ability. Boys' lace-working careers were restricted to hemstitching only.

11 Making a Living with Saba Lace

What kind of living did lace-working women make? There are two ways of looking at this question. If we compare the lives of lace workers in the 1900–1929 heyday to the lives of women in the late nineteenth century, Saba lace brought never-seen-before wealth to the island. If we compare the lives of the lace workers in the first third of the century to the lives of Saban women today, the former worked slave-like hours for pitiful wages.

In the early days, Saba's women often received goods in kind for their lacework. Saban homemakers welcomed pots and pans or skincare products made by employees of the North American companies from whom they solicited business. Saban women, in turn, bartered these items for other goods and services on the island. Later, Saba lace probably brought the first significant amounts of hard currency to the island outside of salaries sent home by men at sea or abroad. While lacework brought cash to Saba, it also had very high overhead costs. Even with help from the likes of Ben Hassell and Eleanor Durner, raw linen remained especially expensive.

In the mid-1960s, a time when lacework fetched higher prices, American anthropologist Julia Crane researched the economy of Saba and found that net earnings for a full day's work were only about fifty-six cents.[5] Additionally, all of this assumes the woman was working with her own buyers. If she was working for someone else, she could expect to be paid about thirty-three cents per day.

Twenty-first-century lace makers often say things like, "You got to do it because you love it, not because you are making any money"; "It's a hobby that helps pay for itself; you really can't make money anymore"; and "I like to see things I have made myself; it is very satisfying." All of these statements suggest that making money is no longer the main reason for doing lacework.

While lacework remained a crucial part of the island's economy until the 1950s, the years 1900–1929 were the golden age of Saba lace. Most of the patterns in use now were developed during this period, and lacework defined the economy and lifestyle of the island. Today, the era is remembered as the time that formed Saba's identity and made it forever the Island of Lace. During this

5 Crane, *Educated to Emigrate*, 1971.

era, island consciousness began to be more important than village identity to Sabans. Lacework emerged as a common experience that helped define Sabans as a people and bring them into the modern world.

In 1930, financial depression swept the world. Places whose economies depended on one luxury export item were hit particularly hard. For most buyers in Saba's largest market, the United States, fancy napkins from the Caribbean plummeted on the list of things they could afford. The customers who did continue to buy lacework paid much less than they had before. Saba's lacework economy collapsed, and Sabans scrambled to save their livelihood. They formed committees to solve the problem, but Saba would have to wait for renewed prosperity elsewhere before it could revive Saba lace. The island was never secluded from the world economy.

During the 1940s, World War II raging in the North Atlantic posed obvious problems for reviving an export economy in the Caribbean. In the 1950s, lacework sales began to recover, but the craft would never dominate Saba to the extent it did in the 1920s. During the middle third of the twentieth century, remittances from men at sea or abroad, especially men working at oil refineries in Aruba, Curaçao and Venezuela, brought the most income to Saba. In the 1960s, a pan-Caribbean tourist boom and an airstrip completed in 1963 began to bring tourist day-trippers from St. Maarten to Saba.

In the latter third of the twentieth century, government salaries for administration, public works projects and services—as well as income from tourists coming to dive, sightsee and hike—emerged as the driving forces of Saba's economy, but lacework held on as an important supplement. Lacework sales to tourists in Saba began to replace the mail-order industry, partly because of the rising costs of postage. Secret addresses in the United States hardly mattered when women could simply go down to the airport and sell their wares to incoming visitors. A very few Sabans still worked for other women, but, for the most part, island tourism cut out the "middlewoman," and lace workers sold their own work in Windwardside and Hell's Gate. Most lace workers gladly took mail orders from tourists who had returned home, but they no longer solicited business abroad. Nevertheless, even today, some still correspond as pen pals with lacework clients from years ago.

From the 1970s to the present, the demand for Saba lace has mirrored the growth of tourism. Lace workers say that sales volume took a drop after the early 1990s recession and has not fully recovered. Demand for lacework remains steady, but, while it is still central to Saban cultural identity and artistic expression, it is now an appendage to the island's economy rather than its pillar. Attitudes and habits bred by their history as lace workers have made

Sabans independent and powerful and have prepared them for success in other pursuits.

Many have worried that Saba lace might die out, fearing that such is perhaps the price of "progress." While lacework certainly does not occupy as many people or as much time as it once did, and Saba women do not often take on projects as ambitious as their mothers used to, drawn thread work is a vital and healthy tradition in Saba. Gladys Hassell of Windwardside taught well-attended Saba lace classes in Windwardside and The Bottom, and Tina Johnson of Hell's Gate once taught a thread work class at the University of St. Maarten. Tourists often ask lace workers to adapt their art to a special idea they have in mind, and drawn thread work artists continue to develop new designs of their own. Both of these circumstances contribute to a living, evolving art form.

Acknowledgments

This is an edited excerpt of a chapter originally published in Eliason, Eric A., and Scott Squire. *The Island of Lace: Drawn Threadwork on Saba in the Dutch Caribbean*. Jackson: University Press of Mississippi, 2019. Reproduction of this text is courtesy of University Press of Mississippi.

Bibliography

Crane, Julia G. *Educated to Emigrate: The Social Organization of Saba*. Anjerpublikaties 13. Assen: Van Gorcum, 1971.

Johnson, Will. "'Saba Lace' – A Time-Honored Craft." Unpublished manuscript, n.d.

Johnson, Will. *Saban Lore: Tales from My Grandmother's Pipe*. Saba: OKSNA, 1989.

CHAPTER 45

Making Up the Rules on My Own

Linda Richardson

Abstract

As writer and founder of the women's theater group The Oualichi Players in St. Maarten, as former minister of education and culture of the government of the Netherlands Antilles and as court interpreter for the Joint Court of Justice of Curaçao, Aruba, Bonaire, St. Maarten, Saba and St. Eustatius, Richardson reflects on her life and involvement in cultural activities and educational policy in the Dutch Windward Islands. The significance of the mother tongue as a vehicle of cultural self-reflection and as a means for social mobility and civic participation is a concern running throughout her work.

Keywords

The Oualichi Players – theater – St. Maarten – mother tongue education – language in judicial system

1 Becoming a Feminist

I learned about feminism as a student in Europe in the 1970s. This was a process of becoming self-aware and conscious of the social roles that women are expected to play. In the late 1960s, as a pupil in a Catholic girls' boarding school in Curaçao, it was in part due to my initiative to bring a male band called The Swinging Scouts to perform during a cultural variety show at my boarding school that men were allowed to enter the convent premises for the first time, an event that was even reported in the local press.[1] When I returned from studying in Europe to the Caribbean in the beginning of the 80s, it seemed like the feminist agenda did not exist in St. Maarten and I felt like I was the first person

1 "Bonte avond in Maria College" [Variety show at Maria College], *Amigoe di Curaçao*, Vol. 84, Issue 23, January 27, 1967, p. 3. The *bonte avond* was a cultural variety show organized as a fundraiser by students residing at the boarding school.

 | DOI:10.1163/9789004690882_047

to address it. To me, this was not simply about copying the European model, for I was also influenced by the activities of the Steering Committee Curaçao, with leaders such as Stella Oosterhof, Maria Liberia-Peters and Stella Pieters Kwiers, among others. There was a branch of the steering committee in St. Maarten, but I do not remember this branch gaining momentum in seriously promoting awareness and conducting activities for women in St. Maarten or of having any clear plan of action on equal rights for women, except for some sporadic initiatives on domestic violence. Even today, I don't think there is any real policy or program on gender equality at the women's desk in St. Maarten. Although policy pays attention to what is referred to as community development, the focus on issues such as domestic violence and the hurdles faced by single mothers is limited. To bring about awareness on the rights of women, I started distributing the women's daily planner, received from the Steering Committee Curaçao, which contained proverbs, quotes and ideas by and for women and was very popular among women on the island. I also promoted the celebration of International Women's Day on March 8, gave talks on women's issues and got invited to various fora, including the Third World Conference on Women held in Nairobi, Kenya, in 1985. Eventually, I started getting involved in theater-making. During the recent COVID-19 pandemic, I ran a weekly live program on Facebook titled "Aging with Grace," in which I shared advice on health and aging.[2]

2 The Oualichi Players: Women's Theater Group in St. Maarten

My involvement with theater started during my student days in Europe. A close actor friend in the Netherlands invited me to numerous performances. In 1977, I traveled from the Netherlands to Nigeria to attend the International Festival of Arts and Culture (FESTAC), paying my way with a job as an interpreter for the Cuban delegation. There, I met my former husband, Fabian Badejo, who had studied in Spain, with whom I worked together in translating works by Cuban writers and poets into English. When we moved to St. Maarten in 1981, Badejo and I decided to organize an arts and cultural festival along the lines of FESTAC, FESTANTIL (Cultural Festival in the Netherlands Antilles) and CARIFESTA (Caribbean Festival of Arts in Barbados), which I had also attended in 1981. Such festivals exhibited a diverse range of talents, including dance, poetry, literature, music, fashion, arts and crafts. As director of the St. Maarten Council on the Arts, Badejo spearheaded the St. Maarten's Festival of Arts and

2 The archives of the show are available via https://www.facebook.com/groups/agingwithgracetv.

Culture (SMAFESTAC), which eventually took place in 1982. Besides participation of local artists and groups, SMAFESTAC was well attended by artists and groups from Curaçao, Aruba and other islands.[3] Seeing that the only theater group in St. Maarten, the Colebay Theater Group, which at that time focused on folklore singing and dancing, had indicated that it would not participate in the festival, I decided to start a theater group myself. That is how The Oualichi Players began in 1982. I liked the name Oualichi and chose it without initially knowing its meaning or origin. It was only afterward that I learned that St. Maarten had two Amerindian names in the Kalinago and Arawak languages respectively, namely Soualiga, "the land of salt," and Oualichi or Qualichi, "the land of brave women." The Oualichi Players was basically a women's theater group, consisting of approximately eight women belonging to different generations, none of whom had any prior acting experience. I invited people I knew to join, wrote the script on my own, did the directing and just made up the rules on my own. I wrote as much as possible in the local language, St. Maarten English, reading aloud what I scripted to the elderly women in the group, who assisted me with fine-tuning the local idioms and phrases. Having spent my early years in Aruba and Curaçao and not having grown up in St. Maarten, I did not have some of the finesses of St. Maarten English, the language mastered by the local population.

The Oualichi Players did something different from what already existed on the island. We performed our first play, *Family Melée*, as an open-air show under the shade of a tree at a restaurant in 1982. It was a play about single parenthood and about the socioeconomic changes on the island in the wake of tourism. The play portrayed three generations of single mothers who spoke to each other about the issues faced by their own generation. The first act of the play started out with children's games and songs. These were melodies in English as well as in Dutch that children and adults in the audience recognized and could sing along with, such as "Zagen, zagen, wiede wagen" and "I went down deh, come on deh." The play also offered a commentary on the effects of the tourist economy in St. Maarten, for instance, on young people who earned a living working in the casino or on the elderly who were moved to senior citizens' homes and faced loneliness and isolation even within their own families.

One scene in the second act was particularly memorable for it humorously displayed an incident at a nude beach on the island. It was based on a news item reported in the local media in which an American tourist went to the

3 See also Rutgers, *Beneden en boven de wind: Literatuur van de Nederlandse Antillen en Aruba* [Beneath and above the winds: Literature from the Netherlands Antilles and Aruba], 1996, p. 385. Editors' note: see contribution by Echteld and Rutgers in this section.

police station in St. Maarten to lodge a complaint about being bitten by a fish on his penis while visiting the nude beach. In the play, the police officer in the scene, who initially refused to believe the tourist and insisted on checking if it were true, eventually told the tourist that the Dutch part of the island was not responsible and sent him to file his complaint on the French side of the island, where the nude beach is located. The audience roared with laughter because they recognized the local references and saw their lives and day-to-day realities reflected in a light and funny manner in the play.

The Oualichi Players became very successful and was, in fact, the second all-female theater group in the Caribbean; the first being the well-known Sistren from Jamaica.[4] Unlike Sistren, which had a seasoned playwright and actresses, The Oualichi Players was just a group of amateurs wanting to have fun and share their observations and comments about the society they lived in. Following the SMAFESTAC event and the staging of *Family Melée*, I wrote and staged several other plays for different occasions, but these productions were skits.

The play *Pregnant Women* was staged in 1983 on International Women's Day.[5] It was a one-act play about women in different stages of pregnancy in a doctor's waiting room. They talk about different myths and prejudices around pregnancy, such as the child being a boy if the belly shape is pointed and a girl if the belly shape is round. I interspersed the dialogues with local expressions such as "pork chops" for girls and "spareribs" for boys. I used incidents from my own experience of pregnancy in St. Maarten, where I learned that women were respected more if their firstborn was a boy. It may no longer be the case, but these ideas used to be prevalent then. The play progresses into a scandal when two of the women in the room find out they are pregnant by the same man. Social commentary and feminist criticism are thus woven into the play.

The Oualichi Players was invited to perform this skit in Anguilla and in Saba. In Saba, *Pregnant Women* was slotted in an evening of poetry, dance and other cultural expressions. I replaced one of the players who did not want to fly to Saba because of the challenges of flights landing on the rocky island. As I happened to be pregnant at the time, it confused the audience as they could not figure out who was really pregnant and who was merely acting. The play was so well received that, after we finished and came for the curtain call, the audience insisted that we repeat the play, so we actually performed it all over again on the same night!

4 Akhter, "Sistren: The Vanguard of Popular Theater in Jamaica," 2008.

5 The unpublished manuscript of the play was stored in the Central Library of Phillipsburg but was unfortunately damaged in the wake of Hurricane Irma in 2017.

The Oualichi Players continued with performances until early 1986 with productions such as *Freedom Song*, *The Prime Minister* and *Mixed Couples*. This last play explored racial prejudices in interracial relationships. The group became known for bringing to the forefront women's voices and women's concerns and raising public awareness in a light and humorous vein. The activities stopped after I became minister of education and culture in the Netherlands Antilles in 1986.

3 Forays into Educational Policy

I never imagined joining party politics to become a minister. In fact, I only joined the cabinet of Don Martina, prime minister of the Netherlands Antilles, in 1986 because I was requested and invited by Senator Will Johnson from Saba to represent Saba and St. Eustatius in Cabinet Martina IV. With Aruba leaving the Netherlands Antilles, it was the first time the smaller islands of the Netherlands Antilles were allotted a ministerial portfolio. They may have gotten the education portfolio because domains such as education and culture are not money-making areas. Another possible reason was the ongoing battle in Curaçao between the very powerful teacher's union SITEK (Sindikato di Trahadó den Edukashon na Kòrsou [Union of Educational Workers in Curaçao]) and the equally powerful school boards, such as the Catholic and the Protestant school boards, on issues such as mother-tongue education and curricular reform. This could have led politicians in Willemstad to hand over what was a conflict-ridden education portfolio to the two smallest islands, represented for the first time in history in a Dutch Antillean Council of Ministers.

As a linguist and keynote speaker at a teacher's conference in St. Maarten in 1981, I met with strong resistance when I argued that Dutch was in fact a dead language in the Dutch Windward Islands, since it was neither spoken by most people nor used in print media, radio or television. I strongly advocated ending Dutch-medium education on the islands, arguing that education in St. Maarten, Saba and St. Eustatius was not characterized by bilingualism, as some educators in St. Maarten claimed, but by semilingualism, implying that neither language was learned, taught or mastered properly.

In 1981, the then minister of education and culture, Mr. Jacques Veeris, appointed me as a policy worker and head of the Windward Islands' section of the Instituto Lingwistiko Antiano (ILA, the Antillean Linguistics Institute). The ideas I was propagating were not necessarily new, as the thinking had indeed been developing for a while already, but they were severely resisted by the powers that be.[6] As early as 1981, the governmental report *Education for One and All / Enseñansa pa un i tur*, aimed at a new education policy for the Netherlands Antilles, advocated education in the mother tongue.[7]

As education minister, I challenged the prevalent idea around language education in schools and insisted on the importance of school education in the language in which children speak, pray, dream and talk to their parents. It was never my intention to wage a war against Dutch but rather to give children the chance to develop their potential fully in the language closest to them. The high rate of school dropouts and repeaters, even at primary school levels, for failing in the Dutch language was disheartening.

Many of those in power at the time were offended by the position I took for it challenged the status of Dutch as the language of governance. In Aruba, Curaçao and Bonaire, there was a lot of resistance to Papiamentu-language education in schools, with arguments about its supposed inferiority or unsuitability for education. Similarly, in the Dutch Windward Islands, it was often claimed that the mother tongue of the children was not standard or "proper" English and that Dutch should be maintained as the language of instruction since it would give the children access to higher education in the Netherlands and future employment in the public sector.

I had to work very diligently to introduce English as a language of instruction in schools in both Saba and St. Eustatius. The conclusion of the report *Breaking the Language Barrier* pointed out the many pitfalls of school education in a foreign language and made it clear that English should be the language of instruction in Saba.[8] Together with the then lieutenant governor of Saba, Wycliffe Smith, also an educator and poet, who had been researching the possibilities of English-medium education in Saba, I went to St. Kitts to speak to our counterparts there and to acquire books and didactic materials for the implementation of English-medium instruction. In our capacities as lieutenant governor of Saba and minister of education of the then Netherlands Antilles respectively, we signed a memorandum putting in place the new language policy in Saba in 1986.

In St. Maarten, the school board of the Methodist Agogic Centre, established by Reverend J. Gumbs, was the first to request and receive permission to

6 Editors' note: for a recent study of national belonging in primary education in St. Maarten, see Halfman, "An educated Sint Maartener? National belonging in a primary school on Sint Maarten," 2020.

7 Ministry of Education of the Netherlands Antilles, *Education for One and All / Enseñansa pa un i tur*: Een visie op het toekomstig onderwijsbeleid [Education for One and All / Enseñansa pa un i tur: A vision for the future of educational policy], December 18, 1981.

8 Smith, Buncamper and Wilson, *Breaking the Language Barrier*, 1986.

continue with English as language of instruction beyond kindergarten and the first two years of primary school. Besides this school, there was a small stream of children in a Dutch public school receiving education in English and achieving excellent results. Notwithstanding these successful instances, there was a lot of opposition by educators to the implementation of English as language of instruction beyond the first two grades of primary education. As a compromise, they demanded the replacement of the Dutch language education system with a bilingual system, thus retaining Dutch while adding English as language of instruction to the curriculum. Although I opposed this idea, arguing that a bilingual education system could only work in a bilingual society, I eventually signed a protocol with the then lieutenant governor of St. Maarten, Mr. Ralph Richardson, establishing a committee aimed at exploring possibilities of a bilingual education system. While signing the protocol, I predicted that, in the not too distant future, the majority of children in St. Maarten would enjoy education in a language they heard and spoke daily. Indeed, this has turned out to be the case. Today, not only do public and government-subsidized schools offer education in English but private schools on the island offer an American or Canadian curriculum as well, attracting many children, including those of native Dutch parents.

As far as St. Eustatius is concerned, English language education was only formally introduced in 2015, while Saba implemented English language instruction almost thirty years earlier in 1987. Many of the politicians in St. Eustatius, who initially vehemently opposed me as minister of education for suggesting that the Statian child would perform better by receiving education in English, later conceded that this was, indeed, the best policy to adopt.[9]

4 Language in the Judicial System

In 1969, I was the first Dutch Antillean student to receive a scholarship to study in Belgium, at the former Higher Institute for Translators and Interpreters (HIVT). At the time, it was not possible to pursue translating and interpreting studies in the Netherlands. I was also the only black student in the entire program. As part of the completion of my studies at the HIVT in 1972, I wrote a thesis on the etymology of the Papiamentu language, titled "Ensayo de la Etimología del Papiamentu," under the supervision of Prof. Raul Römer at the

9 See Drenthe et al, "Haalbaarheidsonderzoek instructietaal Sint Eustatius: 'It Takes an Island to Raise Our Children'" [Feasibility study on the language of instruction in St. Eustatius: "It takes an island to raise our children"], 2014; Faraclas, Kester, and Mijts, *Community Based Research in Language Policy and Planning*, 2014.

University of Amsterdam. This project dealt with the origins of Papiamentu and examined the history and structures of creole languages in the Caribbean. After graduating from the HIVT, I pursued graduate studies in linguistics at the Institute for General Linguistics at the University of Amsterdam.

As a sworn interpreter for the Joint Court of Justice of Aruba, Curaçao, St. Maarten and of Bonaire, St. Eustatius and Saba, I have come to understand that the justice system on our islands is one of the most remarkable expressions of colonial history, the effects of which continue to be felt to the present day. Legal language is a complicated genre in any language, but it becomes even more complicated when people are addressed by the law in a foreign language. I am thus very interested in seeking out changes in criminal proceedings in a way that people are not disadvantaged by the colonial system that underpins it. I have written a reference book, *Trilingual Terminology in Criminal Proceedings*, with legal terms in Dutch and their translations in English and Spanish, with the aim of aiding law enforcement officers, suspects, attorneys, court recorders, probation officers, prosecutors and judges in navigating the language of the criminal justice system.[10]

In response to the lack of court interpreters on the island, I took the initiative to design and organize a course in court interpreting in 2021 with the aim of training interpreters for the court. In doing so, I put together a glossary of terms used in criminal court proceedings in three languages for trainees. This is the basis of the publication, which seeks to familiarize professionals with the terminology related to criminal proceedings. It is not simply a dictionary of terms but a systematization of terminology as well as an outline of the most widespread crimes on the island, along with the relevant terminology pertaining to their legal prosecution. As Dutch is the primary legal language in St. Maarten, St. Eustatius and Saba, but interactions with the courts largely involve English- and Spanish-speaking stakeholders, the book is trilingual. The intention is to expand the publication to Papiamentu and French in the future to enable a broader use across the Caribbean region.

As a legal interpreter, I am often confronted by the fact that, while suspects and defendants are interviewed in English, the official reports are written in Dutch and signed by suspects, witnesses and defendants who have no knowledge of Dutch. Suspects have a right to understand why they are detained, to follow and participate in the legal proceedings and to know the reasons for being convicted. Yet, too often, the defendant in court does not grasp what is happening despite the assistance of an interpreter. In order to improve

10 Richardson, *Trilingual Terminology in Criminal Proceedings*, 2023.

communication with the different stakeholders, I have published another volume titled *Bringing the Court before the People*.[11] This book describes the role of the court interpreter and examines the language used in legal proceedings from the moment someone is arrested or detained until their conviction or acquittal. It also takes inspiration from the international movement to simplify legal jargon and make it accessible to ordinary citizens and simultaneously examines the relation between human rights and the language of the court system in the Dutch Caribbean.

Bibliography

Akhter, Afreen. "Sistren: The Vanguard of Popular Theater in Jamaica." *Signs* 33, no. 2 (2008): 431–6. https://doi.org/10.1086/521058.

"Bonte avond in Maria-College" [Variety show at Maria College]. *Amigoe di Curaçao* 84, no. 23, January 27, 1967, 3.

Drenthe, Tineke, Rose Mary Allen, Wim Meijnen, Gert Oostindie and Monica van Leeuwen-Laan. "Haalbaarheidsonderzoek instructietaal Sint Eustatius: 'It Takes an Island to Raise Our Children'" [Feasibility study on the language of instruction in St. Eustatius: "It takes an island to raise our children"], The Hague/Oranjestad: Ministry of Education, Culture and Science (State Department Caribbean Netherlands), 2014. https://www.eerstekamer.nl/overig/20140619/haalbaarheidsonderzoek/document.

Faraclas, Nicholas, Ellen-Petra Kester, and Eric Mijts. *Community Based Research in Language Policy and Planning: The Language of Instruction in Education in Sint Eustatius*. Vol. 20. Language Policy. Cham: Springer International Publishing, 2014. https://doi.org/10.1007/978-3-030-23223-8.

Halfman, Jordi. "An Educated Sint Maartener? National Belonging in a Primary School on Sint Maarten." *Globalisation, Societies and Education* 18, no. 3 (May 2020): 290–302. https://doi.org/10.1080/14767724.2019.1662280.

Ministry of Education of the Netherlands Antilles. *Education for One and All/ Enseñansa pa un i tur*: Een visie op het toekomstig onderwijsbeleid [*Education for One and All / Enseñansa pa un i tur*: A vision for the future of educational policy]. Report of the Policy Committee of the Ministry of Education of the Netherlands Antilles, December 18, 1981.

Richardson, Linda. *Trilingual Terminology in Criminal Proceedings*. Philipsburg: published by the author, 2023.

11 Richardson, *Bringing the Court before the People*, 2024.

Richardson, Linda. *Bringing the Court before the People.* Philipsburg: published by the author 2024.

Rutgers, Wim. *Beneden en boven de wind: Literatuur van de Nederlandse Antillen en Aruba* [Beneath and above the winds: Literature from the Netherlands Antilles and Aruba]. Amsterdam: De Bezige Bij, 1996.

Smith, Wycliffe, Jacintha Buncamper and Franklin Wilson. *Breaking the Language Barrier.* Report of the Island Government of the Territory of Saba, Netherlands Antilles, 1986.

CHAPTER 46

Fridi Martina: a Brief Biography

Philie van Veen

Abstract

This contribution includes a biographical introduction to the life and works of Fridi Martina, Curaçaoan playwright, poet and theater maker. It also introduces the texts by Martina published in this volume, "Vuurdoop" [Baptism of Fire] and "Baranka Mama" [Mother Rock].

Keywords

Fridi Martina – biography – Curaçao – theater – literary production – postcolonial identity

Fridi Martina was born in Curaçao in 1950. An orphan at the age of nine, she spent much of her youth in a boarding school. As a child, she had the feeling of being judged and treated in a discriminatory way by the nuns. This experience, she often recounted, greatly influenced her determined pursuit to show she could move beyond the profession of a domestic worker. Which she would indeed prove later.

In the early 1970s, when she was twenty-one years old, she left Curaçao for the Netherlands. In those early years, she struggled to find her way, initially working in administrative jobs. Luckily for her, she had the chance to find some fulfillment in amateur dramatics, as she had done during her youth in Curaçao. In 1974, she was accepted into the Academy of Theatre and Dance in Amsterdam, completing her training there as an actor in 1981. In 1987, she qualified as a drama teacher for higher education and was associated with the HKU University of the Arts in Utrecht for ten years.

In her professional life, Fridi Martina worked as an actor, dancer, musician, poet, writer, educator, director and producer. Only days after her death on May 12, 2014, an article about her appeared in the Curaçaoan daily, *Amigoe di*

 | DOI:10.1163/9789004690882_048

Curaçao, with the heading: "The lioness of emancipation is no more ..."[1] The headline says a great deal about her. Her aim was to support people, especially young people, in the process of freeing themselves from a sense of inferiority and experiences of racism and oppression. In her statements about people who get stuck in this process, she often had a sharp tongue but was also able to get people to laugh when they recognized and acknowledged the issues she raised.

Martina left behind a huge and diverse body of work. Prior to her death, she acknowledged the importance of archiving and publishing her work. Her writing includes poems, monologues, dialogues, song lyrics as well as stage and film scripts. She wrote in Dutch, English and Papiamentu. Among her collections are a number of manuscripts written on an old-fashioned typewriter, her very first stage and performance scripts, with accompanying black-and-white photographs. This material is from the late 1970s and early 1980s.

Fridi Martina's work is characteristic because of her choice of subjects, her preferred style and vocabulary. Two clear phases can be distinguished in her work, the first reflecting the twenty-five years she lived and worked in the Netherlands, and the second being the subsequent twenty years after she returned to Curaçao. Her choice of language seems to have depended on her place of residence. In the Netherlands, she primarily wrote in Dutch, but, once in Curaçao, her preference was Papiamentu. Some of her later writing is in English. Most of her texts are in the first person, addressing another who often gives no answer. The other, the "you," assumes many shapes: a lost friend or lover, an adversary, a situation, an event, a country or a community. The first-person narrator often addresses the self and the other in monologue, thinking aloud. The writing revolves around memories, dreams, longings and desires. The characters feel pain and sorrow. There is often the urge to take action or to see others take action. A number of recurring themes in her work are worth noting, such as "the Third World" in its role of victim versus "the First World's" delusion of superiority. Martina is very critical of both worlds and roles. Another theme pertains to how people are programmed and how this goes hand in hand with indoctrination.

She addressed the rigid patterns of our traditions, berating people engaged in an ego struggle compelled by greed and a strong urge to prove themselves. She wrote about denial, concealment, suppression of false pride and other

1 "De leeuwin van de emancipatie is niet meer" [The lioness of emancipation is no more], *Amigoe di Curaçao*, May 12, 2014.

obstructive emotions and people's laziness to not reflect on such things, although such responses indicate that it would be the right time to take action and prove to oneself that it is possible to change. Self-development and the realization of individual potential are important not only on an individual level but also bear crucial societal dimensions in her writing. She incessantly pointed out that the road to equality is a journey in relationships of all kinds, between people, countries and even continents. The motif of an inner dance is significant in her writing, a dance she described as the source of her enduring strength and enthusiasm to continue moving dynamically in this earthly existence. Dance is vocalized through a movement vocabulary of parting, letting go, burning up and transforming.

Martina enjoyed playing with words and a few of those words have come to be regarded as trademark characteristics of her writing.The portmanteau Dutch word *me-schiedenis* (me-story), for example, which she coins to emphasize that there is a history of her own that contrasts with history from above, as it were (*ge-schiedenis*, you-story). And *de mis-der ver-stand*, the "wrongs of the far-away reasoning" (splitting the word *verstand*, which means understanding or reason, to emphasize and reinterpret the prefix *ver* in its meaning as "far"). The cold mind that is so far from the warmth of heart, which is only in the service of power, just like the service, the mass (*mis*), in the Catholic Church is used to repress and exploit.

Over and over again, Martina deals with the process of realizing and embracing where you stand and how you got there, then choosing and deciding how to progress. During her life, she traveled widely, including several times to the African continent. Her writings make occasional references to gods and goddesses of the Yoruba culture of West Africa. She mentions Yemayá(h), for example, goddess of the sea, and Waze, god of the earth. She refers to musical instruments, too, such as the balafon and the *shekere*, both of which she learned to play and used during her performances.

Martina concluded her sojourn in the Netherlands with a text called "Vuurdoop" (Baptism of fire), published in English translation in this volume. In this text, she looked back on her time in the Netherlands, having recently returned to Curaçao. It is not encouraging. She still marveled at the air of superiority and attitude of the Dutch, but she lived up to her own invitation to work with others to turn the tide. Once in Curaçao, she soon realized that Curaçaoan society had been stuck in a great inferiority complex from which it has still not recovered. She found herself bogged down in the treacle of how people present themselves and how they act in general. Her early writings clearly show the frustration and sense of helplessness she felt. Her work became more optimistic as she began to write and perform her song lyrics, always involving young people in the process.

"Baranka mama" (Mother rock), also included in this volume, is one of Martina's more tranquil poems. Returning to the Mother rock is associated with coming home to where she is loved unconditionally, where she finds safety and recognition and can be herself. The protective coat of her spiritual mother gives the authorial figure enough strength to live on without her physical presence, knowing that their connection is everlasting.

Acknowledgments

This is an edited translation of a Dutch text originally published as van Veen, Philie. "Een korte levensbeschrijving van Fridi Martina" [A brief biography of Fridi Martina]. In *Fridi Martina in Good Company: Een meertalige bloemlezing met gedichten, liedteksten en monologen van Fridi Martina* [Fridi Martina in good company: A multilingual anthology with poems, lyrics and monologues by Fridi Martina], 8–11. Curaçao: University of Curaçao; Carib Publishing, 2019. English translation by Marcus Ferley. Reproduction courtesy of Philie van Veen and Carib Publishing.

Bibliography

"De leeuwin van de emancipatie is niet meer" [The lioness of emancipation is no more], *Amigoe di Curaçao*, May 12, 2014.

Van Veen, Philie, ed. *Fridi Martina in Good Company: Een meertalige bloemlezing met gedichten, liedteksten en monologen van Fridi Martina* [Fridi Martina in good company: A multilingual anthology with poems, lyrics and monologues by Fridi Martina]. Curaçao: University of Curaçao; Carib Publishing, 2019.

CHAPTER 47

Baptism of Fire

Fridi Martina

Mother Earth woke me up again today. I so want to talk to you. Tick, tick; tick, tick ... On their morning walk, my eyes encounter the endless horizon. The whole spectrum of colors sets the scene for me. The tapping disappears into the background. An amiable lady, who, through the ether, confessed that she loves me, is playing a waltz. So melancholic that I understand why I'm sitting here: finally back home again.

I communicate with Socrates so that I can remember what I learned yesterday, so that I can translate it for you. But everything's already been said, everything's already been written. How can I sing the translation so that you will listen? Do you want to know who I am? Do you find me so insecure then? Strangely enough, I am, even though I'm sure of myself. Do you understand? Are you ready to experience me as an element of surprise in your existence? An adventure that guarantees the excitement of a new existence.

The mangos are really sweet, the medlar tastes just like honey and the watermelon really does quench my thirst. The hibiscus looks at me so penetratingly. Turned red with a passion, which can pierce my heart.

Do I miss the Netherlands? The people who are dear to me, of course. But not the fight for that right to exist in your life, a right I was given at birth. And I don't miss myself constantly having to convince you that you need not be afraid of me. True, I'm fiery. That comes from the burning sun. Merciless, you could say, so that I feel that I truly exist. Well now, it's this fire that I wanted to use to warm you.

Now, sitting here, I think to myself: What's so different about me that people think a policy is needed to keep us apart? Your leaders speak of me as a threat to this small, wet and cold "frogland" of yours. But your people are still with me and are replenished again and again. They are truly not just here for a visit. No, they've taken the bait and bought a house with me in it, backed up by your government. Here, in my place, you are trading in the shame you call upon us! It's called development, of whom and from what is still a mystery to me!

I speak your language, I use it to teach, and I pay your social security tax so you, too, can have the right to exist. But they still tell me I should swim nine thousand kilometers away, when I can quite easily afford the flight home like any normal person so that I can be sure of landing safely along with your

 | DOI:10.1163/9789004690882_049

people in my own paradise. So much of what is typically Dutch is to be found here on this tropical pinhead on the map, but, oddly enough, there is no outcry against this. Quite the opposite, in fact. How come? Anyway, for how much longer I dare not guess.

Well, all right, I do hear about the various options that your people are offered here to stay adventurous to your heart's content. You may buy a villa from us if you can, and, if you want it, with live-in help for an additional fee, which would be impossible in your country; and our tax authority is friendlier to you than the Dutch one. You see, the structure accommodates these behaviors. I myself have made several attempts with you, to be independent and to be able to stand on my own. One robbed me and another one cheated me. The next one humiliated me, I was put in chains, smeared with slander and dragged through the mud. I stood alone after giving everything I still believe in. That is the immensity of life. I was punished for it. They chose Barabbas.

It lives on in our midst. That fear of really sharing what's meant for everyone. People rummage around in a past that doesn't exist anymore. To avoid feeling it, people think about tomorrow but see only images that cannot be felt. You look at me, then retreat to a safe distance as if you were painting me.

The picture has the properties that people sought when making the painting. You must be thinking: "Theatrical." Yes, so I am, and the theater of my soul is performed of my own free will in order to unchain my heart from denial, cherishing the hope that you know it as well as you have led me to believe. I have resigned myself to the fact of how you see me: a raging bull, someone who is sulking, mean and with no respect for you and yet wanting to take over your space. So I got that part in your theater! Tell me, honestly, are you happy with your creation?

Have I been of service yet again?

Ah, you are of no use to me indeed because I pierce through your masks and see that you are still the beggar. Even if you play the role of the Grande Madame, or Don Juan. The truth is naked as night. That's why you hate me so much. You're still the masochist to the sadist, the courtesan to papa "Giant," who gives you pocket money if you do what his law says. Still the slave of Mr. and Mrs. Intellect.

What am I still doing in your presence? Your inability to see that you have, for ages, been using me to learn, that you crave insight from me, shows me the ruthlessness of the sickness working inside the red blood cells of your society.

You completely destroy the things you yourself often called beautiful. You still don't realize that everything that you value as attractive and interesting has been trapped by yourself in a prison of anthropological curiosity! The sympathy you feel for me has been degraded to an addiction to the drunkenness of oppression. Indeed, I am of no use to you. I got too close and could see that the beautiful sermon, which taught me to love my neighbor, does not apply to you.

See! The magic word is Black! Unseen, unrecognized, unknown.

Illicit feeling. That which can neither be grasped nor manipulated. It is what will flow through the light it begets of itself.

Women prove every time how painful it can be to let this light shine. Often, the pain would rather be held fast. Who still doesn't know that, time and again, pain gives birth to sunshine?

Am I really the great recognition that you dare not let in?

I deeply hope that you will shine when you are healed by my soul and then you will see that my soul is your soul. May the gods and goddesses be with you. Do you actually follow me? Perhaps I ought to explain my process to you.

Look, I was really dissolved in loneliness, I'd sunk through the bottom of the pit. The stairs to the valley seemed endless. My limits were crossed. There was nothing left but to surrender myself to what I didn't know, what I did not even recognize. Silence, there in that black hole. The desire to live got another chance. The music helped me along.

I sank to my knees, head bowed in reverence to the darkness within me, and prayed. "O, black hole, suck me in so that I can feel again. O, Sun of tropical vigor, make this day holy for me. In remembrance of you from whence I came, I will bathe myself under the water of the shower. I will remain faithful to you until my last gasp, and shall be your witness. I offer you my dance, my song and above all my laughter. I'm coming, cleansed of my wounds. I will remain hopeful to welcome your healing." Do you now understand what I really wished to share with you? Not yet?

It is so human, even planetary, this inner transformation. Hope is truly medicine. The miracle occurred! The pain began to abate once I had let it go. But the fear is stubborn. It has also subsided, but it is clearly present. So what is that fear? Fear of what? Fear for what? Caused by what?

From thinking I may never be really successful. I told myself that what people said must be true and I convinced myself that I could see the same truth. Now, that is called objectivity. Even when I felt: "this is deceit," I forced myself to see my own backwardness and the disadvantages of the race, to which I seemed to belong, as the reality. This is what I was always taught. Also, that I must fight and that it was a privilege to imitate the one who denied me by showing complete obedience to his orders, which, today, permeates life, so brilliantly disguised, and makes me think that we're all being traded democratically. But you know what? If I go on like this, I shall end up in pain from all the ever-increasing force I have to use, which wears me out so terribly. And then I can never recharge myself for what I'd like to do! I was so afraid to have faith in those images I dream of and which I see so clearly. I work on that every day. I see it now, how, all those years, I thought I could think because I can speak your language. Because I was an imitation, I could not understand why I always failed to be myself when I was with your people.

I was raised and taught by you and programmed in your image. You formed me, that's true. You are part of me. And Mother Earth, who embodies darkness just as I do, is silent in all languages so that the child, her child, thus I, can unfold.

She is the one who gives us room until she takes away what is not received. Annihilation through irreverence for that which has had the courage to give birth to us all. This is my part in the whole, but you don't want to learn what I have to offer. I mean, really, would you listen to me!! You, then, become so pathetic, and especially weak, which is treated as childishness as if being a child were an insult. A child, so pure and free of fear, completely open to learning. A child, who keeps asking questions when the story gets too complicated.

For years, I've been asking: "How can I manifest who I am?" The answer is: "You can't, so I won't let you." So my fear is the punishment that awaits when I have shown that I can do all that I really want to do. I am so afraid of admitting that I'm the mother of all of you. It is a whole world I am raising. I am like every other woman who is sometimes weak, full of desire to receive something. You know, to recharge, to regain my strength and then to transform into the Mother of the Universe who takes care of everyone again. Do you know what I mean?

If you do this your way it is called work. But I've learned that it is and always will be unthinkable to be rewarded for my achievements. As a result, I no longer have to prove to myself that I can function efficiently. I have learned to see that I am not considered necessary. You've made that clear to me with all those thick reports on me, all done without consulting me. Even if I'm gasping for air, I must stay on my feet here to let you know that I, too, exist. I've realized that, too, from your policy. I have accepted it and am content with myself!

I have learned a great deal from it and I'm thankful for it. I can finally see what was going on in front of me all this time. Myself, in a prison of fear, and of anger, but above all of pain. So afraid to change as if I had to be just one thing, while the movement of Fire that takes shape through everything is the law. So the same thing again! Me, again! Fire destroys and renews form. Those two, the fire and the shape, separated from one and the same Source, always travel together, only I didn't see it. That's why the mirror shattered. I took my leave and prayed again. "Warm me then, O Sacred Fire, and accept every new shape I take, the illusions I myself create. Now well aware that everything is changeable."

The color spectrum of the whole universe is playing out inside me now. The fire is working in my deepest self. It incinerates everything and forces the pain of fear into silence. The order sounds: "LIE DOWN!" You know, resistance to pain, anger and vengeance are true brothers of Fire, necessary for it to function. His job is to transform! To bid farewell to the paralysis seems an unwanted task, but it submits to the law of the Fire.

Would you rather I shut up? Do you want me to forsake the recognition of my own voice, to get used to the idea that there's only one ME in this whole world? This is the knowledge of anyone who recognizes it. Only then can you reflect on things from a position of pure independence.

Form has taught me that it needs me. What is that, then, that me? I can certainly hear what you are thinking. It's the radiance of a force coming from the depths of black. It's just like in the soil: you plant a seed and it grows into a tree of life.

These are the reasons why I want to share consciousness with you. You see? I am willing to explore who you are with you so that you leave me in peace.

See for yourself how it feels, to experience all the things you think of yourself, of me, of everyone you think you can form an opinion of, about whom you let your verdict be felt, you being so sober and matter-of-fact. What you so tirelessly try to make clear to me that I must or must not do. Find out for yourself that it's always just a thought that was once born of yourself. Once upon a time ... unconsciously! Recognize for once that this creation is something other than the essence of who you are. Rid yourself of your creation and dare to experience the source of abundance that you are just as I am. Then create from that source what your deepest self really wants. That's how you'll earn my admiration! It is that simple. And its workings are full of love. It is pure grace! You'll have a sense of humor because you'll live in the moment! That consciousness comes from believing that this is the truth you chose. So I appeal to you, above all to the woman in you, and in me, and in everyone in your society. I urge you to make your fantasies concrete. Now with me! I am ready to show the courage I feel to turn the tide of ignorance with dignity.

In memory of her in me, I set myself in motion and dance the dance of reunion, which makes me speak in a new language. Again, I hope for the birth of humanity in our communication, like the heart of our Mother Earth that makes available to us the element for it, fire. Her beating heart has the character of eternal movement. In this, each of us has a purpose to fulfill.

Whether willingly or not.

Of course we're not equal. Isn't that a blessing? Just imagine! Equality, that's the keyword you're all scared to death of. As if death were that much of a problem. Calvin is dead, let him rest in peace. Raise yourself from the death of condemnation that you pronounce on me again and again because you think that being different makes a difference to setting a value that you also consider lesser. Lesser than what?! You don't even know yourself! Just because I turn out to be as white as you? On the inside, you're just as black as I am. Yes, there, where you'd come to meet me if you had the guts to go there after so many centuries of being with me. You will see yourself reflected in me! Do you follow me?

So, when I say I want to talk to you, I am always referring to the disentanglement of the sickness that still makes slaves of us all, which is also labeled confusion.

Ah, the wayward paths that we keep treading, led by the evil spirits who contaminate our intellect so it does not work properly for us to improve. How proud are you of the images of your advanced technology that has brought misery upon misery to our house?

It is sold to me, and to you, at a profit. They sell it to me, and to you, under the pretext of being state-of-the-art.

You know, it chases me to my beach of clear water. Our fish are in danger of being slaughtered to preserve your well-being yet again. No, I don't miss it. I don't miss the misery. Although I do admit that the invasion of terror, occasioned by hunger for the apparent power of money, inspired by your system, has managed to gain a foothold here too. I don't know, there's so much I want to say, above all to share with you, so that we can think of something together to turn the tide. Please understand that!

Do you think I am preaching nonsense again? So what? For years, centuries, I've listened to your preaching. Then let me now speak once to make my deeds heard. I'll give you a hint to put into practice in your Netherlands that you want me to believe is so overcrowded. Go into yourself, make your music and paint your paintings. Dance with me now that I exist for you. We look upon each other as dead while we are alive.

Acknowledgments

This text was first published in Dutch as Martina, Fridi. "Vuurdoop" [Baptism of Fire]. In *Het vrolijke meisje. Verhalen van vrouwen die putten uit meer dan alleen de Nederlandse cultuur* [The happy girl: Stories of women who draw from more than just Dutch culture], edited by Astrid Roemer, 156—164. Amsterdam: Arena, 1995. Translation by Marcus Ferley. Publication courtesy of Philie van Veen.

CHAPTER 48

Mother Rock [Baranka Mama]

Fridi Martina

Your functional purity
pure with sincere tenderness

Delicate and careful
you molded me to get me back home
where my bed deserved to be
my native country, my rock

Much appreciation I have
for your guts to love me
Only you have known me
unconditionally

Our souls were already acquainted
Your look was the spotless mirror
after every bath,
the clean environment
on my path to become human

No more words
nothing more to say
So although you are absent
and my flesh cannot touch yours
I will not suffer
Although I truly miss you
I will not feel sorry for myself

Bo puresa den funshon,
bo puresa ku sinseridat den bo
ternura
Delikado i kuidadosamente
bo a mansa mi, laga mi yega kas
kaminda mi kuna a meresé di ta
mi tera, mi baranka

Mi apresio ta p'e brio di stima mi
T'abo so a konosé mi
sin buta ni un kondishon

Nos alma ya tabata konosí pa otro
Bo mirada tabata e spil
sin ningun spat
despues di kada un baño
limpiesa di ambiente pa mi a bira
hende

Palabra a kaba
no tin nada mas di bisa
Ta p'esei maske bo n' tei
pa mi karni mishi ku bo
lo mi no pena
Aunke mi ta sinti bo falta
lo mi no pena

 | DOI:10.1163/9789004690882_050

Cause you are my flaming heart
at all times in the air
You are the taste of my homeland
the fragrance of the night queen flower
my bird that sings praises of my cereals
every morning when I wake up and
remember how much light you offered
me

You had such a great existence,
Mother Rock
Now that you left us at last
you are still this vivid woman
in my belly
I send you my blessing on your trip
which seems so lonely

for us humans who stay behind

We will meet again when I
recognize you
during the same trip that is awaiting
me too
to reunite with you
Meanwhile my memory of you will be
the strength of my compassion
Thank you for your protection.

Abo ta mi kandela kurason
den e airu tur momentu
Bo ta e sabor di mi krioyo
e holó di Dama djanochi
mi para ku ta kanta mi papa pa mi
tur mainta ku mi spièrta i kórda
kuantu lus bo a duna mi

Bo a eksistí grandi asina, Mama
Baranka
A la fin bo a bai, ma bo ta muhé bibu
den mi

Bendishon ami ta manda ku bo awor
pa kompañá bo riba e biahe ku ta
parse solitario
serka nos humano ku ta keda atras

Nos enkuentro ta bai ripití na e
momentu ku mi rekonosé bo
durante dje mes biahe ku ta warda

ami tambe pa nos por reuní
Tanten bo memoria ta mi forsa di
kompashon
Danki pa bo protekshon.

Acknowledgments

This poem was originally published in Papiamentu as Martina, Fridi. "Baranka Mama" [Mother Rock]. In *Fridi Martina in good company: een meertalige bloemlezing met gedichten, liedteksten en monologen van Fridi Martina* [Fridi Martina in good company: a multilingual anthology of poetry, lyrics and monologues by Fridi Martina], edited by Philie van Veen, p. 79. Curaçao: Carib Publishing, 2019. English translation by Wernher Suares. Reproduction courtesy of Philie van Veen.

CHAPTER 49

Chakutoe: a Play about the Port Strike of 1922 in Curaçao

Gilbert Bacilio

Abstract

Bacilio's play about Felix Chakutoe, leader of the port strike of 1922 in Curaçao, captures the milieu to which Chakutoe belonged and explores the complex ties between the Church, the state and the community. The play explores the impact of these conditions on the broader society, paying particular attention to the lives of working-class families, especially the women in this milieu. The society depicted in the play is characterized by unemployment, poverty, hunger and exploitation, resulting in the migration of unskilled men, leaving women alone to raise their children. Three scenes have been selected and translated from Papiamentu for the present volume.

Keywords

Felix Chakutoe – playwriting – port strike – Curaçao – literary production

1 Introduction

Felix Chakutoe, remembered as the leader of the Curaçaoan port workers' strike of 1922, was a seafarer who traveled to New York. Upon his return to Curaçao from New York, he found himself involved in the largest harbor strike in the island's history. That year, ship companies lowered the salary for taking in cargo from 50 to 40 cents per hour. When the harbor workers went on strike, they were replaced by migrant workers from abroad who were paid more, causing the protest to intensify. Felix Chakutoe became the leader of the uprising, for which he received a nine-year prison sentence. He was eventually freed following pleas from his mother and mediation efforts by Father Verriet. It is likely that he became politicized and interested in public campaigning as a seafarer and during his time in New York, where he came into

 | DOI:10.1163/9789004690882_051

contact with various international people's civil liberties movements. It was not least through his intervention in the strike of 1922 that the first collective labor agreement in the history of the island was reached. Unfortunately, his role in the uprising was not acknowledged until much later, and he died a poor and forgotten man on September 20, 1967.

Bacilio's play captures the milieu to which Chakutoe belonged and explores the complex ties between the Church, the state and the community. The play explores the impact of these conditions on the broader society, paying particular attention to the lives of working-class families, especially the women in this milieu. The society depicted in the play is characterized by unemployment, poverty, hunger and exploitation, resulting in the migration of unskilled men, leaving women alone to raise their children.

Three scenes have been selected and translated from Papiamentu for the present volume, featuring the 15-year old Tirso, his 17-year old sister Magdalena, their single mother Constancia Schilden, known as Mama Stan, who all belong to a working-class household living in the Otrobanda District of Curaçao, and Father Verriet. Inspired by stories of warriors, martyrs and heroes he hears and reads about, Tirso dreams of becoming a leader. He leaves school to look for work in order to financially support his mother. Unable to find work, he approaches Father Verriet, who takes him under his wing. He becomes an altar boy and does odd jobs in and around the church. Tirso aspires to be a good *Yu di Kòrsou*.[1] Law and order is his motto. He detests the noisy, riotous, macho dock workers and his sister who cheers them on. As he gets to know Chakutoe, he finds himself in a difficult internal battle between the established order and his own awareness of injustice, between the authorities and the workers, between Father Verriet and Chakutoe. In the end he sides with Chakutoe.

Magdalena hates her work as a hat and basket weaver. She prefers staying on the quay among the dock workers. There she encourages them to protest against the circumstances that cost her father his life. When the strike reaches its climax on July 17, 1922, culminating in hard clashes with the police, vandalism and other forms of violence, Magdalena joins the barricades. She is arrested by the police for sedition and vandalism.

As she sinks into deep loneliness, orphaned after her mother is shot by a stray police bullet, without her cherished wish for freedom and equality in this tough masculinist society, she ends up in a psychiatric ward.

1 Editors' note: *Yu di Kòrsou* literally means "Child of Curaçao", a term that has, in the course of time, come to denote someone who belongs to Curaçaoan society, thereby distinguishing them from those who don't.

Her mother, Constancia Schilden, is the widow of the dock worker Daniel Schilden, who died following a fatal work injury while loading the ship Zulia in 1921. She does the housekeeping for the white landowner, *Shon* Katrina, and tries to keep herself above water with odd jobs, leading a pious life. During the climax of the 1922 strike, she dies of a stray bullet while preparing food for her children.

While Chakutoe is the central figure of the play, Bacilio also foregrounds the youth and working-class women who actively mobilized the population to join the agitations and dared to challenge the authority of the Church. The play depicts how parties that refuse to take each other's differing interests seriously, who do not listen to each other, ultimately end up in conflicts predominated by arrogance, wherein people's dependencies are exploited to the extreme. The play shows that when all hell breaks loose, people are prepared to use anything at their disposal to be heard and respected.

Scene 5: **At Mama Stan's house**

Mama Stan is weaving a basket. Tirso is reading a book. Magdalena enters, gets a basket that is halfway done and starts weaving it.

Magdalena: What are we eating today?

Mama: There's a jug with tamarind juice over there.

Magdalena: I asked what we are eating.

Mama: Stave off your hunger with it. I don't have anything else right now. When we sell these baskets we will eat. I will cook something for you with that income.

Tirso: I have a stomach ache. That tamarind juice will not help me right now.

Mama: Take a teaspoon of Emulsion de Scott.

Magdalena: If it's not tamarind, it's *funchi*.[2] If it's not *funchi*, it's tamarind. Or *funchi* with tamarind, *funchi* with milk. *Funchi* with buttermilk. I'm just so fed up.

Tirso: Stop complaining. You're upsetting my stomach even more. Your lament does not eliminate hunger.

Magdalena: It's as if there are rusty needles stuck in every single segment of my fingers, in my entire hand.

Tirso: Take a teaspoon of Emulsion de Scott.

2 Translator's note: *Funchi* is a side dish made of cornmeal.

Mama: Powerful medicine.

Magdalena: Yuck!

Mama: Now that Daddy is no longer with us, may God guard him in his kingdom, the three of us have to struggle to make ends meet. Each one of us must contribute. No pain, no gain.

Magdalena: These damn baskets made my hands look like this. Rough, pale, ugly. Just like a man's hands. Robust.

Tirso: Don't you wanna be like a man. Or do you wish to be a man with soft hands?

Magdalena: I don't want to be a man. I want to be equal to men.

Tirso: Well, your hands have to be equal to a man's hands. Rough. Work hard, by the sweat of your brow, to fill your belly.

Magdalena: I want to have a woman's hands. I want to work hard and fill my stomach. The only thing I can do right now is work hard!

Mama: Look at my hands! Hands that for many years have been cleaning floors, washing, starching, ironing. Not for myself! For you! And you're complaining because your fingers are painful? Hurry up and finish that basket.

Magdalena: I'm not afraid of any kind of work, but I don't want to be stuck forever making baskets and hats. There are other things, grander and more beautiful in life.

Mama: These battered hands are the reason why you're alive today.

Magdalena: Your hands indeed reveal what kind of person you are. You need your hands to work, for sure, but with these same hands, you should be able to help people as well, to guide and caress them!

Mama: Let me starve to death then. Food for *warawara*.[3]

Tirso: Magdaleentje, why is it always the same, huh? Accept your destiny. You'll put a curse on us.

Magdalena: Look here, pastor, you don't get to tell me anything! Look at your hands.

Tirso: Not all male hands are meant to do the same kind of work.

---

3 Translator's note: *Warawara* refers to the crested caracara, a large bird of prey native to the Americas.

Magdalena: Neither are women's hands.
Mama: Come on, hurry up with that basket!
Magdalena: What did you do today? Just reading and more reading. Reading alone will not put food on the table either. Why don't you do something? Velvety hands!
Tirso: While you were snoring in your bed this morning, I was already up, said my prayers and went to help Father Verriet. I prepared everything for tonight's mass.
Magdalena: Look for a proper job. Be careful they don't turn you into a priest.
Tirso: Would that be a crime?
Magdalena: I can already see you walking around in a white skirt.
Tirso: It's not a skirt, it's a cassock.
Magdalena: Or do you wish to wear a skirt?
Tirso: It's not a skirt. Anyways, I worked quite hard already this morning.
Magdalena: Did they pay you?
Tirso: I got a good breakfast: oranges, toasted bread with sweet butter. I could choose between ham, cheese and sausage. I chose all three.
Magdalena: Shame on you!
Tirso: Tea with milk and mixed fruits.
Mama: I thought you had a stomach ache.
Magdalena: His belly is already full.
Mama: You could've saved something for us.
Tirso: Next time.

Scene 7: I'm going to the harbor

Tirso: So we can fill our bellies. Beefsteak!
Magdalena: Hey!
They all get a calabash dish to eat.
Mama: Just in time. The pot is empty today.
Magdalena: Nothing at all.
Tirso: Today the Father indicated how important it is for someone to know what he wants to become in life.
Mama: What did you answer?
Magdalena: A priest, of course!
Mama: Is this true my son?
Tirso: Not a priest. Someone like Christ or Tula.
Magdalena: Hmmm, to become a leader you still need a lot of balls.

Mama: Wash your mouth!
Tirso: Those are the kinds of things she learns in the harbor. Have you been to confession lately?
Magdalena: I will not tell any priest about my life.
Tirso: You should definitely visit the Father, Leentje.
Magdalena: Not me.
Tirso: I don't want the devil to take you. At least go to the Father and confess.
Magdalena: You must be crazy. Just keep chattering with them and you'll see how they'll double-cross you.
Tirso: The Father said that Mama should force you to visit him. He heard too that you are moving around on the wharf.
Magdalena: You are the one who gossiped!
Mama: She's not listening! You need to help me with this, Tirso.
Tirso: If you don't go to the Father, I will stop bringing you his food too.
Magdalena: Don't bring me his food anymore. Because he gives food, I have to do what he wants?
Mama: Where are you going?
Magdalena: To the wharf.
Mama: You have no business on the wharf. The wharf is a man's place.
Magdalena: There's life on the wharf. You hear about history, find out about the news, get to know many things.
Tirso: A lady has no business there.
Magdalena; The wharf is for everybody.
Tirso: Go to the Father, not the wharf.
Magdalena: I'll go wherever I want to go and whenever I wanna go. Nobody can stop me.
Mama: Don't you dare go to these men. You'll most certainly know what these hands you hate so much can do.
Magdalena: He's allowed to go out anytime he wants to, wherever he wants to go to, and I have to sit around and daydream in here, work my ass off. Not fair!
Mama: He never goes to the wharf!

Magdalena wants to go.

Mama: Set the rules, Tirso. You are the man of the house right now.
Tirso: There's nothing out there for you. In here there is everything: Baskets, hats, a floor to be cleaned. Clothes to be washed, starched, ironed. You're destined to do all of this.

Magdalena: A destiny that you men have determined for us.

Tirso: God made man first. Woman came afterwards, taken from our ribs. You're a piece from my rib.

Magdalena: That's a "fairy tale" from the Bible. Do you believe that it's possible to make a woman from a man's rib? Your rib would not be complete then. We're made with our own ribs. We don't need your bones.

Tirso: The Bible itself says that man is the head of the household, women have to serve men.

Magdalena: The Bible was written by people.

Tirso: Inspired by God.

Magdalena: In the days of yore. An old-fashioned way of thinking!

Tirso: God is above time. Time doesn't count for Him. His word is eternal.

Magdalena: God can never agree with women being less than men. We are equal.

Tirso: You're just saying that to flee from your destiny.

Magdalena: I'm older than you.

Tirso: Age doesn't matter.

Magdalena: Go to hell, with your age, baskets, Bible and all!

Mama: Lord God Almighty! Set the rules, Tirso!

Magdalena pushes Tirso away and bolts out of the house.

Tirso: Venomous tongue!

Scene 22: Tirso asks Father to help Magdalena

Tirso enters at Father Verriet's place. The Father hugs him intensely.

Father: How did it go afterwards?

Tirso: Terrible!

Father: I can imagine what you're feeling. It's something terrible. May God give you strength to deal with this hardship!

Tirso: They took Magdalena away.

Father: The Bishop has just informed me.

Tirso: She was in yesterday's riot. She was talking to the workers in action.

Father: Agitating them.

Tirso: Animating them. Giving them strength.

Father: She played with fire until she got burnt.

Tirso: I tried to convince her to quit and come home, but in vain.

Father: You reap what you sow.

Tirso: I admired her courage. I know that she can be quite rebellious, but I never knew that she was so strong.

Father: I've been telling you for a long time now to bring her to me.

Tirso: Father, you know very well how hard we've tried. Please Father, get her out of prison!

Father: I don't have a say in that.

Tirso: She's my sister. Locked up!

Father: It's her own fault. She refused to come to me. She preferred to choose the devil's squad.

Tirso: Talk with Volksbond, with the Bishop, the Governor!

Father: We'll help those who want to be helped.

Tirso: You can, Father, at least if you want to! Or is it that you don't want to?

Father: She has to sit on her blisters.

Tirso: Make an exception. She's my sister. My only sibling. It's Magdalena!

Father: I did everything within my reach, but she turned it down.

Tirso: Don't leave me in the lurch, Father. It's me, Tirso! I've always counted on you, Father. In good and bad times.

Father: There's nothing else I can do about this wrongdoing. If she wants me to visit her in prison and let her confess, I'll do it with all my heart. Nothing else, Tirso.

Tirso: You of all people, Father? You, who has always pointed me to the correct way.

Father: Her way was not the right one.

Tirso: You, who has always taught me how to believe in God, the church, Christ, life, in people, in yourself, Father. Now you give up just like that.

Father: I didn't give up. She surrendered in the arms of the Evil one.

Tirso: We're here to help her!

Father: Every day we were available for her. Day and night.

Tirso: Help my sister right now, Father! She needs us now more than ever.

Father: It's becoming clearer now that your sister was possessed by evil forces.

Tirso: She was a bit rebellious, true, but she's not a bad person. You should've seen her yesterday. Happy, with zeal, determined. Everybody admired her!

Father: Neither you nor your mom could let her understand that she had to come to church for her own good, for her salvation. Let her save herself now.

Tirso: Father? She means well! She's fighting for justice too, in her own way.

Father: In the wrong way, pagan!

Tirso: A bad dream?

Father: No!

Tirso: Jeanne D'Arc?

Father: No!

Tirso: Order from above?

Father gives Tirso a very hard slap in the face. Then he tells him:

Father: Do you wanna eat something?

Tirso bolts out.

Acknowledgments

This is a translated excerpt from the unpublished Papiamentu playscript. The play premiered on March 27, 2019, on World Theatre Day, in Teatro La Tentashon in Curaçao and was directed by the playwright. It was produced by the Teatro KadaKen Foundation, with Maryluska "Lou" Nisbet as Chief Producer. "Chakutoe" has been performed for both schools and the general public in 2019 and early 2020. Translation by Wernher José Suares.

CHAPTER 50

Woman [Muhé]

Imelda Valerianus-Fermina

Hari, muhé, hari tira garganta atras,
Esei pará den bo balkon,
Kaba hari, drenta bo kamber
tapa barika abou riba bo kama bo yora.

Kaba yora, dal e kara un labá
Pasa peña den e kabei …
I sali djingueli asina enfrentá mundu.

Tira ayera tras di lomba
No pensa riba ayera, ya ta tardi,
Mañan si Dios duna bo bida
Ora bo mira e aurora
Di un dia nobo na horizonte.

Habri brasa p´e dia nobo
Bo n´sa kiko e ta trese
Pero bo mester aseptá,
Di pursi ta e mes un wega
Ku mundu ta hunga ku nos,
Nos ta hunga ku mundu.

Laugh, woman, rock with laughter,
standing boldly on your balcony.
The laughing done, enter your room,
fall flat on your bed and cry.

The crying done, wash your face,
comb your hair and leave
sprightly to confront the world.

Throw all those past days behind you,
don't even think of yesterday.
It's late afternoon already,
tomorrow, God willing, you'll see
a new day dawning at the horizon.

Embrace that new day,
you don't know what it brings,
yet comply you must.
After all, it's the same game
the world plays with us,
that we play with the world.

Acknowledgments

This poem was first published in Papiamentu as Valerianus-Fermina, Imelda. "Muhé" [Woman]. In *Mi pensamentunan* [My thoughts], 9. Willemstad, Cultureel Centrum Curaçao, 1985. Revised translation by Aart G. Broek. Reproduction courtesy of the heirs of Valerianus-Fermina.

 | DOI:10.1163/9789004690882_052

Index

If you have any questions regarding this title, please contact:

Koninklijke Brill BV
Plantijnstraat 2
2321 JC Leiden
Email: info@brill.com

Batch number: 08132564